At the Cross

At the Cross

Race, Religion, and Citizenship in the Politics of the Death Penalty

MELYNDA J. PRICE

OXFORD
UNIVERSITY PRESS

Oxford University Press is a department of the University of Oxford.
It furthers the University's objective of excellence in research, scholarship,
and education by publishing worldwide. Oxford is a registered trade mark
of Oxford University Press in the UK and in certain other countries

Published in the United States of America by
Oxford University Press
198 Madison Avenue, New York, NY 10016,
United States of America

Library of Congress Cataloging-in-Publication Data
Price, Melynda J.
At the cross : race, religion, and citizenship in the politics of the death penalty / Melynda J. Price.
p.   cm.
Includes bibliographical references and index.
ISBN 978–0–19–020553–9 (hardback : alk. paper) — ISBN 978–0–19–020554–6
(pbk. : alk. paper) 1. Capital punishment—United States. 2. Discrimination in criminal
justice administration—United States. 3. Racism—United States. 4. Religion and justice.
5. African Americans. I. Title.
HV8699.U5P75 2015
364.660973—dc23
2014046236

For my mother,
Sandra Faye Spates Price,
who taught me in her word and deed how to do the hard work

and

For my son,
James Efrain Price,
who keeps me working hard

Contents

Acknowledgments

THIS BOOK HAS been a long time in the making. Over the years, I have been helped and encouraged by more people than I can remember, let alone acknowledge. I thank them all, but some warrant specific mention.

First and foremost, I would like to thank my mother, Sandra Spates Price, for her unending support. Alone, she raised my sisters and me and stressed the value of education. We have all graduated from college and have a few advanced degrees. Our achievements are as much hers as they are our own. I am also grateful that when she sent us into the world of academia that she entrusted my sister and me to the guidance of Dr. Jewel L. Prestage at Prairie View A&M University. Dr. Prestage had a vision for my life that went beyond anything I knew. From day one at PV, she preached the gospel of graduate education and changed the path of my and my sister's lives.

I would also like to acknowledge the encouragement and support of my older sisters—Sandra, Leslie, Sharon, and the baby—Shawana—for their love and support. They have been more than sisters through this long process— friends, moving women, personal chefs, babysitters, and more. They have also allowed me to love and care for their children in ways that others would consider intrusive and rude. Although they are all grown—Joseph, Melissa, Adrienne, Alicia, Alex, and Leslie—they have been my inspiration and support. I thank my uncle, Joe Louis Spates, who passed shortly before the publication of this book, and my aunt, Mary Spates Gordon; both have always offered a word of encouragement and unwanted lawyer jokes. I have to also thank the others members of my family who were supportive even when they were skeptical about this process, especially my cousins Erica, Wanda, Kathryn, and their children. I always have to thank separately my twin sister and fellow political scientist, Melanye Price. From the very beginning, she has been with me. She has helped me through several cross-country moves and many other transitions.

I owe a debt of gratitude to my dissertation committee, who guided me through the first stages of this project. I met Dan Levine when I visited the University of Michigan as a prospective student. My first lessons in the study of politics occurred around his dining room table in a course on Latin American politics, and some of those lessons are the foundation of this work. Hanes Walton was my link to the historically black college and university (HBCU) and all the things that are so wonderful about those institutions. I can only hope I thanked him enough for his help. Don Herzog encouraged me to think beyond sometimes what I thought were the edges of my intellect. Kevin Gaines was the last member to join my committee, but before I knew him, I knew and was helped by his work.

In my first year at Prairie View, I took an honors colloquium as part of the requirements for being a student in the Benjamin Banneker Honors College. In that seminar I made friends who continue to be my most important and closest relationships today. I can remember the first day I met Salina Gray as if it were yesterday. Together we have weathered riots and other reasons to give up, but we haven't. She and her son, Israel, are my family. I also have to thank Juba Watts-Cain and Phyllis and Sadie Watts. When I met Juba at PV, I could not foresee the way his mother and his entire family would take me in and care for me as if I were their own. I thank them for all the holidays and other days away from my family that I did not have to spend alone.

I must also thank the professors of the Banneker Honors College and Prairie View A&M University (PVAMU) for nurturing my early interest in scholarship and its connection to community. I would like to thank by name Dr. Dennis Judd, Dr. Lisa Aubrey, and the Drs. Barbara A. P. and Mack Jones. My time at PVAMU continues to stand as the most important educational experience of my life and I am, like so many for more than 150 years, indebted to that great institution built from the sweat and hopes of formerly enslaved Blacks who could not imagine the education I have been privileged to receive.

I lived two different lives in the Michigan political science department and I am grateful to those who helped me through difficult subject matter and long winters, particularly Zenzele Isoke, Alana Hackshaw, and Kimala Price. I was very nervous about returning to Ann Arbor after law school, but I was surprised and gladdened by the friends I made and rediscovered—Mariely Lopez-Santana, Kenyatha Loftis, and Tiffiany Howard, Ayanna Sheree Brown, Menna Demessie, and Elizabeth James. Isa Quintana was clearly meant to be my friend even if her own biases toward law students delayed our meeting. I do not know how I would have made it through these many years without her friendship and support.

Kevin Maillard and Jenny Diamond-Cheng encouraged me to attend law school. We all went off to different institutions, but remain an important personal and professional support system for one another these many years later. For his love and support, Kevin has been given the additional duty of godfather with a lowercase "g."

There are two Michigan friends to whom I owe special thanks. Ruth Nicole Brown is a friend of my heart. I thank her for her mother wit, Black girl genius, and keen eye. Lastly, I have to thank Dr. Gina Athena Ulysse, who is one of those friends that make it hard to imagine my life before them. I went to the field with her in Jamaica before I began my research. She helped me to understand the complications and benefits in studying your "own" community.

I entered the University of Texas Law School during the Hopwood years where the number of Black students was the lowest they had been since integration. Wendy Hall Warren was in my first-year section and study group. But, it was her assistance as we learned of the sickness and death of our other beloved classmate and friend—Felecia Shankle-Rogers—that truly showed me the depth and strength of our friendship. Felecia, Wendy, Lewis Hutchison, and I represent the Black students in the class of 2002 at the UT School of Law and being members of that small club has bonded us forever. Through an indirect path, I came to know Emily Armitano and am glad we found each other. John Newton was probably the only person other than my committee who read every page of my dissertation. I will forever appreciate his hand-holding in those critical moments.

In addition to the friends I made, I also had the pleasure of learning the law from truly great professors at the University of Texas. I have to make special mention of Rob Owen and the other professors of the Capital Punishment Clinic at the University of Texas School of Law, who opened my eyes to the complexities of death penalty. I would also like to thank Maurie Levin. An internship at the Texas Defender Service's Austin office under her guidance during my second year of law school is where the seeds were planted for key parts of this work.

Since I began this process I have lost a number of important people, including my uncles Alvin Gordon, George Spates, Alex Spates, and Andrew Spates; my grandmother, Janie B. Mack; my father, Leslie Leroy Price; and my aunt, Gladys Spates Spann. The most important of all was my uncle, James Spates, for whom my son is named. Throughout his life, he was a warrior. First he fought poverty and the degradation of Jim Crow. He—like at least five, but maybe more, of my uncles—fought in Viet Nam. When he returned to the states he battled alcoholism, and then he became a minister of the gospel. It is in this role that I knew him best. He gave unselfishly of his time, his money, and his spirit to the people of his congregation and to my family. I am truly sad that he is not here at the end to see me succeed.

In 2006, I joined the faculty at the University of Kentucky College of Law. I am grateful to my colleagues who have provided me with the space to grow as an intellectual and a teacher, especially Carolyn Bratt, Louise Graham, and Nicole Huberfeld. I am grateful to Melissa Henke for being a willing reader. I also came to know colleagues throughout the university whose generosity helped push me across the finish line, like Wayne Lewis and the "core" faculty of the African American and Africana Studies Program. I must also thank my research assistant Sarah Perlmutter for her deeply curious mind and religious devotion to follow through.

I came to Lexington alone and knew no one. I am now a mother and have a community of family whose support has been invaluable to the last stages of this project. Nikky Finney became my first Kentucky-Black-girl-friend with the added title of Godmama. Kate Black is the rootedness of place and home, and James and I are made better by the steadiness of her love. I am also grateful to Kathi Kern, who holds the highest honors that James bestows, neighbor and fast runner. I am indebted to Allison Connelly and Julie Butcher, who from first days embraced me, and then James, and have not let us go. I owe a load of back babysitting fees to Mekhatansh and Sonja McGuire that will never be paid. They are James's right-on-time girls and he lives comfortably in their love. My newest Lexington friend became quickly one of my best. Thank you Tiea Roper for taking me as I am and for your model of motherhood that provides such balance to mine. I also thank Amaya and Armondi Stallworth for giving James cousins in Kentucky.

Lastly, I thank James for his hugs and tolerance of my big work. He is a love song written in the genetic notes, melodies, and rhythms of all of those who came before him.

Prologue

ON THE DAY before I took the bar exam, my father died. My mother debated about whether to tell me or to wait. All I could do was try to think of the last time I had seen him face to face. I knew it was before I left Houston for Ann Arbor only to return almost home to study law in Austin. This was the last not-doing of the things I needed from a man who had done nothing except help my mother give me life. Now when I think about how this last hoop I jumped through to enter the practice of law is so marked by the death of my father, I know that death had been there from the beginning.

I have always feared the death of my mother. Her life was also mine. From a very early age, I remember anxiety when my mother would not make it home at her usual time. As she ages, she more freely discusses the anxiety she had then about her death and her fear that my sisters and I would be set adrift like she was when her mother died. At these times, I know that my fear was warranted. Even now, as an adult, I find myself holding my breath, if only for seconds, when I know she should be home and she does not answer the phone. Not only I, but also my sisters, live and breathe in her responses. Her breath, her heartbeat, her blood pressure, the fluidity of her joints, her happiness, her wishes are constellations by which we set our course.

My father's life had always been his own. His life had never been a fixed point for he or I. Gone before my twin sister and I, the last of their children, were born, my childhood memories are remote islands of his casual and inconsistent intrusions. He never lingered long enough to fit smoothly into the female form of our family. In middle school, I would see him frequently from the window of my school bus on the way to a better education than my community could provide as he laughed with the other workingmen in the parking lot of the donut shop. Other children on the bus would joke about the men on a street corner wasting time. They did not know who he was and was not to me.

The wasting of time would eventually catch him, age him, cripple him, and then kill him. Even though I knew for years my father was ill, it had not occurred to me that he would die. At one point in my teens, I had explained away the questions about my father's absence with death. I was struck by the fact that this lie to sidestep the reality of our relationship would now hold more unrevealed truths than when first told. The ethics of how, when, and what to tell and feel became entangled in the rules of proprietary and familial law and civil and criminal procedure that faced me the next day.

I made the decision to go to law school as the state of Texas weighed the execution of Karla Faye Tucker. A young woman with the face of an angel who killed two people with a pickaxe made clear to me that my study of religion and politics would lead me back to the place where the roots of my interests first met ground. I returned to Texas to study, and I spent two of my three years in law school working with men on death row. I went to the death chamber. I went to the prison. I spoke with inmates. I was deeply ensconced in the lives of men whose deaths were settled by Texas courts. But these men were not my father. I was not their daughter. Although I was deeply saddened by the deaths of the men whose cases I worked on during that period, I did not mourn them.

I sat at the folding table covered in African cloth that was my desk, holding the telephone while listening to my mother relay the plans for the funeral. She said that I would be OK and that I had to take the test. Until then it had not occurred to me there was a choice in that matter. There were many tests. My mother never sheltered us from death, having lost her own mother in her youth and her father in mine. She had dedicated her life to nursing people with cancer, all haunted by, if not succumbing to, death. So by example, I understood what I had to do. I took a deep breath. I wiped my face. I looked down at my desk. I began reading. For three and a half days, I would not tell my friend and study partner—whose premature death I would grieve three short years later—that the minute we were done I would leave Austin. I would take the two-and-a-half-hour drive to Houston to help bury a man who had been of little help to me.

My life in the law is intimately tied to death. I am a scholar of the death penalty. Like my mother, I have chosen to be a witness to the dying. She says there can be dignity in death. I, with my academic's distance, see only power in death. It is that power that intrigues me, the power of the state or an individual actor to proclaim an end to a life that they feel probably does not deserve much consideration. When I articulate my sincere belief in the inherent moral, legal, and political wrong of this form of punishment, I am often challenged with the truth that these men killed one or more innocent persons. I reply that at various points in time, recent and distant, those whose lives were deserving and innocent was highly situated in the color and class of their bodies. Is there is any more dignity in death when the innocent hang from the end of a noose tied by mob or sheriff?

It is possible that this argument about the innocent and the deserving convinces me because I study the death penalty in Texas, a place that is for me the motherland. My father's family are relative newcomers to Texas. My grandmother arrived as a child from Louisiana still speaking the Creole that would be gone before it could be passed to my father. My mother's family is not new to this place. For five generations, my foreparents, including my mother, picked cotton in the fields of southeast Texas. There is not one experience of African Americans during Jim Crow that they escaped. The story that most haunts me in my academic work is not the heat of the Texas sun or the snakes or the way the cotton bolls made the fingers bleed and swell. It is a simple story of a father's attempt to help his daughter that was made difficult by the time in which he lived, a story in which he, unlike most of the men I have met on death row, narrowly escapes death.

As I remember the story, my great-grandfather, Alex, was a barber in the flats, a low-lying area of town where Blacks could build their homes. One day the son of a white official wandered into this Black section of town and, drunk, made sexual overtures toward my great-aunt. His offer was refused. He became angry and picked up a piece of wood from the ground nearby. Alex, hearing the altercation, stepped in to protect his daughter. As he grabbed the wood from the boy's hand, the boy was cut and began to bleed. Later, a relative who worked in a white home sent a message that they were planning to lynch my great-grandfather. Several men in their Black community smuggled him on a train to Houston. The next day my great-grandmother and her children followed.

They moved to the Fourth Ward, a community just north of downtown Houston that had once been called Freedman's Town because of the number of formerly enslaved Blacks who settled there in the days immediately following emancipation. They lived in Freedman's Town for several years before trusting that the violent intentions of the mob back home had dissipated. The entire family returned and lived as safely as they always had, although my great-grandfather used the name Jack until the day he died, a concession to the racial hierarchy that tolerated his return. In the early 1980s when an auxiliary of white women wrote a history of the town on the centennial of its official incorporation, my great-grandfather was listed, along with his photo, as one of the upstanding Black members of the community, Jack Spates. There was not a telling of how he came to be Jack. In my family's story, he is still Alex, and my uncles, cousins, and nephew are named after him.

This story stays with me because it reminds me of how Black bodies made people guilty and undeserving, therefore subject to violence. The state is, in theory, the antithesis of the mob. It was not so in this case. In the history of the death penalty, the state has been at various times substitute and proxy for, coordinator of, and witness to the mob. I reflect on my personal stories of death and near-death because they are as much a part of my perspective of the death penalty as the court opinions, surveys, trial transcripts, and other forms of data used to analyze the meaning of this form of punishment to African Americans. Biologically, my father died from congestive heart disease brought on by years of self-abuse and self-neglect. Despite my mother's refusal to attend the funeral of a man she had worked hard to separate herself from decades before, she will sincerely question what his life chances might have been had he had not been born Black and poor in the Texas Hill Country.

My mother, my father, my great-grandfather, and all those who, with them, lived with their necks under the foot of Jim Crow understand the power of the state to alter, dislocate, exclude, and kill. I carry with me, through their experiences, an understanding of how in death, or narrow escapes from death, the truth can be submerged and revealed in the personal and public histories of the teller. The identity or experience of the teller is not traditionally foregrounded in the discipline in which I was trained. I begin this book with a story of its origins as a way of providing a more complete portrait of the narratives that influence this work. I am the first of my people to tell.

Introduction

*Our country's national crime is lynching. It is not the crea-
ture of an hour, the sudden outburst of uncontrolled fury,
or the unspeakable brutality of an insane mob. It represents cool calculating deliberation of intelligent people who
openly avow that there is an "unwritten law" that justifies
them in putting human beings to death without complaint
under oath, without trial by jury, without opportunity to
make defense, and without right of appeal.*

—IDA WELLS-BARNETT, "Lynch Law in America" (1900)[1]

*At first they hung them. Now they're just sticking them
with a needle.*

—DENISE, 19-year-old cashier (2004)[2]

TWO DAYS AFTER Anthony Quinn Francois was found guilty of capital murder for killing the three younger sisters of his teenaged ex-girlfriend
Shameka Patterson, I conducted a focus group in a low-income housing community only blocks from where the girls were murdered. One of the focus
group participants, 19-year-old Danielle, did not know Shameka or any of
the Pattersons. They had not gone to the same schools or attended the same
church.

Although Danielle did not know Shameka, she understood the space they
all occupied. She lived with the specter of violence that permeated the lives of
all local residents every day. Danielle and Shameka shared more than a neighborhood and an age group. Their community, like most Black communities,
is dotted with houses of worship that serve as both religious and political
sanctuaries. Modest homes are interspersed with houses used to sell narcot-
ics. There is a visible police presence in the neighborhood, as in many urban
centers, but because this is urban Texas, there are also winding bayous and

pastures where livestock graze. The people and the place are marked by their years as a battlefield in the war on drugs. They also have shared a lived experience of racism and a sense of justice articulated in a language of religion.

On September 11, 2003, Francois crept into Shameka's home with a gun. He vowed that if he could not have her, no one would. Francois shot Shameka in the face. He continued through the house, shooting her three younger sisters—Naikesha, 15; Ashley, 11; and Brittney, 10. Shameka lived, but her sisters did not. He shot two of the girls at close range while they slept in their beds and critically wounded their mother, Sheila Ann. After eight hours of deliberation, a jury sentenced him to death on July 29, 2004. Francois's face revealed no emotion as the judge read the verdict. LaKeyda Patterson, Shameka's 19-year-old cousin, read victim impact statements from family members of the murdered girls, including Shameka. As she read, Francois's eyes shifted to the defense table. Dorothy Patterson, Shameka's grandmother, said in her statement, "I forgive you for what you did. I cannot judge you, only God can do that."

The statements of both Shameka and her mother also expressed a forgiveness based in their faith. Shameka, who was 16 and still a girl herself at the time of the murders, began dating Francois when she was 14, wooed by gifts and attention. Shameka ended the relationship one year later but could not get Francois to stop calling. Francois had already spent time in a juvenile detention facility for murdering another teen and had also spent time in prison for drug possession. When Shameka became involved in another relationship, the threats against her family began. He followed through on that night in September. Shameka wrote, "I know you tried to destroy my life but you didn't. Even though my sisters are in a better place, I'm holding my head up high." Her mother, who had lost three daughters, testified, "I will forgive you for what you did because I know you can never get to Him with hate in your heart."

In the quote that opens this chapter, Danielle describes a racially biased system of capital punishment that has changed over time only in the method of execution. Grief over lost lives does not blind African Americans to the racial and political history of the death penalty. In the murder of three Black girls and a death sentence for one Black man, we see how members of the Black community must deal with the death penalty while also accounting for the history of racially motivated violence through lynching and unfair executions. They look at this issue through the lens that incorporates religious beliefs and places them at odds with the continued use of death as punishment.

This book looks at how Black people understand the death penalty. How do Black people, who live in such close proximity to crime and capital punishment, view this practice, and how do those views inform their relationship to the state? The heavy reliance on religion and religious language in political decision-making among African Americans necessitates an engagement with how faith intersects with other concerns such as race and access to justice. This is a death penalty project that ultimately describes how the death penalty continues to constrain the citizenship of African Americans and their sense of belonging in the larger political body, even as elites tout post–Civil Rights Movement gains.

The concern over how the violence Blacks are subjected to affects their status as citizens is not a new conversation in the African American community. As early as 1900, anti-lynching activist and journalist Ida Wells-Barnett described the organized nature of extralegal executions of African Americans. Her writing challenged the popular view that lynching was the product of uncontrolled mob violence. In the essay from which the chapter epigraph is drawn, Wells-Barnett eloquently outlined the role of lynching and the government's failure to respond to the rampant denial of the citizenship rights of African Americans after the Civil War. Wells-Barnett made this argument not simply from her position as a member of a wronged community but as part of a larger critique of how lynching distorted the meaning of American democracy, especially in the post-Confederate South.

In the face of both violent and nonviolent repression, African American political rhetoric continually embraces and reflects the fundamental tenets of American democracy. The "righteous discontent" of African American activists has been consistently articulated in dialogue with the political and legal context of the times. This makes understanding the religious sentiments of Blacks an exercise in understanding their views of policy and social issues. Regardless of the evolving political and legal doctrines of the appropriate role of race in American society, the articulation of basic citizenship rights by African Americans in the rhetoric of American democracy remains constant, heavily laced with religion. So, for instance, when Martin Luther King Jr., wearing the mantle of minister, stood on the steps of the Lincoln Memorial at the March on Washington in 1963 and declared, "Now is the time to make justice a reality for all God's children," he was drawing on a long line of political claims to rights grounded both in African American and broader American political thought and a well-established tradition of merging religion and politics among African Americans and their leaders.[3]

The research in this book, completed nearly forty years after the death of King and eight decades after the death of Wells-Barnett, tells a story about the lasting and contemporary links between the righteous politics of Black people, state violence, and political inclusion. Regardless of the venue—jury box, focus group, news pages, survey data—the views of African Americans on the form of punishment most politically and rhetorically tied to policing racial boundaries—capital punishment—are voiced with illusions to the divine and a sense of exclusion. When Denise, the 19-year-old focus group participant, drew a link from the lynching of the past to the death penalty of the present, she expressed a consistent theme throughout the data about how the death penalty continues to define individual and community status for African Americans. For everyday African Americans who live where the death penalty continues to be a profound part of the administrations of justice, there is little meaning in the legal efforts to justify and regulate its use or in the work of academics that attempts to situate lynching solely in historical studies of racial politics. The continued practice of executions makes past injustices resonate with contemporary African American concerns about justice.

The Supreme Court, however, has spent decades trying to distinguish the current practice of the death penalty from its racist past. The modern era of the death penalty is marked by the 1972 decision of *Furman v. Georgia*, in which the Supreme Court ruled that death penalty statutes were unconstitutional because they were so inconsistently administered. The Court pointed to what it called a high level of "randomness" in death penalty convictions. But death sentences were not so random for Black criminal defendants. Blacks were disproportionately sentenced to death, especially in cases involving white victims.

In his review of the history of death penalty litigation during the 1960s and 1970s, Stuart Banner commented that the Court was transforming criminal rights and civil rights in cases when it was "confiden[t] in its ability to minimize the effects of racism."[4] He concluded that "'randomness' became in effect a code word for discrimination."[5] So the challenge for several justices writing majority opinions was to take on racism in existing death penalty regimes without doing so explicitly. Since *Furman*, the justice system has struggled, although unsuccessfully, to transform the death penalty process to one that is determined by rules rather than race.

As the times and the justices changed, the Supreme Court stopped attempting to eradicate racism from the process. The Court rejected the statistical analysis in *McCleskey v. Kemp* (1987) that undergirded the NAACP Legal Defense Fund's argument that widespread racial discrimination still existed in the practice of the death penalty. The Court gave up on the work it began in *Furman* and instead asserted that "apparent disparities in sentencing are an inevitable part of our criminal justice system."[6] In an internal memorandum on *McCleskey*, Justice Antonin Scalia wrote, "The unconstitutional operation of irrational sympathies and antipathies, including racial, upon jury decisions and (hence) prosecutorial decisions is real, acknowledged in the decisions of this court, and ineradicable."[7]

When evidence of discrimination arose in the context of a specific case, it would be remedied, but doing away with wide-scale racial discrimination was beyond the Court's reach. *McCleskey* set up decades of continued racial disparity and decreasing oversight by federal courts. Although the written law sees the current death penalty regimes as distinct from their discriminatory origins, racial disparities in capital sentences persist, and social scientists have painstakingly demonstrated the continuing influence of race in the administration of the death penalty.[8]

Yet little attention has been paid to how those who were and continue to be disproportionately subject to this policy have viewed the progression from Wells-Barnett's unwritten law of lynching to written law that accepts levels of discrimination. In the analysis that follows, I, like the Supreme Court, move away from systemic critiques, but not in capitulation to the view that racism is irremediable. Instead, I turn to how historical and contemporary systemic inequities are interpreted and understood by African Americans today.

I began this project by asking which aspects of African Americans' beliefs and identity influence their position on the death penalty in light of changes in the political landscape in the post–Civil Rights period. This question was prompted by scholarship chronicling the increasing importance of religion and religious actors in American political discourse generally and by early observations of the public discussions of the execution of Karla Faye Tucker in the state of Texas. The image of George W. Bush standing on the steps of the Texas capital announcing that he was born again and had consulted his God about the execution of Tucker is representative of the way religion and politics have emerged in conservative politics. Many of the figures—religious and secular—that emerged in the debate over the execution of Tucker made moral claims that they argued were grounded in a "true" reading of Christianity and its religious commitments.

I was extremely curious about how this case and the evolving political grammar—the basic language or system of knowledge for communicating ideas of justice, politics, and political belonging—that incorporated religion were playing among African Americans. By standard measures of religiosity, African Americans are more religious than whites and religious Blacks are more likely to engage in political activity.[9] Since its inception, the Black church has been a political institution, while white evangelicals have begun only recently to use churches as political bases. However, even with these levels of religiosity, racial identity and racial solidarity continue to be the primary arbiter of African American political preferences. As a result, sorting out themes of faith and inequality in public discourse is a task that involves studying intersections as well as divergences.

In the current atmosphere of conservative religious values, racial discrimination, and political posturing, African Americans must make political sense of the death penalty. African Americans must process the external debate in the contexts of the discussion and preferences within the Black community and their individual policy preferences. I used various sites to uncover common discussions and themes about this form of punishment, religion, race, and African Americans' relationship to the state and their sense of political belonging. Throughout this work, I use the term "political belonging" in place of and alongside terms such as "inclusion" and "citizenship." Inclusion and citizenship are terms that by their very definition are determined and policed by the state. There are strong persuasive examples of how African Americans have greater access to and inclusion in the privileges of citizenship than they did before the legislative successes of the Civil Rights Movement, but that access has been uneven across the Black community. African Americans have not always felt as if they fit or that their presence was welcomed. Whether one feels a sense of belonging is defined by the self, or, in the collectivist ideology of Black politics, it is defined by the selves rather than by the state.

The death penalty provides very fertile ground for analyzing political belonging, religious attitudes, and the politics of race. Denise, the 19-year-old focus group participant who is quoted in the chapter epigraph, was born in 1985 and never lived under Jim Crow or its violence. So when a person as young as Denise compares the contemporary practice of lethal injection to the past violence of lynching, it exposes the continuity of African American opinion on the death penalty. If African Americans see the death penalty as part of an unbroken thread of discrimination, this suggests that neither their perception of progress in the racial climate nor religious appeals mitigate or alter their lived experiences of racial and legal inequality. It is clear that African Americans continue to ground their views of equality in the rhetoric of American democracy, but what remains an open question is whether, like Wells-Barnett, they continue to see a departure from the constitutional guarantees of American citizenship in the way the death penalty is applied.

Like any project on state violence, the book also speaks to the broader issue of state power. The legitimacy of state violence has long been a concern of political scientists, but the continued use of capital punishment in a country that considers itself a model of democracy and political sophistication raises fundamental questions about the contemporary meaning of state violence and the relationship between the state and a community that frequently finds itself the object of that violence. During the late nineteenth century, the death penalty was used to police racial boundaries in the political uncertainty created by the emancipation of Blacks from chattel slavery. The racial motives of the past are no longer as explicit as they were during the political and legal activism of the 1960s. But changes in formal legal and political discourse do not necessarily translate to changes in the politics and perceptions of non-elite citizens. The toleration of greater violence against particular communities reveals both the character of a society and the state it has created and the position of those communities relative to the state and others within the society.

This work focuses specifically on the contemporary narratives of the death penalty among African Americans in the Houston metropolitan area and the state of Texas. No community has had more experience with this form of punishment. Since the reinstatement of executions in the late 1970s, nearly 25 percent of the people of the 254 people who have been executed in Texas were convicted in this one county. Harris County—the main county covered by the city of Houston—sends more convicted murderers to death row than most states. This county ranks third behind all of Virginia and the rest of Texas in number of executions. Studies have shown that the majority of death cases come from only 2 percent of counties nationwide.[10] The high rate of capital sentences and convictions in Harris County has resulted in a population that is profoundly familiar with the death penalty and a location where the death penalty is a meaningful part of the criminal justice system. Houston is both structurally and geographically important. The death chamber is a little more than an hour away in Huntsville, making Houston media outlets a primary source of execution coverage statewide. The coincidence of large populations of racial minorities, the site of executions, and the frequency with which the prosecutor's office seeks capital convictions make this a compelling, and arguably unique, location for this study.

The focus on this location allows for analysis of sources that are often underutilized in the study of this community and these subjects. The chapters use media accounts, case analysis, and survey and focus group data. I chose an interdisciplinary approach not only to provide a more thorough picture of African Americans' thinking on the death penalty and issues tangential to it such as equality, gender, and political belonging in post–Civil Rights Movement America but also because the topic forces one to use an interdisciplinary lens. African Americans, like Denise, link history and contemporary death penalty politics together. This long view of the death penalty held by African Americans requires an analysis that draws from history, political science, various theories of race and religion, and the role of memory in constructing policy preferences.

The link between the death penalty and citizenship (as traditionally understood) or political belonging was not a significant part of the book originally. Yet the continuing importance of the death penalty as a metric African Americans in Texas use to measure the value the state places on their collective lives and those of their racial kin makes citizenship and political belonging significant analytical frames in this work. A unifying finding from the various data sources is the persistence of the death penalty in defining groups and defining for groups their location within the society.

The analysis of the cases of Karla Faye Tucker and Gary Graham in chapter 1 serves as an introduction to the complicated public debate over the death penalty in Texas and the role of race and religion in shaping that debate. The cases of Tucker and Graham provide an interesting analytical lens because of the media and political attention they garnered and the legal positioning of each in relation to that attention. The race and gender differences between Tucker, a white woman, and Graham, a Black man, provide a good place to begin our analysis of the role of race and religion in contemporary narratives of the death penalty. These cases point to the connections between specific and abstract views on the death penalty, as well as how race, gender, and religion impacted the outcome of the cases.

The first chapter focuses largely on the discourse of religious and political elites, both Black and white, about these cases and the narratives the inmates themselves used. The data for this chapter are largely media accounts from mainstream local and national newspapers, national African American publications, and archived copies of African American newspapers published in the Houston metropolitan area. The comparison of Tucker and Graham in media accounts and the focus groups I discuss in later chapters highlight not only the legal importance of innocence to African Americans but also how the politics of race and gender affect the value assigned to certain narratives of innocence over others for African Americans.

Chapter 2 assesses views African Americans express on the death penalty in the highly structured space of capital jury selection. Jury participation is important because it is where ordinary citizens put their feet to the fire and make determinations about whether the death penalty should be applied against a particular defendant. Death penalty cases have even greater requirements for jury participation; in such cases, the jury selection process includes investigating attitudes on the death penalty and, in some instances, race. The reality of capital juries in Texas and other jurisdictions with capital punishment is that very few African Americans are seated and the most important mechanisms preventing their participation are peremptory challenges. I focus on the responses of jurors and prosecutors in *Batson* hearings—a procedure during voir dire to determine whether peremptory challenges are racially motivated—to examine how the state acts as a gatekeeper to disproportionately prevent Blacks from entering the jury box. I have long been intrigued by *Batson* hearings. The fascination stems from the important legal, and, I think, political moment they represent in which the state has to, in the very instant, explain how it is not discriminating against a person based on race.

Subsequent chapters shift the analysis of the role of race, religion, and citizenship/political belonging to the collective and individual views of African Americans in the unmoderated space of surveys and racially homogenous focus groups. Chapter 3 utilizes data from the Houston Area Survey (HAS) to demonstrate how surveys may have missed the nuances of African Americans' position on the death penalty. The HAS is an annual survey of Houston residents that began in 1982, at the same time that Texas resumed executions after the Supreme Court upheld the revised death penalty statutes written in response to *Furman*. This chapter explores the theories that have emerged from the broader literature on African American public opinion, a population with significant exposure to the death penalty. The literature posits that views on capital punishment, like other aspects of the criminal justice system, are driven by sentiments of linked fate, but the prediction of the impact of religious attitudes on capital punishment is unclear. The HAS includes several questions on religion and perceptions of discrimination that make it possible to explore how attitudes about the death penalty relate to these variables. All prior studies have shown that Blacks are less supportive of the death penalty than whites, and the data from the HAS reaffirms this finding. However, this finding tells little about the sentiments that underlie the racial differences. This chapter lays a descriptive backdrop for the opinions offered in the focus group data and offers some discussion of the benefits and limitations of the HAS findings.

Chapters 4 and 5 both analyze focus group data I gathered in the Houston metropolitan area. I asked adult African Americans about their perspectives on the death penalty and on the influence of religion on their views. I had planned to ask the participants about their views on the Tucker and Graham cases, but in each group one or both of the cases were raised by the participants. Chapter 4 analyzes what Benjamin Steiner has called the "folk knowledge" of African Americans on the death penalty. According to Steiner, folk knowledge is "the everyday, taken-for-granted understandings and beliefs that shape people's perceptions, actions, and reactions to events and situations."[11] Folk knowledge is important to understanding individual stances on the death penalty because the perceptions of crime and punishment that citizens carry with them can have legal and political consequences. (Chapter 2 provides examples of an instance where preconceived notions impacted legal proceedings.) Often, according to Steiner, this community common sense on the death penalty includes misconceptions and incorrect information. However flawed it may be, this folk knowledge becomes the script by which the state and citizens make sense of the death penalty. Chapter 4, through focus group discussions, maps out the script or scripts among African Americans about the death penalty.

Chapter 5 analyzes the focus group responses to questions about aspects of gender, racial equality, and other aspects of citizenship, such as voting. It begins with theories of democratic inclusion and the connection of these theories to notions of justice. This chapter moves beyond simple questions of support or opposition to the death penalty and looks at how the death penalty interacts with existing theories of Black political preferences and participation such as linked fate. Linked fate is the idea that the political behavior of African Americans is significantly influenced by their perceptions that the plight of other African Americans is intertwined with their own—that their fates are linked. I also explore how the respondents' views on the death penalty frame their connection to larger American society.

The conclusion is a discussion of the findings of the research and how Blacks' perspectives on the death penalty reveal continued contestations for full inclusion in the American political community. The injustices of the death penalty—perceived or actual—distort the meanings of justice and rule of law for African Americans. Where the Supreme Court sees a bright line between the racially biased administration of the death penalty prior to the 1970s and today, African Americans in Texas have not been able see the distinction. Justice, fairness, and inclusion are central to the foundational texts of the United States. The conclusion offers some answers about the impact of race on the shared values and historical legacy of the United States.

I

Can the Souls of Black Folk Be Redeemed? Race, Religion, and the Politics of Public Appeals for Salvation from the Execution Chamber

If you believe in it for one, you believe in it for everybody.
If you don't believe in it, don't believe in it for anybody.
—KARLA FAYE TUCKER[1]

My responsibility is to make sure our laws are enforced
fairly and evenly without preference or special treatment.
—GOVERNOR GEORGE W. BUSH ON HIS REFUSAL TO
GRANT A REPRIEVE TO KARLA FAYE TUCKER[2]

THE FIRST TIME I heard the name Gary Graham, I was standing in the washateria at Prairie View A&M University in the early 1990s. Prairie View is a historically Black land grant university located northwest of Houston that mostly produces teachers and engineers. Since it opened its doors at the end of Reconstruction, it has been a place where young Black people from rural and urban communities have met to be educated in the professions and in the politics of respectability or resistance, depending on the times. In the midst of sorting laundry, I heard the name of a man whose significance would not be known to me until this project. A student whose name I can no longer recall was walking from person to person asking them to call the governor's office to stop the execution of an innocent Black man named Gary Graham. Some were not interested, but others went to the pay phone and dialed the number. I was one of the latter. As I read from a photocopied script, clearly marred from handling, I had my first encounter with race and the politics of the death penalty in Texas. Graham was spared that time, but like many on Texas death row, his life would end at the hands of the state.

This event returned to me as I began to consider whether moral transformation, specifically religious transformation, has legal and political meaning. Because of the research site—Harris County, Texas—the meaning of the death penalty is not limited to the symbolic, as it might be in other states that rarely execute offenders. The relatively high number of executions in Texas in recent years makes the death penalty a lived reality for this state's citizens. The cases of Karla Faye Tucker and Gary Graham show two distinct ways how the death penalty, religion, and race ignited an unprecedented public debate about the death penalty in Texas. These two cases represent somewhat opposing possibilities for understanding contemporary narratives of the death penalty. Both cases demonstrate how capital punishment extends beyond a trial and an execution. For most of the seventy or more people who were executed in the two years between the deaths of Tucker and Graham, there was little more than a blurb on an inside page in the big-city papers. But these two cases broke rank and captured the attention of individual citizens, the media, and political and religious elites, although most clearly by the racial polarization of their supporters.

Looking at these cases can be like looking into a kaleidoscope. The image is complicated, and perceiving which color is the most intense or prominent can be challenging and difficult at any moment. As one looks at the Tucker and Graham cases through a kaleidoscope of race, gender, and religion, the challenge is to deconstruct which of these aspects of their lives colors the politics of their cases most intensely. These two cases are useful for identifying the critical intersections of race and gender in current death penalty narratives and their connection to past justifications for the death penalty. Working to untangle the continuing impact of race and gender also helps us understand how an increased reliance on religious narratives is shaping the larger public debate.

Karla Faye Tucker's quote at the beginning of this chapter seems to be a reasonable claim about how the logic of individual opinions on the death penalty should operate from one case to the next. However, some of arguments made by those supporters who came forward to ask for mercy for Tucker contradict the idea that the identity of the defendant has no bearing on whether one supports or opposes the death penalty. One commentator objected to the fact that people were emphasizing that Tucker was a woman instead of emphasizing what she perceived to be the more important issue—the inherent evil of capital punishment. "The protester who supported her clemency because of her religious conversion will most likely not be there when the next inmate is walked to the death chamber," that commentator predicted.[3] She was partially correct.

Graham, whose execution in 2000 followed Tucker's by almost two years, was the 222nd person to be executed in Texas since 1982, when the brief moratorium after the *Furman* decision was lifted. Racial disparities make the issue of the death penalty even more of a reality for the African American community in Texas, especially those who live in Harris County, where 119 defendants have been executed since 1982.[4] Although this work focuses specifically on the death penalty, all of the data I draw on contain explicit and implicit critiques of the broader relationship between African Americans and the criminal justice system.

The amount of public debate in Texas and across the nation about the appeals and eventual execution of Gary Graham was exceeded only by the amount of debate over the execution of Karla Faye Tucker. Graham and Tucker offer a fragile and problematic dichotomy because of differences in their identities and the fact that Tucker admitted her guilt while Graham insisted he was innocent. We begin with a description of the two cases.

Gary Graham

I would like to say that I did not kill Bobby Lambert. That I'm an innocent black man that is being murdered. This is a lynching that is happening in America tonight. . . . We must do everything we can to outlaw legal lynching in America.

—GARY GRAHAM[5]

Graham, an African American man, was convicted of killing Bobby Lambert, a white man, on the night of May 13, 1981, in the parking lot of a Safeway.[6] A witness named Bernadine Skillern testified at trial that she saw Graham murder Lambert in the grocery store parking lot while she waited in her car for her daughter, who was shopping inside.[7] Skillern was the only one of seven possible witnesses who could identify Graham as the killer, making her testimony critical to the prosecution's case. Despite suggestions by some that she should retract her statements (and she was harassed for not doing so), Skillern remained steadfast in her contention that Graham was the man she saw shoot and kill Lambert.

At the time the Lambert killing took place, Graham was on what newspaper reports described as a seven-day robbery spree. Even though he "pled guilty to 10 other armed robberies in the same week," Gary Graham consistently claimed that he was innocent of the murder of Lambert.[8] The robberies included two nonfatal shootings (one of the victims lost his leg) and the rape of and multiple sexual assaults on a 59-year-old woman.[9] The rape is what actually led to Graham's eventual capture.[10] Seven days after Lambert was killed, Graham approached a taxi driver and asked to be driven to an apartment complex. After the driver took Graham to his destination, he pulled a gun and raped her. Afraid that she would be murdered and never found if she was taken to an unfamiliar location, she convinced Graham to take her to her own apartment. The police arrested Graham as he was passed out in her bed. Graham pled guilty to the robberies and was sentenced to 20 years. Police then noticed that Graham *fit the description* of the perpetrator in the Lambert case and began questioning witnesses from the Safeway that night.

Much of the controversy in the Graham case focused on flaws in the handling of Graham's original trial rather than on the character of Graham himself. Graham's lawyers failed to call to the stand the six other witnesses from the grocery store who could not pick Graham from a photo array, and they failed to call alibi witnesses. They did not call any witnesses during the entire guilt-or-innocence phase of the trial.[11] During the punishment phase, the prosecution called every person Graham had victimized in the robbery spree, including the taxi driver, to testify. The defense called two witnesses, Graham's grandmother and stepfather. Both testified that Graham was respectful. Graham's grandmother, who had cared for him from the time he was three until he was ten, said "He loved the lord, you know."[12] These recollections, which were presented as mitigation evidence, are a hard sell, to say the least, in light of the parade of brutality the prosecutor marshaled.

Gary Graham, who was 39 when he was executed, was convicted of capital murder at age 17.[13] Like Karla Faye Tucker, Graham had a troubled youth. In Graham's case, that youth ended with the perpetration of at least 21 violent crimes and his conviction for murder.[14] Graham not only *fit the description* of the perpetrator of the particular crime for which he was convicted, he also fits the description of what the average American thinks of as a capital murderer—young, Black, male, violent, and a person with previous criminal offenses.[15]

While on death row, Graham had a transformative spiritual experience, although the exact nature of Graham's transformation is unclear from media accounts. Unlike the rich description of Tucker and her transformation, which I discuss later, there is very little documentation of Graham's conversion. When I surveyed national newspaper and magazine articles, for instance, I found many mentions that Graham had changed his name but only one mention of when or why he did so.[16] He became Shaka Sankofa, although legal documents, while acknowledging that his name was changed, continued to refer to him as Graham "for consistency."[17] The fact that descriptions of Graham as a whole person are so few is actually quite surprising, considering the level of attention paid to the case in Houston and across the nation. We are left with major gaps in the story of the person Graham became once he was on death row.

The only discussions of Graham as a transformed person came from Black sources.[18] For instance, the *Houston Defender*, one of two Black newspapers in Houston, was the only source to report the date (1995) and the reason (as a tribute to his African roots) for Graham's name change.[19] Black sources also consistently refer to Graham's new name in articles thereafter. The narratives that Black sources presented offered more than the reasoning behind the adoption of a new name. In an article in *Essence*, a magazine for African American women, Ashanti Chimurenga, a lawyer for Amnesty International who later befriended Graham, quotes Graham describing himself as "a seventeen-year-old young kid who didn't have much of a social conscience."[20] In the same piece, she characterized the Graham on death row as having "overcome a cycle of pain stemming from childhood abuse and neglect that led to adolescent drug addiction and violence."[21]

This characterization of Graham links him to the Black community's shared experience of *fitting the description* of a wide variety of pathologies, especially criminal behavior.[22] As early as his first execution date in 1993, for instance, the Geto Boys, a local rap group with national notoriety, and several other local Black artists began holding benefit concerts for the Gary Graham Justice Coalition. A representative for the coalition said, "We are trying to unite the youth through this effort and raise their consciousness of the situation. . . . The youths will listen to rappers, and we hope to make them aware of what's going on in the judicial system."[23]

Part of the intense interest in Graham within the African American community is a sense of kinship with Graham's precarious relationship to the state. That relationship ended for Graham with his execution on June 22, 2000. Unlike most funerals of executed inmates, Gary Graham's funeral was attended by a large number of people. As one member of the largely Black crowd said, explaining the enormous turnout for Graham's funeral, "There's a lot of us didn't know him personally, but it was like we have seen over the years how innocent people, especially blacks, have been convicted of crimes they weren't guilty of."[24]

At the local level, Graham became a kind of Every Black Man, representing the abuses the Black community experienced at the hands of the criminal justice system. Mainstream news accounts offer nothing that allows the reader to see beyond Graham's crime, rendering him as invisible as the thousands of other young Black men ensnared in the criminal justice system. But Graham asserted that he had a message for young, incarcerated Blacks, a message that they, like him, had the potential to transform "into a force that could uplift mind, spirit, and soul."[25]

The increasing viability of George W. Bush's presidential bid at this time swept Graham and his case up in the media circus that accompanies campaigns. Like Willie Horton in an earlier presidential year, Graham's image became blurred by the need to underline candidate Bush's tough-on-crime attitude. Unlike the Horton ads, which the left assailed because of the implicit racial appeal, the call to save Graham became a tool of the left to embarrass Bush on his death penalty record as governor of Texas.

Local Black activists lobbying for relief in the Graham case were aware of the importance of the death penalty in the presidential campaign. Robert Muhammad, the regional representative of the Nation of Islam for the Southwest, was quoted as saying at a rally in support of Graham, "Don't forget the road to the White House goes through Huntsville."[26] However, the attention to Graham cannot be read simply as electioneering. Calls to stop the execution came from a broad cross-section of national leaders and celebrities such as Danny Glover and Kenny Rogers, figures who held no direct ties to politics.[27] Local Black clergy and Reverend Joseph Fiorenza, the bishop of the Houston-Galveston Diocese, formed another significant group of advocates. Many members of this group had been advocates for Graham through several execution dates. For example, Reverend Jew Don Boney, a minister and activist who would later become a member of the Houston City Council, led the local campaign to save Graham and asked "the spiritual leadership of the community" to pray for and contribute their influence to Graham's cause.[28] Boney argued that "there is a power in the soul force, and that's the kind of power we were trying to exert."[29] At a rally to protest one of the first of Graham's execution dates, Reverend James Dixon, pastor of one of the largest Black Baptist churches in the city, responded to claims that the mid-90 temperatures of the Houston summer made the timing of the rally less than ideal with the statement that "we will sweat for justice."[30]

However, none of these figures could match the media whirlwind associated with Reverends Jesse Jackson and Al Sharpton, who went to Texas to show their support for Graham at what would be his final execution date.

Jackson and Sharpton brought their public notoriety and political clout to the national media campaign, and both spoke at Graham's funeral. The national media configures the dual role of Black ministers as political and religious leaders in the Black community to make them primarily political figures.[31] Unlike Jerry Falwell and Pat Robertson, who brought an aura of (or at the least a façade of) religion and morality when they entered the political fray, Jackson's and Sharpton's identities as religious figures are limited by the prevailing perception of them as primarily political. These limitations also obscure the meaning of religion in the issue at hand. The presence of Sharpton and Jackson, who were frequently mentioned and who were both present at Graham's execution, did not foment any greater attention to religion or to what it was about Graham that warranted their attention. Thus, in Graham's case, religion was subsumed by political considerations in media coverage and Graham and his own religious beliefs were made virtually invisible. This contrasts strongly with what happened in Karla Tucker's case. When Jerry Falwell and Pat Robertson became advocates for sparing her life, a religious spotlight was thrown on Karla Tucker's case and on Karla herself.

The absence of Graham's humanity and the silence about his transformation in mainstream narratives is relevant as we take up the question of how African Americans make sense of the death penalty. In the national media, Graham and his claims of innocence become the background to the main narrative, which was that a murderer was unrepentant. A ready example is the headline in the mainstream press on the day the Geto Boys announced a benefit for Graham: "Local Rappers Plan Concert to Support Murderer Graham."[32]

Karla Faye Tucker

Yes sir, I would like to say to all of you—the Thornton family and Jerry Dean's family—that I am so sorry. I hope God will give you peace with this. . . . I love you all very much. I am going face to face with Jesus now.

—KARLA FAYE TUCKER[33]

The life of Karla Faye Tucker had some of the same tragic themes as Graham's life. Like many of those who have shared her fate in the Texas death chamber and those who continue to reside on death row, she had a dysfunctional childhood, struggled with substance abuse, and was involved in previous crimes before the one that landed her on death row. Her story is simultaneously no different from and totally different from Graham's. The most obvious distinctions are that she was a woman and she was white. Although there is a longer history of executing women in this country than many might guess, the execution of women is still a rarity, even in Texas.[34]

When the author Beverly Lowry met Tucker for the first time, after Tucker had been on death row for nearly five years, her first impression was that "she seemed more like maybe, 13, a transitional girl."[35] This is not the description we expect of someone who was guilty of murdering two people with a pickaxe and who bragged to friends that she experienced sexual pleasure while doing so.[36] By the end of Tucker's life, no one could reconcile the small, beautiful young woman whose conversation was laced with religious praise to the individual who was guilty of the brutal acts she never denied committing.[37] Tucker's admission of guilt was as adamant as Graham's claim of innocence.

On June 12, 1983, Karla Faye Tucker and her accomplice, Daniel Ryan Garrett, entered the home of Jerry Lynn Dean while he and a woman lay sleeping. Tucker bludgeoned both to death with a pickaxe, which she left lodged in the woman's chest.[38] Tucker and Garret would likely not have been caught, but they boasted about the crime to friends. This was the culmination of an extremely troubled life. Tucker had a history of drug use that dated back to preadolescence.[39] By the time she was 14, she had been on the road with rock bands and her mother had encouraged her to become a prostitute.[40] At 23, she was on death row. Charley Davidson, the chief prosecutor of Daniel Ryan Garrett, remembered "seeing [Tucker] . . . and having the gut reaction that she was the embodiment of evil."[41] But after Tucker's spiritual transformation, Davidson stated, "The Karla Tucker who remains on death row is a completely different person who, in my opinion, is not capable of those atrocities."[42]

Davidson's impression of the incarcerated Tucker reflects the view of many of those who lobbied for Tucker's life to be spared. It was as if the Karla Faye Tucker who had lived in the free world was a completely distinct person from the affable woman on death row. On death row, Karla Faye was born again and married a prison minister, Dana Brown.[43] But her astonishing rehabilitation was no salvation from the Texas death chamber. Governor George W. Bush denied her request for a 30-day reprieve, citing his own spiritual reasons.[44] At the press conference announcing his denial, he explained:

Like many touched by this case, I have sought guidance through prayer. . . . I have concluded judgments about the heart and soul of an individual on death row are best left to a higher authority. . . . May God bless Karla Faye Tucker, and may God bless her victims and their families.[45]

Although religion clearly influenced the decision-making of both the governor and Tucker's supporters, the role of religion in this case was not as simple as two sides with differing religious views. It is worthwhile to note that Tucker made an appeal that her life should be spared based on her transformation to a governor who would later parade his own "born-again" experience and state that its impact "made him fit to assume state, national and international leadership."[46] Tucker and Governor Bush used religion to articulate divergent political perspectives. In the end, the legal and political will was aligned with the governor's perspective and Karla Faye Tucker was executed on February 3, 1998, at the age of 39.[47]

In the national media, the Tucker story was one of transformation. Tucker preached that her faith in Jesus had cleansed her soul, but her personal transformation cleansed the perception of her in the public as well. Although her life was not spared, for many her moral reputation was repaired by her renewed dedication to Christianity. The new Karla that Donaldson—the prosecutor quoted above—and the rest of viewing public observed made it very difficult to position her as the "other," as happens in many narratives of death row inmates.[48] One reporter described her as follows:

> Her peculiar little person was all contradiction. She was sunny and nice, and she gave you the creeps. She was an innocent who was a guilty criminal. She was evil, and she was embraced by religious leaders who declared she was good.[49]

Tucker's transformation and her execution were by far the most debated and watched issues in recent Texas and U.S. history. They reveal important racial and gender connotations that were captured in accounts of this case. The high visibility of Tucker's case is anomalous; most death row inmates are invisible. Although religion was central to Tucker's personal metamorphosis and the public reception of the Karla Faye that emerged, so were her race and gender. Tucker was not the first inmate on death row to experience a religious conversion, but she was the first white woman to be executed in Texas history.[50] In striking contrast to the mono-dimensional representation of Graham, the descriptions of Tucker in the media accounts are rich and personal. These descriptions provide the reader with a strong sense of her humanity and the difficulty reporters had with reconciling it with her crime.

We know what she looked like, that she was attractive and young and feminine. Unlike Gary Graham, Tucker was described as the opposite of someone who *fits the description*. There is rarely any mention of her race or its impact in her case. We know the particulars of her crime. She killed two people with a pickaxe and experienced sexual pleasure while doing so, but the reader is told nothing of the proceedings in which she was convicted. Articles on Tucker all inevitably mention her appearance, the pickaxe, and that she was born again. But these are just supporting facts for the articulation of the central story, Tucker's transformation. Everything becomes background to the story of the pretty young woman who murdered two people with a pickaxe and found Jesus on death row. At the end of the day, Tucker was just a vehicle for the narrative that someone who is young, pretty, white, Christian, and female should not be in the reach of the executioner.

Are These the Models? The Benefit of Looking at Concrete Cases

The Graham and Tucker cases present models of how death row inmates may, at least in the public sphere, rehabilitate themselves with religion. Looking at concrete cases is beneficial in spite of profound differences among the cases of death row inmates. I see the Tucker and Graham cases as opposing ends of a spectrum of possibilities of how religion may extend historical narratives about race and gender into the present. Even though the majority of accounts took little note of Tucker's gender and even less of her race, these silences are important to consider relative to accounts of Graham, who, like the majority of death row inmates, was male and a racial minority. The meaning of masculinity, especially Black masculinity, is very different from the gender norms that may have aided the public's acceptance of Tucker's transformation. However, analyzing these cases simultaneously is important because they have fueled the contemporary debate over the death penalty in Texas.

In their analysis of "the power of concrete cases," Sam Gross and Phoebe Ellsworth start with Thurgood Marshall's opinion of the requirements for the constitutional death penalty the regime articulated in *Furman v.* Georgia (1972) would create. Marshall wrote in *Furman* that the constitutionality of the death penalty would be determined by "whether people who were fully informed as to the purposes of the [death penalty] and its liabilities would find the penalty shocking, unjust, and unacceptable."[51] Marshall argued that since the average American knows little to nothing about the actual operation of the death penalty, the resulting state of affairs is "indifference and ignorance."[52]

Gross and Ellsworth argue that this hypothesis has been largely proven incorrect, as "surveys repeatedly show that many Americans believe that the death penalty does not deter murder, that it is administered unfairly and it is used in a manner that discriminates against minorities and poor people—but they support it nonetheless."[53] However, Marshall was partially correct that "in the context of concrete cases, learning about the operation of capital punishment in practice does sometimes shock people's conscience and offend their sense of justice."[54]

The idea that concrete cases viewed in a particular context can influence existing attitudes about the death penalty—even though Gross and Ellsworth were referring to the recent attention given to innocent defendants who had been released from death row on the basis of DNA evidence—argues for a combined analysis of the Graham and Tucker cases in a study of the death penalty among African Americans in Texas.[55] The cases have similarities that make them particularly useful in this discussion. Graham and Tucker were executed within two years of each other and were convicted in the same jurisdiction. The debate over the fairness of their executions played out with the same governor and district attorney and in similar political climates. In addition, the victims in both cases included white men.

These cases also provide a modern window into the historical narratives this project draws upon, the history of and inextricable link between gender and race in the Jim Crow South. The prevailing justification for lynching and executing Black men from the time of emancipation well into the twentieth century was the protection of "virtuous white women." The Supreme Court removed this justification for discriminatory state killing by finding the imposition of the death penalty for rape unconstitutional in *Coker v. Georgia* (1977). However, I argue that the history of Texas and the South generally warrants an examination of race and gender in tandem because these issues arise in cases in this century as well. The treatment of Blacks in the criminal justice system continues to be understood by Blacks, and by social scientists, in relation to the treatment of whites; this is another reason that it makes sense to compare the cases of Graham and Tucker, the two most visible cases in recent years.

The asymmetry of the Tucker and Graham cases points to the racial and gender contradictions embedded in the differing ways religion is woven into these narratives. Karla Faye Tucker and the attention given her case ignited a public debate in a state where regular executions were and remain the order of the day; this debate reached a fevered pitch when the debate over the execution of Gary Graham coincided with the presidential campaign of George W. Bush. Texas continues to be the epicenter of the death penalty. The consistently high level of executions and the state's willingness to take actions that go against emerging trends in this area of law have kept Texas at the center of the death penalty debate beyond the notoriety over these two cases.[56]

It is not easy to predict which capital case will become a cause célèbre. Although Tucker and Graham were able to arrest the public's attention, many death row inmates are invisible to anyone but the state penal institution and the legal system. Though I do not analyze legal advocates and anti–death penalty organizations in this project, I think their role must be noted. Capital defense lawyers fall into a category of lawyers that Austin Sarat calls "cause lawyers."[57] Lawyers, celebrities, and other associates participated in the campaigns to save Tucker and Graham's lives just as much as Karla and Gary themselves did. The analysis that follows describes the narratives that brought Tucker and Graham's cases to visibility, but it also looks at how those who were associated with them and their cases used Tucker and Graham's social and legal positions to advance both their individual interests and the "cause" of ending the death penalty more generally.

At the time of Tucker's impending execution and two years before the execution of Graham, one reporter described the impact of the frequent use of capital punishment on Texas residents: "Since Texas resumed executions in 1982, 145 people have died, and we hardly notice anymore. . . . The following day, the reports will probably tell more about what they ordered for a last meal than about their lives, because Texas executions have become so common."[58] The controversy surrounding Graham and Tucker disrupted the pattern this reporter articulates as the norm. These cases are anomalous in relation to the vast majority of cases of Texas death row inmates. Concrete cases do not necessarily need to be representative to affect the public's perception of the death penalty. For instance, death row inmates exonerated due to DNA evidence represent only about 10 percent of the total persons who are freed, despite public perception to the contrary. The small number and lack of representativeness of DNA-innocence cases has not countered the current fascination with this technology and the way it has undermined the legitimacy of the death penalty. Similarly, although the Graham and Tucker cases are arguably not representative of the vast majority of Texas death penalty cases, that does not diminish their impact as concrete cases that have reshaped the debate. In fact, the Graham and Tucker cases are quite revealing of the way religion operates in the context of contemporary racial inequality.

Gross and Ellsworth raise one caveat about the influence of concrete cases that serves as a caution as I move forward. They ask, "Would many Americans care if they learned that a death row inmate who was in fact guilty of a vicious multiple murder had a defense attorney who never talked to him, or a prosecutor who lied, or was arrested because of his race?"[59] The Graham and Tucker cases demonstrate that most Americans do not care in any systematic way if the processes that result in guilty people receiving the death penalty are flawed *but* that in particular instances they may. In the Houston area, where the deaths of Graham and Tucker would have been nothing out of the ordinary, people cared.

The Difficulty in Comparing These Cases

I believe it is worth addressing the major arguments against comparing Graham and Tucker's cases and understanding how those arguments, if reframed, may actually contribute to the analysis.

Differences in Gender and/or Race

Karla Faye Tucker was a white woman, Gary Graham a Black man. This is an obvious truth about the identity of these people, but what is not obvious is how these differences affected the public debate over their executions. The majority of accounts of the Tucker case, for instance, tend to focus on her gender and her miraculous transformation. The first argument against comparing the Tucker and Graham cases is that the social norms that influence public support for or disapproval of execution are different for men and women. I agree with that argument, but these norms do not exist in isolation. They are part of a larger narrative that ascribes different values to the lives of men and women and Blacks and whites. In the context of the southern historical narrative, race and gender cannot be separated, especially when one speaks of white women, Black men, and the death penalty.

Historians have documented the need to understand the history of race and gender in the post-emancipation South as systems of oppression that operated in tandem. For example, in her work on women and southern politics, *Gender and Jim Crow: Women and the Politics of White Supremacy in South Carolina, 1896–1920*, Glenda Gilmore chronicles her realization that "gender and race were no less intertwined in men's politics than they were in women's" in the South.[60] Gilmore argues that "naturaliz[ing] white women's purity" was as much a part of the southern white supremacist project as "naturaliz[ing] black men's impurity."[61] The need to maintain the racial order meant upholding the purity of white women at all costs. The incontrovertible accusation of rape by white women meant sure and swift death for most accused Blacks, through both legal and extralegal means.

Although no one can be executed for rape under current law, there continues to be a high correlation between the race of the victim and the race of the defendant and the likelihood of conviction. Black offenders who murder white victims in Texas continue to be significantly more likely to receive the death penalty than defendants of other categories who are convicted of capital murder.[62] At this point, I make no arguments about a relationship between the past discrimination that led to the Jim Crow criminal justice system and current racial disparities. I only suggest that we think about these cases together in light of the past linkages between the value of white women and the lack of value of Black men and the perpetuation of this value system through the criminal justice system.

In fact, studies of contemporary Black masculinity also allude to the positioning of African American men, especially young African American men, as problematic, to say the least, within and outside of the Black community. They are largely seen as a danger. A litany of negative statistics is frequently offered to justify the pervasiveness of the perception of African American men as "criminal." The death penalty is a small and extremely meaningful part of a larger criminal justice system that Patricia Hill Collins argues was developed in the post–Civil War period "to curtail the citizenship rights of African American men."[63] In *Black Sexual Politics*, Collins argues that "because the American public routinely perceives African American men as actual or potential criminals," the incarceration and execution of Black men has become normalized. Thus, the execution of Graham was business as usual, but the execution of Tucker was extraordinary. Within the hierarchy of race and gender in the United States, and, to a more heightened level, in the South, Tucker was not within the category of people who are *normally* executed. She did not *fit the description*.

The gender analysis that accompanied the Tucker case tended to ignore race, instead focusing on how she was treated compared to how men are treated in the criminal justice system.[64] Because of the historical entanglement of race and gender in the South, analysis of the Tucker and Graham cases must look at the combined influence of gender and race on the disposition of their cases. Past studies have tended to look at gender without attention to race or at race without attention to gender. One only has to look at the tremendous focus on Tucker's appearance to see why isolated analysis of these factors is incomplete. Coverage of the Tucker case largely overlooked the role her whiteness played in the effort to save her life and focused instead on her attractiveness as a woman.

An El Paso minister asked whether Tucker would have received the support of conservative religious leaders such as Pat Robertson "if she had converted to some other faith, or, for that matter, if she had been of some other race or a man."[65] He is clear that Tucker received so much attention because she was "pretty, young, white and female—four characteristics that tug at the heartstrings of a culture that values them."[66] The value of white femininity is magnified in a southern culture that, at its heart, privileges those who have this identity. That unnamed minister in El Paso asks a question that illustrates how critical it is to read these two cases together: "How many homely, black, male, or older convicts enjoy the defense of such high-profile religious leaders as the Rev. Pat Robertson?"[67]

Questioning the role of identity in formal and informal "hearings" of particular cases is common sense in the context of modern U.S. culture. In Texas, this kind of questioning is a prerequisite for understanding the role of religion and race in legitimating the death penalty as a form of punishment. The El Paso minister quoted above articulated and confronted the value American society places on beauty, whiteness, and femininity. The Tucker case demonstrates how strongly these qualities are valued because they privilege even a woman who has committed heinous acts.[68] Tucker's ability to access this privilege renders her visible and makes it difficult to see her as the "other" and thus eligible for execution.[69]

I am hesitant to use the word privilege, considering the fact that Tucker was still executed, but the outcry that arose about Tucker's impending execution contrasts strongly with the racially charged standoff in the Graham case, highlighting the differing values placed on the lives of these two people. Tucker's lawyer emphasized the nearly predetermined outcome of these cases, given where they originated and the fact that symbolic privileges cannot overwhelm the machinery of death in Texas, when he said: "We all know that Texas doesn't have any mercy.... Mercy is the fragrance that clings to the boot that just crushed Karla Faye Tucker."[70]

The absence of any legal or political relief increases the importance of the narrative that surrounds an individual case. These two people are joined in a common system that has made executions a silent and regular part of the landscape. Yet both were able to break through the silence and force an out-loud debate. Even if the protests could not stop the outcome, there is value in understanding how the individual narratives relate to the political and legal structure and to the values of society. These values led the same prosecutor (a critical cog in the machinery of the law) to change his mind in the Tucker case but argue in the Graham case that "to have Graham as the poster child to end the death penalty is like having Frankenstein for a poster child for the March of Dimes."[71]

What Do You Plea? Post-Conviction Claims of Guilt and Innocence

The other important argument against comparing the Graham and Tucker cases is the postures each took toward their crimes at the time of execution. Graham proclaimed his innocence with his dying breath. In his last statement, which was reported to have lasted six minutes—quite lengthy in comparison to most other final statements—Graham used the words innocent and lynching and/or alluded to his innocence 14 times. Intermingled with thanks to his family, supporters, and the Black community is his repeated claim of innocence. Near the end of the statement Graham proclaims,

> I'm innocent. They've got the facts to prove it. They know I'm innocent. But they cannot acknowledge my innocence, because to do so would be to publicly admit their guilt. This is something these racist people will never do.[72]

In proclaiming his innocence, he also critiqued the system that placed him on that gurney and the individuals who represented that system. His proclamations of innocence become more than a statement of his lack of guilt; they became an act of defiance.

Tucker, on the other hand, admitted her guilt early on and never denied that she was guilty of the murders for which she was convicted. At rallies to spare her life, she called for a change in the death penalty system and "compassion for the people hurting because of the violence done to them."[73] At the time of her execution, she appeared resigned to her fate. Unlike Graham, Tucker seemed to have a positive relationship with her jailers. She said in her last statement, "Warden Baggett, thank all of you so much. You have been so good to me. I love all of you very much."[74] One witness to Tucker's execution said that he "never saw Karla Faye Tucker take the smile off her face."[75] She had a consistent narrative. She was guilty, and then she was born again.

I argue that the differences in Graham and Tucker's claims of innocence or guilt overshadow the fact that they were engaged in the same process. At first glance, the claims of innocence or guilt seem to complicate the comparison because of the importance innocence has played in the debate over the death penalty in recent years. I deconstruct the idea of a singular definition of innocence in narratives of the death penalty later in this chapter. For the moment, let us hold to the vernacular definition of innocence as "you didn't do it." Polls show that even respondents who support the death penalty are troubled by the possibility of executing innocent people—people who did not commit the crime.

By claiming innocence Graham arguably placed himself in a different category than Tucker. Tucker was exactly the kind of person polls show Americans would want to receive the death penalty: the guilty. However, both Graham and Tucker were found guilty and sentenced to death in a court of law. From the time of that death sentence, both pursued every legal option available to spare their lives, including state and federal appeals, clemency petitions, and a media campaign to rally political and public support for their case. The legal system places tremendous value on having been found guilty of murder in trial in a court of law, despite claims of innocence. I would suggest that these cases exemplify that this finding of guilt also carries moral and even religious value.

In *Herrera v.* Collins (1993), the Supreme Court spoke to the weight of legal guilt even when evidence of actual innocence surfaces after conviction.[76] Leonel Herrera was convicted of capital murder and sentenced to death in the state of Texas in 1982. Ten years after his conviction and after his case had completed the state appellate proceedings, Herrera claimed that he was "actually innocent" as his case entered federal habeas (appeals).[77] Most of the Supreme Court decision explored the particularities of federal habeas proceedings,[78] but the Court also discussed at length how claims of actual innocence should be viewed in postconviction proceedings. In the majority opinion, Chief Justice Rehnquist reiterated that once an individual is found guilty, "the presumption of innocence disappears."[79] Conviction in a full and fair trial moves the debate from proof of innocence in federal habeas proceedings to proof of constitutional grounds for remedy from unfair process. In this decision, the Court places all defendants found guilty of capital murder into a single group—the guilty. So Graham's claims of innocence and Tucker's claims of guilt did not alter the fact that they were both "guilty" from the moment they were convicted.

The emphasis placed on Graham's claim of innocence and Tucker's admission of guilt leads to the final argument of this chapter and to the final reason why comparing these two cases is so revealing. Innocence has multiple meanings that are dependent on/entangled in the identities of the person who is at the center of the discussion. The simplistic notion of innocence as whether the defendant did in fact commit the crime ignores the continuance/evolution of the roles of race, religion, and gender in death penalty cases. Indeed, in *Herrera v. Collins* the Supreme Court began the process of fracturing the meaning of innocence by bifurcating legal innocence from actual innocence. *Herrera* suggests at least two types of innocence, but this typology is insufficient to explain the political usages of "innocence" in death penalty cases for which race, religion, and gender are central to the analysis.

Innocence Complicated

Herrera is clear that actual innocence does not guarantee relief. Despite some debate over the legal reasoning employed in *Herrera*, it continues to stand as law.[80] The relevant legacy of the *Herrera* decision, for this analysis, is that it complicates the legal meaning of innocence, which in turn suggests the possibility there may be more meanings of innocence that explain particular positions on the death penalty. Graham and Tucker, both legally guilty, used different innocence narratives in their efforts to rescue themselves from the executioner's needle. The final sections of this chapter discuss some of the alternative meanings of innocence the Graham and Tucker cases suggest.

Social Innocence

We begin with the idea of social innocence. One could argue that Tucker's transformation made her socially innocent. Tucker attempted to return to the protection of the bounded community—or that portion of the community that is protected from state-wielded or -sanctioned violence.[81] More simply stated, she was trying to stay alive. The saliency of race and religion in this region meant that Tucker should have been ineligible for execution in the minds of many of the mostly white supporters who felt her life should be spared. Tucker's previous behavior could be ignored. Religion became a kind of passkey that allowed her to be reframed as someone whose life was worth saving.

By comparison, the Graham case exemplifies how this passkey may not work for African Americans on death row. To become socially innocent, no longer considered a physical or political danger, one has to render themselves free of past behaviors and align their image with those that elevate the individual to a position worthy of political salvation. The pervasive image of the dangerous Black criminal limits the narratives that were available to Graham, but for Tucker, social and political space was created by the prevailing reluctance to execute women and the customary inclination to protect white women.

What is interesting about the strategy of becoming socially innocent is its use as a political strategy by the African American community prior to the Civil Rights Movement. In his essay "Constructing African Americans as Minorities," historian Earl Lewis discusses the evolution of the perception of the African American community from a danger to the public to that of injured citizens.[82] Lewis argues that as far back as 1900, African American institutions "competed to establish blacks as injured citizens rather than dangerous victimizers."[83] He makes special note of the NAACP Legal Defense and Education Fund, which has orchestrated most of the important legal attacks on the death penalty as well as the legal structures that subordinate African Americans.

According to Lewis's reading of African American political history from slavery to the entrenchment of Jim Crow, Blacks were viewed as a threat, a social danger. Before African Americans could seek redress from the denial of the citizenship rights guaranteed to them in the Civil War amendments, they had to become "socially innocent." Religious institutions and social and political organizations played an important role in this transformation.[84] Unlike minorities in other political systems who were fighting to separate from their majority communities, Blacks were fighting for inclusion, integration. But before integration was possible, they had to be viewed as citizens, members of the protected community whose injuries required remedy.

Lewis argues that during this period when extralegal and legal state violence were conflated, such violence was made possible by the public's belief that Blacks were dangerous. Blacks were perceived not only as a physical danger but also as a political danger. The possibility of newly freed Africans entering the political process was a danger to the racial hierarchy of the South, which had been constructed in slavery and reaffirmed in Jim Crow. The systemic violence visited upon Blacks in the South was accompanied by an entire legal and political structure that was dedicated to disenfranchising and alienating Blacks from the political process. In addition, the exclusion of African Americans from the civic and social life of the nation "cemented a racialized public sphere."[85] Within that public sphere, popular culture and its representation of African Americans, in Lewis's analysis, played a key role in further marginalizing African Americans. The presentation of Black men, in particular, as violent criminals and potential rapists allowed "scores to see blacks as the supreme embodiment of danger."[86] The general antidote for this danger was violence—first in the extralegal form of lynching and then with legal executions through state death penalty regimes.[87]

Karla Tucker followed a similar process of moral refashioning. She changed her identity from that of an immoral young woman to that of an injured citizen who could demand political and legal remedy from the unfair imposition of state policies, in this case the death penalty. Tucker credited her last incarnation to the fact that she had been born again. The groundswell of support for sparing Tucker's life was largely attributed to religion, but I argue that the religious transformation was made palatable by her gender and racial identity. Tucker, in contrast to Graham, did not *fit the description* of someone who should be executed in the first place. Just as African Americans were initially prevented from gaining redress because of existing social and legal norms, Tucker's case that she should be seen as socially innocent was supported by the gender and race norms associated with her whiteness and her womanness.

Although the persistence of the role of whiteness and femininity may be part of a continuing historical thread in the South,[88] tracing the role of race in contemporary politics has become more complicated. In *The Boundaries of Blackness: AIDS and the Breakdown in Black Politics*, Cathy Cohen suggests that past strategies for community uplift have been supplanted by fragmentation in African American political advocacy. One result of this, she argues, is the uneven integration of the African American community into the larger social and political community of the United States in the post–Civil Rights period.[89] Cohen contends that this fragmentation has led to a reliance on alternative political alliances for marginalized groups within the African American community (i.e., cross-racial coalitions that have formed, especially among opponents of the death penalty).

I argue that Cohen's work has additional implications for the contemporary meaning of social innocence as part of the politics of respectability death row inmates draw upon. This fragmentation makes the process of becoming socially innocent an individual strategy for African Americans who are marginalized within the Black community. Members of these subgroups—those Cohen categorizes as secondary marginalized groups—may be able to successfully trigger the political resources of their racial community by becoming "socially innocent," even if they are not able to reenter that community.

The Graham case is instructive about the possibility that Blacks on death row can become socially innocent.

Graham, like Tucker, claimed that he had become a changed person, and those around him supported his claim. Jennifer Clebourn, Graham's aunt, said as much: "Gary is a changed person. He has matured since he was 17 [the age when Graham was arrested]. He has had 12 years to think about what he's done wrong. He knows those robberies he did was wrong."[90] But unlike the racial and gender norms that supported the authenticity of Tucker's transformation, the racial and gender norms surrounding Black masculinity worked against the larger society perceiving Graham as anything other than a murderer. Graham's transformation, along with his claims of innocence, did trigger a significant response in the African American community. He received a tremendous amount of support from that community, which in the post–Civil Rights period has not prioritized the death penalty on its political agenda.

Innocence by Lynching

Graham's narrative of innocence and abuse by a racist state leads to another conceptualization of innocence these cases suggest: innocence by lynching. Unlike efforts to render inmates socially innocent, some narratives of the death penalty automatically rehabilitate the subject of the narrative. In vernacular and academic narratives of lynching, the person who is lynched is always articulated as innocent. This type of innocence is distinct in that it is simultaneously a declaration of innocence and a critique of the criminal justice system. Part of the analysis of the data I gathered in focus groups, which I discuss in later chapters, is a question about whether and if so to what degree the lynching narrative continues to resonate for African Americans. Public opinion research shows the substantial effect Clarence Thomas's invocation of lynching during the controversy over his nomination to the Supreme Court had on the attitudes of African Americans.[91] I argue that much of the attention paid to the Graham case resulted from his ability to marry his execution with the lynching narrative.

In the late nineteenth century, anti-lynching activism was one of the highest priorities on the Black political agenda.[92] As early as Reconstruction, Black activists labeled the justifications for mob violence against Blacks as mere façades for political oppression.[93] The rhetoric of anti-lynching campaigns, even those spearheaded by secular Black organizations, sometimes took on a spiritual tone. While James Weldon Johnson was investigating a lynching in which a Black man was burned alive before a white mob, he made this observation:

> I tried to balance the sufferings of the miserable victim against the moral degradation of Memphis, and the truth flashed over me that in large measure the race question involves the saving of black America's body and white America's soul.[94]

Though James Marquart, Sheldon Ekland-Olson, and Jonathan R. Sorensen do not argue that "illegal lynchings were the sole factor" that explains why the death penalty statute in Texas was reformed in 1923, they argue that prior to this period the lines between legal and illegal hangings "were often very thin"; both were "administered as much to maintain the caste-like system of domination as to even the scales of justice."[95] During this period, lynching was coupled with legal executions because both were used as a form of social control, primarily for controlling the formerly enslaved and their descendants.[96] The perceived need for anti-lynching campaigns declined with the passing of Jim Crow and its legal vestiges. Even after Jim Crow had come to an end, some legal groups continued their efforts against the death penalty.

So when Gary Graham invoked the image of lynching, he was simultaneously proclaiming his innocence and making more concrete the tentative relationship between Blacks and the state by calling on the past uses of violence against innocent Black men. Like the innocent victims of lynching in the past, he was being "murdered" by a racist state and signaling to other Blacks the possibilities of a similar fate. Graham said as much in his last statement: "This is a lynching in America tonight."[97] Graham's supporters also used religious language similar to that of Johnson at the turn of the century. When Robert Muhammad was asked whether a month-long fast by Graham's supporters was a hunger strike, he replied, "This is not a hunger strike. A hunger strike is a political statement, and I am not making a political statement. We are making a spiritual statement. . . . We are here to stop the execution of an innocent man."[98] Jesse Jackson described Graham's death as a "political sacrifice"[99] and compared George W. Bush to Pontius Pilate.[100] In Jackson's words, "his spirit will never surrender."[101] Because Graham was able to align his story with the lynching narrative, he was able to activate the African American community in a way that other death row inmates have not.

One of the important limitations of being perceived as innocent by alluding to the lynching narrative is the highly gendered nature of this narrative. The image of lynching is centered on Black men despite the historical fact that Black women were also victims of lynching, as were other racial/ethnic groups.[102] When Billie Holiday sings to a near-moan of "black bodies swinging in the Southern breeze," the horrors in those lyrics tend to conjure images of Black male bodies hanging from trees. The power of this combined narrative of race and gender is affirmed by the near-invisibility of African American women from the discussion of lynching. This invisibility extends into the discussion of capital punishment. For instance, the next woman set for execution after Karla Faye Tucker was an African-American woman, Yvonne Sheppard. There was no Pat Robertson or Jerry Falwell to speak for her, although Jesse Jackson visited her at his request.[103] The comparison between Sheppard and Graham, or even between Sheppard and Tucker, is complicated by the fact that Sheppard was a volunteer, an inmate who gives up their right to appeal, which expedites their execution. Even though Sheppard volunteered, it is important to ask why the passionate critiques of the state and death penalty associated with Graham's case were not activated in her case.

The capacity of the lynching narrative to silence Black women and their experiences is also present in the Graham case. Bernadine Skillern was a Black woman whose eyewitness testimony single-handedly convicted Graham. Skillern was harassed by members of the African American community and the press for her unwavering stance that it was Graham she saw in that parking lot on the night of Bobby Lambert's murder. Graham supporters passed out leaflets in Skillern's neighborhood and near her church identifying her as the witness who convicted Graham. These campaigns resulted in damage to her home and car. Skillern also sued a television news program for harassing her in her home when she refused to open her door and grant them an interview. This incident resulted in a lawsuit against ABC.[104] The primacy of the lynching narrative increased the desire to protect Graham and left Skillern vulnerable. In the eyes of Graham's supporters, her refusal to recant made her complicit with the state in the death of an innocent Black man.

Confession as Innocence

The last type of innocence analyzes the role of confession in public's perception of innocence. It is important to acknowledge that Tucker's repetitive confessions of guilt may have contributed to her public refashioning, just as Graham's professions of innocence and perceived failure to show remorse may have heightened the desire of some to see him executed.

Tucker's guilt became part of her "testimony" that she shared frequently during her numerous encounters with the media. I use the word testimony in the sense of the Pentecostal act of public confession as opposed to the legal act of telling one's story in legal proceedings. Both involve acts of truth-telling, but the religious usage invokes a much more expansive notion. The religious usage asserts that not only is the telling a public good (i.e., a lesson to both listener and teller), but also that it has a cleansing power that can remove the taint of sin or any bad behavior. As a performative act, testimony allows the person giving witness "to specif[y] her social location in the group, and through repeated performance, signal to the community her more advanced status."[105]

Tucker repeatedly used the media to offer her testimony or to testify about her case and tell Governor Bush and the public how she was born again. Tucker's appeal to religious communities placed significant political pressure on Bush, who received much of his support from conservative Christians. In an open letter to Governor Bush, Tucker proclaimed,

> Even though I did murder Jerry Dean and Deborah Thornton that night and did not think anything of it back then, it is now the one thing I regret most in my life and in the frame of mind I am now in it is something that rips my guts out. I felt the pain of that night, and I feel the pain that goes on every day with others because of what I did that night. I know the evil that was in me then, and I know that what took place that night today, and because of who I am today it makes it all the more harder for me to have to think back on that night and after that night, and a lot of things I did while I was not saved.[106]

The letter reiterates Tucker's acceptance of her guilt. To some degree, the public nature of Tucker's campaign posed a significant challenge to the state's authority to execute its judgment because of her direct appeal to Christian sentiments.[107] Tucker appealed to the public's view of the cleansing nature of confession.

In *Troubling Confessions: Speaking Guilt in Law and Literature*, Peter Brooks argues that "the confessional rehearsal or repetition of guilt is its own kind of performance, producing at the same time the excuse or justification of guilt." Further, according to Brooks, "it is the speech-act itself which simultaneously exonerates and inculpates."[108] He points out that "the notion that possible redemption depends on a confession is deeply ingrained in our culture."[109] However, Brooks also argues that "the confessional impulse, considered to be redemptive[,] can in fact produce a sterile, passive, self-satisfied complicity in the negation of the possibility of redemption" among those who hear the confession.[110] The possibility of redemption is undone by the very confession that society desires. Brooks argues that some confessions can actually "affirm the fallen condition" of the confessor and support the violations of individual rights and freedoms.

The Tucker case is a prime example of the ambivalent way confessions of guilt are understood legally and, I would argue, politically. For many, the combined performance of evangelical Christianity, femininity, and continual confession of guilt wiped Tucker's slate clean. The Tucker who killed two people with a pickaxe, according to those most familiar with the details of her crime, was not the Tucker on death row, in spite of her repeated admissions of guilt. The notion that redemption is dependent on confession benefited Tucker. Ultimately, Tucker failed because she was essentially out-confessed by George W. Bush, who had his own story of moral and religious transformation and public redemption. Bush uses Tucker's own words of confession to justify her execution: "Like many touched by this case, I have sought guidance through prayer. . . . I have concluded judgments about the heart and soul of an individual on death row are best left to a higher authority."[111] With these words, any possibility for Karla Tucker's earthly redemption was lost.

Juxtaposing the cultural emphasis on redemption by confession with Graham's ceaseless claims of innocence demonstrates how confession can actually highlight guilt. Every article about Graham repeated his professions of innocence. Graham's claim of innocence became the mantle for his supporters and anti-death penalty activists. Graham was quoted as saying shortly before his death, "I die fighting for what I believed in. Truth will come out."[112] That truth for Graham was his innocence. His perceived failure to show contrition only fueled political support and, according to Brooks's theory, legal and cultural support for his execution. Shortly before Graham's execution, George W. Bush responded to his claim of innocence:

> As far as I'm concerned, there has not been one innocent person executed since I've become governor. I know there is a lot of emotion swirling around the case and I understand that. The death penalty is not an easy subject for folks. I'm going to uphold the laws of the land and if it costs me politically, it costs me politically. No one case is an easy case. Obviously, those that get a lot of public attention increase the degree of difficulty. I'm going to treat this case no differently than any other case that has come across my desk. I'm going to uphold the laws of the land. I believe the system is fair and just.[113]

Bush reaffirmed Graham's guilt and his plans as governor to uphold the legally proscribed punishment. He did not need to "search his heart" or pray on it. The law dictates how to handle the unrepentant guilty. Even though Graham also maintained that he had been transformed, his unwillingness to confess gave the final legal authority, the governor, no reason to hesitate.

I include this notion of innocence last because it is difficult to parse out when this ingrained cultural notion that Brooks discusses is obscured by race and religion. In comparing these two cases, I maintain that the admissions of guilt or innocence are less important than the similarities between the two cases, but it is important to acknowledge the American cultural preference for confession and other markers of contrition. The preference for confession intersects with race and gender in important ways. We continue to litigate cases, in courts of law and public opinion, where Black men have claimed innocence, in some cases even after their death. The intersection of race, injustice, and confession can create and/or limit the power of such stances.

Conclusion

This chapter explores how contemporary explanations for support of the death penalty that rely on religion merge with past narratives of gender and race and other cultural notions of performance connected to religion. The *Herrera* case challenges the notion that innocence is the simple concept that is often discussed in both law and politics. I extend the challenge created by *Herrera* and offer other constructions of innocence woven into the cases of Karla Faye Tucker and Gary Graham: social innocence, innocence by lynching, and confession as innocence. Popular perceptions are often crystallized or shattered by death penalty cases that capture public attention. Analyzing the operation of race, religion, and innocence in these two cases provides a foundation for the analysis that follows and encourages us to extend the search to other locations as we seek to understand this dynamic relationship. The political dynamics of campaigns for life and/or claims of innocence have been shown to have real effects on the public's views on the death penalty. In *The Decline of the Death Penalty and the Discovery of Innocence*, Frank Baumgartner, Suzanna L. De Boef, and Amber Boydstun chronicle how claims of actual innocence or "errors in justice" have led to a national movement that has reshaped American views on the death penalty. The analysis in this chapter shows that the power of some campaigns may be driven by narratives of history or other narratives of identity that are linked to the bodies of the persons at the center of the claim.

2

Performing Discretion or Performing Discrimination? Race, Ritual, and the Denial of Participatory Rights in Capital Jury Selection

You and each of you do solemnly swear (or affirm) that in the case of the State of Texas against the defendant, you will a true verdict render according to the law and the evidence, so help you God.

—OATH OF JURORS IN CRIMINAL CASES, Article 35.22, Texas Code of Criminal Procedure

I believe in justice.

—AFRICAN AMERICAN VENIREWOMAN IN *DEBLANC V. STATE OF TEXAS*

FEW ACTIVITIES REPRESENT the active meaning of citizenship more than serving on a jury. The jury has long been a critical space where citizens stand in judgment of the propriety/impropriety of the behavior of their fellow citizens. But a number of groups, including African Americans, have not had equal access to this actually and symbolically important space. Through litigation, safeguards have evolved to protect the rights of defendants to have juries that reflect the community at large and the rights of citizens to participate in juries. But despite these efforts, African Americans and other racial minorities continue to be underrepresented on trial juries and in the panel of potential jurors. The oath jurors take requires fidelity to truth and the law, concepts that are fluid across individuals and communities. The continued exclusion of African Americans in significant numbers often leads to concern about the meaning of justice in this space.

This chapter focuses on *Batson* hearings, which are explicit attempts to ensure that no discrimination occurs based on race in the use of peremptory or discretionary challenges and to prevent and/or correct discrimination based on race at the point it occurs.[1] *Batson* hearings take place during the jury selection process, which is by its very nature discriminating. How courts police the limits imposed on the selection process by *Batson v. Kentucky*, as defined by the Supreme Court and state courts, are of interest here. Bringing together research in law, the social sciences, and cultural studies uncovers the multiple meanings of this interaction between citizens and the state in this legal moment.

Batson hearings are unique, not only in law but also in the state's administration of its duties. They are one of the few places where a representative of the state is required to stop in the act of doing their job and explain how they have done that job in a race-neutral manner. This repetitive event in criminal trials, particularly capital trials, with their consistent structure and transmission of the state's views of who should participate in the finding of guilt/innocence and life/death, should be understood as a ritual more than as a meaningful legal process. The legal meaning of these hearings is debatable because of the extremely low evidentiary standard the state must meet to show an absence of bias. These hearings are more a ritual than an effective legal instrument to combat improper selection of juries because the state's performance of the process seems to overwhelm the actual selection of a jury without discrimination. The ritual perpetuates a veneer of racial inclusion that is substantively false.

In actuality, *Batson* objections and hearings have not remedied racially discriminatory jury practices. They have instead erected a process that masks the state's continuing discrimination in the use of peremptory challenges. At the time of its invention, this unique performance by the state—which is meant to ensure that litigants are not using peremptory challenges in a racially discriminatory way—appeared to be a progressive and immediate remedy for a violation of the Constitution. The absence of meaningful investigation into prosecutorial motives has meant that everything short of an explicitly racial statement—I do not want this juror because he or she is Black—will be upheld as a race-neutral reason for excluding someone.[2] If *Batson* challenges are not doing what they have been created to do—that is, prevent the removal of potential jurors because of their race—what work may they actually be doing? The answer I offer is that *Batson* hearings allow for the appearance of fairness while requiring little work on the part of courts and prosecutors to alter biased practices.

The state points to these hearings as visible examples of efforts to combat discrimination in jury selection. By examining voir dire responses of African Americans and the way prosecutors interpret those responses, this chapter demonstrates how racial discrimination and race neutrality have become indistinguishable in *Batson* cases. Going through the motions of *Batson* hearings is sufficient to give the proceedings the imprimatur of fairness while legitimating the removal of African American jurors. This chapter is a close reading of *Batson* decisions in the Texas Court of Criminal Appeals (CCA).[3]

Whose Jury and Whose Peers? Race and the Jury Selection Process

The jury system is constructed on the belief that the guilt or innocence of defendants is best determined by the members of a society who are eligible for participation or, in common language, a jury of one's peers. This idea of one's peers does not imply only those who are drawn directly from the defendant's sphere of knowledge, social class, or race. It has origins in democratic norms that link all citizens through jury service to the project of upholding the moral and governmental authority of the legal system. In capital cases, the individual moral views of jurors on the death penalty come face to face with laws that legitimate capital punishment. Because of these democratic origins, as groups have become incorporated in the bounded community of citizenship, systematic bars on their participation in jury service have been perceived as abridgements of the rights—and to some degree, the obligations—of citizenship. When particular groups are barred from capital cases, their values are barred as well.

The fact that the Constitution mentions juries more than once highlights the importance of the jury in the minds of the framers, but the specifics of who is fit for jury service has been negotiated by the courts and litigants and at times by state and federal legislatures. The status of free Blacks during the antebellum period was often highly variable and dependent on the laws of the locale in which they lived. With the passage of the Civil War amendments, all African Americans were legally granted citizenship and Black men were granted participatory rights that included jury service.[4] Jim Crow was the Southern response to this expansion of Black rights. Jim Crow developed as a system to maintain the sociopolitical structure of white subjugation of Blacks that began during chattel slavery. States constructed these laws in various ways. Many were litigated to the Supreme Court with decisions that sometimes protected and sometimes ignored the rights of African Americans created by the Thirteenth, Fourteenth, and Fifteenth Amendments. The critical case involving Black jurors, *Strauder v. West Virginia* (1880), was one of the successes in terms of the Court's willingness to protect this aspect of African American citizenship rights.[5]

Taylor Strauder, a Black man, was convicted of murder and that conviction was later affirmed by the West Virginia Supreme Court. Strauder petitioned the U.S. Supreme Court to overturn his conviction because West Virginia law permitted only white men to serve on juries. This statute, Strauder argued, denied him equal protection of the law. The Supreme Court agreed with Strauder and went further, arguing that this case and several others in the same vein were critical to elevating Blacks' citizenship to that of whites. The Court also explicitly acknowledged that there was a constitutional interest in ensuring that the "habitual discrimination" practiced before the passage of the Civil War amendments did not become entrenched in new legislation by the states. The Court specifically addressed the connection between racially discriminatory jury selection rules and the meaning of citizenship:

> It is well known that prejudices often exist against particular classes in the community, which sway the judgment of jurors, and which, therefore, operate in some cases to deny to persons of those classes the full enjoyment of that protection which others enjoy.[6]

It is important to note that *Strauder* does not guarantee the defendant the right to have members of his or her race seated as jurors; it only guarantees that members of the defendant's race will not be statutorily excluded from the pool of potential jurors.

Strauder represent the beginning of continuing legal wrangling that connects jury service and other forms of the participation of African Americans in civic life to their equal protection as citizens. The landscape of this particular battle for race-neutral selection and administration of juries has been altered in recent decades by new mechanisms and evidentiary standards to police discrimination. With the decision in *Batson v. Kentucky* (1986), the Supreme Court again addressed the harm to defendants when a jury is selected using discriminatory methods and took up the more complicated issue of the role of race in the use of peremptory challenges.[7]

Two types of challenges are used to remove jurors during the selection process—a challenge for cause and the peremptory challenge. A challenge for cause "permit[s the] rejection of jurors on a narrowly specified, provable, and legally cognizable basis of partiality."[8] Peremptory challenges are discretionary challenges that allow jurors to be rejected for "real or imagined partiality that is less easily designated or demonstrable."[9] In selecting which jurors to seat from the venire, each side of the dispute is allowed to remove a limited a number in the venire for cause and a limited number with peremptory challenges. Peremptory challenges give litigants the opportunity to whittle down the number in the venire using their experience, their instincts, and other intangibles gained through the practice of law that cannot be captured in the statutory reasons that constitute cause. There are some boundaries on the use of peremptory challenges. For example, lawyers cannot use peremptory challenges in ways that violate the Constitution, such as discriminating against a juror based on race.

In *Batson*, the Supreme Court reiterated the basic principles of *Strauder*, thus setting standards for showing racial discrimination in peremptory challenges.[10] Before this decision, policing discrimination in peremptory challenges was difficult, if not impossible, because litigants were not required to articulate their reasons for making such challenges. In *Batson*, the Supreme Court created a new process for evaluating the use of peremptory challenges against racial minorities in the instant case where they occur. Justice Powell's majority opinion argued that because the jury's "central position in our system of justice" is to "safeguard a person accused of crime against the arbitrary exercise of power by prosecutor or judge," racial discrimination in the jury process affected the "entire community" by "undermin[ing] public confidence in the fairness of our system of justice."[11]

Batson was a more complicated case to decide than *Strauder*. *Strauder* and its progeny repeatedly stated that racial discrimination in the selection of the panel of citizens summoned for jury duty—the venire, or jury pool— violates the Equal Protection Clause, while *Batson* involves the racially discriminatory use of peremptory challenges. Peremptory challenges, according to Chief Justice Burger in his dissent in *Batson*, had been a part of the U.S. criminal justice system for at least 200 years at the time of this decision.[12] Peremptory challenges acknowledge that lawyers, over time, develop certain intuitive strategies—hunches, instincts—for evaluating whether a juror will be biased or will in some way be detrimental to their side.[13]

In *Batson*, the Court demarcated the line between prosecutors'— historically unfettered—right to use their instincts in the form of peremptory challenges and the purposeful use of race discrimination in peremptory challenges. The Court connected the constitutional prohibition on legislation that excludes members of a particular race from the venire to racially discriminatory peremptory challenges. The significance of peremptory challenges in jury selection makes them necessarily subject to constitutional review, according to the Court. The heightened scrutiny of peremptory challenges reiterated the Court's commitment to removing racial discrimination from every aspect of the jury selection process.

Much of the majority opinion is focused on the Court's previous decision in *Swain v. Alabama* (1965), which held that a "State's purposeful or deliberate denial to Negroes on account of race participation as jurors in the administration of justice violates the Equal Protection Clause."[14] The effect of *Swain* was to allow defendants to claim a violation of equal protection if they could prove that the prosecutor had systematically used peremptory challenges to strike Black jurors. *Swain* had little practical impact because of the high evidentiary standard required to prove constitutional harm. The amount of time and effort involved and the extremely high legal standard created a nearly insurmountable obstacle for a successful objection to a peremptory challenge on the basis of racial discrimination.

Under the reasoning in *Swain*, to demonstrate a prima facie case of racially discriminatory peremptory challenges, a Black defendant was required to show that he was a "member of a cognizable racial group capable of being singled out for differential treatment" and to show evidence of "the prosecutor's systematic use of peremptory challenges against Negroes over a period of time."[15] It is the latter half of this requirement that made *Swain* so ineffectual. For a defendant to prove systematic discrimination, he had to gather data on the use of peremptory challenges in that court over time to support an equal protection violation in their particular case. In his concurring opinion, Justice Marshall pointed to several examples where defendants were able to gather substantial evidence of discrimination, including evidence that in one year the Dallas County, Texas, prosecutor struck 405 out of 467 Black jurors with peremptory challenges.[16] Yet this showing was deemed insufficient proof of racially motivated peremptory challenges under *Swain*. Most defendants could not afford the investigations required to demonstrate systematic discrimination. Even if the defendants could gather the evidence, the Dallas County example suggests it may not have been enough unless perhaps *all* Blacks were removed using peremptory challenges.

Batson decreased the standard of proof and narrowed the inquiry of racial discrimination to the case and the prosecutor before the court, removing the need to prove discrimination across cases and over time. According to the new rule *Batson* articulated, to make a showing of racial bias in the prosecutor's use of peremptory challenges, defendants must demonstrate that (1) they are a "member of a cognizable racial group" and "that the prosecutor has exercised peremptory challenges to remove from the venire members of the defendant's race";[17] (2) "that the prosecutor has exercised peremptory challenges to remove from the venire members of the defendant's race"; (3) that peremptory challenges constitute a jury selection practice that permits "those to discriminate who are of a mind to discriminate";[18] and (4) that these facts and other "relevant circumstances raise an inference" that the prosecutor used peremptory challenges to remove members of the defendant's race from the trial jury.[19]

The result in practice is what is referred to as the *Batson* hearing, where the defendant's lawyer can object if he or she believes the prosecutor is using peremptory challenges to strike jurors based on race. Essentially the proceedings are halted and the prosecutor is questioned about his or her reasons for striking Black jurors. These reasons must be race neutral. Though they were on opposite sides of the *Batson* decision, Justices Marshall and Rehnquist both predicted what would later become the clear problem with *Batson*: proof is very difficult.

Justice Marshall went further than any other member of the Court in proposing solutions to discriminatory uses of peremptory challenges. In Marshall's concurring opinion, the holding that the use of peremptory challenges to remove Blacks from juries violates the equal protection clause is enough to "eliminate" peremptory challenges altogether. Justice Rehnquist, in his dissent, defended peremptory challenges as a historic and valued tool for legal practitioners and argued that as long as peremptory challenges are used to remove jurors of all races in cases where the defendant's and the juror's race are the same, then no equal protection claim is raised. Rehnquist acknowledges that prosecutors "seat-of-the-pants instincts" may be "crudely stereotypical and may in many cases be hopelessly mistaken" but the impact was mitigated by the fact that all racial groups used such flawed information to make judgments.[20] Marshall addressed this point in Rehnquist's dissent directly, arguing that "seat-of-the-pants instincts may often be just another term for racial prejudice."[21] In his view, the potential for racial bias in peremptory challenges is so high that they should be discontinued.

Prosecutors do indeed rely on instincts and past experience to make decisions about which jurors would be best for the state. Peremptory challenges allow both sides to remove jurors based on qualities that do not amount to cause but arouse certain unease in the litigant about their presence on the particular jury in the particular case. But the shallowness of the courts' investigations of the reasons offered by prosecutors render Justice Marshall's concerns a caution unheeded.

Though the Supreme Court has held fast to the constitutional prohibition of racial discrimination in the jury process, implementation of this rule has been inconsistent across history and jurisdictions. African Americans continue to be underrepresented in jury pools, and explanations for this phenomena range from low levels of desire among African Americans to participate on juries to structural obstacles (e.g., exclusive use of voter registration instead of driver's license records). Work on felony disenfranchisement and the loss of citizenship rights in recent decades provides tremendous insight into another important structural obstacle for African Americans in the jury process. The Sentencing Project—a nonprofit organization that advocates for reducing incarceration in favor of alternative policies toward crime—estimates that in some states as many as 40 percent of African American men may lose their voting rights permanently, which also blocks them from jury service.[22] As this line of research develops, so does our understanding of the multifaceted consequences of the overrepresentation of African Americans in the criminal justice system. The structural obstacles that now limit African American participation may overwhelm the Supreme Court's attempts to curb discrimination in other parts of the jury selection process. These issues of race become even more important when one takes into account the heightened considerations for service on capital juries that I discuss later.

Batson *Hearings as a Ritual in Capital Cases:*
Theory and Practice

I have always been intrigued by *Batson* hearings because they represent one of the few places where representatives of the state are required to stop doing their job and explain how they have done that job in a race-neutral manner. The legal meaning of these hearings is debatable because of the extremely low evidentiary standard the state must meet to show a lack of bias. The repetitive, structured hearing in trials of all kinds (especially capital cases) that transmit the state's views on who should participate in finding guilt and in sentencing can be understood as a ritual. Rethinking these hearings as a ritual—in which the state attempts to demonstrate that its jury selection processes are not discriminatory through their performance—moves analysis of the role of African Americans in capital juries toward an understanding of the symbolic meaning of jury participation for the relationship of African Americans to the state and to this state policy.

Why ritual? Over time and across disciplines, the definition of ritual has varied. I draw on the writing of sociologist Robert Wuthnow, who has demonstrated the linkages between culture, religion, morality, and meaning in American social structures, including the law. In *Meaning and Moral Order: Explanations in Cultural Analysis*, Wuthnow defines ritual as "a symbolic-expressive aspect of behavior that communicates something about social relations, often in relatively dramatic or formal manner."[23]

For Wuthnow, acts are symbolic "if they stand for something else, if they communicate meaning rather than being performed purely for instrumental purposes."[24] The activities that make up ritual have meaning that go beyond the superficial performances, and these meanings are often communicated "through subtle and implicit messages."[25] According to Wuthnow, ritual "provides an occasion for making public what one thinks, feels, or intends to do" because of its expressive nature.[26] The fundamental role of ritual is to regulate and define social relations. Rituals do this by clarifying boundaries between social groups, by reminding participants of their relationship to each other, or by sending signals about social positions. Wuthnow compares ritual to a "thermostat" that provides "feedback about how to regulate social behavior so as to better attain the collective goals of that behavior."[27]

Wuthnow's concept of ritual is particularly relevant to *Batson* hearings because of their origins in the Court's desire to prevent racially motivated removal of jurors. The Court has required the judge and legal counsel to act out, in dramatic fashion, this process to communicate that race is not a factor in the jury selection process. The defendant objects to the prosecutor's removal of African American jurors. The judge stops the proceedings. The prosecutor offers race-neutral reasons for removing Black jurors. The judge is significantly more likely to affirm than deny those reasons. The trial continues. In this action, the court can ignore the unconstitutional use of race in peremptory challenges.

Rituals such as trials and hearings are structured so that they are meaningful to both participants and observers. How does the viewer of the *Batson* ritual know that it has fulfilled its role of preventing racially motivated peremptory challenges? The viewer—be that viewer society, the defense attorney, the dismissed juror, or the court clerk—knows because the prosecutor has publicly declared in the authoritative space of the courtroom that motives animated by race are absent in the removal(s) in question. Our understanding of the physical space in which these hearings take place should not be limited to the courtrooms or the courthouses in which these courtrooms are located and the participants should not be limited to the audience or the litigants and the jurors. These courtrooms and courthouses and the human participants in the ritual are located in a legal, political, and cultural context that is steeped in the practices, traditions, and values of the people and the landscape on which they stand.

The legal, political, and cultural backdrop to *Batson* hearings is one where race and racism have been at times determinative and where they continue to be factors in how the death penalty is administered. Texas is ground zero for capital trials and convictions. The citizens of the state of Texas may not each be privy to the individual proceedings in capital cases, but they are aware that such cases occur and are aware of the eventual executions. Texas residents are, however, clearly a large portion of the audience to whom the elected judges and prosecutors play. Despite the history of the state and the well-documented discriminatory practices of its agents, the CCA has found the prosecution's use of peremptory challenges to violate the constitutional rule articulated in *Batson* in only a few cases. The decisions of this highest Texas criminal court have, however, been companion and/or primary cases that have forced the Supreme Court to more clearly define the relationship between peremptory challenges and constitutionally prohibited uses of race.[28] To some degree, one can witness the development of *Batson* hearings and their ritualization in the space of Texas courts. The courts, the agents, and the persons of color who have been unconstitutionally removed from juries in this state represent a critical community for understanding these hearings.

One can—and the courts have repeatedly done so—point to Dallas County as emblematic of how peremptory challenges can be an extremely powerful tool in discriminatory jury selection. The Dallas County prosecutor's office used a training manual for almost two decades that instructed prosecutors to remove "any member of a minority group which may subject him to oppression" because "they [members of minority groups] almost always sympathize with the accused."[29] Nearly two decades after *Swain,* The *Dallas Morning News* published a study in 1986 that found that as a result of the Dallas County Prosecutor's policies, only 2.8 percent of the jurors on capital murder cases from 1980 to 1986 were African American.[30] Prosecutors used peremptory challenges to strike an amazing 92 percent of Black jurors. Dallas was not the only Texas county that was found to use such practices and/or state them explicitly in training manuals.[31] Harris County, where I gathered some of the data for this project, also engaged in such practices and institutionalized the removal of racial and religious minorities with peremptory challenges, albeit informally.[32] Numerous studies have demonstrated the intentional use of peremptory challenges to also remove Latinos, Jews, and the disabled.[33]

The decision in *Miller-El v. Dretke* (2005) reaffirms the importance of Texas courts in the evolution of the *Batson* ritual.[34] In 1985, Thomas Miller-El was sentenced to death by an all-white jury in Dallas, Texas, after the prosecutor dismissed 10 qualified Black jurors by peremptory challenge. The trial court found under *Swain*, the guiding case at the time, no evidence of "systematic exclusion of blacks as a matter of policy." Miller-El, tried prior to *Batson*, was subject to new rules after the new standard was articulated.

The following discussion of *Miller-El* is presented in some detail because the Supreme Court encourages an interpretive approach to evaluating peremptory challenges that is not dissimilar to the analysis I use here. The Supreme Court urges lower courts to look beyond *Batson* hearings to the broader practices of jury selection. *Miller-El* is also a compelling example of how *Batson* hearings can fail to prevent discrimination without significant investigation by the lower courts but in their form can uphold unconstitutional death sentences. *Miller-El* calls for analysis of the cultural context in which jury strikes occur (e.g., the racist history and practices of the Dallas County district attorney), a comparative analysis of differences in treatment between jurors who are seated and jurors who are removed (e.g., comparison of Blacks and whites in the venire), and attention to what is physically taking place in the courtroom (e.g., jury shuffles).[35] As did Justice Souter, who wrote for the majority, I focus on two of the practices used in selecting the *Miller-El* jury because they clearly demonstrate an expressive and dramatic communication by the state of who is a fit juror in capital cases: the first is known in Texas as the jury shuffle; and the second is the provision of different prefatory statements to Black and white members of the venire panel about the death penalty.[36]

The jury shuffle allows either party to request that the clerk of the court literally shuffle the cards bearing the jurors' names.[37] In *Miller-El*, a number of the Black jurors were seated at the beginning of the panel, so the prosecutor requested a shuffle, moving the Blacks at the beginning to the end.[38] The prosecution and the defense spent the next few weeks shuffling the venire panel in a kind of legal musical chairs, trying to move or remove Blacks from the front of the panel, which would have made service unlikely since the seated jury is typically chosen from those at the front of the line.[39] I am not arguing that the Black members of this venire are the metaphorical equivalents of Rosa Parks being forced to the rear of the bus. Despite legal rules that are in place to prevent racial discrimination, the trial court permits, the prosecutors request, and everyone participates in literally moving the entire panel around the courtroom in an attempt to consistently position Blacks for exclusion. The whole performance pivots around the state's desire to exclude

Blacks instead of selecting a fair jury. The motives of the prosecutors are separate from those of the defense in these shuffles because of the prosecutor's role as the state's agent—a difference the Court acknowledges.[40]

The second practice in *Miller-El* that reveals this dramatic and expressive desire for exclusion is the use of different prefatory statements for Blacks and whites when the prosecutor described the role of jurors in capital trials. The statements were offered just prior to questioning jurors' personal views on the death penalty.[41] Ninety-four percent of white jurors heard the following:

> I feel like it [is] only fair that we tell you our position in this case. The State of Texas . . . is actively seeking the death penalty in this case for Thomas Joe Miller-El. We anticipate that we will be able to present to a jury the quantity and type of evidence necessary to convict him of capital murder and the quantity and type of evidence sufficient to allow a jury to answer these three questions over here in the affirmative.[42]

However, 44 percent of African American venire members and 6 percent of the white venire members heard the following more "graphic" statement:

> I feel like you have a right to know right up front what our position is. Mr. Kinne, Mr. Macaluso and myself, representing the people of Dallas County and the state of Texas, are actively seeking the death penalty for Thomas Joe Miller-El. . . .We do that with the anticipation that . . . at some point Mr. Thomas Joe Miller-El—the man sitting right down there—will be taken to Huntsville and will be put on death row and at some point taken to the death house and placed on a gurney and injected with a lethal substance until he is dead as a result of the proceedings that we have in this court on this case.[43]

The state argued that the prefatory statements provided were based on the jurors' ambivalence about the death penalty and were an attempt to expose jurors who were "uncertain" about the death penalty, not the juror's race.[44] However, differential treatment of Black and white jurors to ensure the exclusion of one group is itself a communication that the state views those in the excluded group as less valuable both as jurors and as citizens whose rights are worthy of state protection.

Ambivalence about the death penalty on the part of African American members of the venire is often given as a race-neutral reason for the use of peremptory strikes. However, in *Miller-El*, the Court found that this reason did not fit the facts of the case, given that Black jurors were more likely to hear the latter "graphic" statement about the death penalty than whites, whatever their opinion on the death penalty.[45] Justice Souter wrote that even if the Court based its analysis only on ambivalent jurors, Black ambivalent jurors were still more likely to be presented with the more graphic statements.[46] The Court concluded that the behavior of the prosecutors in the *Miller-El* jury selection, coupled with the Dallas County prosecutor's history of racially discriminatory jury practices, were more than sufficient to reverse the state courts and grant Miller-El relief.[47] In his concurring opinion, Justice Breyer outlined how bar journals, trial consulting firms, and materials from legal organizations had systematized "the use of race- and gender-based stereotypes in the jury-selection"—a point first brought to the Court's attention by Justice Marshall in *Swain*.[48] The view that one must look beyond the dialogue between attorney and juror to determine whether race has been used impermissibly in selecting a capital jury was reaffirmed in the 2008 Supreme Court decision in *Snyder v. Louisiana*.[49]

Until *Miller-El* returned to the Supreme Court a second time, the overwhelming majority of *Batson* objections were unsuccessful. One attorney in Texas summarized the futility of *Batson* claims in state courts with the following,

> The state doesn't have to worry about coming up with *Batson* excuses anymore because it is not politically popular to do anything for a defendant, so the objection is never going to be sustained. In Dallas, where all the judges are Republicans, we still had a judge defeated because he lowered the bond on a defendant where the victim was a well-known person. He's no longer a judge because he did the right thing. And, if the appeals courts do anything to uphold the law, they know the CCA will overturn them, so why should they risk their political careers if the ruling isn't even going to stick?[50]

From 1987 to 2002, the CCA overturned only one case on *Batson* grounds.[51] The disproportionate use of peremptory challenges against African Americans and the failure of state courts to see through the veil of race-neutral explanations the state offered is not unique to Texas. Studies in Florida, Louisiana, North Carolina, and Pennsylvania have pointed to the disproportionate use of peremptory challenges against Blacks.[52] *Batson* hearings have proven to be a weak legal instrument, so the next question is what other purpose can they be fulfilling. Using a framework of ritual, we can analyze *Batson* hearings for what they communicate about the symbolic meaning of the death penalty.

Wuthnow provides us with the logical explanation of the function of this ritual: meaning(s) and the definition of social status. This is not the first application of the concept of ritual to the study of the death penalty. Other analysis has focused on the execution itself.[53] In the study of race and the ritualistic nature of executing, authors have suggested that Black bodies—especially Black male bodies—make a better sacrifice at the altar of state power.[54] I suggest that the analysis of the ritualistic nature of capital punishment needs to be applied at much earlier stages in the process so that we can see the diffuse ways in which the dysfunctional relationship of the state to African Americans manifests itself. The symbolic and literal meaning of the death penalty for African Americans goes beyond the killing of Black bodies; the death penalty is a constant factor in shaping the very definition of African American citizenship.

Batson *Hearings in Texas Capital Cases and the Construction of a Ritual: A Description of the Methodology and the Data*

This chapter surveys capital cases where *Batson* objections were made in the state of Texas. The cases are drawn from the CCA, the highest criminal court in the state. The cases date from 1986—immediately after the *Batson* decision—to 2003. Twenty-three cases with *Batson* objections involving African American venirepersons reach the CCA in this period. This analysis focuses on the cases that made it to the CCA for several reasons. First, the CCA is the final arbiter of the correct application of the Supreme Court's decisions at the state level. Second, because of the number of capital cases adjudicated in this state, Texas courts have an increased opportunity to oversee capital jury selection and *Batson* claims in the context of capital cases. Finally, focusing on the cases that had the strongest claims of discrimination directs attention to the cases that became the models for all other state courts.

Several cases were excluded from this analysis. Many of the CCA's early decisions involving discriminatory usage of peremptory challenges following the Supreme Court decision in *Batson v. Kentucky* were simply working out the legal reasoning and the mechanics of how the trial court should behave when these objections were raised.[55] So, for example, questions about the propriety of the timing of the objection or the exact makeup of a sufficient record dominate these opinions. Because of the CCA's concern for the mechanics of how this new legal process would work, they included very little about the statements of the jurors or the prosecutors in these early cases. Also, many of the excluded cases were overruled because of the lower court's failure to construct a sufficient record for appellate review. In some cases, the CCA remanded these cases so the lower court could make the findings necessary for review. In these instances, the new record was included. Lastly, some cases were excluded because although they involved Black jurors, the legal issues centered on another aspect of the venireperson's identity (e.g., country of origin).[56]

In the analysis that follows, I extracted prosecutors' statements during *Batson* hearings, first-person statements from venirepersons, and objections by defense counsels where there was a sufficient record. In some cases, the decision involved the Black venireperson responding to a question in voir dire followed by the prosecutor's interpretations of the venireperson's response and statements about why these responses made them poor candidates for jury service. The prosecutors' statements are important because they are the street-level agents of the state in the implementation of the death penalty. These interactions in the jury selection process are also of interest to this project because they provide evidence of the contemporary dialogue between African Americans and the state about the death penalty and the implications of this dialogue for African Americans' relationship with the post–Civil Rights state.

Noticeably absent from this analysis are judges and their role in these hearings. The argument could be made that the prosecutor and the defense counsel play their appropriate roles in the adversarial process and that the real gatekeepers in the process are judges. It is the judge in the end who decides whether a prosecutor's statements are race neutral. Although this work focuses on the decision-making of the appeals courts, previous studies have analyzed the implementation of higher court decisions at the lower court level. Malcolm Feely concluded from his review of nearly 1,700 cases that the miniscule amount of time spent reviewing constitutional issues in lower courts indicated that "the courtroom encounter was a ritual in which the judge ratified a decision made earlier."[57] However, it should be acknowledged that it would be difficult for the court to undertake all the requirements of review outlined in *Batson* and its progeny—particularly the comparative analysis required by *Miller-El*—at the time of the immediate judgments of race neutrality in each individual voir dire. The difficulty of this review for judges also supports my conclusions.

"I Believe in Justice": The Voir Dire Response of African American Jurors

This quote is from an African American woman who was removed from a capital jury in *DeBlanc v. State of Texas* (1990). When asked her views on the death penalty she responded, "I believe in justice." This juror's response is interesting because of the particularly heinous nature of the crime in this case. David DeBlanc was convicted of murdering a Catholic priest in his rectory.[58] According to polls, DeBlanc is exactly the kind of defendant those who support the death penalty say should be executed, but all the African Americans in the venire were removed using peremptory challenges based on similar reasons. There is no prohibition against using peremptory challenges for those who oppose the death penalty, but the consistency with which these reasons are offered question findings of race neutrality. First, the African Americans who were removed opposed the death penalty. Second, they were familiar with the defendant. These two reasons reverberate through all the cases in my survey. Even if the African American venirepersons did not all personally know the defendant in a particular case, they had a familiarity with defendants in general because they had relatives or friends who had somehow become entangled in the criminal justice system.

African American responses fall into two basic categories, but in most cases jurors' responses draw from both categories. The first and most common is ambivalence about the death penalty. Twenty-four of the thirty-six African American venirepersons in this set of cases expressed feelings ranging from hesitation to opposition to the death penalty. A Black venireman who had been an employee of the state correctional system, the Texas Department of Criminal Justice (TDCJ), felt that some of the murderers he worked with in the TDCJ "might be innocent."[59] Even an employee of the state correctional system who had significant interactions with convicted murders expressed lingering doubt about their guilt. He also said that he felt that African Americans "disproportionately" received the death penalty and that Governor George W. Bush should have given Gary Graham a stay of execution.[60] This venireman was the only one to mention a previous case in explaining his opposition, but he was not the only one to mention racial discrimination in capital sentencing.

In several cases, the potential jurors based their opposition to the death penalty on religious beliefs. In *Jasper v. State of Texas* (2001), a venireperson responded he could not "play the role of God" and could "send nobody to death." Margaret Sanders, a Black woman, said, "God says vengeance is mine." Three venirepersons in *DeBlanc*, including the one mentioned above, also said that they objected to the death penalty for religious reasons. One quoted the Ten Commandments' prohibition of killing to explain her opinion. Because of the high levels of religiosity among African Americans, political views are often expressed in religious language and/or attributed to religious beliefs or biblical interpretations.[61]

In *Casarez v. State of Texas* (1993), the Court actually distinguished removal for race from removal for religion. Two Black members of the venire in *Casarez* were removed because they were Pentecostals. The defendant made a *Batson* objection, and in the hearing, the prosecutor testified that it was their religion, not their race, that motivated their removal. The bulk of the CCA's opinion in this case is an analysis of whether *Batson* also barred removal for religious views. The final decision was religion should not be treated like race. The court explained its ruling with the following:

> Persons of the same race or sex, on the other hand, are not distinguished by their beliefs, attitudes, or convictions. Because all kinds of political, moral, and religious tenets are commonly shared by people of many different races and by those of both sexes, race and sex clearly do not reveal much of anything about a prospective juror's beliefs. In short, discrimination against race and sex in American history was never based upon the proposition, rational or otherwise, that women and racial minorities subscribe to a disagreeable or undesirable belief system.[62]

This rationale illustrates one way the law could be informed by the study of Black politics. Research has shown that there is a significant coalescing of Black political and moral beliefs around particular positions, including the significant factor of religion. So it is not so clear that Blacks' experiences of racism mean that they share religious beliefs with individuals of other races within the same religion. African American views of the death penalty show that race and experiences of racism can create significant differences between Blacks and whites, even if their religious views might have significant overlap. Public opinion research has demonstrated that similar religious beliefs can lead to completely opposite policy preferences among respondents of different racial backgrounds. The death penalty is one of those instances. Blacks who identify as evangelical are more likely to oppose the death penalty than white evangelicals, who are more likely to support it.[63] Race and religion (and other aspects of identity) are highly correlated with policy preferences.[64] It is not clear how the procedures created in *Batson*, or any process, could adequately disentangle this historical and experiential mix. Thus, removal for religious beliefs could also be a proxy for removal for racial reasons.

In other cases, the venirepersons who were removed using peremptory challenges offered more general opposition to the death penalty. Jurors expressed concern about the frequency of death sentences. In one case, the venireperson did not believe that he could be convinced that a person would commit future acts.[65] This response is important because in order to sentence someone to death in Texas, one of the questions the jury must answer affirmatively is its belief that the defendant would be a future danger. This juror felt that he could not know the answer to this question. Jessie Mae Matthews and Helen Linued, venirewomen in *Cook v. State of Texas* (1993), did not support the death penalty for an accomplice who did not have a gun at the time of the crime. Matthews and Linued expressed opinions ranging from reservations about the death penalty to opposition to it.[66] One African American woman "declared in voir dire that she would falsify her answers to the special issues to avoid the death penalty."[67]

Some potential African American jury members who supported the death penalty were removed using peremptory challenges. Venireman Dreannan, in *Morris v. State of Texas* (1996), responded that he was "strongly in favor of the death penalty."[68] But even so, he was not sure he could give the death penalty to someone who was the 18-year-old defendant because he had a son who was the same age. Additionally, Dreannan testified he had spent a sleepless night worrying about his responses to questions about his views on the death penalty. Charles Brooks, in *Camacho v. State of Texas* (1993), supported the death penalty but felt that the prosecutor was too eager. Another dismissed venireperson in the same case responded, "Although I do not support the death penalty, as long as the law provides for it, I could assess it under the right circumstance."[69] Both these views, if we follow the Court's rules in *Wainwright*, should be within the spectrum of responses that would allow the venireperson to be seated, unlike the African American woman above who said she would falsify her decision to avoid the death penalty. It did not matter whether Blacks opposed or supported the death penalty; they were still subject to removal.

Another significant group of African American jurors was those who had an ambivalent relationship with the state. This ambivalence expressed itself in several ways—uneasy feelings about law enforcement or the criminal justice system, the fact that the venireperson had relatives or friends who were in the criminal justice system, and/or the fact that the person had had some kind of negative experience with the state. Venireman Vines, an African American woman in *Johnson v. State* (2002), was resentful toward the police, whom she felt abused their uniform. She also felt that her 21-year-old nephew, who was "an innocent man," was harassed because of his race, but on further questioning she admitted that she was grateful to the police for putting their lives on the line to protect the public. Margaret Sanders, in addition to her religious objections, also responded that she did not like cops. She told the prosecutor during questioning that "she did not discuss politics, religion or anything to do with the law."[70]

The largest group by far among venirepersons who had an ambivalent relationship with the state was those individuals whom the prosecutor challenged because of their connection to the criminal justice system, either personally or through friends and relatives. The example with the closest kinship ties to the criminal justice system is that of Leo Sterling, a venireman in the *DeBlanc* case, whose son had been tried for capital murder. But the level of offenses—committed by the jurors and/or friends and relatives—varied from driving with a suspended license to transporting whiskey in a dry county to a multiple-decade felony sentence. Ten of the cases involved some version of this scenario. Typically the venireperson had a brother,[71] a nephew, or some other—typically male—relative who was incarcerated or awaiting trial. For example, veniremen Earl (*Simpson v. State*) and Vines (*Johnson v. State*) both had nephews who were in Texas Department of Criminal Justice.

Links to the criminal justice system are second only to an ambivalent view about the death penalty as the most frequent reason for using peremptory challenges to remove African American jurors. As the rate of incarceration continues to increase among African Americans, the experience of being jailed or imprisoned is a factor in abridging not only the rights of African American felons but also the rights of other African Americans who are connected through filial and social networks. There may be legitimate—or strategic—legal reasons for removing those who are tangentially connected to those who are facing some punitive aspects of the criminal justice system, but this does not negate the consequences it may have for African American citizenship rights or the verdict in cases involving racial minorities defendants.[72] Moreover, the exclusion of African Americans with a connection to the criminal justice system also reinforces perceptions of linked fate and, in turn, African Americans' sympathy for criminal defendants.

"More Intuitive Than Rational, So Long as It Is Race
Neutral": Prosecutorial Interpretations of African
American Responses in *Batson* Hearings

In *Sauls v. State of Texas* (2001), four African Americans were removed from the jury for cause and one was removed using a peremptory challenge. When the prosecutor used his peremptory challenge to remove James Bell, the remaining African American, from the jury, the defense counsel raised a *Batson* objection. The prosecutor gave the following reasons for removing Bell:

(1) He was the only man in the pool wearing an earring
(2) He was the only man wearing more than one ring that was not a wedding ring, and
(3) He had on a gold medallion surrounded by at least twelve diamonds, which the prosecutor claimed was "an outward manifestation of his liberal tendencies."[73]

Defense counsel argued that dismissing Bell for wearing jewelry was racist. According to the defense, young African American men have a propensity to wear "bling."[74] Furthermore, he argued, "Wearing a lot of jewelry is not I think a valid reason to strike someone. But I do know that wearing earrings and wearing gold chains is something that a lot of young African American men do. I don't think it is a valid reason to strike." The CCA found no evidence for the defense's jewelry theory, but this case raises an interesting question about appearances. Appearance plays a pivotal role in how the prosecutors in these cases construct a race-neutral scheme for removing Black jurors.[75]

What does a death-qualified African American juror look like? In *Fuentes v. State*, the CCA upheld the removal of five African Americans through peremptory challenges, accepting the prosecutor's perception that the jurors did not appear "particularly state-oriented" as a race-neutral reason.[76] *Fuentes* demonstrates how legitimate concern over "the fairness of the criminal justice system" positions African Americans for discretionary removal.[77] Again, it is not just the bodies of Black people but also their collective experience of the criminal justice system and its biases that is being turned away from capital juries. In *Chamberlain v. Texas*, the prosecutor actually gave "her instincts" as the reason why an African American man would not make a good juror. The CCA agreed with the prosecutor, saying that "peremptory challenges may be more intuitive than rational, so long as it is race neutral." The CCA, however, failed to consider the possible connection of intuition to racist attitudes, as Thurgood Marshall did in *Swain* and several justices did in the cases that followed.

The prosecutor's perceptions of the intelligence or character of Black venirepersons is very important in jury selection. Another common justification for removal is the prosecutor's perception of a venireperson's social and intellectual abilities. In *Jasper v. State of Texas* (2001), the prosecutor testified that "he noticed mannerisms that demonstrated some uncertainties" without any explanation of what those mannerisms were. Venireperson Calvert, in *Staley v. Texas* (1994), "was nervous," according to the prosecutor. She was unable to "follow the law" and "although she worked in a restaurant, she expressed no feeling about a capital murder committed in a restaurant." She was "hesitant." She was "weak willed" and "unable to maintain any opinion in the face of questioning or challenge." According to the prosecutor in *Chambers v. State of Texas*, a litany of factors made venirewoman Cox a bad juror. She was young, she was unemployed, and she had a brother with mental problems, which, by the prosecutor's estimations, made her more sympathetic to the defendant. The prosecutor "believed [that the venirewoman] was intimidated during the individual voir dire and would not admit earlier statements" and thus would not admit the true extent of her opposition to the death penalty.[78] Two jurors completed their juror questionnaires incorrectly.[79] Henry Nichols, in *Tennard v. State* (1990), had "trouble understanding questions" and, according to the prosecutor, was of "limited intelligence."[80] Another venireman in this case was also of "low intelligence," according to the prosecutor, "such that he agreed to whoever questioned him at the time."

The most frequent reason prosecutors offered for striking jurors in the cases analyzed is that they vacillated on the death penalty. A venirewoman in *Chambers* stated, "I don't think I could vote for death" but later admitted that she could follow the law. In the same case, another African American woman "vacillated" about the death penalty. According to the prosecutor in *DeBlanc*, a venirewoman altered her views depending on whether the prosecution or the defense was questioning her. Joann Smith, in *Tennard*, "initially indicated she was opposed to the death penalty and could not vote to impose the death penalty," but later she stated that she could follow the law despite her views. In some cases, the jurors vacillated about the level of proof the state would have to mount.[81] For instance, Leo Sterling in *DeBlanc* did not believe in circumstantial evidence. In the same case, Tommy Crosby required a higher level of proof than reasonable doubt, according to the prosecutor. (In the focus group data that I discuss in the chapters that follow, this belief that the level of proof for a death conviction should be higher than the traditional standard of beyond a reasonable doubt is prevalent among those who support or are most ambivalent about the death penalty.) Finally, the use of the word "vacillate" stands out because of the Supreme Court's articulation of a rule that those who had not resolved their views about or had uncertainties about the death penalty should be included on capital juries if they could follow the law.

The implications of African Americans' familiarity with the criminal justice system through personal experience of prosecution or policing or the experiences of those in their social and or familial networks are quite pronounced in analysis of the prosecutors' explanations for removal. In *Herron v. Texas*, the CCA upheld a juror strike against a Black venirewoman for both familiarity with "defendants" and vacillating on the death penalty. The prosecutor "discovered through an out-of-court investigation" the basis for its strike. He testified that this investigation revealed that

> [she] had a reputation at her workplace for being stubborn and close-minded. . . . She had confrontations with her supervisors and co-workers. An investigator with the sheriff's office who knew [the venirewoman] advised the State that she "had a chip on her shoulder," that she would likely let race influence her verdict, and that she was not someone they wanted on the jury. The prosecutor also informed the judge that the father of [the venirewoman's] children had an extensive criminal record. In fact, [the venirewoman] had been investigated for assaulting that man. Finally, the prosecutor explained that [the venirewoman] apparently had numerous domestic relations problems which indicated a level of instability in her life.[82]

Based on the subjective view of someone outside the litigation process, the CCA was willing to accept that this venirewoman was hostile, biased, and potentially incompetent. Despite failing to demonstrate that the venirewoman was unfit under the cause analysis that allows for removal of incompetent jurors, the court upheld the peremptory strike as race neutral.[83]

In *DeBlanc*, several of the jurors knew the defendant or his family intimately, as did venirepersons in other cases. In *DeBlanc*, one venireperson also knew the accomplice the prosecutor planned to put on the witness stand in the defendant's trial. The prosecutor challenged the juror because he "felt any who knew [the accomplice] too well would not believe his testimony." In *McGee v. State of Texas*, most of the Black members of the jury panel asked to be excused because of their "familiarity" with the defendant. Defense counsel questioned one of the Black jurors about the impact of this refusal on the appellant's trial: "If all the Black people in the community asked to be excused, do you think [McGee] would get a fair trial?" The venireman replied:

> No, sir, I don't, but only if they didn't know him. If they don't know the people that's involved in it . . . maybe they could do it. But, I mean

you know, I been here twenty-six years and I went to the Laundromat with the victim. I know him. And I have seen this man walk around and I just can't do it. This is too much on me, your honor. It is.

Indeed, in several cases, members of the jury panel actually knew the defendant.

This may appear, at first reading, to rebut the argument that prosecutors are not removing African American jurors because of race but are rather removing jurors whose close proximity to the crime and the victims make them less willing to participate. I would disagree. Since *Strauder*, the Supreme Court has made clear that jury participation is an obligation of citizenship. Allowing Blacks to remove themselves from that obligation because of the difficulty of the task runs counter to the clear principle articulated in *Strauder* and reaffirmed in later cases. In *Snyder v. Louisiana*, a 2008 case involving race and peremptory challenges, the Supreme Court paid specific attention to a prosecutor's use of a peremptory challenge to remove an African American juror who expressed concern that service would interfere with another obligation.[84] The Court made clear that even reasons jurors themselves offer for why they should be excused from participation are subject to the comparative review called for in *Miller-El*.[85] Several of the cases where Black jurors literally knew the defendant were tried in small communities where it is likely that non-Black members of the community were also familiar with the defendants and/or the victims. *Snyder* stands for the principle that the difficulties imposed by jury service do not constitute a race-neutral reason for peremptory strike unless all jurors, regardless of race, are struck for similar reasons.[86]

When we consider the meanings of *Batson* hearings, the question becomes whether this type of intimate contact with defendants signals to African American venirepersons something more than the commitment of the state to race-neutral jury selection. In my discussion of the Gary Graham case in the previous chapter, I explored how not only death row inmates but also many (if not most) African American men are entangled in the criminal justice system, particularly through racially motivated police stops and police procedures such as stop-and-frisk. The frequency of these experiences gives African Americans a particular understanding of their relationship to the state and a familiarity with the experience of being under the scrutiny of law enforcement. Removing African Americans from jury pools because they express hostility toward the state and its agents is not race neutral.

Deconstructing the Batson *Ritual*

Batson hearings can be categorized as rituals because there is a visible pattern to the responses African Americans and prosecutors offer. African Americans are ambivalent about the death penalty and suspicious of the state. Prosecutors are unwilling to accept African Americans' vacillation about the death penalty, skeptical of their ability to be good jurors, and unquestioningly leery of their proximity to the criminal justice system. The beliefs prosecutors express constitute more than an assessment of the ability of a particular juror to be fair and impartial in a particular case; they constitute a rejection of the very reality of the African American experience and what it could bring to weighing evidence in capital trials.

If these are the messages, how then do we understand their meaning? There is a very strong argument to be made that *Batson* hearings are a merely symbolic gesture toward sanitizing the jury selection process of discriminatory ills such as racism. The meaning of a symbolic gesture depends on "its relationship to a set of objective truths, the sincerity of the speakers involved, the degree to which comprehensible language is used and its legitimacy to social norm and circumstances," according to Robert Wuthnow.[87] *Batson* hearings have become a visible presence in capital trials that allow the state to dissimulate continued discriminatory practices in the exercise of legal discretion. The objective truth of the jury selection process is that few African Americans sit on capital juries. The absence of Blacks from juries does not equal racist decision-making, but systematic removal of Black jurors increases the importance of race, or at least the perception of race, in the selection of jurors in capital cases.

If we accept that the integrity of the criminal justice system requires the setting of some minimal requirements for participation, then the disparate treatment of African Americans in the use of discretionary tools, such as peremptory challenges, helps push those acts to something more than merely institutional racism. The court has placed a lot of emphasis on the oath by arguing that taking an oath to be truthful in their ability to decide innocence or guilt and life or death should be sufficient validation of sincerity.[88] The court believes that the sincerity of the oath should make the race of either the juror or the defendant irrelevant. If the oath is as powerful as the Court suggests, why continue to use such a problematic legal instrument as the peremptory challenge? Justice Marshall's suggestion that we abandon peremptory challenges altogether appears to be the best course of action if the parties are truly interested in removing race or racism as a factor in discretionary challenges.[89]

One could push the Court's logic further by acknowledging that the behavior of prosecutors—as agents of the state and members of the bar—is regulated by multiple codes of conduct, including one that requires them to make sincere efforts to uphold the law.[90] If we continue to allow prosecutors (and defense attorneys, for that matter) to disguise racially biased jury selection with a race-neutral performance, it is not just the oaths of jurors that are in question but also the oaths taken by those who are charged with ensuring the fairness of the process.[91] Ultimately, the process itself is called into question.

However, one important question that arises from this aspect of ritual is: Does common language equal common meaning? In each presentation of a performance, the same words and movements are repeated. There may be changes in tone and inflection, but essentially the performances are the same. Yet it is not clear that each of the spectators is hearing them the same way and/or making the same interpretations. The possibility that the words mean different things to different participants even though they share the same language is significant. A generous reading of prosecutors' reasons for striking jurors could be that they are using only their discretion to remove jurors who have connections and opinions unfavorable to their case and that correlations of these factors to race are incidental. Yet it is possible that when African American potential jurors speak, some prosecutors hear and see only hostility to the state and its position. All too often, the result of *Batson* hearings on peremptory challenges is that even African Americans who meet the minimal criteria for participation suffer the taint of crime and exclusion because of the behavior of other members of their racial community.

Yet in a pervasively racial society it is always possible that the meanings of words differ when translated across racial lines. Do you believe in the death penalty? Yes or no? Do you believe in the death penalty for a person who was involved but did not pull the trigger? Yes or no? The monosyllabic response solicited by the question does not offer depth of meaning, but if we look at the patterns of response of multiple prospective jurors, meaning becomes clearer. So, for instance, a pattern of negative responses to questions about the death penalty by potential African American jurors could mask a more complicated relationship with the state, one that sees the state as the sometime persecutor of Black communities that are concerned about escalating violence in their neighborhoods instead of as their protector. The possibility of interracial misinterpretation, particularly in the gray area of discretionary challenges, only adds to the constitutional concerns raised by discriminatory uses of peremptory challenges.

The latter part of Wuthnow's theory about the meaningfulness of rituals—performances that provide legitimacy in relation to social norms and circumstances—is the most informative for our understanding of *Batson* hearings. The death penalty is an area of law where the Supreme Court has paid tremendous attention to "community" consensus, but it has not deconstructed the meaning of community in any meaningful way. For the last three decades, watershed decisions in capital cases have referred to polls that show that the majority of Americans support the death penalty as part of the Supreme Court's interpretation of the Eighth Amendment prohibition of cruel and unusual punishment.[92] Truly, the only place where color-blind community exists is in the fictive community constructed in the Supreme Court's death penalty decisions.[93] The death penalty is legal in 32 states and the federal government. However, a 2007 poll by the Pew Research Center found that 55 percent of African Americans opposed the death penalty; only 39 percent approved of it.[94] If we focus on Houston, we find that fewer African Americans in that city favor the death penalty than the national average.[95] A 2001 survey of residents in Harris County, one of the counties that constitute the Houston metropolitan area, found that only 32 percent of African Americans supported the death penalty (compared to 71 percent of whites).[96]

Despite significant differences in support among Blacks and whites, the Supreme Court continues to speak of community consensus for the death penalty as if community were monolithic. In fact, the Supreme Court's view of an inclusive community obscures the history of the death penalty itself as a tool that has been used to control the behavior of groups who were deemed to be outside the protected "community" because of racial or other prejudices.[97] One can point to the high incarceration rates of and the disproportionate use of the death penalty against Black and brown people today to suggest that these legal proceedings are taking place in a racialized context in which different communities have different levels of legitimacy. One of the conundrums of the criminal justice system is that African Americans bear the brunt of overpolicing and state crime policies while longing for better, safer communities, particularly those in lower socioeconomic strata.[98]

Lastly, *Batson* hearings, similar to subsequent appellate processes and the execution itself, have become ritualized steps performed in service to legitimizing the process instead of ensuring that verdicts in capital cases represent a just outcome. Understanding *Batson* hearings as a performance links it to other ways that current jurisprudence on the administration of the death penalty has focused more on procedural than on substantive justice. The view of courts as protectors of a fallible and all-too-human process has brought routine checks into the process. *Batson* hearings seem to be upholding current inequities rather than fulfilling their intended role as substantive reviews of behavior that is highly suggestive of unconstitutional practices. A good example of this transition is Supreme Court decisions concerning actual innocence in capital cases.[99] The Court has separated the underlying question (Is the defendant guilty of the crime for which he or she has been sentenced to death?) from the performance of the trial (Was the process fair?). One has to question the utility of such disconnections when the consequence in cases of actual innocence and in *Batson* violations is the failure to ensure that the objective of trial and appellate courts is fulfilled—preventing or correcting wrongful convictions and preventing or correcting impermissible uses of race in jury selection. We are left with the question of what this emphasis on form over substance means for the fairness and justice that we purport are the foundations of the entire process. *Batson* rituals leave us with a process that is less fair and just than it could be because Blacks and their views are systematically excluded from the adjudicative process.

Conclusion

The jury is a place where individual identities and values negotiate with the state over appropriate behavior and appropriate punishment. Peremptory challenges are a long tradition in litigation. The predictions by Justices Scalia and Marshall that these endeavors would involve difficult issues have been borne out in the cases that followed. The criminal justice system is an important public transcript because of its very real use of state power. The increasing connections of African Americans to the criminal justice system—directly and indirectly—make them all too familiar with this aspect of power. Most of the focus on this connection has tended to highlight how it weakens African American voting strength through the disenfranchisement of felons. This analysis reveals the other, less visible ways that African Americans are affected.

The use of *Batson* hearings with little consideration of the rights of Black jurors in capital cases in Texas courts makes a strong case for reading the hearings as little more than performance. Studies commonly point to the disproportionate representation of Black men on U.S. death row without acknowledging that the presence of Black men in other processes of the criminal justice system has important connections to their representation on death row. Moreover, the meaning of the death penalty and its discriminatory use has implications for the entire African American community. Focusing on jury selection as performance exposes those implications. African Americans are ambivalent about the death penalty largely because they are ambivalent about their relationship to the state and about the state's ability to be fair and impartial in cases involving Black defendants. The implications for the Black community become clearer as we think about how these other processes communicate the relationship between African Americans and the state.

3

Do Blacks Die Alone? The Role of Collective Identities in Individual African American Views of the Death Penalty

THIS CHAPTER BEGINS with a simple question grounded in decades of public opinion research and even more decades of the history of Black people in the United States. Do Black people die alone when their bodies are part of ritualized killings through lynchings or executions? If we were speaking only of the impact of death on the physical body, the answer might be clear that death is something that happens to all human beings. This chapter looks at the larger meaning of the legal and extralegal killing of Black people to the Black community. These techniques of violence have been used historically to control the Black community and communicate their lesser status in the body politic. In studies of Black politics, the question posed in the chapter title is a critical concern because of the way African Americans have tended to view their social, political, and economic fates as inextricably linked to each other.

In addition to the role of linked fate, this chapter also explores the way religion impacts African Americans' views of the death penalty in the contemporary racial context. Studies have shown individuals on both sides of the death penalty view their position as unequivocally supported by the Bible.[1] Even in this moral discourse, race continues to be a factor that demarcates who supports the death penalty and who does not.[2] Differences in interpretation of religious edicts and perceptions of discrimination have typically been analyzed as separate issues.[3] This chapter brings these issues together. It asks and answers a very basic question: When asked their opinion of the death penalty, are African Americans' views correlated with religion, with race, with some hybrid of the two, or with something else altogether?

The previous chapters have focused on the relationship between race, religion, and capital punishment in the media and the courts. This chapter and the chapters that follow look at individual responses to questions on these topics from both survey and focus group data. I begin the discussion of the individual-level data with survey data that identifies trends among the African American population in the Houston metropolitan area. This quantitative analysis is offered as a backdrop to the discussion of the findings in later chapters and to highlight how the data interact with dominant theories in Black politics.

Houston as Signifier: The Data and Its Utility and Limitations

The data for this chapter and the larger project draw from the Houston metropolitan area. Houston is by all metrics the epicenter of the death penalty in the United States. It leads nationally in capital convictions and is the jurisdiction of origin for cases that have culminated in executions. Six of the top ten counties in number of executions since 1976 are in Texas. Harris County, the main county covered by the city of Houston, leads the state and the nation in executions during that time period and it leads the number two county (Dallas) by more than twice as many executions (116 versus 50). The sheer number of executions has also made it an important source of cases that drive Supreme Court jurisprudence and national politics on the death penalty. Houston also has the fifth largest African American population in the United States. The combination of a concentration of executions and a large Black population make the views of this community particularly important when exploring the ideas presented in this book. In the area of capital punishment, Houston is a signifier of the racial, legal, and political complications of the continued used of this form of punishment.

The data for this chapter were taken from the Houston Area Survey (HAS).[4] I use this survey because of the breadth of its questions and because it includes a significant sample of Blacks. This survey has been conducted in February and March of each year since 1982 and is comprised of representative samples of Harris County residents. The HAS is a telephone survey (using both land lines and cell phones) that uses multistage random digit dialing to identify respondents. The survey is given to adults over 18. Since 1990, the sample size has ranged from 650 to 750. The survey reported a cooperation rate of 80 percent in its early years, but recently participation has declined.

Beginning in 1994, the survey oversampled Houston's ethnic communities with the exception of one year (1996).

The survey questions participants on a broad cross-section of issues that include poverty, ethnic relations, school quality, religious participation, political behavior, and crime and public safety. Not every question is asked every year, but most are asked consistently enough to allow for analysis across time. So, for instance, the questions, "How would you rate police protection, in terms of living in the Houston area? Would you say: excellent, good, fair, or poor?" were asked every year from 1982 to 2005 but only a few years after that. The fact that it does not ask the same questions each year is a limitation of the survey. The question of whether respondents support or oppose the death penalty was only asked six times in the period of interest—1993, 1998, 1999, 2001, 2003, and 2005—although questions relating to the death penalty were asked every year.[5]

Across the years, 5,758 African Americans were surveyed. The pattern of questioning narrows the pool of African Americans at various points in the analysis. The quantitative analysis in this chapter relies heavily on cross-tabulations to create a richer description of the African American population in Houston. The pool of respondents I analyzed included over 2,000 African Americans. I used some logistic regression analysis to draw inferences between the variables and the death penalty, but given the constraints discussed above, the model is limited. The regression analysis uses a smaller pool of 761 respondents who were simultaneously asked about death penalty support, religiosity, and perceptions of discrimination. Even with the loss of cases in the regression analysis, the sample represents a significant pool of African Americans.

Even with its limitations, the HAS is useful because it includes relevant socioeconomic variables and questions about political participation. In addition to providing information about respondents' age, education, and the other demographic variables, the HAS includes questions about residential patterns and perceptions of other ethnic groups. The richness of the data provides an opportunity to learn more about the meaning of the death penalty for African Americans in this locale and African Americans more generally. Although my geographic focus is narrow, this single locale has a broad impact on the politics of the death penalty nationally.

I used age, gender, income, and education as the basic demographic variables; I modified age and education into categorical variables.[6] A little more than 20 percent of the respondents were in the middle-age categories (24–45 and 46–55), while 14.5 percent were members of the youngest age group (18–24) and 11.5 percent were members of the oldest age group (over 65). Slightly more than 58 percent of the African American respondents were female. Some 75 percent had some college or less; respondents having only a high school diploma represented the largest cohort. Of those who had completed college, the majority had undergraduate degrees and 9 percent had graduate and professional degrees. Almost 74 percent of the Black respondents reported having attended religious services other than a wedding or a funeral in the previous thirty days. As expected, 69.3 percent self-identified as Democrats, compared to 5.2 percent who identified as Republican. Despite the prevalence of Democrats in this group, more than three-fourths of the respondents identified as either moderates (36.7 percent) or conservatives (39.4 percent). Interestingly, respondents identifying as liberals represented the smallest group.

For or Against? African American Support for the Death Penalty in the Houston Area Survey

Among the African Americans surveyed in the HAS, almost 52 percent opposed the death penalty and 48 supported it (Table 3.1).[7] Support for the death penalty was not even across age groups. The oldest participants were the least likely to support it.[8] Of the respondents who were 45 to 65 years old, 53.5 percent opposed the death penalty; of those over 65, a full 60.5 opposed the death penalty. The youngest cohort showed slightly higher levels of opposition than those between the ages of 24 and 45.[9] Respondents who were 45 in the 2005 survey would have been born in 1959 and come of age during the political unrest of the 1960s and 1970s. It is possible that the perspective of

Table 3.1 African Americans for or against the Death Penalty by Age[1]

Age	18–24	24–35	35–45	45–65	65 +	Total
Against	165	238	211	349	176	1,139
	50.5%	48.2%	49.9%	53.5%	60.5%	52.1%
For	162	256	212	303	115	1,048
	49.5%	51.8%	50.1%	46.5%	39.5%	47.9%
Total	327	494	423	652	291	2,187
	100%	100%	100%	100%	100%	100%

1. Pearson's Chi-square = 0.012.

Source: Houston Area Survey, 1993, 1998, 2001, 2003, and 2005.

this group and those who are older was influenced by these experiences and memories of past race relations in the United States. In the focus group data discussed in the chapters that follow, the oldest cohort was also the most emphatically opposed to the death penalty.

The education levels of the older cohort may also have some influence. One of the focus groups was comprised of all elderly women at an activity center for senior citizens. All but one of these women had not finished high school or had only a high school diploma. In the HAS data, Blacks with the lowest levels of education had the greatest opposition to the death penalty. Of Blacks who did not finish high school, 55.9 percent were against the death penalty and only a slightly smaller proportion of those with only a high school diploma (55 percent) were against it. The highest level of support for the death penalty came from Blacks with a college degree (54 percent). Black respondents with graduate or professional degrees had greater opposition to the death penalty than those with only an undergraduate degree (48.9 percent) but showed less opposition than those with a high school diploma or less (as shown in Table 3.2).

The older cohort's views might also be explained by income. Respondents with the lowest household incomes had the strongest opposition to the death penalty; the highest opposition came from respondents with a household income of less than $15,000 annually. Income and education are highly correlated generally, and that is the case in this sample (as shown in Table 3.3).

The majority of African American female respondents (55.3 percent) were against the death penalty, but only 47.1 percent of African American

Table 3.2 African Americans for or against the Death Penalty by Education[1]

	No high school diploma	High school diploma	Some college	Undergrad degree	Graduate or professional degree	Total
Against	162	333	416	172	97	1,180
	55.9%	55.0%	50.9%	46.0%	51.1%	51.8%
For	128	272	401	202	93	1,096
	44.1%	45.0%	49.1%	54.0%	48.9%	48.25
Total	290	605	817	374	190	2,276
	100%	100%	100%	100%	100%	100%

1. Pearson's Chi-square = 0.044.

Source: Houston Area Survey, 1993, 1998, 2001, 2003, and 2005.

Table 3.3 African Americans for or against the Death Penalty by Income[1]

	Less than $15,000	$15,000 to $25,000	$25,001 to $35,000	$35,001 to $50,000	$50,001 to $75,000	More than $15,000	Total
Against	195	214	179	174	129	107	998
	62.1%	55.7%	53.0%	47.8%	44.3%	46.1%	51.9%
For	119	170	159	190	162	125	925
	37.9%	44.3%	47.0%	52.2%	55.7%	53.9%	48.1%
Total	314	384	338	364	291	232	1,923
	100%	100%	100%	100%	100%	100%	100%

1. Pearson's Chi-square = 0.000.

Source: Houston Area Survey, 1993, 1998, 2001, 2003, and 2005.

men were opposed. This gender gap was quite significant (as shown in Table 3.4). This finding seems odd in light of the emphasis in African American political discourse on African American men and the male slant of the African American political agenda.[10] In spite of the domination of men in the discourse and agenda of the African American community, it has been theorized that the unique position of African American women's experience of "interlocking systems of oppression" of race and gender has "produce[d] a powerful dynamic of activism that is absent from the political behaviors of African American men and attitudes of White women."[11] This difference is seen in higher registration and voting rates among African American women than among Black men.

**Table 3.4 African Americans for or against
the Death Penalty by Gender[1]**

	Male	Female	Total
Against	460	722	1,182
	47.1%	55.3%	51.8%
For	517	584	1,101
	52.9%	44.7%	48.2%
Total	977	1,306	2,283
	100%	100%	100%

1. Pearson's Chi-square = 0.000.

Source: Houston Area Survey, 1993, 1998, 2001, 2003, and 2005.

African American women also show stronger support for feminist principles than white women.[12] This increased political participation and identification with freedom struggles may cross over to other perceived locations of oppression. The combination of the complexity of gender norms and discourse in the African American community and past connections between the death penalty and Black masculinity would suggest that there is more here than a simple gender gap or the outcome of increased political participation.

Linked Fate and the Collective Effects of the Death Penalty

The prevailing theory of Black political preferences and behavior is grounded in African American collectivist sentiments in the form of linked fate, the idea that the political identities of African Americans are shaped by feelings of closeness to other African Americans and that their individual futures are tied to the futures of the whole group.[13] Though the belief in linked fate has its origins in past marginalization, it persists because of the daily oppression of African Americans.[14] Linked fate has been used to explain political behavior in the Black community. The racial solidarity embodied in the concept of linked fate is incubated in African American religious institutions.

In her study of ideology in Black discursive spaces, *Barbershop, Bibles, and BET*, Melissa Harris-Lacewell adds the idea of a "black common sense" to the study of Black public opinion, "the idea among African Americans that blackness is a meaningful political category" and that those that adhere "to a black common sense tradition perceive blackness as identifiable, persistent over time, and relevant to making personal life decisions." Harris-Lacewell's idea of "black common sense" is not dissimilar to the theory of folk knowledge I use in the next chapter. This chapter examines two of the most salient factors in African American political behavior and opinion—linked fate and religiosity—and looks at how they relate to attitudes about the death penalty.

Linked fate continues to be a powerful theory because of Blacks' perceptions of racial discrimination. The HAS asks respondents how often they personally felt discriminated against and how often they felt that members of their ethnic group were discriminated against. Thus, I was able to cross-tabulate two measures of perceptions of discrimination with support for or opposition to the death penalty. Both of these cross-tabulations demonstrate a significant relationship between perceptions of discrimination and support for or opposition to the death penalty (as shown in Tables 3.5 and 3.6). Blacks who reported feeling discriminated against very often had a high level of opposition to the death penalty

Table 3.5 African Americans for or against the Death Penalty
by Feelings of Personal Discrimination Because of Ethnicity[1]

	Never	Rarely	Fairly often	Very often	Total
Against	109	276	188	137	710
	48.2%	45.2%	50.4%	55.9%	48.8%
For	117	334	185	108	744
	51.8%	54.8%	49.6%	44.1%	51.2%
Total	226	610	373	245	1454
	100%	100%	100%	100%	100%

1. Pearson's Chi-square = 0.037.

Source: Houston Area Survey, 1993, 1998, 2001, 2003, and 2005.

(55.9 percent). Opposition to the death penalty decreased as the respondents feel little to no personal discrimination. Most telling in the analysis of these measures is that opposition to the death penalty is even higher for African Americans who felt that members of their ethnic group were discriminated against very often (58.9 percent).

These results suggest that perception of group discrimination is more important in determining opposition to the death penalty than perceptions of individual discrimination. The range in opposition to the death penalty between individuals who felt they were very often personally discriminated against and those who felt they were only fairly often the objects of discrimination was 5.5 percent. However, the range more than doubles, to 12.8 percent, when opposition to the death penalty for those who felt members of their ethnic community were very often discriminated against is compared to the views of those who felt their community was only fairly often discriminated against.

These results are important because they allow us to analyze the impact of linked fate on African American attitudes toward the death penalty. Traditional analysis of belief in linked fate uses the question, "Do you think what happens to black people in this country will have something to do with what happens in your life?"[15] This question was asked in each year of the National Black Election Study Series.[16] Because the HAS was constructed to look at large sociological, economic, and political issues, the variables that measure perceptions of discrimination are the closest proxy for linked fate this survey provides. The HAS asks, "How often are [members of respondent's ethnic group] discriminated against in Houston?" Respondents could reply very often, fairly often, rarely, or never. This question alone would be an

Table 3.6 African Americans for or against the Death Penalty by Feelings of Group Discrimination[1]

	Never	Rarely	Fairly often	Very often	Total
Against	9	82	228	269	588
	42.9%	48.5%	46.1%	58.9%	51.5%
For	12	87	267	188	554
	57.1%	51.5%	53.9%	41.15	48.5%
Total	21	169	495	457	1142
	100%	100%	100%	100%	100%

1. Pearson's Chi-square = 0.000.

Source: Houston Area Survey, 1993, 1998, 2001, 2003, and 2005.

insufficient proxy for measuring linked fate, but the HAS also asks respondents about their perceptions of discrimination against themselves. Thus, it is possible to cross-tabulate answers about a respondent's own discrimination with perceptions about discrimination against other members of his or her group. The fact that perceptions of group discrimination yield higher opposition to the death penalty is strongly suggestive that the group dynamic has a greater influence on respondents' opposition to the death penalty.

Katherine Tate and Michael Dawson theorize that the origins of beliefs in linked fate lie in people's lived experiences of race and class oppression.[17] Dawson uses the term "black utility heuristic," which he defines as follows:

> My framework is based on two assumptions. First, it is quite clear that, until the mid-1960s, race was the decisive factor in determining the opportunities and life chances available to virtually all African Americans, regardless of their own or their family's social and economic status. Consequently, it was much more efficient for Americans to determine what was good for themselves individually, and more efficient for African Americans to determine what was good for the racial group, both relative and absolute, as a proxy for individual utility.[18]

My analysis of the data in the HAS finds a greater influence of perceptions of group discrimination than personal discrimination in determining attitudes toward the death penalty. This is aligned with Dawson's reading of the group dynamics of the African American community. These levels of perception of discrimination are key to understanding the strains of collectivist sentiment other research has found among African American survey respondents and its impact on attitudes about the death penalty.

The contemporary meaning and relevance of linked fate has come under scrutiny as a result of the fragmented successes of African Americans in the post–Civil Rights period. Looking at the relationship between income and perceptions of discrimination can help piece together the puzzle of how to understand and analyze the persistence of beliefs in linked fate. The majority of the African American respondents in the HAS in the three highest income brackets felt they were "rarely" discriminated against, but the majority in the low-income brackets felt they were discriminated against fairly often. The highest percentage of the respondents who felt they were discriminated against very often was among those in the lowest income bracket as seen in Table 3.7. If we look at perceptions of group rather than personal discrimination, the picture is quite different. Although those in the lower income brackets reported that those in their ethnic group experienced higher levels of discrimination, the majority of respondents in each income bracket felt that members of their ethnic group were discriminated against often. This finding suggests that even though a small proportion of respondents reported experiences of personal discrimination, many more respondents were willing to acknowledge or identify group-level discrimination.

Table 3.7 Income of African Americans by Perceptions of Group Discrimination[1]

	Less than $15,000	$15,000 to $25,000	$25,001 to $35,000	$35,001 to $50,000	$50,001 to $75,000	More than $75,000	Total
Never	8	9	3	8	2	2	32
	2.2%	2.1%	0.6%	0.6%	0.5%	0.6%	1.35%
Rarely	51	72	55	84	48	52	362
	13.9%	17.2%	11.7%	16.7%	11.7%	16.0%	14.5%
Fairly often	124	170	200	217	199	167	1077
	33.7%	40.6%	42.6%	43.1%	48.5%	51.2%	43.1%
Very often	185	168	211	195	161	167	1025
	50.3%	40.1%	45.0%	38.7%	39.3%	51.2%	41.1%
Total	368	419	469	504	410	326	2496
	100%	100%	100%	100%	100%	100%	100%

1. Pearson's Chi-square = 0.000.

Source: Houston Area Survey, 1993, 1998, 2001, 2003, and 2005.

Race, Religion, and Perceptions of the Death Penalty

Previous studies of the death penalty have used survey data to show that although the majority of Americans support the death penalty, the majority of African Americans do not.[19] Local surveys have found that support for the death penalty among African Americans in the Houston metropolitan area is lower than the national average for African Americans and for Americans generally. The lower level of support could be explained by the frequency with which state officials seek the death penalty in this jurisdiction, but the values and norms that drive African Americans' objections to the death penalty cannot be summed up by proximity to a hostile criminal justice system.[20]

The levels of incarceration among African Americans in the United States illustrate the increasing entanglement of Blacks in the nation's criminal justice systems. Incarceration rates generally have steadily increased even though the crime rate has leveled off. Jeff Yates and Richard Fording reiterate the political nature of incarceration policies and suggest that "we might reasonably consider the relative imprisonment rates as a political outcome in which blacks have not fared well."[21] By the late 1990s, an African American was eight times more likely to be incarcerated than a white person—the largest disparity in recent history.[22]

Yates and Fording measured the political environment of state politics and its impact on racial disparities in incarceration. They found that "while the relative imprisonment rates of blacks and whites may have certain root causes in common, there are important differences in the determinants of imprisonment rates between the two races."[23] Their most significant finding is that "conservative elite political environments operate to disproportionately amplify the imprisonment rates of blacks."[24] Yates and Fording conclude with this description of the double bind that increasing rate of imprisonment creates for African Americans:

> First, the law and order policy of conservative political officials yield increased (and relatively disproportionate) imprisonment rates for blacks. Second, imprisonment often leads to disenfranchisement, and thus, blacks are in jeopardy of becoming increasingly politically marginalized and unable to elect the officials who could possibly serve to improve their relative lot in criminal justice policy outcomes.[25]

With this work, Yates and Fording show the effect in states of the increased use of the "race card" in presidential campaigns that play to white racial resentment.[26] Tali Mendelberg demonstrates how presentations of crime with a Black face can be used to wage successful electoral campaigns.[27]

Jon Hurwitz and Mark Peffley point to the sad truth that political scientists have paid little attention to race and crime.[28] These coauthors are the first to give substantial empirical attention to comparative analysis of Blacks' and whites' views of the criminal justice system. Others had focused on the effect of attitudes about the justice system in individual communities but not in ways that allowed for the comparative analysis by racial groups.[29] Most instructive for this project is Hurwitz and Peffley's work on how racial and nonracial arguments against the death penalty are received or resisted across racial lines. They find that African Americans are much "more responsive to persuasive appeals that are both racial and nonracial (i.e., innocence) in nature" because they are predisposed to believe that "the criminal justice system is racially unfair." Although it has been known for a long time that views on the death penalty diverged among Blacks and whites, even Hurwitz and Peffley were "startled" to find "many whites became more supportive of the death penalty upon learning that it discriminates against blacks." They found that whites "seem immune to persuasion and, in the case of the racial argument [against the death penalty], exhibit a response in the direct opposite of the message."[30]

Yet increased support for punitive policies does not lead to death in many states. In Texas, death is a form of punishment that is used much more often than in other states that may have large death rows but few executions. In Texas, the death penalty is supported by both elected officials and public opinion. The mixture of norms and values that has led Texas to become the center of the modern American death penalty goes beyond secular political beliefs; the values that have led to this phenomenon involve beliefs about life and death that are profoundly influenced by religion. Religious rhetoric that both state officials and African Americans use tells us much about the entanglement of religion and politics on this issue in Texas and, I suspect, elsewhere.

In his study of religious orientation, race, and attitudes about the death penalty using the General Social Survey, Robert L. Young found that the evangelical emphasis on "concern and compassion for others" was more pronounced among Black Americans and that the fact that these collectivist tendencies were supported by Black religious institutions led to lower support for the death penalty.[31] The Black church is by all accounts the most important political institution in the African American community, but its impact on African Americans' preferences on policy issues is unclear.[32] Young analyzes attitudes about fairness and race and correlates his findings with evidence of support for the death penalty in previous work.[33]

Young's analysis provides a fruitful direction for my own work. The HAS asks several questions on religious participation and identity. My own research uses variables similar to those Young used to measure respondents' prioritization of religion, beliefs in Biblical literalism, and church attendance.[34] The HAS respondents primarily identified themselves as fundamentalists (56.5 percent).[35] The next largest group identified themselves as religious progressives (35 percent), and a small number of respondents identified themselves as secularists (8.5 percent). Identification as fundamentalist declined as the household income increased. In the lowest income bracket, 67.4 percent of the respondents identified as fundamentalist, while 46.3 percent of those in the highest income bracket identified in this way.

The respondents also have a high level of church attendance; 73.6 percent reported having attended a religious service other than a wedding or funeral in the previous 30 days. Church attendance was correlated with income and age. The higher the income bracket, the higher the number of respondents who reported attending a religious service in the previous 30 days that was not a funeral or wedding. The respondents in the lowest income brackets reported having attended church significantly less than those in the highest bracket.

The survey results show significant gender differences in the reporting of religious importance. African American men were more likely to identify as religious progressives and secularists than African American women. Among African American women, 61.7 percent identified as religious fundamentalists compared to 49.1 percent of African American men. The gender gap between those identifying as religious progressives was much smaller: 32.6 percent of women and 38.4 percent of men identified in this way. African American men were more than twice as likely to identify as secularists as African American women—12.6 percent compared to 5.7 percent.

The gender difference might be explained by the increased participation of African American women in Black religious institutions, but this difference in participation should not be read to mean that these institutions are reflective of the interests or political attitudes of the women who participate in them.[36] Similar to Young's analysis of General Social Survey data, my research finds that African Americans who identify as fundamentalist show less support for the death penalty than those who identify as religious progressives or secularists. However, in my research the cross-tabulations of the religious variables were not significant.

I was interested in how the Black respondents in the HAS rated on other measures associated with political conservatism generally and religious conservatism specifically. The increased participation of white Christian evangelicals in the public sphere since the early 1980s is driven by views on particular issues such as prayer in schools, abortion, and views on homosexuality. African Americans in the HAS reflect conservatism on these issues similar to the conservatism of white Christian evangelicals and Blacks in other locations. Among African American respondents in the HAS, 86 percent supported religious prayer at official school functions. Sixty-one percent said they believed that abortion was morally wrong and slightly more than 67 percent supported a law requiring parental consent before a female under 18 could have an abortion. Similarly, 68 percent of African American respondents believed that homosexuality was morally wrong. However, these views did not always translate into the policies that are normally aligned with them. Even though a majority of the African American respondents in the HAS felt that homosexuality was wrong, 69 percent agreed that gay marriages should be given legal status equal to that of heterosexual marriages and supported efforts to guarantee civil rights for homosexual men and women.

There was a significant correlation between opposition to the death penalty and party identification in the cross-tabulation and the regression analysis discussed below. The respondents who identified as members of the Democratic Party had the greatest opposition to the death penalty as seen in Table 3.8. Those who identified as Republicans had the least opposition to the death penalty. The majority of African Americans are Democrats and vote for Democratic candidates, but the strength of identification with this party is not enough to

Table 3.8 African Americans for or against the Death Penalty
by Party Identification[1]

	Independent	Republican	Democrat	Total
Against	158	43	825	1,026
	48.0%	36.8%	53.4%	51.5%
For	171	74	720	965
	52.0%	63.2%	46.6%	48.5%
Total	329	117	1,545	1,991
	100%	100%	100%	100%

1. Pearson's Chi-square = 0.001.

Source: Houston Area Survey, 1993, 1998, 2001, 2003, and 2005.

explain increased opposition to the death penalty. Michael Dukakis's opposition to the death penalty led to a sound beating in the 1988 presidential campaign that was attributed to his "soft-on-crime" position.[37] This soft-on-crime position did not diminish support for the Democratic Party among Black voters. Clinton took the exact opposite approach and is beloved by the Black community. However, similar soft-on-crime narratives did not emerge in the 2004 election, despite John Kerry's opposition to the death penalty. This may have marked some change in the symbolic meaning of the death penalty, but we would need to observe more election cycles to know. The nuanced position of Barack Obama on the death penalty, although he is still in favor of it, may support the assertion that strong support of the death penalty is no longer a requirement in national electoral politics.

African Americans' affiliation with the Democratic Party is very complicated. Before the 1960s, African American support for both parties shifted more times than is acknowledged in current discussions of party alignment. When the parties became hostile to the interests of the Black community, there were always slippages.[38] Since 1964, Black party support has been consolidated in the Democratic Party and this consolidation has been consistent and stable. This stability is demonstrated not only in the voting behavior of African Americans but also in their consistent view of the Democratic Party as working harder for Black interests than the Republican Party.[39] This perception may include a perception that the Democratic Party is most responsive to the community's concerns about the death penalty and other issues related to the criminal justice system. This correlation was statistically significant, implying that African Americans who oppose the death penalty believe that the Democratic Party is more likely to represent their interests on these issues.

The Death Penalty and the Interactive Effects of Modern Political Contexts: The Regression Model and Its Implications

The significant relationship between perceptions of community-level discrimination and opposition to the death penalty suggests that sentiments of linked fate influence African Americans' positions on the death penalty. Racial discrimination against one African American signals to those who may or may not have had the same experiences the possibility that any member of their community, including themselves, could be treated that way. This is the power of lynching and reminders of lynching, such as a lynching tree or even a noose hung in a public square. The current rates of incarceration have created a state of affairs where many members of the African American community have some connection through familial or friendship networks to persons involved in the criminal justice system. It is likely that these conditions amplify the influence of linked fate in attitudes about the death penalty and other criminal justice policies.

As a way of better understanding the possible interactions among the variables in the HAS, I tested the variables using logistic regression. The model includes the variables of age, gender, education, income, religious importance, church attendance, party identification, political ideology, fear of crime, and feelings of personal and community discrimination. In my logistic regression, I analyzed all of these variables together to create an approximate measure of linked fate. The five significant variables for this regression are income, church attendance, partisan identification, fear of crime, and perception of group discrimination. The discussion that follows takes up the significance of each of these variables.

The probability of support for the death penalty was 20 percent higher for those in the highest income category than for those in the lowest category

Table 3.9 Logistic Regression of Model of Support for the Death Penalty

Variable	Coefficient	Marginal Effect for Significant Variables
Age	0.005	
Gender	−0.099	−0.0629
Education	0.020	
Income	**0.165**[1]	**0.203**
Religious importance	−0.202	
Church attendance	**−0.381**[1]	**−0.095**
Party identification	**−0.449**[1]	**0.110**
Political ideology	0.013	
Fear of crime	**0.131**[2]	**0.098**
Perceptions of individual discrimination	−0.052	
Perceptions of group discrimination	**−0.252**[1]	**−0.186**
Constant	1.53	
−2 log likelihood	1,018.002	

1. $p < 0.05$; N = 761.
2. $p < 0.10$.

Source: Houston Area Survey, 1993, 1998, 2001, 2003, and 2005.

(as seen in Table 3.9). In *The Boundaries of Blackness*, Cathy Cohen argues that the consensus issues that fit neatly into existing community narratives often overshadow cross-cutting issues that affect subpopulations of the Black community. *The Boundaries of Blackness* analyzes the failure of Black political institutions to respond to the HIV and AIDS crisis, but the larger argument of her work is that the presence of members of the Black community who are somehow blighted by moral or legal taint (and I would add poverty) is antithetical to the dominant political discourse of moral and economic uplift among African Americans. Although Blacks who commit capital crimes arguably suffer from both the moral and legal taint of criminality and imprisonment, the broader concern about incarceration and issues of racial injustice in the criminal justice system tend to keep capital punishment on the list of political concerns of the Black community.

This could explain how cross-cutting issues that have a visible impact on some members of the African American community can motivate members who are not directly affected to become politically active on their behalf, at least in certain moments, such as when Gary Graham used the lynching narrative to describe his case. It can also explain why Blacks in lower income groups show higher opposition to the death penalty. Major works, largely in other disciplines, have already begun to connect what is now being called hyperincarceration (rather than mass incarceration) and the criminalization of the Black body today to political projects that reach as far back as Reconstruction or are as recent as the War on Drugs.[40] Hyperincarceration is linguistically and empirically accurate way to describe how heightened incarceration has disproportionately impacted poor Black men (but increasingly also poor Black women) and have left most of the rest of American society "untouched[,] including middle- and upper-class African Americans"—the Blacks who have seen the most progress post–Civil Rights.[41]

The difference in perceptions of both personal and group discrimination among the various income groups adds to Cohen's claim that subpopulations have fragmented the post–Civil Rights politics of the African American community. Not only do the respondents in the lower income brackets have higher opposition to the death penalty, they also attend church less and feel more personal and group discrimination. Church attendance was a significant predictive variable; there was a significant increase in opposition to the death penalty among those who attended church services. The probability of opposition to the death penalty was 9.5 percent higher for those who attended church than for those who did not.

Cohen and Dawson have shown that Blacks living in communities with higher concentrations of poverty tend to be more socially isolated and have greater suspicion of other groups in American society.[42] My findings suggest that this group of African Americans is not only isolated from the larger American community but also from institutions that are indigenous to the African American community. The poorest members of the African American community see themselves as vulnerable in ways that may explains their higher levels of opposition to the death penalty. They may feel more subject to it, and accurately so.

Blacks who believed that Blacks were discriminated against often were 18.6 percent less likely to support the death penalty than those who believed that Blacks were never discriminated against (as seen in Table 3.9). Those with lower incomes felt that they experienced higher levels of discrimination than those on the higher end of the income spectrum and also had a greater fear that they or their family members would be victims of crime. In this analysis and in the focus group data, the facts that most homicides are intraracial and that Black killers of Black victims receive the lightest sentences seem to be left out of their conceptualization of their vulnerability. The data also suggests that others in the Black community see no utility in helping them become less vulnerable.

Neither the multivariate nor the bivariate analysis showed any significant relationship between importance of religion and support for or opposition to the death penalty. Young's study also found no significant relationship between fundamentalist views and Blacks' attitudes toward the death penalty. The duplication of this finding is important because it suggests that the opinions of African Americans in Harris County may be reflective of Black opinion in other parts of the country on these variables. This finding is not surprising; past studies have argued that a person's relationship to the Black church does not sufficiently predict their political activism. Allison Calhoun-Brown most strongly demonstrates this in her study of the context and content of the rhetoric of Black churches. She finds that it is not whether or not Blacks attend church or participate in religious activities but whether or not they attend and participate in activities at political churches that predicts how going to church affects political views.[43] Tamelyn Tucker-Worgs and Eric McDaniel have expanded the work of Calhoun-Brown and others to explain how a church's pastor, members, organization, and environment impact the likelihood that a churchgoer will engage in political activity.[44] Their data does not distinguish the actual character of the religious institutions in which respondents participate, but some of the links between church rhetoric and views on the death penalty will be explored in the focus groups.

Black Support for the Death Penalty and the Need to Understand Black Racial Resentment: Space for Critical Investigations

One aspect of the questions about race and support for the death penalty that has not been addressed is why a significant portion of the Black community in Houston and in other locales supports the death penalty. It is hard from the HAS data to identify why this is so, but it does offer some insight into who might be in the minority group of Blacks who support the death penalty. The literature on Black resentment and conservatism within the Black community provides helpful guidance for speculating about why these attitudes exist in the face of clear demonstrations of bias in the use of capital punishment. It is possible that the cohort of Blacks who support the death penalty are made up of these two groups—Black conservatives and Blacks who hold high levels of Black racial resentment—with the possibility of some overlap between the two. I am not asserting that all Blacks who support capital punishment hold anti-Black sentiments or are politically conservative, but am suggesting that this might be a place to consider the way such sentiments might work in the analysis of criminal justice policies like the death penalty.

Blacks are not immune to the negative stereotypes that Blacks are criminals and are prone to violence that have created heightened support for capital punishment among other racial groups. In *Dreaming Blackness: Black Nationalism and African American Public Opinion*, Melanye Price argues quite successfully that the focus on linked fate as the primary measure of Black racial attitudes has overemphasized areas of racial solidarity and largely ignored the policy preferences of Blacks who have internalized negative attitudes of their racial community.[45] Current work on Black racial resentment might allow us to parse those Blacks who have internalized negative stereotypes about other Blacks and those Blacks who hold conservative, or simply contrary, political views to the larger Black community.

Byron D'Andra Orey's work examines the operation of racial resentment and conservatism among African Americans. Orey points to both how racial resentment structures conservatism in the Black community and how high levels of racial resentment impact the policy preferences of some Blacks.[46] Orey grounds his explanation of Black conservatism in the debates about the form and substance of Black protest in the writings of Booker T. Washington and then moves forward to more recent writing in political theory. As Orey eloquently puts it, "To be sure, African American conservatives have provided support for traditional conservative issues like welfare reform and abortion (i.e., pro-life positions); however, it appears that some of this conservatism may be a function of resentment toward other African Americans."[47] But at this moment, we cannot distinguish when Black conservatism is linked to Black racial resentment.

In more recent work, Orey, Craemer, and Price move us further along in our understanding of implicit racial attitudes among Blacks. This research direction is relevant to this project not only because it helps us understand policy preferences among Blacks but also because lawyers who represent persons on death row have recently become interested in studies that measure implicit racial attitudes.[48] Lawyers have latched on to this type of research because it offers a clear and systematic explanation of the how implicit racial bias impacts decision-making in criminal cases, particularly among jurors. Studies using implicit attitude testing have demonstrated how race impacts juror's perceptions of defendant's death-worthiness, cross-racial identification in eyewitness testimony, and how race leads to the dehumanization of Black defendants.[49] A 2013 article in the *New York University Law Review* showed that death-qualified jurors are more likely to harbor implicit racial bias that leads them to believe that Black lives were worthless and white lives were more valuable.[50] Work on implicit racial bias has provided insight into the operation of race in spaces where the law does not allow lawyers to interrogate.

However, Orey and his colleagues highlight one of the flaws of previous studies of implicit racial attitudes. Most of the studies have relied almost exclusively on white subjects. Orey, Craemer, and Price argue that both of the probable reasons for near-uniform exclusions of Black subjects are "problematic because [they] treat black racial attitudes as a monolith."[51] The measures used in these studies were developed to assess the social desirability among whites of biased attitudes toward Blacks, and the studies did not see anti-Black sentiments among Blacks as particularly important. The presence of such biases among Blacks is important because they are indicative of opposition to policies—such as affirmative action, welfare, reparations—which others in their racial community view as favorable to the group. If we couple the absence of Blacks in this increasingly important area of research with the dearth of Blacks in national surveys, we are left with a rather limited understanding of how anti-Black sentiments within the Black community impact policy preferences among Black people.

However, I think we have enough data to make some speculations about the impact of anti-Black sentiments and Black conservatism on capital punishment. We know from a previous study that Black conservatism is intimately linked to class and that it "dovetails quite nicely with the long-standing white supremacist notion that the unequal position of blacks is due neither to racism nor to systemic economic conditions but to the inappropriate behavior of blacks themselves."[52] We know that there is greater support for the death penalty among Blacks in the HAS who identify as Republican. Blacks who report rarely or never experiencing either personal or group discrimination also have higher levels of support for the death penalty. More Black men support the death penalty than Black women. Blacks in higher income brackets are more likely to support the death penalty than those with lower incomes. A higher proportion of Blacks with only an undergraduate degree support the death penalty than those in other education categories.

Most of these factors have been linked to conservatism and higher levels of racial resentment. Association with the Republican Party is a clear marker of conservatism among Blacks and whites.[53] Education is not just a measure of ideology among Blacks; it is also a measure of class.[54] When you couple that with the finding that Blacks with higher incomes were also more likely to support the death penalty, we find greater support for the suggestion that there may be a class story that explains why Blacks support the death penalty. Although I am using questions on perceptions of group and individual discrimination as proxies for the traditional measure of linked fate, we also see more support for the death penalty among those who never or rarely experience discrimination and those who believe that other Blacks never or rarely experience discriminate. This suggests that they see themselves and their experiences as less linked to those of other Blacks. However, lower levels of perception that one's fate is linked to that of other members of his or her race do not necessarily mean higher levels of racial resentment or conservatism. Within the limitations of the survey, I am able to construct a proxy for linked fate, but the question of racial resentment is simply beyond reach with the data resources to which I have access.

Conclusion

Future empirical investigation should allow for more specific analysis of the variables used in this survey. The very basic statistical analysis discussed in this chapter could be greatly augmented with the addition of several questions to the HAS and new waves of the National Black Election Survey. First, it would be useful to see data on responses to more specific questions about religious institutions than questions that limit themselves to what type of religion respondents identify with and whether or not the respondents participate in the religion they identify with. Calhoun-Brown and McDaniel have demonstrated the need to distinguish between personal religious sentiments and the effects of religious institutions in the Black community. Additionally, more direct measures of ideology would help us ascertain the impact of ideology on attitudes about the death penalty. Future research may explore the interaction of African Americans' ideologies with other parts of the criminal justice system and the correlation of measures of ideology with measures of opinions about the death penalty. Finally, it is very important to include questions about the implicit racial attitudes of African Americans. This knowledge will help us understand the policy preferences of Blacks and whether the theories that have been derived from existing studies about implicit racial attitudes are applicable to the Black community.

4

———

What We Tell Each Other: African American Folk Knowledge of the Death Penalty

THE ORAL TRADITION in Black American community has been an instrument of both survival and resistance. The communication of knowledge from one to another was necessitated by the circumstances of chattel slavery and the attempts of repressive states—and some citizens—to continue those conditions and control after emancipation. Not all communication was a life-and-death matter, but when life and death were at stake, networks were essential to protect individuals and communities. The poem excerpted in the epigraph of this chapter could be read simply as a fictional telling of the very real attempts of enslaved women to exercise reproductive control by the passing of information and roots. That reading is an important one. In the context of this work, this poem also tells the corporeal reality of Black women's bodies in relationship to unchecked white supremacy and state injustice. The collective wisdom of Black people has operated broadly as sword and shield in circumstances where Black people found their rights and bodies to be in critical conflict with the state. The death penalty is a life-and-death issue. This chapter gets us to the root of what information is passed among African Americans about the death penalty.

The previous chapters have analyzed race and religion using public narratives about the death penalty and individual responses to survey questions. This chapter looks at informal conversations in which African Americans reveal their collective wisdom or folk knowledge about the death penalty. It asks what Black people tell each other about this form of punishment and how race, religion, and citizenship inform those conversations. The law, especially criminal law, has long been understood as the state's attempt to regulate the behavior of its citizens or anyone within reach of its jurisdiction. The legislature codifies laws after some debate and compromise, but individual citizens rarely know the specific details of what is written. Perceptions of the law vary widely across time and communities as the law shifts from the page to the tangible aspects of social control. How citizens understand the law, its requirements, and the penalties of failing to meet those requirements becomes the informal or *folk knowledge* of a community.

Legal theory has taken "folk knowledge" to mean "the everyday, taken-for-granted understandings that shape people's perceptions, thinking, actions and reactions to events and situations."[1] I argue that this common-sense knowledge of the law also influences the political actions of individuals. Folk knowledge, like all knowledge, is situated within a cultural, political, legal, and geographic context. Previous discussions have made clear that for African Americans almost everything that relates to state policy is filtered through the lens of race. The folk knowledge of African Americans about the death penalty is similarly filtered. Cultural studies scholars have also pointed to the primacy of the spoken word because of the oral tradition in the Black community. Jordie, Mondie, Lou, and the other women in Nikky Finney's poem provide an example of the power of word of mouth in Black life and survival. In *Culture and African American Politics*, Charles Henry argues that investigation of African American attitudes "must begin with the oral tradition."[2] In Henry's analysis, knowledge in the African American community continues to be passed orally "through folklore, music, proverbs and religion" and tends to "unite religion with all other aspects of life."[3] The analysis that follows takes seriously the import of what African Americans say when they speak to each other about the death penalty.

Folk Knowledge and Its Racial and Religious Contours

The primary relevance of folk knowledge to this project on the death penalty is its recognition of moral authority outside the state and its agents. In his articulation of the connection between folk knowledge and legal action, Benjamin Steiner argues that "we [citizens] are not merely the inert recipients of law's external pressures. We make laws in our daily lives, in our expectations, in our norms, in our knowledges."[4]

In Steiner's view, individuals' everyday experiences shape the law and their knowledge of the law. Whether knowledge is gained, Steiner contends, is contingent on such factors as "cultural institutions" or the understandings that make up that community's "truths." Although there are some "truths" or "claims that may be held broadly throughout society," particular subgroups may have their own "truths."

African Americans have a high level of individual experience with the criminal justice system, ranging from being stopped by the police because of their race to incarceration, which is now at epidemic levels among the Black community. These and other factors have led to high levels of mistrust of the criminal justice system among African Americans.[5] As Jon Hurwitz and Mark Peffley summarized the findings of their study of perceptions of fairness among Blacks and whites, "The differences, by any criterion, are enormous: while whites see a justice system that is essentially egalitarian, African Americans do not."[6] Controversial verdicts coupled with individual experiences with discrimination and the criminal justice system "contribute heavily in creating in much of the African-American community a profound understanding that the justice system is inherently biased against them."[7] Hurwitz and Peffley point not only to incarceration but also to the death penalty as sources of African Americans' fundamental distrust of the criminal justice system.[8]

These experiences make the criminal justice system a constant issue of concern for individual African Americans and African American political elites. The idea of individual experiences leading to collective truths is extremely important in studying African Americans because of their historical marginalization in politics. If we add linked fate to the idea of folk knowledge, understanding the narratives that are internal to the Black community is essential for understanding African Americans' policy preferences or political outcomes on issues.[9] These narratives are negotiated and transmitted in an alternative sphere of politics that is often referred to as the Black counterpublic.[10] In this counterpublic, African Americans create hidden transcripts of meaning and action in the face of perceived and real inequality.[11]

It should be noted, however, that there is no single articulation of preferences, identity, or any other matter of political or legal interests within African American political spaces.[12] The idea of a monolithic Black community has been challenged for more than two decades by social scientists even as the political ties that bind African Americans lead to high levels of cohesion around certain polices and in electoral politics. This questioning has led to a rich literature that asserts that even though African Americans vote in a bloc, multiple ideological differences exist in the Black community. What exists is a dynamic and evolving sphere where Blacks' political views are honed through discussion and transmission of political values and messages in Black public spaces, including messages about the death penalty. This explains the differences in the news accounts of the Graham case discussed in chapter 1.

The Black church continues to be the most important and persistent example of the Black counterpublic in contemporary politics.[13] Research on the Civil Rights Movement points to the Black church as one source of information networks, financial resources, and indigenous leadership, but in addition to its structural role, the Black church provides a forum for debate and discussion.[14] The importance of religious forums, structures, and practices infuses African Americans' political rhetoric with religion, though a vibrant debate remains over whether a reliance on religion—rhetorically or institutionally—stifles or encourages political participation. In her analysis of everyday talk among African Americans, Melissa Harris-Lacewell argues that the Black church is significant because it provides a primer to its members that they use "[to] make sense of the world outside of the church."[15]

Whether one calls it folk knowledge, narratives of the Black public sphere, or everyday talk, the internal dialogues of African Americans have a significant effect on their politics and their views of the law. The link between knowledge structures and legal or political action unites these theoretical frames. Simply put, what people believe and say—whether they are grounded in fact or represent misinformation—has meaning. The focus group discussions highlighted in this chapter illustrate some of what African Americans tell each other about the death penalty and the role of religion in those articulations.

The Tellers: Description of the Focus Groups

I conducted a series of peer focus groups in the Houston metropolitan area in the summer of 2004. Peer focus groups are a variation on the traditional focus groups method. They use participants who have a social connection to one another. Peer focus groups are organized by identifying one person and getting that person—an insider—to gather a small group of friends, relatives, and/or co-workers for a discussion. To identify insiders, I posted flyers in community centers, public libraries, and businesses located in predominantly African American communities and downtown Houston. I talked with employees, visitors, and clients of businesses in Black communities. I explained that I was seeking participants for a study on politics. I did not tell them the subject of the study, but I did let them know that there would be a small gift for participating.[16] Once an insider was identified, we agreed on a time and place to meet. Each focus group took an average of two hours and was both audio and video recorded.

A total of 21 people participated. Each participant completed a questionnaire that asked for key demographic information and asked other questions related to the project. I attempted to recruit participants of various ages, genders, classes, and levels of education. There was good variety with each of these variables in the focus groups with the exception of gender. Of the total participants, only four were men and three of those men participated in the same focus groups. This gender imbalance is a limitation of the findings of these groups, but the responses are valuable because they reflect the existing gender imbalance in political participation among African Americans. Also, every one of the participants voted Democratic in the prior presidential election. There is generally little variation in which party African Americans vote for or identify with.

The average age of the participants was 42; however, one of the participants—Ms. Helen Mae—was 92 years old. If we remove Ms. Helen Mae, the average age drops to 31. The youngest was 19. Seven of the participants had only high school diplomas and three did not complete high school.[17] The remainder all had some college and three had college degrees. Two of the participants were married, two were divorced, and four were widowed. The others were single.

Since religion is of such significance in this analysis, the questionnaire asked about religious participation. All of the participants were Christian, and 13 were Baptist. The various Baptist denominations collectively have the largest number of adherents in the state of Texas. All of the participants, with the exception of three, attended services at least twice a month, and many attended more. Only one participant reported attending no services at all. This level of church attendance is in line with the level of church attendance among African American respondents in the Houston Area Survey sample.

The average annual income was $21,000; the highest was $52,000 and the lowest was $6,000. The occupations of the participants ranged from daycare worker to teacher to pharmacist. One of the focus groups occurred at a day center for seniors. Another focus group took place in a local pharmacy, and as a consequence all of the participants were pharmacy employees. The remaining focus groups took place in the homes of the contact people. Their occupations ranged from assistant principal to truck driver to housewife to data entry clerk.

All of the participants reported watching television news broadcasts or reading the newspaper on a daily to weekly basis.[18] The final question of the questionnaire asked if they had a close relative who had been a victim of a violent crime. Four participants answered yes. I did not ask if they had relatives who had committed violent crimes. Reflecting on the responses, I now see this would have been valuable information. However, most of the participants indicated that they had friends and/or relatives who had been incarcerated for reasons they did not specify.[19]

Finally, the use of one insider and individuals from their social circles allows the unit of analysis to move from the individual to the conversation, which, as William Gamson observes, allows us to "observe the process of people constructing and negotiating shared meaning, using their natural vocabulary."[20] Like Gamson, I was interested in analyzing the way the participants understood the meaning of the death penalty both individually and within the negotiated space of community. Similar to what we can learn from natural conversation, peer focus groups help us understand why participant think as they do.[21] The structure of these groups creates a space where the folk knowledge Steiner speaks of can be revealed because, as Gamson notes, "people bring to bear many popular beliefs that transcend the specific issue."[22] The participants' introduction of what Gamson calls "popular wisdom" can often lead to the introduction of lived experiences to "make the same point concrete." The focus groups in this study conversed in ways that were similar to what Gamson described. Unlike Gamson, however, I was not concerned about whether working-class Black participants would be able to carry on sustained conversation about an important political and legal issues, for several reasons.[23] First, African Americans have a long-standing oral tradition that includes political discussion. Second, this population has a tremendous amount of exposure to the death penalty and the surrounding debates. My reasoning was borne out in the conversations. The participants were extremely well versed on the death penalty. They were very articulate about their opinions and attitudes and offered examples to illustrate them.

Who among You Can Judge? Religion, Race, and Views on the Death Penalty

The first question I asked in the focus groups was: What is your position on the death penalty? It was very easy to predict that the majority of the participants in the focus groups would be opposed to the death penalty. Given what I knew about African Americans' opposition to the death penalty, especially African Americans in Texas, it was very easy to predict that the majority of the participants in the focus groups would be opposed to that punishment. My original hypothesis was that African Americans would articulate their opposition in religious language. This hypothesis proved to be correct for some, but not all, of the participants. Religion as the main reason for opposition to the death penalty among these focus group participants was often trumped by a belief that the criminal justice system is inequitable and fallible.

Thou Shall Not Kill: Religion and Views on the Death Penalty

Faye, Denise, and Pumpkin were all residents of a low-income housing community when these focus groups were conducted. Two of the women were employed full time in low-wage jobs. When they were asked to share their views on the death penalty, they did not hesitate. Pumpkin, a 28-year-old child-care worker, stated her views in a two-word declarative sentence, "It sucks." Denise, a 19-year-old cashier, parroting her cousin Pumpkin, said, "It sucks," but continued with, "It's not right. It's really not. I mean, how can a man choose, you know, the death of some other person? I thought that was God's stuff." Faye, a 33-year-old secretary, added the following:

> I'm against it. Because in my religious beliefs thou shalt not kill. So whether I committed a vicious crime or violent crime or whatever, the Bible still say "Thou shalt not kill." So are you going to kill me because I did something wrong? I should be punished but I don't think the death penalty.

At some point, all of these women had been regular churchgoers, although Pumpkin and Denise were not attending regularly at the time the focus groups were conducted.

All the women agreed that religion informed their views, but it was not the only basis for their positions. For them, religion was part of a mixture that included perceptions of discrimination and fairness. As the discussion progressed, the women revealed that a capital trial that had received substantial news coverage was for a murder that had taken place in their neighborhood—the trial of Anthony Quinn Francois that I discussed in the introduction. Their connection to the death penalty was not very distant.[24] Both the victims and the accused murderer lived in their community. The physical proximity of these women to this type of crime exemplifies the proximity of the African American community in Texas to the very real consequences of the death penalty.

Ms. Helen Mae, at 92 years old, was the oldest participant in the focus groups. She summed her opposition to the death penalty with, "'cause the Bible says, 'Thou shalt not kill.'" Her words echo the views of Faye, nearly six decades her junior. The focus group in which Ms. Helen Mae participated was conducted at a day center for senior citizens. Like Denise—the youngest participant—and Faye, the older cohort of women believed decisions about life and death are best made by God. For Emma, a 67-year-old housewife, "God's the only somebody give life." Genevieve, a 68-year-old who described herself as unemployed and whose participation was largely limited to utterances of agreement, made one of her few full statements when she described her view of the death penalty with, "I think the Lord giveth, the Lord taketh away. Thus saith the Lord."

Devon, a 25-year-old data clerk, also felt that life-and-death decisions were to be made by God. Devon explained her view this way:

> I think that—I think it does but I'm not sure what it is. But I think it's one that God will deal with them, you know? Don't—you can't make judgment on no one else, off of what someone else does because that person—one sin is not higher than another sin and you know God will deal with that. That's not for you to, you know, judge or, you know, say that someone needs to die for that.

Three other participants in that focus group—Sarita, Celina, and Takeisha—agreed that religion was the basis for their views on the death penalty. Celina, a 51-year-old secretary, felt that the "mortality" of those handing out the punishment made them the wrong persons to make such decisions. In another focus group with employees at a local pharmacy, Brad also pointed to religion and morality as the basis for his view:

> I've been swinging on both sides of the fence of that issue because morally I don't think you should take a man's life 'cause taking a man's

life is something you can't give back. And if you're not 100 percent sure—you're not going to be 100 percent sure. That's a decision you have to make and a man shouldn't make a decision of who lives or dies. God chooses.

Even when participants opposed the death penalty based on the fact that the state makes mistakes, they repeated that human beings are ill suited to determine who lives or dies. Like the humans that comprise it, the state, in their view, is fallible.

Although the majority of participants opposed the death penalty, not all did. In the focus group at the senior center, one of the participants strongly favored the death penalty. Charlene, a 72-year-old retiree, once shared her peers' feelings about the death penalty. Everything changed when her 16-year-old grandson was shot and killed. When she expressed how and why her views changed, the other women challenged the benefit of such punishment for her and her grandson. Charlene held to her position in the following exchange:

CHARLENE: I didn't, I didn't agree but after my grandson was killed, I do. I do! I changed! Just like that.

EMMA: I don't agree with it 'cause what good's it gonna do? You can't get—I don't care how many people you put to death, won't bring your relative back.

CHARLENE: Yeah, it won't but I just—my mind just changed.

EMMA: Just leave it in the hands of God.

GENEVIEVE: Yeah, that's what you do, but then let him work it out.

Despite their sympathy for Charlene and their condemnation of her grandson's murderer, the other women held to their religious conviction that the death penalty was not right. This older cohort of women most consistently referred to God and the Bible in support of their attitudes about the death penalty. Unlike Faye, Denise, and Pumpkin, who transitioned into reasoning based on fairness and discrimination that was not articulated in religious terms, for the older women, it always came back to religion. This reversion to religious rhetoric also made theirs the shortest focus group session.

A Fate Worse than Death? Life as an Alternative to Death

For those who did not rely on religion, their opposition to the death penalty was based on discrimination in the assessment of punishment, the possibility of error, and/or their belief that life imprisonment was a more significant punishment than a death sentence. The latter reason is best exemplified by the response of Monifah, a 29-year-old college student who worked part-time at the pharmacy:

> I don't agree with the death penalty. I don't agree because I think it's an easy way out for them. I feel like if they killed somebody, they should have to be—they should have to deal with that from then on. I mean, if they decide that they want to take their lives or something, you know. We shouldn't take their lives, like, for example, Timothy McVeigh. He was asking to die because he wanted to die so he would not think about it every day. He needs, to me,—they need to think about it every day and they need to—if they decide that they want to kill themselves, then that's fine, but I don't think that we should take on the responsibility of doing it.

Monifah was not the only participant to express an opinion that death was too "easy." In addition to their religious views, Maggie and her friends at the senior center also felt that a death sentence was light punishment. This was their exchange:

MAGGIE: I don't even. Even with Hussein—
INTERVIEWER: Saddam Hussein.
MAGGIE: I don't think he ought to be killed. I think he ought to be locked up and made to work hard, hard, hard. Every day of his life.
GENEVIEVE: Punish him real good!
HELEN MAE: And give him cornbread every meal! [Laughter] Something like that.
MAGGIE: And if that—death . . . it's an easy way out for him now.

Several women in the focus group of senior citizens spent their early years working in the agricultural sector of rural Texas. So when Ms. Helen Mae says that suitable punishment would be to "give him cornbread every meal," she is both critiquing the death penalty and linking the experience of those on death row to past hardships she and her community had experienced. Later in the same discussion, the women discussed the fact that prisoners on the prison farms that ring Houston now use tractors to harvest cotton crops. The women noted the ease of this task compared to the time they spent picking cotton by hand in the same area when they were younger.

The women from the low-income housing community had a similar exchange. They, like the older women and Monifah, were concerned about the ability of the death penalty to truly punish. They responded:

PUMPKIN: That's what—I mean, they're convicted of capital murder, that's what they get but it's ways of going along instead of, you know, like the death penalty and it's ways of—you could, like, torture—not saying "torture" but you could—[laughter] you give them life. I mean, you could give them life but you could kind of like fix it to where they could relive, you know, like kind of fix it where they could realize what they had done, you know? It doesn't make sense to take them—
DENISE: Let them die a natural death.
FAYE: The death penalty is the easy way out.
ALL: Yeah!
FAYE: Yeah, because if I kill you, I mean, you don't—you don't feel no pain, no remorse or anything, for what you did—
DENISE: You go to sleep!
FAYE: —you just—you just dead. I mean, but if you spend life in prison—
DENISE: You can think about it.
PUMPKIN: It's rewinding over and over in your head, like, "If I didn't do this, see, I wouldn't be in this three-by-five cell block," you know.

Faye also relayed a story she heard on the radio of a death row inmate who claimed his execution would be cruel and unusual punishment because his execution would require surgical intervention. Years of intravenous drug use had compromised the veins in his arm to the extent that a surgeon would have to make a deep incision to facilitate lethal injection. She commented:

FAYE: There was one case. I can't remember whether the person was Black or white. I was listening—
INTERVIEWER: Can you describe it?
FAYE: Yeah. I was listening to the radio and they had this case, this guy was on death row and then wanted to—they didn't want to do it because he was a drug user.
INTERVIEWER: Yes.
FAYE: And they said that—
INTERVIEWER: They couldn't get any veins.
FAYE: Yeah, but, and then when they—he said, if you got one—
INTERVIEWER: You would have to do a deep incision.

FAYE: And they would hurt him and it would be cruel and—what are we trying to do? Kill him, right? And so I was like, okay, why would you put him on death row then? You know what I'm saying? If you know, he's a drug addict, well, I don't even know why he was on death row. I didn't know what he did. But now you can't get no veins and you going to be just, that's cruel to him and it's going be cruel and unusual punishment, I think he said. Really, but the death row is just that to me! It's cruel and unusual. You shouldn't be killed for something wrong you did. You should really be just locked up. Maybe for eternity?

Whether she is simply regurgitating the language of the media report or the comments stem from her familiarity with the Eighth Amendment prohibition against cruel and unusual punishment, Faye's comments demonstrate a clear opposition to the death penalty as a form of punishment based on a sense of morality and law. She is also presenting a ground-level application of the Eighth Amendment prohibition of just such punishment.

The majority of the focus group participants knew one or more persons who were or had been incarcerated. Familiarity had not diminished the specter and meaning of imprisonment in the eyes of these women. In each focus group there was a discussion of the impact of incarceration on someone the participants knows or knew. This is not surprising in Texas, which has large public and private prison systems. In Texas, more than 40 percent of the state prison population is Black, even though the Black community constitutes only 12 percent of the state's population.[25]

"A Necessary Evil": Perspectives on Race in the Implementation of the Death Penalty

Among the three men and two women in Monifah's focus groups, she was the only person who absolutely opposed the death penalty. Other participants, such as Willie, expressed hesitation about the death penalty because of biases in sentencing, not because of actual objections to the methods of punishment. Willie's position was defined by the role of race in meting out sentences. The way he saw it, the death penalty was "a necessary evil." However, racial discrimination in the implementation of the death penalty led him to question its use:

Black people have been so taken advantage of over the history that—we see in Chicago, I think it was, Illinois, revoked the death penalty, overturned all these death penalty sentences because the technology that they used at the time was screwed. If you wanted to get somebody, you planted the evidence. So who's to say that most of the people that have been killed aren't innocent?

Willie is pointing to the 2003 decision by the Governor George Ryan of Illinois to commute several sentences because of the number of inmates on the state's death row who had been shown to be innocent. Willie's response goes beyond the differential treatment of Blacks and whites by the criminal justice system to another recurring theme in these focus groups—the incompetence of the state in the handling of death penalty cases, especially those with Black defendants. The belief that Blacks are unfairly convicted of capital crimes in comparison to whites surfaced in each of the focus groups.

The heightened concern over unfair convictions affected the attitudes of the participants in two ways. Either the concern led the respondents to assert that they would support the death penalty if the state could meet an inordinately high level of proof or it affirmed existing opposition to the death penalty. One of Willie's counterparts, Frederick, explained the conditions that would have to be met for him to sentence someone to death:

> I believe in it, as long as you have—once you have 100 percent proof of evidence, I mean, that's a very, very reliable witness or like caught them straight up on videotape. I mean, I don't think you should give them a death penalty based on what, like, six or eight people say on a jury, you know, because they may have their own personal vendetta against someone, there can be someone on the jury who's real strung up and speaks out real strongly who can persuade the jury to lean one way or the other, so I don't believe it should be based on a jury decision unless jurors provided just like straight evidence, like 100 percent evidence. Okay, you see them on camera actually hitting someone on the head and run, killing someone or making—other than that, you can't really, you know, other than that, you're choosing whether a person lives or dies. . . . So without 100 percent, what I would call 100 percent evidence, on a camera, I mean, 10,000 people saw it—you know. You know, but I do believe that if those were the cases they should die.

Frederick, similar to the Black venirepersons in the *Batson* hearings, had a hard time believing he could truly be convinced by the state that someone deserved to die without overwhelming proof. This level of proof goes substantially beyond the existing standard of beyond a reasonable doubt. Pumpkin, who opposed the death penalty, used the following analogy to describe the way bias in the criminal justice system affects whites and Blacks differently,

> This to me is racial because I have heard to where white people have killed more Black people—or not more Black people, sorry, more people. They're doing their thing and so you watch, see, they get less time than a guy that goes and rob a store, Black guy goes, rob a store, will get 50 years to a white-collar white man just stole a million dollars from the job and, you know, he gets, what, two years' probation?[26]

The women at the senior center agreed with Pumpkin, Willie, and Frederick. For these women, race and other factors connected to race—such as poverty—made it more likely that Blacks would receive stiffer penalties generally. They outlined their views with the following exchange:

EMMA: You don't have money, get the high-powered attorneys when you Black.
MAGGIE: And then I don't think you are always—
GENEVIEVE: You don't get treated equally.
MAGGIE: —I don't think you really don't get—
EMMA: That's right, don't get a fair shake.
GENEVIEVE: You don't say—
MAGGIE: I don't think the jury are always people of your peers either—
GENEVIEVE: You're not equal—Because of your color. That's true.
EMMA: That's what we think any way—
GENEVIEVE: That's for sure, that gonna die in me. [Laughter]
MAGGIE: And it sure does count depending on what color you kill.
EVERYBODY: Um-hum.
EMMA: Well, you already know, if you kill a white person, you already doomed.
CHARLENE: Yeah.
EMMA: You can kill us all the time! You get, what, five, seven years?
GENEVIEVE: Maybe not that long.
EMMA: Sometime you can get off.
JESSIE: That's true!

In the course of the focus group, Charlene pointed to the impending release of her grandson's murderer after he had served only 15 years in prison. However, even Charlene, who supported the death penalty after the murder of her grandson, agreed that race played a significant role in which defendants received death sentences.

Charlene was not alone among the participants in her support of the death penalty. Malik supported the death penalty because he wanted the punishment to be available if he ever faced a situation similar to that of Charlene. He posited the following scenario, which continued his support for the death penalty:

> Let's say if something happened to someone I love, I think if you've committed a crime against them that was so severe that it cost them their life or something along those lines, I think it's necessary.

Samantha, a 41-year-old pharmacy student and full-time employee of the pharmacy, also supported the death penalty. She offered a very common reason—the prevention of crime and the excessive cost of housing prisoners. In her view, the death penalty was "most likely morally wrong." However, the realities of crime led her to believe that

> there is a conundrum for us in America because we have more people in jail than we can afford to take care of. And since we are not finding any other ways to deal with the problem, we have to figure out something. What do you do with somebody who is a serial killer or somebody who has had four or five chances? Do we keep letting them out to take other people's lives? So I think it's a necessary evil.

Frederick also supported the death penalty, contingent on the state's ability to meet the aforementioned evidentiary requirements. Takeisha said she supported the death penalty as well, but her support "depend[ed] on the crime."

The Impact of Religious Leadership on Individual Perspectives of the Death Penalty

One of the interesting findings of the focus groups was the response to the question of how the position of their affiliated religious institution influenced the participants' position. Takeisha actually stated a position that was different from her understanding of her church's doctrine on the death penalty. She was one the only person to state an opposition to the death penalty with an eye to a religious institution. She responded,

> I belong to the Church of Christ, and they're strongly against it. But my own views, I guess, and my own judgment is why I'm kind of for it.

Unanimously, the focus group participants stated the leaders of or the institutional position of their church did not influence their views on the death penalty. The women at the senior center, who most consistently and directly attributed their views to religion and the Bible, had the following exchange:

INTERVIEWER: But does it matter to you if your church had a position on the death penalty?
EMMA: Well, depend on what the position was. [Laughter]
MAGGIE: I would still hold—
EMMA: Even if the church said "kill"—
MAGGIE: Even if the Baptists said we should believe in the death penalty, I would still be against the death penalty. That's right.
EMMA: Can't change my mind on account of what they say. What I believe, I believe.
[Several speakers at once]
GENEVIEVE: That's right! Each man has his own beliefs.

In another focus group, Frederick nicely summed up the sentiment of the participants with, "I make my own decisions. I'm still a man." Willie, a member of the same focus group, made the following argument to explain the low level of significance he gave to the position of his church or its elites:

In the twenty-first century, I don't think in the twenty-first—the twenty—the new millennium—that we are as much controlled as in the past by what the church leaders believe, you know?

The way these African Americans disconnected their political views from the doctrine of their denomination and the views of their religious leaders has interesting intersections with recent work on religion and politics. The focus groups took place in a community that had been under the leadership of George W. Bush at both the state and national level. Bush was known for his appeal to religious conservatives and his willingness to use his personal narrative of spiritual transformation as a tool of political persuasion. In his study of faith-based politics in the era of George W. Bush, John C. Green found that "the fact that religion plays a significant role may be less important than the ways that religion has been politicized."[27] Green points specifically to cultural issues, which include policies such as the death penalty. The question of how faith impacts views of leadership extends beyond religious institutions to raise interesting questions of how the focus group participants assess political leadership as well.

For What Purposes Death? Participants' Perspectives on the Utility of the Death Penalty

All of the focus group participants were asked about their thoughts on why the death penalty continues to be used as punishment. Because I anticipated opposition to the death penalty among the participants, I asked this question to elicit the participants' perceptions of the state's reasoning for using such an objectionable punishment. I was interested in the participants' explanations of, speculations about, and theories about why the state in which they lived so actively pursued a form of punishment they found objectionable. The participants' explanations coalesced around the connections between the death penalty, racial politics, the politics of incarceration, and, at times, the interconnectedness of these issues.

As they did with the other questions, the women at the senior center immediately used religious logic to explain the state's behavior. They remained faithful to their narrative that the death penalty is wrong because of biblical prohibitions against killing and the primacy of God as the legitimate seeker of retribution. Ms. Helen Mae gave the following response when the question was asked: "We shouldn't have because the Bible said that 'Vengeance is mine.'" Another woman suggested that there must be some state response to violations of the law and she quickly responded, "That's man-made law because the Bible says killing is wrong." The women were also aware of the differences in how they and others may interpret religious texts. Genevieve says, "They go by the Bible! They go by the Bible that they want to go by and that's the wrong Bible!," to which Ms. Helen Mae agreed with an emphatic, "Yes." Studies have found that African American Protestants, a group that includes these women, "are more likely to embrace biblical literalism than are mainline Protestants, Catholics, or adherents of other faith traditions."[28] For these women, biblical law exists above all laws of the state. Religion is the primary source of their views on the death penalty.

In their discussions, Denise and the other members of her group laid out what became the persistent narrative that explained the state's continued use of death as punishment:

Society is racist. Black people are not valued. If the state did not execute Blacks, then the state would incarcerate them.

This project does not have sufficient data to make causal claims, but the focus group participants made a strong claim that the criminal justice system targets Blacks. Pumpkin and Faye gave these responses to the question of the purposes of the death penalty:

> PUMPKIN: So that was just another excuse to say, "Well, you know, they're already killing Black folks so just go ahead, give the death penalty. That be one less Black nigger!" As they say, in the society.
> FAYE: I don't know why they did that. Because if they don't kill them, they going lock them all up! So they don't be out here!

This response and similar responses were repeated in the other focus groups.

Michael, the only person in his focus group to absolutely support the death penalty, began his response to the question with a deterrence argument:

> I mean, you have to have something in place that says if you do something that's just over the line, then we're going to give you the ultimate punishment. You don't want the ultimate punishment to be life in prison because I think the crime rate would go up. I mean, you need something to say that if you go this far, then, dude, we're gonna kill you.

But even Michael believed that the death penalty targets Blacks. He later made the following statement:

> I think that—like they were saying earlier, I think that it really has to do with our system. It's just the Deep South, when you go to court, more times than not the people are going to be telling you what to do and what's gonna happen to you, determining your fate, they're gonna be white. They're not going to live in the inner city, they're going to be commuting in and passing all these judgments, this judgment, and they gonna commute out at the end of the evening. And so because of that, I think that has do with why it's so many brothers being accused of all of this stuff that some of them not doing.

For Michael, the physical disconnect between white suburbanites and the Black inner city has real consequences for Blacks and how they are treated in the criminal justice system.

Takeisha, like Denise, connected her perceptions of the death penalty today to the discrimination of previous periods and viewed the connection as seamless. She said, "Times, they changed a little bit, but we still have, you know, the racism. It's still strong." Takeisha and Michael were romantic partners who lived in a middle-class suburb of Houston. Takeisha was an assistant principal at an elementary school and Michael owned a small trucking company. Their material success and education did not mitigate their view that in Houston and in the South generally, decisions about the death penalty were racially motivated. Michael described his perceptions in this way:

> Because if you think about the way Houston is made up, as a Black man in Texas, I couldn't live anywhere other than a major city because of the rights I feel like I'm due as a Black man and so like if I just moved—no different than when I was commuting back and forth from [an affluent suburb] and that's not even really out of the city. Once you get out to the suburbs, then it's a whole 'nother thing going on and like we live in [another affluent suburb][29] now but we live in a part of [another affluent suburb] that's brand new. But if we go on the other side of [another affluent suburb] then it's a whole 'nother ballgame and the South is still—the old South, when people think of Houston and you drive into Houston, you don't want to be really thinking about all of the rural areas before you get to Houston. You just thinking of Houston when you drive in and you know, you can drive 30 minutes anywhere out of this city and be right there in the old South. I mean, they don't necessarily have outhouses but the mentality is the same, you know. You got white people there with him that ain't seen niggers in two weeks. You know, they haven't!

Michael supported the death penalty, but he was not immune to the feeling that race continued to drive the use of the death penalty.[30]

When Michael offered his opinion on the importance of geography to the continued use of death as punishment, Celina, Sarita, and Devon were reminded of a recent incident on an interstate, where they passed a "bus full of Klan." Celina declares, "There's racism and it's real." Each of the participants agreed with this position. This was, for these three women, visual confirmation that some aspects of society had changed very little or not at all.

Because of their age, the women at the senior center were the only participants who were adults before the social and political changes of the Civil Rights Movement. Ms. Helen Mae, at 92, was the oldest participant by decades. She and her cohort's experience with Jim Crow provided some insight into the possible evolution of perceptions about the death penalty. Have the substantial changes after the activism of the 1960s altered African American perceptions of the death penalty? The thin line between legal and illegal execution would have been part of these women's lived experience, in contrast to the younger participants, whose experience of such would have been indirect or learned. During the focus group these women participated in, I asked specifically about past experiences with the death penalty. Here is how the women responded:

EMMA: Oh, back—well, back then, I don't think they gave you a trial. They took you to a tree and hung you up. And a lot—and some of those men were found innocent, and what happened? They were still dead.

HELEN MAE: They—they—they was already dead!

EMMA: They were dead, and hung them on a tree!

HELEN MAE: Oh, yeah.

EMMA: Then they had no trial, no nothing.

EVERYBODY: Um-hum.

EMMA: Just 'cause they said you did it.

HELEN MAE: Yeah, because you remember the boys that was hung in Columbus?

EMMA: I heard about them up there in Alleyton.[31] They had a tree in a road, the hanging tree.

[Several speakers at once]

MAGGIE: The tree is still there!

HELEN MAE: All right, they hung them. But after they were dead, then somebody else come and confess.

EMMA: Somebody on their deathbed, though.

HELEN MAE: That's—it was a white man come and confess that he did it.

EMMA: But they was still dead.

HELEN MAE: But they was still dead, them Black boys was still dead.

GENEVIEVE: Never blamed them people doing that.

MAGGIE: And no restitution for the family at all, the other person.

EMMA: No. You just lost your child—

HELEN MAE: And I go under that tree often and every time I go by that tree, I think about it.

MAGGIE: It is still there? Should be chopped down!

Even Charlene, who supported the death penalty, affirmed these descriptions of the conflation of lynching and the death penalty prior to the Civil Rights Movement. In this description of lynching, the participants pointed out the lack of due process for African American lynching victims, the victimization of the innocent, and the irreparability of death as a sentence. Chapter 1 points to the "innocent victim" as a central figure in the lynching narrative, and the centrality of that figure is repeated in the dialogue of these older women.

The length and significance of these memories led to a second question on the impact of sociopolitical changes on the attitudes of these women who had witnessed the transformation:

INTERVIEWER: What do you think about when people make those same comparisons? Do you think they're legitimate comparisons? Do you think they're unfair comparisons to executions today when they compare it with lynching?

The women answered with the following,

MAGGIE: Let me say, Let me say, I can't remember white people being lynched. I can't remember—
EMMA: I can't, either.
MAGGIE: I don't think I have heard telling of white people being lynched. So that form of execution was mainly for Black people.
JESSIE: Um-hum.
MAGGIE: And—but now, with the lethal injection—
EMMA: Everybody—everybody can get the death penalty now.
MAGGIE: It's not as brutal but—
EMMA: Of course, when someone gets stays and all these here stuff. It's still for Blacks, more so.

These women see a distinct difference between lynching and the current implementation of the death penalty. The increased numbers of whites who are executed symbolizes a perverse equality in this policy area. Second, the use of lethal injection is less brutal than lynching in the eyes of these women. This view is aligned with the Texas state legislature's reasons for transitioning to lethal injection in 1977: its members saw injection as "more humane than the physically traumatic and visually offensive electrocution."[32] In spite of the views that the current death penalty was used against "everybody" and was less brutal, the perception that Blacks were disproportionately penalized persisted.

Understanding how African Americans mark political change or lack of change can be a significant tool in uncovering their sense of political belonging and the qualitative meaning of citizenship today. One of the interests of this project is how the death penalty and its entanglement with other criminal justice policies shape the relationship between African Americans and the post–Civil Rights state. I asked the women at the senior center the questions I recorded above because the first analogy of the death penalty to lynching was raised by the youngest participant—19-year-old Denise—in the first focus group. Born in 1985, she would not have any personal memory of Jim Crow, though this does not mean she has not had her own experiences with racism and an oppressive state. When I asked the participants of her focus group why we still had the death penalty, Denise replied, "At first they hung them. Now they're just sticking them with a needle." For this respondent, who was born into a different political epoch, the thread between lynching and the death penalty is seamless. The view of this young woman goes against the progress narratives associated with other studies of change in post–Civil Rights politics.

If Denise were the only one of the younger participants who expressed such a view, it could be treated as anomaly. But other participants connected pre– and post–Civil Rights criminal justice policies, particularly when they discussed the links between the death penalty and the regional and local racial history of Texas. Similar to the hanging tree in the dialogue between the women at the senior center, repetitive exposure to the imagery of past racial discrimination and the real experience of present racism affects the views of Black Texans who have come of age in post–Civil Rights America. Blacks and whites in Texas are highly polarized in their support for or opposition to the death penalty. How the continuous negotiation of race and the death penalty is affected by geography and historical memories is a question this project cannot answer fully, but certainly it raises the question of how the geography—the physical proximity to the sites of subordination—influences the retention or intensity of certain attitudes. The polarization of attitudes about the death penalty among Black and whites may also suggest oppositional historical narratives among these communities. These narratives may also be influencing the politics of the death penalty. The historical connection may be seamless for these respondents because the very landscape in which they live is a relic of past oppression and current discrimination enacted by the state and its policies.[33]

Conclusion

Understanding the folk knowledge of the Black community is key to understanding Black politics. In studies of the law, this knowledge has very real implications for the outcome of proceedings and the translation of state policy by the citizenry. This chapter looks at how the focus group data provides answers to two basic questions about the death penalty: (1) What are African Americans' opinions of the death penalty? and (2) How do African Americans understand the continued use of death as a form of punishment? The focus group respondents, like African Americans in polls, were overwhelmingly opposed to the death penalty. In part, this may be because of the history of the region. The South plays a significant role in the formation of these participants' views on the death penalty. Another explanation could be the negative connection of this community to the state and other aspects of the criminal justice system, particularly prisons.

Religion did not inform the views of several participants, but, for most, religion was the one factor that was most often coupled with perceptions of racial discrimination. This finding fits well with the findings from the Houston Area Survey, but that inquiry is limited by the survey's lack of specificity on certain key questions. Of the participants who absolutely supported the death penalty, one had lost a relative to murder and the other believed in the death penalty as a deterrent. The responses to this question suggest the need for greater interrogation of attitudes on crime, perceptions of discrimination, and beliefs about incarceration and how these attitudes shape the views of African Americans about the death penalty.

When I asked respondents why they felt the death penalty was used as punishment, their answers took two (sometimes intersecting) paths. The first view was that the death penalty particularly and the criminal justice system generally are highly influenced by race. Some participants framed their views on race in a historical context, while others saw the past as quite present in their current experiences and perceptions of the death penalty. The second view was connected to the high levels of incarceration of African Americans. The number of incarcerated African Americans in the United States has significantly impacted the politics of the African American community. Heightened opposition to the death penalty may be one of the many ways incarceration affects Blacks' political views. The focus groups participants were keenly aware of the power of the criminal justice system. Some participants linked these two views, making the argument that African Americans are especially targeted for imprisonment and the racially discriminatory use of the death penalty. Both of these opinions reinforce the concept that the views of African Americans are shaped by a sense that their fate is linked to that of their community.

5

Something Less Than Equal but the Same: The Death Penalty and the Inversion of Equality in African American Politics of Punishment

IN THEIR ANALYSIS of the death penalty in Texas from 1923 to 1990, James Marquart, Sheldon Ekland-Olson, and Jonathan R. Sorensen conclude:

> The source of this Southern concentration of both illegal lynchings and state-sanctioned executions is rooted in a cultural readiness to engage in what we call the logic of exclusion. . . . When we legitimize capital punishment, and where we tolerate lynching, we engage in a kind of logic of exclusion whereby the life being terminated is placed outside the security of the "bounded" community.[1]

Marquart and his colleagues begin their analysis at the end of the Civil War, with the battle for legitimate authority over both the meaning of justice and the meaning of the economic and political bodies of newly emancipated Blacks. Although they acknowledge efforts by the state to create new legal paradigms for the treatment of excluded Blacks—the Thirteenth, Fourteenth, and Fifteenth Amendments—it is clear from their work that "a culture of exclusion . . . is not easily extinguished."[2] Incidents of illegal executions, or lynchings, subsided in Texas and throughout the South in the early part of the last century, but the decline in the number of illegal lynchings blurred into a state-controlled system of execution that continued previous racial disparities. This history has had a lingering impact on the politics and beliefs of African Americans in Texas, especially as those beliefs relate to the death penalty. The logic of exclusion created by the legacy of slavery in the South is largely thought to have been reversed by the legal and political successes of the Civil Rights Movement. This assertion, as is evinced in the responses of focus group participants, may be overstated.

This chapter illuminates the impact of continued exclusion on African American attitudes about the death penalty and other political issues. Theorists have spent considerable time trying to understand what the various prerequisites are for full inclusion in democratic societies. The concept of democracy includes the notion of a public defined by a national civic identity, and a multiplicity of values, cultures, and political views are sometimes thought to be inconsistent with the formation of a singular "public."[3] In addition, at times difference has meant differences in power and in the weight given to the voices of those marked as "others" in democratic societies. The othering of particular groups in the United States has created the need for alternative spaces for political discussion.

The focus group data reveal how perceptions of, and the lived reality of, discrimination, particularly when discussing the death penalty, invert the fundamental meaning of the core democratic value of equality for African Americans. I have already argued that African American citizenship is impacted by the state's perceptions of where African Americans stand on the death penalty, as exemplified by their exclusion from capital juries. Participatory rights, such as jury service, are one aspect of citizenship, a form of inclusion that is defined and determined by the state. The data from my focus groups provide some insight into the level of belonging African Americans feel—the degree to which an individual or a community feels they are included. The Civil Rights Movement was a profound redefinition of citizenship and of African Americans' understandings of their connection to the nation. The focus groups offered an opportunity to investigate how those whose inclusion was gained by protest and not invitation define belonging.

Although African Americans were largely excluded from voting and jury service in the Jim Crow South, they were engaged in democratic practices within the confines of their churches, schools, fraternal organizations, and other civic groups. The contemporary reliance on the vote in particular ignores the long history of other democratic activities in the African American community, such as political debate and discussion. By the time African Americans have access to the vote and by extension the jury box, ideas about equality, democracy, and belonging had been nurtured, cultivated, constructed, and deconstructed in the ordinary conversations internal to the Black community. The next section discusses the way theorists of various kinds have explained democratic deliberations among African Americans, and how those deliberations relate to the death penalty.

Race, Democratic Deliberation, and the Death Penalty

The peer focus groups in this study, to a certain degree, replicated Iris Marion Young's idea of deliberative democracy based on political discussion. The illusion that understanding is shared may be one of the reasons Blacks and whites tend to moderate their political views during interracial political discussions.[4] Political discussion that includes both Blacks and whites serves to mask the full range of Black political discourse. We also know from the study of "black everyday talk" that most respondents to the National Black Political Survey reported having talked to family and friends—essentially their peers—about politics.[5] In *Barbershops, Bibles, and BET*, Melissa Harris-Lacewell found that for both Black men and women, informal conversations about politics "reinforce both a sense of black linked fate and a belief in black self-reliance."[6] Racially homogenous peer focus groups allow for unmediated responses from African Americans and offer glimpses of how narratives of the death penalty are incorporated into other political narratives of everyday Black talk. Additionally, understanding the narratives of single groups "can serve to explain to outsiders what practices, places, or symbols mean to the people who hold them and why they are valuable."[7] During the course of this project, the responses of the focus group participants led me to ask questions about the practices, meanings, and symbols of justice in this community.

Continuing racial polarization over the death penalty is one illustration of how the degree to which a person feels included in democratic society shapes that person's ideas about justice. Political scientists have noted that "it is hardly an overstatement [to say] that blacks and whites inhabit two perceptual worlds."[8] The idea that African Americans have different experiences and interpretations of American society than whites do goes back to W. E. B. Du Bois's explication of the veil in *The Souls of Black Folk*.[9] These different perceptual worlds are further contrasted by African Americans' feelings that they are excluded because of present-day discriminatory practices and that the criminal justice system plays a major role in maintaining the separation between the races.[10] Incidents of crime and criminal prosecutions in the last several decades have provided significant support for African Americans' perceptions of their out-group status—from the outcome of the trial of Los Angeles Police Department officers for the beating of Rodney King and the resulting riots to the assault of Abner Louima and the shooting of Amadou Diallo by New York police to the police brutality against African Americans that led to riots in Cincinnati in 2003 to the shooting of Sean Bell in 2006 and Oscar Grant in 2009 and Michael Brown in 2014 by law enforcement officers to the release of George Zimmerman for the murder of Trayvon Martin. In each instance, the reaction to the state's use of power varied significantly by race.

However, it is more than these events that have led to the current state of affairs.[11] This research was conducted in the midst of significant increases in the levels of incarceration generally and among African Americans in substantial numbers. Using data from the 1993–1994 National Black Politics Study, Michael C. Dawson found that 70 percent of African Americans "believe that the society and legal system are unfair to blacks."[12] Other studies have shown that perceptions of the efficacy of the legal system stem from a person's evaluation of the process, not necessarily from their assessment of the outcomes.[13]

Young's theory about how the politics of difference inform ideas about justice is again instructive. She argues that for excluded groups, the "new left social movements of the 1960s and 1970s" redefined oppression to mean "the disadvantage and injustice some people suffer not because tyrannical power coerces them but because of the everyday practice of a well-intentioned liberal society."[14] This definition focuses on aspects of everyday life that act as barriers to full inclusion. Young analyzes oppression based on her typology of its five essential attributes—exploitation, marginalization, powerlessness, cultural imperialism, and violence. Young also uses the concept of the "other" and how the othering of particular groups places them in a position of both invisibility and deviance. The othering of groups also makes them acceptable targets of violence, as has been suggested by scholars who study the death penalty.[15] Invisibility and deviance are intermingled for African Americans when it comes to their assessment of the death penalty and the political debate that surrounds it.

As discussed in previous chapters, polling shows that African Americans view the death penalty as racially biased. African American views are silent in the legal and legislative processes, which in recent years have reaffirmed each institution's commitment to maintaining the death penalty with only a few notable exceptions. The legal affirmations of the death penalty are strong examples of Young's concern that the shared assumptions are equated with the views of dominant. The Supreme Court decision to uphold the death penalty—while exempting particular groups such as those with intellectual disabilities ("mental retardation") and minors under the age of 18—bear out Young's concerns. The decisions in cases with defendants in these categories are based on the Supreme Court's view of "national consensus" in support of this form of punishment. Consensus, in the Court's assessment, was measured by polling data and the policy positions of state legislatures, where the desires of individual residents are necessarily filtered through the lawmaking process. This construction of consensus obscures real opposition to the death penalty in the Black community. Dominant support for the death penalty overwhelms Black opposition even when Blacks have good reason for that opposition. Sam Gross and Phoebe Ellsworth show that the "majority of Americans" support the death penalty despite the fact that "surveys repeatedly show that many Americans believe that the death penalty does not deter murder, that it is administered unfairly and it is used in a manner that discriminates against minorities and poor people."[16]

African Americans' experiences of exclusion and constrained inclusion and their higher vulnerability to violence shape what justice means to them.[17] This has required a kind of flexibility in African Americans' understanding of justice that allows for some appreciation of even small measures of fairness while advocating for greater allotments of the kinds of justice available to dominant populations. Young defines justice as "perspectives, principles, and procedures for evaluating institutional norms and rules."[18] She sets out the following test of the justice of social and political norms,

> Every valid social and political norm and rule (every law) must meet the condition that the foreseeable consequences and side effects the general observance of that law (norm) exacts on the satisfaction of the needs of each and every individual would be accepted by everyone concerned, and the claim of the norm to actualize the universal values of freedom and/or life could be accepted by each and every individual, regardless of the values to which they are committed.[19]

Young's definition of justice as the creation of rules, or laws in this instance, whose "foreseeable consequences and side effects" do not unduly burden the freedom of any individual regardless of identity or ethical commitments is synchronized with African Americans' historical political struggle for "universal freedom."

After analyzing several historical and political definitions of freedom, Hanes Walton Jr. and Robert C. Smith argue that the struggle of African Americans in the United States is characterized by a simultaneous call for collective deliverance from various formal and informal structures of white supremacy and a fight for the freedom of all people.[20] Dawson argues that the way African American critiques have helped shape and reshape American democracy are significantly overshadowed by the focus on African Americans' claims to freedom or rights grounded in American liberalism. Thurgood

Marshall's remarks in a speech commemorating the bicentennial of the Constitution underscores the latter process:

> Nor do I find the wisdom, foresight, and sense of justice exhibited by the framers particularly profound. To the contrary, the government they devised was defective from the start, requiring several amendments, a civil war, and momentous social transformations to attain the system of constitutional government, and its respect for the individual freedoms and human rights, we hold as fundamental today. When contemporary Americans cite "The Constitution," they invoke a concept that is vastly different from what the framers began to construct two centuries ago.[21]

The same critiques of the framers' failure to live up to their principles of egalitarianism are today being levied against the African American community by subgroups within it because of its failure to be more inclusive of women and members of the lesbian, gay, bisexual, and transgender community. These questions about how African Americans deal with notions of justice and equality within their own communities must be discussed in light of discussions of equality in the larger democratic community about equality.

The definition of equality has always been a moving target in a society where widespread formal and informal discrimination has been a part of its political and economic structures. The next sections discuss the impact of the suppression of African American views on the death penalty on how they view equality. The next section also explores how the focus group participants reconciled the dominance of other views on the death penalty and their own politics. The ways the internal mechanism of silencing operates within the Black community can be seen in these discussions. In a sense, the remainder of this chapter outlines how these African Americans understand the injustice/justice of the death penalty.

A "Peculiar" Equality: Evaluations of the Karla Faye Tucker and Gary Graham Cases and the Meaning of Equality

The language of the heading for this section of the chapter is borrowed from historical writing on the death penalty and race relations generally. Those writings referred to the "peculiar form of chivalry" the state and mobs exercised in the Jim Crow South.[22] Scores of African American men were lynched and executed for rape in the chivalric protection of the virtue of white women. After emancipation, Black men were perceived as animalistic in their sexual desires and white women (unlike Black women, who were presumed to be naturally licentious), were viewed as vulnerable to the desires of newly freed Black men. Nationally, 455 men were executed for rape from 1930 to 1972, and the overwhelming majority were African American.[23] Of those executions, 97 percent took place in former Confederate states. In a similar period, 99 men, 82 of them Black, were executed for rape in Texas, "more than in any other state."[24] Of the men who found themselves on the Texas death row during this period, there was only one offender for raping a Black victim and that offender was also Black.[25] The execution of these men illustrate how the meaning of chivalry—in which notions of justice are embedded—was perverted by and for the purpose of maintaining the racial hierarchy most patently exemplified in Jim Crow laws. The distortions of racial differences contributed to the distortions of justice, gender norms, and all other values of southern society in that time.

One of the more interesting patterns in the focus group discussions was how the death penalty affected the way participants defined and understood equality. After I asked questions about why they believed the death penalty continues as a form of punishment and what the role of religion played in their views, I asked participants what they thought about the cases of Karla Faye Tucker and Gary Graham, both of whom were executed in the Houston area. The questions about Tucker and Graham opened up discussions of how race, religion, and gender contribute to the meaning of cases where the individuals represent the modern embodiment of the intersection of these factors and the death penalty. They also helped me understand how these factors influence other ideals such as equality and justice for African Americans.

In all the focus groups save one, at least one participant knew of both Graham and Tucker and the facts of their cases as well as the controversy surrounding them.[26] The participants had a greater familiarity with Graham's case than with Tucker's, but African American residents of Houston are extremely well versed on the death penalty and readily provided specific cases as examples of their beliefs.[27]

Before entering the complexities the Graham and Tucker cases posed, I first asked the participants what their impressions were of inmates who experienced religious conversions while on death row and whether these conversions mattered in their estimation of the offenders and the outcome of their cases. I also asked them about conversions to Islam versus conversions to Christianity. This particular path of conversion is very common for incarcerated African Americans and contributes significantly to the ranks of both non-Christian Blacks and Muslim Americans. These are important questions for both the participants and for the larger Black community. In part, the impact of both Graham and Tucker's cases is weighted by one's reception to or belief in claims of transformation based on religious conversion. This question allowed some insight into the participants' general sense of the validity of such conversions and an exploration of how these claims of conversion meshed with the respondents' own religious and political views.

The responses to the questions about conversion—whether the participant supported or opposed the death penalty—ranged from profound skepticism to disbelief. The following exchange was typical of the responses to this question,

TAKEISHA: Some of them, I think is fraudulent.

SARITA: I'm skeptical.

[Several speakers at once]

[Laughter]

MICHAEL: I've had—I've had four cousins that I've known well before they went [to prison], kind of had conversations with them while they were out, and saw the results of all of that after. And, oh, they all turned religious! When you get locked up—

CELINA: You don't have no choice.

MICHAEL: The first thing, they start talking about reading the Bible. You know, I don't have a lot of faith in that.

SARITA: The Bible. They don't have nothing else to do.

MICHAEL: Right.

TAKEISHA: They become Muslim while they in there. When they get out, they eat pork!

MICHAEL: The minute they get out, they can't seem to find a mosque when they get out.

The skepticism of these respondents stemmed from the intimate knowledge African Americans have of family members and/or acquaintances who have been incarcerated. Though none of the participants had been incarcerated, they relayed stories of people they knew who had been. Pumpkin responded, "I think it's a joke! I mean, for real, I think it's a joke because like she [Denise] said, why? Why wait 'til you get locked up?" Faye added:

I think—part of it is jailhouse talk. Depend on who it is. And some of it, I believe, could be sincere. Because you know, I know someone that went to prison but he was at a young impressionable age so him going to prison and, you know, immediately started reading the Bible or whatever, I believe he was sincere. I believe he's sincere. But then when you go and come out and two days later and do the same thing— You tripping again.

The other participants echoed the skepticism of Faye and those quoted above. This skepticism over the validity of death row—or any "jailhouse"—conversions continued into the discussion about Graham and Tucker. Takeisha was at university in Huntsville—the location of all executions in Texas since 1923—at the time Karla Faye Tucker was executed, so of all the participants, she had the greatest recollection of the case and the subsequent protests. She described the Tucker case for her fellow participants as follows,

TAKEISHA: Karla Faye Tucker was a woman that was chopping up a man with an axe, chopped up a person with an axe. I was in Huntsville when they executed her.
CELINA: Was that her husband or was that just—
INTERVIEWER: It wasn't her husband; I think it was a friend.
TAKEISHA: A friend or boyfriend. . . . If you were in Huntsville, I mean, there was a big thing in Huntsville. Everybody was there because a lot of people, religious people were there, you know, trying to vouch for her and trying to get her a stay of execution and I think—I don't know, I can't really talk about that because who's to say if she really changed or not? But she did commit the crime, she was proven to have committed the crime and I think if they killed her—well, they did kill her—but I don't know. She still committed the crime so whether you changed or not, I think—

Takeisha witnessed the controversy firsthand, but others who were physically distant from the controversy remembered the basic facts of the case. In a separate focus group, Willie described the case:

WILLIE: Karla Faye went to jail and she found the Lord. When her time came up . . . which was. Bush was governor then . . . [28]
FREDERICK: She Black or white?
WILLIE: She was a white woman, she had the support of a number of highly—highly thought-of pastors but in the end, she accepted her death. She said, "I found the Lord and so I might as well go home to the Lord." She didn't ask for this, people outside asked if she could stay.[29]

Even for those who did not remember the Tucker case with this level of detail, they remembered the brutality of the crime.[30]

The controversy over the execution of Gary Graham, on the other hand, was much more present in the minds of the participants. Chapter 3 outlines the broad and varied support Graham received in Houston's Black community. Willie's fellow participants described him as "an encyclopedia of everything," and he was the person in their group who could recount the facts of the cases of both Tucker and Graham. His group could not relay very many details about Graham other than that he was Black and that the evidence was questionable.[31] Willie described Graham in the following interchange,

WILLIE: Um, Gary Graham—

BRAD: Did he change his name when he—

INTERVIEWER: He changed his name, yeah.

WILLIE: He did something about 30 years ago. I know that he was Black—

SAMANTHA: He broke into somebody's house, didn't he?

INTERVIEWER: No.[32]

WILLIE: The Black leaders were up in arms because he had been wrongly accused.

BRAD: There was evidence.

WILLIE: He had a lot of evidence to support him. They had eyewitnesses changed their testimony—

SAMANTHA: Saying that he wasn't there.

WILLIE:—that said that it was not him.

BRAD: Yeah. And he was put to death.

FREDERICK: And so—who was—who was the supporter? Who was the supporter? Was it Quanell X[33] and them?

WILLIE: No. No, it was some of them—The Rainbow Coalition,[34] I can't even think of his name—

BRAD: Yeah.

MONIFAH: He also had, like, the celebrities—

WILLIE: A lot of the—he had you know, the actor—

MONIFAH: Danny Glover.

In the last focus group, Gary Graham was offered as a counterexample to Tucker before I asked specific questions about the two cases. Takeisha, who was at university in Huntsville at the time of Tucker's execution, was still in

school when Graham was executed. She offered the following description of
what she saw:

> Gary Graham, yeah. And they executed him in Huntsville. That was
> a big controversy. But they still executed this brother and to me, the
> evidence wasn't there because they had a woman that said she saw him
> and another woman that said she didn't remember.

Takeisha and her fellow participants described Graham's case as follows:

CELINA: I think they were wrong because my husband was with the defense.
They were saying that the one—they was gonna kill him or it's a possibility that he didn't do it.[35]

DEVON: Right.

CELINA: Everyone was looking at, but he did all of this other stuff. But the
law states that you can't do that. I mean, if you gonna kill him—

TAKEISHA: No double jeopardy.

CELINA: Right. Kill for what he—but everybody was looking at his past and
again, I say, if he was white, it would have been a whole different thing as
to how many people was down in Huntsville, but it wasn't.

TAKEISHA: It was like—it was a lot of people at Huntsville for him but not
like whatchacallit—

CELINA: No, not like Karla Faye Tucker.

TAKEISHA: Come all the way down—Danny Glover had—And all the
Black—the new Black Panther Party—

DEVON: Yes, right, exactly, because the Christian people were not down there
for him and if you—[36]

TAKEISHA: Because he chose to become Muslim so all of his Muslim brothers and—

DEVON: They want to make it like, "Oh, it's a Black man. They trying to
keep another Black man from dying." And I think because it became—it
almost became violent when Gary Graham was getting executed because,
remember, the Black Panther Party came with guns and they were protest-
ing on a college campus. It just—it brought a lot of bad attention to him.

CELINA: He fought.[37]

TAKEISHA: And he fought all the way there. And I think—not to say that
that's wrong, 'cause who wouldn't fight all the way there, you know?

For these women, Graham's protest was justified. All of the participants in
the focus group remembered at least Graham's name and his execution. The

predominant image in their responses was a basic sketch of Gary Graham as a Black man who was unfairly executed. The picture they drew is not dissimilar to the sketchy accounts of Graham's case in the media, but these participants come to very different conclusions about Graham and the meaning of his case.

At times, even in the same conversations, respondents expressed conflicting views about the meaning of equality and justice based on their experiences or their perceptions of oppression and justice. They have already learned from their experiences that for African Americans, an expression of religious transformation or contrition is not enough to overcome public perceptions of guilt or a life worth saving in spite of guilt. For instance, although the women at the senior center were the most emphatic about the biblical basis for their objections to the death penalty, even they responded ambivalently to questions about Karla Tucker.

MAGGIE: I still don't think she should have been released because—just because she found God! I mean—
EMMA: You can't get released on something like that!
MAGGIE: God could be with her there in that prison just like he could be on the outside; somebody has to pay for her crime.
EMMA: That's not—that's not a way to get released—
MAGGIE: You still have to pay.
EMMA: When you find God.

These women, who explained nearly every response using religion, articulated a notion of justice contrary to their stated opposition to the death penalty for the sake of a system of punishment that metes out the same treatment no matter what the defendant's race. The women follow this exchange with a discussion of how both Black offenders and victims are unjustly treated in the criminal justice system. They argued that the skin color of the defendant and the victims is the only thing that matters when death sentences are handed down. Although the older women perceived the process today as better than it was in their pre–Civil Rights experiences, their views are still acutely defined by their experiences and perceptions of discrimination. Although they relied heavily on religion as the basis for their objections in earlier parts of the discussion, the strength of their religious views could not overwhelm their desire to see some sort of parity in the treatment of Black and white offenders and in the state's prosecution of the murderers of Black and white victims.

The young women who lived in the low-income housing community most clearly exemplify what I call an inversion of equality. By inversion of equality

I mean that some of the participants are willing to orient their definition of what is just toward the lower standard applied by the state in certain circumstances. This willingness stems from their perceptions of discrimination. African Americans are willing to invert their larger view of equality as all persons receiving the justice to one that constitutes something far less. They essentially advocate for parity over equality. They have the following exchange:

FAYE: I believe if you go to prison and you found guilty, whatever sentence you get—
PUMPKIN: Yes, that's what you—
FAYE:—you need to serve it.
INTERVIEWER: But you just said that you thought—
FAYE: But I'm not for the death penalty.
INTERVIEWER: Um-hum.
FAYE: But my opinion is if—my opinion is if whoever's making these rules, and they say, "Okay, you guilty. Your sentence is the death penalty."

Faye further elaborates,

> Because even though she converted to Christianity, she got born again, okay, so she's saved. I mean, you know what I'm saying? So my religion, she would go to heaven, okay? You going to go to heaven. You going serve your—you did your crime, you asked for forgiveness, okay. You can't stop what they doing to you because you was already guilty. . . . I believe if it was a Black person, it wouldn't have no—it wouldn't have been even no question.

Tucker's transformation appealed to Faye's religious beliefs. Although she insisted that she was opposed to the death penalty, the transition in her narrative implied that in her opinion, sameness of treatment is a more satisfactory outcome than an outcome that is in line with her beliefs. The women were consoled by the fact that Tucker rededicated herself to Christianity, but they felt that Tucker's punishment should not have been adjusted because "if she had been Black" her fate "wouldn't have been a question."[38] Her race raises a question, in these women's perspective of the state's administration of the death penalty, where there would not have been one if the defendant were Black.

The participants in the focus group that consisted of the employees of a local pharmacy were the most ambivalent about their support of the death penalty. Only one person, Monifah, objected to the death penalty absolutely.

Unlike other participants, she remained consistent in her position on the death penalty despite her feelings and the insistence of the other participants that race was the most important factor in the outcome. Monifah compared her own behavior to that of Tucker, whose crime was committed in a haze of drugs and alcohol. The following discussion about race and its impact on the consequence of criminal punishment ensued:

MONIFAH: I think of it like—I would want jurors to have sympathy on me if that's—if the situation was reversed. I would want somebody to say, "Well, damn! It's bad they got on those drugs. They got on those drugs and I'm sad they got on those drugs and they shouldn't have done those drugs," you know, but I remember last week when I did some stuff that I didn't have no business and when I drove home and I had four, five drinks. And I had no business doing it but I know I did it. And it if it came down to it, I ran over somebody, I would want somebody to say damn.

SAMANTHA: You should have the same consequences as anybody.

MONIFAH: You know, I would want someone to do it and I would want somebody to come up to my defense.

WILLIE: Two weeks before her death, there was a Black man who had killed a white couple who was on drugs. He found God and that didn't sway anybody to spare his life.[39]

SAMANTHA: Nobody ran up there, "Oh, save the Black man! Ooh, save him!"

MONIFAH: But what are you all talking about, it's a Black-white issue or—

SAMANTHA: I'm going to tell you that there should be consequences, period.

WILLIE: Of course it's a Black and white issue, that's it—

SAMANTHA: Period!

FREDERICK: No, no, no! It's always a race issue because, I mean, the reason it drew the attention was because she was white. Had she been Black or even Hispanic—or even Asian—

MONIFAH: He is just asking if the death penalty was right or wrong. I mean, I mean, what I'm saying is—

FREDERICK: But it doesn't matter. Doesn't matter!

MONIFAH: There's no—I'm saying, there's no way you can make—there's no unbiased person. I don't care what race, no unbiased person . . . no unbiased person, so therefore you should not be able to judge whether or not my crime is any different than your crime. You shouldn't even have the authority to do that.

WILLIE: That's the law's business.

For this group, Tucker's religious beliefs were of no consequence: the only issue that mattered was her race. Race trumps other aspects of Tucker's identity in questions of fairness and justice among the participants.

The women in the low-income housing community were the first to make comparisons between Tucker and other white women and between Tucker and Black women. This discussion brought to the participants' minds the case of Andrea Yates. Yates, a Houston mother who drowned five of her children in a bathtub, was tried for capital murder and sentenced to life in 2002.[40] This was their conversation:

PUMPKIN: You know what this reminds me? This here reminds me of when this case against that white girl, the white lady who drowned her kids, how the way her case was more controversial. She was being real sobby-like, you know?

INTERVIEWER: Andrea Yates.

FAYE: Yates. She was depressed.

DENISE: Yeah, she was depressed.

PUMPKIN: If it had been a Black woman, it would have been guilty, no question,

DENISE: It was stress and she couldn't deal with her children, she couldn't take care of kids, so she just killed them. I mean, it would have been—She went through a lot of psychological evaluations and stuff, but—

PUMPKIN: If it was a Black woman, guilty![41]

Similar to Frederick above, these women recognize differences in Tucker and Graham's cases based on both gender and race. The respondents expressed a complicated definition of equality from the perspective of both gender and race. Two of the women in the low-income housing community were single mothers who identified with the stress of parenting and Yates's struggle with postpartum depression. However, they felt deeply that had they been driven to the extremes of Andrea Yates, their fates would have led them straight to death row instead of a hospital for the criminally insane.

The comparisons of Tucker and Graham also raised questions about the impact of the perceptions of discrimination on the behavior of African Americans. Again, the women in the low-income housing community had strong feelings about the implication of these cases for the Black community.

FAYE: Yeah, if they hadn't have killed that woman [Karla Faye Tucker], they probably would have burned Huntsville down.

INTERVIEWER: Who? Who are "they"?

[Laughter]

DENISE: Karla Faye Tucker, she—you saying she should have died.

FAYE: I believe—you say ain't nobody gone see this but you. I believe Black folks would have burned that place down.[42]

INTERVIEWER: Really?

PUMPKIN: Because—I—they have to kill one of they own.

FAYE: Because I'm saying she did—[Soft speech, probably directed to the child].[43] I just believe, you know, and I really try to hope and pray my brothers and sisters that come a long way—

INTERVIEWER: Which brothers and sisters?

FAYE: The Black ones.

INTERVIEWER: Oh, okay.

FAYE: But I believe had they not killed that white woman because she was talking about she was religious—well, she might have found God, I don't know her heart. I don't know the conversation her and God had, her and Jesus, her and Allah, whoever she found, I don't know. She could be sincere, you know, but had they not killed that lady, you know, I think it would have been unjust. It would have been awful.

PUMPKIN: Yeah, I think that Black people would have been unjust—

DENISE: Because they killed—how many Black people did they kill that year to white people?

FAYE: I don't even remember, but it would have been—

PUMPKIN: They killed quite a few of them and so I guess like the female, they picked her, you know, to come up there 'cause they had to kill at least a female, you know?

Tucker's execution is seen as a symbolic slaying to maintain the stability of the accepted racial imbalance in executions. These women viewed Tucker's execution as necessary for the sake of the appearance of equality—or simply some attempt at parity. Tucker's execution was necessary because of the state's failure to recognize the religious conversions of other (presumably Black) offenders.

The predictions of other participants of how Blacks would have reacted had Tucker's case ended differently were not as extreme, but they do identify race as a distinguishing factor between the outcomes in Graham and Tucker's cases. In their discussion of the distinctions, the pharmacy employees debated which was more significant, race or class.

SAMANTHA: We know that if you white, it makes a difference. We all know that. We live with it every day, everywhere we go. When we look in the mirror and get ready to walk out the door, we say, "God bless America, but America has two different shades, one a color and one that don't have color." And they judge you different from the time they see you to the time you walk out the room and that's something that we just have to—we have to learn to deal with it. It's not gonna go away. It—no matter how un-racially biased a person says they are, we all deal with some prejudices.

FREDERICK: The darker you are, the more guilty you are.

WILLIE: The similarity is that these both were poor folks. They had a court-appointed lawyer, didn't have access to the legal system that O. J. Simpson or those two brothers that killed their mother and father.

INTERVIEWERS: The Menendez brothers?

WILLIE: The Menendez brothers, or this guy that supposedly killed his wife—

SAMANTHA: The one in—

INTERVIEWER: [Scott] Peterson.

SAMANTHA: Peterson, yeah.

WILLIE: Getting off on all types of technicalities. He's going free. He already knows it.

MONIFAH: It's not technicalities, it's the law.

WILLIE: Technicalities! The DA said, the DA's planting evidence, you know, all kinds of stuff now, you know. But poor folk, minorities, be it trailer trash white people, niggers, spics, Hispanics, whatever they want to call you, poor folks do not have that access. . . . And without equal access to the law, there won't be equal justice under the law.[44]

The opinions of the participants that emerged in their discussions of the death penalty were sophisticated and closely mirrored the constitutional principles of equal protection and procedural fairness.

This reflection of traditional American values is in line with Hanes Walton and Robert Smith's reading that African Americans have historically been committed to the broad notions of freedom in the words, if not in the deeds, of the founding documents, tempered by an understanding that discrimination has rendered those notions largely unmet. These respondents' discussions of the death penalty show how African Americans continue to grapple with these concepts and their experiences/understanding of racism and their concerns about poverty and social class. Many of the participants see race as more influential than other factors, but separating issues of race and class in the politics of African Americans is difficult. The political and economic subjugation of African American was "forged during the historical experiences that linked a general subjugation of black life with economic domination of blacks by whites."[45] Race and class are intermingled with and have shaped the meaning of equality in the politics of African Americans.

The Death Penalty as a Meaningful Marker of African American Citizenship

The final section of the chapter is a discussion of the links the focus group participants made between other markers of inclusion and the death penalty and how they define the political. The participants saw the use of the death penalty as political, and they were very aware of the politics that have clouded the state's connection to this form of punishment across historical periods.

The women in the low-income housing community made a very strong and clear connection between voting and their perception that the death penalty is a policy that targets African Americans. The interchange began with the following,

INTERVIEWER: Do you think race is the most important factor—
PUMPKIN: Right, it's always been the most—it's always been the number one most factor—look at it even with the politics, schools, everything. Race is the number one cause of everything. And Blacks are still today getting treated like crap. And they going always will be.
FAYE: Unless we train our children as sisters and brothers and tell them to get up and go vote! We could make a difference together! Because no— because have we had more of us voted when Bush went out there—

During the majority of the voting lives of these young women, George W. Bush was the governor of Texas. In the five or so years that Bush was governor, he oversaw the executions of 137 prisoners, the highest rate of executions per year at that time.[46] That rate of execution may also explain why these focus group participants were so knowledgeable—if not always completely accurately—about the administration of the death penalty.

Denise disagreed with Faye's reading of Blacks' failure to participate in electoral politics, and the other women responded accordingly,

DANIELLE: But we did!
FAYE:—it wouldn't have been that close!
DENISE: But we did!
FAYE: More of us voted, but if everybody that's a registered voter have voted, it would not have been as close.

PUMPKIN: The other thing, think about it, Bush got it set up, too, is what I'm saying, with all the felonies and the ones who's been convicted of crimes, the majority of the Black men, they can't vote. But they wanted to vote.

FAYE: They can vote after they off paper. And first of all, if you wouldn't get on the paper—

DENISE: Yeah.

INTERVIEWER: What do you mean by "off paper"?

FAYE: When you get off parole or whatever. Because, see, now, like a couple of people that I know,[47] closely related to, they won't go vote because the white man is keeping them down. But now you not on paper, you don't have no reason not to vote—

PUMPKIN: 'Cause I ran to the polls!

FAYE: And to make it easier for you, I went to register you to vote! But you won't go vote. But you want to sit and talk about what Bush did, he sending all our boys over there to kill up they selves over there in Iraq, but you not helping 'cause you don't want to go and do nothing!

In this conversation, the women extended their observations beyond statements that the outcome of the 2000 presidential election might have been different had there been higher voter turnout among African Americans. They also pointed to the impact of military service and the disenfranchisement of felons on the voting strength of the Black community. After these comments, I asked if the women considered the lack of voting to be related to the death penalty.

FAYE: It's related to—the—the people that's in charge of the death penalty because the people that's in charge of the death penalty as we see it are out to kill our boys but we keep voting them in by not voting.

INTERVIEWER: Who are these people?

FAYE: The government, the—

INTERVIEWER: You mean the prosecutors, the president, and all those people—

FAYE: Yeah.

INTERVIEWER: All those people?

FAYE: Right. They're in charge and they're putting the death penalty—

PUMPKIN: And it's not really just the white men, too, because some are uppity Black people are keeping their own people—Down!

DENISE:—down. But then you can't always blame it on the white man. All the white man—

FAYE: [Speaking over the first speaker] Some of this stuff is our own self-doing. You went out and kill James Doe or raped Bobby Blue Bland or whoever. Nobody handed you the pipe to smoke to go kill—

DENISE: The white man didn't tell you to do this.

FAYE: You did it your own self, but when you do get the opportunity to get out as a race, we need to get it together!

These young women recognized the political currency of the death penalty for elected officials. Their critique of "uppity Blacks"—which could mean politicians or Blacks with higher incomes—reflects Dawson's description of the economic schisms between poor and middle-class Blacks.[48] The older women, whose comments were usually similar in theme to these younger women, were silent on the political nature of the death penalty, but in every other focus group the connection between politics and the death penalty was a point of discussion.

Among the pharmacy employees, the issue of reliance on the death penalty for political success generated an extended discussion that also included the issues of the economy, race, and the politics of incarceration. It began with a question about why we have the death penalty.

FREDERICK: Political reasons. I think it's all political.

BRAD: America's always had the death penalty from what I've heard in history.

INTERVIEWER: Political in what way?

FREDERICK: I think it's political. I think because you gonna have—you gonna have—you always gonna have that group of people that, you know, are pro–death penalty and those—just like abortion, you know, abortion. It's the same thing to me. You want those votes. Or maybe so, you gonna either choose one side or other and you're going to get those—I think it's political! I mean, now that it's come down to political, it's come to political.

WILLIE: I think the trouble is—

FREDERICK: I mean, 'cause I mean, killing someone? I mean, you can always build new jails. I mean, you can go all the way out to Alaska and build a jail. I mean, they don't need the best part—you don't need the best of things. You go to Hawaii, build a jail there. I mean, there's enough—you can build enough prisons. Build one that's this big, we can have a cubicle. Who cares what they feel like? They're in prison, you know?

WILLIE: Back in 1971—

FREDERICK: So I mean, basically—I'm not going like I was saying—basically, you know, it's just—it's like—it's a political thing, it's a cop-out, you know, to satisfy those people who feel that—I don't know, it's just all political to me. If you want to build enough jails, there's enough room in America to build jails if you—I mean, if it come down to it. I mean, 'cause small towns, you know, like you said, small town before will welcome jails because they bring jobs and everything.

SAMANTHA: Yeah, but that's basically an economic reason now.

FREDERICK: Give them lettuce and oatmeal and water. I mean, we have a lot of people who are not eating anything and have not committed not one crime. So just give them the bare essentials to live! No TV, let them just sit there with just four walls around them.

As it was for the women in the low-income housing community, for the pharmacy employees, life imprisonment was a viable and potentially crueler option than the death penalty. This group considered the impact of prisons on local economies. The city of Houston is ringed by correctional facilities, and municipal and county governments have lobbied to locate new prisons in their towns because of the economic benefit they will bring. Samantha articulated the economic impact of prisons: "The death penalty, let's just say this. Our prison system is nothing but an economic—it's business. It's economics." For Samantha, the politics of imprisonment represent a continuation of the economic subjugation of past periods. The link Samantha made between slavery and the pressing of Blacks into labor through the prison system was not unlike historian David Oshinsky's analysis that Parchman Farm in Mississippi was an expression of whites' desire to control Black labor after emancipation.[49]

In the final focus group, Takeisha made a direct connection between electoral politics and the death penalty. She says,

> I think yeah, it is, as far as the death penalty and I think it brings in a lot of political views. It's a seller! The death penalty is a seller! People get on the bandwagon. Politics is a big issue, especially during voting time, like now. Everybody's jumping on it. The death penalty is one of the hot topics too, as well as the war.

She, like Faye, saw the war in Iraq and the death penalty as issues politicians can use to distinguish themselves in a competitive electoral field. For Michael, the political value of the death penalty is captured in his view of the sentiments of politicians who take pride in the exceptionalism of Texas in the administration of the death penalty in the United States: "The people in power here? I think they're proud of the fact that we're [Texas] leading the nation."

Sarita defined the political character of the death penalty as less an electoral issue than a way for politicians to garner media attention:

You don't hear about them [executions] unless it's their turn for execution or there's something political, somebody political or something, this person gets involved in their case. The other ones you really don't hear about, unless they have some kind of political backing or some other thing, somebody that's a superstar that's backing them or whatever. Or if a superstar is backing them we don't hear about, you know?

The participants' commentary on the markers of citizenship such as voting and participation in electoral politics suggests that the views of African Americans on their exclusion from American society generally are connected to their views about the criminal justice system and the increased rate of incarceration of Blacks. The fact that the criminal justice system is being used as a tool of exclusion is not a new phenomenon in the political history of African Americans, but scholarship on racialized political inclusion has tended to focus on voting as the sole metric of African American citizenship. For example, one could argue that the economic, political, and legal vulnerability of the young female residents of the low-income housing community made them more likely to connect the current implementation of the death penalty with forms of political participation like voting. However, the majority of the other participants also connected the death penalty to some aspect of electoral politics. Voting is a very clear political act, but this project shows how the death penalty limits African Americans' access to other participatory acts.

Conclusion

African Americans' experiences of everyday discrimination have led them to identify with each other strongly and to distance their political perceptions from those outside their community. Exploring African Americans' perceptions of the death penalty can further elucidate the divergence of the perceptual worlds that Blacks and whites inhabit and the residual effects of this divergence on their respective politics and values. This study shows one of the important divergences—the ways that experiences of discrimination distort the meaning of equality for African Americans. Dawson argues that although Black liberalism is still the dominant and most supported ideology among African Americans, the increasing levels of disillusionment with their status in American society is leading—or driving—African Americans to less liberal and more radical ideologies. His research found that over 80 percent of African Americans do not believe that they receive equal treatment before the law and believe that they are farther away from the American Dream than they were the decade before the study was conducted.[50] The responses of the focus group participants in my study suggest that compromised citizenship may lead African Americans to change their beliefs about the underlying concepts and values that define citizenship, beliefs in concepts such as equality, for example. The focus group participants' suggestion that the execution of Karla Faye Tucker was a sacrifice by the state to maintain the stability of current racial inequities and that Tucker's salvation might have been met with violence by African Americans seems to support Dawson's finding that African Americans' views of American society are perhaps becoming more extreme.

Marquart, Ekland-Olson, and Sorensen see early perpetrations of state violence as a way to define which citizens were included within the bounds of "community"—safe from the executioner.[51] The threat of the Black economic and political power after emancipation prompted other legal and extralegal methods of distinguishing Blacks from that "community" through lynching, coupled with and then exclusively through the death penalty.[52] The responses of the focus group participants in this study suggest that African Americans feel that the death penalty may still be one of the many factors that distinguishes them from "bounded" American society. I do not have the data to measure the intensity of the respondents' beliefs about the death penalty, so where they would prioritize the death penalty among the various issues facing the Black community cannot be known in this sample. What we do know is that when asked, African Americans in Texas viewed the death penalty as an electoral tactic that is deployed at their expense.

Even when they discussed the most visible marker of citizenship—voting—the participants disagreed about the efficacy of their participation in electoral politics. The one aspect of voting that they did agree on was that politicians are buoyed during elections by their support for the death penalty. The competitiveness of politicians who support the death penalty in local and national campaigns was central to the participants' understanding of the political nature of the death penalty. The participants also suggested that the increased rate of incarceration of African Americans, especially African American men, represents a form of political currency. The difficult relationship between African Americans and law enforcement officials has been captured quite well elsewhere, but the responses of these participants show that African Americans' critique of the state's enforcement of laws goes beyond their attitudes toward police. The participants saw the prevalent use of the death penalty as an instrument of a discrimination that permeates the legal and justice systems of America: it begins with overpolicing, but that practice is reinforced by racially biased prosecutors and the people who elect them, most of whom they assume are not African American. Even with the multiple connections the participants made, most failed to note the fact that the state does not adequately protect members of their racial community, for example, the state routinely gives less severe sentences to killers who murder African Americans. The scope of this project did not allow for the investigation of African American views of white citizens' support for the death penalty. The data shows, however, that Blacks perceive the state and its officials as hostile to their interests. Incarceration—both the rate of incarceration and conditions of incarceration—is the evidence the participants offered most often, but they also saw the death penalty as a clear and not insignificant part of the criminal justice system.

Electoral politics are important to the participants because of the impact of incarceration generally on the voting strength of the African American community. The disenfranchisement of felons has made the treatment of African Americans in the criminal justice system an important issue for both ordinary African Americans and African American political elites. It is not clear if the connections these participants made between the death penalty and incarceration is an outgrowth of this concern or of the fact that these participants live in the county that executes the most prisoners in America or some combination of both. The response of the participants in these focus groups suggests that even the rather fragile domain that African Americans inhabit in Texas is being further encroached upon by incarceration, the death penalty, the association of Blacks with criminality, and the continuously present factor of economic marginalization. Finally, the participants in these focus groups see themselves in opposition to the state and question whether they or others like them fully belong in American society.

Conclusion

THE DEATH PENALTY
AND THE SHARED LEGACY OF RACE

ALMOST A DECADE after his conviction, Anthony Quinn Francois is awaiting execution on the Texas death row. If you go to the Death Row Information page of the Texas Department of Criminal Justice website, you can find a lot of information about Francois. His height, his highest level of educational attainment, his race, his gender, and even his eye color are publicly accessible details. The one-line summary of his crime reads: "On 09/11/2003 in Harris County, Texas, Francois fatally shot five black females."[1] Francois is one of the 117 Black men who collectively make up 40 percent of the population of death row in a state where Blacks are less than 12 percent of the state population. These facts do not tell us about the little girls—Naikesha, Ashley, and Brittney—who died in September. We do not know how Shameka Patterson, Francois's ex-girlfriend, and her mother, who were both also victims that day, have fared in this last decade. The information provided by the Texas Department of Criminal Justice does not give us details about the lingering impact of this crime on the neighborhood and the residents where this crime took place. The missing details are exactly the factors that form African American perspectives about the death penalty.

To simply say that individual African Americans are more subject to the death penalty in criminal cases, particularly if they are poor, does not tell the whole story of the relationship between the death penalty and race in American politics. I do not argue that the current death penalty regime operates in the same way it did in the past, but the findings of this research demonstrate how the racial inequity in the meting out of death sentences has legal and political externalities that affect large numbers of African Americans. Curing systemic inequalities in the criminal justice system is an unfinished task of the Civil Rights Movement. No part of that system highlights this truth more than the current implementation of the death penalty.

This book has looked at the meaning of the death penalty to and for African Americans by using various points of analysis. I have focused on how the media, both Black and white, frames death row inmates as they campaign to stay alive. The Tucker and Graham cases illustrate the importance of looking at both race and gender in representations of the religious transformations of death row inmates. I have analyzed the responses of African Americans and prosecutors in the jury selection process and how the state understands and responds to attitudes of African Americans in that process. As a backdrop to the more detailed focus group responses, I analyzed survey data of a much larger pool of Black Houston residents that showed that perceptions of group discrimination and levels of income are more salient factors than religious affiliation and practices on shaping the positions of African Americans about the death penalty. The analysis ends with explorations of the folk knowledge of African Americans about the death penalty and how the death penalty reinforces African Americans' feelings or beliefs that they are excluded from mainstream U.S. society.

Several major arguments arise from this study. First, the political strategy of achieving social innocence—the strategy African Americans used after emancipation to reframe their public image as citizens worthy of full legal and political rights—continues to be a part of the way African Americans attempt to overcome racial inequality. However, it has moved from a collective to an individual strategy. At the turn of the twentieth century and into the early 1920s, African Americans used strategies of social uplift to counteract public narratives that described them as dangerous or threatening. The entire Black community is no longer perceived as a dangerous presence the way it was in the early twentieth century. So although there is significant public opposition in the Black community to racially motivated traffic stops, which affect all Blacks regardless of class, the community has been virtually silent about its opposition to the disproportionate use of the death penalty against mainly poor Black men. In efforts to spare their lives, Black defendants must continually overcome the equation of Blacks with crime and violence in public discourse. Cases such as those of Graham and Tucker demonstrate that race and gender can work together to both expand and limit the narratives inmates can draw upon to reframe their image in the public eye. In their efforts to spare their own lives, Graham and Tucker's claims of innocence and transformation were either thwarted or buoyed by existing social narratives that frame Black men as criminal and dangerous and white women as valuable and in need of protection. Although pursuing social innocence might not have the capacity to permit Black death row inmates to change the opinions of mainstream media makers and politicians, it can trigger support from political resources within the Black community. Graham's case is an example of how employing particularly salient narratives, such as lynching, can motivate substantial activism regarding the death penalty despite the relative inactivity on the issue within the Black community.

Second, public performances of racial neutrality in capital jury selection through *Batson* hearings mask the continued exclusion of African Americans from this important political and legal space. The judicially crafted process, an attempt to remedy racial discrimination, has opened the door for prosecutors to remove African Americans for juries for reasons closely associated with race. Patterns in the responses of prosecutors in *Batson* hearings demonstrate, most importantly, that the effects of increased incarceration rates in the Black community extend beyond those who have been convicted of crimes; they also compromise access to this basic right of citizenship for African Americans. As the rates of incarceration trend upward, scholars of Black politics have focused on the impact of incarceration on the voting strength of the Black community. This study shows the need to look at the connection between incarceration rates and the political and legal rights of African Americans who are only tangentially connected to the criminal justice system through familial and social networks. The performative nature of these hearings demonstrates how changes in legal structures have not been able to reverse unconstitutional racial discrimination and the exclusion of African American voices and policy perspectives.

The third theme that arises is the influence of local and even regional narratives on the politics of African Americans. The South has important meaning for African Americans and brings to mind images of racial oppression and injustice, likely even for African Americans who have not lived there for generations. The associations between the death penalty and lynching linked the past with the present in the minds of the participants in this study's focus groups. The history of the death penalty cannot be erased from the memory of those who live at sites where it is primarily practiced simply because the Supreme Court drew a line in the sand between the current administration of the death penalty and past death penalty practices. Separate rules for Blacks and whites are a vestige of "southern justice." The Court's view of racism as ineradicable leaves African Americans, and others similarly situated, to deal with the consequences of legal inaction on their own. Additionally, Blacks' attitudes toward the death penalty are further amplified by the priority they give to the experiences of African American men and the importance of gender in the histories of execution and lynching.

The final theme the evidence from this study produces is that the death penalty exposes fractures in American democracy that create perceptions among Blacks that they are excluded from mainstream civil society. The elements of a shared understanding of "American" values are still being negotiated. So when religious conservatives pitch their traditional values platform to African Americans, they ignore something that African Americans do not: the fact that one of the traditional values of the United States is racial discrimination. For some of the respondents in this study, their understanding of Jim Crow comes from lived experience. Yet, the younger respondents also point to this history as a factor that shaped their views. The reliance of younger respondents on their understanding of Jim Crow communicates the failure of contemporary society to fully incorporate African Americans into the larger legal and political community of the nation.

The Death Penalty, Race, and Defining Shared Values

These findings raise profound questions about which political values Americans share in post–Civil Rights America. The legislation of the mid-1960s—the 1964 Civil Rights Act and the 1965 Voting Rights Act—was for many Americans "the defining moment in U.S. political history . . . because it honor[ed] the potential for democratic government to achieve outcomes."[2] Yet by the middle of the 1990s, 65 percent of African Americans "believed that racial progress in America would either not be achieved in their lifetime or would never be achieved."[3] By 2000, this number had risen to 71 percent.[4] Even though the African American community is ideologically diverse, each strain of thought is marked by its "decisive rejection" of what Michael Dawson calls "the shared heritages of American political thought." African Americans' declining belief in the possibility of racial progress and their view and experience of the state as unjust lead them to perceive themselves as members of an out-group.

For some African Americans living in Texas, a continuous line connects the death penalty of the past with the death penalty of today. This perception is driven in part by their actual knowledge of the administration of the death penalty, but to a greater degree it is driven by the beliefs that the policy is useful to politicians and that it is a holdover from past injustices that have yet to be completely remedied. In her study of the influence of race in the contemporary administration of the death penalty, Sheri Lynn Johnson points to racial disparities in prosecutors' decisions to seek the death penalty, cross-racial identifications in eyewitness testimony, jury misconduct, and biased conduct of trial participants as common sites where racial bias is introduced in capital cases.[5] The discrimination that scholars of capital sentencing have recorded could explain lower support for the death penalty among African Americans. However, those kinds of discrimination are often invisible to those outside the criminal justice system. African Americans bring their own assessments of the death penalty and the meaning of justice in this country to the table when they form opinions about the legitimacy of the death penalty.

Through familial or friendship networks and/or personal experience, more and more African Americans have become eyewitnesses to the workings of the criminal justice system. In the past, public narratives about Blacks presented them as a danger to society. This cultural process is increasingly being accomplished by criminal justice policy. The stamp of criminality marks Blacks as a danger and therefore subject to exclusion. My research shows that the effects of the increasing involvement of African Americans with the criminal justice system are not confined to those who are convicted of crimes. All of the members of the focus groups drew upon the experiences of friends, relatives, and/or romantic partners with law enforcement and incarceration. They might not have understood the complicated relationship between race and capital sentences, but their experiences and the experiences of those they knew led them to believe that race alters the rules. They were not free of the effects of criminal justice policy simply because they were not behind bars.

African Americans' belief that race alters the rules challenges their definition of equality and justice. This was evident among focus group participants who reversed their stated opinion when I asked them about their views about the treatment of whites in death penalty cases. Respondents would ardently state their objections to the death penalty and then later make a case for the primacy of enforcing "the law" in cases involving whites. This simple reversal points to a much more complicated problem related to finding the common ground that is a part of every political campaign for racial harmony. The criminal justice system signals to Blacks their exclusion. This sense of exclusion in turn distorts the meaning of democracy while also defining African Americans' citizenship in the larger political community.

The ways that current death penalty practices shape African Americans' understandings of citizenship have very important implications for legal and political studies that define civil rights legislation as the marker of full inclusion of African Americans as citizens. Unless the issue at hand is voting, contemporary legal and political scholars often assume that African Americans have full citizenship rights. But I argue that in terms of citizenship rights, African Americans are more similar to other groups whose rights are not fully protected, such as immigrants, than they are to white Americans. Are the criminal rights outlined in the Bill of Rights extended to African Americans in a fair and unbiased way? This question cannot be answered by reviewing statutes and constitutional theory; it can only be answered by analyzing the everyday on-the-ground interactions between African Americans and the state. The findings of this study would suggest that they are not. The heightened protection of political rights, like voting, is not sufficient to overcome the vestiges of the entrenched discrimination that was part of every aspect of the Jim Crow state. Addressing the racial inequities of the criminal justice system is critical to incorporating African Americans fully into the community of citizens that is protected from intentional and arbitrary state violence.

Though religion did not prove to be as significant as I hypothesized, African Americans use religious language to articulate discrimination and critique the state. The fact that African Americans resort to religious language to talk about political issues seems to suggest that they cannot fully communicate their political and legal status in the language of citizenship. Religion cannot fully link African Americans to other groups because they bring to politics, including religious politics, the experiences of discrimination and exclusion that continue to distinguish Blacks as a social and political group.

A prominent discussion of race in the academy focuses on the social construction of racial categories. Although this discussion is useful, issues like the death penalty point to the fact that African Americans' very real concern for their bodily integrity continues to shape their relationship to the state and their status as citizens. Lynn Sanders argues that the very definition of citizenship cannot be detached from the body.[6] Much like the way the focus group respondents and African American venirepersons reject the notion that capital punishment is fairly and equally administered even when Supreme Court justices have argued that it is, Sanders concludes that the fundamental principles of American democracy are not "transcendent and enduring"[7] but are instead "objects of contestation" that have been "invoked in American struggles to overcome and to re-establish racial hierarchies."[8] Sanders focused on Reconstruction Era debates over the meanings of freedom and equality. If the Civil Rights Movement ushered in a second Reconstruction, then this book advances the argument that in the post–Civil Rights era, some policies are reestablishing racial hierarchies.

The Supreme Court has actually proven to be a significant obstacle to those who would make the case for racial discrimination in capital sentencing. Since at least the early 1980s, the Supreme Court has promoted what Sanders calls "a mistaken notion that the American Creed transcends political conflicts and endures even through pernicious episodes."[9] In the past three decades, the Court has prioritized a notion of equality that has focused on race neutrality. This is a departure from previous decades, when the Court was an active participant in attempting to root out the vestiges of slavery and Jim Crow. The Court has essentially created a body of legal decisions based on a fictive America. The recent decisions of the Court about the death penalty ignore long-standing cleavages—especially those based on race—for the sake of promoting a definition of equality that does not consider race. As Stuart Banner's history of the death penalty outlines, the modern review of the death penalty reaches the Supreme Court at a time when the Court is attempting to create fair legal structures that diminish the influence of race without explicitly using the language of racial discrimination. Avoiding the language of race does not wipe away the continued importance of race in this area of law. This has led to a presumption that as long as the rules are "fair," a certain amount of racial discrimination is acceptable, a presumption that raises the question of what an "acceptable" amount of discrimination is. To whom is such discrimination "fair"—those who do the discriminating or those who are discriminated against? As the focus group respondents demonstrated, they may be aware of the difficulty involved in rooting out racism, but they do not accept that racial discrimination can be part of a "fair" justice system.

To some degree, the Supreme Court is permitting and affirming the continued exclusion of African Americans from the community of citizens who are protected from the excesses of the state. The findings of this project raise important questions. How does the law construct meanings of equality and community? What is the measure of consensus in a country where a clear fracture along racial lines has contributed to differences in policy attitudes and a vastly disproportionate representation of Black men on death row? African Americans' exclusion from the "bounded" community has led them to strongly oppose the death penalty. The language of the Supreme Court seems oblivious to this racial fracture and assumes a singular notion of justice and fairness arising from universal principles. The Court's silence about racial divisions is dangerous because their incomplete picture of the world is memorialized in their decisions. These decisions, due to the rules of precedent, only replicate the same narratives that exclude the policy preferences of African

Americans. This pattern by the court creates space for death penalty practices that in effect mark certain groups in American society.

The debate over the meanings of fairness, inclusion, and justice is not taking place exclusively between Blacks and those outside their community. An ongoing negotiation is taking place within the Black community about these issues. The political behavior of African Americans is marked by high levels of solidarity with other African Americans—a solidarity that is usually conveyed using the concept of linked fate. However, the solid surface of African American public opinion has at times masked calls for greater equality within the Black community. When Graham claimed that he was being lynched, the power of his words stemmed from their invocation of a dominant theme in the politics of African Americans: the vulnerability of Black men in American society. Gender is one cleavage, but the mark of criminality is another. The influence of linked fate separates subgroups, of all kinds, in the Black community from access to political resources.

In 1995, one year after the end of apartheid, the South African Supreme Court unanimously voted to abolish the death penalty in a decision that relied heavily on U.S. Supreme Court decisions.[10] The South African justices took a path U.S. justices could have taken but did not. The South African Court concluded that the disproportionate impact of the death penalty on Blacks and its use as part of a larger legal structure that denied the humanity and citizenship of the country's Black population made its continuance as a system of punishment untenable. Understanding that African Americans do not agree with dominant articulations of shared values is critical to understanding Black political preferences on both the specific issue of death as punishment and the larger issue of inclusion in the body politic. African Americans articulate alternative paths to equality and justice born of their ongoing experiences of discrimination and exclusion, even if they are the only ones who are listening.

Epilogue

TROY, TRAYVON, AND THE TREND(?)
TOWARD ABOLITION

IN THE YEARS since I began this research I have become a parent. Within weeks of finding out I was pregnant, I knew in my heart my child would be a boy. By the time I reached the sonogram in the 24th week, when the sex can be verified, I had already chosen his first name. I named him James for my mother's third brother and my first substitute father. I was elated when science confirmed what my heart knew. In less than 24 hours that elation would transform into intense worry.

My son was conceived in Texas, a place where my family has lived in relatively the same place for nine generations. Texas is the place where my family's home and labor and blood are built in the soil, where their race had for most of those generations determined their destiny. James was also conceived in "the field," what social scientists call the places where we conduct our research. I had returned to Texas for one year to immerse myself in this place where my intellectual efforts, if not my body, are always toiling. I visited death row. I attended hearings. I sat next to lawyers who were my teachers and models for how to be a lawyer with the ability to change and save lives. I read. I wrote. I conceived a child.

Even though I was submerged in the history and sadness of the death penalty, I had not connected that part of my life to the part that was about to be a parent until the day the sonographer said, "It is definitely a boy." Happiness became worry when I thought about the Black men I had met in prisons, jails, and other unproductive places over the years. I thought about how easy it can be for Black men to be caught up in a system that does not value their survival or preservation. I thought about the first day he would be pulled over by the police for performing the ordinary task of driving an automobile. I thought about the intraracial contests of masculinity that have led some young Black men to become their own worst enemies. I thought of how, because he is my child and will surely have my sharp tongue, the public school system will try to pathologize what I know to be precociousness. I thought about my father, who died as I began my dissertation work. All I could see were the negative statistics about the lives of Black men I have studied in my professional life.

This project is bookended by the death of my father and the birth of my son. The life-and-death concerns discussed in this project reflect my long interest in how communities and individuals on the peripheries of American politics understand and articulate the meaning of their citizenship. What does it mean to be both Black and a citizen of the United States in this particular political moment? How are these identities further complicated by other identities such as gender, socioeconomic status, and region? How do both state violence and the unwillingness of the state to redress the violence perpetrated against Black people continue to constrain feelings of belonging among African Americans? Just as they are for me, these questions are both intimate and open for many African Americans. They are individual and interconnected. They are grounded in immediate experience and in the long history of race and place.

These questions continue to be relevant because of the way the present mirrors and or reminds African Americans of their past exclusion or vulnerability. The 2011 execution of Troy Davis by the state of Georgia and the 2012 murder of Trayvon Martin by George Zimmerman have forced both state violence and the value of Black life to the front of the minds of many African Americans. The old-school narratives of unjust state prosecution of Blacks while the taking of Black life goes unpunished have now been validated once again by twenty-first-century martyrs. Martin and Davis are not alone. They keep company with other African American women and men, boys and girls who have been at the center of media controversies related to the violent excess of the state and the absence of repentance on the part of white perpetrators over the last few years.

It is not just the loss of life or unjust prosecution that are at play in the public grieving and calls for actions, it is also a sincere questioning of belonging and value within the social order. In the faces of Sybrina Fulton, the mother of Trayvon Martin, as well as Lucia McBath, the mother of Jordan Davis, another murdered Florida teen, I and other African Americans see Mamie Till weeping for her boy Emmitt and numerous unknown Black women and men whose grief went unnoticed. As I began this project, I was most interested in the meaning of state power in post–Civil Rights America, but I am now also interested in the political meaning of Black mothers' tears and the fluidity of time in African Americans' understanding of their political and social location.

Since the election of Barak Obama, hope has been a tricky word to use in political conversation. Hope is a powerful sentiment that has driven the righteous protest of African Americans for centuries in this country. Hope as a belief in the possibility of something better or a desire for the elusive in African American political rhetoric and life goes far beyond the sloganeering of electoral contests. In the area of capital punishment there is reason to have concrete hope that there may be some steady progress in efforts to end the use of this form of punishment. In the course of this work, New York (2007), New Mexico (2009), Connecticut (2012), and Maryland (2013) abolished the death penalty and a nearly successful referendum to do the same in California in 2012.

These are not enough cases to make a systematic claim that we are moving toward abolition universally, but it is enough to be hopeful. The deep entrenchment of the death penalty in states such as Texas, Virginia, and Florida and the willingness of these states to fight for retention of the death penalty suggest that the legal structures that support this form of punishment cannot easily be undone. The African Americans in this study tell us that as long as this form of punishment and other discriminatory practices associated with the criminal justice system continue, so will African Americans' questions about when they will be included in notions of protection and justice, when they will be valued as members of society, and when they will have access to their full rights as citizens.

Data on Attitudes about the Death Penalty Among African Americans from the Houston Area Survey, Selected Years

Year	Against	For	Total
1993	102	174	276
	37%	63%	100%
1998	196	166	362
	54.1%	45.9%	100%
1999	174	198	372
	46.8%	53.2%	100%
2001	230	169	399
	57.6%	42.4%	100%
2003	216	215	431
	50.1%	49.9%	100%
2005	264	179	443
	59.6%	40.4%	100.0%
Total	1,182	1,101	2,283
	51.8%	48.2%	100%

This table shows the fluctuations in support for the death penalty among African Americans in Houston across time. The 1993 results are unclear, but after the HAS began oversampling African Americans in 1999, the numbers stabilized on the side of opposition to the point where in 2005 almost 60 percent of African Americans opposed the death penalty. The changes in levels of support for the death penalty from 1998 to 2001 seem to support some of the findings of this study. The execution of the

Karla Faye Tucker took place as the 1998 wave of data was being gathered. At that time, the majority of African Americans opposed the death penalty. In the following year, African American support for the death penalty increased. In 2000, the debate over the execution of Gary Graham took place and was used as a political tool in the presidential election. After this point, the views on the death penalty among African Americans who responded to the Houston Area Survey remained on the side of opposition to the death penalty.

Additional Cross-Tabulations Utilizing Houston Area Survey Data (see Chapter 3)

Income of African Americans by Church Attendance in the Last 30 Days[1]

	Less than $15,000	$15,000 to $25,000	$25,001 to $35,000	$35,001 to $50,000	$50,001 to $75,000	More than $75,000	Total
No	210	194	189	171	119	771	960
	33.4%	29.7%	26.2%	24.8%	21.4%	8.0%	26.1%
Yes	418	459	532	518	438	350	2,715
	66.6%	70.3%	73.8%	75.2%	78.6%	82.0%	73.9%
Total	628	653	721	689	557	427	3,675
	100%	100%	100%	100%	100%	100%	100%

1. Pearson's Chi-square = 0.000.

Source: Houston Area Survey, 1993, 1998, 2001, 2003, and 2005.

Age of African Americans by Religious Affiliation[1]

	18–24	25–35	35–45	45–65	Over 65	Total
Fundamentalists	366	669	599	858	405	2,897
	51.6%	53.1%	54.8%	57.0%	68.9%	56.2%
Religious Progressives	226	480	395	557	163	1,821
	31.9%	38.1%	36.1%	37.0%	27.7%	35.3%
Secularists	117	110	100	89	20	436
	16.5%	8.7%	9.1%	5.9%	3.4%	8.5%
Total	709	1,259	1,094	1,504	588	5,154
	100%	100%	100%	100%	100%	100%

1. Pearson's Chi-square = 0.000.

Source: Houston Area Survey, 1993, 1998, 2001, 2003, and 2005.

Variables and Questions from the Houston Area Survey

AGE	How old were you on your last birthday? (82–05)[1]
GENDER	Gender of the respondent, recorded by the interviewer. (82–05)
ETHGROUP	Are you Anglo, Black, Hispanic, Asian, or of some other ethnic background (specify)? If R names more than one ethnicity: Which ethnic group do you generally identify with? (82–05)
EDUC	What is the highest grade of school or year of college that you've completed? Open-ended: Coded into nine categories. (82–05)
INCOME8	Please stop me when I reach the category that includes your total household income in [the past year]; that is, the income for all members of the household during the past year. Eight categories. (03–05)
INCOME6	Please stop me when I reach the category that includes your total household income in [the past year]; that is, the income for all members of the household during the past year. Six final categories. (90–05)
MYETHDIS	How often are [R's ethnicity] discriminated against in Houston? Would you say: very often, fairly often, rarely, or never? (97, 99–04)
SELFDISC	How often have you personally felt discriminated against in Houston because of your ethnicity? Would you say: very often, fairly often, rarely, or never? (93–97, 99, 01–04)
DEATH4	For/Against: What about the death penalty for persons convicted of murder? (93, 98, 99, 01, 03, 05)
RELIG1	What is your religious preference, if any? Open-ended: Five categories. (82–05)

DENOM5	If "Protestant" (RELIG1): What specific denomination is that, if any? Open-ended: Nine final categories. (89–05)
BIBLE	Which one of these three statements comes closest to describing your feelings about the Bible?—"The Bible is the actual word of God, and it should be taken literally, word for word"; "The Bible is the inspired word of God, but it was written by men and contains some human errors"; or: "The Bible is an ancient book of history and legends; God had nothing to do with it." (83–05)
RELIMP	How important would you say religion is in your life? Would you say: very important, somewhat important, or not very important? (83–05)
NEWRELIG	Computed variable: Combining BIBLE and RELIMP into three categories of religiosity: "Fundamentalists," "Religious Progressives," and "Secularists." (83–05)
CHURCH1	In the past 30 days, did you attend a religious service, other than a wedding or funeral? (82, 86, 90, 91, 96–05)
PARTY	What is your political preference? Would you call yourself a Republican, a Democrat, an Independent, or something else? (82–05)
POLITICS	Do you think of yourself as conservative, moderate, or liberal in your politics? (82–05)

Focus Group Questions and Participant Questionnaire

What do you think of the death penalty?

Does your religion have a particular position on the death penalty?

Does it matter to you where your church stands on the death penalty?

What do you think of the people charged with crimes? With murder? With capital murder?

Does it matter if while on death row they become devoutly religious? (If they say yes, ask in what way it matters. If the response is in favor of mercy, ask what if they convert to a different religion like Islam.)

What if a person on death row claims to be innocent?

Can you think of some reason why a person found guilty of capital murder should not be put to death?

Do you remember the Karla Faye Tucker case? (If someone doesn't remember the case, ask someone in the group to explain. Record the description. If no one knows of the case read description provided.)

Do you remember the Gary Graham case? (If someone doesn't remember the case, ask someone in the group to explain. Record the description. If no one knows of the case read description provided.)

How are these cases the same? Different?

Do you think the defendant's race was important in these cases?

Do you think the defendant's race influences whether or not they receive the death penalty generally?

QUESTIONNAIRE FOR FOCUS GROUP PARTICIPANTS

Age: _______

Occupation: _______________________________

Race: _______________________________

Sex: _______

Marital Status: _______________________________

Income: _______________________________

Education Level: _______________________________

Where were you born? _______________________________

Religion: _______________________________

How often do you attend services? _______________________________

Which political party do you vote for primarily? _______________________

Have you or a close relative ever been a victim of violent crime? _______________________
If so, when? _______________________

Do you watch the news? _______ How often? _______________________________

Do you read the newspaper? _______________ Which newspaper? _______________________________

Notes

INTRODUCTION

1. Ida Wells-Barnett, "Lynch Law in America" (1900), in *Words of Fire: An Anthology of African American Feminist Thought*, ed. Beverly Guy-Sheftall (New York: The New Press, 1995), 70.

2. Focus Group #2, July 30, 2004.

3. A very good example of the juxtaposition of these two patterns of thought can be found in Martin Luther King's fourth annual report on the state of the civil rights struggle, published in the *Nation* in 1964. At various points, King points to the Emancipation Proclamation, the post–Civil War civil rights legislation, and existing federal voting laws as opportunities for the government to make good on its promises of equality by enforcing its own laws and regulations. M. L. King Jr., "Hammer on Civil Rights," *Nation* 198 (March 9, 1964): 230–234, reprinted in *A Testament of Hope: The Essential Writings and Speeches of Martin Luther King Jr.*, ed. James M. Washington (San Francisco: Harper San Francisco, 1986). Also see the long discussion of various conceptualizations of rights among African Americans in Hanes Walton Jr. and Robert C. Smith, *American Politics and the African American Quest for Universal Freedom* (New York: Longman, 2003).

4. Stuart Banner, *The Death Penalty: An American History* (Cambridge, Mass.: Harvard University Press, 2002), 265. It is also important to note that this confluence is not completely unrelated. Many of the criminal rights and civil rights cases are being championed and litigated by the NAACP Legal Defense and Education Fund.

5. Ibid.

6. Scalia to conference, January 6, 1987, Box 425, Folder 7, Thurgood Marshall Papers, Library of Congress.

7. David C. Baldus, George Woodworth, and Charles A. Pulaski Jr., *Equal Justice and the Death Penalty: A Legal and Empirical Analysis* (Boston: Northeastern University Press, 1990), 154.

8. Since the *McCleskey* (1987) decision there have been numerous reports documenting the role of race in who receives death sentences, which death row inmates are executed, and how the court chooses those who make the decisions in death penalty cases. Nonprofit organizations like the Death Penalty Information Center, The Texas Defender Service, and others have compiled studies analyzing data across the ensuing decades that indicate the continuing influence of race in all aspects of capital punishment. See, e.g., Richard Dieter, *The Death Penalty in Black and White: Who Lives, Who Dies, Who Decides* (Washington, D.C.: Death Penalty Information Center, 1998); William J. Bowers et al., "Death Sentencing in Black and White: An Empirical Analysis of the Role of Jury Racial Composition and the Juror's Race," *University of Pennsylvania Journal of Constitutional Law* 3 (2001): 171, 193; and Isaac Unah and Jack Boger, *Race and the Death Penalty in North Carolina An Empirical Analysis: 1993–1997* (The Common Sense Foundation North Carolina Council of Churches, April 16, 2001).

9. The measures of religiosity at the base of this claim are frequency of church attendance and prayer and a subjective identification with God. See Robert Smith and Richard Seltzer, *Race, Class and Culture: A Study in Afro-American Mass Opinion* (Albany: State University of New York Press, 1992), 126–128.

10. Richard C. Dieter, *The 2 percent Death Penalty: How a Minority of Counties Produce Most Death Cases at an Enormous Cost to All* (Washington, D.C.: Death Penalty Information Center, 2013), http://deathpenaltyinfo.org/twopercent.

11. Benjamin D. Steiner, "Folk Knowledge as Legal Action: Death Penalty Judgments and the Tenet of Early Release in a Culture of Mistrust and Punitiveness," *Law and Society Review* 33, no. 461 (1999): 462.

CHAPTER 1

1. E. R. Shipp, "Where Was Pat Robertson for Other Executions?" *Austin American Statesman*, February 1, 1998, H3.

2. R. G. Ratcliffe, "The Execution of Karla Faye Tucker; Bush Prayed for Guidance before Denying Tucker's Appeal," *Houston Chronicle*, February 4, 1998, A10.

3. Julie H. Patton, "The Lost Issue in the Tucker Debate; Karla Faye Tucker's Execution Was Unjust Because the Death Penalty Is Unjust, Not Because She Is a Women Who Found God," *Texas Lawyer* 36 (February 16, 1998), 44.

4. A total of 517 men and women have been executed in Texas since 1982, when the death penalty was reinstated after the moratorium. Harris County, one of the counties that encompasses the city of Houston, accounts for 122 of those executed offenders. This number is even more significant when one realizes that

there are 254 counties in the state of Texas and only about 44 of those counties account for all execution. The significance of Harris County's numbers are magnified even further when one considers the county with the next highest number of executions, Dallas County, has executed only 32 people. Of the 275 inmates currently on death row in Texas, 97 are from Harris County. See Texas Department of Criminal Justice, "County of Conviction for Executed Offenders," https://www.tdcj.state.tx.us/death_row/dr_county_conviction_executed.html, accessed April 8, 2014.

5. Excerpts from Gary Graham's last words from Texas Department of Criminal Justice, "Last Statement of Gary Graham," https://www.tdcj.state.tx.us/death_row/dr_info/grahamgarylast.html, accessed April 30, 2014.

6. Anna Quindlen, "Public & Private: Dead Man Walking," *New York Times*, May 26, 1993, A21; Guillermo Garcia, "Texas Inmate Struggles to the End: Courts Deny Last Minute Civil Lawsuit," *USA Today*, June 23, 2000, 3A.

7. Bernadine Skillern, who was 30 to 40 feet away from Graham, testified that she saw him shoot Bobby Lambert, while several other witnesses who were nearer to the shooting claimed that it was not Graham. Andrea Greene, "Catholic Group Backs New Trial for Inmate," *Houston Chronicle*, May 31, 1993, A34. Skillern also twice failed to pick Graham in a photo array.

8. Ibid.

9. Even though his son was not killed in the robbery Graham perpetrated, Franklin C. Jones wrote a letter to the editor of the Houston Chronicle that said, "if anyone deserves the ultimate penalty for his actions, Graham qualifies." Jones's son lost his leg and almost bled to death as a result of injuries sustained in the robbery. Jones was one of a small cadre of victims of the robberies who also spoke publicly in support of Graham's execution. Franklin Jones, "Should Gary Graham Get New Trial? He Deserves the Ultimate Penalty," *Houston Chronicle*, July 23, 1993, A31.

10. Amy Dorsett and Katy Hunger, "Capital Questions: As Execution Date Nears, Proof of Houston Man's Guilt in Slaying Hinges on a Single Witness," *San Antonio Express-News*, June 11, 2000, 1A.

11. Ibid.

12. Ibid.

13. There was also significant post-conviction litigation over the trial court's denial of allowing the jury to consider Graham's age at the time of the trial as a mitigating factor. See, e.g., *Graham v. Lynaugh*, where Graham unsuccessfully argued that "his death sentence violate[d] the eighth amendment because he was seventeen at the time of the offense." 854 F.2d 715, 717 (1988).

14. By the time he arrived on death row, Graham had fathered two children. His son Gary Hawkins, who was two when his father went to death row and with whom Graham had little contact, was also convicted of capital murder during the year before his father's execution. Bruce Nichols, "Death Row Inmate's Son Faces

Judgment: He Could Join Father Gary Graham in Prison If Convicted in Capital Case," *Dallas Morning News*, April 13, 2000, News 1A.

15. In their research on race and media, Entman and Rojecki argue that the overrepresentation of Black perpetrators, the underrepresentation of Black victims, and the overrepresentation of white victims in local news intensifies negative stereotyping of Blacks and "promotes anxiety and hostility in the audience." Robert Entman and Andrew Rojecki, *The Black Image in the White Mind: Media and Race in America* (Chicago: University of Chicago Press, 2000), 81–82. This anxiety is fed by the news media, which "presents a face of black criminalizing and victimization that compares unfavorably to whites" (209).

16. In an extensive search of hundreds of articles from national and local newspapers and magazines and transcripts of news programs, I found one article that discussed this change or really any characterizations of Graham as a person at the time leading to his death.

17. See, e.g., *Graham v. Johnson*, 168 F.3d 762n.1 (1999).

18. This finding is compatible with research on Black counterpublics that finds separate institutional spaces for Black political debate, of which the most important are the Black church and the Black press. See Michael Dawson, *Behind the Mule: Race and Class in African-American Politics* (Princeton, N.J.: Princeton University Press, 1994). However, in *Black Visions: The Roots of Contemporary African-American Political Ideologies* (Chicago: University of Chicago Press, 2001), Dawson complicates his earlier analysis, arguing that "the dismantling of the formal barriers of segregation combined with the sharpening of economic divisions within the black community also problematized black political discourse" by highlighting existing cleavages once the unifying goal of ending segregation was removed (39).

19. Michica Guillory, "Execution for Graham: Date Would Be Set for June," *Houston Defender*, May 7–13, 2000. Two Black Houston newspapers—the *Houston Defender* and the *Forward Times*—are archived at the Houston Public Library. Lexis-Nexis includes the *Houston Chronicle*, which has been Houston's only daily for more than a decade, as well as *Essence* and *Jet*, publications geared to a Black audience.

20. Ashanti Chimurenga, "I Remember Shaka," *Essence* (September 2001), 114.

21. Ibid.

22. Ibid.

23. Earnest L. Perry, "Local Rappers Plan Concert to Support Murder," *Houston Chronicle*, May 23, 1993, B23; Sheila Rule, "Rap to the Rescue," *New York Times*, June 2, 1993, C16.

24. Bruce Nichols, "Protests Mark Graham's Service: High Profile Guests Assail the Death Penalty," *Dallas Morning News*, June 29, 2000, News 23A.

25. Chimurenga, "I Remember Shaka," 113.

26. Huntsville is where the execution chamber is located. Michica Guillory, "Graham Faces Execution: Rallies and Vigils Planned January 11th," *Houston Defender*, January 10–16, 1999.

27. Though the events were reported only in the *Houston Defender*, Glover actually went to Texas nine times between 1993 and 2000 to advocate on Graham's behalf. Michica Guillory, "Glover Back to Defend Graham: I Thought His Life Had Been Spared," *Houston Defender*, February 21–27, 1999.

28. Susan Warren, "Graham Supporters Renew Attention as Two Key Court Rulings Are Pending," *Houston Chronicle*, March 12, 1994, A29.

29. Ibid.

30. Ibid.

31. The perception of Black clerics as primarily political figures when they enter mainstream politics may be encouraged by the clerics themselves in attempts to make their message palatable to a wider audience. In his analysis of Jesse Jackson's speaking style during the 1984 presidential campaign, Charles Henry argues that Jackson "moved from an African-American preacher-cum-American politician to an American politician utilizing the expressive characteristics of black sermon performance to achieve his goals"; Charles Henry, *Culture and African American Politics* (Bloomington: Indiana University Press, 1990). Black politics scholar Adolph Reed has criticized the role of Jackson as both a religious and a political figure. In his critique of Jackson's 1984 presidential campaign, Reed rejected the predominant view that religion encourages political participation among Blacks and argues instead that "Afro-Christianity" encourages "political quietism" among Blacks. Adolph Reed Jr., *The Jesse Jackson Phenomenon: The Crisis of Purpose in Afro-American Politics* (New Haven, Conn.: Yale University Press, 1986). In his seminal work on religion and African-American political activism, *Something Within*, Fred Harris wrote that Reed sees the reliance on ministers for political leadership "as authoritarian and the tradition of the black church as antidemocratic"; Frederick C. Harris, *Something Within: Religion in African-American Political Activism* (Oxford: Oxford University Press, 1999), 6. The argument over the impact of clerical leadership on African-American political behavior goes back to Du Bois, Frazier, and Lincoln, who all agreed that religion was impacting Black political participation but make separate claims about the actual impact. See W. E. B. Du Bois, *The Souls of Black Folk* (Chicago: A. C. McClurg, 1903); E. Franklin Frazier, *The Negro Church in America* (New York: Schocken Books, 1963); C. Eric Lincoln, *The Black Church since Frazier* (New York: Schocken Books, 1974). More recent studies show that the scholars who asserted that Black religion led to political quietism were partially correct. Recent work by Allison Calhoun-Brown has found that church attendance is not what determines religious participation among Blacks but whether they attend a political church. See Allison Calhoun-Brown, "African American Churches and Political Mobilization: The Psychological Impact of Organizational Resources," *Journal of Politics* 58, no. 4 (1996): 935–953.

32. Earnest L. Perry, "Local Rappers Plan Concert to Support Murderer Graham," *Houston Defender*, May 7–13, 2000, B23.

33. Excerpt from Karla Faye Tucker's last words; Texas Department of Criminal Justice, "Last Statement of Karla Faye Tucker," http://www.tdcj.state.tx.us/death_row/dr_info/tuckerkarlalast.html, accessed April 30, 2014.

34. Karla Tucker was the first white woman to be executed in the history of the state of Texas. See Ellen Goodman, "Karla Tucker Gave Death Row a Human Face," *Houston Chronicle*, February 15, 1998, Outlook 6.

35. Beverly Lowry, *Crossed Over: A Memoir, a Murder* (New York: Knopf, 1992), 25.

36. Marianne Means, "No Gender Lines Exist in Use of Death Penalty," *San Antonio Express-News*, January 20, 1998, B7.

37. See Lowry, *Crossed Over*, 242: "Karla never removes herself from blame or responsibility."

38. "Tucker continued to hack at her victims long after they were dead and left the pickax sticking out of the woman's chest. Hardened police officers were haunted for years afterward by the carnage." Gregory Curtis, "The Texas Twenty: Forgiveness and the Law," *Texas Monthly* 26, no. 9 (September 1998).

39. See Lowry, *Crossed Over*, 121–122. See also Christy Hoppe, "Woman's Execution Looms, Stirring National Discussion: Gender, Rehabilitation Add to Debate in Texas Case," *Dallas Morning News*, January 13, 1998, 1A ("A heroin abuser at age 10, Ms. Tucker became a teenage prostitute").

40. See ibid., 124–125.

41. Kathy Walt and T. J. Milling, "Karla Faye's Last Chance; Words on Life or Death," *Houston Chronicle*, February 1, 1998, A14.

42. Ibid.

43. Christy Hoppe, "State Urged to Spare Karla Faye Tucker Minister, Married to Killer, Rock Singer's Ex-Wife Lead Call for Clemency," *Dallas Morning News*, January 18, 1998, 24A. Karla Faye Tucker was married to Dana Brown, whom she met through a prison ministry.

44. Ratcliffe, "The Execution of Karla Faye Tucker."

45. Ibid., A10.

46. Paula M. Cooey, "Women's Religious Conversions on Death Row: Theorizing Religion and State," *Journal of the Academy of Religion* 70, no. 4 (2002): 700.

47. See Texas Department of Criminal Justice, "Executed Offenders," http://www.tdcj.state.tx.us/death_row/dr_executed_offenders.html, accessed April 30, 2014.

48. See Francine Banner, "Rewriting History: The Use of Feminist Narratives to Deconstruct the Myth of the Capital Defendant," *New York University Review of Law and Social Change* 26 (2000): 580.

49. Gregory Curtis, "Because of Her, the Whole World Took a Second Look at the Death Penalty," *Texas Monthly* (September 1998): 135.

50. Tucker was only the second woman to be executed in Texas history. The last woman executed before Tucker was an innkeeper named Chipita Rodriguez.

Rodriguez was hanged for the murder of one of her patrons, whose body was found floating in the Arkansas River. In 1985, the legislature passed a bill clearing her name. See Goodman, "Karla Tucker Gave Death Row a Human Face."

51. *Furman v. Georgia,* 408 U.S. 238, 361 (1972).

52. *Id.* at 361n.145.

53. Samuel R. Gross and Phoebe C. Ellsworth, "Second Thought: Americans' Views on the Death Penalty at the Turn of the Century," in *Beyond Repair? America's Death Penalty,* ed. Stephen P. Garvey (Durham, N.C.: Duke University Press, 2003), 38.

54. Ibid., 39.

55. Gross and Ellsworth note the fact that DNA has played a role in only about 10 percent of the cases in which innocent defendants have been exonerated and that this fact continues to go unnoticed. Whether they are true, false, or slightly misinformed, the accounts of the Tucker and Graham cases illustrate the discussion at the time and how race, religion, and gender play out in those accounts. Ibid.

56. The most notable recent example of this is the execution of Napoleon Beazley. Napoleon was convicted of capital murder at the age of 17. There is considerable legal debate in the United States about the execution of children. It is also condemned internationally. The state of Texas moved forward with the execution of Napoleon Beazley despite a movement by the Supreme Court to review the issue of execution of children in the following session. See Stephanie Simon, "Court Puts Age, Crime on Scales; Law: Issue Is Whether It's Just to Execute Criminals Who Were Young at the Time of Their Offenses. A Supreme Court Decision Could Help Settle It Soon," *Los Angeles Times,* June 9, 2002, A20.

57. See Austin Sarat and Stuart Scheingold, *Something to Believe In: Politics, Professionalism, and Cause Lawyering* (Stanford, Calif.: Stanford University Press, 2004).

58. Carlos Guerra, "We Hardly Blink at Executions Anymore," *Austin American Statesman,* February 6, 1998, A13.

59. Gross and Ellsworth, "Second Thought: Americans' Views on the Death Penalty at the Turn of the Century," 39.

60. Glenda Elizabeth Gilmore, *Gender and Jim Crow: Women and the Politics of White Supremacy, 1896–1920* (Chapel Hill: University of North Carolina Press, 1996).

61. Ibid., 73.

62. William J. Bowers and Glenn L. Pierce, "Racial Discrimination and Criminal Homicide under Post-*Furman* Capital Statutes," in *The Death Penalty in America,* 3rd ed., ed. Hugo Adam Bedau (New York: Oxford University Press, 1982).

63. Patricia Hill Collins, *Black Sexual Politics: African Americans, Gender and the New Racism* (New York: Routledge, 2004), 219.

64. See, e.g., Chimene I. Keitner, "Victim or Vamp? Images of Violent Women in the Criminal Justice System," *Columbia Journal of Gender and Law* 11 (2000): 38–89.

See also Jenny E. Carroll, "Images of Women and Capital Sentencing among Female Offenders: Exploring the Outer limits of the Eighth Amendment and Articulated Theories of Justice," *Texas Law Review* 75 (1997): 1413–1453; Melinda E. O'Neil, "The Gender Gap Argument: Exploring the Disparity of Sentencing Women to Death," *New England Journal on Crime and Civil Confinement* 25 (1999): 213–234; and Andrea Shapiro, "Unequal before the Law: Men, Women and the Death Penalty," *American University Journal of Gender Social Policy and Law* 8 (2000): 427–470.

65. Cal Thomas, "Flawed Reasoning in Sparing Tucker," *San Antonio Express-News*, January 26, 1998, A11.

66. Ibid.

67. Ibid.

68. Each time I mention Tucker as advantaged or privileged, it seems important to mention that despite any social or gender advantage Tucker may have had, she was still executed. Making such comparisons of advantage or status in the area of capital punishment is extremely difficult because where or how one marks the meaning of advantage is still unclear, to me at least.

69. The concept of othering is borrowed from analysis of the death penalty that joins ideas of marginalization in feminist theory with analysis of the types of narratives used to justify the death penalty. See Banner, "Rewriting History," 580. Others are those groups "whose marginality defines the boundaries of the mainstream, whose voice and perspective—whose consciousness—has been suppressed, devalued, and abnormalized"; Nancy L. Cook, "The Call to Stories: Speaking in and about Stories," *University of Cincinnati Law Review* 63 (1994): 102, quoting Richard Delgado, "Storytelling for Oppositionists and Others: A Plea for Narrative," *Michigan Law Review* 87 (1989): 2412. See also Keitner, "Victim or Vamp?," 38.

70. Nancy Donisi, "Tucker's Lawyer Still Backs Death Penalty: Attorney Speaks at Arlington Seminar," *Dallas Morning News*, February 7, 1998, A1.

71. Sam Gideon Anson and David Cogan, "A Death in Texas," *LA Weekly*, June 30, 2000, http://www.laweekly.com/2000-07-06/news/a-death-in-texas/.

72. Texas Department of Criminal Justice, "Last Statement of Gary Graham."

73. Hoppe, "State Urged to Spare Karla Faye Tucker."

74. Texas Department of Criminal Justice, "Last Statement of Karla Faye Tucker."

75. Vincente Arenas, a Houston television reporter, made these statements. See Sue Anne Pressley, "Texas Executes Killer Karla Faye: 'Baby, I Love You,' She Tells Husband," *Toronto Star*, February 4, 1998, A1.

76. See *Herrera v. Collins*, 506 U.S. 390 (1993).

77. Herrera claimed that the eyewitness testimony used to convict him at trial was improperly admitted. He also submitted an affidavit from his nephew, who claimed that he was in the car at the time his father and his uncle, Raul Herrera, killed the two deputies. Also, a longtime friend of the Herrera brothers submitted an affidavit saying that Raul Herrera, not Leonel, confessed to the murder.

Corroborating statements were also offered by a former cellmate and by a lawyer of Raul Herrera Sr. See *id.* at 393–397.

78. Habeas is "a writ employed to bring a person before a court, most frequently to ensure that the party's imprisonment is not illegal." Death penalty cases can go through both state and federal habeas proceedings. See Bryan A. Garner and Henry Campbell Black, eds., *Black's Law Dictionary* (Minneapolis, Minn.: West Group, 1996).

79. *Herrera v. Collins*, 506 U.S. at 399.

80. For more discussion, see Arleen Anderson, "Responding to the Challenge of Actual Innocence Claims after Herrera v. Collins," *Temple Law Review* 71 (1998): 489–520; Vivian Berger, "Herrera v. Collins: The Gateway of Innocence for Death-Sentenced Prisoners Leads Nowhere," *William and Mary Law Review* 35 (1994): 943–1023.

81. For more discussion, see James Marquart, Sheldon Ekland-Olson, and Jonathan R. Sorensen, *The Rope, the Chair, and the Needle: Capital Punishment in Texas* (Austin: University of Texas Press, 1994), 17.

82. Earl Lewis, "Constructing African Americans as Minorities," in *The Construction of Minorities: Cases for Comparison across Time and around the World*, ed. André Burguiére and Raymond Grew (Ann Arbor: University of Michigan Press, 2001).

83. Dorsett and Hunger, "Capital Questions: As Execution Date Nears, Proof of Houston Man's Guilt in Slaying Hinges on a Single Witness," 1A.

84. See, e.g., Henry, *Culture and African American Politics*; Paula Giddings, *When and Where I Enter: The Impact of Black Women on Race and Sex in America* (New York: William Morrow, 1984); and Kevin K. Gaines, *Uplifting the Race: Black Leadership, Politics, and Culture in the Twentieth Century* (Chapel Hill: University of North Carolina Press, 1996).

85. Harris, *Something Within*, 9.

86. Lewis, "Constructing African Americans as Minorities," 24.

87. Ibid.

88. Even though I include Houston in the South in this analysis, there are some who might challenge the categorization of Texas as part of the South. I agree with them that it would be harder to use general southern historical analysis in an analysis of the death penalty statewide, but Houston and other parts of north, east, and southeast Texas actually fit relatively smoothly into "the South." Political scientist Chandler Davidson, who has studied Houston politics for decades, argues that Houston and the counties that border traditionally southern states such as Arkansas and Louisiana should be considered part of the "rim south"— areas of states that are not traditionally considered southern that share a historical, economic, and political culture with the Deep South. Chandler Davidson, *Biracial Politics: Conflict and Coalition in the Metropolitan South* (Baton Rouge: Louisiana State University Press, 1972).

89. For more discussion of past strategies of racial uplift, see Lewis, "Constructing African Americans as Minorities." For a discussion of the historiography of Black nationalism and racial uplift, see Gaines, *Uplifting the Race*.

90. Andrea Greene and Valerie Godines, "Killer's Supporters Seek to Prevent His Execution," *Houston Chronicle*, June 1, 1993, A16.

91. Jane Mansbridge and Katherine Tate, "Race Trumps Gender: The Thomas Nomination in the Black Community," *PS: Political Science & Politics* 25, no. 3 (1992): 488–492.

92. See, e.g., Giddings, *When and Where I Enter*.

93. See the analysis of how Black leaders responded to lynching in Gaines, *Uplifting the Race*, 86.

94. James Weldon Johnson was the field secretary for the NAACP from 1916 to 1920. Johnson made this observation while investigating the lynching of Ell Persons in 1917. Hazel Carby viewed this observation as an improvisation on "the multiple meanings of Du Bois's declaration that 'the problem of the Twentieth Century is the problem of the color line.'" Hazel Carby, *Race Men* (Cambridge: Harvard University Press, 1998), 46.

95. Marquart, Ekland-Olson, and Sorensen, *The Rope, the Chair, and the Needle*, 12.

96. Ibid., 2

97. For Graham's last statement, see Texas Department of Criminal Justice, "Last Statement of Gary Graham."

98. Michica Guillory, "Graham Supporters Ready for Final Fight," *Houston Defender*, May 28–June 3, 2000, 1.

99. "Capital Punishment: Many Will Continue to Doubt Graham's Guilt," *Houston Chronicle*, June 23, 2000, A36.

100. Jackson was criticized in an editorial in the *National Review* for this comparison that compared Graham to Jesus Christ. See "Capital Punishment: Lifeless Debate," *National Review* 52, no. 13 (2000): 16–17.

101. "Capital Punishment: Many Will Continue to Doubt Graham's Guilt," *Houston Chronicle*, June 23, 2000, A36.

102. See, e.g., Crystal N. Feimster, *Southern Horrors: Women and the Politics of Rape and Lynching* (Cambridge, Mass.: Harvard University Press, 2009); Kerry Segrave, *Lynchings of Women in the United States: The Recorded Cases, 1851–1946* (Jefferson, N.C.: McFarland, 2010); and Evelyn Simien, ed., *Gender and Lynching: The Politics of Memory* (New York: Palgrave Macmillan, 2011).

103. Mike Ward, "Jesse Jackson Asks to Visit Condemned Woman: Unlike Tucker—Before," *Austin American Statesman*, March 21, 1998, B2.

104. Norma Martin, "Witness against Graham Files Harassment Suit: Behavior of TV Crew Is 'Outrageous'," *Houston Chronicle*, May 20, 1993, A26.

105. J. Stephen Kroll-Smith, "The Testimony as Performance: The Relationship of an Expressive Event to the Belief System of Holiness Sect," *Journal for the Scientific Study of Religion* 19, no. 1 (1980): 18. The performative aspects of Tucker's testimony are discussed later in this chapter.

106. Karla Faye Tucker to Gov. George W. Bush and the Texas Board of Pardons, reprinted in *Houston Chronicle,* January 21, 1998, A25.

107. For greater discussion of the role of religion and conversion, see Cooey, "Women's Religious Conversions on Death Row," 700.

108. Peter Brooks, *Troubling Confessions: Speaking Guilt in Law and Literature* (Chicago: University of Chicago Press, 2000), 22.

109. Ibid., 112.

110. Ibid., 166.

111. Ratcliffe, "The Execution of Karla Faye Tucker."

112. "Capital Punishment: Many Will Continue to Doubt Graham's Guilt," *Houston Chronicle,* June 23, 2000, A36.

113. Michica Guillory, "The Graham Case: What Does It All Mean?," *Houston Defender,* June 25–July 1, 2000, 1.

CHAPTER 2

1. *Batson v. Kentucky,* 476 U.S. 79 (1986).

2. It is not clear that the Court always intended such a low threshold in evaluating race-neutral reasons offered by prosecutors. However, with the decision in *Hernandez v. New York,* the Court makes two points clear that are important to later evaluations of *Batson* claims. First, the showings of race neutrality required to overcome claims of bias are low. Second, a demonstration that peremptory challenges disproportionately impact a single group is not necessarily an inference of discrimination. *Hernandez v. New York,* 500 U.S. 352, 360, 362, 372 (1991).

3. In Texas, there is only one intermediate appeals court (the Texas Court of Appeals), but the highest courts are bifurcated. The Texas Supreme Court hears civil cases and the Court of Criminal Appeals hears criminal cases. See "Texas Court Structure," Texas Courts Online, http://www.courts.state.tx.us/, accessed May 1, 2014.

4. It is always important to mention that this right of citizenship was not fully extended to African American women at this time and that for all women, the right to participate on juries would not be expanded until the 1970s. For example, Louisiana excluded women from jury service unless they filed a declaration saying they wanted to be considered for service. At the time of the petitioner's trial in *Taylor v. Louisiana,* 419 U.S. 522 (1975), the Court found that there were no women on the venire even though they were 53 percent of the population in the judicial district. In 1979, The Supreme Court ruled that a Missouri law that permitted women to be exempted from jury duty if they wished was unconstitutional. As a result of that law, only 14.5 percent of the post-summons venire included women, and the petitioner claimed that the paucity of women in the venire denied his right to have his case heard by a fair cross-section of the community; see *Duren v. Missouri,* 439 U.S. 357 (1979). The Supreme Court did not recognize female jurors of all races as having the right not to be discriminated against on the basis of sex

in the use of peremptory challenges until *J. E. B. v. Alabama ex rel. T. B.*, 511 U.S. 127 (1994). Even after they had attained suffrage, women were barred from jury service completely in many states. Alabama was one of the last states to recognize the specific jury rights of women, in 1966. *Id.* at n.3.

5. *Strauder v. West Virginia*, 100 U.S. 303 (1880).

6. *Id.* at 309.

7. 476 U.S. 79 (1986).

8. "While challenges for cause permit rejection of jurors on a narrowly specified, provable, and legally cognizable basis of partiality, the peremptory permits rejection for a real or imagined partiality that is less easily designated or demonstrable"; *Swain v. Alabama*, 380 U.S. 202, 221 (1965).

9. In *Swain*, the court explained peremptory challenges in this way: "The essential nature of the peremptory challenge is that it is one exercised without a reason stated, without inquiry and without being subject to the court's control." *Id.* at 221.

10. *Id.*

11. *Batson*, 476 U.S. at 87–88.

12. *Id.* at 112 (Burger, C. J., dissenting).

13. I say prosecutors here because *Batson* is silent about the racially discriminatory use of peremptory challenges by the defense. See *Batson,* at 89n.12. Also, this analysis focuses on the interaction between Black citizens and the state as represented by the prosecutor.

14. *Swain v. Alabama*, 380 U.S. 202, 203–204, my emphasis.

15. *Id.* at 227. This part of the rule was first articulated in *Castaneda v. Partida*, 430 U.S. 482, 494 (1977).

16. The Dallas County prosecutor also used a handbook for jury selection that encouraged prosecutors to eliminate "any member of a minority group." An earlier jury selection treatise that was circulated in the same county instructed prosecutors: "Do not take Jews, Negroes, Dagos, Mexicans or a member of any minority race on a jury, no matter how rich or how well educated." Quoted in *Dallas Morning News*, March 9, 1986, 29.

17. This part of the rule is from *Swain* and was first articulated in *Castaneda,* 430 U.S. at 494–495.

18. This part of the rule is now considered an indisputable fact in the legal analysis of the use of peremptory challenges to remove racial minorities. In *Avery v. Georgia*, the Supreme Court held that once a defendant makes a prima facie case of discriminatory jury selection, it is the responsibility of the state to disprove the discrimination. In Georgia at that time, jury commissioners would print the names of whites on white paper and Blacks on yellow paper. The slips were placed in a box and a judge would pull them out and hand them to the sheriff. The sheriff would give them to a clerk to type and arrange. In Avery's case, the judge pulled 60 slips from the box. The judge testified that he did not discriminate when selecting the slips from the box, but no African Americans were on the panel.

Justice Frankfurter, in his concurring opinion, concluded that "the mind of justice, not merely its eyes, would have to be blind to attribute such an occurrence to mere fortuity." *Avery v. Georgia*, 345 U.S. 559, 561–562, 564 (1953).

19. *Batson*, 476 U.S. at 96.

20. *Id.* at 138 (Rehnquist, J., dissenting).

21. *Id.* at 106 (Marshall, J., concurring).

22. Forty-eight states have laws that temporarily or in some cases permanently disenfranchise citizens who commit felonies. Approximately 13 percent of all Black men are disenfranchised in the United States. See, e.g., "Felony Disenfranchisement Laws in the United States," The Sentencing Project, Washington, D.C., 2003, http://www.sentencingproject.org/detail/publication.cfm?publication_id=15, accessed May 1, 2014.

23. Robert Wuthnow, *Meaning and Moral Order: Explanations in Cultural Analysis* (Berkeley, Calif.: University of California Press, 1987), 109.

24. Ibid., 99

25. Ibid.

26. Ibid., 104.

27. Ibid.

28. *Swain* and *Miller-El* (see below) are only the most recent examples of the involvement of Texas state courts in the evolution of constitutional law on jury discrimination. As early as 1940, the U.S. Supreme Court unanimously overturned a Texas statute that systematically excluded Blacks from juror lists. In *Smith v. Texas*, the Court used statistical analysis to show that in Harris County, where the defendant was convicted, the population of African Americans numbered more than 20 percent. Despite the estimated three to six thousand eligible Blacks, only five were seated on grand juries from 1931 to 1938. *Smith* began nearly six decades of the Supreme Court's attempt to regulate and rectify racial discrimination in jury selection in this one state. See *Smith v. Texas*, 311 U.S. 128–129 (1940).

29. Steve McGonigle and Ed Timms, "Race Prejudice Pervades Jury Selection: Prosecutors Routinely Bar Blacks, Study Finds," *Dallas Morning News*, March 9, 1986, 28A. See also *Batson,* 476 U.S. at 104n.3 (Marshall, J., concurring).

30. McGonigle and Timms, "Race Prejudice Pervades Jury Selection."

31. Similar practices were found in other Texas counties. See, e.g., Ex Parte *Brandley*, 781 S.W. 2d. 886, 926 (Tex. Crim. App. 1989).

32. A study by the Texas Defender Service, a nonprofit legal defense organization, published the testimony of several former prosecutors from Harris County and counties around the state who had witnessed such practices post-*Batson*. See Texas Defender Service, *A State of Denial: Texas Justice and the Death Penalty* (Houston: Texas Defender Service, [2000]), 54–59, http://www.texasdefender.org/tds-publications/, accessed May 1, 2014.

33. Texas Defender Service, *A State of Denial,* 54–59; Bruce J. Winick, "Prosecutorial Peremptory Challenge Practices in Capital Cases: An Empirical Study and

a Constitutional Analysis," *Michigan Law Review* 81, no. 1 (1982): 39; David Baldus, George Woodworth, David Zuckerman, Neil Alan Weiner, and Barbara Broffitt, "The Use of Peremptory Challenges in Capital Murder Trials," *University of Pennsylvania Journal of Constitutional Law* 3, no. 1 (2001): 10; Mary R. Rose, "The Peremptory Challenge Accused of Race or Gender Discrimination? Some Data from One County," *Law & Human Behavior* 23, no. 6 (1999): 695, 697; Billy M. Turner, Rickie D. Lovell, John C. Young, and William F. Denny, "Race and Peremptory Challenges During Voir Dire: Do Prosecution and Defense Agree?" *Journal of Criminal Justice* 14, no. 1 (1986): 61, 63; Holly Becka, Steve McGonigle, Tim Wyatt, and Jennifer La Fleur, "Disputed Practice Still a Courtroom Fixture; Peremptory Challenges Survive Calls for Reform, Decades of Controversy," *Dallas Morning News,* August 23, 2005, 11A.

34. See *Miller-El v. Dretke*, 545 U.S. 231, 235, 237, 252 (2005).

35. *Id.* at 252–266.

36. See, e.g., *id.* at 253: "The first clue to the prosecutors' intentions, distinct from the peremptory challenges themselves, is their resort during *voir dire* to a procedure known in Texas as the jury shuffle." See also 255: "Some of these prefatory statements were cast in general terms, but some followed the so-called graphic script, describing the method of execution in rhetorical and clinical detail."

37. Either defense counsel or the prosecution can make requests to shuffle the jury. The procedure is conducted under the Texas Code of Criminal Procedure, article 35.11 (Vernon Supp. 2004–2005).

38. *Miller-El*, 545 U.S. at 254.

39. The record reflects that both the prosecution and defense asked for shuffles. The Court finds the fact that the defense actually asked for more shuffles than the prosecution irrelevant. *Id.* at footnote 14. Justice Souter wrote that the uses of the jury shuffle by the defense did not negate a suspicion of racial discrimination on the part of the prosecutor. *Id.* at 253.

40. *Id.* at 253. Akhil Amar argues that racially motivated peremptory challenges, "even in the hands of a defendant, violate the Fifteenth Amendment." Akhil Reed Amar, "Reinventing Juries: Ten Suggested Reforms," *U.C. Davis Law Review* 28 (1995): 1169, 1178.

41. *Miller-El*, 545 U.S. at 255.

42. *Id.* at 255–256.

43. *Id.* at 256.

44. *Id.* at 257.

45. The majority and minority opinions in *Miller-El* turn on the justices' different characterizations of the venire members' responses to the jury questionnaire. The majority opinion in footnote 17 says as much:

> The dissent has conducted a similar statistical analysis that it contends supports the State's argument that the graphic script was used to expose the true feelings of jurors who professed ambivalence about the death penalty on their

> questionnaires. A few examples suffice to show that the dissent's conclusions rest on characterizations of panel members' questionnaire responses that we consider implausible.

Id. at n.17. The fact that the Court, which has the primary responsibility for articulating the rules on the use of peremptory challenges, is divided on how the individual responses of jurors should be interpreted is a telling aspect of the vagaries of evaluating discrimination in the peremptory challenges.

46. *Id.* at 258.

47. *Id.* at 264–266.

48. *Swain,* 380 U.S. at 220, 222.

49. *Snyder v. Louisiana,* 128 S. Ct. 1203 (2008). The Court looks at the dialogue between prosecutor and the venire person and other aspects of selection, including the handling of other jurors who offered similar testimony. The entirety of the jury selection process is used to determine whether the reasons proffered are truly race neutral.

50. To completely understand this perspective, it is important to mention that judges in Texas, including those on the highest courts, are elected through partisan elections. Excerpt from interview with Attorney Fred Tinsley in Texas Defender Service, *A State of Denial,* chapter 4, 58.

51. *Chambers v. State of Texas,* 742 S.W.2d 695 (Tex. Crim. App. 1988).

52. This article offers studies before and after *Batson* that point to the decreased representation of Blacks on juries where discriminatory peremptory challenges were a significant reason. Baldus et al., "The Use of Peremptory Challenges in Capital Murder Trials."

53. See, e.g., Timothy V. Kaufman-Osbourne, *From Noose to Needle: Capital Punishment and the Late Liberal State* (Ann Arbor: University of Michigan Press, 2005).

54. Ibid.

55. Many of the cases where the appellant was convicted either immediately before or after *Batson* were remanded to the trial court with instructions on how to proceed when new objections were raised. See, e.g., *Keeton v. State of Texas,* 724 S.W.2d 58 (1987); and *DeBlanc v. State of Texas,* 732 S.W.2d 640 (1987).

56. See, e.g., *Wamget v. State,* 67 S.W. 3d 861 (Tex. Crim. App. 2001). In this case, a Black venireperson was removed because she was from Liberia. The court upheld the prosecutor's assertion that venirepersons who were from places where violence was quite frequent such as New York City or Liberia could be removed based on geography despite a bar against removing a person strictly because they are naturalized citizens. There may be some connection between geographic exclusion and race, but that is outside of the scope of this book.

57. Malcolm M. Feeley, *The Process Is Punishment* (New York: Russell Sage, 1979), 11.

58. In March 2005, DeBlanc's sentence was commuted to life. DeBlanc is one of a number of death row inmates whose sentences were commuted after the Supreme

Court ruled in *Atkins v. Virginia*, 536 U.S. 304 (2002) that mentally retarded individuals could not be executed. DeBlanc's high school records indicated he had an IQ of 56. See Cindy Horswell, "Commutation for Priest's Killer: A 2-Decade-Old Sentence Changes after a Court Finds He Is Retarded and Can't Be Executed," *Houston Chronicle*, March 17, 2005, B1.

59. *Simpson v. State*, 119 S.W.3d 262 (Tex. Crim. App. 2003).

60. Gary Graham's case, which was tried in Houston, was extremely controversial. Gary Graham became a national symbol of many of the failures of the Texas death penalty regime. His case is discussed in chapter 1 and later in the discussion of the focus group data.

61. See, e.g., Charles Henry, *Culture and African American Politics* (Bloomington: Indiana University Press, 1990).

62. *Casarez v. State of Texas*, 913 S.W.2d 468, 494 (1995).

63. See Robert L. Young, "Religious Orientation, Race and Support for the Death Penalty," *Journal for the Scientific Study of Religion* 31, no. 1 (1992): 76–87.

64. Ibid.

65. *Trevino v. State of Texas*, 864 S.W.2d 499 (Tex. Crim. App. 1993).

66. See responses of Evelyn Guillory and Joann Smith in *Tennard v. State*, 802 S.W.2d 678 (Tex. Crim. App. 1990); see also Jeanetta Chaney in *Keeton v. State of Texas*, 724 S.W.2d 58 (1987) and venireperson Calvert in *Staley v. State*, 887 S.W.2d 885 (Tex. Crim. App. 1994).

67. *Cook v. State of Texas*, 858 S.W.2d 467, 472 (Tex. Crim. App. 1993).

68. *Morris v. State of Texas*, 940 S.W.2d 610 (1996).

69. Response of venireman Johnny Crowder in *Camacho v. State of Texas*, 864 S.W.2d 524, 529–531 (Tex. Crim. App. 1993).

70. *Johnson v. Texas*, 68 S.W.3d 644, 649 (Tex. Crim. App. 2002).

71. In *Chambers v. State of Texas* (1993), jurors Mosley and Kennedy had relatives who were incarcerated and had been prosecuted by the prosecutor in the case. It is not uncommon in small communities for the jury panel to know—or at least be aware of—the defendant and/or the prosecutor. The prosecutor claimed that the family of juror Kennedy, a woman who's family rioted at the courthouse, held a grudge against him. In *Staley v. State,* the defense counsel's father was the employer of one of the African American jurors; *Staley*, 887 S.W.2d at 898 n.3.

72. A reason that is both legitimate and strategic may be that those who have connections to the criminal justice system may be biased in favor of the state and be less willing to hear the evidence put forth by the state.

73. *Sauls v. State of Texas,* Nos. 05–00–00,538-CR, 05–00–00,539-CR, 05–00–00,638-CR, 2001 WL 406,582, at 1 (Tex. Ct. App. Apr. 23, 2001).

74. The word bling was chosen because it alludes to a particular kind of aesthetic originally associated with young Black men. Bling is hip-hop slang for expensive jewelry and other accoutrements.

75. For research on the role of nonverbal cues in the jury selection process, see, e.g., Jim Goodwin, "Articulating the Inarticulable: Relying on Nonverbal Behavioral Cues to Deception to Strike Jurors during Voir Dire," *Arizona Law Review* 38 (1996): 739–761.

76. *Fuentes v. State*, 991 S.W.2d 267, 279 (Tex. Crim. App. 2002).

77. This is a quote from one of the African American jurors in *Fuentes. Id* at n.5.

78. *Chambers v. State of Texas*, 866 S.W.2d 9 26 (1993).

79. *Casarez v. State of Texas* (1993).

80. *Tennard,* 802 S.W.2d at 681.

81. Good examples of this are Tommy Crosby in *Keeton v. State of Texas* and James Doyle and Henry Nichols in *Tennard v. State.*

82. *Herron v. Texas*, 86 S.W.3d. 621, 631 (2002).

83. *Id.*

84. *Snyder v. Louisiana*, 128 S. Ct. 1203 (2008). In *Snyder,* juror Jeffrey Brooks was peremptorily challenged. Defense counsel raised a *Batson* objection. The prosecutors argued that Brooks appeared to be nervous because he feared sequestration, which would take him away from his student teaching obligations. *Id.* at 1208. Brooks's concern for his schooling, in the prosecutor's view, made him more inclined to find for one of the lesser-included offenses that took less time to adjudicate. *Id.* The Court found that this reason failed the race-neutral requirement because of the prosecutor's acceptance of white jurors who expressed concerns about other obligations that were more substantial than those of Brooks. *Id.* at 1211.

85. *Id.* at 1208: "In *Miller-El v. Dretke,* the Court made it clear that in considering a *Batson* objection, or in reviewing a ruling claimed to be *Batson* error, all of the circumstances that bear upon the issue of racial animosity must be consulted. 545 U.S., at 239, 125 S. Ct. 2317, 162 L. Ed. 2d 196."

86. *Id.* at 1209–1212.

87. Wuthnow, *Meaning and Moral Order*, 140.

88. *Wainwright v. Witt,* 469 U.S. 412 (1985).

89. Since Marshall's call in *Batson* for the elimination of peremptory challenges, several other justices have made similar arguments or raised serious questions about whether the current line of decisions will allow for the practice to continue. See, e.g., *Miller-El v. Dretke,* 545 U.S. at 267 (Breyer, J., concurring); and *Georgia v. McCollum,* 505 U.S. 42, 60 (1992) (Thomas, J., concurring).

90. A good example of the prosecutor's obligation is the requirement that the prosecutor notify the defense of possibly exculpatory evidence under *Brady* even if it is detrimental to the state's case. See *Brady v. Maryland*, 373 U.S. 83 (1963).

91. Prosecutors and defense attorneys are what Amar calls "repeat-player regulars." The regularity of the presence of these figures allows for greater opportunities "to manipulate demographics and chisel an unrepresentative panel out of a cross-sectional venire." Amar, "Reinventing Juries," 1178, 1182.

92. A good example of this reliance is *Atkins v. Virginia*, where the Court points to polls conducted by news organizations and religious groups to support its view of a community consensus against execution of the mentally retarded. *Atkins v. Virginia*, 536 U.S. at n.21.

93. Indeed, recent work on contemporary manifestations of racism argues that claims of color-blind views of race are a "justification" whites offer for continued racial inequality. See Eduardo Bonilla-Silva, *Racism without Racists: Color-Blind Racism and the Persistence of Racial Inequality in the United States*, 2nd ed. (Lanham, Md.: Rowman and Littlefield, 2006).

94. Robert Ruby and Allison Pond, "An Enduring Majority: Americans Continue to Support the Death Penalty," The Pew Forum on Religion & Public Life, Washington, D.C., December 19, 2007, http://pewforum.org/docs/?DocID=272, accessed October 31, 2009.

95. Allan Turner, "Bloodthirsty Image at Odds with Local Poll," *Houston Chronicle*, February 3, 2001, A1.

96. Ibid.

97. James Marquart, Sheldon Ekland-Olson, and Jonathan R. Sorensen, *The Rope, the Chair, and the Needle: Capital Punishment in Texas* (Austin: University of Texas Press, 1994).

98. To some degree, poor Blacks also suffer the brunt of underpolicing. Murderers of Black homicide victims receive far less punishment than murderers of other victims.

99. In *Herrera v. Collins*, the Court made a distinction between legal and actual innocence. *Herrera v. Collins*, 506 U.S. 390, 398–400 (1993): "A person when first charged with a crime is entitled to a presumption of innocence, and may insist that his guilt be established beyond a reasonable doubt. . . . Once a defendant has been afforded a fair trial and convicted of the offense for which he was charged, the presumption of innocence disappears."

CHAPTER 3

1. Robert M. Bohm, "American Death Penalty Attitudes: A Critical Examination of Recent Evidence," *Criminal Justice and Behavior* 14, no. 3 (1987): 380–396.

2. Robert L. Young, "Religious Orientation, Race and Support for the Death Penalty," *Journal for the Scientific Study of Religion* 31, no. 1 (1992): 76–87.

3. See, e.g., ibid.; and Rosalee Clawson, Elizabeth Kegler, and Eric N. Waltenburg, "Supreme Court Legitimacy and Group-Centric Forces: Black Support for Capital Punishment and Affirmative Action," *Political Behavior* 25, no. 4 (2003): 289–311.

4. The founder and principle investigator of the Houston Area Survey is Stephen L. Klineberg, a professor of sociology at Rice University.

5. In 1982, survey also included items that asked whether the death penalty should be reinstated. This was during the time when Texas resumed executing inmates after the Supreme Court decision in *Gregg*, which overturned the unofficial

moratorium initiated by the *Furman*. It periodically includes questions related to specific political or legal happenings related to capital punishment. When Texas was debating whether to include a life-without-parole option, the survey asked a question on that specific issue.

6. The AGE variable in the original survey was recoded to AGECAT, which had five age categories—1 (18–24), 2 (25–34), 3 (35–45), 4 (46–65) and 5 (over 65). The education variable EDUC was recoded to EDUCAT: 1 (no high school graduation), 2 (high school graduation), 3 (some college), 4 (undergraduate degree), and 5 (some graduate and professional schooling).

7. The data in this chart represent the results of all the respondents. The table in Appendix A shows the results across years.

8. When these variables were cross-tabulated, there were slightly fewer respondents than in the frequency for the for/against the death penalty variable. Among those compared in this cross-tab, 52.1 percent opposed the death penalty and 47.9 percent supported it. This difference should not be read as significant, because cross-tabs only analyze the respondents who answered both questions. Pearson's chi-squared test was significant at 0.012 for this cross-tabulation.

9. The difference is indeed slight. Among 18- to 24-year-olds, opposition was 50.5 percent, compared to 48.2 percent for 24- to 35-year-olds and 49.9 percent for 35- to 45-year-olds.

10. Evelyn Simien, "Race, Gender, and Linked Fate," *Journal of Black Studies* 3, no. 5 (2005): 529–550; Patricia Hill Collins, *Black Feminist Thought.* (New York: Routledge, 1990); bell hooks, *Feminist Theory: From Margin to Center* (Boston: South End Press, 1984).

11. Simien, "Race, Gender, and Linked Fate."

12. For discussions of voting and registration patterns among Black men and women, see Sandra Baxter and Marjorie Lansing, *Women and Politics: The Visible Majority* (Ann Arbor: University of Michigan Press, 1983); S. L. Williams, "Black Political Progress in the 1980's: The Electoral Arena," in *The New Black Politics*, ed. Michael B. Preston, Lenneal Henderson, and Paul Puryear (New York: Longman, 1987), 97–131. For discussion of support for principles of feminism among Black and white women, see Jane Mansbridge and Katherine Tate, "Race Trumps Gender: Black Opinion on the Thomas Nomination," *PS: Political Science & Politics* 25, no. 3 (1992): 488–492.

13. Michael Dawson calls this idea the Black utility heuristic; see Michael C. Dawson, *Behind the Mule: Race and Class in African-American Politics* (Princeton, N.J.: Princeton University Press, 1991); Katherine Tate, *From Protest to Politics: The New Black Voters in American Elections* (Cambridge: Harvard University Press, 1994); Gerald Jaynes and Robin Williams, *A Common Destiny: Black and American Society.* (Washington, D.C.: National Academy Press, 1989).

14. For a discussion of the impact of linked fate on African American political participation, see Tate, *From Protest to Politics*; and Dawson, *Behind the Mule.* For

a discussion of Black public opinion in the Reagan-Bush era, see Hanes Walton Jr., *African American Power and Politics* (New York: Columbia University Press, 1997), 135–153; Patricia Gurin, Shirley Hatchett, and John Jackson, *Hope and Independence: Blacks' Response to Electoral and Party Politics* (New York: Russell Sage Foundation, 1989); and Mary Herring, Thomas B. Janowski, and Ronald E. Brown, "Pro-Black Doesn't Mean Anti-White: The Structure of African-American Group Identity," *Journal of Politics* 61, no. 2 (1999): 363–386.

15. Dawson, *Behind the Mule*; and Michael C. Dawson, "African American Political Opinion: Volatility in the Reagan-Bush Era," in *African American Power and Politics*, ed. Hanes Walton Jr. (New York: Columbia University Press, 1997), 135–153.

16. Much of the quantitative analysis of Black political behavior is based on the National Black Election Survey, a series of surveys conducted by the Program for Research on Black Americans at the Institute for Social Research at the University of Michigan. Over the course of several years, the survey received funding from the Ford Foundation, the Rockefeller Foundation, and the Carnegie Corporation. These national-level surveys were conducted before and after elections in the presidential election years of 1984, 1988, and 1996.

17. Tate, *From Protest to Politics*; Dawson, *Behind the Mule*.

18. Dawson, *Behind the Mule*, 10.

19. Robert L. Young, "Race, Conceptions of Crime and Justice, and Support for the Death Penalty," *Social Psychology Quarterly* 54, no. 1 (1991): 67–75.

20. A 2005 survey fielded by the Houston Chronicle and directed by the University of Houston Center for Public Policy found that 57.9 percent of African Americans opposed the death penalty, compared to 23.9 percent of whites. See Mike Tolson, "A Deadly Distinction: Harris County Is a Pipeline to Death Row," *Houston Chronicle*, May 22, 2005, A1.

21. Jeff Yates and Richard Fording, "Politics and State Punitiveness in Black and White," *Journal of Politics* 67, no. 4 (2005): 1100.

22. Ibid. For greater discussion of the historical context of current incarceration rates and race, see Michael Tonry, *Malign Neglect: Race, Crime, and Punishment in America* (New York: Oxford University Press, 1995).

23. Yates and Fording, "Politics and State Punitiveness in Black and White," 1118.

24. Ibid.

25. Ibid., 1119.

26. Tali Mendelberg, *The Race Card: Campaign Strategy, Implicit Messages and the Norm of Equality* (Princeton, N.J.: Princeton University Press, 2001).

27. Tali Mendelberg, "Executing Hortons: Racial Crime and 1988 Presidential Campaign." *Public Opinion Quarterly* 61, no. 1 (1997): 134–157.

28. Melynda Price, "Are We Imprisoned in Narratives of Progress: The Work of Hanes Walton and Its Lessons for an Afrofuturistic Black Politics," *Politics, Groups and Identities* 1, no. 4 (2013): 577–588; Jon Hurwitz and Mark Peffley,

"Explaining the Great Divide: Perceptions of Fairness in the U.S. Criminal Justice System," *Journal of Politics* 67, no. 3 (2005): 762–783.

29. Paul M. Sniderman and Edward G. Carmines, *Reaching beyond Race* (Cambridge: Cambridge University Press, 1997); Dawson, *Behind the Mule*; Vesla M. Weaver, *Frontlash: Civil Rights, the Carceral State and the Transformation of American Politics* (Cambridge University Press, forthcoming); and Khalilah Brown-Dean, "Permanent Outsiders: Felon Disenfranchisement and the Breakdown of Black Politics," in *The Expanding Boundaries of Black Politics: The National Political Science Review*, ed. Georgia A. Persons (New Brunswick, N.J.: Transaction Publishers, 2007).

30. Mark Peffley and Jon Hurwitz, "Persuasion and Resistance: Race and the Death Penalty in America," *American Journal of Political Science* 51 no. 4 (2007): 1006.

31. This finding is in line with the theory of linked fate, the leading theory of Black political behavior and public opinion. Young argues that Blacks' high level of concern for the treatment of prisoners is related to "their tendency to make situational rather than personal attributions, and to the relative skepticism with which they view the American criminal justice system." Young, "Religious Orientation, Race, and Support for the Death Penalty," 85. This finding also could be attributed to the very well-documented existence of linked fate among Blacks.

32. C. Eric Lincoln and Lawrence H. Mamiya, *The Black Church in the African American Experience* (Durham, N.C.: Duke University Press, 1990); Clyde Wilcox and Leopoldo Gomez, "Religion, Group Identification and Politics among American Blacks," *Sociological Analysis* 51, no. 3 (1990): 271–285; Evelyn Brooks Higginbotham, *Righteous Discontent: The Women's Movement in the Black Baptist Church, 1880–1920* (Cambridge, Mass.: Harvard University Press, 1993).

33. Young, "Race, Conceptions of Crime and Justice, and Support for the Death Penalty."

34. The biblical literalism variable (BIBLE) asked, "Which one of these three statements comes closest to describing your feelings about the Bible?: The Bible is the actual word of God, and it should be taken literally, word for word; The Bible is the inspired word of God, but it was written by men and contains some human error; or The Bible is an ancient book of history and legends; God had nothing to do with it." The religious importance variable (RELIMP) asked, "How important would you say religion is in your life? Would you say: very important, somewhat important, or not very important?" The measures of biblical literalism and religious importance were combined in the survey data to create a single variable (NEWRELIG) with three categories—fundamentalist, religious progressive, and secularist.

35. These are common terms for the typology of religious groups but there is always the possibility that multiple or different meanings could be at work among these respondents.

36. For a more detailed discussion of the role of women in the Black church, see Higginbotham, *Righteous Discontent*.

37. I refer to Tali Mendelberg's work on the use of crime policy and the William "Willie" Horton ad as a mechanism for priming white racial resentment. See Mendelberg, "Executing Hortons." The connection between the use of crime policy as a way to communicate racial norms and the use of the death penalty as a way of demonstrating a politician's attitudes on crime, and the impact of this on individual attitudes on both crime and race, has yet to be explored in this work.

38. Hanes Walton Jr., *Black Political Parties* (New York: Free Press, 1972).

39. Dawson, *Behind the Mule*, 110.

40. Michelle Alexander's work on mass incarceration has received a tremendous amount of attention. Alexander lays out in great detail the way increased rates of incarceration have created a new system of racial caste comparable to previous periods in U.S. history. See *The New Jim Crow: Mass Incarceration in the Age of Colorblindness* (New York: The New Press, 2010). She is not the only one to make these arguments; works in history, geography, sociology, and the popular press have also made them. See, for example, Douglas A. Blackmun, *Slavery by Another Name: The Re-Enslavement of Black Americans from the Civil War to World War II* (New York: Random House, 2009); Ruth Gilson Gilmore, *Golden Gulag: Prison, Surplus, Crisis, and Opposition in Globalizing California* (Berkeley: University of California Press, 2007); Heather Thompson, "Why Mass Incarceration Matters: Rethinking Crisis, Decline, and Transformation in Postwar American History," *Journal of American History* 97, no. 3 (2010): 703–734.

41. Loïc Wacquant, "Class, Race & Hyperincarceration in Revanchist America," *Daedalus* 139, no. 3 (2010): 74–90.

42. Cathy J. Cohen and Michael C. Dawson, "Neighborhood Politics and African American Politics," *The American Political Science Review* 87 (1993): 286–302.

43. Allison Calhoun-Brown, "African American Churches and Political Mobilization: The Psychological Impact of Organizational Resources," *Journal of Politics* 58, no. 4 (1996): 935–953.

44. See Tamelyn N. Tucker-Worgs, *The Black Megachurch: Theology, Gender and the Politics of Public Engagement* (Waco, Tex.: Baylor University Press, 2012). See also Eric L. McDaniel, *Politics in the Pews: The Political Mobilization of Black Churches* (Ann Arbor: University of Michigan Press, 2008).

45. Melanye T. Price, *Dreaming Blackness: Black Nationalism and African American Public Opinion* (New York: New York University Press, 2009).

46. Byron D'Andra Orey, "A Research Note on White Racial Attitudes and Support for the Mississippi State Flag," *American Politics Research* (January 2004): 102–116; Byron D'Andra Orey, "Explaining Black Conservatives: Racial Uplift or Racial Resentment," *Black Scholar* (Spring 2004): 18–22; Byron D. Orey, "The New Black Conservative: Rhetoric or Reality?," Faculty Publications, Paper 16,

Department of Political Science, University of Nebraska, 2003, page 39, http://digitalcommons.unl.edu/poliscifacpub/16.

47. Orey, "The New Black Conservative: Rhetoric or Reality?," 39.

48. Byron D'Andra Orey, Thomas Craemer, and Melanye Price, "Implicit Racial Attitude Measures in Black Samples: IAT, Subliminal Priming, and Implicit Black Identification," *PS: Political Science & Politics* 46, no. 3 (2013): 550–552.

49. See, for example, J. L. Eberhardt, P. G. Davies, V. J. Purdie-Vaughns, and S. L. Johnson, "Looking Deathworthy: Perceived Stereotypicality of Black Defendants Predicts Capital-Sentencing Outcomes," *Psychological Science* 17, no. 5 (2006): 383–386; and J. L. Eberhardt, P. A. Goff, V. J. Purdie, and P. G. Davies, "Seeing Black: Race, Crime, and Visual Processing," *Journal of Personality and Social Psychology* 87, no. 6 (2004): 876–893.

50. Justin D. Levinson, Robert J. Smith, and Danielle M. Young, "Devaluing Death: An Empirical Study of Implicit Racial Bias on Jury-Eligible Citizens in Six Death Penalty States," *New York University Law Review* 89, no. 2 (2014): 513–580.

51. Orey, Craemer, and Price, "Implicit Racial Attitude Measures in Black Samples."

52. Lucius J. Barker, Mack H. Jones, and Katherine Tate, *African Americans and the American Political System*, 4th ed. (Upper Saddle River, N.J.: Prentice Hall, 1999), 99.

53. See Tasha Philpot, *Race, Republicans, and the Return of the Party of Lincoln* (Ann Arbor: University of Michigan Press, 2007); and Michael K. Fauntroy, *Republicans and the Black Vote* (Boulder, Colo.: Lynne Rienner, 2008).

54. Dawson, *Behind the Mule*.

CHAPTER 4

1. Benjamin D. Steiner, "Folk Knowledge as Legal Action: Death Penalty Judgments and the Tenet of Early Release in a Culture of Mistrust and Punitiveness," *Law and Society Review* 33, no. 2 (1999): 461–505.

2. Charles P. Henry, *Culture and African American Politics* (Bloomington: Indiana University Press, 1990), 7.

3. Ibid.

4. Ibid.

5. Jon Hurwitz and Mark Peffley, "Explaining the Great Divide: Perceptions of Fairness in the U.S. Criminal Justice System," *The Journal of Politics* 67, no. 3 (2005): 762–783.

6. Ibid., 778.

7. Ibid., 781.

8. Ibid., 765.

9. For lengthier discussion of linked fate, see the previous chapter.

10. Michael C. Dawson, *Behind the Mule: Race and Class in African-American Politics* (Princeton, N.J.: Princeton University Press, 1994); Melissa Harris-Lacewell,

Barbershops, Bibles, and BET: Everyday Talk and Black Political Thought (Princeton, N.J.: Princeton University Press, 2004).

11. James C. Scott, *Domination and the Arts of Resistance: Hidden Transcripts* (New Haven, Conn.: Yale University Press, 2005).

12. Dawson, *Behind the Mule*; Katherine Tate, *From Protest to Politics: The New Black Voters in American Elections* (New York: Russell Sage Foundation, 1994).

13. See C. Eric Lincoln and Lawrence H. Mamiya, *The Black Church in the African American Experience* (Durham, N.C.: Duke University Press, 1990); Clyde Wilcox and Leopoldo Gomez, "Religion, Group Identification and Politics among American Blacks," *Sociological Analysis* 51, no. 33 (1990): 271–287; and Evelyn Brooks Higginbotham, *Righteous Discontent: The Women's Movement in the Black Baptist Church, 1880–1920* (Cambridge, Mass.: Harvard University Press, 1993).

14. See Doug McAdam, *Political Processes and the Development of Black Insurgency, 1930–1970* (Chicago: University of Chicago Press, 1982); and Aldon Morris, *The Origins of the Civil Rights Movement* (New York: Free Press, 1984).

15. Harris-Lacewell, *Barbershops, Bibles, and BET*, 76.

16. The token was a gift card to local grocery and retail stores valued at 10 or 15 dollars.

17. I was not sure how to categorize Ms. Helen Mae's educational attainment. She had only completed the 11th grade, but she said that that was the highest grade in the school at the time.

18. Earlier in the project, I thought of working more with participants' perceptions of media coverage and imagery of the death penalty. So I asked in the questionnaire and in the focus group about the media and media coverage. This data may be analyzed at a later date but it is not a part of this project.

19. The focus group questions, flyers, and questionnaires can be found in Appendix D.

20. William A. Gamson, *Talking Politics* (New York: Cambridge University Press, 1992).

21. David L. Morgan, *Focus Groups as Qualitative Research* (Newbury Park, Calif.: Sage, 1998).

22. Gamson, *Talking Politics*, 123.

23. Gamson writes, "We were concerned with the threatening nature of the task for working people who do not normally carry on sustained conversation about public issues." Ibid., 17.

24. This revelation came in a discussion of media coverage. The conversation went as follows,

> INTERVIEWER: So all of you indicate that you watch the news. So what do you think of news coverage of Black people who are convicted of crimes or Black people who are convicted of capital crimes that have been a very prominent case in the news?

PUMPKIN: Actually, I didn't really watch the news because it has been depressing
so—

DENISE: It's this guy who, he tried to get back at his girlfriend by killing her two
little sisters and her mother.

PUMPKIN: Oh, dear, I remember that. That Black dude.

FAYE: That was around here somewhere.

DENISE: That was over in Williams Square.

PUMPKIN: Yeah.

FAYE: It was in the area, yeah.

INTERVIEWER: So how do you think the news portrays—do you think it portrays Black people and white people differently?

DENISE: It makes Black people look ignorant. It makes us look real ignorant and
real—

FAYE: And guilty!

DENISE: Right, and guilty.

FAYE: We're guilty from the jump.

DENISE: When that man went out and shot that girl because, what, they weren't
talking or something or whatever? When he just went out and shot, that made
him look real ignorant. Then too, a white man, "Oh, well, she was cheating
on him!"

PUMPKIN: You know what this reminds me? This here reminds me of when
this case against that white girl, the white lady who drowned her kids,
how the way her case was more controversial, being real sobby-like, you
know?

This led to a discussion of the Andrea Yates case, which I discuss later.

25. This is the percentage of the Texas Department of Criminal Justice offenders "on
hand." "On hand" does not include offenders out on a bench warrant or in a pre
parole transfer/work release facility. In 2004, those not on hand accounted for
nearly 4,000 offenders. Texas Department of Criminal Justice, *Statistical Report
Fiscal Year 2005,* http://www.tdcj.state.tx.us/documents/Statistical_Report_
FY2005.pdf, accessed May 17, 2014.

26. These focus groups were conducted the summer after the collapse of Enron, a
Houston-based company. The trials of Enron executives were in the newspaper
and television news daily. All of the participants in the focus groups said they
watched TV news and a smaller number read the paper, so Pumpkin may have
been primed to make this comparison. The larger point is still clear.

27. John C. Green, "American Faith-Based Politics in the Era of George W. Bush,"
European Political Science 8, no. 3 (2009): 326.

28. Laura R. Olson and Adam L. Warber, "Belonging, Behaving, and Believing: Assessing the Role of Religion on Presidential Approval," *Political Research Quarterly* 61, no. 2 (2008): 200.

29. The names of the suburban communities have been removed to maintain the respondents' anonymity.

30. Melvin Williams's work chronicles the continued racial struggles of the Black middle class in an attempt to explain why there continues to be strong identification between poor and middle-class Blacks. Melvin Williams, *The Black Middle Class and Social Transformations: The Production and Reproduction of Social Inferiority* (Ann Arbor: University of Michigan Press, 1992).

31. The women in the senior center were either friends or relatives who knew each other from their upbringing in rural Texas. I suspect from the location of their hometown that they were referring to a lynching in Colorado County in 1935. I could not find the name of the case, but a documentary produced in 1995 of African Americans living in this area showed interviews of African Americans relaying the story of the lynching of two teens; see *Coming through Hard Times* (1995). The writer and producer of the film, Patsy Craven, has a book about the events: Patsy Craven, *Leavin' a Testimony: Portraits of Rural Texas* (Austin: University of Texas Press, 2006).

32. James Marquart, Sheldon Ekland-Olson, and Jonathan R. Sorensen, *The Rope, the Chair, and the Needle: Capital Punishment in Texas* (Austin: University of Texas Press, 1994), 132.

33. Ruth Wilson Gilmore, "Fatal Couplings of Power: Notes on Racism and Geography," *The Professional Geographer* 54, no. 1 (2002): 15–24.

CHAPTER 5

1. James Marquart, Sheldon Ekland-Olson, and Jonathan R. Sorensen, *The Rope, the Chair and the Needle: Capital Punishment in Texas, 1923–1990* (Austin: University of Texas Press, 1998), 17.

2. Ibid.

3. Iris Marion Young, "Communication and the Other: Beyond Deliberative Democracy," in *Democracy and Difference: Contesting the Boundaries of the Political*, ed. Seyla Benhabib (Princeton, N.J.: Princeton University Press), 121.

4. Lynn M. Saunders, "The Racial Legacy of American Values" (PhD diss., University of Michigan, 1995); and Lynn M. Saunders, "What Is Whiteness? Race of the Interviewer Effect When All the Interviewers Are Black," 1995, unpublished paper in author's possession.

5. Melissa Harris-Lacewell, *Barbershops, Bibles, and BET: Everyday Talk and Black Political Thought* (Princeton, N.J.: Princeton University Press, 2004), 99.

6. Ibid.

7. Iris Marion Young, *Inclusion and Democracy* (Oxford: Oxford University Press, 2000).

8. Lee Sigelman and Susan Welch, *Black Americans' Views of Racial Equality: The Dream Deferred* (New York: Cambridge University Press, 1991).

9. See W. E. B. Du Bois, *The Souls of Black Folk* (1903; repr., New Jersey: Gramercy Books, 1994).

10. The findings in Chapter 4 demonstrate the clear connection between perceptions of discrimination by African Americans in the Houston metropolitan area and their opposition to the death penalty. Another good example of the ways in which criminal justice policies have led to two oppositional experiences for Blacks and whites is the discrepancy in sentencing under the Federal Crack Cocaine Law of 1986 (21 U.S.C. 841), which gave the same prison sentence for possessing large quantities of powder cocaine and significantly smaller amounts of crack cocaine.

11. The videotaped beating of Rodney King, the verdict in the trial of the accused officer, and the subsequent unrest in Los Angeles are examples of an early fissure in attitudes of Blacks and whites about state power and police behavior. The behavior of law enforcement officers in specific locations fueled the divergent sentiments of Blacks and whites. Abner Louima, a Haitian immigrant, was severely beaten and sodomized with a toilet plunger by New York City police officers in 1997. The same department was scrutinized two years later for its treatment of Black residents after Amadou Diallo was shot 41 times by officers who claimed to have mistaken his wallet for a gun. Black residents of Cincinnati, Ohio, rioted in 2001 after what they saw as the final straw in a series of incidents of police brutality against Black residents. In Texas, the dragging death of James Byrd in 1998 also brought the brutality of lynching to the forefront of the memories of generations old and new. The most recent cases of Trayvon Martin, Jordan Davis and Eric Garner and the protests that followed are demonstrative of the continued concern of African Americans around state power and police behavior. We have yet to see the power and impact of the emerging #BlackLivesMatter movement, but the constant call to the simple idea of black lives having value is indicative of where we currently stand.

12. This belief among African Americans was coupled with a belief that the "economic system is unfair to poor people." See Michael C. Dawson, *Black Visions: The Roots of Contemporary African American Political Ideologies* (Chicago: University of Chicago Press, 2001), 83.

13. See, e.g., Tom R. Tyler, "Social Justice: Outcome and Procedure," *International Journal of Psychology* 35, no. 2 (2000): 117–125.

14. Iris Marion Young, *Justice and the Politics of Difference* (Princeton, N.J.: Princeton University Press, 1990), 41.

15. Timothy V. Kaufman-Osbourne, *From Noose to Needle: Capital Punishment and the Late Liberal State* (Ann Arbor: University of Michigan Press, 2002); Marquart, Ekland-Olson, and Sorensen, *The Rope, the Chair, and the Needle.*

16. Samuel R. Gross and Phoebe C. Ellsworth, "Second Thought: Americans' Views on the Death Penalty at the Turn of the Century," in *Beyond Repair? America's Death Penalty,* ed. Stephen P. Garvey (Durham, N.C.: Duke University Press, 2003), 38.

17. Young is referring to a much broader notion of violence than the death penalty. Her work also analyzes random and irrational violence. She also discusses issues of harassment and the social context in which the violence take place. See Young, *Justice and the Politics of Difference,* 61–63.

18. Ibid., 33.

19. Young borrows this test from Agnes Heller. See ibid., 34, quoting Agnes Heller, *Beyond Justice* (New York: Basic Books, 1987), 240–241.

20. Hanes Walton Jr. and Robert C. Smith, *American Politics and the African American Quest for Universal Freedom,* 2nd ed. (New York: Longman, 2003), 2–3. The idea of collective deliverance is taken from Richard King's analysis of the idea of freedom articulated in the Civil Rights Movement. Collective deliverance was "understood as the liberation of a group from external control—from captivity, slavery, or oppression"; Richard King, *Civil Rights and the Idea of Freedom* (New York: Oxford University Press, 1992), 26–28.

21. Address by Justice Thurgood Marshall at the annual seminar of the San Francisco Patent and Trademark Association, May 6, 1987, reprinted as "Racial Justice and the Constitution: A View from the Bench," in *African Americans and the Living Constitution,* ed. John Hope Franklin and Genna Rae MacNeil (Washington, D.C.: Smithsonian Institution Press, 1995), 315.

22. Glenda Elizabeth Gilmore, *Gender and Jim Crow: Women and the Politics of White Supremacy, 1896–1920* (Chapel Hill: University of North Carolina Press, 1996); Marquart, Ekland-Olson, and Sorensen, *The Rope, the Chair, and the Needle*; Kevin K. Gaines, *Uplifting the Race: Black Leadership, Politics, and Culture in the Twentieth Century* (Chapel Hill: University of North Carolina Press, 1996); C. Vann Woodward, *The Strange Career of Jim Crow,* 3rd rev. ed. (New York: Oxford University Press, 1974).

23. Stuart Banner, *The Death Penalty: An American History* (Cambridge, Mass.: Harvard University Press, 2002); Marquart, Ekland-Olson, and Sorensen, *The Rope, the Chair and the Needle.*

24. Marquart, Ekland-Olson, and Sorensen, *The Rope, the Chair and the Needle,* 39.

25. Ibid., 64.

26. In the focus groups at the low-income housing community, two of the participants said they remembered Tucker's names but not the details of the case. They all knew of Gary Graham. In that focus group, the following exchange took place,

> INTERVIEWER: Do you remember this case about this woman—you're probably too young, Denise, but I don't know how old—well, you're probably a little young, but this case of this woman named Karla Faye Tucker. Do you remember that case?
>
> DENISE: No, I—
>
> INTERVIEWER: Do you remember, Faye?

FAYE: I remember. I don't—

PUMPKIN: Karla Faye Tucker?

INTERVIEWER: She was this white woman who was convicted of murdering two people with a pickaxe and while she was in prison—

FAYE: Oh, yeah.

INTERVIEWER:—she converted—she found—she was saved and she was born again and so there was this big controversy over whether she should be executed.

FAYE: Right, I remember that.

INTERVIEWER: It was in 1998 so you're probably a little young. I mean, probably don't remember it at all. You remember that? [This question was addressed to Denise, who was 19 at the time of the focus group.]

PUMPKIN: I remember that.

DENISE: I probably do remember—I mean, like, but I was like eight—

These women were the youngest participants of all the focus groups. Even though Denise was eight at the time of Tucker's execution, both she and Pumpkin lived in Huntsville at the time, so the case was vaguely familiar to them. In the other focus groups, the members were adults at the time and a participant recounted the facts.

27. The other case that was more commonly mentioned as a counterexample to the treatment of Blacks—and was mentioned spontaneously and not in response to a specific question—was the case of Andrea Yates. Andrea Yates was found guilty in 2002 of the drowning deaths of her five children. She alleged that her acts were motivated by postpartum depression. Due to extremely misleading testimony by an expert witness, Yates was granted a new trial in 2005. During Yates's first trial, the state's sole mental health expert testified that Yates may have been motivated by an episode of the *Law and Order* TV series that depicted a mother who mounted an insanity defense after murdering her children. It was later discovered after her trial that no such show existed. Peggy O'Hare, "Jury Selection to Begin in New Trial for Yates: Five Years Later, Experts Say Lack Of Death-Penalty Component Could Work in Her Favor," *Houston Chronicle*, June 19, 2006, B1.

28. This is the portion that was left out of the formal text:

SAMANTHA: That's not the spider woman, is it?

WILLIE: No, this one—that one's still on death row.

MONIFAH: He gave her a stay, or what?

BRAD: Did he give her a stay?

SAMANTHA: She died.

WILLIE: No, she died. Yeah, she died in the hands of the state. She got the injection, lethal injection.

29. Willie's impression that Karla Faye Tucker's religious transformation led her to accept her fate and to refuse to participate in the efforts to spare her life is the perception that I am partially addressing in chapter 1. Tucker was very much a participant in the fight to save her life, but her performance of contrition made this less obvious to the public observations.

30. Emma, one of the women at the senior center, said as much: "[I] thought it was a brutal way to kill somebody."

31. This quote is from Samantha.

32. I was incorrect in saying "no" on this point. As the description in chapter 1 relays, Graham did actually take a woman hostage and rape her.

33. Quanell X is the leader of the Houston chapter of the New Black Panther Party and is a former minister of the Nation of Islam. He has been very active in recent years in death penalty cases and cases of alleged police brutality. See, e.g., Robert Crowe and Peggy O'Hare, "Quanell X Helps Pair of Fugitives Turn Selves In: Two Are Wanted for Questioning in Woman's Death," *Houston Chronicle*, November 20, 2004, B7.

34. The Rainbow Coalition is the organization founded and headed by Jesse Jackson.

35. I am not sure to what extent Celina's husband participated in Graham's defense. I know he was not an attorney or a law enforcement officer. As I have previously suggested, Graham's case spawned a tremendous amount of grassroots activism in the Black community. Celina was not the contact person for this peer focus group, so I was not aware of her connection to Graham's case beforehand.

36. It is hard to know whether Devon is referencing the "Christian people" who supported Tucker or "Christian people" generally.

37. Graham mentioned in his last statement that he was fighting and alluded to a possible beating by prison officials. Texas Department of Criminal Justice, "Last Statement of Gary Graham," https://www.tdcj.state.tx.us/death_row/dr_info/grahamgarylast.html, accessed May 1, 2014.

38. This is a quote from Faye.

39. It is not clear which case Willie is referencing, but here he uses it as an example of the differential treatment of Blacks and whites, specifically where religious transformation is involved. Willie was by far the most informed participant in all the focus groups, but in this study, perception is of more interest than individual accuracy.

40. Her original sentence was overturned on appeal. In 2006, she was retried and found not guilty by reasons of insanity. Andrea Yates suffered from severe postpartum depression at the time of her crime.

41. In actuality, Andrea Yates was found guilty of capital murder in her first trial.

42. As with most qualitative research, I informed the participants that their identity would be concealed. I videotaped and audiotaped the focus group sessions. Faye is reaffirming my earlier statement that I (and maybe my committee members) would be the only people to see the video, assuring her anonymity.

43. Two of the women in this focus group had children. The children were playing in a bedroom while the focus group was conducted. Periodically the children would come in to ask their mothers questions.

44. The summer these focus groups were conducted, the Houston Police Department (HPD) Crime Lab was being investigated for serious flaws in the handling of evidence. The HPD Lab was accused of tainting evidence. Two inmates were released after a review of old evidence and some undiscovered evidence showed them innocent of the crimes for which they were convicted. The issue was in the local news almost every day and it was mentioned in each focus group. Forty-five cases were being reviewed after flaws were found in the handling of evidence by the HPD crime lab, and the reviewers were considering extending the review to other cases. Roma Khanna and Steve McVicker, "45 Crime Lab Cases Will Get Legal Reviews: Faulty Evidence Needs Scrutiny, Project Innocence Co-Founder Says," *Houston Chronicle*, March 15, 2006, B1.

45. Michael C. Dawson, *Behind the Mule: Race and Class in African-American Politics* (Princeton, N.J.: Princeton University Press, 1994), 48. See also Earl Lewis, *In Their Own Interests: Race, Class and Power in Twentieth-Century Norfolk, Virginia* (Berkeley: University of California Press, 1991).

46. Mike Tolson, "Fewer Killers Getting Sentenced to Death: Sharp Drop Seen across the Nation, Including Texas," *Houston Chronicle*, May 22, 2005, A1. Texas Governor Rick Perry passed Bush's record in 2011. At the time, Perry had overseen 234 executions. Robert Barnes, Rick Perry Holds the Records on Executions, *Washington Post* (August 23, 2011) at http://www.washingtonpost.com/politics/rick-perry-holds-the-record-on-executions/2011/08/17/gIQAMvNwYJ_story.html

47. Faye's ex-husband, the father of her young son, had been incarcerated at some point in the relationship. The other women also knew men who had been incarcerated. At one point in the focus group, they had a discussion about whether long-term incarceration is worse than the death penalty.

PUMPKIN: I feel that's a punishment, sitting in jail because you get to—Every time they think about it and it's in they head every day, every day, "I shouldn't have, I shouldn't have did this, I shouldn't have killed this person."

FAYE: Can't go nowhere, can't do nothing, can't talk to nobody.

PUMPKIN: That's punishment.

FAYE: And nine times out of ten, you going to be moved from your home, you going be way out, you know, somewhere they're going keep moving you around so your family's not going to come. You going to be sitting in jail, no commissary, 'cause after two, three days of that, they going to get tired of sending you money. You know? So to me, it's more punishment in jail than it is . . .

DENISE: in your life.

FAYE: And depending on what cell block you in, who in the cell block, I mean, they just do stuff to people, you know, whatever they—mental cruelty, physical cruelty, whatever, to people 'til—you know, to me, you get more punishment in jail. And they nasty. [Laughter]

DENISE: I feel like to me, jail for them is hell. That's their punishment.

PUMPKIN: It is!

DENISE: That's their hell.

INTERVIEWER: You mean men?

FAYE: Women, too! I mean—

PUMPKIN: Women too.

FAYE:—when you got to sit—from what I've heard, I've never been to jail, let's put that on tape. You got to go in the bathroom right with everybody and you know, it's just to me—

These women were extremely familiar not just with persons who were incarcerated but also with the experience of incarceration.

48. Dawson, *Black Visions*, 40.

49. Though his work is on Mississippi, David Oshinsky's *Worse than Slavery: Parchman Farm and the Ordeal of Jim Crow Justice* (New York: Free Press, 1996) is a very good history of the connection between prisons and the racial politics of the South.

50. Dawson, *Black Visions*, 310; Michael C. Dawson, "Globalization, the Racial Divide, and a New Citizenship," in *The New Majority: Toward a Progressive Popular Politics*, ed. Theda Skocpol and Stan Greenberg (New Haven, Conn.: Yale University Press, 1997), 264–278.

51. Marquart, Ekland-Olson, and Sorensen, *The Rope, the Chair, and the Needle*.

52. When I discussed my research with Professor Roberta Harding at the University of Kentucky College of Law, she suggested that I should not be so quick to exclude lynching from contemporary discussions of violence and African American citizenship. She asked, "Wasn't James Byrd lynched?" The 1998 dragging death of James Byrd Jr. in Jasper, Texas, has all the earmarks of a lynching, but the trial and conviction of his white assailants seem to at least distinguish it from how I conceptualize lynching. However, I do think the question Harding raises is valid given the facts of the Byrd case.

CONCLUSION

1. Texas Department of Criminal Justice, "Death Row Information: Offenders on Death Row," https://www.tdcj.state.tx.us/death_row/dr_offenders_on_dr.html, accessed May 16, 2014.

2. Taeku Lee, *Mobilizing Public Opinion: Black Insurgency and Racial Attitudes in the Civil Rights Era* (Chicago: University of Chicago Press, 2002), 5.

3. Michael C. Dawson, *Black Visions: The Roots of Contemporary African American Political Ideologies* (Chicago: University of Chicago, 2001), 318.

4. Charles Henry, *Long Overdue: The Politics of Racial Reparations* (New York, NY: New York University Press, 2009), 109.

5. Sherry Lynn Johnson, "Race and Capital Punishment," in *Beyond Repair? America's Death Penalty*, ed. Stephen P. Garvey (Durham, N.C.: Duke University Press, 2003), 133.

6. Lynn M. Sanders, "The Racial Legacy of American Values" (Ph.D. diss., University of Michigan, 1995), 44.

7. Ibid., 183.

8. Ibid.

9. Ibid., 184. Sanders is speaking specifically of the pernicious episode of slavery, but I think her point also extends to periods of obvious and harmful racial discrimination.

10. *S. v. Makwanyane and Another*, Constitutional Court 1995 (6) BCLR 665 (CC), 06/06/1995 (South Africa).

APPENDICES

1. The numbers after each variable and or question indicate the years that question was asked.

Bibliography

Alexander, Michelle. *The New Jim Crow: Mass Incarceration in the Age of Jim Crow.* New York: The New Press, 2012.

Allen, Richard L., Michael C. Dawson, and Ronald E. Brown. "A Schema-Based Approach to Modeling and African American Racial Belief System." *American Political Science Review* 83, no. 2 (1989): 421–441.

Amar, Akhil Reed. "Reinventing Juries: Ten Suggested Reforms." *U.C. Davis Law Review* 28 (1995): 1169–1194.

Anderson, Arleen. "Responding to the Challenge of Actual Innocence Claims after *Herrera v. Collins.*" *Temple Law Review* 71 (1998): 489–520.

Anderson, David C. *Crime and the Politics of Hysteria: How the Willie Horton Story Changed American Justice.* New York: Times Books, 1995.

Anson, Sam Gideon, and David Cogan. "A Death in Texas." *LA Weekly*, June 30, 2000. http://www.laweekly.com/2000-2007-06/news/a-death-in-texas/.

Baldus, David C., Charles Pulaski, and George Woodworth. "Comparative Review of Death Sentences: An Empirical Study of the Georgia Experience." *Journal of Criminal Law and Criminology* 74, no. 3 (1983): 661–753.

Baldus, David C., George Woodworth, and Charles A. Pulaski Jr. *Equal Justice and the Death Penalty: A Legal and Empirical Analysis.* Boston: Northeastern University Press, 1990.

Baldus, David C., George Woodworth, David Zuckerman, Neil Alan Weiner, and Barbara Broffitt. "The Use of Peremptory Challenges in Capital Murder Trials: A Legal and Empirical Analysis." *University of Pennsylvania Journal of Constitutional Law* 3 (2001): 3–170.

Banner, Francine. "Rewriting History: The Use of Feminist Narratives to Deconstruct the Myth of the Capital Defendant." *New York University Review of Law and Social Change* 26 (2000): 569–614.

Banner, Stuart. *The Death Penalty: An American History.* Cambridge, Mass.: Harvard University Press, 2002.

Barker, Lucius J., Mack H. Jones, and Katherine Tate. *African Americans and the American Political System*. 4th ed. Upper Saddle River, N.J.: Prentice Hall, 1999.

Baron, Jane B., and Julia Epstein. "Is Law Narrative?" *Buffalo Law Review* 45, no. 1 (1997): 141–188.

Baxter, Sandra, and Marjorie Lansing. *Women and Politics: The Visible Majority*. Ann Arbor: University of Michigan Press, 1983.

Becka, Holly, Steve McGonigle, Tim Wyatt, and Jennifer La Fleur. "Disputed Practice Still a Courtroom Fixture; Peremptory Challenges Survive Calls for Reform, Decades of Controversy." *Dallas Morning News,* August 23, 2005, 11A.

Bedau, Hugo Adam. "American Attitudes toward the Death Penalty." In *The Death Penalty in America*, 3rd ed., ed. Hugo Adam Bedau, 65–68. New York: Oxford University Press, 1982.

Bedau, Hugo Adam, and Paul G. Cassell. *Debating the Death Penalty: Should America Have the Death Penalty*. New York: Oxford University Press, 2005.

Bell, Jeanine. *Policing Hatred: Law Enforcement, Civil Rights, and Hate Crime*. New York: New York University Press, 2002.

Benhabib, Seyla, ed. *Democracy and Difference: Contesting the Boundaries of the Political*. Princeton, N.J.: Princeton University Press, 1996.

Berger, Vivian. "*Herrera v. Collins*: The Gateway of Innocence for Death-Sentenced Prisoners Lead Nowhere." *William and Mary Law Review* 35 (1994): 943–1024.

Billingsley, Andrew, and Cleopatra Howard Caldwell. "The Church, the Family and the School in the African American Community." *Journal of Negro Education* 60, no. 3 (1991): 427–440.

Blackmun, Douglas A. *Slavery by Another Name: The Re-Enslavement of Black Americans from the Civil War to World War II*. New York: Random House, 2009.

Bohm, Robert M. "American Death Penalty Attitudes: A Critical Examination of Recent Evidence." *Criminal Justice and Behavior* 14, no. 3 (1987): 380–396.

Bonilla-Silva, Eduardo. *Racism without Racists: Color-Blind Racism and the Persistence of Racial Inequality in the United States*. 2nd ed. Lanham, Md.: Rowman and Littlefield, 2006.

Bowers, William J., and Glenn L. Pierce. "Racial Discrimination and Criminal Homicide under Post-*Furman* Capital Statutes." In *The Death Penalty in America*, 3rd ed., ed. Hugo Adam Bedau, 206–224. New York: Oxford University Press, 1982.

Bowers, William J., Marla Sandys, and Thomas W. Brewer. "Death Sentencing in Black and White: An Empirical Analysis of the Role of Juror's Race and Jury Racial Composition." *University of Pennsylvania Journal of Constitutional Law* 3 (2001): 171–274.

———. "Crossing Racial Boundaries: A Closer Look at the Roots of Racial Bias in Capital Sentencing When the Defendant Is Black and the Victim Is White." *DePaul Law Review* 53 (2004): 1497–1538.

Breur, Jennifer. "Habeas Corpus—Limited Review for Actual Innocence." *Journal of Criminal Law and Criminology* 84 (1994): 943–974.

Bright, Stephen. "Counsel for the Poor: The Death Sentence Not for the Worst Crime but for the Worst Lawyer." In *The Death Penalty in America: Current Controversies*, ed. Hugo Adam Bedau, 275–309. New York: Oxford University Press, 1997.

Brock, Deon, Nigel Cohen, and Jonathan Sorensen. "Arbitrariness in the Imposition of Death Sentence in Texas: An Analysis of Four Counties by Offense Seriousness, Race of Victim, and Race of Offender." *American Journal of Criminal Law* 28 (2000–2001): 43–74.

Brooks, Peter. *Troubling Confessions: Speaking Guilt in Law and Literature*. Chicago: University of Chicago Press, 2000.

Brown, Ronald, and Monica Wolford. "Religious Resources and African-American Political Action." *National Political Science Review* 4 (1993): 30–48.

Brown-Dean, Khalilah. "Permanent Outsiders: Felon Disenfranchisement and the Breakdown of Black Politics." In *The Expanding Boundaries of Black Politics: The National Political Science Review*, ed. Georgia A. Persons, 103–119. New Brunswick, N.J.: Transaction Publishers, 2007.

Calhoun-Brown, Allison. "African American Churches and Political Mobilization: The Psychological Impact of Organizational Resources." *Journal of Politics* 58, no. 4 (1996): 935–953.

"Capital Punishment: Lifeless Debate." *National Review* 52, no. 13 (2000).

"Capital Punishment: Many Will Continue to Doubt Graham's Guilt." *Houston Chronicle*, June 23, 2000, A36.

Carby, Hazel V. *Race Men*. Cambridge, Mass.: Harvard University Press, 1998.

Carroll, Jenny E. "Images of Women and Capital Sentencing among Female Offenders: Exploring the Outer Limits of the Eighth Amendment and Articulated Theories of Justice." *Texas Law Review* 75 (1997): 1413–1454.

Carson, Clayborne. *In Struggle: SNCC and the Black Awakening of the 1960s*. Cambridge, Mass.: Harvard University Press, 1981.

———. *Malcolm X: The FBI File*. New York: Carroll and Graf Publishers, 1991.

Cassanova, Jose. *Public Religions in the Modern World*. Chicago: University of Chicago Press, 1994.

Chimurenga. Ashanti. "I Remember Shaka." *Essence*, September 2000, 114.

Clawson, Rosalee A., Elizabeth R. Kegler, and Eric N. Waltenburg. "Supreme Court Legitimacy and Group-Centric Forces: Black Support for Capital Punishment and Affirmative Action." *Political Behavior* 25, no. 4 (2003): 289–311.

Cohen, Cathy J. *The Boundaries of Blackness: AIDS and the Breakdown of Black Politics*. Chicago: University of Chicago Press, 1999.

Cohen, Cathy J., and Michael C. Dawson. "Neighborhood Politics and African American Politics." *American Political Science Review* 87 (1993): 286–302.

Cohen, E. G. "Expectation States and Interracial Interactions in School Settings." *Annual Review of Sociology* 8 (1982): 209–235.

Collins, Marjorie. "How Americans Voted: A Political Portrait." *New York Times*, November 7, 2004, 4:1

Collins, Patricia Hill. *Black Feminist Thought: Knowledge, Consciousness, and the Politics of Empowerment*. New York: Routledge, 1990.

———. *Black Sexual Politics: African Americans, Gender and the New Racism*. New York: Routledge, 2004.

Cooey, Paula M. "Women's Religious Conversions on Death Row: Theorizing Religion and State." *Journal of the American Academy of Religion* 70, no. 4 (2002): 699–718.

Cook, Nancy L. "The Call to Stories: Speaking in and about Stories." *University of Cincinnati Law Review* 63 (1994): 95–164.

———. "Outside the Tradition: Literature as Legal Scholarship." *University of Cincinnati Law Review* 63 (1994): 95–164.

Craven, Patsy. *Leavin' a Testimony: Portraits of Rural Texas*. Austin: University of Texas Press, 2006.

Crowe, Robert, and Peggy O'Hare . "Quanell X Helps Pair of Fugitives Turn Selves In: Two Are Wanted for Questioning in Woman's Death." *Houston Chronicle*, November 20, 2004, B7.

Curtis, Gregory. "Because of Her, The Whole World Took a Second Look at the Death Penalty." *Texas Monthly* 26, no. 9 (September 1998): 135.

———. "The Texas Twenty: Forgiveness and the Law." *Texas Monthly* 26, no. 9 (September 1998).

Dao, James. "Democrat Wins Top Job in G.O.P. Stronghold." *New York Times*, November 8, 2005, A1.

Davidson, Chandler. *Biracial Politics; Conflict and Coalition in the Metropolitan South*. Baton Rouge: Louisiana State University Press, 1972.

Dawson, Michael C. *Behind the Mule: Race and Class in African-American Politics*. Princeton, N.J.: Princeton University Press, 1994.

———. "African American Political Opinion: Volatility in the Reagan-Bush Era." In *African American Power and Politics*, ed. Hanes Walton Jr., 135–153. New York: Columbia University Press, 1997.

———. "Globalization, the Racial Divide, and a New Citizenship." In *The New Majority*, ed. Theda Skocpol and Stan Greenberg, 264–278. New Haven, Conn.: Yale University Press, 1997.

———. *Black Visions: The Roots of Contemporary African-American Political Ideologies*. Chicago: University of Chicago Press, 2001.

Dawson, Michael, Ronald Brown, and Richard Allen. "Racial Belief Systems, Religious Guidance and African American Political Participation." *National Political Science Review* 2 (1990): 22–44.

Delgado, Richard. "Storytelling for Oppositionists and Others: A Plea for Narrative." *Michigan Law Review* 87 (1989): 2411–2441.

Dieter, Richard C. *The 2% Death Penalty: How a Minority of Counties Produce Most Death Cases at an Enormous Cost to All*. Washington, D.C.: Death Penalty Information Center, 2013. http://deathpenaltyinfo.org/twopercent.

DiMaggio, Paul, John Evans, and Bethany Bryson. "Have American's Social Attitudes Become More Polarized?" In *Culture Wars in American Politics: Critical Reviews of a Popular Myth*, ed. Rhys H. Williams, 63–100. New York: Aldine de Gruyter, 1997.

Donisi, Nancy. "Tucker's Lawyer Still Backs Death Penalty: Attorney Speaks at Arlington seminar." *Dallas Morning News*, February 7, 1998, 1A.

Dorsett, Amy, and Katy Hunger. "Capital Questions: As Execution Date Nears, Proof of Houston Man's Guilt in Slaying Hinges on a Single Witness." *San Antonio Express-News* June 11, 2000, 1A.

Dow, David. *Executed on Technicality: Lethal Injustice on the Texas Death Row.* Boston: Beacon Press, 2005.

Du Bois, W. E. B. 1994. *The Souls of Black Folk.* 1903; repr., New York: Gramercy Books, 1994.

Eberhardt, J. L., P. G. Davies, V. J. Purdie-Vaughns, and S. L. Johnson. "Looking Deathworthy: Perceived Stereotypicality of Black Defendants Predicts Capital-Sentencing Outcomes." *Psychological Science* 17, no. 5 (2006): 383–386.

Eberhardt, J. L., P. A. Goff, V. J. Purdie, and P. G. Davies. "Seeing Black: Race, Crime, and Visual Processing." *Journal of Personality and Social Psychology* 87, no. 6 (2004): 876–893.

Ellsworth, Phoebe. 1989. "Are Twelve Heads Better Than One?" *Law and Contemporary Problems* 52, no. 4 (1989): 205–224.

Ellsworth, Phoebe C., and Samuel R. Gross. "Hardening of the Attitudes: Americans' Views on the Death Penalty." *Journal of Social Issues* 50, no. 2 (1994): 19–34.

Entman, Robert M., and Andrew Rojecki. *The Black Image in the White Mind: Media and Race in America.* Chicago: University of Chicago Press, 2000.

Fauntroy, Michael K. *Republicans and the Black Vote.* Boulder, Colo.: Lynne Rienner, 2008.

Feeley, Malcolm M. *The Process Is the Punishment: Handling Cases in a Lower Criminal Court.* New York: Russell Sage Foundation, 1979.

"Felony Disenfranchisement Laws in the United States." The Sentencing Project. 2003.http://www.sentencingproject.org/detail/publication.cfm?publication_id=15. Accessed January 23, 2015.

Foner, Eric. "Reconstruction and the Black Political Tradition." In *Political Parties and the Modern State*, ed. Richard S. McCormick, 53–70. New Brunswick, N.J.: Rutgers University Press, 1984.

Foucault, Michel. "Intellectuals and Power." In *Language, Counter-Memory, Practice: Selected Essays and Interviews by Michel Foucault*, trans. Donald F. Bouchard and Sherry Simon, 205–217. Ithaca, N.Y.: Cornell University Press, 1977.

Frampton, Mary Louise, Ian Haney López, and Jonathan Simon, eds. *After the War on Crime: Race, Democracy, and a New Reconstruction.* New York: New York University Press. 2008.

Frazier, E. Franklin. *The Negro Church in America.* New York: Schocken Books, 1974.

Gaines, Kevin K. *Uplifting the Race: Black Leadership, Politics, and Culture in the Twentieth Century.* Chapel Hill: University of North Carolina Press, 1996.

Gammel, H. P. N. *The Laws of Texas, 1822–1897.* Vol. 1. Austin, Tex.: The Gammel Book Company, 1898.

Gamson, William A. *Talking Politics.* New York: Cambridge University Press, 1992.

Garcia, Guillermo. "Texas Inmate Struggles to the End: Courts Deny Last Minute Civil Lawsuit." *USA Today,* June 23, 2000, 3A.

Garland, David. *The Culture of Control: Crime and Social Order in Contemporary Society.* Chicago: University of Chicago Press, 2002.

Garner, Bryan A., and Henry Campbell Black, eds. *Black's Law Dictionary.* Pocket Edition. St. Paul, Minn.: West Publishing Company, 1996.

Garrow, David J. *The FBI and Martin Luther King, Jr.* New York: Penguin Books, 1981.

Gay, Claudine, and Katherine Tate. "Doubly Bound: The Impact of Gender and Race on the Politics of Black Women." *Political Psychology,* 19, no. 1 (1998): 69–184.

Gibbs, Jack P. *Crime, Punishment, and Deterrence.* New York: Elsevier, 1975.

———. "Preventive Effects of Capital Punishment Other Than Deterrence." In *The Death Penalty in America: Current Controversies,* ed. Hugo Adam Bedau, 103–116. New York: Oxford University Press, 1982.

Giddings, Paula. *When and Where I Enter: The Impact of Black Women on Race and Sex in America.* New York: Morrow, 1984.

Gillers, Stephen. 1985. "Proving the Prejudice of Death Qualified Jurors." *University of Pittsburgh Law Review* 47 (1985): 219, 238.

Gilmore, Glenda Elizabeth. *Gender and Jim Crow: Women and the Politics of White Supremacy, 1896–1920.* Chapel Hill: University of North Carolina Press, 1996.

Gilmore, Ruth Wilson. "Fatal Couplings of Power: Notes on Racism and Geography." *The Professional Geographer* 54, no. 1 (2002): 15–24.

———. *Golden Gulag: Prisons, Surplus, Crisis, and Opposition in Globalizing California.* Berkeley: University of California Press, 2007.

Goodman, Ellen. "Karla Tucker Gave Death Row a Human Face." *Houston Chronicle,* February 15, 1998, Outlook 6.

Goodwin, Jim. "Articulating the Inarticulable: Relying on Nonverbal Behavioral Cues to Deception to Strike Jurors during Voir Dire." *Arizona Law Review* 38 (1996).

Green, John C. "American Faith-Based Politics in the Era of George W. Bush." *European Political Science* 8, no. 3 (2009): 316–329.

Greene, Andrea. "Catholic Group Backs New Trial for Inmate." *Houston Chronicle,* May 31, 1993, A34.

Greene, Andrea, and Valerie Godines. "Killer's Supporters Seek to Prevent His Execution." *Houston Chronicle,* June 1, 1993, A16.

Greene, C. Jennifer, and Valerie Caracelli, eds. *Advances in Mixed-Method Evaluation: The Challenges and Benefits of Integrating Diverse Paradigms.* San Francisco: Jossey-Bass, 1997.

Greenhouse, Linda. "Court to Review Using Death Penalty in Juvenile Cases." *New York Times*, January 27, 2004, A1.

Gross, Samuel R. "American Public Opinion on the Death Penalty—It's Getting Personal." *Cornell Law Review* 83 (1998): 1448–1475.

Gross, Samuel R., and Pheobe C. Ellsworth. "Second Thought: Americans' Views on the Death Penalty at the Turn of the Century." In *Beyond Repair? America's Death Penalty*, ed. Stephen P. Garvey, 8–57. Durham, N.C.: Duke University Press, 2003.

Gross, Samuel R., Kirsten Jacoby, Daniel J. Matheson, Nicholas Montgomery, and Sujata Patil. "Exonerations in the United States, 1989 through 2003." *Journal of Criminal Law & Criminology* 95, no. 2 (2005): 523–553.

Guerra, Carlos. "We Hardly Blink at Executions Anymore." *Austin American Statesman*, February 6, 1998, A13.

Guillory, Michica. "Glover Back to Defend Graham: I Thought His Life Had Been Spared." *Houston Defender*, February 21–27, 1999, 1.

———. "Graham Faces Execution: Rallies and Vigils Planned January 11th." *Houston Defender*, January10–16, 1999.

———. "Execution for Graham: Date Would Be Set for June." *Houston Defender*, May 7–13, 2000.

———. "The Graham Case: What Does It All Mean?" *Houston Defender*, June 25–July 1, 2000, 1.

———. "Graham Supporters Ready for Final Fight." *Houston Defender*, May 28–June 3, 2000). 1.

Gurin, Patricia, Shirley Hatchett, and James S. Jackson. *Hope and Independence: Blacks' Response to Electoral and Party Politics*. New York: Russell Sage Foundation, 1989.

Haney, Craig. *Death by Design: Capital Punishment as a Social Psychological System*. New York: Oxford University Press, 2005.

Hans, Valerie P., and Neil J. Vidmar. *Judging the Jury*. New York: Plenum, 1986.

Harris, Fredrick C. *Something Within: Religion in African-American Political Activism*. New York: Oxford University Press, 1999.

Harris-Lacewell, Melissa. *Barbershops, Bibles and BET: Everyday Talk and Black Political Thought*. Princeton, N.J.: Princeton University Press, 2004.

Heller, Agnes. *Beyond Justice*. New York: Basic Books, 1987.

Henry, Charles P. *Culture and African American Politics*. Bloomington: Indiana University Press, 1990.

Herring, Mary, Thomas B. Janowski, and Ronald E. Brown. "Pro-Black Doesn't Mean Anti-White: The Structure of African-American Group Identity." *Journal of Politics* 61, no. 2 (1999): 363–386.

Higginbotham, Evelyn Brooks. *Righteous Discontent: The Women's Movement in the Black Baptist Church, 1880–1920*. Cambridge, Mass.: Harvard University Press, 1993.

hooks, bell. *Feminist Theory: From Margin to Center*. 2nd ed. Cambridge, Mass.: South End Press, 1984.

Hoppe, Christy. "State Urged to Spare Karla Faye Tucker: Minister Married to Killer, Rock Singer's Ex-Wife Lead Call for Clemency." *Dallas Morning News*, January 18, 1998, 24A.

———. "Woman's Execution Looms, Stirring National Discussion: Gender, Rehabilitation Add to Debate in Texas Case." *Dallas Morning News*, January 13, 1998, 1A.

Horswell, Cindy. "Commutation for Priest's Killer: A 2-Decade-Old Sentence Changes after a Court Finds He Is Retarded and Can't Be Executed." *Houston Chronicle*, March 17, 2005, B1.

Howe, Adrian. *Punish and Critique: Towards a Feminist Analysis of Penality*. New York: Routledge, 1994.

Hurwitz, Jon, and Mark Peffley. "Explaining the Great Racial Divide: Perceptions of Fairness in the U.S. Criminal Justice System." *Journal of Politics* 67, no. 3 (2005): 762–783.

Jamieson, Kathleen Hall. *Dirty Politics: Deception, Distraction, and Democracy*. New York: Oxford University Press, 1992.

Jaynes, Gerald David, and Robin M. Williams, eds. *A Common Destiny: Black and American Society*. Washington, D.C.: National Academy Press, 1989.

Johnson, Dirk. "No Execution in Illinois until System Is Repaired." *New York Times*, May 21, 2000, National Desk 20.

Johnson, Sherry Lynn. "Race and Capital Punishment." In *Beyond Repair? America's Death Penalty*, ed. Stephen P. Garvey, 121–143. Durham, N.C.: Duke University Press, 2003.

Jones, Franklin. "Should Gary Graham Get New Trial? He Deserves the Ultimate Penalty." *Houston Chronicle*, July 23, 1993, A31.

Kaufman-Osbourne, Timothy V. *From Noose to Needle: Capital Punishment and the Late Liberal State*. Ann Arbor: University of Michigan Press, 2002.

Keitner, Chimene I. "Victim or Vamp? Images of Violent Women in the Criminal Justice System." *Columbia Journal of Gender and the Law* 11 (2002): 38.

Kelley, Robin D. G. *Race Rebels: Culture Politics and the Black Working Class*. New York: Free Press, 1994.

Kepel, Giles. *The Revenge of God: The Resurgence of Islam, Christianity, and Judaism in the Modern World*. University Park: Pennsylvania State University Press, 1994.

Khanna, Roma, and Steve McVicker, "45 Crime Lab Cases Will Get Legal Reviews: Faulty Evidence Needs Scrutiny, Project Innocence Co-Founder Says." *Houston Chronicle*, March 15, 2006, B1.

"Killer Executed after Clinton Denies Clemency." *New York Times* May 8, 1992, A17.

King, M. L., Jr. "Hammer on Civil Rights." *Nation* 198 (March 9, 1964): 230–234. Reprinted in *A Testament of Hope: The Essential Writings and Speeches of Martin Luther King Jr.*, ed. James M. Washington. San Francisco: Harper San Francisco, 1986.

King, Richard. *Civil Rights and the Idea of Freedom*. New York: Oxford University Press, 1992.

Kirkpatrick, D. David. "Black Pastors Backing Bush Are Rarity, but Not Alone." *New York Times*, October 5, 2004, A15.

Khanna, Roma, and Steve McVicker. "45 Crime Lab Cases Will Get Legal Reviews: Faulty Evidence Needs Scrutiny, Project Innocence Co-Founder Says." *Houston Chronicle*, March 15, 2006, B1.

Kroll-Smith, J. Stephen. "The Testimony as Performance: The Relationship of an Expressive Event to the Belief System of Holiness Sect." *Journal for the Scientific Study of Religion* 19, no. 1 (1980): 16–25.

Lee, Taeku. *Mobilizing Public Opinion: Black Insurgency and Racial Attitudes in the Civil Rights Era*. Chicago: University of Chicago Press, 2002.

Lempert, Richard O. "Desert and Deterrence: An Assessment of Moral Bases for the Case of Capital Punishment." *Michigan Law Review* 79 (1981): 1177–1231.

Levinson, Justin D., Robert J. Smith, and Danielle M. Young. "Devaluing Death: An Empirical Study of Implicit Racial Bias on Jury-Eligible Citizens in Six Death Penalty States." *New York University Law Review* 89, no. 2 (2014): 513–580.

Lewis, Earl. *In Their Own Interests: Race, Class and Power in Twentieth-Century Norfolk, Virginia*. Berkeley: University of California Press, 1991.

———. "Constructing African American as Minorities." In *The Construction of Minorities: Cases for Comparison across Time and around the World*, ed. André Burguière and Raymond Grew, 15–38. Ann Arbor: University of Michigan Press, 2001.

Lin, Ann Chih. "Bridging Positivist and Interpretivist Approaches to Qualitative Methods." *Policy Studies Journal* 26, no. 1 (1998): 162–180.

Lincoln, C. Eric. *The Black Church since Frazier*. New York: Schocken Books, 1974.

Lincoln, C. Eric, and Lawrence H. Mamiya. *The Black Church in the African American Experience*. Durham, N.C.: Duke University Press, 1990.

Lowry, Beverly. *Crossed Over: A Memoir, A Murder*. New York: A. A. Knopf, 1992.

Mansbridge, Jane, and Katherine Tate. "Race Trumps Gender: Black Opinion on the Thomas Nomination." *PS, Political Science & Politics* 25, no. 3 (1992): 488–492.

Marquart, James W., Sheldon Ekland-Olson, and Jonathan R. Sorensen. *The Rope, the Chair, and the Needle: Capital Punishment in Texas, 1923–1990*. Austin: University of Texas Press, 1994.

Marshall, Thurgood. Address Given at the Annual Seminar of the San Francisco Patent and Trademark Association, May 6, 1987. Reprinted as "Racial Justice and the Constitution: A View from the Bench." In *African Americans and the Living Constitution*, ed. John Hope Franklin and Genna Rae MacNeil, 315. Washington, D.C.: Smithsonian Institution Press, 1995.

Martin, Norma. "Witness against Graham Files Harassment Suit: Behavior of TV Crew Is 'Outrageous.'" *Houston Chronicle*, May 20, 1993, A26.

McAdam, Doug. *Political Process and the Development of the Black Insurgency, 1930–1970*. Chicago: University of Chicago Press, 1982.

McDaniel, Eric L. *Politics in the Pews: The Political Mobilization of Black Churches*. Ann Arbor: University of Michigan Press, 2008.

McGonigle, Steve, and Ed Timms. "Race Prejudice Pervades Jury Selection: Prosecutors Routinely Bar Blacks, Study Finds." *Dallas Morning News*, March 9, 1986, 28A.

McKay, Jordan. "Sign of the Times: How a 2 Year Old Texas Murder Case Became a National Service." *Texas Monthly* 27, no. 1 (1999): 16–18.

McMullen, Cary. "Reed Speaks at GOP Rally; Ex-Christian Coalition Director Emphasizes Religious, Moral Values." *The Ledger* (Lakeland, Fla.), September 25, 2004.

Means, Marianne. "No Gender Lines Exist in Use of Death Penalty." *San Antonio Express-News*, January 20, 1998, B7.

Mendelberg, Tali. "Executing Hortons: Racial Crime and 1988 Presidential Campaign." *Public Opinion Quarterly* 61, no. 1 (1997): 134–157.

———. *The Race Card: Campaign Strategy, Implicit Messages and the Norm of Equality*. Princeton, N.J.: Princeton University Press, 2001.

Moraes, Lisa de. "Kanye West's Torrent of Criticism, Live on NBC." *Washington Post*, September 3, 2005, C1.

Morgan, David L. *Focus Groups as Qualitative Research*. Newbury Park, Calif.: Sage, 1998.

Morris, Aldon D. *The Origins of the Civil Rights Movement: Black Communities Organizing for Social Change*. New York: The Free Press, 1984.

Muhammad, Khalil Gibran. *The Condemnation of Blackness: Race, Crime, and the Making of Modern Urban America*. Cambridge, Mass.: Harvard University Press, 2010.

Myrdal, Gunnar. *An American Dilemma: The Negro Problem and Modern Democracy*. New York: Harper & Brothers, 1944.

National Association for the Advancement of Colored People. *Thirty Years of Lynching in the United States, 1889–1918*. 1919, repr., New York: Arno, 1969.

Nichols, Bruce. "Death Row Inmate's Son Faces Judgment; He Could Join Father Gary Graham in Prison if Convicted in Capital Case." *Dallas Morning News* April 13, 2000, News 1A.

———. "Protests Mark Graham's Service: High Profile Guests Assail the Death Penalty." *Dallas Morning News*, June 29, 2000, News 23A.

O'Hare, Peggy. "Jury Selection to Begin in New Trial for Yates: Five Years Later, Experts Say Lack of Death-Penalty Component Could Work in Her Favor." *Houston Chronicle*, June 19, 2006, B1.

Ogletree, Charles, and Austin Sarat. *From the Lynch Mob to the Killing State: Race and the Death Penalty in America*. New York: New York University Press, 2006.

Olson, Laura R., and Adam L. Warber. "Belonging, Behaving, and Believing: Assessing the Role of Religion on Presidential Approval." *Political Research Quarterly* 61, no. 2 (2008): 192–204.

O'Neil, Melinda E. "The Gender Gap Argument: Exploring the Disparity of Sentencing Women to Death." *New England Journal on Criminal and Civil Confinement* 25 (1999): 213–244.

Orey, Byron D'Andra. "The New Black Conservative: Rhetoric or Reality?" Faculty Publications, Paper 16, Department of Political Science, University of Nebraska, 2003. http://digitalcommons.unl.edu/poliscifacpub/16.

———. "Explaining Black Conservatives: Racial Uplift or Racial Resentment." *Black Scholar* (Spring 2004): 18–22

———. "A Research Note on White Racial Attitudes and Support for the Mississippi State Flag." *American Politics Research* 32, no. 1 (January 2004): 102–116.

Orey, Byron D'Andra, Thomas Craemer, and Melanye Price. "Implicit Racial Attitude Measures in Black Samples: IAT, Subliminal Priming, and Implicit Black Identification." *PS: Political Science & Politics* 46, no. 3 (2013): 550–552.

Oshinsky, David. *Worse than Slavery: Parchman Farm and the Ordeal of Jim Crow Justice.* New York: Free Press, 1996.

Patton, Julie H. "The Lost Issue in the Tucker Debate: Karla Faye Tucker's Execution Was Unjust Because the Death Penalty Is Unjust, Not Because She Is a Women Who Found God." *Texas Lawyer*, February 16, 1998, 36.

Peffley, Mark, and Jon Hurwitz. "Persuasion and Resistance: Race and the Death Penalty in America." *American Journal of Political Science* 51 no. 4 (2007): 996–1012.

Perkinson, Robert. *Texas Tough: The Rise of America's Prison Empire.* New York: Metropolitan Books/Henry Holt, 2010.

Perry, Earnest L. "Local Rappers Plan Concert to Support Murder." *Houston Chronicle*, May 23, 1993, B23.

Philpot, Tasha. *Race, Republicans, and the Return of the Party of Lincoln.* Ann Arbor: University of Michigan Press, 2007.

Powe, Lucas A., Jr. *The Warren Court and American Politics.* Cambridge, Mass.: Belknap Press of Harvard University Press, 2000.

Pressley, Sue Anne. "Texas Executes Killer Karla Faye, 'Baby, I Love You,' She Tells Husband." *Toronto Star*, February 4, 1998, A1.

Preston, Michael B., Lenneal J. Henderson, and Paul L. Puryear, eds. *The New Black Politics.* 2nd ed. New York: Longman, 1987.

Price, Melanye T. *Dreaming Blackness: Black Nationalism and African American Public Opinion.* New York: New York University Press, 2009.

Price, Melynda. "Are We Imprisoned in Narratives of Progress: The Work of Hanes Walton and Its Lessons for an Afrofuturistic Black Politics." *Politics, Groups and Identities* 1, no. 4 (2013): 577–588.

Quindlen, Anna. "Public & Private: Dead Man Walking." *New York Times*, May 26, 1993, A21.

Ransby, Barbara, and Tracye Matthews. "Black Popular Culture and the Transcendence of Patriarchal Illusions." *Race and Class* 35 (1993): 57–68.

Ratcliffe, R. G. "The Execution of Karla Faye Tucker; Bush Prayed for Guidance before Denying Tucker's Appeal." *Houston Chronicle*, February 4, 1998, A10.

Reed, Adolph L., Jr. *The Jesse Jackson Phenomenon: The Crisis of Purpose in Afro-American Politics.* New Haven, Conn.: Yale University Press, 1986.

Regnerus, Mark D., David Sikkink, and Christian Smith. "Voting with the Christian Right: Contextual and Individual Patterns of Electoral Influence." *Social Forces* 77, no. 4 (1999): 1375–1401.

Riessman, Catherine Kohler. *Narrative Analysis*. Newbury Park, Calif.: Sage Publications, 1993.

Robinson, Deborah Marie. "The Effect of Multiple Group Identity among Black Women on Race Consciousness." PhD diss., University of Michigan, 1987.

Rose, Mary R. "The Peremptory Challenge Accused of Race or Gender Discrimination? Some Data from One County." *Law & Human Behavior* 23, no. 6 (1999): 695–702.

Rosenberg, Gerald N. *The Hollow Hope: Can Courts Bring about Social Change?* Chicago: University of Chicago Press, 1991.

Ruby, Robert, and Allison Pond. "An Enduring Majority: Americans Continue to Support the Death Penalty." The Pew Forum on Religion & Public Life, Washington, D.C., December 19, 2007. http://www.pewforum.org/docs/?DocID=272, accessed October 31, 2009.

Rule, Sheila. "Rap to the Rescue." *New York Times*, June 2, 1993, C16.

Sanders, Lynn M. "The Racial Legacy of American Values." PhD diss., University of Michigan, 1995.

———. "Against Deliberation." *Political Theory* 25, no. 3 (1997): 347–376.

Sarat, Austin, and Stuart Scheingold. *Something to Believe In: Politics, Professionalism, and Cause Lawyering*. Stanford, Calif.: Stanford University Press, 2004.

Saunders, Lynn M. "What Is Whiteness? Race of the Interviewer Effect When All the Interviewers Are Black." 1995. Unpublished paper in author's possession.

Schneider, Anne, and Helen Ingram. "Social Construction of Target Populations: Implications for Politics and Policy." *American Political Science Review* 87, no. 2 (1993): 334–347.

Scott, James C. *Weapons of the Weak: Everyday Forms of Peasant Resistance*. New Haven, Conn.: Yale University Press, 1985.

———. *Domination and the Arts of Resistance: Hidden Transcripts*. New Haven, Conn.: Yale University Press, 2005.

Segrave, Kerry. *Lynchings of Women in the United States: The Recorded Cases, 1851–1946*. Jefferson, N.C.: McFarland, 2010.

Shapiro, Andrea. "Unequal before the Law: Men, Women, and the Death Penalty." *American University Journal of Gender, Social Policy and Law* 8 (2000): 427–470.

Shaw, Theodore M. "Confronting Justice." 2006. http://www.naacpldf.org/landing.aspx?sub=67. Accessed June 17, 2006.

Shipp, E. R. "Where Was Pat Robertson for Other Executions?" *Austin American Statesman*, February 1, 1998, H3.

Sigelman, Lee, and Susan Welch. *Black Americans' Views of Racial Equality: The Dream Deferred*. New York: Cambridge University Press, 1991.

Simien, Evelyn, ed. "Gender Difference in Attitudes toward Black Feminism." *Political Science Quarterly* 119, no. 2 (2004): 315–338.

———. "Race, Gender and Linked Fate." *Journal of Black Studies* 35, no. 5 (2005): 529–550.

———. *Gender and Lynching: The Politics of Memory*. New York: Palgrave Macmillan, 2011.

Simon, Stephanie. "Court Puts Age, Crime on Scales; Law: Issue Is Whether It's Just to Execute Criminals Who Were Young at the Time of Their Offenses. A Supreme Court Decision Could Help Settle It Soon." *Los Angeles Times*, June 9, 2002, A20.

Simpson, Andrea. *The Ties That Bind: Identity and Political Attitudes in the Post-Civil Rights Generation*. Philadelphia, Pa.: Temple University Press, 1998.

Smith, Robert C., and Richard Seltzer. *Race, Class and Culture: A Study in Afro-American Mass Opinion*. Albany: State University of New York Press, 1992.

Sniderman, Paul M., and Edward G. Carmines. *Reaching beyond Race*. Cambridge: Cambridge University Press, 1997.

Steiner, Benjamin D. "Folk Knowledge as Legal Action: Death Penalty Judgments and the Tenet of Early Release in a Culture of Mistrust and Punitiveness." *Law and Society Review* 33 (1999): 461–505.

Steiner, Benjamin D., William J. Bowers, and Austin Sarat. "Folk Knowledge as Legal Action: Death Penalty Judgments and the Tenet of Early Release in a Culture of Mistrust and Punitiveness." *Law and Society Review* 33, no. 2 (1999): 461–505.

Sunstein, Cass R., and Adrian Vermeule. "The Ethics and Empirics of Capital Punishment: Is Capital Punishment Morally Required? Acts, Omissions, and Life-Life Tradeoffs." *Stanford Law Review* 58 (2005): 703–750.

Swidler, Ann. "Culture in Action: Symbols and Strategies." *American Sociological Review* 51, no. 2 (1986): 273–286.

Tate, Katherine. *From Protest to Politics: The New Black Voters in American Elections*. New York: Russell Sage Foundation, 1994. http://www.courts.state.tx.us/publicinfo/crt_stru.htm.

Texas Defender Service. *A State of Denial: Texas Justice and the Death Penalty*. Houston: Texas Defender Service, 2000. http://www.texasdefender.org/publications.htm. Accessed September 12, 2011.

Texas Department of Criminal Justice. "Executed Offenders." http://www.tdcj.state.tx.us/stat/executedoffenders.htm. Accessed May 4, 2011.

———. "County of Conviction for Executed Offenders." https://www.tdcj.state.tx.us/death_row/dr_county_conviction_executed.html. Accessed April 8, 2014.

———. "Death Row Information: Offenders on Death Row." https://www.tdcj.state.tx.us/death_row/dr_offenders_on_dr.html. Accessed May 16, 2014.

———. "Last Statement of Gary Graham." https://www.tdcj.state.tx.us/death_row/dr_info/grahamgarylast.html. Accessed April 30, 2014.

———. "Last Statement of Karla Faye Tucker." http://www.tdcj.state.tx.us/death_row/dr_info/tuckerkarlalast.html. Accessed April 30, 2014.

———. *Statistical Report Fiscal Year 2005*. http://www.tdcj.state.tx.us/documents/Statistical_Report_FY2005.pdf. Accessed May 17, 2014.

The Pew Research Center for People and the Press. "Religion, Belief, and Policy, Religion and Politics: Contention and Consensus." http://people-press.org/reports/. Accessed May 17, 2004.

Thomas, Cal. "Flawed Reasoning in Sparing Tucker." *San Antonio Express-News*, January 26, 1998, A11.

Thompson, Heather. "Why Mass Incarceration Matters: Rethinking Crisis, Decline and Transformation in Postwar American History." *Journal of American History* 97, no. 3 (2010): 703–734.

———. "Downsizing the Carceral State: The Policy Implications of Prison Guard Unions." *Criminology and Public Policy* 10, no. 3 (2011): 771–779.

Tocqueville, Alexis de. *Democracy in America*. Trans. Arthur Goldhammer. New York: Library of America, 2004.

Tolson, Mike. "A Deadly Distinction: Harris County Is a Pipeline to Death Row." *Houston Chronicle,* February 4, 2001. http://www.chron.com/content/chronicle/special/01/penalty/index.html. Accessed March 20, 2006.

———. "Fewer Killers Getting Sentenced to Death: Sharp Drop Seen across the Nation, Including Texas." *Houston Chronicle*, May 22, 2005, A1.

Toner, Robin. "Dukakis Makes Strong Response to G.O.P.'s Ads." *New York Times*, October 20, 1988, B11.

Tonry, Michael H. *Malign Neglect: Race, Crime, and Punishment in America*. New York: Oxford University Press, 1995.

Tucker, Karla Faye. "Letter to Gov. George W. Bush and the Texas Board of Pardons." *Houston Chronicle*, January 21, 1998, A25.

Tucker-Worgs, Tamelyn N. *The Black Megachurch: Theology, Gender and the Politics of Public Engagement*. Waco, Tex.: Baylor University Press, 2012.

Turner, Allan. "Bloodthirsty Image at Odds with Local Poll." *Houston Chronicle*, February 3, 2011, A1.

Turner, Billy M., Rickie D. Lovell, John C. Young, and William F. Denny. "Race and Peremptory Challenges during Voir Dire: Do Prosecution and Defense Agree?" *Journal of Criminal Justice* 14, no. 1 (1986): 61–69.

Tyler, Tom R. "Social Justice: Outcome and Procedures." *International Journal of Psychology* 35, no. 2 (2000): 117–125.

U.S. General Accounting Office. "Death Penalty Sentencing: Research Indicates Patterns of Racial Disparities." General Accounting Office document GAO T-GGD-90-37. May 3, 1990. http://archive.gao.gov/t2pbat11/141293.pdf. Accessed May 1, 2006.

Wacquant, Loïc. "Class, Race & Hyperincarceration in Revanchist America." *Daedalus* 139, no. 3 (2010): 74–90.

Walt, Kathy. "Death Penalty's Support Plunges to 30-Year Low." *Houston Chronicle*, March 15, 1998, A1.

Walt, Kathy, and T. J. Millin. "Karla Faye's Last Chance: Words on Life or Death." *Houston Chronicle*, February 1, 1998, A14.

Walt, Kathy, and John W. Gonzalez. "Despite Doubts, Most Texans in Poll Support Death Penalty." *Houston Chronicle*, June 22, 2000, A17.

Walton, Hanes, Jr. *Black Political Parties: An Historical and Political Analysis*. New York: Free Press, 1972.

———. *African American Power and Politics: The Political Context Variable*. New York: Columbia University Press, 1997.

Walton, Hanes, Jr., and Robert C. Smith. *American Politics and the African American Quest for Universal Freedom*. New York: Addison Wesley Longman, 2003.

Ward, Mike. "Jesse Jackson Asks to Visit Condemned Woman: Unlike Tucker—Before." *Austin American Statesman*, March 21, 1998, B2.

Warner, R. Stephen. *New Wine in Old Wineskins: Evangelicals and Liberals in a Small-Town Church*. Berkeley: University of California Press, 1988.

Warren, Susan. "Graham Supporters Rally at City Hall." *Houston Chronicle*, July 11, 1993, A24.

———. "Graham Supporters Renew Attention as Two Key Court Rulings Are Pending." *Houston Chronicle*, March 12, 1994, A29.

Wasby, Stephen L. *Small Town Police and the Supreme Court: Hearing the Word*. Lexington, Mass.: Lexington Books, 1976.

Weaver, Vesla M. "Frontlash: Civil Rights, the Carceral State and the Transformation of American Politics." *Studies in American Political Development* 21 (Fall 2007): 230–265.

———. "Frontlash: Race and the Development of Punitive Crime Policy." *Studies in American Political Development* 21 (Fall 2007): 230–265.

Wells-Barnett, Ida. "Lynch Law in America." [1900]. In *Words of Fire: An Anthology of African American Feminist Thought*, ed. Beverly Guy-Sheftall. New York: The New Press, 1995.

Weisberg, Robert. "The Death Penalty Meets Social Science: Deterrence and Jury Behavior under New Scrutiny." *Annual Review of Law & Social Science* 1 (2005): 151–170.

Wilcox, Clyde. "Black Women and Feminism." *Women and Politics* 10 (1990): 65–84.

———. "Racial and Gender Consciousness among African American Women: Sources and Consequences." *Women and Politics* 17, no. 1 (1997): 73–94.

Wilcox, Clyde, and Leopoldo Gomez. "Religion, Group Identification and Politics among American Blacks." *Sociological Analysis* 51, no. 3 (1990): 271–285.

Williams, Melvin D. *The Black Middle Class and Social Transformations: The Production and Reproduction of Social Inferiority*. Ann Arbor: University of Michigan Press, 1992.

Williams, S. L. "Black Political Progress in the 1980's: The Electoral Arena." In *The New Black Politics*, ed. Michael B. Preston, Lenneal Henderson, and Paul Puryear, 97–131. New York: Longman, 1987.

Wing, Bob. "The White Elephant in the Room: Race and Election 2004." *The Black Scholar* 35, no. 1 (2005): 16.

Winick, Bruce J. "Prosecutorial Peremptory Challenge Practices in Capital Cases: An Empirical Study and a Constitutional Analysis." *Michigan Law Review* 81, no. 1 (1982): 1–98.

Woodward, C. Vann. *The Strange Career of Jim Crow*. 3rd rev. ed. New York: Oxford University Press, 1974.

Wuthnow, Robert. *Meaning and Moral Order: Explorations in Cultural Analysis*. Berkeley, Calif.: University of California Press, 1987.

Wyatt, Kristen. "GOP Hopes Black Candidates Help Break Democratic Lock: Party Officials Concede Goal Won't Happen Overnight." *Houston Chronicle*, May 21, 2006, A18.

X, Malcolm. *Malcolm X Speaks: Selected Speeches and Statements*. New York: Grove Press, 1965.

Yates, Jeff, and Richard Fording. "Politics and State Punitiveness in Black and White." *Journal of Politics* 67, no. 4 (2005): 1099–1121.

Young, Iris Marion. *Justice and the Politics of Difference*. Princeton, N.J.: Princeton University Press, 1990.

———. "Communication and the Other: Beyond Deliberative Democracy." In *Democracy and Difference: Contesting the Boundaries of the Political*, ed. Seyla Benhabib, 120–136. Princeton, N.J.: Princeton University Press, 1996.

———. *Inclusion and Democracy*. New York: Oxford University Press, 2000.

Young, Robert L. "Race, Conceptions of Crime and Justice, and Support for the Death Penalty." *Social Psychology Quarterly* 54, no. 1 (1991): 67–75.

———. "Religious Orientation, Race and Support for the Death Penalty." *Journal for the Scientific Study of Religion* 31, no. 1 (1992): 76–87.

Zangrando, Robert. *The NAACP Crusade against Lynching, 1909–1950*. Philadelphia: Temple University Press, 1980.

COURT CASES

Atkins v. Virginia, 122 S. Ct. 2242; 153 L. Ed. 2d 335 (2002)

Avery v. Georgia, 345 U.S. 559 (1953)

Batson v. Kentucky, 476 U.S. 79 (1987)

Bean v. State, 816 S.W.2d 115 (Tex. Crim. App. 1991)

Brady v. Maryland, 373 U.S. 83 (1963)

Brown v. the Board of Education, 347 U.S. 483 (1954)

Butler v. State of Texas, 872 S.W.2d 227 (1994)

Camacho v. State of Texas, 864 S.W.2d 524 (1993).

Casarez v. State of Texas, 913 S.W.2d 468 (1995)

Castaneda v. Partida, 430 U.S. 482 (1977)

Chambers v. State of Texas, 742 S.W.2d 695 (Tex. Crim. App. 1988)

Chambers v. State of Texas, 866 S.W.2d 9 (1993)

Cook v. State of Texas, 858 S.W.2d 467 (1993)

DeBlanc v. State of Texas, 732 S.W.2d 640 (1987)

Duren v. Missouri, 439 U.S. 357 (1979)

Ex Parte Brandley, 781 S.W.2d. 886 (Tex. Crim. App. 1989)

Fuentes v. State, 991 S.W.2d (Tex. Crim. App. 2002)

Furman v. Georgia, 408 U.S. 238, 309; 92 S. Ct. 2726 (1972)

Georgia v. McCollum, 505 U.S. 42 (1992)

Graham v. Johnson, 168 F.3d 762 (1999)

Graham v. Lynaugh, 854 F.2d 715 (1988)

Gregg v. Georgia, 428 U.S. 153; 96 S. Ct. 2909 (1976)

Hernandez v. New York, 500 U.S. 352 (1991)

Herrera v. Collins, 506 U.S. 390 (1993)

Hovey v. *Superior Court of Alameda County*, 28 Cal. 3d 1 (1980)

In re Kimmler, 136 U.S. 436 (1890)

Jasper v. State of Texas, 61 S.W.3d 413 (2001)

J. E. B. v. Alabama ex rel. T.B., 511 U.S. 127 (1994)

Johnson v. State, 68 S.W.3d 644 (Tex. Crim. App. 2002)

Jurek v. Texas, 428 U.S. 262 (1976)

Keeton v. State of Texas, 724 S.W.2d 58 (1987)

Ladd v. State, 3 S.W.3d 547 (Tex. Crim. App. 1999)

Lockhart v. McCree, 476 U.S. 172 (1986)

McCleskey v. Kemp, 481 U.S. 279 (1987)

Edwin Ray McGee v. State of Texas, 817 S.W.2d 810 (1991)

Richard Jewell McGee v. State of Texas, Tex. Crim. Appeals 105 (1989)

Miller-*El v. Dretke*, 125 S. Ct. 2317 (2005)

Morris v. State of Texas, 940 S.W.2d 610 (1996)

Neal v. Delaware, 103 U.S. 370 (1880)

People v. Carpenter, 13 Ill. 2d 470 (2004)

Powell v. Alabama, 287 U.S. 45 (1932)

Roper v. Simmons, 125 S. Ct. 1183 (2005)

S. v. Makwanyane and Another, Constitutional Court, 1995 (6) BCLR 665 (CC), 06/06/1995 (South Africa)

Satterwhite v. Texas, 858 S.W.2 412 (Tex. Crim. App. 1993)

Sauls v. State of Texas, Tex. Ct. App. (Apr. 23, 2001)

Simpson v. State, 119 S.W.3d 262 (Tex. Crim. App. 2003).

Snyder v. Louisiana, 128 S. Ct. 1203 (2008)

Staley v. State, 887 S.W.2d 885 (Tex. Crim. App. 1994)

Strauder v. West Virginia, 100 U.S. 303 (1880)

Swain v. Alabama, 380 U.S. 202 (1965)

Taylor v. Louisiana, 419 U.S. 522 (1975)

Tennard v. State, 802 S.W.2d 678 (Tex. Crim. App. 1990)

Texas ex. rel. Tim Curry v. Bowman, 885 S.W.2d 421 (1993)

Trevino v. State of Texas, 864 S.W.2d 499 (Tex. Crim. App. 1993)

Wainwright v. Witt, 469 U.S. 412 (1985)
Wamget v. State, 67 S.W. 3d 861 (Tex. Crim. App. 2001)
Witherspoon v. Illinois, 397 U.S. 1070 (1968)

STATUTES

Tex. Code Criminal Procedure Annotated, Article 35.11 (Vernon Supp. 2004–2005)
Federal Crack Cocaine Law of 1986 (21 U.S.C. 841)

Index

122 skepticism re jailhouse conversions

125 inversion of equality   142

129 Tucker's execution as symbolic: maintain appearance of equality

136 becoming more radical, extreme

138 impact of crime: missing details

139 reinforces feelings of exclusion

139 Arguments / themes
        achieving social innocence remains a strategy
          but moved from collective to individual strategy

141 raise profound questions

143 more similar to immigrants

143 Religion not as significant
144 S ct as obstacle, oblivious, dangerous

158   517 executions in Texas since 1982

53 Texas conservatism: politically risky to favor defendants
54 Blacks as ritual sacrifice
56 exclusion of blacks for opposition to DP
57 Removal for religious reasons: can be proxy for race
58 qualified opposition to DP
58 exclusion b/c of links to CJ system
60 removal for bias
63 Removal for hostility to state: not race-neutral
64 message: reject reality of black experience
64 Rely on oath not peremptory challenges
65 oath of prosecutors; calls process into que.
66 55% of blacks oppose DP   72 52% oppose, 48% support
67 less fair + just b/c of bias
78 Houston as epicenter of DP
72 52% of blacks oppose DP
73 more women than men oppose
75 discrimination → opposition to DP, esp. group discrim.
78 more report group discrim than personal
79 Lower support for DP in Houston
79 Higher levels of black incarceration
86 Black killers of black victims: lightest sentences
87 clear demonstrations of bias in cJ
     why do many blacks support it? Anti-black
     internalized negative stereotypes?   ?
89 Higher social class: more support for DP
93 Black fundamental distrust of CJ system
94 No monolithic black community
94 2004 focus groups
99 Religious basis for opposition to DP
100 Death as too easy
102 Texas: 40% of prison pop. black
           Blacks: 12% of population

112 continuity of post-civil rights state

113 overwhelmingly opposed   ?

114 Logic of exclusion / legacy of slavery
115 Inversion of equality
117 National consensus = views of dominant group
119 Lynching as 'peculiar chivalry'

60 Black jurors not state-oriented, concerns re fairness
61 concerns about low intelligence
63 Even difficulties must be race-neutral
64 Baton as merely symbolic
64 Not racist, but increases perception of race
69 Blacks see fates as linked

2 see only power in death
3 sincere belief in wrongness
3 desert vs. innocence situated in color, class
4 Black bodies make people guilty
   state not diff. from mob
6 Black view of death penalty
   Heavy reliance on religion   — cf. 143
8 lynching & death penalty
8 SCt gave up on eradicating racism
9 accepts levels of discrimination
   Focus on how inequities are seen by blacks
10 continuity of opinion: 0 unbroken thread of discrm.
11 Houston as unique location
12 DP as metric of black citizenship
12 Tucker & Graham: white woman, black man
12 media accounts, focus group
21 Jackson, sharpton: portrayed as political not religious
24 Tucker: young white woman shouldn't be executed
25 Americans support DP despite knowing its flaws
25 asymmetry of Tucker, Graham cases
   Racial & gender contradictions
27 diff. values to lives of women men, black & white
29 Tucker coverage focused on her gender, not race
29 Beauty, whiteness, femininity.
28 white women's purity
29 outcry at Tucker's execution, unlike Graham's
32 deconstruct simple notion of innocence
32 social innocence: blacks perceived as dangerous
36 invoking lynching as claim of innocence
   gendered idea, tho women lynched too
37 Black woman witness convicts Graham
34 Bush; judgments about soul of person on death row
41 Blacks lack equal access to justice
42 Batson hearings: more ritual, veneer of racial inclusion
44 Strander: cannot exclude jurors based on race
47 Batson hearing: defendant can demand
48 multiple reasons for low black participation
49 Ritual: regulate & defme social relations
50 rarely find evidence of discrm. in Batson
50 Dallas: remove any oppressed minority: too sympathetic
      Latinos, Jews, disabled
51 jury-shuffle used to move blacks to end
52 diff. peremptory statements for blacks & whites

8 'illusions'

11 underutilized sources
   interdisciplinary

!! not judgments in
   courtroom?

שְׁמַע בְּנִי, מוּסַר אָבִיךָ; וְאַל-תִּטֹּשׁ, תּוֹרַת אִמֶּךָ.

Hear, my son, the instruction of thy father, and forsake not
the teaching of thy mother

Proverbs 1:8

Contents

Acknowledgments

It was my good fortune to have written this book while teaching at The Jewish Theological Seminary. I was able to ask my colleagues questions about areas where their own expertise far exceeded mine. Some of the persons who assisted me include Professors Ben Sommer, Leonard Levin, Eitan Fishbane, Judith Hauptman, David Marcus, and my doctoral student, Rabbi Geoffrey Claussen. I have also profited from frequent discussions with Professors Lenn Goodman and David Novak. Both of them, as persons and as scholars, have inspired and challenged me over the years. Their friendship and support have enriched my life. I have also profited from conversations with my friends Professors Steven Grosby, Jonathan Jacobs, Hartley Lachter, Abraham Melamed, Leora Batnitzky, and Michael Morgan. I wish to thank as well my assistant, Bobbi Raphael, who helped in the preparation of the manuscript. Needless to say, I bear sole responsibility for any errors the book might contain. My wife, Patti Mittleman, encouraged me every step of the way, as she has done with all my writing. Without her, nothing would be possible. My children, Ari and Joel, no longer minors, suffered no parental neglect during the writing of this book, unlike several previous ones. From afar, their humor and filial love buoyed me during the sometimes lonely endeavor of writing. This book is dedicated to the memory of my mother, Shirley Leah (Goldberg) Mittleman, who passed away in the spring of 2010. Her long decline into Alzheimer's pressed me to think about the moral meanings of respect and love for a person whose personhood has ebbed away. May her memory ever be a blessing.

Introduction

When I was in graduate school, many years ago, I had the good fortune to come upon Alasdair MacIntyre's *A Short History of Ethics*. I found this book insightful and useful; I still consult it with profit today, even though MacIntyre has distanced himself from the sort of study the book represents. More of that in a moment. I wondered back then whether a similar study could be written on Jewish ethics. This book is an attempt to respond to my decades-old query.

There are a number of formidable problems in thinking about Jewish ethics as a conceptual category, let alone in organizing a presentation of Jewish ethics along historical lines. I will try to work through some of these problems in the pages that follow.

As mentioned, MacIntyre himself repudiated the kind of historical presentation of Western moral thought he achieved in his *Short History of Ethics*.[1] He abandoned the view that each of the great moral philosophers whom he treated was talking about the same kind of thing such that one could see them as existing within a single, ongoing tradition. He came to the view that Western moral thought – down to the most fundamental issues of what morality can be said to include – is so irreducibly variegated that it cannot be held to constitute a single tradition. Rather, there is a congeries of traditions of "moral enquiry." Criticizing a famous nineteenth-century Victorian predecessor in the business of writing histories of ethics, MacIntyre writes:

> Sidgwick's falsifying history thus projected back into the past the conceptual structuring of the author's present and thereby suggested that Plato and Aristotle,

A Short History of Jewish Ethics: Conduct and Character in the Context of Covenant, First Edition. Alan L. Mittleman.

> Hobbes, Spinoza, and Kant and Sidgwick himself were all offering accounts, albeit rival accounts, of the rational status of one and the same timeless subject matter.[2]

MacIntyre came to believe that these variegated traditions of inquiry into morality are so different from one another as to be incommensurable. Between Nietzsche and Aquinas, say, such "irreconcilable division" and "interminable disagreement" reign that there is no way to interpolate both figures into a single tradition of inquiry. "So general is the scope and so systematic the character of some at least of these disagreements that it is not too much to speak of rival conceptions of rationality, both theoretical and practical."[3]

Having abandoned an approach that construes the major moral philosophers as all speaking to the same subject matter, albeit in different ways, MacIntyre puts in its place characterizations and analyses of discrepant, incompatible traditions of "moral enquiry." "When I speak of moral enquiry," he writes, "I mean something wider than what is conventionally, at least in American universities, understood as moral philosophy, since moral enquiry extends to historical, literary, anthropological, and sociological questions."[4]

These concerns speak directly to the methodological problems of Jewish ethics. First, it is very helpful that MacIntyre should parse moral thought into complex, historically articulated traditions rather than flatten it into a series of texts which one might take to be doing the same thing, namely philosophical ethics. As we shall soon see, Jewish ethics seldom presents itself in an official philosophical uniform. One must ferret it out of legal texts, stories, commentaries, wise sayings, and so on. If one looks for Jewish ethics in a form comparable to that of the Western philosophical treatise, one will find very little. And yet one ought not to deny that Jewish thinkers reflected seriously and with great sophistication on the demands of conduct and the ideals of character. Locating and analyzing that reflection is the work of an historical presentation of Jewish ethics. That MacIntyre complicates and pluralizes the philosophical tradition opens a space for traditions of Jewish moral reasoning to display their own patterns of rationality.

Second, the idea of tradition is itself quite helpful. Jewish moral thinkers located themselves within the broad normative traditions of the Jewish people. They made constant reference to the Bible and to the foundational texts of the ancient rabbinic sages. While some of these normative traditions pull in different directions, so much so that a prominent modern scholar prefers to talk of "Judaisms" rather than Judaism, the incommensurability of traditions may be less of a problem for Jewish ethics than for Western ethics, on MacIntyre's telling. What we have in Judaism are traditions of moral reasoning, of intellectual engagement with conduct and character, going back millennia. The sustained reference to prior foundational texts, such as the Bible, builds a common denominator into the Jewish moral project, without depressing its internal diversity.

Third, MacIntyre's idea of inclusive "moral enquiry" as an improvement on stringently philosophical analysis suits the sources of Jewish ethics which we must explore. The tools of literary analysis, anthropology, sociology, moral philosophy per se, political theory, and jurisprudence all bear on the identification and understanding of Jewish ethics.

This last point implies another significant problem. To put it baldly: What is our subject? What is Jewish ethics? If Jewish ethics requires all of these approaches, does it actually exist as a distinct domain? Is it a native category for Judaism or is it a Procrustean bed, an attempt to make Jewish texts answer to Western categories? Dissenting from the assumption that Jewish ethics is a legitimate domain, the contemporary theologian Michael Wyschogrod writes, "Ethics is the Judaism of the assimilated."[5] For Wyschogrod, the urge to construe Judaism along the lines of ethics is typical of liberal, non-observant modern Jews. Jewish law, halakha, is the operative authentic category of Jewish self-understanding. The Jewish ethics project of liberal modernity is an attempt to substitute something purely rational, universalizing, cross-culturally intelligible, and respectable for the highly particular, divinely revealed law to which pre-modern Jews gave their allegiance, come what may. Jewish ethics is, on this view, a kind of political statement, a polemic on behalf of a reconstructed non-offensive Judaism.

Wyschogrod has a point. One sees in contemporary American Judaism, especially that of the large Reform stream, a dethroning of Jewish law and a coronation of Jewish ethics as the sovereign category of Jewish representation both to insiders and outsiders. That is an historic break with classical and medieval models of Jewish self-understanding. Contemporary denominational politics aside, however, the deep and abiding problem is whether the category of Jewish ethics has a legitimate conceptual role to play, given the vast scope and power of law in traditional Judaism. Any construction of Jewish ethics has to make sense of the relationship between ethics and law. Nor is this simply a problem for acculturated modern Jews. There are legitimate conceptual issues here which must be freed from the ideological framework in which they are embedded.[6] Part of what is wrong with the ideological framework is its underlying facile assumption that we know what "ethics" and "law" mean. Rather than carry us more deeply into a fundamental inquiry into the nature of normativity, ideology arrests investigation.

To begin to grasp the problem, consider Deuteronomy 6:18: "Do what is right and good in the sight of the LORD that it may go well with you and that you may be able to possess the good land that the LORD your God promised on oath to your fathers."[7] Doing what is "right and good" (*ha-yashar v'ha-tov*) may be taken as an indicator of ethical conduct and yet it is *commanded by the law* or rather it is enunciated as a divine command. What foothold can ethics get here? Is law, in the sense of divine command, not the master category, indeed, not the exclusive category? (Let us leave aside the Kantian problems presented by the text such as whether divine commandment or the prudential motive of possessing the land vitiates ethics. The problem we need to focus on here is one of fundamental categorization.) Sensing the problem of categorization, the great thirteenth-century exegete, Moshe ben Naḥman (Naḥmanides), finds a foothold for ethics in this text. As comprehensive as the law is, it cannot cover every future case. Therefore, we need to develop good judgment and the willingness to compromise; we need to see our fellow's point of view and restrain ourselves from asserting our legal rights to the limit. Doing the right and the good is required by the law but it complements and completes the law. Persons can be commanded but personhood needs to be nurtured; the law cares for the character of its adherents. Duty and virtue hang together.[8] This play in the joints of the commandments seems to be Naḥmanides' version of how ethics may relate to law. Naḥmanides invokes the concepts of *peshara* (compromise) and *lifnim me-shurat ha-din* (roughly: going beyond the letter of the law) to indicate the supererogatory standards which life according to law itself requires. For the law to work, one must go beyond the law.

But how far beyond the law does one go if the law commands that one go there? There is a hefty debate among contemporary scholars of Jewish ethics as to whether *lifnim me-shurat ha-din*, insofar as it is commanded by the law itself, can be thought of as in some way extra-legal and thus foundational for the category of Jewish ethics.[9] Similarly, there are debates between scholars of Jewish law as to whether the law per se is answerable to extra- or pre-legal normative standards or whether those standards are necessarily immanent in the law itself. This debate tracks roughly speaking that between natural law theorists and legal positivists. The natural law position – that there exists discernable normativity prior to and abidingly over and against halakha – opens up a conceptual space for Jewish ethics. But on the positivist view, Jewish ethics cannot become a stable category; it is stillborn rather than viable.[10] Although these debates are of some philosophical interest, what I want to argue for here is a way of moving beyond them.

MacIntyre provides a clue. In his *Short History of Ethics* he noted, and in his later writings came to question, the notion that morality is a distinct phenomenon separable from, for example, the ritual purity taboos of archaic societies.[11] The very act of distinguishing an identifiable domain labeled "morality" to be studied by a conceptually discrete method known as "ethics" is a matter of historical contingency. MacIntyre's dissent goes back perhaps to Elizabeth Anscombe, who made this point half a century ago in her celebrated "Modern Moral Philosophy."[12] Not all societies have made this move, nor is there any rational necessity that they should have done so.

That what we have come to call ethics is held to be distinct from what we have to come to call law need not reflect badly on cultures which have not cut that distinction. Nor is this a putative failing of intellectually immature cultures. Recently, the view that moral phenomena are conceptually distinctive, requiring their own language and evaluative logic, has also been attacked, from a different philosophical point of view than MacIntyre's, by Philippa Foot. Her *Natural Goodness* argues for the non-uniqueness of moral predicates such as "good" when applied to good actions or intentions vis-à-vis other forms of evaluation ("That's a good dog." "Joe has good vision.").[13] The details of Foot's argument need not concern us. I want simply to note her project: ethics may be a naturalized inquiry; it may have to do with what enables us to flourish as a species, different yet not inseparable from animal species.[14] Bernard Williams and Raymond Geuss have made comparable arguments. This represents a massive dethroning of the categoricity and autonomy of ethics, so crucial to the work of Kant and his followers. Insofar as the standard debate among Jewish scholars as to the relation between law and ethics seems to presuppose a well-formed, if largely tacit, conception of ethics, it likely presupposes too much.

The search for a categorically distinct domain of ethics, Jewish or otherwise, may be misguided from the outset. One might also add that construing the rule-following traditional Jewish way of life (halakha) as law might also entrain a conceptual baggage that misleads as much as it illumines.[15] Halakha is surely comparable to uncontroversial cases of legal systems in some respects but it is incomparable in others. Its claim to divine origin, its articulation and endurance under conditions of exile and lack of political sovereignty, its failure to be recognized as binding by many if not most Jews in the present age, and, most notably for our purposes, its enshrining of aspirational, virtuous ideals distinguish it from the legal systems of secular societies.[16] Jewish law is no less problematic as law than Jewish ethics is problematic as ethics. To seek categorical distinctions in these matters may be methodologically foolish. To try sharply to distinguish between law and ethics may be rewarding conceptual work in a system where those distinctions are incipient or explicit but may be misguided when applied to Jewish thought. A picture, as Wittgenstein might have said, holds us captive. The picture of a hard disjunction between law and ethics is the wrong picture to apply to Judaism.

Rather than treat these concepts as timeless designations that refer extensionally to definitely described items, we should treat them as related, contrastive terms. Law and ethics hang together, partially defining the domain of the other in a fluid, culture-bound way. They gain their meaning intensionally from their semantic interplay. Yet, there is something below the level of semantics. "Law" and "ethics" point toward human impulses for normative ordering. Perhaps we should say that human beings go in for norms as they go in for language. Normativity per se, just as much as speech, is native to us; it is part of our evolutionary biology, the diversity of its culture-bound expressions notwithstanding. (To gesture toward an explanation of the normative in this way is not, of course, to engage in a normative argument.)

If there is an underlying capacity and potential for normativity, one could say that law and ethics, as well as custom, are its, by no means mutually exclusive, modes. "Law" and "ethics" describe overlapping and inter-penetrating kinds of norm. Terms such as "custom" or "constitution" describe other modalities of the normative. We should not expect hard distinctions between these terms any more than we should expect hard distinctions between culturally embedded linguistic phenomena such as poetry and prose.

The fluid, contrastive interplay between law and ethics is exemplified by numerous Jewish texts, which suggest a relationship of mutual dependence between norms answering at least prima facie to the two categories. Thus, Jewish tradition itself tries to draw some distinctions. Hebrew has a term – *musar* – which if not strictly coterminous with "ethics" nonetheless points in that direction. In biblical Hebrew, *musar* signifies "chastening," "discipline," or "exhortation."[17] In the Middle Ages, a genre of musar literature develops which extends down to modern times, even giving rise to a movement in the nineteenth century.[18] This literature looks to both conduct and character; to what ought to be done as well as to the dispositions, attitudes, values, and intentions of the doer. It is concerned with what we would call moral psychology, with motivation, *akrasia*, attention and inattention, attitude, indecision, focus and distraction; it is the Jewish equivalent, in broad terms, of the study of virtue. Classic works of musar, such as the eleventh-century *Book of the Direction of the Duties of the Heart* by Baḥya ben Joseph ibn Paquda, work in tandem with overtly legal texts. Baḥya presents a good example of trying to develop a contrast between "law" and "ethics" while nonetheless holding them together. He distinguishes between the customary halakhic "duties of the limbs" and the *equally* halakhic but more elusive (and, according to his plaint, frequently neglected) "duties of the heart." The latter correspond to what we might think of as ethics, but they are no less "legal" than the former. Nonetheless, a working phenomenological distinction has been made. Maimonides also sees no rift between enjoining the development of practical and intellectual virtues and the behavioral stipulations of halakha. His great code, the *Mishneh Torah*, begins with elucidations of metaphysical, epistemological, and ethical matters along broadly Aristotelian lines as a prolegomenon to the codification of Jewish law. And yet these matters are themselves matters of law; the law requires that Jews be metaphysicians and moral philosophers up to a point.[19] Indeed, the Mishnah itself includes in the order dealing with civil and criminal law an exhortatory, musar-oriented tractate, *Pirke Avot*

(*The Chapters of the Fathers*, often interpretively rendered *The Ethics of the Fathers*). The placement of the tractate by the second–third century CE editors of the Mishnah seems to indicate that its purpose is to help form what we would call "judicial temperament" in those who would interpret and apply the law stipulated in the surrounding books. All of this is to suggest that although theorizing a bright-line distinction between law and ethics in the manner of Western philosophy may be a dead end for Jewish thought, there are still distinctions to be made. Those distinctions inhere in the material as such. A conceptually and historically sensitive treatment will try to highlight the contrasts felt by the authors themselves.

Can we then propose a way of thinking (I hesitate to call it a definition) about Jewish ethics, which is warranted by the evidence of texts and yet guides the interpretation of those texts in a heuristic, intellectually productive way? I suggest that an historical inquiry into Jewish ethics attend to *Jewish reflection on conduct and character*. This is sufficiently minimal and broad as to avoid on principle labeling and excluding relevant material. (That's law, not ethics! Ethics is what supplements, complements, or even underlies law!) Nor is it so broad as to be vacuous; not everything reflects on conduct and character. The term "reflection" is also important. While looser than "analysis" or "argument," it still marks an intellectual engagement with the problems of conduct and character. That engagement could be manifest in a legal text or it could be found in a poem. There is no reason to stipulate in advance what will count as ethics and what will not. Nonetheless, reflection implies cognitive content, a real grappling with an issue relevant to conduct and/or to character. Although a study of Jewish ethics cannot be, as argued above, a strictly philosophical inquiry, it must nonetheless expose patterns of thought, as well as the questions that motivated the thought and the justification for the answers moved by the texts. The historical study of Jewish ethics should be descriptive, normative, and metaethical – the latter even in the absence of strictly philosophical source materials. All serious reflection makes a case and seeks to justify its position. I aim here to expose those intellectual transactions.

The idea of Jewish ethics as reflection on conduct and character suggests that Jewish ethics attends to two foci at once. I would like to call this dual focus, using Greek-derived terms, an *aretaic–deontic pattern*.[20] Virtue and rules work together in a mutually reinforcing way. Both are necessary. The idea that duty, obligation, or justice – the tissue of a legal system or of a deontological concept of ethics – requires a complement in virtue is as old as Plato and Aristotle. (Insofar as this is the biblical view, it is, of course, even older.) In the *Nicomachean Ethics* (Book X, Chapter 9 1179b 32), Aristotle is not content to leave the inculcation of those dispositions and habits that comprise the virtues to the vagaries of custom. He would charge the laws of the city with the task of shaping the souls of men. Thus the

Ethics flows into the *Politics*, into the study of constitutions and the sort of person, virtuous or vicious, whom they produce. In Aristotle's case, the vast majority of his analysis is devoted to the virtues; law enters as a necessary if subsidiary appendix. *Arete* trumps *deon*. In Kant, by contrast, deontology rules. Even Kant, however, develops a doctrine of the virtues as a necessary adjunct to his duty-oriented system. Virtue, in *The Metaphysics of Morals*, is a kind of internal, private law-giving; virtue facilitates that self-legislation which is constitutive of normativity for Kant. The virtuous person is inclined to duty on purely internal grounds. Virtue entails developing oneself in the direction of holiness, of willing unmediated compliance with the moral law. Kant takes over the classic aretaic ethics of antiquity and domesticates it to a duty-bound framework.[21]

Contemporary Kant-inspired thinkers, such as John Rawls, have scanted virtue, fearing that any comprehensive vision of the good life, from which virtues as means toward achieving human flourishing draw their intelligibility, will be anti-democratic. Rawls' exclusively justice-oriented "Kantian constructivism" led to a backlash on behalf of the virtues, both among communitarians and among liberals, such as Stephen Macedo and William Galston, who sought accounts of "liberal virtues."[22] Onora O'Neill's work seeks explicitly to integrate justice and virtue, arguing that "concern for justice and for the virtues can be compatible, indeed that they are mutually supporting ..."[23]

None of this would seem foreign to generations of Jewish thinkers. Indeed, the modernist divorce between justice and the virtues is what would call out for vindication. What accounts for this? The naturalness of the aretaic–deontic framework for Jewish thought is arguably to be traced to the covenantal origins of Judaism, indeed, of the Jewish people. The Bible portrays Israelite origins in two modes. On the one hand, Israel is presented as an extended family descended biologically from a single patriarch, Abraham. On the other hand, Israel is presented as a nation constituted at least in part by the non-primordial ties of consensual religious identification, acceptance of a common constitution, political cooperation and solidarity, etc. It is both consanguineous and voluntary: one can be born into it or one can choose to identify with it. The vehicle by which the latter possibility is effectuated is the covenant (*berit*).[24] Masses of non-consanguineous people chose to identify with Israel when the latter was liberated from Egypt. The people as a whole gained the full stature of their nationhood by the acceptance of a constitution (the Torah) at Mount Sinai. The narratives of Exodus and especially of Deuteronomy frame the encounter between God and the people in covenantal terms: the people voluntarily accept God's rule and God's teaching. They enter into a relationship with Him, as He desires a relationship with them. They consent to serve Him in response to His choice of them. By so doing, they become a full, if unique nation. Not all texts in the Bible reflect a covenantal perspective, but that perspective has shaped the whole as well as all subsequent Jewish self-understanding.[25]

A key consequence of the radically foundational nature of covenant is that law must be thought of as chosen, not imposed. Although the God of the Hebrew Scriptures is famously stern, He is not tyrannical. Israel entered into a relationship, which, however unequal the parties to it, is still mutual. The lives of the Jews and of God, as it were, are henceforth and forever joined. Law must be understood within the context of a shared form of life devoted both to justice and to the good. Covenant, unlike compact or contract, is about the whole of life. The individuality of the covenanting parties is retained but the relationship works a transformation on both of them. God wants Israelite society to instantiate norms of respect, friendship, kindness, compassion, and equity. He also wants Israelites to manifest holiness, saintliness, self-sacrifice, empathy, and courage. (As to the transformation of God, Moses repeatedly dissuades Him from obliterating Israel, bringing out, as it were, the better angels of His nature.) Deontic and aretaic considerations are inseparable here. The theological–moral–political framework which covenant is resists reduction for other than ideal-typical analytic purposes into disjunctive categories such as ethics vs. law.[26]

This is due in part to the comprehensiveness of the covenantal framework. Judaism is not, in a crucial sense, a religion if by religion we mean a discrete, separable dimension of belief and ritual supervening on a secular way of life. The Torah, understood classically, is the way of life of a holy, yet politically instantiated nation. Unlike Christianity, which was born in the cities of the Roman Empire, Judaism was born, on its own telling, in the wilderness. There was no civil authority to order the political functions of the society. The Israelite project was civilizational: everything had to be included. Although the Jews developed distinctions between civil and religious authorities, these were not as sharply formulated as they were among Christians. There is no Jewish St Augustine.

The archaeological discovery of Hittite treaty documents in the early twentieth century suggested to biblical scholars that ancient Israel understood its relationship with God along the lines of a "suzerain–vassal treaty" or covenant. Later, political and social thinkers, most notably Max Weber, saw that covenant described not only the "vertical" relationship between God and Israel but also defined the "horizontal" relationship among Israelites.[27] Israel was a federal (from the Latin *foedus*, covenant) polity. Individual clans and tribes federated by oath into a political superstructure. A feature of the Hittite treaties, which continues strongly into Israelite covenantalism, is that the vassal is enjoined to love the suzerain. In the Bible, this becomes *ḥesed* – covenant love/loyalty. God wants not only the obedience of Israel, but their love for Him. Indeed, God wants Israel to be like Him, insofar as that is possible for human beings. Here again, a substantial internal, "ethical" dimension is built into life under the constitutive "legal" obligations of the covenantal relationship. As Jon Levenson remarks, "… *all* law codes in the Torah were ascribed to the revelation to Moses on Mount Sinai. That is to say, all law in Israel, whether casuistic or apodictic in form, has been embedded within the context of covenant."[28] The mutually supportive interplay of duty, especially of legally stipulated duty, with the aspiration toward goodness is native to the covenantal framework of biblical Israel and hence of subsequent Judaism.

This book is an historical study of the unfolding of the aretaic–deontic pattern across a diachronic range of Jewish sources. By "historical" I mean something not much more than "chronological." As was the case with MacIntyre in his *Short History of Ethics*, my concern is for conceptual analysis of reasoning rather than intellectual history. I don't pay more attention to influences, sources, continuities, innovations, cultural or political contexts, and other standard preoccupations of historians than I have to. Jewish Studies is heavily populated by intellectual historians. I want here to take a somewhat different tack. I take my cue both from MacIntyre and from Stanley Cavell, who writes of his own approach that "my idea of the history of philosophy is that it can be approached only out of philosophizing in the present."[29] Although the majority of the texts we will consider are not overtly philosophical, all of them qua reflections on conduct and character make an argument, present a vision, or affirm the value of a way of life. I try to evoke, describe, analyze, and sometimes criticize these arguments and affirmations. Each chapter tries to uncover and reconstruct patterns of reasoning about conduct and character, neither scanting the strangeness of that reasoning in the eyes of modern readers nor romantically consigning it to the exotic or primitive. I try to find reasons for the positions taken by historical thinkers and, whenever possible, to consider whether they are good reasons. Although the task is primarily interpretive, I am also concerned to display the aretaic–deontic framework as a well-formed conceptual approach to the moral life. One might say that it is a traditional conceptual approach to the moral life, shared by Jews and non-Jews alike. A full theoretical defense of such an approach lies beyond this work. I hope, at least, to provide some resources from the Jewish tradition for anyone who would undertake that worthy end.[30]

In **Chapter 1**, we explore biblical ethics in terms of Karl Jaspers' paradigm of the "Axial Age." The biblical literature is the primary source for the development of Jewish moral concepts and ethical reflection over the ages. This chapter explicates some of the main ethical issues in this highly variegated literature both within its own historical context and in order to show how later Jewish thought interprets, transforms, and preserves earlier views. We consider the relationship between cultic, "religious" orientations and "ethical" orientations, the nexus of law and ethics, the nature of moral agency and constraint, including a biblical approach to the problem of free will and determinism, and the tensions between a naturalistic and a revealed grounding for ethics. Insofar as our framework is the Axial Age rather than biblical civilization per se, we also consider the fusion of overtly philosophical, Hellenistic ethics and biblical ethics in *Aristeas* and Philo.

Chapter 2 looks at ancient rabbinic understandings of conduct and character. Judaism reads the Bible through the eyes of the post-70 CE leadership collectively known as the Sages. How did the Sages interpret and transform the moral teachings found in the ancient literature that they canonized as "written Torah"? This chapter explores aspects of rabbinic legal and non-legal exegesis, focusing on texts that are alive to ethical considerations. It explores what constitutes exemplary character and moral motivation through a study of aggadic (non-legal) interpretations of the patriarch Abraham. It looks as well at the question of the limits of ethics: could religious considerations suspend or cancel ethical considerations? The chapter then explores the issue of reward and punishment as a ground for moral motivation. It engages the complex of issues surrounding the Kantian dichotomy of autonomy and heteronomy. It argues that the Sages were alive to the moral nobility of autonomy but were also concerned to moderate the demand for autonomy given their theistic context. Finally, the chapter turns to an analysis of the concept of justice, as refracted by the rabbinic discussion of the lex talionis. The Talmud's effort to read an "eye for an eye" as a "civil" rather than a "criminal" matter, as a matter of financial compensation rather than mutilation, reveals a subtle appreciation of how ideal norms of justice must be adapted to the contingencies of the social world.

A self-consciously philosophical treatment of ethics emerges in the Middle Ages. This development is explored in **Chapter 3**. Prior to the ninth century only the Greek Jewish writer Philo wedded an external philosophical system to Jewish tradition. Jewish participation in the "medieval enlightenment" restored this intellectual opportunity. This chapter considers the genuinely philosophical ethics produced by Jewish thinkers in the Muslim orbit including Saadya Gaon, Baḥya ben Joseph ibn Paquda, and Moses Maimonides. What new elements did the absorption of philosophy add to Jewish moral thought? What tensions did philosophy introduce into Jewish ethics? What permanent influences did philosophy wield on Judaism? How did traditional Jewish moral teaching shape the philosophical concepts and methods adopted by Jewish thinkers?

Alongside philosophical work, a popular version of ethical instruction developed. Rabbinic authors of the Middle Ages and early modernity produced numerous works of moral instruction utilizing different literary genres. Several of these popular, non-philosophical books (although often indebted to their philosophical predecessors) are explored in **Chapter 4.** In addition to popular pious moralizing, ethical works drawing from the mystical teachings collectively known as kabbalah emerged by the thirteenth century. The chapter considers rabbinic ethical works exemplifying several of these genres, including Naḥmanides' *Sermon on the Words of Ecclesiastes* (*Drasha al Divrei Kohelet*), Rabbi Jonah Gerondi's *Gates of Repentance* (*Sha'are Teshuvah*), Baḥya ben Asher's *Jar of Flour* (*Kad ha-Kemach*), Isaac Aboab's *Lamp of Illumination* (*Menorat Ha-Maor*), and Moses Cordovero's *The Palm Tree of Deborah* (*Tomer Devorah*). We will also look at a parallel development, the mystical pietistic movement of medieval Franco-German Jewry, the Hasidei Ashkenaz. The focus will be on a late medieval work influenced by this trend, the anonymous *Ways of the Righteous* (*Orḥot Tzaddikim*). In addition to describing and analyzing some of the arguments and vision of these works, the chapter reflects on the gaps between the medieval moral imagination and the modern horizon of Jewish thought.

In **Chapter 5,** we explore the impact on Jewish ethical thought of those fundamental changes to Jewish life in Europe brought on by Emancipation and Enlightenment in the West and by the spread of Hasidism in the East. Spinoza stands at a watershed, in some ways negating all of Judaism, in others suggesting, albeit inadvertently, how Judaism might go forward. A great classic of Jewish ethics, Moshe Hayyim Luzzatto's *The Path of the Just* (*Mesillat Yesharim*), although falling chronologically within this period, takes little account of the growing Enlightenment. It represents an attempt to continue the old, pietistic–mystical trend. Within a few years of Luzzatto, Moses Mendelssohn and his followers reintroduced philosophical ethics to Jewish thought and re-envisioned a new basis for Judaism, which gave ethics an extraordinarily prominent role. In the East, hasidic homilies and treatises revivified traditional patterns of moral aspiration. The Lithuanian reaction to Hasidism also gave rise to a new emphasis on ethics, the Musar movement. This chapter considers examples of these various trends. We then consider the development of a highly philosophical, albeit apologetic, presentation of Judaism as an ethical monotheism in German-speaking central Europe, focusing on the work of Moritz Lazarus, Hermann Cohen, Franz Rosenzweig, and Martin Buber.

We turn then to the diverse forms of Jewish ethical writing that have flourished in the past several decades, looking first at Emmanuel Levinas and then noting areas of applied ethics. We note also the philosophical ethics of such scholars as David Novak, Elliot Dorff, Lenn Goodman, and Eugene Borowitz.

In the **Conclusion,** we raise questions about the uses of the Jewish moral tradition and its prospects.

Notes

1   MacIntyre's criticisms and corrections appear in the Preface to the second edition (1998) of *A Short History of Ethics* (Notre Dame: University of Notre Dame Press, 1998). The first edition was published in 1967.

2   Alasdair MacIntyre, *Three Rival Versions of Moral Enquiry* (Notre Dame: University of Notre Dame Press, 1990), p. 28.

3   MacIntyre, *Three Rival Versions*, p. 13.

4   MacIntyre, *Three Rival Versions*, p. 8.

5   Michael Wyschogrod, *The Body of Faith: God in the People of Israel* (San Francisco: Harper & Row, 1989), p. 181.

6   For a sketch of the ideological context (that is, the division between Orthodox, Conservative, and Reform approaches to Judaism) in which the ethics/law relation is configured, see Menachem Marc Kellner, ed., *Contemporary Jewish Ethics* (New York: Hebrew Publishing Co., 1978), p. 17.

7   All biblical references, unless otherwise noted, are from the New Jewish Publication Society (NJPS) translation.

8   Ethics, on this account, is not identical with virtue qua corrective to pure legalism. Virtue and duty interpenetrate; you can't have one without the other. Ethics is found in the virtuous observance of the law. This point of view pervades Jewish texts. Part of the burden of this book is to exemplify this claim, to account for it, and to argue that it offers a valuable way both to think about ethics *and* to live an ethical life.

9   Aharon Lichtenstein, "Does Jewish Tradition recognize an Ethic Independent of Halakha?" in Kellner, ed., *Contemporary Jewish Ethics*, pp. 102–123. In this classic article Rabbi Lichtenstein argues for an expansive understanding of halakha, which includes an ethical dimension that is analytically distinguishable but not finally separable from law (*din*). A natural ethic or morality exists but its relevance is circumscribed, post-Sinai, for Jews. For a review and synthesis of this debate, see Louis Newman, *Past Imperatives: Studies in the History and Theory of Jewish Ethics* (Albany: State University of New York Press, 1998), esp. Chapter Two. See also Jonathan Jacobs, *Law, Reason and Morality in Medieval Jewish Philosophy* (Oxford: Oxford University Press, 2010), Chapter Seven.

10   Representative figures in this debate are, on behalf of positivism, Marvin Fox, "Maimonides and Aquinas on Natural Law," *Dine Israel* 3 (1972), reprinted in Marvin Fox, *Interpreting Maimonides* (Chicago: University of Chicago Press, 1990). On behalf of natural law, David Novak, *Natural Law in Judaism* (Cambridge: Cambridge University Press, 1998). For a review of and an original contribution to the debate, see Jonathan Jacobs, "Natural Law and Judaism," *Heythrop Journal*, Vol. 50, No. 6, pp. 930–947.

11   MacIntyre, *Three Rival Versions*, p. 28.

12   Originally in *Philosophy*, 33 (1958), reprinted in G. E. M. Anscombe, *The Collected Philosophical Papers of G. E. M. Anscombe*, Vol. III (Minneapolis: University of Minnesota Press, 1981), pp. 26–42.

13   Philippa Foot, *Natural Goodness* (Oxford: Clarendon Press, 2001), see especially Chapter 2. Another formidable critic is the late Bernard Williams.

Williams attacked what he termed "the morality system" – the post-Kantian common wisdom as to what constitutes the distinctive sphere of moral obligation. Williams contrasted a broader field of "ethical considerations" with the narrower morality system. He sees morality as entailing a false understanding of practical necessity, interests, value, freedom, character, and so on; the morality system is the false religion of godless modernity. In its place, he would reintroduce a modest, rather culture-bound ethics. See Bernard Williams, *Ethics and the Limits of Philosophy* (Cambridge, MA: Harvard University Press, 1985), Chapter 10. See also Raymond Geuss's genealogy of modern philosophical ethics in Raymond Geuss, *Outside Ethics* (Princeton: Princeton University Press, 2005), Chapter 3. On Geuss's view, the central question of philosophical ethics – what ought I to do? – derives from a medieval world in which doing God's will was the paramount human task. With the loss of that world, a secularized equivalent takes its place. Ethics becomes an ever more total domain, compensating for the absence of the divine. It is difficult, although worthwhile for Geuss, to get "outside" ethics.

14 Note the application of this, broadly speaking, evolutionary paradigm to rationality per se in Robert Nozick, *The Nature of Rationality* (Princeton: Princeton University Press, 1993), especially Chapter IV.

15 For a view of the conceptual complexities of distinguishing a legal system from other socially articulated forms of normativity, see Martin Golding, *Philosophy of Law* (Englewood Cliffs: Prentice Hall, 1975), Chapter One.

16 For a further consideration of these matters, see Alan Mittleman, *The Scepter Shall Not Depart from Judah: Perspectives on the Persistence of the Political in Judaism* (Lanham: Lexington Books, 2000), Chapter 8.

17 See Ludwig Koehler and Walter Baumgarten, *A Bilingual Dictionary of the Hebrew and Aramaic Old Testament* (Leiden: Brill, 1998) s.v. *musar* for extensive text references, p. 503.

18 For a good general overview of musar literature (*sifrut ha-musar*) see *Encyclopedia Judaica* (Jerusalem: Keter Publishing, 1974), Vol. 6, pp. 922–932. For the Hebrew reader, see the Introduction to Isaiah Tishbi, *Mivḥar Sifrut Ha-Musar* (M. Newman: Jerusalem, 1970).

19 The twentieth-century Jewish philosopher, Leo Strauss, took the integration of philosophy into law to be a mark of the superiority of the "medieval Enlightenment" over the modern Enlightenment. For Strauss's classic statement on this subject, see his *Philosophy and Law: Contributions to the Understanding of Maimonides and his Predecessors*, trans. Eve Adler (Albany: SUNY Press, 1995).

20 *Arete* is ordinarily translated as "virtue." Its semantic range covers goodness, excellence, perfection, merit, fitness, bravery, and valor. *Deon* implies "what one must do." For a caution regarding the latter term, see Bernard Williams, *Ethics and the Limits of Philosophy* (Cambridge, MA: Harvard University Press, 1985), p. 16.

21 Immanuel Kant, *The Metaphysics of Morals*, trans. Mary Gregor (Cambridge: Cambridge University Press, 2009), Part II, Metaphysical First Principles of the Doctrine of Virtue.

22 Stephen Macedo, *Liberal Virtues: Citizenship, Virtue, and Community in Liberal Constitutionalism* (Oxford: Oxford University Press, 1990). William Galston, *Liberal Purposes* (Cambridge: Cambridge University Press, 1991). An early communitarian critic of Rawls who argued contra Rawls for the priority of the good over the right is Michael Sandel. See his *Liberalism and the Limits of Justice* (Cambridge: Cambridge University Press, 1982).

23 Onora O'Neill, *Towards Justice and Virtue: A Constructive Account of Practical Reasoning* (Cambridge: Cambridge University Press, 1996), p. 10.

24 The life's work of the late political scientist, Daniel J. Elazar, was devoted to analyzing the moral and political consequences of the idea of covenant. See Daniel J. Elazar, "Covenant as the Basis of the Jewish Political Tradition," in Daniel J. Elazar, ed., *Kinship and Consent: The Jewish Political Tradition and its Contemporary Uses*, 2nd edn (New Brunswick: Transaction Publishers, 1997). See also Daniel J. Elazar, *Covenant and Polity in Biblical Israel*, Vol. I of *The Covenant Tradition in Politics* (New Brunswick: Transaction Publishers, 1998).

25 On the dangers of over-extending the category of covenant, see Jon D. Levenson, *Sinai and Zion: An Entry into the Jewish Bible* (San Francisco: Harper & Row, 1987), p. 50.

26 An excellent discussion of the usefulness of the concept of covenant for theorizing Jewish ethics may be found in Newman, *Past Imperatives*, Chapter 3.

27 For Weber's contribution to an understanding of the moral and political implications of covenanting, see Mittleman, *The Scepter Shall Not Depart from Judah*, pp. 59–68. See also, Alan Mittleman, "Judaism: Covenant, Pluralism and Piety," in Bryan Turner, ed., *The New Blackwell Companion to the Sociology of Religion* (Oxford: Wiley-Blackwell, 2010).

28 Levenson, *Sinai and Zion*, p. 49.

29 Stanley Cavell, *Cities of Words* (Cambridge, MA: Belknap Press of Harvard University Press, 2004), p. 327.

30 O'Neill, *Justice and Virtue*, Chapter I.

1
Ethics in the Axial Age

The Bible is not a philosophical text. It does, however, provide rich content for philosophizing. Although it does not, therefore, provide formal or rigorous arguments on behalf of its ethics, it does provide broad patterns of reasoning about proper conduct and character. It does not simply assert and command; it invites the engagement of our reason. Despite its modern reputation as a blunt record of divine commands, it often appeals to our intellect and conscience. In Deuteronomy, for example, the Israelites are told that other nations will admire their wisdom and wish to emulate them: "Surely, that great nation [Israel] is a wise and discerning people" (Deut. 4:6; cf. Isa. 2:1–3). The Israelites will be thought to model a way of life that non-Israelites will find appealing. The eighth-century prophet Isaiah has God imploring the Israelites to "come, let us reach an understanding" (Isa. 1:18). The literary mode of this prophetic discourse, the lawsuit (*riv*), suggests a dialogue between parties who can rise above their passions and prejudices and seek a reasonable solution. The ethics of the Hebrew Bible is typically not presented as a purely human affair but it is nonetheless answerable to shared, rational criteria of evaluation. Abraham famously challenged God, when he learned of God's impending judgment of Sodom and Gomorrah, "Shall not the Judge of all the earth deal justly?" (Gen. 18:25). The text assumes a natural apprehension of justice, which Abraham and God both share.[1] The significance and range of ethical naturalism in the Bible will be considered below.

The biblical literature has much to say about the ensemble of human excellences that constitute the best life for human beings. It ensconces its teaching in narratives, poetry, law, and wise sayings, examples of which we

A Short History of Jewish Ethics: Conduct and Character in the Context of Covenant, First Edition. Alan L. Mittleman.

will presently explore. It is concerned as well with the best ordering of society, of economic life, and of political matters. In none of these domains is its vision systematic or deductive. It is often suggestive and casuistic, asserted rather than explicitly argued. The Bible's style, although differing by genre, is typically laconic. It does not dwell, as Homer did, on the elaboration of pictorial detail, nor does it develop in its narratives reports of the psychological states of its characters.[2] One would love to know what Abraham and Isaac, for example, thought during their three-day trek to the mountain where Abraham would attempt to sacrifice his son. But we are told nothing; the lacunae are filled by later imaginative Jewish (and Christian) literatures.

The collection of, according to the traditional Jewish enumeration, 24 books that constitute the canonical scriptures came into being over a span of almost a millennium.[3] (Nor is the process by which some books were included in the canon and others excluded clear or easily datable.) The Bible's earliest constituent texts reflect, although probably do not derive from, a late Bronze Age Near-Eastern civilization. Its latest text, usually assumed to be the Book of Daniel, comes from a second-century BCE Hellenistic world for which the Bronze Age was a remote antiquity. The Bible expresses not only a stream of Israelite and Judean-Jewish creativity stretching over centuries, it also expresses a continual reworking of inherited textual materials, symbols, literary motifs, beliefs, and values; a history of intra-biblical development and commentary. It is as if the English-speaking world continued to rewrite and develop Shakespeare for twice the amount of time that has elapsed since the Elizabethan Age. Beyond this, the biblical literatures themselves represent a radical reworking and revolutionary challenge to earlier, non-literary forms of Israelite and Judean religion.[4] The Bible is a polemic against what came before, against an Israelite and Judean culture that was hardly distinguishable from the "pagan" cultures in whose orbit it lived. The remnants of that banished form of life are half-veiled in the biblical text and partially revealed by archaeology. An historical account of ethics has to take this development into account.

The world of biblical religion, as opposed to its Israelite–Judean precursor, comes into being in the so-called Axial Age, a term of art that comes not from the vocabulary of the archaeologist but from that of the philosopher and social theorist. The Axial Age refers to a set of developments in the major civilizations of the world – Greece, China, India, Persia, and Israel inter alia – with roughly overlapping features. It represents a major shift in beliefs, values, religious consciousness, social and political thought, as well as in the social structures and centers of authority that fomented and sustained these shifts. The term was coined by the German philosopher Karl Jaspers. Jaspers contrasted the Axial Age with its predecessor "mythical age." The Axial Age represents the triumph of "logos against mythos."

"Rationality and rationally clarified experience launched a struggle against the myth; a further struggle developed for the transcendence of the One God against non-existent demons, and finally an ethical rebellion took place against the unreal figures of the gods. Religion was rendered ethical, and the majesty of the deity thereby increased."[5]

In pre-Axial Age, "mythic" civilizations, there was a sense of a distinction between the mundane and trans-mundane spheres. Animistic forces or, where present, gods penetrated mundane experience. The forces and gods were distinguishable but not radically different from human beings. Shamans crisscrossed the realms; magicians influenced the trans-mundane to assist human beings in their quest for purely mundane goods such as health, fertility, victory, and survival. Society was typically organized in clan and tribal structures. Authority was traditional or charismatic. With the rise of the Axial Age, a new relationship between the mundane and what Jaspers called the trans-mundane occurs. The trans-mundane ceases to be a rather more charged version of the ordinary world of experience and becomes fully transcendent. There is now a "sharp disjunction" between worlds.[6] In Israel, for example, the God who earlier "moved about in the garden during the breezy time of day" (Gen. 3:8) became an inconceivably austere sovereign who speaks and the world comes into being (Gen. 1:3). The creation account that features this sovereign as its main character, Genesis chapter 1, although the most famous in the Bible, is only one of many. Other accounts, preserved as fragments rather than fully fleshed-out literary narratives, speak of that older conception of the deity. In texts such as Psalms 74:12–17 and 104:6–9, Isaiah 51:9–11, or Job 38:8–11 are preserved cultural memories of a more mythological God fighting primordial monsters and suppressing the forces of chaos.[7] This God is much closer to his Babylonian analogues than the God of Genesis, chapter 1. With the rise of an intellectual class, the literary prophets of the eighth century, God became fully transcendent rather than trans-mundane. The sixth-century anonymous prophet known as Deutero-Isaiah gives pointed expression to this sense of radical transcendence when he proclaims: "For My plans are not your plans, Nor are My ways your ways, declares the LORD. But as the heavens are high above the earth, So are My ways high above your ways" (Isa. 55:8–9).

The fully transcendent God is increasingly revealed through word, law, and the cognition of value rather than through adventitious experiential, especially visual, encounters.[8] No longer are archaic experiences of God, conveyed by such texts as Genesis 18:1–14 and 32:24–30, Exodus 4:24–26 and 33:23, Joshua 5:13–15, or Judges 6:11–23 and 13:2–24, possible. God comes increasingly to be conceived as pure spirit; without a body, there is nothing to see. Where there is something to see, it is not God but a mediated presence (Isaiah, chapter 6; Ezekiel, chapter 1). The experience of God, to the extent that it is possible, requires levels of mediation. In the popular religious imagination, angels come into being as designated intermediaries. In earlier Israelite religion, as in some of the texts just cited, angels, divine messengers, are not stable entities. They have no fixed identity – God and His messengers are one and the same. In mature biblical religion God is distinct and radically unique. As God's transcendence grows, the "space" between the mundane and the transcendent is increasingly populated by a heavenly host. The religious imagination abhors a vacuum.

The challenge of the Axial Age, in all of the world civilizations, was to align the mundane order with the newly envisaged transcendent order.[9] Social and political life, once timelessly organized along traditional tribal and clan lines, became an intellectual and a practical problem. How can the social and political realm reflect the eternal order of transcendence? For Israel, this problem had two interrelated solutions. The first was found in the concept of covenant, the conceptualization of the relationship between the nation of Israel and its transcendent sovereign along juridical and moral lines.[10] The second was found in the reorganization of the social sphere under a divinely legitimated monarchy. In pre-Axial civilizations, deities were more powerful versions of humans but similar in nature. The totems or gods of the clan brought fertility, successful hunts or growing seasons, victory in battle, etc. The relationship between the group and its trans-mundane counterparts was natural, organic, and mutually beneficial. With the development of the Axial civilization, the social group – now orders of magnitude more complex than a clan-based or tribal society – becomes accountable to the god or, more precisely, to the eternal, transcendent values that the god represents. The higher order, in the Israelite case represented by terms such as justice (*mishpat*) and righteousness (*tzedek*), must be appropriately actualized in the mundane realm. God is now known as one who wills *tzedek* and *mishpat* for his people; who is approached through acts of *tzedek* and *mishpat*. The relationship between people and deity is no longer natural and organic but juridical and moral: they are linked to God through a deliberate acceptance of a mode of life in which *tzedek* and *mishpat*, which are willed by the divine, become operational.

The prophets, themselves ethicized and intellectualized descendants of earlier shamanic figures from Israelite–Judean religion, are the carriers of this consciousness of accountability. The prophets speak in the name of a universal God, uniquely revealed to (albeit frequently ignored by) Israel, and at the same time lord of all the world. As a mature, Axial Age phenomenon, prophecy arraigns the Israelite and Judean elites for their failures to instantiate *tzedek* and *mishpat* in the life of society and state.

Prophecy develops in tandem both with monarchy and with increasing disparities of wealth in society. Its terms of reference are grounded in covenant, both the presumptive nation-founding covenant of Sinai and the political-founding covenant of Zion, which established the legitimacy of David and his descendants. As in the case of national existence per se, political rule is legitimate only if it accords with transcendent norms of justice and righteousness. The prophetic enterprise is oriented toward reminding the king that his authority is conditional on his fidelity to norms underwritten by a higher authority. The political is subsidiary to the moral and the juridical. There are evidences of a "political ethics" along the lines of realpolitik in the Bible but the dominate voice subordinates realist decision making to transcendent religious-ethical norms.[11] When kings follow *raison d'état*, they usually do what is evil in the eyes of the Lord.

Covenant establishes a set of moral referents in some ways reminiscent of the culture of constitutionalism in the modern West. (This should not be surprising in light of the fact that biblical covenantalism lies at the roots of Western constitutionalism.[12]) Constitutions, especially written ones such as the Constitution of the United States, appeal to some prior normativity such as natural right while also standing on their own voluntaristic, contractual character.[13] The covenant of God with Israel at Sinai reflects this dual foundation. In part, the covenant rests on the normative claims of the divine per se. God is that goodness that ought to be chosen.[14] There is something ineluctable about the claims God makes on us, in the Bible's view. Yet unlike the pure contemplation of the good in Plato, the Bible presents the human encounter with divinity as requiring choice, response, consent. There is a recognizable, practical picture of moral agency in the Sinai story. Israel is offered a choice. Perhaps not a fully free choice – a powerful God has just liberated her from bondage and brought her to a barren wilderness. Neither ingratitude nor abandonment is a desirable option. Nonetheless, the choice is real, if constrained – like most morally significant choices in life. Under these circumstances, Israel chose to bind herself to the One who showed her favor, who liberated her from slavery. Israel met God's offer of relationship with a rational response of gratitude and a pledge of fidelity (Exod. 19:7–8). The imperatives of biblical law are contextualized within a narrative that emphasizes consent, rather like the social contract tradition that it anticipates. The law is also tied to, in the sense of requiring and promoting, the virtues of gratitude, fidelity, and love. Law must not be seen in purely deontological terms, nor should it be framed solely by reference to heteronomous commands. The covenant entrains its own distinctive virtues.

Once articulated, both constitutions and covenants function as models for the subsequent guidance of practical reasoning. Constitutions generate their own traditions of moral wisdom and culture. Once on the scene, a constitution is neither a sheer piece of positive law nor a transparent symbol of natural law. It is its own inflected, particular order, both generative of positive law and dependent on deep, thematic sources of normativity.[15] So it is with the covenantal framework of the Hebrew Bible, expressed most paradigmatically in the Book of Deuteronomy, the leading covenantal text in the Bible. Although Deuteronomy per se may only have come to light in the seventh century BCE, much of what becomes canonical scripture was recast to accord with it.[16] It shapes the subsequent "deuteronomic history" (the books of Joshua, Judges, Samuel, and Kings), and the prophets, particularly Jeremiah, but it also influenced the outlook of the other books of the Pentateuch. The Torah's modes of understanding human relations as well as the relation between the divine and the human were reframed along covenantal lines.[17]

Just as constitutions should not be read as codes of law but as frameworks for the development of a normative form of life, so too should biblical covenants. The concept of covenant is not comprised by a set of rules but by the aspiration to achieve a just ordering of communal life and an ideal of individual character. This dimension of the phenomenon of covenant mitigates somewhat the rule-oriented appearance of biblical legal texts. One must keep in mind the larger normative and aspirational context in which those texts inhere. The philosophical paradigm of an ethics of divine command does not quite suit the great number of "thou shalt" and "thou shalt not" statements of the Bible. Within a covenantal context such statements are less flat rules than they are occasions for enacting a form of life, which has been entered into for rational and defensible reasons. As H. L. A. Hart pointed out, legal systems not only command, they enable. Laws not only constrain liberty, they create opportunities for its exercise.[18] So too, the covenantal framework, although it contains rules, also opens possibilities for the growth of the soul, as it were. Laws – in later Judaism – become opportunities for the enactment of virtues such as fidelity, gratitude, and love, as well as an apparatus for the development of character.

The other device of Israel's Axial Age civilization for instantiating *tzedek* and *mishpat* in society is kingship. Kingship is also framed as a covenantal institution, along the lines of a constitutional monarchy. The Book of Deuteronomy absorbs and transforms earlier understandings of kingship inherited from the ancient Near East. Kings in Ugarit or Babylon were understood to have been adopted by the god (cf. Ps. 2:7), endowed with special judicial wisdom (cf. Ps. 72:1), charged with administering justice (Ps. 72:4), which ought to carry across their entire reign (cf. I Kings 10:9); they were as well to maintain the cult and temples (cf. I Kings, chapters 1–8) and lead the army personally to war (I Sam. 10:27–11:15).[19] In Deuteronomy, however, the king's role as the dispenser of justice is minimized – a professional, rationalized judiciary is to be set up "in each of your city gates" (Deut. 16:18). The powers of the king are tightly circumscribed (Deut. 17:14–20). He is subordinated to the Torah-constitution. Nor does he have any role vis-à-vis the religious cult. Individual Israelites are responsible for their religious lives (Deut. 16:11, 14). The king does not officiate at religious ceremonies or mediate divine grace. Deuteronomy thus represents a sharp, utopian rejection of the prevailing royal ideology-theology of the ancient Near East, including that of earlier Israel. So sharp a break was never fully instituted, as numerous contradictions between Deuteronomy's program and the reports of kingship in the subsequent books of (deuteronomic!) history indicate. Nonetheless, we have here a tendency toward ethicizing and rationalizing the norms of society and state, as well as a tendency against reliance on charisma and political authority made sacred. The attempt of covenantal thinkers to subordinate political rule to the Torah-constitution grounds all subsequent attempts in the West to deconstruct what Ernst Cassirer called "the myth of the state."

Another significant achievement of the Axial Age was the ethicization of the cult. The Bible has an important strand of priestly writing (P), which appears in Genesis, the last sections of Exodus, all of Leviticus, and some of Numbers. P is heavy with ritual texts, typically focusing on purity, impurity, and sacrifice. Its dominant theme is the presence of God (*kavod*) in the midst of Israel and the consequences of that incursion of the sacred. The indwelling of God's *kavod* requires a shrine, initially the Tabernacle, the ritual achievement of purity, and expiatory sacrifices centered on the ritual use of blood. P reworks earlier Israelite and Judean popular religion, also under the impress of covenantal thought. Most significantly, P responds to the growing prophetic movement by modifying antique categories of purity and impurity along ethical lines. Some scholars refer to a priestly school that stresses holiness (H) in a moral cum ritual mode. Thus, a central text of Leviticus, the Holiness Code (Leviticus, chapters 17–26) seamlessly interweaves purely "ritual" with "moral" injunctions. This interdependence of the "religious" with the ethical becomes decisive and typical for subsequent Judaism. We shall explore this in the next section.

Alongside these processes of rationalization and ethicization evident in narrative, legal, prophetic, and ritual texts there is a relatively "secular" ancient Near Eastern tradition of wisdom (*ḥokhmah*). Wisdom – found in the books of Proverbs, Job, Ecclesiastes, several Psalms, and elsewhere – focuses on individual virtue, the development of appropriate habits and traits of character and their employment in successful action. Wisdom is an achievement of the unassisted human mind. Desirable traits and wise decisions can be acquired through the observation of nature; the best human patterns can be inferred from the patterns of the natural world. This tradition, which reflects a mode of inquiry and assertion common to several ancient Near Eastern cultures, especially Egypt, is thus significantly different from the deliverances of prophets or the revelation of divine law. In general, wisdom is worldly and success-oriented. The wise person achieves material prosperity and security in Proverbs. This easy equation of wisdom and merit is challenged, famously, by the Book of Job. The usefulness of wisdom overall is thrown into question by the Book of Ecclesiastes. Wisdom cannot, therefore, be said to be a single coherent literary tradition. It is, nonetheless, marked off from other genres by its individual (vs. national) focus and by its relatively secular perspective. Given the antiquity of Egyptian wisdom texts (e.g. 1200–1100 BCE for the *Instruction of Amenemope*, which Proverbs resembles), sustained attention to *ḥokhmah* precedes the Axial Age.

With these considerations in mind, let us turn to some biblical texts that exemplify these various literary genres, that show the development of biblical thought in the direction of rationalization, and that indicate the Bible's manner of dealing with selected ethical problems.

Moral Realism and Divine Command

A key question for ethics in a theistic mode is the relation of God to value. Does God affirm a good, which is independent of him, and then command us to follow it because it is per se good? If the good is per se good and, crucially, accessible to human beings through moral reason, then God's command may be superfluous. Or is the good itself *constituted* by God's command; is something good because God *says so*?[20] This problem was famously raised by Plato in the *Euthyphro*, a dialogue between Socrates and the character for whom the dialogue was named. Socrates pointedly asks Euthyphro "Is what is holy holy because the gods approve it or do they approve it because it is holy?" (10a). Socrates wants to argue the latter point against Euthyphro, who wants to maintain a pure voluntarism or divine command ethics: x is holy or good because the god N wills it to be so. Euthyphro in effect claims that the good, the just, and the holy comprise the set of actions that the gods love. When we engage in acts that conform to what the gods desire then we engage in good, just, or holy acts. These values are contingent on extrinsic divine approval rather than on any qualities intrinsic to the acts. Socrates shows Euthyphro that his definition is incoherent. In a polytheistic context, the gods in fact differ in their appraisals of what is good, holy, or just; such differences lead to violent conflicts among the gods of myth. What one god considers just, another finds outrageous. Socrates tries to wean Euthyphro from his traditional piety toward a more transcendent, rational perspective – the kind of move we associate with the Axial Age. He wants to ground ethics in abstraction, to free ethics from the arbitrariness of saga and traditional authority.[21] Plato, in works such as the *Protagoras*, will later try to found a science of ethics that has an exactitude and a rational structure similar to mathematics. But here Socrates only gestures. He points toward a rational or natural goodness. Both gods and men delight in and defer to a perfection that is independent of, while rationally accessible to, them. The implications of this intuition, far from fully fleshed out in the *Euthyphro*, become thematic for the *Republic*, with its Platonic theory of the Good as the form of forms.

These views suggest what contemporary philosophers (earlier philosophers called it natural law) call moral realism: the view that moral facts are facts about the world; that "values" exist in some way independently of those who make evaluative judgments. We needn't locate values in a reified Platonic realm of Forms. Realism claims, with greater metaphysical modesty, that fact and value are so mutually implicated that evaluation is intrinsic, not secondary, to description.[22] When we talk about value, moral and otherwise, then we are talking about matters available to all rational beings and at the same time in some manner independent of them. The *Euthyphro* raises the issue in a peculiar way: as a question of the status of value vis-à-vis gods and men. The possibility of moral realism – that value could be independent of the gods – raises theological problems for a traditional faith. For Plato, the Good takes on the role of God. For biblical monotheists, that is both appealing and problematic.

The dialogue between Abraham and God in Genesis, chapter 18 raises some of the same questions that Plato much later addressed, albeit in a non-philosophical, narrative form. God appears to Abraham in the form of three men who approach his camp by the "terebinths of Mamre." Abraham practices exemplary Near Eastern hospitality, hastening with his wife and servants to prepare a feast for them. (Later Jewish interpretation notes both the verbs indicating alacrity and the proximity of this pericope to the previous one in which Abraham was circumcised. His generous hospitality is made all the more vivid by having to overcome the pain of his recuperation. In this way, biblical stories become paradigmatic for subsequent Jewish virtue ethics.) The men/angels/God – note the instability of identity typical of pre-Axial Age reports of divine–human encounter – tell the aged and barren Sarah that she will have a child. She laughs at the news, as at an absurdity, and then dissembles in fear, telling God, when He asks, that she did not laugh (and therefore doubt Him). God replies tartly "You did laugh." But then God considers, in the subtle manner of biblical narrative, whether He ought to dissemble too, hiding from Abraham what He is considering with regard to the wicked cities of Sodom and Gomorrah.

> "Shall I hide from Abraham what I am about to do, since Abraham is about to become a great and populous nation and all the nations of the earth are to bless themselves by him? For I have singled him out, that he may instruct his children and his posterity to keep the way of the LORD by doing what is just and right, in order that the LORD may bring about for Abraham what He has promised him." (Gen. 18:17–19)

God's question may be genuine or it may be rhetorical. (Given who Abraham is going to be, how could I *not* tell him?) Abraham and his line are uniquely destined to keep the way of the LORD, to do what is just and right. A significant demonstration of justice – the deserved punishment of the wicked inhabitants of Sodom and Gomorrah – should not be hidden from him. He should see how divine justice operates in the world, especially as he is to be the founder of a "great and populous nation."

Abraham, however, does not seem to need an object lesson in divine justice. He already grasps, in a natural and rational way, as it were, the concept of justice and its implications. "Abraham remained standing before the LORD. Abraham came forward and said 'Will you sweep away the innocent along with the guilty?'" (Gen. 18:22b–23). "Standing" here refers to the behavior of a litigant, entering a lawsuit to plead for justice. Abraham makes bold to confront "the Judge of all the earth" to "deal justly" (v. 25). He both asserts his claim to speak in the name of a justice to which God too is accountable, and apologizes for his temerity, for he is but "dust and ashes" (v. 27). Abraham poses a basic moral question to God: "Will you sweep away the innocent along with the guilty? What if there should be fifty innocent within the city?" (vv. 23–24a). The concept of justice rests on the idea of desert. Justice entails giving persons, indeed, giving all beings their due.[23] To punish the wicked, on a suitable definition of wickedness, is just; to punish the innocent is unjust. Abraham does not need God to tell him this. This basic insight into the workings of desert is natural or rational. To know persons is to know their value; personhood is a value-laden fact about the world. What Abraham has yet to learn is how his natural cognition of the value of persons fares when it is enlarged to comprise a political body (the city). As Leon Kass argues, this is a story about Abraham's education in political justice.[24]

Thus, Abraham goes farther. He asks "will you then wipe the place out and not forgive it for the sake of the innocent fifty who are in it? Far be it from you to do such a thing, to bring death upon the innocent as well as the guilty, so that innocent and guilty fare alike" (vv. 24b–25). Abraham is making a case about public justice. Individuals should get what they deserve, but the embeddedness of individuals in a common life complicates the logic of desert. Persons are not just individuals but social beings ensconced in a political context where the possibility of "moral man and immoral society" emerges. How does Abraham address this social fact? He argues that the putative presence of innocents should not only prevent the destruction of the city but spare the wicked as well. It would be unjust for the innocent to receive the same treatment as the guilty; but it would be unjust for the guilty, under the circumstances, to be punished at all. Why? Given Abraham's concept of collectivity, the innocents cannot be separated from the guilty. The intermingling of all in the city is ineluctable. Deserts cannot be apportioned in a selective way; it's all or nothing at all with bodies politic. This should preempt God's exaction of justice. Abraham is not arguing that the innocent redeem the guilty; he is arguing rather that their presence complicates an otherwise just process of recompense.

Abraham then famously pushes God to withhold punishment if there were to be as few as 10 innocent people in the city. The sordid story that follows, illustrating the inhospitality and rapine of the inhabitants (Genesis, chapter 19), justifies God in destroying Sodom and Gomorrah. Presumably, God accepts Abraham's moral argument about the conditions of public justice. The facts of the case, however, allow that argument no traction. There are no innocents in the cities. After the destruction, Abraham "hurried to the place where he had stood before the LORD, and, looking down toward Sodom and Gomorrah and all the land of the Plain, he saw the smoke of the land rising like the smoke of a kiln" (Gen. 19: 27–28). Abraham accepts God's moral argument, as well.

Abraham may have a natural, rational, or moral realist apprehension of justice but he must discover its implications through application to actual cases. The story raises the issue of how justice in a public context differs from justice among private persons. Abraham's assumption, which is to say, the Bible's assumption in its earliest strata, is that groups are to be judged collectively. The social condition of human beings implies collective guilt (or innocence). The criteria by which collective guilt or innocence is determined are unclear. Some threshold of majoritarian and/or intergenerational wickedness must be crossed. This is clear in both versions of the Decalogue (Exod. 20:5; Deut. 5:9), which indicate that an impassioned God will visit "the guilt of the parents upon the children, upon the third and upon the fourth generations of those who reject" him. He will, as well, show "kindness to the thousandth generation of those who love" him. The guilt or innocence of parents is determinative of the deserts of their descendants. Belonging to a collectivity determines what one deserves – a view surely troubling to persons who live in an age that prizes individuality and valorizes autonomy. This view was, however, found wanting *within* the biblical literature itself. Already within the Pentateuch, Deuteronomy rejects it. "Parents shall not be put to death for children, nor children be put to death for parents: a person shall be put to death only for his own crime" (24:16). The prophet Ezekiel is even more forthcoming. He rejects the exiled Judeans' complaint that their ancestors were wicked but they are paying the price. Ezekiel condemns the consoling but pernicious saying, "the fathers have eaten sour grapes and the children's teeth are set on edge." He categorically asserts: "The person who sins, only he shall die" (Ezek. 18:4).[25] Here we see an Axial Age breakthrough toward a heightened concept of individuality, moral agency, and responsibility. The hold of the clan, of the collective, has been weakened. There is a theological corollary as well: the concept of repentance moves to the forefront. If one is now fully responsible for one's desert and cannot explain it by reference to one's collective situation, then one needs to examine one's ways, repent, and return to God's path.

> Yet the House of Israel say, "The way of the Lord is unfair." Are My ways unfair, O House of Israel? It is your ways that are unfair! Be assured, O House of Israel, I will judge each one of you according to his ways – declares the LORD God. Repent and turn back from your transgressions; let them not be a stumbling block of guilt for you. Cast away all the transgressions by which you have offended, and get yourselves a new heart and a new spirit, that you may not die, O House of Israel. For it is not My desire that anyone shall die – declares the LORD God. Repent, therefore, and live! (Ezek. 18:29–32)

Interestingly, this bright-line delineation of personal responsibility is addressed to the collectivity, the "House of Israel." The balance between the "lonely man of faith" and the *ben berit*, the member of a covenanted community, remains labile in subsequent Judaism.

To return to where we began, this story seems to assume the reality and accessibility of independent and objective moral knowledge, available both to God and man. Its metaethics, as it were, is realist. Whether the idea that moral value is embedded in creation, available to Israelites and non-Israelites alike, rises to a theory of natural law is debatable. What is more certain is that pure positivism, whether that of Marvin Fox or Karl Barth, misreads the biblical text. Precisely where we might expect positivism to gain the most traction, in prophecy where God speaks and commands, we immediately encounter a problem. The eighth-century prophet Amos, for example, inveighs against Israel and Judah's gentile neighbors for their barbaric conduct in war against one another (Amos 1:3–2:3). Amos castigates non-Israelites for violating what are assumed to be generally accepted moral norms of conduct. The nations have neither been commanded by God (within the universe of the text) nor subject to the covenantal stipulations of biblical law. Yet they are expected to know the relevant moral norms, presumably on the basis of their own natural moral sense.[26]

This approach to moral realism short circuits the Euthyphro problem, to an extent. What differentiates it from Socrates' position is that, for the Bible, God has made the world as it is, so moral knowledge is still dependent on God, as His creation. (Wisdom, personified, in Proverbs 8:22 declares "The LORD created me at the beginning of His course, as the first of His works of old.") Once created, however, it takes on, like all created things, a life of its own. Moral knowledge or wisdom comes in an agonistic way to human beings. It is not exactly God's free gift – He did, after all, proscribe Adam and Eve from eating the fruit of the tree that bestows it. There is a Promethean aspect to humanity's reception of moral discernment. The serpent seduces Eve with the promise that were she to eat of the fruit of the Tree of Knowledge "your eyes will be opened and you will be like divine beings who know good and bad" (Gen. 3:5). Moral knowledge mediates between humans and the divine; in being able to distinguish good from bad, humans become like God, who wrought order from chaos in creating the world and repeatedly determined that the world is good. (For example, "God said, 'Let there be light'; and there was light. God saw that the light was good, and God separated the light from the darkness" (Gen. 1:3–4).) Goodness comes from God, as does the ability to discern it. Value – although it has its remote source in God's creative act – is not presented by biblical texts as arbitrary, a product of mere fiat or divine whim. Even Job, who in the end must suspend his impassioned inquisition of God's apparent injustice, accepts God's will as bound by a higher, inscrutable justice rather than by no justice at all. The frame story of the book of Job sets forth a rationale for Job's suffering; Job will be tried so that God may demonstrate his merit. That may be cruel, but it is not senseless.

Value is embedded in nature qua creation. The knowledge of value and the capacity for evaluative judgment are primordial to human nature. They link the human to the divine. Out of this nexus arises the possibility of theomorphic action: man is to emulate God. Although radically distinct ontologically, God and the human may share such values as compassion, justice, fidelity, and generosity. Rabbinic Judaism, as we shall see in the next chapter, develops a virtue ethic, augmented by a legal framework, of imitatio dei. This is made fully systematic in the Middle Ages by Maimonides. That ethic is already established in the biblical literature, however, although not without complications and contradictions, as we shall now see.

Holiness, Goodness, and the Emulation of God

God proclaims, in one of the most oft-cited verses in the Bible: "You shall be holy, for I, the LORD your God, am holy" (Lev. 19:2). Can human beings emulate God; can they emulate God's holiness? God is holy, which as Rudolf Otto argued means "wholly Other," a *mysterium, tremendum et fascinans*, uncanny and often terrifying.[27] We typically think of holiness today in moral terms, roughly equivalent to saintly behavior, an extraordinary and consistent goodness. The Bible itself moves in that direction but it also contains something more discordant to modern ears – holiness as immense unpredictable power, which can wound and destroy as much as it can energize and vitalize.[28] In II Samuel 6:7, King David's servant, Uzzah, grabs the Ark of God as it was about to fall out of the cart carrying it up to Jerusalem and was instantly struck down, as if he had been hit by lightning. (Compare the narrative of Aaron's sons, who are eradicated by a burst of fire due to their unauthorized infringement on holy space in Lev. 10:1–2.) Holy things – things that belong to the divinity or are closely tied to His being (e.g. his Name, Exod. 3:14–15) – hold the power of life or death; they must be kept separate from ordinary things. Hence, biblical law records a great deal of conceptualization and regulation of purity and impurity, conditions which either allow for the divine presence, holiness, to be in the midst of Israel or to remain aloof from it. The dichotomy of purity and impurity (*taharah* and *tumah*) is not the same as the dichotomy of holy or sacred (*kadosh*) and profane (*ḥol*). The former facilitates or retards the presence, status, or property of the latter.[29]

In Mesopotamian societies, impurity was thought to be occasioned by demons. Demonic activity, invasion, or possession rendered one impure. The Bible, whose texts reflect the ethicizing perspective of the Axial Age, virtually eliminates the role of demonic forces (as well as malevolent deities, Fate, or necessity – the other divine and meta-divine forces of the pagan world). As Jacob Milgrom puts it:

> The Priestly theology negates these premises. It posits the existence of the supreme God who contends neither with a higher realm nor with competing peers. The world of demons is abolished; there is no struggle with autonomous foes, because there are none. With the demise of the demons, only one creature remains with "demonic" power – the human being. Endowed with free will, human power is greater than any attributed to humans by pagan society. Not only can one defy God but, in Priestly imagery, one can drive God out of his sanctuary. In this respect, humans have replaced demons.[30]

Impurity in Israel is basically harmless for those subject to it. It prevents their entrance into the holy place, first the wilderness Tabernacle and then the Temple, but it does not harm them. Impurity follows organically or mechanically from certain contingent events, such as scale diseases of the skin, as well as comparable eruptions in fabrics or on the walls of houses (Leviticus, chapters 13–14), chronic genital flows (Leviticus, chapter 15), or touching a corpse. Persons or places that have these disorders must be separated until they pass (and appropriate sacrifices are brought) lest they prevent the holy from abiding within the people Israel and, eventually, its land. In this literature, there is a mechanical, almost karmic quality to this process. The divine is envisioned not as a personal, moral being but as an impersonal, amoral, purely energetic force. The symbolism which underlies the selection of impure conditions has to do with death. The impurity laws, in their entirety, have to do with the antipode to the life-giving force of divine holiness. They indicate that the force of life (semen, blood), which is dissipated in genital discharge, or the healthy intactness of the body, which is violated by wasting disease at its boundaries (scales, earlier erroneously translated as "leprosy"), is being vanquished by the pull of death. The restoration of sufferers from these conditions reenacts a creation-like victory of life over chaos, disorder, and death. "No wonder," Milgrom writes, "that reddish substances, the surrogates of blood, are among the ingredients of the purificatory rites for scale-diseased and corpse-contaminated persons (Lev. 14:4; Num. 19:6). They symbolize the victory of the forces of life over death."[31]

Earlier generations of scholars, as well as Christian readers over the centuries, saw in the purity laws something primitive and alien, the very antithesis of ethics. That rabbinic Judaism developed and codified these laws into an even more elaborate system earned it an additional measure of scorn. Jesus' ethicizing teaching "not what goes into the mouth defiles a man, but what comes out of the mouth, this defiles a man" (Matt. 15:11) seemed to give the coup de grâce to the entire system of purity and impurity with respect to diet (*kashrut*), which remains at the core of Jewish practice and continues the logic of Leviticus' symbolism. Contemporary scholars are more understanding. The work of the anthropologist Mary Douglas, for example, established that purity and pollution rules cannot be radically divided from moral rules; there is no hard dichotomy between ritual and ethics, even when the rituals deal with the most foreign and inassimilable material. Analyzing the social function of Nuer pollution rules, Douglas shows how such rules can marshal "moral disapproval when it lags." "… when the sense of outrage is adequately equipped with practical sanctions in the social order, pollution is not likely to arise. Where, humanly speaking, the outrage is likely to go unpunished, pollution beliefs are likely to be called in to supplement the lack of other sanctions."[32] In Douglas's view, beliefs and practices related to purity and impurity are powerful adjuncts to the basic moral-normative dimensions of a given society. Typically, purity and impurity have to do with the intactness of categories and the disturbing presence of anomalies, particularly on the body. The body is thought to symbolize society as a whole; guarding the soundness of its boundaries (e.g. skin) is tantamount to guarding the uniqueness, solidarity, indeed, the holiness of the collective.[33]

The conceptual interweaving of purity and impurity, holiness, and ethics finds expression in the extension of *taharah* and *tumah* to moral matters per se. Ritual impurity, such as corpse defilement, is not sinful. But eventually the commission of grave sins such as murder (Num. 35:33–34), idolatry (Lev. 19:31; 20:1–3) or impermissible sexual acts (Lev. 18:24–30) is assimilated to the category of impurity; these sins are held to be "abominations" which defile those that commit them, the Land of Israel as a whole, and the sanctuary.[34] The accumulated impurity of such acts will result in the expulsion of the people from the Land. The Land, as a holy place, must be separated from polluting–defiling forces. The Holiness code, Leviticus chapters 17–26, shows precisely this intermingling of the ritual and the ethical, the extension of the penumbra of the purity–impurity dichotomy, as well as the complexity of biblical concepts of holiness.

The Holiness source or H represents, according to Israel Knohl, a priestly response to the ethically charged work of the prophets, especially of Isaiah.[35] Priestly theology per se reveals the marks of an Axial Age perspective. As already mentioned, the demonic had been banished and natural processes as well as human choices were thought to account for impurity. The God of priestly theology is remote, non-personal, and, according to Knohl, amoral. God is more like gravity or electromagnetism than father or judge. This reflects a high sense of transcendence, of macro-level cosmic order within which human significance is meager. The work of priests is to keep the energy flowing, as it were, to repair the breaches in the wall of purity such that God can remain connected to his sanctuary and endow his holy land and people with life. The God of H remains transcendent but is drawn into another paradigm: the God of the covenant, the God who enters into morally recognizable relations with human beings. Henceforth, holiness will have to do with more than the separation of sacred objects, persons, places, and times from the profane; it will have to do with moral life, with the quality of actions and intentions. Thus, Leviticus, chapter 19 applies considerations of holiness seamlessly to "moral" as well as to "ritual" matters. The whole range of Israelite life (and of Israelites – holiness is no longer the exclusive concern of priests) is drawn into a sacred register.

Leviticus, chapter 19 begins, as we have seen, with an injunction to *all* the Israelites to be holy, for God is holy. Immediately, a crucial "ritual" observance, the Sabbath, is linked to a "moral" one, revering father and mother (19:3). Injunctions as to the proper conduct of sacrifice (19:5–8) are juxtaposed with procedures for harvesting one's field so that produce remains for the benefit of "the poor and the stranger" (19:9–10). (These norms become foundational for the later, extensive Jewish concern with the welfare of marginal classes.) Stealing, deceptive commercial practices, fraud, retention of a worker's wages, mocking, taking advantage of or treating cruelly the deaf or the blind are related to the holiness of God. To deal falsely is equivalent to swearing falsely "by My name, profaning the name of your God" (19:12). The text is regularly punctuated with the reminder "I am the LORD" to underscore how much is at stake. God becomes an affected party in every human interaction. There is no conduct purely *inter homines*. Whether the implications of divine holiness are recognizably moral in modern terms ("Love your fellow as yourself: I am the LORD" 19:18) or rather alien to modern sensibilities ("You shall not make gashes in your flesh for the dead, or incise any marks on yourselves: I am the LORD" 19:27), correct action enables and protects God's presence in the world. Unholy action banishes it.

Later Jewish tradition took the significance of "be holy, for God is holy" to mean: be Godlike insofar as that is possible for human beings. Emulate the moral attributes of God such as compassion, forgiveness, patience, and truthfulness. "It is comparable to the court of a king. What is the court's duty? To imitate the king!"[36] But it is questionable that this is precisely what emulative holiness means in Leviticus. The overtly moral notes are clear, but so is the distinctively ritual dimension. Taking holiness in its full ritual–moral/purity–impurity complexity, the text calls for Israel's separation from the practices of its pagan neighbors. Just as God is separate, so should Israel be separate – especially from the enduring temptations of paganism, real and notional, in its own midst. Later Judaism, of course, sensed this dimension very keenly. The rabbinic halakhic midrash to Leviticus, Sifra, interprets *kedoshim tihyu* (You shall be holy) as "Israel's behavior is different from that of other nations."[37] The practice of the distinctive stipulations of the covenant, the mitzvot, renders Israel distinct from the nations. By living according to the mitzvot, Israel brings holiness qua separation into the world and creates a space for the vitalizing power of God to make its presence felt.

On this view of holiness, not only are ritual and ethics thoroughly mixed and mutually supportive but God and ethics are inextricable – and not merely as a theology of the divine nature but as a strong claim as to the presence of God. Holy acts bring divine holiness into the world. Holiness, as a concept, is incoherent without the idea of divine presence. It is the idea of God's actual presence in the sanctuary which gives purity and impurity, and consequently holiness, traction. Absent these metaphysical beliefs, the system becomes wholly symbolic, a fading metaphor for values and significance more properly conceived at another ontic level.[38] Trying to keep some strong version of holiness, call it metaphysical holiness, alive against demythologizing and ethicizing trends remains a preoccupation of subsequent Judaism. We will encounter it again in Chapter 3 on medieval Jewish ethics and in Chapter 5 on modern Jewish ethics.

Agency, Free Will, and Responsibility

Human agency is central to the Bible. Theologically minded readers, such as Abraham Joshua Heschel and, before him, Leo Adler, have accordingly argued that the Bible is less about God than about man, less about theology in the sense of a doctrine of God than about a normative anthropology.[39] The commandments presume that ought implies can; that human beings can follow them. "Surely this Instruction [Torah], which I enjoin upon you this day, is not too baffling for you, nor is it beyond reach. It is not in the heavens, that you should say, 'Who among us can go up to the heavens and get it for us and impart it to us that we may observe it?' ... No the thing is very close to you, in your mouth and in your heart, to observe it" (Deut. 30:11–14). Human beings are thought to be the authors of their own deeds. They are responsible, within limits, for the consequences of their actions, thoughts, and desires; they are able to discern and choose the right path and ought to do so.

But how far do these very robust assumptions about moral agency go? Given the evolution of a heightened sense of individual agency and responsibility in the Axial Age, does Scripture show awareness of constraints on agency, such as ungovernable passions, mental illness, inadvertence, and, more theoretically, the problem of free will and determinism?[40] Biblical law and narrative recognize some of these constraints. Deuteronomy 19:4–5 recognizes the constraint of pure contingency: Two men are cutting wood and, by accident, the handle flies off the axe of one and kills the other. The survivor is not a murderer, but neither is he free from guilt. He has killed inadvertently and has to flee to a "city of refuge" where the family member of the deceased (the "blood avenger") is not allowed to hunt him down. I Samuel 1:12–19 recognizes that drunkenness, while shameful, would account for and excuse puzzling behavior. Extreme passion can lead to vicious behavior, such as rape (II Samuel, chapter 13). King David, although not his son Absalom, apparently excused Amnon's rapine because of his deranged emotions. (Absalom later had him murdered.) In each of these cases, the Bible acknowledges that we are not always in full control of ourselves. An adequate law and ethics needs to account for such constraints on agency. It needs to diminish responsibility for acts where constraints are in play.

But what if the constraints are not merely adventitious but structural? What if they are routinely built into the way things are such that responsibility is thrown radically into question? The conceptual problem of freedom in a putatively deterministic, fated cosmos does not come into clear focus until the Stoics. We should not, of course, expect a rigorous examination of it in the biblical literature. Nonetheless, the free will/determinism problem does make an appearance. This should not be surprising, as it grows out of the natural human awareness that sometimes action is more or less compelled, more or less restrained. As alluded to above, passions, drives, hunger, lust, as well as kings and commanders, friends, and God can compel us to act. One can naturally imagine a contrast between action under constraining conditions and action in a context of greater liberty. One need not be a philosopher to recognize oneself as a moral agent within these different orders of condition. There is no reason to doubt that biblical Israelites shared this moral imagination.

As we have seen, mature biblical religion rejects inter-generational punishment for misdeeds. Both Deuteronomy and Ezekiel assert that every individual accounts only for his or her own sins. That mature view increases moral agency and responsibility. Yet dissonant notes remain. Jeremiah, a reluctant prophet, is told "Before I created you in the womb, I selected you; Before you were born, I consecrated you; I appointed you a prophet concerning the nations" (Jer. 1:5). The issue here is neither sin nor punishment but ranges of condition that limit freedom of choice. Jeremiah's choices in life were severely constrained, to say the least. Here something like fate enters the picture, a constraint on freedom of agency so deep as to be structural. (The more common case, however, is of the reluctant prophet who fears to accept his call. Consider Jonah, for example, who fled the divine charge to rebuke Nineveh and wound up in the belly of a "huge fish" for three days and three nights (Jon. 2:1). God's intentions for the prophet are irresistible. This also suggests an awareness of "metaphysical" constraints on moral agency.)

The problem of metaphysical or structural constraints on an agent's range of choice, and hence on his accountability and responsibility, is raised by the Exodus narrative of Moses and Pharaoh. In the course of telling Moses to go to Pharaoh and plead with him to let the Israelites go, God famously "hardens Pharaoh's heart" and constrains his choices. This immediately raises the moral conundrum, which gives the freedom/determinism problem its human significance, of whether God is punishing Pharaoh unjustly. If he cannot choose to let the Israelites go, in what sense is it just to punish him for his refusal?[41]

When God commissions Moses to go before Pharaoh and demand that he release Israel from bondage, God announces that:

> I will harden Pharaoh's heart, that I may multiply My signs and marvels in the land of Egypt. When Pharaoh does not heed you, I will lay My hand upon Egypt and deliver My ranks, My people the Israelites, from the land of Egypt with extraordinary chastisements. And the Egyptians shall know that I am the LORD ... (Exod. 7:3–5)

God appears to deny Pharaoh freedom of choice; even if he wanted to repent, he would not be able to do so. He would not have, as contemporary philosophers say, liberty of indifference; that is, he would not be able to choose among possible options. He would be constrained to choose only one – refusal to let Israel go. Does this not count against God's justice? Furthermore, God intends to use Pharaoh, as Kant might put it, as a means rather than an end. God will make a display of Pharaoh so that the Egyptians will know who is really in charge. God has not only removed Pharaoh's freedom of choice; He has made Pharaoh an unwilling tool of divine pedagogy.

At first glance, the text seems innocent of the moral complications it engenders, as if the loss of Pharaoh's moral agency were not an issue. But that may not be the case. As the medieval Jewish exegetes noticed, the motif of heart-hardening is artfully arranged and the arrangement is no doubt significant. It occurs precisely 20 times. Pharaoh hardens his own heart 10 times (Exod. 7:13, 14, 22; 8:11, 15, 28; 9:7, 34, 35; 13:15) and God hardens it (or announces He will harden it) another 10 (Exod. 4:21, 7:3, 9:12, 10:1, 20, 27; 11:10, 14:4, 8, 17). Crucially, God's hardening of Pharaoh's heart does not begin until the sixth plague. "For the first five plagues," Nahum Sarna writes, "the pharaoh's obduracy is a product of his own volition."[42] Even after the first instance where God directly stiffens Pharaoh's heart (9:12), we read that once again Pharaoh is responsible for hardening his own heart (9:34–35). Only afterwards does his agency decline. In this subtle narrative way, the writer seems to give us a clue to his awareness of the moral problem and to the solution for it. Pharaoh brought his calamity upon himself. Later Jewish exegetes will pick up this clue: having made himself guilty through his invidious choices, the hardening of Pharaoh's heart is not a prelude to his punishment, it *is* his punishment. He is the author of his own hopeless situation. Being unable to repent, to atone for one's deeds, to be trapped without possibility of release in a vicious way of life is its own punishment. It is a choice against life, in the sense of full human flourishing; it is a choice for death.

Pharaoh's is an extreme case where the constraint on desire, choice, and action is purely internal to the agent. More typically, constraint on agency comes in the form of difficult circumstances, some of them engineered by God, which circumscribe and limit one's range of choice. The fact that the Bible portrays God as a character, working behind the scenes to challenge human beings, need not dismay the skeptical reader. What is important here is not the cause of constraint but the reality of it and the challenge it poses to successful moral deliberation and choice. Biology (and God) has prevented Sarah or Rachel or Hannah from conceiving but what is really important is the quality of their understanding of, and response to, their hardship. Up against these discouraging situations, they show their mettle, anger, hope, despondency, impatience, or courage. Without internal, psychological depiction, the Bible nonetheless reveals the complexity of its characters, as well as their moral stature, virtues, and failures. The tense, intricate narrative of the competition between Jacob's wives, Leah and Rachel, for example, in Genesis, chapter 30, reveals in just a few strokes how human beings cope with the adversities of a "step-motherly nature." Rachel emerges as both petulant and pious, conflicted and joyous – the very model of a realistic human being. The Bible's portrayal of its characters, especially in Genesis, emphasizes their flawed humanity. They grope to do the right thing, the good thing, untutored by anything other than their own resources of experience and tradition, and occasionally by the illumination of the deity. Later tradition garbs these characters with the cloak of saintliness; the Bible covers them with rougher garments. It paints them in vivid, contrasting colors rather than the pastel hues of subsequent faith.[43]

The Bible's representation of human agency remains robust, perhaps unrealistically so. Contemporary cognitive neuroscience has brought the old philosophical problem of free will and determinism back into the intellectual spotlight. How can a complex physical system – the human brain – generate a realm of consciousness or experience which seems to float above the laws of physics, which govern physical systems? How could a gap arise between neurobiological matter, subject to the laws of physics, and consciousness, which seems from our internal, first personal perspective to be at least relatively independent of cause and effect considerations, at least of cause and effect considerations of a physical kind?[44] If it could be shown, as many contemporary physicalists think, that there is no gap, that the laws of physics govern mental phenomena all the way down to their chemical and electrical origins, then robust accounts of desire, choice, and agency look naïve. The Bible's metaphysics of morals, as it were, would be shown to be unrealistic. God's charge to Israel to keep His law, the prophets' ceaseless call to Israel to change its ways, and the Wisdom literature's prudential nostrums for how an Israelite should conduct him or herself would all be based on an overly sanguine assessment of human freedom. As one neuroscientist puts it, we don't have freedom of will, we have "freedom of won't."[45] That is, we cannot control the wellsprings of our intentionality. By the time thought, desire, and so on reach our conscious awareness, they have already been causally determined and we have already been set on a certain path by them. What we can do is filter, sort, censor, and defer some of these impulses and intentions. But the ability to do so may itself be biologically determined. Thus, on a neurobiological account, it's not that we could not walk in God's ways. It is that some would be constitutionally more able to do so than others. Some would have greater native ability to assess, evaluate, and respond relevantly than others. Just as some are able to do mathematics, paint, or learn languages better than others, so too deep biological factors might constrain moral intelligence and facility. We are much less the authors of our own deeds than we think. The Bible might speak well to the internal, first personal psychological framework within which we understand ourselves as ethical beings, but it would not speak at all to the underlying neurobiological conditions of which the psychological framework is a higher-order expression. Ignorant of the deep existence conditions which make moral psychology possible, a biblical understanding of human agency quickly reaches or overshoots its limits. On this view, the biblical emphasis on a strong version of agency and responsibility would severely circumscribe its relevance to the challenges of a twenty-first-century ethics.

A fuller account than can be offered here might further qualify the strength of moral agency and complicate the picture. We have already seen how the Bible presents responsible moral agency against a backdrop of constraint.

Consider another example of this. In Genesis 4:6–7, Cain is told by God, when he is disheartened that his offering was not accepted, "Why are you distressed, and why is your face fallen? Surely, if you do right, there is uplift. But if you do not do right sin couches at the door; its urge is toward you, yet you can be its master." Here we have a keen sense that wayward intentions and desires (personified as sin couching at the door) are native to us; their sway over us is almost ineluctable. We are constituted in a way that makes our aspiration to goodness fragile. Yet we are not powerless over its power; we can still choose to do right. Genesis, like Freud, in full recognition of the darkness within and around us would still give reason, however halting or thin, a role in our moral regeneration. We can, challenged though we are, still choose to do right. This hope, of course, does not answer the challenge of neurobiology. But it does show awareness of how recalcitrant the nature of our humanity is. That the Bible can grasp that and still come down on the side of hope for the possibility of moral regeneration, without naïveté, has had a profound impact on the history of Jewish ethics, as well as on the moral thought of the West.

Discernment and choice remain at the center of biblical ethics. The world, as a created order wrought from primordial chaos, is good. We are equipped to discern the good and to enact it. The value embedded in the world, qua creation, already limns the outlines of a best way of life for human beings. The world is so arranged that human beings can flourish within it if they follow this way. The way can be discerned. It is available to non-Israelites, through moral reason. Its most basic principle is one of respect, reciprocity, and limit: "Whoever sheds the blood of man, by man shall his blood be shed" (Gen. 9:6). (In subsequent Judaism, the best or morally appropriate life for non-Jews is elaborated on the basis of this and other postdiluvian verses. Non-Jews are thought to be in a covenant initiated by God with Noah. Their covenantal framework is called the Noaḥide Laws.[46]) For Israelites, however, the way of life acquires specificity and determination as it is progressively revealed by a concerned God who would adopt Israel as His special possession. But moral reason, choice, and agency do not drop out of the picture after God enters it. The way is broadly mapped by God's teaching and example, by the emulation of God's holiness – by fidelity to the relationship with God framed by the stipulations and spirit of the covenant – but Israelites have to discern it and choose it, both initially and continuously. (Note, for example, the prevalence of covenant renewal occasions in the Bible.[47]) The way is thus discovered and revealed, revealed and discovered yet again. Moral consciousness precedes the giving of the Torah. But the Torah gives further definition and determination to a primordial awareness of the good and the right. The Torah, once accepted, needs to be reaffirmed on the basis of a moral reason that has itself been educated and refined by the Torah. The Torah both evokes and demands the continuous exertion of moral reason. And the Torah itself grows in the light of it.

The emphasis on agency, choice, and responsibility works in tandem with the basic trope of covenant. In a covenantal relationship, the parties retain their individual existence; they join their lives together, but they remain ontologically distinct. They appeal to the best in one another, transforming themselves in the direction of moral perfection, without shedding their distinctive personae. The world is not an illusion. Atman is not Brahman. Persons are real and durable. Time and space, history and land are realities that enable and constrain human action, the doing of which enacts God's goodness or drives it from the world. The bridge between the ultimate and the human is not notional, it is actionable. It requires constant attention, dedication, and assent. Thus, Deuteronomy thematizes choice:

> See, I set before you this day life and prosperity, death and adversity. For I command you this day, to love the LORD your God, to walk in His ways, and to keep His commandments, His laws, and His rules, that you may thrive and increase, and that the LORD your God may bless you in the land that you are about to enter and possess. But if your heart turns away and you give no heed, and are lured into the worship and service of other gods, I declare to you this day that you shall certainly perish; you shall not long endure on the soil that you are crossing the Jordan to enter and possess. I call heaven and earth to witness against you this day: I have put before you life and death, blessing and curse. Choose life – if you and your offspring would live – by loving the LORD your God, heeding His commands, and holding fast to Him. For thereby you shall have life and shall long endure upon the soil that the LORD swore to your ancestors, Abraham, Isaac, and Jacob to give to them. (Deut. 30:15–20)

Would the Israelite flourish because he follows the divine command qua command, that is, because he does God's will and is rewarded for doing so? Or would he flourish because the way of life which the text enjoins him to choose is intrinsically excellent? There is a tension here between two types of ground for a life in which one can "thrive and increase"; are they natural or revealed? The above text seems to come down hard on the side of revelation. If God did not desire that the Israelites "walk in His ways" and "keep His commandments" then there would be no advantage for them to do so. Another less encumbered way of life might be best for them. On this view, the law is simply positive. It has no intrinsic merit. The various incipient reasons that the Torah provides for observance, for example, the Decalogue's "Honor your father and your mother, that you may long endure on the land that the LORD your God is assigning to you" (Exod. 20:12), are meaningful only insofar as they please God. If God had decreed that you should dishonor your father and mother, then that would be the condition for long endurance upon the land. This form of pure voluntarism had its advocates in subsequent Jewish thought, but the sounder tradition is the one that exemplifies the Axial Age orientation.[48] The gods of myth are capricious. The God of Israel, albeit ineradicably mysterious, is a god of justice whose ways can be known and emulated ("The Rock! His deeds are perfect, Yea, all His ways are just" Deut. 32:4.) His commandments, although not reducible to an ethics, can pass muster before the bar of moral reason.

Nonetheless, there is distance between the open-ended Socratic question of how one is to live (*Republic* 352d) and the biblical answer that one is to live by walking in God's ways, where those ways are seen through the prism of a law understood by the biblical authors to be heaven-sent. The Bible does not relax this tension. It invites rational inquiry into its ethics. The canonical text even contains traditions of purely prudential, international, and secularly oriented moral teachings in the form of the Wisdom literature. (For example, Prov. 4:20–23: "My son, listen to my speech; incline your ear to my words. Do not lose sight of them; keep them in your mind. They are life to him who finds them, healing for his whole body. More than all that you guard, guard your mind, for it is the source of life." Mind (literally, heart) as the source of life!) The Bible does not restrict appropriate moral life and correlative human flourishing to the recipients of a particular divine revelation. Nonetheless, it puts that revelation in the foreground of its vision of the good life for man. It remains for the inheritors of the biblical traditions of moral reason *and* of Greek ethics, the Jews of the Hellenistic world, to explore this tension and to build a theoretical bridge between its two poles.

Hebraism and Hellenism

The Jews of Alexandria, whose community dated from the founding of the city by Alexander the Great in 332 BCE, used the language of Greek thought to articulate, indeed, to theorize the ethics of Scripture. In their writings, something like a self-consciously philosophical ethics emerges. The opposition between "Hebraism" and "Hellenism" became a standard trope among Victorians – Matthew Arnold wrote a famous essay sensitively contrasting the two as competing but ultimately complementary worldviews – but ancient Greco-Jewish authors found more complementarity than competition.[49] Let us consider briefly how the *Letter of Aristeas* and Philo of Alexandria attempt to synthesize biblical and Hellenistic approaches to ethics.

The *Letter of Aristeas*, as it has come to be known, is a pseudepigraphic work claiming to have been written by a councilor and diplomat in the service of King Ptolemy II Philadelphus of Alexandria, who reigned from 285 to 247 BCE.[50] Aristeas is not Jewish, but is a friend of the Jews. The king dispatches him on a mission to Jerusalem to ask the High Priest to send Jewish sages, "six from each tribe," to translate the Bible into Greek, so that it might take an honored place in the library of Alexandria. Aristeas recounts his diplomatic mission (including acting beneficently on behalf of some enslaved Jews in Ptolemaic Egypt before he leaves), his trip to Jerusalem, gift-giving and dialogue with the High Priest, and finally return to Alexandria. Much of the book is taken up by Aristeas' dialogue with the High Priest, Eleazar, and by the king's dialogue with the Jewish sages who have returned with Aristeas. The latter dialogues occur over the course of several days in the context of symposia, that is, philosophical banquets. The conversations between Aristeas and Eleazar, and between the king and the sages, are full of ethical considerations. It is here that biblical thought is framed in categories intelligible to Greeks. The book goes on to describe the translation of the Bible into Greek, known as the Septuagint, and its joyous acceptance by the Jewish community in a public reading reminiscent, perhaps deliberately, of the covenant renewal ceremonies of the Bible. For our purposes, however, the dialogues are most significant.

Unlike biblical literature, *Aristeas* propounds a distinctly philosophical ethics. The Law as a whole has a purpose: to inculcate monotheism (132).[51] The general principles of God's oneness, sovereignty, and omniscience – "principles of piety and justice"(131) – are made real in Jews' lives through deeds. The lawgiver, Moses, devised a code that would promote wise and temperate action. The Law follows the mean ("and that is the best course"), a clear reference to Aristotle (122). The other nations follow false gods, principally ancient worthies who have been foolishly divinized by their credulous followers. (Our author adopts here the theory of the origins of religion propounded by the Greek thinker Euhemerus.[52]) Moses, accordingly, had to keep the Jews from mingling "with any of the other nations, remaining pure in body and in spirit, emancipated from vain opinions, revering the one and mighty God above the whole of creation" (139). A basic purpose of the Law then is to separate the Jews from all others so that their contemplation of the One God and their just actions will not be corrupted. *Aristeas* explicates this theory with reference to the dietary laws, whose deepest purpose reinforces this ideal. "These laws have all been solemnly drawn up for the sake of justice, to promote holy contemplation and the perfecting of character" (144). Each prohibited animal has an allegorical meaning. Prohibited animals tend to exhibit especially violent traits. Hence by abstaining from eating carnivores, the lawgiver has taught the Jews "that they must be just and achieve nothing by violence, nor, confiding in their own strength, must they oppress others" (148). In addition to moral virtues such as gentleness and justice, the dietary laws also inculcate intellectual virtues. Eating only mammals that part the hoof and chew the cud "to thinking men clearly signifies memory." "For the chewing of the cud is nothing else than recalling life and its subsistence, since life appears to subsist through taking food" (154).[53] The extensive use of allegory, a Hellenistic hermeneutic technique first used to adapt Homer to an age that no longer shared Homeric values, appears again in Philo. Later Judaism treats allegory with great caution in reaction to the heavy employment of it by the Church. (We will, however, see the use of allegoresis in the service of finding rational significance in the commandments again when we explore Maimonides in Chapter 3.)

The odd thing about this teaching is that the medium by which it is ostensibly given is at odds with its content. The High Priest here is expounding the meaning of the Law in general and *kashrut* in particular to the purported gentile author of the letter. The very premise of separation, which the Law aims to enhance, is subverted by the friendly philosophical exchange between appreciative gentile and philosophical Jew. Indeed, the text presents an almost utopian meeting of minds – a sympathetic gentile philosopher-monotheist for whom "Zeus" is just the Greek name for the One the Jews know as God, tolerant, expressive sage-like Jews, who are eager to expound their law in Hellenistic terms, a righteous philosopher king, eager to learn and greatly approving of the Jews' wisdom. Habermas could not have imagined a more ideal communication situation. This separation cum subversion intensifies as the text moves to the philosophical dialogue between the king and the sages. The dialogues take place over food, prepared by the royal court in accordance with the dietary requirements of the Jewish guests – a far cry from medieval prohibitions on commensality even if dietary specifications are satisfied.

As a sovereign, the king is a public person interested not only in how to be a good man but in how to be a good king. The sages, therefore, tailor their presentation of Jewish moral wisdom to the needs of political ethics. Insofar as all of the norms of the law "have been regulated with a view to justice and that nothing has been set down through Scripture heedlessly or in the spirit of myth" (168), the Law already has a political cast. Moses has given the constitution of an ideal society along the lines of Plato's fictional philosopher king. The sages basically counsel the king to imitate God (to act as Jews ideally seek to act). This means that he must practice patience, gentleness, and justice toward his subjects, "dealing with those who merit punishment more gently than they deserve" (188). He must, like God, set an example of righteousness for his people. He will by so doing "turn them from wickedness and bring them to repentance" (188). He must be impartial in speech, never arrogant or tyrannical. He must understand that all human beings share the same capacity for flourishing as for suffering. Once this truth is grasped, he will find himself in solidarity with others and find courage therein (197). Mutual respect reaches its apogee in the negative formulation of the golden rule: "Just as you do not wish evils to befall you, but to participate in all that is good, so you should deal with those subject to you and with offenders, and you should admonish good men and true very gently, for God deals with all men with gentleness" (207).

The ethics of *Aristeas* is to some degree naturalistic, if by naturalism we mean something as capacious as one would find in the Stoics. God has made us and our world in a certain way: to seek Him, to be able to contemplate His power and wisdom, to live in light of truths about His nature, the upshot of which is that our souls should be well ordered, that we should seek the mean in all of our acts, and that we should have a great deal of fellow feeling for one another. This is not an outlook that depends heavily on revelation, but neither is it self-sufficiently secular in a modern sense. Consciousness of God's governance and judgment is fundamental to this outlook, but it rests at the level of a philosophical premise shared by both philosophical gentile and Jew. The emphasis is on the perspicacity and insight of the Lawgiver, Moses, not on the miraculous deliverance of a Law from heaven. Indeed, in *Aristeas'* account of the translation of the Bible the miracle story of 70 isolated sages translating the text in exact accord with one another, as reported by Philo and others, is missing. The only miracle in *Aristeas* is the extraordinarily high degree of friendship between Jew and Greek. Nonetheless, it is true that for *Aristeas*, as for other works of Greco-Jewish synthesis, the Torah remains superior to philosophy. The reconstruction of the Torah along the lines of a philosophical wisdom, however, qualifies this doctrinaire confidence.

Philo of Alexandria (c.20 BCE–50 CE) was a prolific author, whose many works were lost to Judaism but preserved by the Church. If a leading scholar of his work, Harry Austryn Wolfson, is correct, Philo is to be credited with inventing a tradition of religious philosophy that shaped the thought of the West down to its dismantling by another Jewish thinker, Spinoza.[54] Philo had an immense impact on Christianity but none on post-Hellenistic Judaism. Alexandrian Christian Fathers such as Origen and Clement learned from his work. Later, Eusebius and Jerome cite him and attest to his influence. Were it not for affinities between his thought and nascent Christianity, his work would have disappeared. The chief affinity is to be found in Philo's doctrine of the Logos, a mediating presence between the unknowable God, which Philo calls *To On*, The Existent One, and the ideas of God which we can entertain as earthbound yet soul-infused creatures.[55] Philo relies heavily on the concept of the Logos, which, in accord with the evolution of Platonism, is reified into something like a spiritual entity. The Logos is both conceived by mind and has independent extra-mental existence. In this Platonized Judaism, the Logos is a gift and expression of God's providence:

> To his chief messenger and most venerable Logos, the Father who engendered the universe has granted the singular gift, to stand between and separate the

creature from the Creator. This same Logos is both suppliant of ever anxiety-ridden mortality before the immortal and ambassador of the ruler to the subject. He glories in this gift and proudly describes it in these words, "And I stood between the Lord and you" (Deut. 5:5), neither unbegotten as God, nor begotten as you, but midway between the two extremes, serving as a pledge for both; to the Creator as assurance that the creature should never completely shake off the reins and rebel, choosing disorder rather than order; to the creature warranting his hopefulness that the gracious God will never disregard his own work. For I am an ambassador of peace to creation from the God who has determined to put down wars, who is ever the guardian of peace.[56]

In the order of ideas, the intelligible world, the Logos is the image of the essentially unknowable God. At the next level, the world of perception, the sensible world per se is the image of the Logos.[57] The Logos made flesh in John's Gospel expresses a similar, if more extreme, version of this process of hypostasis. Law, virtue, knowledge, and wisdom (the latter stage representing the Torah's supremacy over philosophy, however elevated) instantiate the work of the Logos.

Philo, like Plato, theorizes a highly dichotomized universe where the truly human, the rational soul derived from the divine and expressive of the Logos, is trapped in the material shell of the body. The goal of life is communion with the divine source, achieved through a rational mysticism structured by Jewish law and wisdom. The Bible is read allegorically as instruction on the journey of the soul back to its divine source. Some of the characters of the Bible are ancient heroes and villains, but they are also, more importantly, symbols of human experience and its possibilities. Sarah, who is a pure symbol not an actual person, is the virginal divine wisdom, the Logos, with whom Abraham, rising from the nescience and materiality of Haran, eventually mates.[58] Philo interprets God's call to Abraham to "go forth from your native land and from your father's house to the land that I will show you (Gen. 12:1)" as an allegory of spiritual growth. The soul is bidden to journey beyond body and sense perception ("native land"), as well as beyond speech ("father's house").

If then, my soul, a yearning comes upon you to inherit the divine goods, abandon not only your land, that is, the body, your kinsfolk, that is, the senses; your father's house (Gen. 12:1), that is, speech, but escape also your own self and stand aside from yourself, like persons possessed and corybants seized by Bacchic frenzy and carried away by some kind of prophetic inspiration. For it is the mind that is filled with the Deity and no longer in itself, but is agitated and maddened by a heavenly passion, drawn by the truly Existent and attracted upward to it, preceded by truth, which removes all obstacles in its path so that it may advance on a level highway – such a mind has the inheritance.[59]

The thorough, extreme application of allegory seems arbitrary to a modern reader but was standard fare in the Stoic circles of Hellenistic antiquity. Philo was not the first to apply the technique to Scripture but he was its most outstanding practitioner. Where Philo draws the line on allegory, however, is when its use would obliterate the observance of Jewish law. The Sabbath and holidays, for example, are understood symbolically but that does not dissolve their binding, normative character. Philo's extensive project of what rabbinic Judaism calls *ta'amei ha-mitzvot*, searching for "reasons for the commandments," disallows a rationality which would undermine the mitzvot themselves.[60]

Philo's sharp soul/body dualism undergirds his ethics. Abraham's journey provides a model for how the soul frees itself from the shackles of materiality and sensuality, rising to pure contemplation of the Logos. The intellectual and moral virtues prepare and enable the soul that seeks ultimate wisdom to reach its perfection. Moses' project of philosophic constitutionalism establishes an ethical–political order where the devotee of wisdom can lead a flourishing life. Israel, under the guidance of the eternally valid order of its philosopher king, shows humanity the ideal form of the Megalopolis – the great polity that unites the cosmos. Israel under the Torah is the model for the life which best accords with nature.

Philo does not scant revelation, although given his epistemology and metaphysics of the Logos, it is not quite clear how miraculous a process revelation is. Nonetheless, he is at pains to argue for the naturalness of the ethics and law of the Torah. Turning again to his allegory of Abraham:

> We are told next that "Abraham went forth as the Lord had spoken to him" (Gen. 12:4). This is the end celebrated by the best philosophers, to live in agreement with nature; and it is attained whenever the mind, having entered on the path of virtue, treads the track of right reason and follows God, mindful of his ordinances, and always and everywhere confirming them all both by word and deed. For "he went forth as the Lord spoke to him": The meaning of this is that as God speaks – and he speaks in a manner most admirable and praiseworthy – so the man of virtue does everything, blamelessly making straight his life-path, so that the actions of the sage differ in no way from the Divine words.[61]

The patriarchs, living before the time of Moses, perfectly exemplify the laws of nature. "For they were not pupils or disciples of others, nor were they instructed by tutors what to say or do: They were self-taught and were laws unto themselves, and clinging fondly to conformity with nature, and assuming nature itself to be, as indeed it is, the most venerable of statutes, their whole life was well ordered."[62] These laws are unwritten. Mosaic, that is, written law is comprised of detailed, special "copies" of the unwritten law. The Mosaic constitution and polity replicate, through statute, what the patriarchs lived, in their untutored way, namely, a life conforming to the highest standards of natural normativity.

The Logos guides through right reason, exemplified to the greatest extent by Abraham and Moses. The positive laws of cities, in all of their diversity, originate from right reason but diverge from it in equal measure. Only the law of Israel, which is eternal, partakes fully in right reason, which accords with nature. Philo, in keeping with his Hellenistic reconstruction of Judaism, does not see the Lawgiver, Moses, fundamentally as a commander. Moses works by teaching and admonition, not by the application of external force and authority. The Law appeals to the Logos, the image of divine reason resident in each man. The epistemic element is primary. Although not wholly abandoning the foundational idea of covenant, these Hellenistic sources shift the emphasis from covenant to constitution, an intentional rational design for a polity in which human beings may flourish.

Space does not permit a detailed study of Philo's ethics. This brief survey should indicate, however, the extent to which he (and *Aristeas*) strove to present Jewish ethics as compatible with contemporary constructions of rationality. Nature and reason are not the sole grounds of Jewish ethics. Nonetheless, whatever has been disclosed to Israel by the Existent One must give an account (a *logos*, in the original non-metaphysical sense) of itself in which it renders itself intelligible before the bar of nature, reason, and civil virtue. This philosophical impulse was not shared by rabbinic Judaism, at least to so marked an extent. We will probe the possibilities and limits of a naturalistic and rational construction of Jewish ethics, as understood by the sages of midrash and Talmud, in the next chapter.

Notes

1   A sophisticated analysis of Abraham's argument with God as a possible example of a shared moral understanding is found in Michael J. Harris, *Divine Command Ethics: Jewish and Christian Perspectives* (London: Routledge Curzon, 2003), pp. 59–66. Harris postulates a range of nuanced positions from an utterly heteronymous divine command morality on the one hand to a Euthyphro-style normativity independent of God on the other. It is in the middle range of this polarity where the implicit moral grounding of biblical texts seems to lie. As analytically precise as Harris's typology is, one wonders whether it is *too* precise for the materials under consideration. His methodology raises, for me at least, a caution about the extent to which the full rigor of analytic philosophy can profitably be brought to bear on traditional Jewish texts. Compare Cyril Rodd, *Glimpses of a Strange Land: Studies in Old Testament Ethics* (Edinburgh: T&T Clark, 2001), p. 65: "But the writer of the story of Abraham and perhaps the aggrieved men of Judah whose questioning Ezekiel recorded, were sufficiently bold to posit an ethics to which even God had to submit, for if he did not he would have been guilty of injustice."

2   Erich Auerbach, *Mimesis: The Representation of Reality in Western Literature*, trans. Willard R. Trask (Princeton: Princeton University Press, 1953), Chapter 1.

3   The number 24 is arrived at as follows: five books constitute the Pentateuch; the Prophets – counting Samuel and Kings as one book each and the minor prophets, from Hosea to Malachi, as one book – comprise eight, plus 11 in the Writings.

4   Stephen Geller, "The Religion of the Bible," in Adele Berlin and Marc Zvi Brettler, eds, *The Jewish Study Bible* (New York: Oxford University Press, 2004), pp. 2021–2040. The schematic presentation of biblical religion which follows is based on that of my colleague, Prof. Geller, in this trenchant article. This presentation, in keeping with the historical perspective of this book, brackets out theological claims about revelation. This should not be taken to imply a disinterest in, or disregard for, this important issue. If I were writing a theology of Jewish ethics, rather than a history, I would have taken a different approach.

5   Karl Jaspers, *The Origin and Goal of History* (New Haven: Yale University Press, 1953), p. 3. For Jaspers, this profound global intellectual transformation came about as "consciousness became … conscious of itself, thinking became its own object" (p. 2). The immediacy and naïveté of the world of myth was irreparably broken. As a methodological note, I would add that the concept of the Axial Age is not per se explanatory; it is descriptive.

6   S. N. Eisenstadt, ed., *The Origins and Diversity of Axial Age Civilizations* (Albany: State University of New York Press, 1986), p. 3.

7   For the classic scholarly account of this process, see Jon Levenson, *Creation and the Persistence of Evil: The Jewish Drama of Divine Omnipotence* (Princeton: Princeton University Press, 1994).

8   On encounter with God on the most archaic understanding of the divine in the Hebrew Bible, see James L. Kugel, *The God of Old: Inside the Lost World of the Bible* (New York: The Free Press, 2003), Chapter 2.

9   Eisenstadt, *The Origins and Diversity of Axial Age Civilizations*, p. 8. For a general theory of normativity in the Axial Age vis-à-vis its predecessor epochs, see Eric Voegelin, *The New Science of Politics* (Chicago: University of Chicago Press, 1987), Chapter 2.

10   It is controversial whether the concept of covenant arises relatively late or relatively early in the history of the religion of Israel. Wellhausen thought it late; many but not all twentieth-century scholars, under the influence of the discovery of ancient Near Eastern treaty texts, thought it to be an early phenomenon. A contemporary exposition of the view that covenant becomes an organizing concept no earlier than literary prophecy may be found in Ernest W. Nicholson, *God and His People: Covenant and Theology in the Old Testament* (Oxford: Oxford University Press, 1988), p. 191.

11   See for example Saul's attempt to exercise rational discretion, against a divine command of total proscription, I Samuel 15:7–13.

12   See the four-volume work of Daniel J. Elazar, *The Covenant Tradition in Politics*, which systematically traces the influence of biblical covenanting on the political forms of the West. See also Eric Nelson, *The Hebrew Republic: Jewish Sources and the Transformation of European Political Thought* (Cambridge, MA:

Harvard University Press, 2010) and Gordon Schochet, Fania Oz-Salzberger, and Meirav Jones, eds, *Political Hebraism: Judaic Sources in Early Modern Political Thought* (Jerusalem: Shalem Press, 2008).

13 In the case of the United States, the Constitution invokes the presumed right of the American people to form a "more perfect union." This assumes the legitimate foundation of that people, in the Declaration of Independence, under the laws of nature and nature's God.

14 Alan Mittleman, "The Durability of Goodness," in Jonathan Jacobs, ed., *Judaic Sources and Western Thought: Jerusalem's Enduring Presence* (Oxford: Oxford University Press, 2011).

15 William F. Harris II, *The Interpretable Constitution* (Baltimore: Johns Hopkins University Press, 1993), p. ix. For more on the parallels between covenant and constitution, see Alan Mittleman, *The Scepter Shall Not Depart from Judah*, Chapter 8.

16 The modern scholarly consensus is that the core of Deuteronomy is what was discovered in the Temple and promulgated by the seventh-century Judean monarch, Josiah, as presented in II Kings, chapters 22–23.

17 For the broad impact of Deuteronomy and its covenantal religion on biblical religion, see Geller, "The Religion of the Bible," pp. 2031–2033. For the ideal, utopian character of Deuteronomy per se and the attempts both to implement and scale back its most aspirational claims in the subsequent deuteronomistic literature, see Bernard M. Levinson, "The Reconceptualization of Kingship in Deuteronomy and the Deuteronomistic History's Transformation of Torah," *Vetus Testamentum*, Vol. LI, No. 4 (2001), pp. 511–534.

18 H. L. A. Hart, *The Concept of Law* (Oxford: Oxford University Press, 1997), p. 39.

19 See Bernard M. Levinson, "The Reconceptualization of Kingship in Deuteronomy and the Deuteronomistic History's Transformation of Torah."

20 A useful discussion of this topic, under the rubric of "divine commands or natural law," may be found in John Barton, *Ethics and the Old Testament* (Harrisburg: Trinity Press International, 1998), pp. 58–76. I agree with Barton's assessment that "The biblical writers often argue not from what God has declared or revealed, but from what is apparent on the basis of the nature of human life in society" (p. 61).

21 Lenn Goodman argues that the alleged dilemma in the *Euthyphro* is more apparent than real. The dialogue "hints at a complementarity of divine commands with human moral insights. Values are constitutive in ideas of divinity and monotheism affirms only goodness in God." See Lenn E. Goodman, "Ethics and God," *Philosophical Investigations*, Vol. 34, No. 2 (April 2011), pp. 135–150.

22 See, for example, Hilary Putnam, "Beyond the Fact/Value Dichotomy," in Hilary Putnam, *Realism with a Human Face* (Cambridge, MA: Harvard University Press, 1990), pp. 135–141, as well as in many of his later works.

23 For a philosophical account of justice shaped from biblical and rabbinic sources, see Lenn E. Goodman, *On Justice: An Essay in Jewish Philosophy* (Portland, OR: The Littman Library of Jewish Civilization, 2008). Goodman's scheme of justice involves the consideration of the deserts of all beings; being itself makes claims.

24   Leon Kass, in his close and subtle reading of this story, sees it as a divine instruction in political, as opposed to personal, justice. Abraham as a political founder requires an enlarged conception of public justice. See Leon Kass, *The Beginning of Wisdom: Reading Genesis* (New York: The Free Press, 2003), p. 321.

25   See also Jeremiah 31:29–30. The modern Jewish philosopher, Hermann Cohen, makes a great deal of Ezekiel's claim. He sees it as the first successful attempt to ground individual moral responsibility. See his magisterial *Religion of Reason out of the Sources of Judaism*, trans. Simon Kaplan (Atlanta: Scholars Press, 1995), p. 194.

26   See the argument of John Barton on behalf of a rudimentary natural law orientation to biblical ethics in his *Ethics and the Old Testament*, p. 62. The Amos text distinguishes between the sins of the nations, who have violated natural moral norms, and the sins of Israel and Judah, who have violated covenantal norms (Amos 2:4–16). This distinction lends weight to the thesis that biblical authors were aware of a pre- or meta-Sinaitic normativity that retained significant axiological consequences, at least for non-Israelites. For a sympathetic critique of Barton, see Cyril S. Rodd, *Glimpses of a Strange Land*, pp. 63–64. Rodd sees divine command, with its correlate of obedience, as the dominant note in "Old Testament" ethics but he does allow, although to a lesser extent than Barton, a role for something akin to natural law. The major work in the area of natural law and Judaism is David Novak, *Natural Law in Judaism*. This work is a sustained scholarly attempt to demonstrate the presence and significance of natural law thinking in biblical and subsequent Jewish thought.

27   Rudolf Otto, *The Idea of the Holy*, trans. John Harvey (Oxford: Oxford University Press, 1958).

28   Consider Exodus 33:17–23 as a text that moves in the direction of an ethicized conception of holiness. Moses asks to see God's tangible presence (*kavod*) but God tells him that no one can see His presence and live. He shelters Moses in a cleft in the rock of Mount Sinai and causes His goodness (*tuv*) to pass before him. Here "goodness" has some of the reified actuality of "presence" yet is not as dangerous or uncanny. For a study of holiness in the Pentateuch, see Baruch Schwartz, "Israel's Holiness: The Torah Traditions," in M. Poorthuis and J. Schwartz, eds, *Purity and Holiness* (Leiden: Brill, 2000). I am indebted to my colleague, Prof. Elsie Stern, for calling this article to my attention. It is unsettling to think that early Israelites had conceptions of God that placed the divine and the good in tension. What counts, I think, is not where these notions start out but where they arrive. Just as in the evolution of creation stories, the Bible records a process of maturation and refinement in Israel's understanding of God and goodness.

29   Path-breaking interpretive work on purity/impurity vis-à-vis holiness has been done by Prof. Jonathan Klawans. For an easily accessible précis of his work, see Jonathan Klawans, "Concepts on Purity in the Bible," in Berlin and Brettler, eds, *The Jewish Study Bible*, pp. 2041–2047.

30   Jacob Milgrom, *Leviticus: A Book of Ritual and Ethics, A Continental Commentary* (Minneapolis: Fortress Press, 2004), p. 9. On the long development toward a sovereign, unopposed God see Jon Levenson, *Creation and the Persistence of Evil*.

31   Milgrom, *Leviticus*, p. 12.

32   Mary Douglas, *Purity and Danger: An Analysis of the Concepts of Pollution and Taboo* (London: Routledge, 1989), p. 132. Douglas offers a comprehensive table of the morally adjunctive functions of pollution, that is, purity and impurity beliefs, on p. 133.

33   Douglas, *Purity and Danger*, p. 52.

34   Klawans, Concepts of Purity in the Bible, p. 245.

35   Israel Knohl, *The Divine Symphony: The Bible's Many Voices* (Philadelphia: Jewish Publication Society, 2003), p. 63. Isaiah, for example, proclaimed that "The LORD of Hosts is exalted by judgment, the Holy God proved holy by retribution" (Isa. 5:16). The extension of divine holiness to moral activities (judging, making retribution) was a profound "conceptual revolution" for Knohl, which the priests could not resist. The prior isolation of holiness to purely ritual, purity/impurity matters left the priests and pious if ethically lax Israelites open to prophetic critique. These themes are developed at greater length in Israel Knohl, *The Sanctuary of Silence: The Priestly Torah and the Holiness School* (Minneapolis: Fortress Press, 1995). Knohl admits, however, that it is impossible to say who came first. Prophets such as Isaiah and Amos may have been inspired by the conceptual revolution within the priestly circle.

36   Sifra Kedoshim para. 1:1, cited in Milgrom, *Leviticus*, p. 219. Cf. *B. Shabbat* 133b for the locus classicus in rabbinic literature for imitatio dei.

37   Sifra Kedoshim para 1.1, in Milgrom, *Leviticus*, p. 219.

38   What is riding on the relationship of holiness to ethics? If holiness as a concept can resist reduction to ethics, without being contra-ethical, it can secure a place for religion. One way of doing this is Kierkegaard's "teleological suspension of the ethical." But that falls prey to a diminution of ethics, to the contra-ethical. A leading moral philosopher, the late Bernard Williams, argues that religion has no place in the mature ethical consciousness; to the extent that religion has to justify itself before ethics, it has lost any raison d'être as an independent force. Holiness, if it could be constituted as overlapping with but not reducible to ethics, would refute Williams's argument. See Williams, *Ethics and the Limits of Philosophy*, pp. 32–33. The modern Jewish philosophers Moritz Lazarus and Hermann Cohen, whom we will encounter in Chapter 5, try to do just this.

39   Leo Adler, *The Biblical View of Man*, trans. Daniel R. Schwartz (Jerusalem: Urim Publications, 2007), p. 6. Abraham Joshua Heschel, *God in Search of Man* (New York: Farrar, Strauss and Giroux, 1995) p. 412.

40   For a detailed discussion of the constraints upon action and thereby upon responsibility implied by ignorance, error, and passion, see David Daube, *The Deed and the Doer in the Bible*, ed. Calum Carmichael (West Conshohocken, PA: Templeton Foundation Press, 2008), Chapters 3–4.

41   This discussion draws from Alan Mittleman, "Free Choice and Determinism in Jewish Thought: An Overview," in Robert Pollack, ed., *Neuroscience and Free Will* (New York: Center for the Study of Science and Religion, Columbia University, 2009): http://www.columbia.edu/cu/cssr/ebook/FreeWill_eBook.pdf.

42   Nahum M. Sarna, *Exploring Exodus* (New York: Schocken Books, 1986), p. 65.

43   One scholar of ancient Jewish literature, Burton Visotzky, argues that the very gap between Genesis's disturbingly realistic portrayal of its protagonists and the

softer, more pious portrayals enshrined by later tradition is itself a stimulus to ethical reflection. How could such flawed characters become ethical exemplars to subsequent Judaism and Christianity? Ethical development, Visotzky claims, takes place in the attempt to address his conundrum. See his *Genesis of Ethics* (New York: Three Rivers Press, 1996).

44   Some philosophers have responded to this problem by reducing consciousness to an ensemble of structures and functions for which purely biological explanations can or likely will be given. Others have claimed that consciousness is a basic phenomenon, not reducible to phenomena explicable by the laws of physics. For an example of the latter view, see David J. Chalmers, "Facing up to the Problem of Consciousness," *Journal of Consciousness Studies*, Vol. 2, No. 3 (1995), pp. 200–219.

45   Michael Gazzaniga, *The Ethical Brain* (New York: Dana Press, 2005) p. 93.

46   The formulation of the Noaḥide laws occurs, inter alia, at *B. Sanhedrin* 56a. My equation of the "best" with the "morally appropriate" life for man was not casual. As far as I can see, the Bible does not entertain the skeptical point of view, which Plato attempts to defeat, that the best or most natural life for man is amoral or contra-moral. For a comprehensive study see David Novak, *The Image of the Non-Jew in Judaism: An Historical and Constructive Study of the Noaḥide Laws* (New York: Edwin Mellen Press, 1983).

47   See Deuteronomy, chap. 27; Joshua, chap. 24; Nehemiah, chap. 9. The practice of public assembly and covenant renewal occurs later at Qumran. It is more difficult to locate in rabbinic Judaism. For a discussion, see Mittleman, *The Scepter Shall Not Depart from Judah*, Chapter 3.

48   A systematic discussion of the problem of whether the commandments are rationally perspicuous or arbitrary may be found in Isaac Heinemann, *Ta'amei Ha-Mitzvot be-Sifrut Yisrael* (Jerusalem: Jewish Agency, 1966). For a review of the arbitrary or irrational tradition in rabbinic thought, see pp. 22–25. This book has recently been translated into English, see Isaac Heinemann, *The Reasons for the Commandments in Jewish Thought: From the Bible to the Renaissance*, trans. Leonard Levin (Brighton, MA: Academic Studies Press, 2008).

49   For an analysis of those elements in Greek philosophical culture which enabled diaspora Jews to find common ground with Greek thought, see Harry Austryn Wolfson, *Philo*, Vol. I (Cambridge, MA: Harvard University Press, 1947), Chapter 1.

50   The weight of scholarly opinion dates the letter much later than Ptolemy's reign and ascribes it to Jewish provenance. See Moses Hadas, ed. and trans., *Aristeas to Philocrates (Letter of Aristeas)* (New York: Harper & Brothers, 1951). See Hadas' Introduction for a thorough discussion. Hadas dates its composition to 130 BCE.

51   All references in parentheses are to line numbers in the Hadas translation of *Aristeas*.

52   For the broader Jewish Hellenistic context, see Wolfson, *Philo*, Vol. I, p. 14.

53   For a comparable, albeit deeper treatment, see Philo, *De Specialibus Legibus* 4:103–115, cited in David Winston, ed. and trans., *Philo of Alexandria: The Contemplative Life, The Giants, and Selections* (New York: Paulist Press, 1981), pp. 282–284.

54 Wolfson, *Philo*, Vol. 1, pp. 155–163.

55 Samuel Sandmel, *Philo of Alexandria: An Introduction* (New York: Oxford University Press, 1979), p. 91.

56 From Philo's *Quis Rerum Divinarum Heres Sit* (205), cited in Winston, *Philo of Alexandria*, p. 94.

57 Winston, ed. and trans., *Philo of Alexandria*, p. 23.

58 Sandmel, *Philo of Alexandria*, p. 113ff. For texts, see Winston, ed. and trans., *Philo of Alexandria*, pp. 212, 215.

59 *Quis Rerum Divinarum Heres Sit* (68–70), cited in Winston, ed. and trans., *Philo of Alexandria*, p. 169.

60 Philo took a position between the literalists, non-philosophers who thought that allegory was unnecessary and did not regard the Torah as containing an inner, spiritual meaning, and extreme literalists. See Wolfson, *Philo*, Vol. I, pp. 55–77.

61 *De Migratione Abrahami* (127–130), cited in Winston, ed. and trans., *Philo of Alexandria*, p. 198.

62 *De Abrahamo* (2–6), cited in Winston, ed. and trans., *Philo of Alexandria*, p. 199.

2
Some Aspects of Rabbinic Ethics

Rabbinic literature is a vast field.[1] Attempts to generalize about its ethically salient dimensions soon come to grief. Although it emerges from a distinctive stream of ancient Judaism, the origins of which are still not completely clear, the literature of this movement is too ramified and too diverse in genre, provenance, date, and purpose to allow for confident generalizations. Additionally, the post-70 ce rabbis – who referred to themselves as sages (*ḥakhamim*) or disciples (*talmidei ḥakhamim*) – were committed to the preservation of conflicting opinions. Even texts presumably emanating from the same circles are full of principled disagreement. In a famous articulation of the commitment to recording disagreement, discrepant opinions ("both these and those") are held to be "the words of the living God" (*B. Eruvin* 13b). Authentic disagreement for "the sake of heaven" is prized. This is in itself an ethically salient fact.[2] However, it makes generalizing about rabbinic ethics all the more difficult.

It was once common to produce anthologies of rabbinic literature in which rabbinic beliefs, including those touching upon moral thought, were compiled and presented as accounts of Jewish ethics. A. Cohen's *Everyman's Talmud* (1932) is a good example of this. In its section "The Moral Life," rabbinic teachings are grouped under such headings as "imitation of God," "brotherly love," "humility," honesty," etc.[3] A great many texts are marshaled to exemplify what are held to be core rabbinic values. The reader emerges with a sympathetic attitude toward a humane body of moral wisdom. As academic scholarship on rabbinic literature has progressed, however, synthetic treatments such as this are no longer in favor. The works of Cohen, of Claude Montefiore and others, were, of course, popular books. But even

A Short History of Jewish Ethics: Conduct and Character in the Context of Covenant, First Edition. Alan L. Mittleman.
© 2012 Alan L. Mittleman. Published 2012 by Blackwell Publishing Ltd.

highly scholarly treatments, such as Ephraim Urbach's *The Sages* or Solomon Schechter's *Aspects of Rabbinic Theology*, are no longer fashionable (although, I would say, no less great). The project of synthesis elides or erases too many significant differences among and within texts, such as those in provenance or period or in rhetorical aims and strategies. Synthesizing approaches may scant the different strata within a given text as well as the problems of transmission and redaction. All of these scholarly concerns are too easily homogenized by an anthological or synthetic approach. Collecting and organizing the concepts and beliefs of the sages according to a modern sense of thematic coherence also ignores the inherent architectonic of rabbinic texts. The sages had their own way of organizing and articulating topics.[4] Contemporary scholars believe themselves to be on firmer ground by treating texts individually or in kindred groups such as Mishnah and Tosefta, tannaitic midrashim, amoraic biblical commentaries, etc. In this way, the scholar can attend to the text as redacted, can try to tease out its edited layers, and can in the end regard the text as an integrated canonical whole. There is no need to assume or postulate a putative coherent unity for all of rabbinic literature. On the other hand, some scholars worry about over-particularizing. The impulse to avoid macroscopic generalization may be salutary, but an overly microscopic approach is not helpful either.[5] For an inquiry such as ours, which looks to the philosophical significance of the texts under discussion, we need not let these concerns weigh too heavily. I do want to be mindful of them, however, and avoid overly broad as well as vanishingly narrow statements. With this in mind, we will look at a few significant topics through the lenses of individual rabbinic texts.

Midrash: Virtuous Character and Conduct

The Bible presents its characters as complex, flawed persons. The sages tend both to deepen these characters and also in a sense to simplify them. The Bible presents Esau, for example, as an aggrieved, cheated, violent, but also (possibly) generous and forgiving man. Rabbinic midrash sees him as the epitome of evil, a cipher for wickedness.[6] His apparent gestures of generosity are tricks and deceptions. Esau becomes symbolic first of pagan and then of Christian Rome. He is beyond redemption. Positive figures, such as the patriarchs, become archetypal Jews. They are interpreted as models of rabbinic character and conduct, standards for proper expectations of how a Jew should think, feel, act, and live. The patriarchs are interpreted according to the idea of "what happens to the fathers is a sign for the sons" (cf. Naḥmanides on Gen. 12:6).[7] Abraham's experiences anticipate those of his descendants.[8] Abraham's migration to Egypt, for example, anticipates later exiles and the vulnerability and hardship they will entail. Beyond its function of making sense of contemporary history through typology, the midrash establishes a moral kinship among the generations. Abraham, although extraordinarily righteous, is sufficiently like us to be emulated. He is present, not merely historically prior. The father's deeds are a sign for his sons, in the dual sense of a pattern that will, come what may, be replicated *and* of a way that ought to be chosen. Abraham's life, in Clifford Geertz's terms, is a model of (a replica) and a model for Jewish life in the sense of a template.[9]

Ancient biblical commentary, both non-rabbinic and rabbinic, presents Abraham as a supremely righteous man, but not necessarily as a Jew. There are two traditions about Abraham. In one, Abraham and the other patriarchs are righteous Noahides – they are bound by the seven commandments which God gave to Noah after the Flood. In rabbinic thought, these are the minimum standards to which non-Jews need to conform to be in covenant – the covenant of Noah – with God.[10] Abraham is considered by apocryphal books like *Sirach* and by some rabbinic sources to be a Noahide who has the additional commandment of circumcision. Other sources, including the non-rabbinic *Book of Jubilees* as well as some rabbinic texts, see Abraham as fully observant of Mosaic law, standing within the covenant between God and Israel deriving from Mt Sinai.[11] The sages fold time and treat "early" as "later." Abraham's covenant of circumcision is imaginatively interpreted to include all of the other commandments, understood by the sages to number 613. The upshot of this is that it is unresolved whether Abraham is a Jew or a Noahide. On the view that he is a Noahide, he stands out to an even greater extent for his moral exemplarity. If Abraham's conduct cannot be thought to be entirely regulated by Torah law, it is easier to describe him in ethical terms. To the extent that we wish to maintain a distinction between ethics and law, Abraham as Noahide gives us an opportunity to do so. In any case, Abraham, as interpreted by the sages, is a locus for moral excellence.

Abraham's moral exemplarity begins with his birth. An old tradition, found in both rabbinic and non-rabbinic sources, asserts that Abraham withstood 10 trials, each one increasingly demonstrating his trust in God. The first was that assassins tried to murder him as an infant.[12] The last, which established his enduring merit, was what medieval Jewish tradition calls "the binding (*akedah*) of Isaac." In Genesis, chapter 22 Abraham responds with complete trust and obedience to the divine call to sacrifice his son, Isaac. The call comes suddenly, threatening to tear from Abraham everything he had hoped for and thought that he had secured:

> Some time afterward, God put Abraham to the test. He said to him, "Abraham," and he answered, "Here I am." And He said, "Take your son, your favored one, Isaac, whom you love, and go to the land of Moriah, and offer him there as a burnt offering on one of the heights that I will point out to you." So early

next morning, Abraham saddled his ass and took with him two of his servants and his son Isaac. He split the wood for the burnt offering, and he set out for the place of which God had told him. On the third day Abraham looked up and saw the place from afar. Then Abraham said to his servants, "You stay here with the ass. The boy and I will go up there; we will worship and we will return to you." (Gen. 22:1–5)

In the context of the biblical text, it is immediately puzzling why the Abraham who resisted God's plans for the destruction of Sodom and Gomorrah in Genesis, chapter 18 does not raise a peep of resistance to the commanded slaughter of his own son. In Genesis, chapter 18 Abraham challenges God with the charge to do justice – what if there were righteous persons in the city who should not be destroyed along with the wicked? Here, he silently acquiesces to God's dreadful charge. Only the subtle expression of hope in verse 5 – "we will return to you" – suggests that he might doubt he would really have to go through with the terrible deed. Modern Jewish exegetes have often seen this text as functioning to overthrow definitively the primitive or pagan belief in child sacrifice. They have presented this text as a great moral breakthrough. The Harvard biblical scholar, Jon Levenson, dissents. On his reading, early strata of the Hebrew Bible present God as having a *right* to first born children (see Exod. 22:28–29); sacrifice of them is something God can legitimately require on a literal reading of the Exodus, chapter 22 text. Later in the history of Israelite religion, redemption of first born humans (albeit ongoing destruction of first born animals) replaces the possibility of sacrifice (see Exod. 13:2, 11–13). At an even later stage, the memory of legitimate child sacrifice has been completely erased (see Deut. 15:19–23; Jer. 19:5). If Levenson's reconstruction is correct, Abraham doesn't oppose God's demand because he recognizes its legitimacy. This is precisely the kind of thing God can require.[13] The Bible, as suggested, eventually sublimates that view. Both later strata of biblical literature and post-biblical literature view child sacrifice as deviant, not as heroic. Indeed, they view it as profoundly violative of the norms of justice and righteousness, which Abraham exemplified when he pled on behalf of Sodom and Gomorrah.

Genesis (or in Hebrew, *Bereshit*) *Rabbah*, the amoraic midrash on Genesis, inherits the problem of how to understand Abraham's silent acquiescence to God's horrific demand.[14] The midrash, with typical inventiveness, solves the problem by eliminating Abraham's silence: Abraham attempts to counter God's demand. The midrash puts words in Abraham's mouth, taking advantage of stylistic peculiarities in the primary biblical text.

And He said: Take, I pray thee, thy son, etc. (Gen. 22:2). Said He to him: "Take, I pray thee – I beg thee – thy son." "Which son?" he asked. "Thine only son," replied He. "But each is the only one of his mother?" – "Whom thou lovest." – "Is there a limit to the affections?" "Even Isaac," said He. And why did He not reveal it to him without delay? In order to make him [Isaac] even more beloved in his eyes and reward him for every word spoken (*Bereshit Rabbah*, 55:7).[15]

God's iteration of locutions for Isaac raises the curiosity of the rabbinic reader. Such surface irregularities give the midrash a foothold. The first nuance the midrash seizes upon is a particle (*na*) following the verb in Hebrew, all but obscured in the English translation "take, I pray thee" (*kakh na*). The particle indicates a polite, deferential shading of the imperative "take!" It softens the imperatival tone. God is begging Abraham to grant his request. Even though God is putting Abraham to the test, God dearly wants him to pass it. Were Abraham to fail the test, God's own reputation in the world would suffer. His investment of love in, and concern for, Abraham would have been for naught. God is not a distant tyrant, cruelly ordering Abraham to obey (despite the harshness of his request); He is a covenant partner asking for Abraham's consideration.

And Abraham is a covenant partner willing to push back, just as he did for Sodom and Gomorrah. Abraham tries to blunt or thwart God's request at every turn, throwing up verbal challenges and obstacles. As at Sodom, he tries to deter and defer the inevitable. When he has no recourse left, he consents. Abraham tests the bounds of resistance. He deploys reasons to preserve a rational commitment to a mutually intelligible justice. But eventually, like Job, he accepts. God's desire becomes his own. Subsequent midrashim portray Abraham (and Isaac!) as single-minded to fulfill God's will. Isaac, who in the biblical narrative is almost completely silent, forcefully states:

> "Father, I am a young man and am afraid that my body may tremble through fear of the knife and I will grieve thee, whereby the slaughter may be rendered unfit and will not count as a real sacrifice; therefore bind me very firmly." Forthwith, "he bound Isaac": can one bind a man thirty seven years old without his consent? (*Bereshit Rabbah* 56:8)

Isaac shares his father's conviction that covenant loyalty, love for God, requires his willing consent. This does not, however, diminish his grief – and Abraham's – at the awful act that awaits. The midrash continues with a touching scene in which Abraham's tears, dripping from his face as he wields the knife, flow into Isaac's eyes.

Once set on his path, Abraham will not be dissuaded. Another well-known midrash details a dialogue between Abraham and a Satan-like figure, the evil angel, Samael, in which the latter is the voice of moral reason or, at least, of prudential self-interest.

Samael went to the Patriarch Abraham and upbraided him saying: "What means this, old man? Hast thou lost thy wits? Thou goest to slay a son granted to thee at the age of a hundred!" "Even this I do," replied he. "And if He sets thee an even greater test, canst thou stand it?" ... "Even more than this" he [Abraham] replied. "Tomorrow He will say to thee, 'Thou art a murderer, and art guilty,'." "Still am I content," he [Abraham] rejoined. (*Bereshit Rabbah* 56:4)

Samael appeals first to Abraham's self-interest. He is about to throw away everything he has hoped and worked for. He then plays on Abraham's fears; this awful test may not yet be the end. There may be even worse ahead. Finally, he implies that God Himself will judge him harshly. God will tell him that he is, in fact, a murderer. But Abraham remains unmoved. Even if God were to return to conventional moral judgment, Abraham would accept the charge. His devotion to God is absolute, heedless of consequences and costs. "Love," as Bereshit Rabbah says in another midrash, "upsets the natural order" (*Bereshit Rabbah* 55:8).

I began with the suggestion that, within the frame of the biblical narrative at least, God's request and Abraham's compliance are not incompatible with *tzedek* and *mishpat*. God has a right to Isaac, as it were. But the Bible itself and the post-biblical literature drive a wedge between intelligible norms of justice and righteousness and human sacrifice. The midrash tries to bridge the gap by having Abraham resist. Abraham tries, again as at Sodom, to reason with God.[16] When that fails, Abraham submits. Indeed, he rises to the grim task with an enthusiasm bordering on, the evil angel implies, irrational fanaticism. What has happened to *tzedek* and *mishpat* here? Can Abraham's deed be made to conform to any rational understanding of justice or does ethics simply come to an end, yielding to some allegedly higher "teleological suspension," as Kierkegaard put it?

One possible resolution should be quickly put out of bounds. The midrash itself indicates that God did not immediately clarify His request so that Abraham could be rewarded "for every word spoken." Reward clearly plays an important role in these texts. Abraham's trial was so great and he passed it with such majestic determination that God rewards him with eternal merit (*zekhut*). The theological concept of the merit of the fathers (*zekhut avot*) plays a major role in rabbinic thought. The virtue of the patriarchs, while emulable, is so beyond the achievement of ordinary mortals that God remembers it and endows the descendants with vicarious worth on account of it.[17] Nonetheless, the midrash *does not* present Abraham as ever taking reward into account. That is God's mysterious business; it plays no role in Abraham's decision. Like Bernard Williams's "one thought too many," Abraham does not weigh his options and decide on the basis of some abstract principle or consequence. He chooses categorically, hard though it is to understand. Abraham chooses categorically against his self-interest.

Nor is there anything in either the biblical or midrashic text which suggests that Abraham fears being punished by God for non-compliance. God asks for consent, not blind submission, and Abraham consents out of covenanted love. Indeed, the midrash portrays Abraham as driven to the utmost extreme: even after God stays his hand, Abraham wishes to continue (*Bereshit Rabbah* 56:7).

Is Kierkegaard correct then? Does ethics yield to a higher stage of religious consciousness, one where holiness is no longer coordinate with morality, where amoral or immoral action is justified? Even to ask the question is problematic. How can injustice be *justified*? We cannot get out of a moral point of view if we want to speak as human beings.[18] We find ourselves in a world that is already saturated with ethical value. Our own thoughts and acts already form within a moral framework. As to the matter at hand, there is no neutral or non-moral perspective from which ultimately to evaluate human sacrifice. We can suspend moral judgment (itself a kind of moral judgment) but not indefinitely. To say that radical devotion to God suspends devotion to more common moral norms is not to step outside the sphere of ethical considerations. It is to privilege one moral value, one valued object (devotion to God), over another (the sanctity of human life). It is not to abandon a moral perspective but to make a deeply troubling choice within it.

Abraham is presented as one who makes such a choice. He gives up everything for God. As Maimonides argues, the point of the story is to depict an ultimate limit. God wished to show the world just how much might be demanded in His service. The purpose of Abraham's "trial" is to establish forever what the maximum fidelity to God – what the love and fear of God – could mean. God, on Maimonides' view, is not running an experiment, waiting to see whether Abraham will obey. Being omniscient, He already knows. The trial is to make a public statement, to fix the norm for heroism in the divine service.[19] The midrash does not seem to be encumbered by philosophical assumptions about the divine epistemology. God does seem open to the possibility that Abraham may fail his test and therefore anxious that he should pass it ("Take I pray thee – I beg thee – thy son"). God wants to reward Abraham for his action, his patience, his trust, his openness to divine direction. Another midrash notes the parallelism between God's staged iteration of His request that Abraham leave his country in Genesis 12:1 ("Go forth from your native land and from your father's house") and the deferral of identifying Isaac as the sacrificial victim (*Bereshit Rabbah* 39:9).[20] God spoke in stages to place "the righteous in doubt and suspense" so that they can prove their mettle. God judges not this or that act, but the whole of a life.

These texts suggest that there is a limit to ethics. But what is that limit? I resist the idea that holiness constitutes a stage beyond goodness or that religion requires a "suspension of the ethical." That invites such malign possibilities as violence in the name of God. The text does not so much suspend the ethical as reconfigure it. God ultimately wants to reward Abraham for his devotion. That devotion is proven over the course of an entire life. I would suggest that the midrash invites us to think holistically about life, rather than atomistically about deeds. The moral life is to be evaluated within the context of an extended narrative, not on a moment-by-moment basis as a series of discrete actions open to moral judgment. The classic moral question "what ought I to do?" is too narrow. The Socratic question "how should I live?" may be the more fitting one.[21] The self has no sense without a narrative context. What must be assessed is the narrative of a life always more complex than the ethical evaluation that could be brought to bear on any of its moments. The answer to "how should I live?" is not an amoral matter but neither can it be parsed into discrepant domains of right and wrong.[22] Abraham's deed, considered in isolation, shocks us. But his life, considered on the whole, is intelligible to us and, for traditional Judaism, paradigmatically worthy. The sages present Abraham's life as a series of trials and triumphs. We cannot diminish the horror of Abraham's attempted act but we can expand the framework of evaluation in which we attempt to make sense of it. That is what the midrash seeks to do.

Bible and midrash do more, of course, than ask Socratic questions. God plays a role in these texts far in excess of his role in Plato. The Good for Plato may function as God, but the Good is not a person. It is the origin and goal of reason, but it has no will of its own. The God of Israel may function as the Good, endlessly drawing humans to contemplate, emulate, and revere the divine being. But God is also father, judge, lover, friend – an active partner in the private and public life of a covenanted people. One need not take these designators literally but one must not argue them away. Jewish ethics has an irreducibly theological dimension. Nonetheless, abstraction is permissible. To recast God's role in more abstract terms, we might say that God functions in the narrative as a representation of the most comprehensive point of view. He alone knows whether in the end Abraham has lived up to his own ideals of *tzedek* and *mishpat*. The dialogue with God reveals to Abraham that his life of trial has triumphed. The midrash presents this last trial as decisive: "[it] was as weighty as all the rest together, and had he not submitted to it, all would have been lost" (*Bereshit Rabbah* 56:11).

From this most comprehensive point of view, ethics makes an ultimate claim on us; to be human is to participate in a moral cosmos. But to be human is not ultimate. It is to be subordinate to an always ineradicable mystery. God is the emblem of that mystery. We cannot fully grasp ourselves in the abiding perplexities of our natality and mortality. We cannot dispel the sheer uncanniness of existence, the abiding obscurity, despite the great gains in our science, of our origins and endings. Our various human points of view, although aspiring to objective knowledge, remain fragmentary and full of yearning. God, in the Jewish tradition, functions as a transcendent point of reference, as an epistemological promise that sense can be made of life if not yet now then in some beckoning future.

To say that Abraham was worthy of reward in God's eyes is to say that his life on the whole and all things considered was a worthy life *in absolute terms*. It is to make a strong statement of what the Jewish tradition expects of those who would devote themselves to it. To follow Abraham is to take enormous risk – and to expose one's children to risk. No wonder that a male baby's life as a Jew begins with circumcision, the covenant of Abraham, on its eighth day. He undergoes both a moment of pain – the sting of life – and the loving embrace of family and community, the sweetness of life. The reality of covenant as a protective, mediating barrier against the stings of life is felt in the flesh. The ritual of circumcision lends narrative structure to the pri-mordial human experiences of pain and relief, isolation and sociality, indi-viduation and mutuality. Although Abraham's willingness to sacrifice Isaac remains scandalous and impenetrable at one level, it is accessible on another. Few generations of Jews did not experience the extreme precariousness of Jewish life. Raising Jewish children in as recently as, say, the 1930s in Europe was to expose them to unimaginable risk. The binding of Isaac, although it had no further resonance in the Bible per se, resounds strongly throughout the texts of biblical commentary and the folk imagination of the Jewish people.[23] It spoke to their experience, commitment, devotion, vulnerability, and, often enough, to their fate. It spoke to the heroism of the ideal-typical Jew, as well to the breakdown of the connection between righteousness and desert. Jewish life can be Joban. Life can constitute a trial with no clear resolution. Cultivating the virtue of steadfast commitment to a holy way might lead to no manifest utility beyond the way itself. Virtue might have to be its own reward. The midrashic retelling of the *aqedah* pushes the limits of ethics; it strains against the moral sense-making that is our birthright.

In the end, however, the midrash abandons neither ethics nor moral sense-making.[24] Kierkegaard's view is firmly rejected. On the other side of the mountain, so to speak, Abraham reverts to his old, rational, argumentative self. In *Bereshit Rabbah* 56:8, Abraham accuses God of astonishing inconsistency. God had promised, in Genesis 21:12, that "it is through Isaac that offspring will be continued for you." But then, Abraham charges, God retracted His promise and said "take your son." And now God has just said to Abraham "do not raise your hand against the boy" (Gen. 22:12). God is not supposed to act in such a capricious, inconstant manner. God's reply, in divine self-defense, first invokes a verse from Psalm 89:5 attesting to the constancy of His intention. Then God throws the ball back into Abraham's court, by using a creative misreading of the original Hebrew in Genesis. The verb that Genesis 22:2 uses (*ha'alehu*) means "make him a burnt offering (*olah*)" but it could also be misread as "bring him up," since the root *'a-l-h* has the sense of "elevate." Thus, God claims that He merely meant bring Isaac up to the mountain while Abraham interpreted the command as "slaughter him." In this midrash, God disowns any such intention, implicitly accuses Abraham of excessive zealotry, and orders him to take Isaac down from the mountain. Later tradition echoes this sense of horror at Abraham's deed. The next chapter of Genesis begins suddenly with the death of Sarah. The lack of an evident reason for her death invites the midrashic imagination to bridge the gap. Thus, the medieval commentator Rashi ascribed her death to having heard a rumor about Abraham's attempted murder of their son. When she heard such terrifying news, her soul departed from her (Rashi on Genesis 23:2).

Abraham's act must not be emulated but his conduct – sacrificial devotion to God – and his character, shaped by the virtues of loyalty, love, and fidelity to God, are to be embraced. They are to be emulated within the bounds of moral accountability.

Ethical Tractates: Moral Motivation

Rabbinic literature contains a number of anthologies of wise sayings and moral maxims, the most prominent of which are *Pirkei Avot* (*Fathers*) and an ancient commentary thereon called *Avot de-Rabbi Natan* (*The Fathers According to Rabbi Nathan*).[25] These anthologies emanated from and circulated within the study halls of the sages in Roman Palestine. Their overall aim was to refine and reshape the personalities of aspiring sages. As such, they are very much concerned with ethical transformation – with such subjects as moral motivation, internal impulses, desires, emotions, and with their improvement. Their primary audience was the world of the sages; they are thus concerned with boundary-marking and the cultivation of highly developed traits of mindfulness, self-awareness, modesty, dignity, circumspection, and rigor. Nonetheless, these texts became popular, gave rise to numerous commentaries, and eventually were printed in editions of the Talmud, where they had an ancillary role. *Fathers* was already studied in the synagogue on Sabbath afternoons in medieval times and found its way into emerging editions of the prayer book. It is standard practice to study it on Sabbath afternoons in the springtime period between Passover and the Feast of Weeks (Shavuot).

What constitutes proper moral motivation? We have already seen, in the midrashim on Abraham, that the concepts of reward and punishment play an important role in rabbinic thought. If Abraham withstands his trial, God will know that he is worthy of blessing. Is expectation of reward or benefit a proper motivation for moral and broadly for religious behavior? This is surely not a question that would puzzle a utilitarian. That acts should engender positive consequences, including benefit for the agent, is a fundamental premise of a consequentialist ethics such as utilitarianism. We will turn shortly to the question of the extent to which Jewish ethics is consequentialist (although not necessarily utilitarian). In a religious context, however, this is a fraught topic. Two millennia of Christian critique of Judaism, beginning with Paul, have charged Judaism with profound and systemic spiritual failure. The Christian knows, so the argument runs, that no human action can induce, buy, coerce, manipulate, or secure God's blessing. Human beings, in their post-lapsarian state, are utterly unworthy of divine favor. The delusion of the Law is that certain approved actions are pleasing to God and that those who do them will be blessed and those who spurn them will be cursed. Paul argued, however, that the Law itself is a curse. Jews think that they are repairing the breach in their relationship with God by doing the works of the Law. In fact, they are widening it and making their condition all the more hopeless. Only the free, self-sacrificial, unmerited, atoning death of Jesus restores the relationship between humans (at least those who accept Christ's sacrifice as decisive; who die to their old selves and rise again with him) and God. God saves us through His grace, not through our works. The punctilious observance of Jewish law is a mark of estrangement from God rather than the enactment of a covenantal intimacy with Him. Elements of this view are found in the Gospels and non-Pauline letters. Modern scholarship has revealed much of the complexity and ambiguity of Paul vis-à-vis early Judaism and one shouldn't oversimplify or retroject Luther's theology onto Paul.[26] Nonetheless, this is, roughly speaking, the kind of accusation which Judaism has faced.

The context in which these concerns are salient is not ethics per se but theology. The core issue has to do with salvation. Salvation cannot be earned or merited. It is God's free gift. This conflicts with the plain sense of much of Hebrew Scriptures. When Deuteronomy affirms "Obey, O Israel, willingly and faithfully, that it may go well with you and that you may increase greatly in a land flowing with milk and honey" (Deut. 6:3) it surely seems to fix a relationship between performance and desert. Furthermore, it interpolates a ground for motivation: you should obey because you wish to flourish in the land and be blessed with "issue of womb and produce of your soil, your new grain and wine and oil, the calving of your herd and the lambing of your flock" (Deut. 7:13). And you want to avoid the cost of disobedience: "like the nations that the LORD will cause to perish before you, so shall you perish – because you did not heed the LORD your God" (Deut. 8:20). The New Testament's concern – for individual post-mortem life – is not identical with the collective this-worldly flourishing on display in Deuteronomy. While rabbinic Judaism develops a concept of an afterlife, a "world to come," it never loses hold of the Bible's this-worldly orientation. Indeed, rabbinic Judaism's distinctive concept, the bodily resurrection of the dead, extends the horizon for this-worldly life, albeit through a kind of supernatural life-extension.[27] Rabbinic Judaism affirms a collective corporeal resurrection for the worthy of Israel in eschatological time. To disbelieve in the resurrection of the dead (as did the Sadducees and their apparent sub-sect, the Boethusians) renders one a heretic, according to the Mishnah. Jews praise God, who gives life to the dead, in daily prayer. They want more, not less, of the goodness of this world.[28]

In some ways, Jews and Christians have been talking past each other at those times when disputations and acrimony about these matters were constant facts of life. The concern for personal salvation, while not unknown to Judaism, is less vital than the hope for collective redemption and eternal peace under the providence of the God of the covenant. The covenantal framework of biblical and rabbinic religion militates against too fine-grained a focus on individual salvation.

These theological concerns are important, not only in and of themselves, but as background to ethical considerations. It is not a big leap from Christian theological anti-Judaism to Kantian philosophical anti-Judaism. The Kant who infamously wrote "the euthanasia of Judaism is pure moral religion" was nurtured by a theological tradition.[29] It is Kant's view that action from any prudential, self-regarding, even other-regarding motives, from any motives other than reverence for the moral law as such, fails categorically to be moral.[30] Such action, however noble its motivation, as for example in the case of altruism, originates in drives, interests, anticipations of benefit, or avoidance of injury. It seeks worldly flourishing, whether along the lines of classical eudemonia or biblical blessing. It originates in a sphere where humans are not free, are less than human. Drives and interests stem from our animal nature, which dwells in a deterministic universe understood along Newtonian lines. Only by rising in transcendence from such a world, by assimilating ourselves to a world of freedom signified by an absolute dedication to the moral law, do we have the possibility of realizing, however briefly, the holiness of the good will. A person should expect nothing, least of all happiness or worldly flourishing. One should wish at most to be worthy of happiness by living in conformity with the moral law. Subordination to what is inherently right solely because it is right is all that counts.

Kant mischaracterizes Judaism as a deformed (pseudo-) moral system wholly governed by anticipation of reward and fear of punishment. Judaism is governed by pure heteronomy rather than by the valorous autonomy which provides a key criterion for true morality under the Kantian dispensation. God either seduces or tyrannizes immature minds under this system. Human beings are not yet able to choose the right solely because it is right. They need, like children, to have extraneous inducements to correct behavior. As in Paul, a focus on personal salvation through a rather mystical identification with a transcendent power negates concern for the inherited norms of public conduct. A transcendent freedom liberates us from the bondage of the public and the political. (Even the slightest shading of the truth for purposes of civil interaction, for example, would be impermissible in Kant's view.) Unlike Judaism, the kingdom is not of this world. We can construct new communities, such as the ecclesia or the Kingdom of Ends on the basis of a shared status vis-à-vis the transcendent, but the old worldly community of the nation, rooted in history, generativity, memory, and law, has no role in the new social ontology. To want to further the project of one's people, to find one's place among an historic collectivity, to want one's group to flourish and oneself to flourish within one's group falls far short of the cosmopolitanism of Paul or Kant.

Unlike Paul, Kant is not antinomian. His pronomian stance earned him many Jewish followers, his actual anti-Judaism notwithstanding. But law for Kant, in the sense of moral law, is a sublime abstraction, a criterion for forming courses of action, not an actual code of conduct. His disdain for Jewish law and for the (pseudo-) ethical premises which he thought lay at its base was vast. In this, it seems to me, he shares in the legacy of Christian anti-Judaism. But cultural tradition or milieu is less important than philosophical argument. How might Jewish ethics respond to a Kantian moral critique? First, it might try to meet it on its own ground. Second, it might try to argue against the cogency of that ground as such.

The key issue for Kant, as noted above, has to do with freedom. To act for any motive other than selfless devotion to the law per se undermines the possibility of a kind of sublime liberty. We must live in two worlds at once, the phenomenal world and the noumenal one. Only in the latter are we free. Our phenomenal selves, partly disclosed to us in self-awareness and partly (and permanently) obscured to us, impinge on our potential for rising to pure moral motivation. Judaism is a capitulation to that melancholy condition, to that "radical evil" which keeps human beings focused on the phenomenal world.

Pirkei Avot (hereafter *Avot*) meets Kant at least halfway. *Avot* 6:2 comments on the verse from Exodus, "The tablets were God's work, and the writing was God's writing, incised (*ḥarut*) upon the tablets" (Exod. 32:16). "Do not read incised (*ḥarut*) but freedom (*ḥerut*)," *Avot* asserts, imaginatively exploiting the ambiguity of Hebrew's consonantal alphabet. "For no one is free," the mishnah continues, "unless he is engaged in the study of Torah." Torah study elevates and transforms one. It enables one to refine one's perspective and view the world sub specie aeternitatis, giving all persons and things their due. It distances one from drives and impulses, allowing one to channel the primordial energy of life, the *yetzer*, into appropriate projects and pursuits. Law, far from being a heteronymous or burdensome imposition, enables the most sublime liberty. The Torah, the sages asserted in *Bereshit*

Rabbah 1:4, was created before the world came into being; God used it as a blueprint for subsequent material reality, just as an architect uses a plan for a building. The Torah, as a normative order, a nomos, is the plan of the cosmos.[31] Reality reflects its underlying normativity. Hence, one who studies the Torah is not simply engaged in the study of a peculiar positive nomos-cum-narrative, but in the inner truth of the world as such. A premise such as this informs *Avot* as well. Torah is more than story and law; it is the inner pulse of reality.

Against the background of this ontology, acts commanded by God through Torah (mitzvot) have both instrumental and intrinsic value. Instrumentally, mitzvot are opportunities to manifest devotion to and love of God. They are concrete performances which enact, sustain, or instantiate the covenantal order. They are moments of world-construction and maintenance. "A mitzvah leads to [another] mitzvah; a transgression leads to [another] transgression" (*Avot* 4:2). The mitzvot form a skein. Performance of mitzvot transforms the overall character of one's life. Whether one is oriented toward transcendence (the Kingdom of God) hinges on accepting the "yoke of the kingdom of heaven," the life of mitzvot. Habituation to the practices of rabbinic Judaism must not become mere habit. Ideally, habit shapes a disposition toward constant awareness of the divine presence. "Know before Whom you labor" (*Avot* 2:14; cf. *Berakhot* 28b, "Know before Whom you stand"): a consciousness of the divine should always be on one's mind. The mitzvot are vehicles for enlivening and refining that consciousness. In addition to whatever actual good they do in the world (as in honoring father and mother, supporting the poor, comforting mourners, visiting the sick, etc.), they change the quality of one's inner life.

The mitzvot can also be understood to have intrinsic worth. In the mishnah cited above, where one mitzvah is thought to entrain another, the text continues "the reward of a mitzvah is a mitzvah and the reward of a transgression is a transgression" (*Avot* 4:2).[32] This suggests that one should not look to the extrinsic consequences of one's actions; mitzvot are inherently right, transgressions are inherently wrong. The only "reward" that one gets for a religiously observant way of life is the continuity of that way of life. That is, of course, a consequence, a gain in utility, but it is intrinsic to the practice as such. One gets to live within the covenantal order, within the normative cosmos. One has intimacy, as it were, with the Creator of that order in its full breadth and depth. This text suggests that the life of mitzvot is inherently excellent, whatever excellent consequences it might produce. The good produced is secondary to the inherent goodness of the way of life that has produced it. This resonates with classical teaching on virtue. Courage, for example, is both good in itself (life would not be good without it) and good for what it produces (victories in battle, for example).[33] Virtues are both instrumentally and intrinsically valuable.

So far our discussion of Kantian deontology (acting out of reverence for the moral law) and consequentialism (acting on the motive of maximizing the good) has focused on the instrumental and intrinsic value of the commandments. But what of the farther reaches of consequentialism, accruing merit for or avoiding punishment in the afterlife, which Kant especially deplored? There is no question that rabbinic texts are concerned for the future felicity of the moral agent in the world to come. The question is how much weight this concern has and what is its specific character. Even Kant introduced theological considerations of a kind in his *Critique of Practical Reason*. He argued, on practical rather than metaphysical (by his lights) grounds, for the immortality of the soul and the existence of God. He needed some version of post-mortem individual perdurance to underwrite the validity of the principle "ought implies can." (One lifetime is never enough to fulfill the demands of the moral law. If we ought to fulfill them, we must be able to do so; we must have enough time to achieve conformity between the will and the law.[34])

A striking text, found in *Avot* (1:3) with commentary in *Avot de-Rabbi Natan* (chapter 5), first repudiates any interest in divine reward and urges the doing of mitzvot in a purely self-abnegating way but then struggles with this view and qualifies it. I shall cite the version in *Avot de-Rabbi Natan* in full. (The italicized sentences constitute the mishnah as found in *Avot*.)

> *Antigonus of Soko took over from Simeon the Righteous. He used to say: be not like slaves that serve their master for the sake of compensation; be rather like slaves who serve their master with no thought of compensation and let the fear of heaven be upon you*, so that your reward may be doubled in the age to come.
>
> Antigonus of Soko had two disciples who used to study his words. They taught them to their disciples, and their disciples to their disciples. These proceeded to examine the words closely and demanded: 'Why did our ancestors see fit to say this thing? Is it possible that a laborer should do his work all day and not take his reward in the evening? If our ancestors ... had known that there is another world and that there will be a resurrection of the dead, they would not have spoken in this manner.'
>
> So they arose and withdrew from the Torah and split into two sects, the Sadducees and the Boethusians: Sadducees named after Zadok, Boethusians after Boethus. And they used silver vessels and gold vessels all their lives – not because they were ostentatious but the Sadducees said, 'It is a tradition amongst the Pharisees to afflict themselves in this world; yet in the world to come they will have nothing.'[35]

The immediately striking thing about this text is that *Avot de-Rabbi Natan* adds a line to the original mishnah in *Avot*, which undermines or at least heavily qualifies Antigonus's central teaching. Whereas the Antigonus of *Avot* disclaims any interest in post-mortem reward, the editors of *Avot de-Rabbi Natan* claim that disinterest in reward will double one's reward! This clearly evidences rabbinic ambivalence about the wisdom of the otherwise unknown Antigonus. And yet, with characteristic rabbinic indulgence of competing opinions the teaching is preserved, weighed, and challenged.[36]

The text then offers a story about the rise of heresy in early Judaism. The Sadducees, opponents of the Pharisees from whom, presumably, rabbinic Judaism at least in part descended, began in reaction to Antigonus's teaching. How could Antigonus have taught that one should not expect a reward after death? It goes against logic and experience. No one works without thought of compensation. If Antigonus and those who transmitted his teaching had known about a world to come they could not have said such an illogical and counterintuitive thing. Therefore, they must not have known about a world to come. Therefore, given the wisdom of the ancestors, the world to come must not exist! The Pharisaic teaching of the resurrection of the dead must be false (as the Sadducees claimed). Therefore, the Pharisaic way of life, which is premised on future rewards, is senseless. There is no reason to deprive oneself of the comforts of this world, this world being the only world that there is.

The status of Antigonus's teaching remains ambiguous. The rabbis do not fully repudiate it. They revise and qualify it. They might be said to agree with it in the sense that one is not entitled to serve God solely on the motivation of receiving compensation (*peras*). (The term *peras* seems to imply a food allowance that employers would give employees or perhaps high-ranking slaves.) That is "one thought too many." Nonetheless, it is not wrong to expect a deferred reward (*sekhar*) in the world to come. The rabbis read Antigonus's dictum to support this distinction. Immediate compensation – out; ultimate reward – in. The cosmos is so designed or governed as to support the expectation of just desert, albeit adjusted by divine mercy and grace. That the erring disciples, who founded the deviant sects of the Sadducees and Boethusians, reject rabbinic teaching on this matter and conclude that there is no future reward shows the consequences of rejecting rabbinic teaching. Antigonus was not a heretic; he was misinterpreted by them. There is a world to come; it is proper to expect ultimate reward (and punishment). The rabbis claim him, once suitably qualified, as one of their own. (It is worth noting that in the *Avot* version, there is no qualification. Antigonus's teaching is allowed to stand as is.)

Neither *Avot* nor *Avot de-Rabbi Natan* rejects hope for a reward as an improper form of moral motivation. "Rabbi Jacob used to say: This world is like a vestibule before the world to come; prepare yourself in the vestibule that you may enter into the banquet hall" (*Avot* 4:16).[37] The trope of relativizing the value of this world vis-à-vis the world to come may also be found in *Avot* 2:15–16. "Rabbi Tarfon said: The day is short and the task is great and the laborers are idle and the wage is abundant and the master of the house is urgent. He used to say: it is not your part to finish the task, yet you are not free to desist from it. If you have studied much Torah much reward will be given to you and faithful is the taskmaster who shall pay you the reward of your labor. And know that the recompense of the reward of the righteous is for the time to come."

Texts such as these admit hope for future reward as a legitimate, even necessary motive for moral action. They do not imply, however, that it should be the *sole* motive or that one's relationship with God should be construed along contractual lines. They are part of an ensemble of proper motivations, originating within the context of a covenantal, reciprocal relationship. Rather than attesting to the narrow, self-interested, strictly prudential character of motivation, belief in a future reward attests to confidence in the benevolence of God. It attests to mutuality. The God of the covenant will not abandon His people. He wishes them to flourish. Even when they sin, He waits for them to return even up to the hour of their deaths (as the liturgy puts it). Belief in future reward attests as well to convictions about the significance of agency, accountability, responsibility, and justice. We are responsible to a high degree for our own fates; our acts will be met by just deserts.[38] The just expectations of God are to be internalized. Thus a rabbi says: "Consider three things and you will not fall into transgression: know what is above you – a seeing eye and a hearing ear and all of your deeds written into a book" (*Avot* 2:1). We are to view ourselves, our thoughts and deeds, sub specie aeternitatis, as if from God's point of view. The belief in reward and punishment then is a belief in divine justice rather than in our own rights, claims, or interests. Those matters have at least prima facie validity, given a scheme of justice that embraces both God and man. But our claims must constantly be judged by God's standards. And they will always fall short. Thus, Jews pray to be judged *not* by what they deserve but by what a merciful father would graciously grant them.[39]

None of this would lessen a Kantian (let alone a Freudian!) critique. Kant would have us act only out of acknowledgment of the inherent rightness of the moral law. *Avot* would have all our actions "done for the sake of heaven" (*Avot* 2:12). Kant would have us act as self-legislating free agents. *Avot* would have us act as free covenantal partners of our Creator. There are superficial resemblances here but also deep differences. Kant would have us act without regard to consequences; purity of will is the controlling criterion. *Avot* would have us strive to bend our will to God's will (*Avot* 2:4), but *Avot* also hopes that God's will might incline toward our will. We expect good conduct and character to have, on the whole and all things considered, good consequences. *Avot*'s consequentialist orientation, although it is sometimes defeated by the contingencies of real life, remains a natural way of reasoning about ethics. Rabbinic ethics, despite the foreignness of some of its concerns and, from the point of view of secular ethics, its dubious theological assumptions, corresponds better to our ordinary moral experience than Kantian ethics. It is hard to imagine sustaining the moral world that Kant wants to sustain without a belief that good conduct is good at least partly because of its consequences: because it benefits others, is integral to personal flourishing, and has ameliorative effects on the social world as such. Indeed, Kant cannot banish such considerations. It is difficult for him to integrate them, however.[40]

Kant is much impressed by how reality can defeat good intention. All that we can freely control in the end is the disposition of our will. Kant is thus almost entirely focused on "what ought I to do?" More precisely, on what ought I to intend or desire to do. The Socratic question, "how should I live?" requires cultivating virtues that will allow me to live well. For Kant, virtues reduce to one: non-resistance to the categorical demand of the moral law. The rest make one too vulnerable. The ancients recognized the large role that vulnerability, contingency, and luck play in eudemonia. They sought to minimize and control luck but they could not eradicate it.[41] Kant eradicates it by training moral decision and action onto a sphere far above the messy contingencies of historical existence. Yet that very messiness gives ethics its point and purpose. A society of angels, of disembodied noumenal wills self-legislating universal law for perfectly rational agents, would lack occasion to apply the moral law in the first place. Do such putative beings have business transactions or secrets to keep or temptations to embarrass others or decisions to reach about the moral status of fetuses or end-stage Alzheimer's sufferers? (The knowledge of good and evil, after all, expels one from paradise.) Kant is arresting as a theoretical account of normativity but frustrating as a guide for actual moral decision.

Rabbinic ethics aspires to transform persons into saints but at the same time revels in the complex messiness of decision situations. Although we have been considering wise sayings and stories, aphoristic encapsulations of moral wisdom, much of the work of rabbinic ethics goes on under the framework of legal discussion and analysis. Here the choices forced on moral reason by historical contingency or competing principles are most acute. We turn now to a discussion of the nature of justice in the Talmud where the sages cope with the implications of a problematic biblical rule.

Talmud and Talion

The Talmud is full of bold rabbinic interpretations of problematic biblical tropes and rules. In Scripture, for example, if a man "seizes" and "lies with" a virgin, who is not engaged to another man, "the man who lay with her shall pay the girl's father fifty [shekels of] silver, and she shall be his wife. Because he has violated her, he can never have the right to divorce her" (Deut. 22:29). This law, which has a parallel in Exodus 22:15–16, protects the woman in the sense that the offending male cannot abandon her. Were she abandoned by him she would probably not have the opportunity to marry anyone else, because of her compromised status, and would be permanently disadvantaged in biblical society. Nonetheless, the prospect of being wed forever to someone who might have raped her – the text is unclear as to whether the sexual encounter was forced or consensual – is grim. In the Talmud's construction of this law, the sages find the woman's consent to be *necessary*. Based on some curious linguistic features of the biblical verses, they empower her to decide her own future (*B. Ketubot* 39b). She cannot be married to him unless she wants to, although he must still pay a fine to her father.[42] One can view this development as rooted in a deep process beginning with the biblical text itself, as well as the social world that lies behind it. Deuteronomy's version of various laws about marriage already shows a departure from an understanding of marriage as a purely contractual phenomenon to an understanding of marriage as a morally weighted condition.[43] One could point as well to the rabbinic restrictions on the "war bride," the female captive with whom an Israelite soldier had sexual relations (Deut. 21:10–14). The biblical text already shows concern for the female captive; it seeks to regulate the soldier's conduct and protect the woman from wanton cruelty. The Talmud deepens this dynamic, adding additional prohibitions that give the woman time to adjust to her new situation, and to consider whether she wants to become a Jew, so that she has full rights and status (*B. Kiddushin* 21b–22a). Indeed, the conduct of war as such was reframed and regulated by the rabbis, albeit in an historical context which made their just war theory purely speculative. The harsh biblical injunctions of total war against the seven Canaanite nations (Deut. 7:1–5) were radically transformed by the sages. The Bible is explicit: "you must doom them to destruction: grant them no terms and give them no quarter" (Deut. 7:2). Nonetheless, the midrash portrays Moses as deciding to offer the Amorites terms of peace. The midrash portrays God as assenting to Moses' decision and, in effect, overturning, out of deference to Moses, his own categorical instruction (*Deuteronomy Rabbah* 5:13).[44]

The unmistakable trend toward further humanization, alive in the biblical process and deepened by the rabbis, failed to mitigate the harsh Christian and secular criticism of the Talmud. Such critics have compared Jewish ethics with Christian ethics and found the former wanting. Its stress on justice is sometimes thought to be both too obsessive and too harsh. A locus classicus for discussion, both condemnatory and apologetic, has been the various formulations of the law of retaliation (*lex talionis*, in Roman jurisprudence) in Exodus 21:23–25, Leviticus 24:17–22, and Deuteronomy

19:21. The main rabbinic discussion of this topic is found in the Mishnah, *Baba Kamma* 8:1 and in the Babylonian Talmud, tractate *Baba Kamma* 83b–84a. As this text displays the subtle moral casuistry of rabbinic thought and is, as well, of inherent moral interest for what it says about justice, we will follow its argument as an example of ethical reasoning in a legal setting.

The version in Leviticus gives us the fullest biblical statement of the *lex talionis*.

> If anyone kills any human being, he shall be put to death. One who kills a beast shall make restitution for it: life for life. If anyone kills his fellow, as he has done so shall it be done to him: fracture for fracture, eye for eye, tooth for tooth. The injury he inflicted on another shall be inflicted on him. One who kills a beast shall make restitution for it; but one who kills a human being shall be put to death. You shall have one standard for stranger and citizen alike: for I the LORD am your God. (Lev. 24:17–22)

Unlike Mesopotamian law codes, which have parallel formulations, biblical law does not peg punishment to social status. Leviticus says nothing about whether the human being killed by another is a slave or social inferior.[45] Those considerations brook large in Hammurabi, for example, so the biblical rule, "life for life," although stringent, assumes the equal value of life in a way that the Mesopotamian codes do not. Continuing that tendency, the law must apply to Israelite and resident non-Israelite alike. One standard (*mishpat*) of justice applies to all in the land, as one God has rule over the moral cosmos.

The understanding of justice embodied in this text is one of strict reciprocity, which does not take account of mitigating circumstances. Already in Numbers, chapter 35 an important range of qualifiers is introduced. Unintentional homicides as well as aggravating conditions with respect to the manner in which the killer struck the victim and the prior history between them are considered. The ideal of strict reciprocity, although it has conceptual elegance, is unworkable under actual conditions. A more subtle understanding of justice, scaled to the particularity of circumstances, is needed. The curious interplay in the text between talion for the range of cases involving human beings and financial compensation for the cases involving animals will capture the attention of the rabbis and help build their argument that, with respect to injury (albeit not death), forms of financial restitution replace corporal punishment.

The first level of the Talmud, the Mishnah (*Baba Kamma* 8:1), lays down a fivefold scheme for how one who has injured another must compensate him. The Mishnah does not even reference any of the biblical texts which stipulate "eye for eye" and so on; it simply assumes the norm of compensation rather than retaliation. (The five forms of compensation include: depreciation, pain, healing, loss of time, and degradation.) Much of the work of the Gemara, the commentary on the Mishnah which (together with the Mishnah) constitutes the Talmud, has to do with warranting the law of the Mishnah and the opinions of mishnaic teachers (known as *Tannaim*). The Talmud begins its argument with the incredulous question "Why [pay compensation]? Does the Divine Law not say '*Eye for eye*'? Why not take this literally to mean [putting out] the eye [of the offender]?"[46] How can this massive departure from the plain sense of the biblical text be justified? The Gemara's first move is to argue that the verbal architecture of the Leviticus passage itself gives support to compensation rather than talion. The juxtaposition of language about restitution in the case of damaged animals and language about corporeal damage in the case of human beings implies that human beings should be compensated, just as the owners of animals are compensated. Yet sensing the possible inadequacy of this hermeneutic argument, the Gemara immediately introduces another line of argument. The verse in Numbers 35:31, which prohibits taking ransom for the life of a murderer (there "life for life" must apply), is read narrowly to imply that ransom, that is, financial compensation, must be taken for all damages which fall short of murder.

The Gemara goes on to question what biblical verses, since several are in play, really support these conclusions. It then raises a general interpretative point. "What is your reason for deriving the law of man injuring man from the law of smiting a beast and not from the law governing the case of killing a man [where retaliation is the rule]? I would answer: It is proper to derive [the law of] injury from [the law governing another case of] injury, and not to derive [the law of] injury from [the law governing the case of] murder." The similarity of injury to a man and injury to a beast should outweigh the dissimilarity of man and beast. On the other hand, the Gemara wants to validate the intuition that there is something unseemly about deriving procedure for human injury from the case of injury to animals. That is why another line of argument – the narrow reading of Numbers 35:31 – was brought into the discussion. The Gemara now explores some implications of the verse from Numbers in conjunction with the verses from Leviticus. It draws out two. The first is a rule that you cannot both execute a man for murdering another *and* fine him for damaging the principal limbs of his victim. The death penalty suffices for justice to be done. Second, damages *must* be paid. If the Numbers verse were considered in isolation, it could be inferred that the malefactor has the option to pay compensation for, say, his victim's eye with his own eye. Given the analogous case of the beast, however, where financial compensation must be paid, so too here corporal punishment, even if (perversely) chosen by the guilty party, is not allowed.

This dense discussion does not settle the matter. The question is now raised again in the name of a tanna, R. Dosthai ben Judah: What if actual corporal retaliation, eye for eye, really is meant? Rather than rely on a hermeneutic strategy, the Gemara now introduces a purely rational argument. Against R. Dosthai's presupposition that perhaps an actual eye is meant, the Gemara argues that eyes come in different sizes – there are large and small eyes. If, say, the victim's eye was small and the offender's eye was large, how can this be fair? Did not the Torah say, in the same portion of Leviticus (24:22), "You shall have one standard …"? (The verse is abbreviated and taken out of context – nothing unusual in a creative rabbinic reading.) But – and here the view is countered – "one standard" should not be read to imply "eyes of the same size" but rather capacity for sight per se. In the Torah's law about "life for life" we are not concerned if a dwarf has killed a giant or a giant has killed a dwarf. What is salient here is life as such, not superficial differences pertinent to the agents. None of this, however, answers the root question of why monetary compensation rather than corporal punishment should prevail. Indeed, the preceding discussion might be taken to give added credence to talion.

The question is raised again and is given a more nuanced reply by the Gemara. If you claim that an eye for an eye literally means what it says, what would you do in the case of an offender who was already blind in one eye or lame in one hand or foot? Putting out his eye or cutting off his hand or foot would cause damage to him disproportionate to the damage he caused to his victim. The Gemara attempts a counterargument. Why not say that where proportionate corporal punishment is possible, inflict it? Where it is not possible, as in the above cases, do not inflict it. The Gemara, in support of this view, brings in a case from tractate Sanhedrin (78a) where a person with a fatal organic disease (known as a *treifah*) who kills another cannot actually be put to death himself. Why not apply that principle of law to these instances?

No decisive answer is given to this question or to the basic question of why financial compensation is the valid reading of "eye for eye." More attempts to deduce the compensation reading from subtle features of the biblical language are adduced. One has particular ethical interest. The language of Exodus 21:23–24 is slightly different from the language in Leviticus. In Exodus, the phrase "life for life" occurs and precedes "eye for eye." The amora Abbaye, citing a tradition, maintains that life for life and eye for eye, separately phrased as they are, are meant to be kept separate as instances of punishment. It might happen that, in the course of affecting putative corporal punishment, taking out an eye could result in a death. Then, instead of life for life and eye for eye, one would have a case of "life and eye for eye." Although corporal punishment *was* intended, capital punishment might inadvertently result. The risk of such gross injustice undermines the feasibility of talion, therefore the Torah must intend financial compensation. The Gemara counters that there need not be a difficulty here.

Competent authorities can make an estimation of whether the offender can withstand the rigors of corporal punishment. If he can, then removal of his eye can proceed. (And if he can't? Is he to be released? This question is not answered by the Gemara.) If he does die in the course of the punishment, no liability ensues. Apparently the authorities acted in good faith and are not guilty of negligence or malpractice. The discussion now turns to justifying the various mishnaic categories of compensation (depreciation, pain, healing, etc.), in the course of which a final proof is introduced to resolve the problem of fully excluding talion and justifying financial recompense. Recall that an initial concern was that cases involving injury to beasts should not provide the analogical basis for cases involving injury to humans. The Gemara finds a verse in Deuteronomy (22:29) where a rapist must pay the father of his victim an amount of silver for the harm that he has done. The text in Deuteronomy uses an "x for x" phrase that grammatically mirrors the relevant phrases in Leviticus and Exodus. Thus, at last, financial compensation can be justified by analogy to a case of conduct among persons rather than one involving animals. The matter is apparently settled. The densely textured text, the conceptual twists and turns, and thrusts and parries, are entirely typical of the Talmud's style. Some find its complexity fascinating; others find it maddening. It has, at any rate, given generations of Jewish learners a keen appreciation for intellectual subtlety. As noted in the Introduction, the line – if any – between law and ethics is hard to draw in Judaism. The argumentation we have just sampled blurs any such putative line.

The Bible records both mutilation and compensation as modes of punishment. The sages move toward a compensation-only system. Whether they wholly retroject their own teaching onto the written Torah or whether they have a reliable tradition from earlier times is unclear. In terms of the pious understanding of oral Torah as coeval with written Torah, this question would not arise. Even bracketing pious belief, however, it is not clear that biblical justice demanded retribution through mutilation. Ancient Near Eastern law codes have examples of compensation systems, often tied to social status. The biblical societies may have practiced compensation as well. Perhaps the bald "eye for an eye" texts are meant to state a principle of justice as strict reciprocity rather than a working rule for what actually is to be done. At any rate, the questions and counterexamples raised by the Gemara might have been raised in very early times as well. They are natural questions that one would raise about justice when difficult cases arise.

The understanding of justice encoded in the biblical text is one of symmetry. A balance exists between act and consequence. In rabbinic language, this is captured by the phrase "measure for measure" (*middah k'neged middah*). The earliest chapters of Genesis evince this symmetry. Cain murders Abel, whose blood cries out to God from the ground (Gen. 4:10). Thus, Cain, the first farmer, will be banished from working the ground, condemned to be a restless wanderer over the earth (Gen. 4:12). The world itself emerged from watery chaos; the corruption wrought by man's wickedness destroys all life and returns the world to the watery chaos of the Flood (Gen. 6:7). The sense of justice as symmetry is brought out by a phrase in Genesis 9:6, which in Hebrew approximates a palindrome: "Whoever sheds the blood of man, by man shall his blood be shed" (*shofekh dam ha-adam b'adam damo yishafekh*). The simple symmetry of eye for eye and life for life encapsulates this large narrative trope and applies it as a nomos. This seems to be the way divine justice works: sin begets a fitting, measured punishment, while good deeds occasion a measured reward. In rabbinic literature, the Mishnah perfectly exemplifies this conception of justice in Sotah, a tractate treating the wife suspected of adultery (based on Numbers, chapter 5). The mishnaic text begins with a statement of general interpretive principle: "according to the measure that a person measures with it do we measure him" (*b'middah she adam moded bo moddedin lo*).[47]

> She adorned herself for transgression, [therefore] God made her disgusting.
>
> She uncovered herself for sin, [therefore] God caused her to be uncovered.
>
> She began her sin with her thigh and afterward [with] the belly, [therefore] her thigh will be afflicted first and afterward her belly (M. Sotah 1:7).[48]

The next mishnah (Sotah 1:8) provides classical examples of the same kind of symmetry. Samson went astray after the desire of his eyes, therefore the Philistines put out his eyes. Absalom gloried in his hair, therefore he was hanged by his hair; he raped 10 of his father's concubines and therefore was thrust through by 10 spears. The symmetry entails matters of both quantity and quality. God's divine justice, working through human events, recompenses bad deeds in an exactly scaled way.

The symmetry is skewed, however, for good deeds. Here God insures that the benevolent actor gets more than his or her due. In Sotah 1:9, Miriam waited for an hour to see what would happen to the infant Moses when set adrift on the Nile (Exod. 2:4), thus Israel waited for seven days until Miriam was healed from her scale disease (Num. 12:15). Joseph buried his father. Then Moses, who was greater than Joseph, buried him (Exod. 13:19). For this, God buried Moses (Deut. 34:6). Justice in these instances is enhanced by mercy. Nonetheless, the notion of symmetry still governs the basic transaction. Act is balanced by consequence in as mirrored a way as possible. Although the author of Job provided a powerful objection to this schema, it remained the dominant view enshrined in the biblical literature. The Mishnah continues to affirm it. It is only in midrash and in the Babylonian Talmud that serious objections are raised against it.

Our text struggles with the symmetrical conception of justice within its own idiom. One issue that arises immediately is whether injury to human beings is like injury to beasts. What should count here – the analogous fact of bodily injury or the disanalogy between humans and animals? Given the unique value of the human, would it not make more sense to set corporeal damage on a continuum with murder as an endpoint? Corporeal damage could be conceptualized as having less gravity than murder but being on the same continuum with it. If that were the right context in which to judge what is to count as just punishment, then the literal meaning of eye for eye, etc. has force. The argument on behalf of monetary compensation, which draws its nerve from the case of animals, falls in the face of human uniqueness. The text struggles with the claims of sacred human value on the one side and of meliorating a harsh, albeit symmetrical, punishment on the other.

The Gemara's struggle to ground financial compensation in conduct *inter homines* reflects a desire to affirm the uniqueness of the human and to ameliorate a troubling biblical rule, ostensibly using the resources of ancient traditions as well as abstract hermeneutic reasoning. Moral reasoning in the halakhic sphere of the Talmud is casuistic; it is anchored in case law. It appraises received texts and traditions with laser-like critical scrutiny, weighing competing constructions of meaning and interpretation. It juxtaposes argument against argument, often leaving the rival claims of competing positions unresolved, thereby inviting future generations to reenact the dialogue. Even where the issues are more or less resolved, as in our case, the issues remain alive. Even where the debates involve issues less ethically fraught than capital punishment or civil and criminal liability, there is always moral significance to be gleaned from the text. Recent efforts to retrieve casuistry as a form of moral reasoning from early modern ignominy would do well to consider the Talmud as an example.[49]

Just as God recompenses good deeds with a greater measure of reward than they, from the point of view of strict desert, warrant, so too Jews are supposed to err on the side of generosity. The Talmud asserts that one should seek the most favorable interpretation of one's fellow's deeds, even when one has a reason to interpret them uncharitably (Shabbat 127a). Such charitable interpretation is one of the six things whose fruits one enjoys in this world and whose stock remains meritorious for the world to come.[50] The Talmud illustrates this virtue with a story.

> Our Rabbis taught: He who judges his neighbour in the scale of merit is himself judged favourably. Thus a story is told of a certain man who descended from Upper Galilee and was engaged by an individual in the South for three years. On the eve of the Day of Atonement he requested him, 'Give me my wages that I may go and support my wife and children.'

'I have no money,' answered he. 'Give me produce,' he demanded; 'I have none,' he replied. 'Give me land.' – 'I have none.' 'Give me cattle.' – 'I have none.' 'Give me pillows and bedding.' – 'I have none.'

[So] he slung his things behind him and went home with a sorrowful heart. After the Festival his employer took his wages in his hand together with three laden asses, one bearing food, another drink, and the third various sweetmeats, and went to his house. After they had eaten and drunk, he gave him his wages.

Said he to him, 'When you asked me, "Give me my wages," and I answered you, "I have no money," of what did you suspect me?' 'I thought, Perhaps you came across cheap merchandise and had purchased it therewith.' 'And when you requested me, "Give me cattle," and I answered, "I have no cattle," of what did you suspect me?' 'I thought, they may be hired to others.' 'When you asked me, "Give me land," and I told you, "I have no land," of what did you suspect me?' 'I thought, perhaps it is leased to others.' 'And when I told you, "I have no produce," of what did you suspect me?' 'I thought, Perhaps they are not tithed.' 'And when I told you, "I have no pillows or bedding," of what did you suspect me?' 'I thought, perhaps he has sanctified all his property to Heaven.'

'By the [Temple] service!' exclaimed he, 'it was even so; I vowed away all my property because of my son Hyrcanus, who would not occupy himself with the Torah, but when I went to my companions in the South they absolved me of all my vows. And as for you, just as you judged me favourably, so may the Omnipresent judge you favourably.'[51]

The story describes an instance of extraordinary generosity of interpretation by an employee of the motives of his employer. While it would have been natural to believe that the employer was cheating the employee of his wages, the employee sought to justify his employer's conduct, even though it was to his immediate detriment to do so. He went back to Galilee with a sorrowful heart. In a sense, he judged his employer as God might judge, not with a strict accounting but with a gracious attitude evocative of empathy. Later, it emerges that the charitable assumptions the employee made about the employer's situation were correct. The excuses that he made for his employer's conduct were warranted. The employer both recompenses the employee and blesses him; may God judge you as favorably as you judged me. The story thus illustrates the principle of "enjoying the fruits of one's action in this world and having merit remain for one in the world to come."

We can see here how strictly legal or deontic considerations fuse with the considerations of virtue to form an integrated approach to justice. As in the classical tradition, justice is both a virtue of persons, of well-ordered souls, and a quality of laws and constitutions. The practice of the virtuous man sustains and is sustained by the just laws of a good society. Deontic and aretaic considerations complement one another. Our story does not explore what might have happened had the employee taken his employer to court; he certainly had that right under Jewish law. It does not suggest that one should suffer losses in saintly resignation. Had the employee good reason to believe that there were no exculpatory circumstances affecting his employer, he need not have borne the loss with equanimity. He could have sued him. He stopped himself from doing so, we may infer, because he found reason to excuse or even justify his conduct. We may conclude therefore that the virtue of judging one's fellow favorably cannot be separated from a context of public justice, from a society ordered by laws that protect contracts, for example. Private virtue needs good public institutions to flourish. The order of the soul, so to speak, needs to be mirrored in the order of society.

The Talmudic ethical/legal principle of "going beyond the limits of the law" (*lifnim me-shurat ha-din*) illustrates this dual emphasis.[52] The principle entails the virtue of self-restraint. One has a right under law to a specific quantity of a specific benefit, for example, but rather than take all of what one is legally owed, one restrains oneself. One's claim ends within (*lifnim*) the limit of the law, before its boundary, so to speak. One takes less than one's rightful share, often for the purpose of benefiting another. God too can practice *lifnim me-shurat ha-din*, extending to Israel more mercy than their deeds, from the perspective of strict desert, require (Berakhot 7a). One can see in this principle a device for ameliorating social conduct. If relations between persons, even in the sphere properly governed by law, were only controlled by strict exchange, life would be harsh. The kind of sympathy properly at home in intimate and familial relations cannot be transferred, nor should it be transferred, to fully public settings. Nonetheless, the world of contractual and civil relations should be tempered by virtues, such as friendliness, more fully at home elsewhere (*Avot* 1:15). In societies where a covenantal understanding of public life is alive this comes more naturally than in those where a more procedural understanding of social contract prevails. As a covenantal order, Judaism envisions a community where people are both responsible for one another and love one another as much as they love themselves (Lev. 19:18).[53] To have a well-ordered soul is to have the capacity to love another, to understand what another needs. To be capable of a moral point of view, one has to recognize one's fellow as a being fully comparable in worth and capacities to oneself. What one finds hateful should not be done to another (Shabbat 31a). A person incapable of empathetic moral imagination at this level is stunted in his or her personhood. A text from *Avot* reveals rabbinic thinking about the achievement of moral personhood. *Avot* (5:10) teaches that

> There are four types among men: he that says, 'What is mine is mine and what is thine is thine' – this is the common type and some say that this is the type of Sodom; [he that says] 'What is mine is thine and what is thine is mine' – he is an ignorant man; [he that says] 'What is mine is thine and what is thine is thine

own' – he is a saintly man; [and he that says] 'What is thine is mine and what is mine is mine own' – he is a wicked man.

The ambivalence of the text as to whether common propriety – what is mine is mine and what is yours is yours – is acceptable or venial is interesting. On the view that this is an average or common character trait (*midah beinonit*) we need not worry about benefiting one another. Your circumstances are not my problem nor are my problems your problems. An atomized, formal social ontology pertains. Relations between persons are strictly contractual. Relationships between such libertarian individuals must be of their own choosing. If one chooses not to be involved with another, no fault or blame may be ascribed. If one chooses to be so involved, the involvement is regulated by a symmetrical, contractual balance of rights and obligations – no more, no less. On the view that this is a recipe for the extreme moral corruption of Sodom, however, this attitude is thought to lead to something much worse. As a classic commentator to the Mishnah suggests, the conventional attitude tends toward promoting a Sodom-like attitude (*midat sodom*) as one becomes habituated to selfishness. Even in the case where "one benefits and the other loses nothing" he will not want to benefit his neighbor. This epitomizes the characteristic of Sodom. Even when the earth and its riches stretched out before them, they would not welcome guests into their midst.[54] The commentator here invokes the legal concept of one benefits from another's action and the other suffers no loss (*zeh neheneh v'zeh lo ḥaser*). The classic case of this is where a landholder has a field adjacent to another field and he wants to sell one of them. His neighbor, whose own plot would be expanded by the purchase, has the right of first refusal. The seller has to offer it to the buyer who would have most to gain by the sale. Everyone benefits, no one suffers loss. If, however, the seller does not want to sell to his neighbor, the court can force him to do so because it can compel a Jew not to act like the people of Sodom (*kofin 'al midat-Sodom*) (Baba Batra 12b). Here a moral principle is given legal teeth. Does that eviscerate the virtue of friendliness by, in a sense, enforcing it on the recalcitrant or does it enable a society to enhance fellowship (*re 'ut*) among its inhabitants? The rabbis, seeking to sustain a covenantal order, had higher expectations than we have for the degree and kind of involvement that persons should have in one another's lives. Whether this is compatible with the high degree of personal liberty that citizens of modern societies expect is worth pondering.

The idea of compelling people not to act in the manner of Sodom entails more than preventing them from being gratuitously selfish. It means educating persons in a correct and humane conception of justice. The sages depict the people of Sodom as wicked precisely because their conception of justice was overly strict and literal and therefore perverse; they used justice as a screen for malevolence. Among the many stories the sages tell of Sodom, the following captures their approach to justice:

> In Sodom there were four judges: Shakrai ("liar"); Shakrurai ("archdeceiver"); Zayyefai ("forger"); and Matzle-dina ("perverter of justice).

> When a man struck his neighbor's wife and caused her to miscarry, the husband would be told, "Give her to this man to impregnate her again."

> When a man cut off the ear of another man's donkey, the aggrieved owner would be told, "Give the donkey to this man to keep until its ear grows back."

> When a man wounded another, the victim would be told, "Pay the man a fee for having bled you."

> When a man crossed a bridge, he would be charged four *zuz*; but if he waded through the water to avoid the toll he would be charged eight *zuz*.[55]

The aggadah portrays the systemic perversion of public justice, mirrored by a cynical and heartless attitude. The law is insensitive to the victims of wrongdoing. It facilitates their continued oppression. Further, it encourages malice and shamelessness in others – all in the name of a warped understanding of justice.[56]

The rabbinic project aims at the education of enlightened persons who accept upon themselves, as individuals and as a people, the "yoke of the kingdom of heaven." The yoke of the kingdom of heaven is comprised of norms of conduct and ideals of character. It envisions a life oriented to the service of God through inner transformation and disciplined practice. Although vastly complex and open-ended as an interpretative and legislative project, the sages' Torah allowed for pithy generalization. The Talmud itself tried to encapsulate the meaning of the Torah in a broadly ethical manner. Rabbi Simlai claimed that the laws of the Torah numbered 613: 365 negative ones, corresponding to the days of solar year, and 248 positive ones, corresponding to the number of joints (on the sages' anatomical reckoning) in the human body. King David came and reduced them to 11 (following Psalm 15). These included such norms as walking uprightly, speaking the truth, and refraining from slander, inter alia. The prophet Isaiah came and reduced the 11 to six (see Isa. 33:15–16). Then the prophet Micah came and reduced them to three: to do justice, to love goodness, and to walk modestly with God (Mic. 6:8). Isaiah returned and reduced them to two: observe what is right and do what is just (Isa. 56:1). The prophet Amos reduced them to one: "Seek Me and you will live" (Amos 5:4).[57] The sages were alive to the salience and power of moral-legal principles, giving them emphasis without losing the particularity of detailed rules. We turn now to a post-Talmudic literature that elevated the clarification of those principles to its highest concern.

Notes

1   The term "rabbinic literature" itself is problematic, as its creators did not call themselves rabbis, nor did they see themselves as authors, nor did they see their "literature" as comparable to anything that moderns would designate by that name. Nonetheless, the term – a product of the nineteenth-century academy – has stuck and modern scholars opt to stick with it. For a helpful, sophisticated overview of the main works of rabbinic literature in their historical contexts, see the Introduction to Charlotte Elisheva Fonrobert and Martin S. Jaffee, eds, *The Cambridge Companion to The Talmud and Rabbinic Literature* (New York: Cambridge University Press, 2007).

2   The Babylonian Talmud, in particular, records such principled disagreements on virtually every page, often without definitive resolution. For an acute modern study of the significance of such a stance, see Avi Sagi, *The Open Canon: On the Meaning of Halakhic Discourse* (New York: Continuum, 2008).

3   A. Cohen, *Everyman's Talmud* (London: J. M. Dent & Sons, 1949). See also C. G. Montefiore and H. Loewe, *A Rabbinic Anthology* (New York: Schocken, 1974).

4   A forceful critique of this older style of academic synthesis is Jacob Neusner's review essay of Ephraim Urbach's *The Sages*. See Jacob Neusner, *A History of the Mishnaic Law of Purities*, Vol. 18 (Leiden: Brill, 1974), pp. 206–220.

5   Jonathan Wyn Schofer, *The Making of a Sage: A Study in Rabbinic Ethics* (Madison: University of Wisconsin Press, 2005), p. 23.

6   An introduction to midrash as a genre may be found in Steven D. Fraade, "Rabbinic Midrash and Ancient Jewish Biblical Interpretation," in Fonrobert and Jaffee, eds, *The Cambridge Companion to the Talmud and Rabbinic Literature*, Chapter 5. For a study that is sensitive to theological and literary concerns, readers may also consult Michael Fishbane, *The Exegetical Imagination* (Cambridge, MA: Harvard University Press, 1998).

7   Midrash Tanhuma, Lekh Lekha, 9.

8   *Genesis Rabbah*, Chapter 40: midrash 6. A leading scholar of rabbinic literature, Jacob Neusner, sees Genesis Rabbah as a rabbinic response to the conversion of Constantine and the rise of imperial Christianity. Just as Eusebius gave a Christian theology of history, oriented toward the Christianization of Rome, so too *Genesis Rabbah* is the sages' attempt to provide a Jewish theology of history which makes sense of the massive change in political circumstances. "The events in Genesis served as types," Neusner writes, "prefiguring what would happen to Israel in the future. Just as the Christians read stories of Genesis as types of the life of Christ, so the sages understood the tales of Genesis in a similarly typological manner." In Jacob Neusner, *Judaism and Christianity in the Age of Constantine* (Chicago: University of Chicago Press, 1987), p. 30.

9   Clifford Geertz, *The Interpretation of Cultures* (New York: Basic Books, 1973), Chapter 4.

10   The Noahide laws are a rabbinic creation unknown to post-biblical books such as Jubilees. The rabbis, through biblical exegesis, give mitzvah-like content

to God's covenant with Noah. The seven laws comprise six negative command-ments prohibiting idolatry, blasphemy, shedding blood, unchastity (e.g. incest), theft, and tearing a limb from a living creature, and one positive law enjoining the establishment of courts of justice. For Talmudic sources on the seven laws, see *B. Sanhedrin* 56a–60a; *B. Avodah Zarah* 3a–b, 64b. For an important study of the laws, which is a work of Jewish moral philosophy in its own right, see David Novak, *The Image of the Non-Jew in Judaism: An Historical and Constructive Study of the Noahide Laws* (New York: Edwin Mellen Press, 1983).

11   See Joseph Schultz, "Two Views of the Patriarchs," in Michael Fishbane and Paul Flohr, eds, *Texts and Responses: Studies Presented to Nahum N. Glatzer* (Leiden: Brill, 1975). On Abraham's knowledge of all the commandments, see *Bereshit Rabbah* 49:2, 64:5.

12   *Pirkei de Rabbi Eliezer*, Chapters 26–30. Cf. *Pirkei Avot*, 5:3.

13   Jon D. Levenson, *The Death and Resurrection of the Beloved Son* (New Haven: Yale University Press, 1993), Chapter 1.

14   For a scholarly analysis of *Genesis Rabbah* as a response to the Christianization of the Roman Empire, see Neusner in note 8 above.

15   English translation is found in H. Freedman, trans., *Midrash Rabbah: Genesis*, Vol. 1 (London: The Soncino Press, 1983), p. 486.

16   A famous midrash (*Bereshit Rabbah* 38:13) presents Abraham as reasoning his way toward a monotheistic belief. Abraham is a proto-philosopher, rather than the passive recipient of divine revelation as presented in Genesis, chapter 12. Abraham, once he arrives at his warranted belief, tries to teach it to others, such as his father. This puts him on a collision course with the evil king, Nimrod. Abraham's suffering under Nimrod is one of his trials. The midrashic emphasis on Abraham's rationality heightens the drama of his eventual submission to divine authority.

17   A classic study of the role of merit in rabbinic thought is Solomon Schechter's essay, "The Zachuth of the Fathers," in his *Aspects of Rabbinic Theology: Major Concepts of the Talmud* (New York: Schocken Books, 1961), Chapter 12. Schechter's work was originally published in 1909. Schechter points out that, while the covenant between God and the patriarchs endures forever, on some views the *zekhut* of the patriarchs came to an end. Consequently, Israel as a nation and Jews as individuals cannot draw from merit not their own. And as their own merit is negligible, they must rely ultimately on divine grace. See Schechter, *Aspects*, p. 177.

18   See David Wiggins, "Truth, Invention, and the Meaning of Life" in Geoffrey Sayre-McCord, ed., *Essays on Moral Realism* (Ithaca: Cornell University Press, 1988), p. 154. But see against this the "obligation out, obligation in" view of the ineluctability of morality, Bernard Williams, *Ethics and the Limits of Philosophy* (Cambridge, MA: Harvard University Press, 1985), Chapter 10.

19   The second purpose of the trial is to establish the reliability of prophecy. Had Abraham not believed that the commanding voice, given to him in prophetic revelation, was God's he would not have done something so utterly abhorrent and contrary to human nature. Maimonides stresses the rational, considered, deliberate nature of Abraham's decision. It must, therefore, have been based on

certainty about the prophetic status of the command. See *Guide* Part III, Chapter 24.

20 The Hebrew for Genesis 12:1 actually has three locutions, which the English translation cited here elides into two. More literally, the biblical text enjoins: Go forth from your land (*me-artzekha*) and from your kin (*u'me-moladtekha*) and from your father's house (*u'me-bet avikha*). These three parallel the three locutions for Isaac in Genesis 22:2.

21 On the difference between these two questions and its consequences for moral inquiry, see Bernard Williams, *Ethics and the Limits of Philosophy*, Chapter 1.

22 Relevant here is Harry Frankfurt's essay on caring. The analysis of "what we care about" is not reducible to a moral analysis of the rightness or wrongness of actions. See Harry G. Frankfurt, *The Importance of What We Care About* (Cambridge: Cambridge University Press, 2009), pp. 80–94.

23 For a classic study of the history of Jewish interpretation of the binding of Isaac, see Shalom Spiegel, *The Last Trial* (Philadelphia: Jewish Publication Society, 1967). The chapter of Genesis narrating the binding is read in the synagogue, as part of the daily liturgy, every morning. Thus, Jews constantly invoke Abraham and Isaac's conduct in the liturgical dimension of their common life.

24 On the persistence of biblical, rabbinic, and mystical sources to fit experience into the paradigm of sin and punishment, reward and blessing, see Gershom Scholem, "On Sin and Punishment," in J. M. Kitagawa and C. H. Long, eds, *Myths and Symbols: Studies in Honor of Mircea Eliade* (Chicago: University of Chicago Press, 1969), pp. 163–177.

25 For an expert overview of this literature and analysis of its purposes, style, and themes see Jonathan Wyn Schofer, "Rabbinical Ethical Formation and the Formation of Rabbinical Ethical Compilations," in Charlotte Elisheva Fonrobert and Martin S. Jaffee, eds, *The Cambridge Companion to the Talmud and Rabbinic Literature* (New York: Cambridge University Press, 2007). For a detailed study of *Avot de-Rabbi Natan*, see Jonathan Wyn Schofer, *The Making of a Sage: A Study in Rabbinic Ethics* (Madison: University of Wisconsin Press, 2005). Schofer's work is the most theoretically astute analysis of rabbinic ethics in late antiquity available.

26 For works of post-Holocaust scholarship which attempt to see Paul working within a Jewish context and thereby diminishing the distance and hostility between him and first-century Judaism, see, e.g., E. P. Sanders, *Paul and Palestinian Judaism* (Philadelphia: Fortress Press, 1977) and Krister Stendahl, *Paul Among Jews and Gentiles* (Philadelphia: Fortress Press, 1979).

27 For the biblical origins of the concept of bodily resurrection, see Jon D. Levenson, *Resurrection and the Restoration of Israel: The Ultimate Victory of the God of Life* (New Haven: Yale University Press, 2006). A fascinating Jewish-Christian theological dialogue in a scholarly mode on this theme may be found in Kevin J. Madigan and Jon D. Levenson, *Resurrection: The Power of God for Christians and Jews* (New Haven: Yale University Press, 2008).

28 Is drawing a limit to the desire for life then anti- or non-Judaic? For a provocative meditation on this theme in the context of bioethics, see Leon Kass, "*L'Chaim* and its Limits: Why not immortality?" in Kass, *Life, Liberty and the Defense of Dignity* (San Francisco: Encounter Books, 2002), pp. 257–276.

29   Immanuel Kant, *The Conflict of the Faculties*, trans. Mary J. Gregor (New York: Abaris Books, 1979), p. 95. I don't mean to imply that Kant's view is an orthodox Christian view or that there is no distance between Kantianism and Christianity. There is a great deal of distance, as the censorship of the *Conflict of the Faculties* by the Prussian authorities attests. (Not that I want to portray the Prussian state as a guardian of authentic Christianity!) Nonetheless, I don't see how anyone can seriously deny that the anti-Judaism of the Enlightenment, in all its various hues, continues classic anti-Jewish tropes of its Christian predecessor cultures.

30   Immanuel Kant, *Groundwork to the Metaphysics of Morals*, trans. H. J. Paton (New York: Harper Torchbooks, 1964), p. 99.

31   A classic reflection on the connections among nomos, cosmos, and narrative with respect to Jewish thought is Robert M. Cover, "Nomos and Narrative," *Harvard Law Review*, Vol. 97, No. 4 (1983).

32   *Avot de-Rabbi Natan* adds an interesting gloss which reveals some moral psychology: "If you have carried out one commandment and do not regret having done so in the end it will lead to many commandments (to be carried out); if one commits one transgression and does not regret having done so, in the end it leads to many transgressions." *The Fathers According to Rabbi Nathan*, trans. Judah Goldin (New York: Schocken Books, 1974), Chapter 25, p. 110. (I have modernized Goldin's language.)

33   Alisdair MacIntyre, *After Virtue* (Notre Dame: Notre Dame University Press, 1984), p. 181ff.

34   Immanuel Kant, *Critique of Practical Reason*, trans. Lewis White Beck (Upper Saddle River: Prentice-Hall, 1993), p. 128.

35   *The Fathers According to Rabbi Nathan*, Goldin, trans., p. 39.

36   The words translated by Goldin as "compensation" (*peras*) and "reward" (*sekhar*) are not exactly parallel. *Peras* is a word of uncertain etymology, perhaps derived from Greek, while *sekhar* is standard rabbinic Hebrew, as in "the reward of a mitzvah is a mitzvah" (*sekhar mitzvah, mitzvah*). That the editors of *Avot de-Rabbi Natan* add a terminological change to their gloss further domesticates Antigonus's radical teaching to more standard rabbinic theology. For a close reading of this passage, see Schofer, *The Making of a Sage*, pp. 54–55. I follow Schofer's interpretation below.

37   But note the teaching in the next mishna (4:17), which is in part the polar opposite: "He used to say: Better is one hour of repentance and good works in this world than all the life of the world to come; and better is one hour of calmness of spirit in the world to come than all the life of this world." This mishna both contradicts *Avot* 4:16, in its initial valuation of the worth of this world, and then contradicts itself. Like religious teaching in other traditions, Jewish sources tolerate, even celebrate, paradox.

38   It is interesting in this connection to observe how strongly the sages in the Talmud try to deflect the force of criticism against divine justice in the Book of Job. For an analysis of their attempt to read Job as confirming rather than challenging a theodicy of reward and punishment, see Alan Mittleman, "The Job of Judaism and the Job of Kant," *Harvard Theological Review*, Vol. 102, No. 1 (2009), pp. 25–50.

39   The traditional morning prayer implores God to consider that "it is not on account of our own righteousness that we offer our supplications before thee, but on account of thy great compassion. What are we? What is our life? What is our goodness? What is our righteousness? What our helpfulness? What our strength? What our might? What can we say in thy presence, Lord our God and God of our fathers? Indeed, all the heroes are as nothing before thee, the men of renown as if they never existed, the wise as if they were without knowledge, the intelligent as though they lacked understanding; for most of their doings are worthless, and the days of their life are vain in thy sight; man is not far above beast for all is vanity." The prayer then invokes the only worthy traits that Israel can bring before God: "However, we are thy people, thy people of the covenant, the children of Abraham thy friend, to whom thou didst make a promise on Mount Moriah; we are the descendants of his only son Isaac, who was bound on the altar ..." The text makes use of the concept of vicarious merit, as mentioned above. See Philip Birnbaum, trans., *Daily Prayer Book* (New York: Hebrew Publishing Co., 1949), p. 24.

40   Part of the work that universalizability (under the Categorical Imperative) is supposed to perform is world maintenance, the maintaining of the moral order. Agents are, for example, categorically forbidden to commit suicide as the death of all agents would result in the collapse of the moral order per se. Could the moral order be sustained if all agents believed that there is no connection between good will and consequential action or that reciprocal transactions, such as gift giving, were morally vacuous? For Kant's rather awkward attempt to retrofit a consequentialist assessment of action to his moral philosophy, see his "Idea for a Universal History with a Cosmopolitan Purpose," in H. S. Reiss, ed., *Kant: Political Writings* (Cambridge: Cambridge University Press, 2007).

41   An excellent study of this theme may be found in Martha Nussbaum, *The Fragility of Goodness*: *Luck and Ethics in Greek Tragedy and Philosophy* (Cambridge: Cambridge University Press, 2001).

42   I am grateful to my colleague, Prof. Judith Hauptman, for calling my attention to this text.

43   "The editors' placement of these laws," Bernard Levinson writes, "suggests their concern to establish sex and family law as an independent moral category. In so doing, the authors of Deuteronomy depart from the earlier legal system of the Covenant Collection. There, the law of the seduced virgin (Exod. 22:15–16) came at the end of a sequence of property law (Exod. 21:35–22:14), implying that the daughter was seen as an extension of her father's estate." In Berlin and Brettler, eds, *The Jewish Study Bible*, p. 417. For a modern feminist reading of these laws, see Rachel Adler, *Engendering Judaism*: *An Inclusive Theology and Ethics* (Boston: Beacon Press, 1998), Chapter V.

44   The medieval commentators and legists are divided on whether the offer of peace does in fact apply to the Canaanites. Maimonides emphatically includes them. Rashi does not, commenting that the offer of peace applies only in the case of "permitted wars." (The war against the Canaanites is considered an "obligatory" or commanded war.) See Avraham Chill, *Ha-Mitzvot v'Ta'ameihen* (Jerusalem: Keter, 1988), pp. 298–299 for a synopsis of the argument. (It is a pleasant duty to recall the memory of Rabbi Chill, my first teacher in Hebrew

school in Providence, RI, and to express belated gratitude for his instruction.) For a history of the biblical understanding of war and its development from a cult and holiness conceptual framework to an ethics- and justice-oriented framework, see Susan Niditch, *War in the Hebrew Bible: A Study in the Ethics of Violence* (New York: Oxford University Press, 1995).

45   See The Code of Hammurabi, in James Pritchard, ed., *The Ancient Near East*, Vol. I (Princeton University Press, 1973) p. 162. If an Israelite slave owner, by contrast, strikes his slave and he dies there and then, he must pay with his own life. If his slave survives for a time and then dies, however, he need not be avenged. The idea here seems to be that had the master wanted to kill the slave initially, he would have done so. Thus, his intention was to punish, not kill him. The un-nuanced rule of Leviticus 24:17 and of Exodus 21:23 is qualified by Numbers 35:31. Here a distinction is made between an intentional murderer and one guilty of manslaughter (unintentional homicide). A murderer must be put to death; a man-slaughterer may flee to a city of refuge. One may not accept ransom (*khofer*) for the life of the murderer, who is guilty of a capital crime. Nor may one accept some form of compensation in the case of manslaughter; he must abide in a city of refuge until the death of the high priest. Priestly concerns for blood defiling the purity of the land are in play throughout these texts.

46   Citations from *Baba Kamma* are taken from the Soncino translation, ed. Israel Epstein (London: Soncino Press, 1935).

47   David C. Kraemer, *Responses to Suffering in Classical Rabbinic Literature* (New York: Oxford University Press, 1995), p. 56. The citation of the mishnah follows Kraemer's translation. By "interpretive principle" I mean to suggest that the Mishnah uses this concept in a hermeneutic application rather than as a principle for generating or controlling law. The relationship between legal rules and principles, as in any legal system, is complex. For an illuminating article on the highly restricted role that moral principles play in governing halakha, see Gerald Blidstein, "Moral Generalizations and Halakhic Discourse," in *S'VARA*, Vol. 2, No. 1 (1991), pp. 8–12.

48   The Babylonian Talmud, remarking on the Jewish courts' inability to prosecute due to the destruction of Jewish institutions with the power of capital punishment, nonetheless sees divine justice working its course, measure for measure, through circumstance. Thus, "One who is liable to be stoned either falls from the roof or a wild animal tramples him. One who is liable to be burned either falls into a fire or a snake bites him. One who is liable to be killed [by the sword] is either captured by the [foreign] government or is attacked by bandits. One who is liable to be strangled either drowns in the river or dies by choking" (Sotah 8b. Cited from Kraemer, *Responses to Suffering in Classical Rabbinic Literature*, p. 156).

49   Casuistry, which became tied to the Jesuits, never quite recovered from the criticism of Pascal. See, e.g., *The Provincial Letters*, letters five and six. An argument for a contemporary attempt to retrieve casuistry may be found in Albert R. Jonsen and Stephen Toulmin, *The Abuse of Casuistry: A History of Moral Reasoning* (Berkeley: University of California Press, 1990). An attempt to represent Talmudic casuistry as a form of moral reasoning especially responsive to conflicts of values may be found in the still unpublished work of Nina Redl.

50   The complete list includes hospitality to guests, visiting the sick, meditative concentration in prayer, early attendance at the house of study, raising one's son to study Torah, and judging one's fellow favorably (*dan l'kaf zekhut*). Another version, which the Gemara tries to reconcile with the above six items, is honoring of father and mother, deeds of lovingkindness, and making peace between man and his fellow (Shabbat 127a). The study of Torah, on the second account, exceeds them all.

51   *B. Shabbat* 127b (Soncino translation, ed. Israel Epstein (London: Soncino Press, 1935)).

52   Louis E. Newman, *Past Imperatives: Studies in the History and Theory of Jewish Ethics* (Albany: SUNY Press, 1998), Chapter 1.

53   For an important contemporary study of the philosophical dimensions of Leviticus 19:18, see Lenn E. Goodman, *Love Thy Neighbor as Thyself* (New York: Oxford University Press, 2008).

54   Comment ad loc of Rabbi Ovadiah Bertinoro.

55   Sanhedrin 109b, cited in Hayim Nahman Bialik and Yehoshua Hana Ravnitzky, eds, *The Book of Legends: Sefer Ha-Aggadah*, trans. William G. Braude (New York: Schocken Books, 1992), p. 36.

56   The aggadot about Sodom make clear that its system of justice was cruel to both outsiders and insiders. Although many of the aggadot deal with the plight of hapless sojourners, many deal with internal relations among citizens. No one, rich or poor, among the Sodomites was safe from the depredations of others. Unlike Hobbes' state of nature where life is famously nasty, brutish, and short, however, Sodom was portrayed as a polity where the rule of law was in place. Perhaps this entails a contradiction. A system that reliably benefits no one would be too incoherent to survive. On the other hand, perhaps it intuits the possibility of truly vicious systems, such as totalitarianism, where even the presumptive beneficiaries are unsafe and can never count on their own survival.

57   Makkot 24a. The text ends with another theocentric reduction to one principle in the name of the prophet Habakkuk, Habakkuk 2:4.

3
Medieval Philosophical Ethics

In the Islamic civilization of the Middle Ages, philosophically minded rabbis, influenced by Muslim theology and philosophy, brought disciplined theoretical perspectives to the tradition of Talmudic Judaism. Unlike the Talmud, with its eclectic and endlessly varied expressions of belief about all matters of Jewish intellectual and practical life, the philosophers sought a high degree of coherence and rigor. At the heart of this enterprise is a concern for ethics, for rationally explicating and justifying Jewish traditions of conduct and ideals of character. Nonetheless, the boundary – if there is one – between philosophical and popular-pious moral literature (*sifrut ha-musar*) is hard to draw. With the exception of Maimonides' *Guide for the Perplexed*, the philosophical literature is not necessarily an elite literature. The first philosophical work in Hebrew, Abraham Bar Ḥiyya's *Meditations on the Soul* (*Hegyon ha-Nefesh*), a moral analysis of repentance, was delivered as a series of homilies on the High Holidays. The philosophical works sought to bring order, a comprehensive perspective, and meta-level sense-making to the inherited body of Jewish moral norms. But popular works in the Spanish-Portuguese and Provencal Jewish cultures did this as well, albeit without the ramified and technical philosophical apparatus of Jewish rationalism. A key philosophical classic which we will look at in this chapter, Baḥya ibn Paquda's *Book of Directions to the Duties of the Heart*, also became an enduring popular classic.

What then distinguishes Jewish philosophical from popular or, after the thirteenth century, kabbalistic ethics? Philosophical writers seek to ground Jewish ethical norms on the deepest, rationally explicable or discoverable sources of normativity available. If they rely upon revelation – as all Jewish

A Short History of Jewish Ethics: Conduct and Character in the Context of Covenant,
First Edition. Alan L. Mittleman.
© 2012 Alan L. Mittleman. Published 2012 by Blackwell Publishing Ltd.

normative discourse does – for the authority of the beliefs and practices under discussion, they in turn seek to give a rational account of revelation. They are aware of the possible tension between a revelation-based analysis of the good, for example, and an analysis conducted by reason without recourse to revelation. They resist sheer assertions of authority; they understand that they need to warrant their claims as to the authority of Torah and tradition through arguments based on metaphysics, epistemology, or philosophical anthropology. This stance requires both courage and confidence. The root of their courage and their confidence is the conviction that God's truth is indivisible. The authenticated findings of science are not to be spurned or scanted. Obscurantism in the service of Torah is no virtue. Contradictions between contemporary scientific learning and Judaic doctrines must be faced and resolved – and the resolutions will not always be in favor of maintaining unvarnished and naïve inherited beliefs.[1]

This philosophical moment of medieval Judaism flourished between the tenth and fifteenth centuries. It began in earnest with work of Saadya Gaon in Baghdad and declined in the last century of Jewish life on Iberian soil. The catastrophic persecutions of the Jews in Spain at the end of the fourteenth century, followed by their expulsion a century later, signaled the demise of medieval Jewish philosophy. The tide of rabbinic opinion turned against it, as communal leaders blamed philosophy for weakening the faith of those many Jews who converted in the persecutions of the 1390s. Henceforth, ethical writing was couched in more particularistic modes of discourse, especially that of kabbalah. Philosophy was thought to be alien to Judaism and traditional Jewish piety, a symptom of acculturation and diminished loyalty. To the extent that modern Jews find these views objectionable, the high medieval battle over the propriety of philosophy in conjunction with faith continues to be fought.

Theories of Virtue and Obligation

The philosophical impulse is native, not alien to Judaism. One has to admit, however, that the forms by which that impulse gained expression were learned in specific cultural contexts. One finds concerns to understand, order, justify, explain, theorize, and reflect on normative matters early on. Rabbinic Judaism has an internal concern to justify its approach to law. Although statements of law in the Bible and subsequently in the Mishnah are often apodictic, laid down without justification, the tradition gives rise to literatures which seek justification through argument and dialectic. To an extent, this begins within the Bible itself. So-called "motive clauses" provide incipient reasons for the commandments.[2] The pre-Sinaitic commandment, we noted in the last chapter, which proscribes murder ("Whoever sheds the blood of man, by man shall his blood be shed" Gen. 9:6a), ends with a justification: "For in His image did God make man" (Gen. 9:6b). The version of the Decalogue in Deuteronomy adds an important motive clause to the verses prescribing Sabbath observance, which the presumably earlier Exodus version (Exod. 20:8–11) lacks. After tracking mostly the same language as Exodus, Deuteronomy introduces an overtly moral rationale:

> … so that your male and female slave may rest as you do. Remember that you were a slave in the land of Egypt and the LORD your God freed you from there with a mighty hand and an outstretched arm; therefore the LORD your God has commanded you to observe the sabbath day. (Deut. 5:14b–15)[3]

Reasons are appended to other commandments of the Decalogue, as well. The honoring of father and mother, for example, will allow the Israelites to "long endure … and fare well in the land that the LORD your God is assigning …" (Deut. 5:16). Indeed, both versions of the Decalogue begin with an historical prologue announcing who this God is. Insofar as He liberated Israel from the house of bondage He has a legitimate claim to Israel's love and loyalty. Israel ought to enter into a covenant with Him.[4] The historical prologue of the covenant form itself provides a compact rational argument on behalf of the justification of the covenantal relationship and its provisions.

The Midrash expands upon the Bible, pervasively introducing reasons for biblical assertions. A famous midrash (*Leviticus Rabbah* 30:12) explains that the four species which God commands the Israelite to take up on the festival of Sukkot (Lev. 23:40) correspond to four different types of person. Binding these branches and fruit together symbolically represents binding all of the different types of Jews together to make a single community. Symbolic explanations of this kind are not uncommon.[5] Finally, the Gemara provides massive argumentative support for the statements of the Mishnah. Reasoning about the law is the heart and soul of the Talmud. Altogether, rabbinic Judaism displays what David Weiss Halivni called a "predilection for justified law."[6] Authority, whether divine or human, requires the giving of reasons. Political authority, so to speak, relies on epistemic authority. Pure power is never enough. It must be transformed into legitimate authority able to give an account of its own normative claims.

The most famous story in the Talmud, the contest between Rabbi Eliezer and Rabbi Joshua over whether a certain oven is ritually clean or unclean, exemplifies this need for reason-giving (*Baba Metzia* 59b). When Rabbi Eliezer's arguments failed to persuade his colleagues in the academy that his position – the oven was clean – was correct, he resorted to supernatural proofs. Through magical power, presumably, he caused a carob tree to be uprooted and flung a long distance. He caused a stream to flow backwards.

He caused the walls of the academy to bend and threaten to collapse. None of these signs were acceptable as none of them constituted proper evidence for his view. Finally, Eliezer commanded a voice to issue from heaven which proclaimed "How dare you oppose Rabbi Eliezer whose views are everywhere [correct] halakha!" At this point, Rabbi Joshua rose to his feet and quoted scripture to the heavenly voice: "The Torah is not in heaven!" (Deut. 30:12). The force of this is that since God has already given the Torah to the Jewish people (it is no longer in heaven), matters of Torah are to be decided by the rational procedures of debate and majority rule, rather than by appeal to prophetic inspiration, miraculous signs, or heavenly voices. (In the denouement of the story, God laughs and says that His children have defeated Him. This is not the end, however. Rabbi Eliezer is banned and the formidable magical power he showed in the academy wreaks havoc on the land. He finally dies, crushed by the rejection of his colleagues.[7]) Although the story establishes the supremacy of rationality, in the sense of the need for reason-giving, it does not entirely consign the supernatural and the charismatic to the ash heap. Nor does it scant the power of emotion. It binds all of these together, giving reason its due without, however, disenchanting the world. My point in mentioning this aggadah is both to emphasize the premium put on procedures of rational deliberation in the Talmud and also to show their limits. The Sages wrest reasoned discourse from a context where magical views of the world were widespread and far from discreditable. Rationality must prevail within appropriate contexts, although rationality does not enjoy an exclusive monopoly. That aspiration (or fiction?) must wait for a more self-sufficiently secular age.[8]

The process of reason-giving, of rational justification, meets another limit in rabbinic literature. Although the Sages were keen to record the argumentation by which they reached decisions about the law, they were often disinclined to speculate about the fundamental rationality of the law per se. Some Sages clearly believed that the law was simply a decree of the God of Israel and had to be followed whether it made sense or not. Indeed, following laws that did not make apparent sense (such as not mixing linen and wool in garments or meat and milk in food or proscribing pork) was more meritorious than following laws that were transparently intelligible (such as refraining from theft, adultery, or murder). The laws need not be of benefit to us, nor should any personal considerations of pleasure, utility, significance, or intelligibility enter into our practice of them. The Jewish way should be one of pure obedience.[9] (A modern Jewish thinker, Yeshayahu Leibowitz, has made radical obedience and the repudiation of searching for underlying rationality the basis of his theology.[10]) Even these Sages, however, did not think that God was arbitrary or tyrannical. God intends only good for his creatures. The commandments provide us with occasions to trust God and then to reciprocate his love, regardless of the intelligibility of the contents of his commands. The system as a whole makes some kind of sense.[11]

Other Sages pushed farther into the territory of sense-making. The conviction that God, as Israel's covenant partner, intends Israel's good was developed into a rudimentary theory of the mitzvot. Rabbi Ḥananya ben Akashya said, "The Holy One, Blessed be He, wanted to increase Israel's merit, therefore He increased for them Torah and mitzvot." On this view, the commandments were a gift to Israel. God wanted to give them opportunities for continuously showing their devotion and increasing their worth in His eyes. Rav said, "The mitzvot were not given other than to purify human beings. How could it matter to the Holy One, Blessed be He, whether one ritually slaughters from one part of the neck or another?" (*Bereshit Rabbah* 44:1). The specific halakhic details of the mitzvot are less important (but not unimportant) to God than their divinely intended purpose: to purify human beings and transform them. The system as a whole has a teleological rationale. And yet the end should not be separated from the means. Just as virtue is acquired by the performance of virtuous actions, human refinement is not unrelated to the performance of ritually oriented mitzvot.

A crucial distinction introduced by the Sages has to do with mitzvot that are not immediately intelligible to reason (*huqim*) and those that are intelligible to reason (*mishpatim*). This distinction, rooted in the Bible, allows the Sages to focus the problem of meaning on specific commandments and to speculate about them as a category.[12] Commenting on Leviticus 18:4, "My rules (*mishpatei*) alone shall you observe, and faithfully follow My laws (*huqotei*)," *Sifra* expounds: "'My rules' – these are matters written in the Torah which even had the Torah not been written, it would have been fitting to inscribe them as law, for example, theft, incest, idolatry, blasphemy and murder. 'My laws' – these are the matters which the evil inclination and the nations of world repudiate such as not eating pork, not wearing mixed garments, the procedure for rejecting levirate marriage, ritual purification of one with a scale disease, the red heifer, and the scapegoat. Scripture states, I the LORD decreed [these], you are not permitted to repudiate them." The reasons for the *huqim* are not revealed (at least to any but Moses and Rabbi Akiba[13]). Some Sages feared that inquiry into the reasons for the *huqim* could undermine the authority of these commandments. Others believed, however, that searching for the reasons would meet with divine approval. The philosophers, as we shall see, belonged solidly to the latter camp. To deepen understanding of the Torah through speculative reason, when rightly guided toward faithful ends, increases the majesty and power of the Torah – that is the faith of philosophers. Intellectual excellence, the highest human virtue, is coupled with the practical excellence of a law affirming life. In this way, virtue and obligation reinforce one another.

The philosophical project of the Middle Ages, especially in the hands of its master thinker, Maimonides, seeks to provide a rational foundation for the life of Torah. It theorizes that life to a much greater extent than did the intellectual trends that came before. It picks up threads from the Bible and the Sages but carries them forward with greater intellectual coherence, rigor, and reflexivity. The philosophers have a scientific interest in grounding the truths of the Torah. They are responsive to the intellectual canons of their day. This, of course, creates certain tensions. One is a problem concerning the source and nature of normativity. The Sages had said that "the world goes according to its custom" (*Avodah Zarah* 54b), by which they meant to indicate the regularity and order of the natural world. The philosophers took this seriously and accordingly had to assess what that incipient naturalism implies for belief in a divine Creator, who has revealed a perfect Torah, and will redeem and judge the world in time to come. How far can one go in asserting the fundamental rationality of the world, and of the Jewish way of life, before one has made revelation otiose? To what extent is normativity discoverable by unassisted reason or by reason shaped within culture and tradition? To what extent can reason discern a normative way of life based on nature? What is the interplay of reason and revelation in the matter of fixing and understanding proper conduct and character? The philosophers of medieval Judaism theorize about these fundamental questions.

Their mode of philosophizing about ethics, despite systemic differences among them, is captured by Stanley Cavell's phrase "moral perfectionism." Moral perfectionism, as Cavell characterizes it, has to do with the realization, often born in spiritual crisis, that both self and world are not as they should be, either in themselves or in relation to one another. Yet both are malleable and can be transformed. A better self, albeit never a perfect self, can be attained. The soul "is pictured as on a journey from spiritual slavery to perfectionist enlightenment."[14] Cavell means to get at the wholeness of the moral life, which "is not constituted solely by consideration of isolated judgments of striking moral and political problems but is a life whose texture is a weave of cares and commitments in which one is bound to become lost and to need the friendly and credible words of others in order to find one's way ..."[15] The books that we will presently consider function as "friendly and credible words," the words of masters directed to searching disciples, who are perplexed and need steady guidance. The goal is not completed perfection but the wholeness (*shlemut*) possible for human beings, an ever-greater integration, focus, directedness, and attention to the rational love and service of God. The focus is on the journey of the self, where the self is thought to be typical, not idiosyncratic or strongly unique. And the journey is through a territory which requires metaphysical analysis as much as ethical or psychological exploration. All of these thinkers conceive of both the Torah and philosophical analysis to be therapeutic, to be a kind of medicine or regimen which can restore a sick soul to health and help a healthy soul reach its divinely intended telos.[16]

Saadya Gaon

Saadya Gaon (882–942), the first philosopher or philosophical theologian of real substance since Philo, wrote his magnum opus, *The Book of Doctrines and Beliefs*, in Baghdad in 933.[17] Saadya was a major rabbinic leader, the head (Gaon) of the academy of Sura, one of the Jewish institutions of learning which produced, centuries before, the Babylonian Talmud. Saadya had already translated the entire Bible into Arabic, written a philosophical commentary on an ancient mystical text, and successfully fought against the Karaites, a Jewish sect which rejected rabbinic authority. Saadya's time was one of vigorous debate within and among religious groups, freethinkers, Indian philosophers, and others. Islam was riven by debate between orthodox theologians (Asharites) and rationalist theologians (Mutazilites).[18] The former were pure voluntarists. They pinned all normativity on divine fiat. The latter were more critical rationalists, who tied divine law and judgment to antecedently available moral norms. Saadya was influenced by the Mutazila, as well as by currents of Hellenistic philosophy such as Neo-Platonism, which were increasingly available to literate persons due to an ambitious translation project sponsored by the caliphate. Unlike his successor, Maimonides, Saadya was not fully aware of the work of Aristotle. Accordingly, Saadya's project of harmonizing Jewish tradition with contemporary rationalism does not completely engage Aristotle's philosophy, with its rejection of creatio ex nihilo. The Aristotelians' postulate of the eternity of the world raised profound difficulties for the Jewish, Christian, and Muslim belief in its created nature. The threat of depriving God of his role as Creator would force a substantial reconfiguration of what the concept of God could mean. Later Jewish Aristotelians were critical of the work of their pre-Aristotelian predecessors. Saadya has a robust confidence in the full convergence or compatibility of religion and reason. He does not evince the agon of Maimonides, who was driven to write esoterically when Aristotelianism and Torah pulled too strongly in opposite directions. (Metaphysics aside, however, Saadya's ethics show an Aristotelian tendency toward the mean.) On the whole, Saadya's work represents a formidable achievement. He brings a level of insight, integration of philosophical and biblical/rabbinic sources, and systematic coherence to the entirety of the Jewish tradition that was, and in some ways remains, unprecedented.

Saadya grounds Torah in a pervasive rationality. Rational speculation (*iyun*, in ibn Tibbon's medieval Hebrew translation[19]) will confirm that the basic outlines of Torah are necessary. Saadya enumerates four points where right reason confirms the logic of the laws of the Torah:

1) I maintain that Reason bids us (*ha-sechel meḥayev*) respond to every benefactor either by returning his kindness if he is in need of it, or by offering thanks if he is not in need of recompense. Now since this is a dictate of Reason itself, it would not have been fitting for the Creator (be He exalted and glorified) to waive this right in respect of Himself, but it was necessary that He should command his creatures to worship Him and to render thanks unto Him for having created them.

2) Reason further lays down that the wise man should not permit himself to be vilified and treated with contempt. It is similarly necessary that the Creator should forbid His servants to treat Him in this way.

3) Reason further prescribes that human beings should be forbidden to trespass upon one another's rights by any sort of aggression. It is likewise necessary that the Wise should not permit them to act in such a way.

4) Reason, furthermore, permits a wise man to employ a workman for any kind of work and pay him his wages for the sole purpose of allowing him to earn something; since this is a matter which results in benefit to the workman and causes no harm to the employer.[20]

The Reason which obligates (*meḥayev*) here is a practical form of reason; a rationality inherent in the transactions of human moral life, of conduct *inter homines* (*bein adam l'ḥavero*). Saadya takes this moral rationality as universal and necessary. He does not draw a strong distinction, as Maimonides does, between practical and theoretical reason. He assumes the naturalness and necessity of moral normativity and abstracts from it to stipulate our stance vis-à-vis the divine (*bein adam l'maqom*). Saadya assumes the necessity of a moral point of view. He is not troubled, as an ideal-typical modern might be, by the presumed cleft between fact and value. There is no value-free, stone-cold universe of brute facts onto which human beings project normativity like so many pebbles thrown against the sky. The naturalness of value is assumed as a correlate of a world created by a God who is Himself characterized, to an extent, by moral terms.

Saadya ascribes rational necessity to features of the moral order, such as gratitude to benefactors, respect, legitimate claims (i.e. rights), and the regulation of relations by justice. That the entire purpose of creation is to express God's justice is a central theme of Saadya's project.[21] (Saadya's view is compelling. It is hard to see how one could have a moral order unless these elements were in place. The necessity of a moral order per se is another question, however. Moderns are far more troubled by this than medievals. Saadya did have to contend with Epicureanism, however, which offered the prospect of a godless or at least god-abandoned, uncaring universe.) These features are instantiated in duties. The duties, all of which are rational, ground the four types of law that comprise the Torah. The duty of gratitude entails that we know and serve God with a sincere heart. The duty of respect entails that we refrain from blasphemy against God. The duty to respect the legitimate claims of others gives rise to the provisions of civil and criminal law. These three spheres of duty ground all of those laws of the Torah which the Sages characterized as *mishpatim*, rules that would be apparent even if the Torah had not been given. The naturalness and rational necessity of such norms did not require revelation. Saadya includes items in this broad category that would strike a modern reader as stipulated only by religion, such as divine worship, humility before God, the proscription of idolatry or swearing falsely in God's name. Saadya finds these as transparently rational as the practice of justice, truth-telling, fairness, love of neighbor, and the avoidance of murder, theft, deceit, etc. All of these things are agreeable to and in conformity with reason. They are commanded by the Law and revealed by revelation, but God has made them appear natural and acceptable to our reason.

The second category of law, corresponding to the rabbinic *ḥuqim*, elicits neither the approval nor the disapproval of reason. God has multiplied such laws for Israel so as to increase their happiness and reward. These matters are not inherently good or evil but contingently so; they become good or evil through divine ascription. Just as a human master hires a workman in a just transaction, so the God of the covenant has employed the Jews for his service. They will be rewarded in the end, even though the precise nature of their tasks is not entirely clear to reason. The laws of divine service are reasonable in broad teleological terms but cannot be fully justified item by item. Justification comes with context. As Goodman writes, "What might have seemed arbitrary in itself becomes morally right or wrong when commanded by God, not merely (as in Ashʿarite theology) *because* it is commanded, but because it is made part of a system of virtues and vices by which we are to be perfected and rewarded or corrupted and destroyed."[22] (To think of this in secular terms, consider that a practice takes its meaning and value within the context of a system of norms of which it is a part. Goods are thought to be such by the significance and weight a community ascribes to them. In a community with a bus or subway system, for example, it is often a matter of law, custom, or morality to give one's seat to an elderly or disabled person. That practice becomes an appropriate expression of norms of respect, assistance, and attentiveness to the needs of others.

One might imagine that in another kind of society, one would not only relinquish one's seat but bow before such a person, etc. The value of practices is tied to social contexts and the narratives that underlie them.[23])

As Saadya's discussion develops, he modifies the preceding typology somewhat and introduces a key distinction between rational commandments (*mitzvot sikhliyot*) and revelational or, more literally, received commandments (*mitzvot shemiyot*). This categorization, once again, tracks the *mishpatim/ḥuqim* distinction of the Sages but introduces epistemological criteria not previously found in the tradition.[24] Saadya explicates the first class, rational commandments, in terms of their logical coherence. Rather like Kant's proscription of suicide as incompatible with the categorical imperative, Saadya argues that murder, adultery, theft, and lying all contradict those fundamental purposes for which human beings exist in the first place.[25] Kant's claim was that if suicide were universalized, there would be no human beings left to be subject to the moral law. Saadya's claim is that if murder were allowed, human beings would annihilate one another and no one would be left to fulfill God's purposes for humanity. The violation of each category of rational commandment is shown to contain a fatal contradiction. This violation of an epistemic norm (here, the principle of non-contradiction) implies a failure of practical reasoning as well.

Particularly interesting in this regard is Saadya's Platonic argument against hedonism. If, pace Thrasymachus and Adimantus, the good is pleasure and acting in a violent, promiscuous, and wanton manner brings the agent pleasure, then violence, etc. is good. Saadya argues that although it may seem good from the point of view of the hedonistic agent, it will surely not seem good from the point of view of his victim. The fact that the same act can be described as both good and evil indicates a contradiction. (Saadya is no perspectival relativist.) The act must be rejected as incoherent; wisdom and folly cannot coexist simultaneously. The ethical upshot of this epistemological point is that one cannot benefit oneself at the cost of harming another person. The concept of benefit could not even apply under those conditions.[26]

Saadya goes on to indicate schematically how *mitzvot shemiyot*, received or revelational laws, also admit in a broad way to rational explanation. The master narrative is that God wishes to benefit Israel by giving them opportunities to demonstrate their fidelity to Him, in the course of which they can perfect themselves. Self-perfection is not achieved simply by fidelity, however; the *mitzvot shemiyot* are *not* simply arbitrary vehicles but have a measure of inherent worth as well. There is a local benefit to be derived from each sub-class of revelational commandment. Designating holy times, such as Sabbath and festival, allows people to gather and learn from one another. Rest is restorative and offers time for study and sharing, enhancing the mind, and the arts of civility. The prohibition of eating certain foods militates against divinizing animals, as idolaters do, and misplacing sacredness onto beings less elevated than God. Laws against incest prevent the deterioration of family life. Proximity and sexual availability would otherwise create a moral hazard. Saadya also claims that directing one's sexual attention only to permitted persons militates against frivolous and superficial sexual attraction. "Another purpose is to prevent men from being attracted only by those women who are of beautiful appearance and rejecting those who are not, when they see that their own relatives do not desire them."[27] Overall, the revelational commandments attune us to heightened moral sensitivity, discipline, and perspective on matters of value.

The revelational commandments contribute essentially, not merely contingently, to our self-perfection. We could not develop in the direction of self-perfection if we did not have *these* commandments to study and practice. Saadya works out a psychological theory which explains how the practice of the commandments (or their disregard) conditions one to virtue (*zekhut*) (or vice – *ḥovah*). Appropriate obedience is virtuous; scornful disregard is vicious. These dispositions create habits of the heart, as it were, which confer benefit or disadvantage. The more one becomes habituated to an antinomian way of life, the more difficult it is to return to virtue and make progress toward that integration of intellectual excellence and practical conduct which constitutes the goal of perfection. This habituation is more than behavioral, however. Saadya advances a kind of psychological theory. He understands the soul to be a "rational and pure substance [*'etzem sikhli zakh yoter*], surpassing in purity the substances of the planets and the spheres" such that we are not able to perceive it with our senses. God, as its artisan, however, knows and examines the soul. He perceives the impressions that good or evil deeds make on the soul. When good deeds predominate, "the soul becomes bright and shining … If, however, the evil deeds are predominant, the soul becomes dim and clouded."[28] Here the soul is materially, if that word is not misleading, affected by actions. It is as if good or bad deeds were like a drug, substantially affecting the neurophysiology of the brain. The perfectionist quest is purgative. One must heal oneself from the toxic influences of one's way of life.

Saadya argues, in the last chapter of *Doctrines and Beliefs*, for a moderate, balanced way of life.[29] His argument begins with metaphysics and ends in perfectionist ethics. Because God is One, in the sense of an absolutely unique unity, creation is necessarily plural and composite. Anything which we call "one" is one in a numerical sense only; materially it is composite. Saadya derives from this metaphysical generalization a kind of ethical implication: a proper way of life harmonizes diverse character traits and values. Any given trait or value, if torn from a context of integration and coordination with other traits and values, becomes invidious. Human beings run into trouble when they absolutize character traits or objects and desire and elevate them into the sole focus of their projects. Thus, food and drink, sexual intercourse, separation from other human beings, contemplative rest, political rule, constructive activity such as farming or building, the acquisition of wealth, etc. all have positive value but when ascribed exclusive value they diminish and distort human life. Saadya argues in a rational, scientific key, buttressed by supporting verses from Scripture, against extremism and exclusivism in the realm of values. The ideal way of life for humans is rationally discernable; the middle way, veering neither toward extreme asceticism nor toward extreme worldliness, manifests itself in bodily and mental health.[30]

We began with the problem of what the function of revelation is, given a generous role for a naturalistic approach to normativity. To put it more baldly than could actually be the case for Saadya, what role does ethics leave for theology? Saadya goes extraordinarily far in accommodating revelation to the contours of rationality. Persons in his own society claim "that men do not need prophets, and that their Reason is sufficient to guide them aright according to their innate cognition of good and evil."[31] This certainly goes too far, in his view. Saadya has several retorts, the most significant of which is that reason gives us *principles* but prophets, communicating specific laws, give us *rules* for putting principles to work. The rational response of gratitude, for example, needs to be particularized: What form should gratitude take? What times and gestures pertain? The traditional Jewish prayers give shape to this rational impulse. This is true for all of the other fields of rational discovery in regard to conduct and the transformation of character. We need guidance in application. Were each of us left to our own devices, we could never reach agreement and form a religious community. Revelation concretizes and applies principles, grounding a public sphere in which the diachronic existence of the Jews, as a nation formed on account of its law, is possible.[32]

Saadya categorically rejects the idea that man does not need revelation. As large a role as he grants to reason, he is mindful of its debilities. Reasoning takes time and ability and persons are differentially qualified in the latter respect. If time is lacking, persons won't drive their account of intellectual matters to the end. Stopping short, they will be filled with doubt and stumble. Also, had God left it to human reason to discover all of the relevant moral truths, human beings would have been without the truth for many years (as reasoning takes time). Thus, God sent reliable messengers, prophets, to save us from bewilderment and confusion.[33] We ought to trust them because – an interesting consequentialist argument – if we do not trust reliable reports, in this case religious tradition, then we will not trust anything and society cannot exist without social trust.[34] Once again, Saadya is alert to the social and political dimensions of religion as a community-building and sustaining force. Reason can atomize and privatize; revelation gives our lives a public reality.[35]

Revelation comes from God via prophets but prophets are not legitimated by the miracles they perform. Rather, prophetic revelation derives its authority from its conformity with moral reason. As important as revelation is, it must be coordinate with rationality.

> For the reason of our belief in Moses lies not in the wonders and miracles only, but the reason for our belief in him and all other prophets lies in the fact that they admonished us in the first place to do what was right, and only after we had heard the prophet's message and found that it was right did we ask him to produce miracles in support of it.[36]

Saadya, although not as rigorously demythologizing as Maimonides, de-centers the miraculous and stresses moral reason, if not as an autonomous force then as a dependent variable. God has given us the truth but we are obligated to make it our own through speculation, which if pursued vigorously will confirm privately and personally what we know publicly and traditionally.[37] An even stronger statement of the epistemic priority and moral significance of reason is found in the next great Jewish medieval moral thinker, Baḥya ibn Pakuda.

Baḥya ibn Pakuda

Little is known about Baḥya ben Joseph ibn Pakuda. His approximate dates are 1050–1156. He was a judge (*dayyan*) of a Spanish rabbinical court, perhaps in Cordova or Saragossa.[38] Baḥya's book was written in Arabic. It is known and beloved by generations of later Jews in its Hebrew translation, *Hovot Ha-Levavot, The Duties of the Heart.* Yehudah ibn Tibbon, who also translated Saadya, translated this text around 1160. Since then, the book has been translated into the major European languages. It also circulated in a Yiddish translation. As in Saadya, Baḥya's ethical theory is grounded in metaphysics. He is at pains, however, to keep the metaphysics at a minimum so that it does not deter his non-specialist readers. Nonetheless, it would be a mistake to extract the purely pious, devotional elements from Baḥya, as some traditional readers do, and scant the rationalist substructure.

Baḥya introduces a distinction between two types of commandment: the duties of the limbs and the duties of the heart. The latter, a key concept undergirding the entire work, refers to commandments that are performed purely through intentionality. He gives as examples of outward duties of the limbs "prayer, fasting, almsgiving, learning His book and spreading the knowledge of it, fulfilling the commandments concerning the tabernacle, the palm branch, the fringes, the doorpost, the railing on the roof, and the like, all of which can be wholly performed by man's physical body."[39] This list is rather surprising, since Jews are accustomed to think that some of these commandments, such as statutory prayer or Torah study, ought not to be rote exercises but should be accompanied by *kavannah*, that is, mindfulness, intention, attentiveness.[40] But that is not Baḥya's distinction. "Duties of the heart" are not comprised of those commandments that require *kavannah* but rather are a special class of commandment which are prior to and productive of *kavannah*. *Kavannah* is indeed critical but it can only be brought to bear on the duties of the limbs once the heart is inwardly converted in a fundamental, all-encompassing way. The duties of the heart are comprised by belief in the unity of God and in the Torah, "in constant obedience to Him and fear of Him, in humility before Him, love for Him and complete reliance upon Him, submission to Him and abstinence from the things hateful to Him."[41] All of our acts should flow from a profound inner obedience to God, which integrates the entirety of one's being and the whole of one's conduct. Baḥya writes:

> These obligations are upon us constantly, everywhere and at all times, accompanying every hour, every minute, every situation, as long as our minds and souls are yet with us. This is like the case of a servant ordered by his master to do two kinds of work. Indoors he must tend to the house, outdoors he must cultivate the soil at certain fixed times. If he misses the right time or is unable to do his work in the field, the obligation to work outdoors is cancelled. But he cannot be freed of his responsibilities indoors as long as he remains in the house and is serving his master. When he is undisturbed, the obligation to work indoors binds him constantly. In the same way, O my brother, the duties of the heart are binding upon us without any excuse, and nothing really prevents us from performing them except the love of this world and our ignorance of God ...[42]

The "obligation to work outdoors," to perform the duties of the limbs, is clearly subsidiary to and dependent on the "obligation to work indoors." The latter is fundamental.

It is also pervasively rational. One cannot fulfill the duties of the heart without the full engagement of reason. Baḥya opposes those who take refuge in traditionalism. Although not all are capable of speculative rationality and logical demonstration – and for them the mere acceptance of tradition must suffice – those who are capable ignore it at their peril. They fail to fulfill the duties of the heart, which are the foundational commandments of the Torah, as well as – more on this in a moment – of the human mind as such. "In other words, after having accepted these things by way of tradition, which means all the religious commandments, both roots and branches, you must continue to speculate upon them with your mind, your understanding, and with well measured logic, until truth is evident and falsehood is driven out ..."[43] The duties of the heart are not primarily about contemplation; they are about *ratiocination.* Hence, Baḥya's book begins with metaphysical arguments establishing the existence, incorporeality, and unity of God, the creation of the world from nothing and the purposive, teleological thrust of reality. The second treatise provides a philosophical anthropology, which situates the human microcosm within the ordered macrocosm of creation. The third treatise, which we shall explore here, looks at the principal ethical expression of the duties of the heart, radical obedience to God. The next seven treatises develop various topics salient to the relationship of the human being and God, such as reliance upon God alone, dedication of our lives and acts to God, humility, repentance, self-evaluation, asceticism, and love. The book is thus arranged in terms of "10 roots" or "10 pillars," a framework followed in some subsequent ethical treatises.

Baḥya grounds radical obedience to God on a purely rational appraisal of the human condition. Saadya had earlier invoked the self-evidence of showing gratitude to one's benefactors.[44] Baḥya, after offering metaphysical arguments on behalf of God's existence, unity, and gracious founding of the world, goes on to argue the rationality of responding with gratitude, thanksgiving, and obedience to the One who brought us into being. He dramatizes his point through a contrast between human and divine benefaction. Analyzing why human beings in various situations (e.g. parents toward children, rich toward poor, etc.) bestow favors on one another, he claims that no benefaction is purely altruistic. Human beings always have some self-interest working through their gestures of generosity. (The father, for example, has invested all of his hopes for continuity in his son. Hence, his provision for his son is self-interested. Baḥya's point, while canny, is overdrawn.) Yet that checkered reality notwithstanding, it is still morally axiomatic to show gratitude for favors done to one. A fortiori, how much more appropriate is it to show gratitude toward the One whose beneficence *is* without any self-interest. "How much, then, should a man obey, praise, and thank the Creator of all benefaction and benefactors, whose beneficence is infinite, permanent, and perpetual, done neither for His own benefit nor for driving away misfortunes, but is all-loving kindness and grace towards men."[45]

God's greatest benefaction is the creation of reason, of mind (*sekhel*, in ibn Tibbon's Hebrew translation). The abilities of the mind require time to develop; human beings come to full cognition only as they mature. They come to full recognition of their duty of obedience to their Creator over time. Furthermore, their rational ability to discern their duty is hampered by other dimensions of their soul such as their inordinate desire for the pleasures and goods of the world, which obscure their consciousness of God. The very constitution of a human being militates against the supremacy of reason. The coarse substance of the desiring functions of the soul is akin to the coarse material of the world; the fine substance of the rational function of the soul, the *sekhel*, is "not only a stranger in this world, but has nothing to support it and nothing to keep it company. Rather is everything against it."[46] To guide us before we come to reason, however unsteady and embattled, God has provided us with the Torah, which is a medicine against the constitutional infirmities of the complex hybrid that is the soul. The Torah's revealed commandments, most of which are duties of the limbs, curtail the appetites, discipline the appetitive dimensions of the soul, and prepare it for the emergence of reason. When one is under the tutelage of the Torah, without yet having achieved true understanding through rational speculation and demonstration, one acts on the basis of fear of punishment or hope for heavenly reward. This is merely propaedeutic. The ideal, which mature persons can achieve, is autonomous rather than heteronomous obedience to God. "Submission through alertness of the mind and through logical demonstration is better in God's eyes, preferable and more pleasing ..."[47] Baḥya enumerates seven reasons in favor of the higher value of autonomy. Particularly striking is the fifth reason. The commandments of the Torah, according to the Talmudic enumeration, are finite – 613. The commandments arising from reason, however, are infinite insofar as knowledge is infinite. With every addition to our knowledge about the world, we have a new occasion to offer our gratitude to God and to renew our obedient devotion to Him. Thus, a rational and autonomous stance vis-à-vis God is superior to one imposed through the prophetic exhortations and laws of the Torah. Nonetheless, the Torah is necessary. The differences among people with respect to cognitive abilities, spiritual sensitivity, etc. require a common denominator, which the law provides. It provides specificity and definition in the expression of duty, as well. Unlike Saadya and Maimonides, Baḥya, in keeping with the near-exclusivity of his focus on the divine–human relationship, does not endorse a political framework for explicating the law. A profoundly apolitical thinker, he sees one who understands the law politically to occupy a lower level than one who comprehends it in a purely vertical, spiritual manner.[48]

The third treatise of *The Book of Direction to the Duties of the Heart* features an extended philosophical dialogue between "the mind" (*sekhel*) and "the soul" (*nefesh*), where soul is understood in opposition to mind as the appetitive, willful dimension of the human person.[49] The soul is aware of its cravings, desires, lusts, and attachment to the world. It asks the mind to administer a "therapy of desire." In the course of the dialogue, the mind explores the sources of the soul's akrasia – the soul knows what it should do but lacks the will to do it. Baḥya portrays the Torah as a strong, therapeutic medicine in the context of a moral anthropology.

What then accounts for the soul's cognitive grasp of the virtue and duty of radical obedience to God over/against its inability to realize that orientation? The soul begs the mind to illumine its painful, dichotomous condition. The mind replies that there is a rational self-evidence to the duties of the heart. All right-thinking human beings, including those who lived before the revelation of the Torah, can grasp the "commandments of the mind."

> God has planted in men's minds: praise of the true and blame of the false, preference for justice and avoiding of iniquity, rewarding of the good with goodness and thankfulness, and requiting of the bad with evil and reproof, as well as the wish to deal with others in peace, to their benefit, matching their favors with our gratitude and their good deeds with a fit reward, as we match bad deeds with due punishment, and also the realization that one reward is better than another, one punishment worse than another, and that we should pardon the sinful who repent truly.[50]

Why should this natural awareness (natural, that is, insofar as God has implanted it in our nature) become obscured or feckless? The mind, at its best, realizes the universality and necessity of these principles but runs into a host of impediments, such as wavering certainty induced by skepticism. Moments of uncertainty entrain the diminution of desire to live according to formerly stable but now jeopardized principles. Skepticism and indifference form a vicious circle, a feedback loop, which must be broken by both cognitive and behavioral therapy. The most radical impediment, however, is a kind of pleasure-principle. The overwhelming desire of the soul for worldly pleasures, such as food, drink, and sexuality, derange the mind. Furthermore, the desire for less physical but no less worldly goods such as fame, power, and honor also diminish the soul's grasp of the universal moral norms. The mind exhorts the soul to consider these systemic derailments of reason as comparable to a diseased limb which requires amputation. An attitudinal-behavioral adjustment is needed; these values must be excised from one's normative orientation toward the world.

Baḥya endorses a moderate asceticism within the limits of the law.[51] Acquiring an attitude of Stoic indifference toward worldly goods and values is propaedeutic to a radical reorientation of the soul. The problem of the soul is one of pervasive egocentricity. The soul realizes that obedience to God is both virtue and duty – gratitude is noble and obligatory, given the manifold benefactions of Creator to creature. Yet even in the midst of obedient gratitude, the soul encounters the impediment of egocentrism. It has an *interest* in thanking God for His goodness, namely that the goodness should continue and endure.[52] This fundamental, prudential self-interest undermines the purity of gratitude, infecting it with hope that blessing will endure and fear that it will cease. An angst haunts the soul and stands in the way of the purely rational, self-transcending dedication counseled by the dispassionate mind. Baḥya diagnoses this condition as a compound of emotion and ignorance. He criticizes the attitudes of hope and fear, analyzing them in terms of cognitive failure. The soul has convinced itself that it knows more and cares more for itself than God does. A dispassionate rational analysis would show that there is need for neither hope nor fear: God knows better than egocentric, passionate man what he needs. Accepting this conceptual truth needs the support of behavioral modifications. The mind prescribes distinct actions for the soul to realize, such as mentioning "the graces God has shown you with your tongue, thanking Him frequently, and you should be grateful to Him in your heart, as well as in your spoken words."[53] Thus, the duties of the heart and the duties of the limbs work together to further conceptual clarity and moral improvement.

The final anxiety that affects the soul also arises from a conceptual problem – but in this case the problem is based on more than error. The problem seems intractable and the soul craves illumination and release from its paradox. The problem is that of free choice and determinism. Scripture, as cited by the soul, indicates *both* the power and sovereignty of God over all of His creation *and* an apparent exception in the case of human beings, the possibility of free choice. For medievals these capacities are hard to reconcile. God's power seems curtailed by the zone of indeterminacy implied by free choice. Yet the justice of God, which hinges on reward and punishment for actions freely undertaken, is undermined if free choice is illusory. The Jewish tradition had a long history, arguably going back to the Exodus narrative about the hardening of Pharaoh's heart, as we saw in Chapter 1, dealing with this problem. Baḥya's answer is strikingly reminiscent of Kant's.

As the mind reviews prior Jewish opinion, it claims that there were rabbis who believed in strict indeterminism as well as strict determinism. The indeterminists, of course, had no problem with affirming God's justice since reward and punishment are fully contingent on free human choice. The determinists, however, had to assert that God's justice, given the absence of freedom of choice, is opaque to us. Nonetheless, we must agree that God is just but "our minds are too weak" to make sense of that justice (and wisdom, and grace). Baḥya then makes a surprising assertion:

> Still others decided to believe in both schools, that is, to believe in both divine justice and in predetermination, claiming that whoever examines these matters too closely cannot escape sin and failure, no matter how he does it. They said, "The right way is to act in the belief that man's actions are entrusted to him, so that he earns reward or punishment, and to try to do everything that may benefit us before God both in this world and the next. On the other hand, we should rely on Him with the submission of those who know that all actions, movements, benefits, and misfortunes lie under God's rule and power and depend on His permission and decree, for He has the decisive argument against man, but man has no argument against his Creator."[54]

At first it seems that Baḥya's rabbis are simply hedging their bets: either view could be the correct one, so it is prudent, if incoherent, to maintain both. His position is deeper than that, however. Baḥya believes, like Kant, that both views are necessary; both are powerful, if irreconcilable, descriptions of the way things are. Our ultimate situation vis-à-vis the way things are is one of ignorance, but this ignorance is blessed. Coming up against the limits of pure reason, to use a Kantian term, we turn back to practical reason. Our metaphysical ignorance frees us to pursue a moral path, to work on the duties of the heart. Baḥya's view is thus a bit similar to Kant's, albeit within his own medieval pietistic idiom. For Kant we are both organisms, subject to mechanical causality, and persons, subject to the "causality of freedom." For Baḥya, we are both part of a great chain of divinely regulated beings and individuals who must develop their own interior bond with God.

The assets of the body and soul, when directed by the rational intellect, are not allowed to follow their own material dynamic but are harnessed toward the goal of ultimate enlightenment, the disinterested love of God. The mind should direct the character traits, emotions, dispositions, and virtues toward the highest end. A sublime teleology should order the values connected with this world and with our embodied, corporeal condition. Mind can bring joy and sorrow, fear and hope, bravery and cowardice, shame and impudence, contentment and anger, mercy and cruelty, vanity and humility, love and hatred, generosity and avarice, and idleness and industry into an overall integration. All of these have their place and moment. They must be used in the right way, at the right time, for the right end. In Baḥya's version of the *phronemos*, the virtuous Jew does not transcend the passions into apatheia; he orders them with reference to the whole and the goal. This strongly perfectionist and intellectualist project prepared the way for the greatest of the medieval Jewish rationalists, Maimonides.

Maimonides

Rabbi Moshe ben Maimon, known by his traditional acronym as the Rambam or Maimonides (the name ascribed to him by the West), lived both in Spain and North Africa from 1138 to 1204. Victims of persecution by fanatical Muslims, the Maimon family left their native Cordoba and migrated across the Maghreb, stopping in the land of Israel and eventually settling in Egypt. Maimonides rose to become physician to the sultan and the leader of the Egyptian Jewish community. He is the dominating figure of the Jewish Middle Ages, author of the most comprehensive code of Jewish law (the *Mishneh Torah*) and of the most profound work of Jewish philosophy (the *Moreh Nevukhim* or *Guide of the Perplexed*). The *Guide* is undoubtedly the most studied work of Jewish thought among modern scholars of Jewish philosophy; a vast secondary literature analyzes and comments upon it. Its bold engagement with science has made it a kind of icon of intellectual integrity and authenticity, especially appealing to Jews who, since the Enlightenment, have tried to navigate the claims of cultures in tension with one another. Prior to writing both his great code and the *Guide*, he wrote, in Arabic, a commentary on the Mishnah. A free-standing introduction to his commentary on *Avot*, known as the *Eight Chapters* (*Shemoneh Perakim*), is a rich source for Maimonides' moral theory. So too is the second volume of his code, known as the *Laws of Character Traits* (*Hilkhot Deot*). A large-scale integration of these theoretical efforts occurs in the *Guide*, especially in Part III, chapters 51–54. In the following sketch, we will draw on all of these sources, with special attention to the argument of the *Eight Chapters*.

As noted above, Maimonides, unlike Saadya, was heir to the teachings of Aristotle (albeit in a manner shaped by Neo-Platonism, the fusion of the two streams already having occurred in late antiquity). Maimonides, like the Muslim philosophers of his age, struggled with Aristotle's teaching of an uncreated, eternally existing cosmos. In Part II, chapter 25 of the *Guide* Maimonides confesses that, had Aristotle proved his theory of the uncreatedness of the world, the Torah would have to adapt itself to this truth. The apparent teaching of Genesis, that the world was created from nothing, would have to be allegorically reinterpreted to accord with scientific truth. Such is the power that Maimonides ascribes to scientific or philosophical rationality. Maimonides does not believe, however, that Aristotle succeeded in producing an infallible demonstration of his claim. A Jewish philosopher, intent on upholding a pillar of the law, that is, Moses' teaching of the createdness of the world, can point out the weaknesses of Aristotle's position. He cannot, however, prove his own position (*Guide* Part I, Chapter 71) with any more deductive necessity or with any fewer vulnerable premises than had Aristotle. Maimonides dismisses the arguments of Kalam and of Kalam-influenced Jews (respectfully, he does not mention Saadya by name) as too supposititious. They depend on fallacious views of time and infinity according to Maimonides. If Aristotle is to be defeated, he must be defeated on the ground of his own (superior) physics and metaphysics, and not by the suppositions of (inferior) Kalam atomism. This leads Maimonides to, on the one hand, a kind of coherentist argument on behalf of creation. Creation is not contrary to reason, although neither can it be impeccably demonstrated by reason. Insofar as creation is coherent with everything else that we can know – and insofar as a great deal of the Torah, such as the power and freedom of God and the authority of the law, is riding on it – it makes sense to affirm it. That is the overt or exoteric affirmation of the *Guide*.

On the other hand, since Maimonides is an "esoteric" thinker, someone who masks his true views from all but the most astute philosophical reader, it is likely that his apparent acquiescence in the Mosaic position is not his true position. Some interpreters – including medieval rabbis who fought against philosophy – have thought that his Aristotelianism was thorough and radical. If so, two possibilities arise. The first is that Aristotle and the Torah are in deep agreement with each other, despite surface dissimilarities. The second is that Aristotle undermines the Torah and that Maimonides uneasily holds that disturbing truth together with professions of piety. A famous modern interpreter, Leo Strauss, did much to promote this highly subversive reading. Strauss thought that Maimonides wrote exoterically for political reasons and esoterically for metaphysical ones. That is, Maimonides' ultimate views about the nature of reality were directly at odds with the moral-political world of the Torah, which he wanted and needed to maintain. In light of his ultimate, albeit well-hidden theoretical views, his "practical" views concerning the law are strategic, politically calibrated, and deliberately misleading. According to this hermeneutic of suspicion, Maimonides becomes somewhat more of an Athenian than a Jerusalemite. The highest life is one of solitary contemplation of divine unity. The Torah is an instrument for our self-perfection. But once we reach the highest stage, once we leave the Platonic cave as it were, we leave ethics and politics, the world of the mitzvot, behind. Strauss sees Maimonides as anticipating Spinoza by consigning the law to a primarily political and subsidiary function and elevating the intellectual love of God to the highest virtue. Unlike Spinoza, however, Maimonides retains a loyalty to Torah as the blueprint for a future, messianic politics of Jewish restoration and world-renewal. The *Mishneh Torah*, as a comprehensive code, is the constitution of a messianic state.

Needless to say, not all agree with Strauss's reading of Maimonides (nor would all agree with my synopsis of Strauss). Some find Maimonides to represent a skepticism about what reason can ultimately prove and know. Some find him to embody the irreducible tensions inherent in a commitment to revelation and to reason. Few believe that he harmonized science and religion, philosophy and Judaism in any straightforward way. The implication of this discussion for our purposes is that there is a tension among the presumptive highest ends of life and that that tension has something to do with the contrast between Athens and Jerusalem. The immediate question is, given the tension between the theoretical and the practical, how are intellectual excellence and moral excellence related?

In the *Eight Chapters*, Maimonides endorses a broadly Aristotelian account of moral psychology and of the virtues. The soul has five faculties, ranging from the nutritive to the rational. Proper and improper conduct originate in the sensitive faculty (i.e. the senses, which gather the basic data of the world) and in the appetitive faculty (which forms reactions of attraction or repulsion, desire for or aversion to objects tendered by the senses). Maimonides allows that the highest faculty, the rational faculty, also plays a role insofar as beliefs frame the epistemic context in which judgments regarding the desirability or undesirability of objects, goals, courses of action, and so on are made.[55] Given this psychology, Maimonides stipulates that virtues (*ma'alot*, in ibn Tibbon's Hebrew translation from the original Arabic) are of two kinds: intellectual (*ma'alot sikhliyot*) and moral (*ma'alot ha-middot*).

> The intellectual virtues belong to the rational faculty. They are (1) wisdom, which is the knowledge of the direct and indirect causes of things based on a previous realization of the existence of those things, the causes of which have been investigated; (2) reason, consisting of (a) inborn, theoretical reason, that is, axioms, (b) the acquired intellect, which we need not discuss here, and (c) sagacity and intellectual cleverness, which is the ability to perceive quickly, and to grasp an idea without delay, or in a very short time. The vices of this faculty are the antitheses or the opposites of these virtues.
>
> Moral virtues belong only to the appetitive faculty to which that of sensation in this connection is merely subservient. The virtues of this faculty are very numerous, being moderation (i.e. fear of sin), liberality, honesty, meekness, humility, contentedness …, courage, faithfulness, and other virtues akin to these. The vices of this faculty consist of a deficiency or of an exaggeration of these qualities.[56]

Maimonides' moral psychology aims to bring the moral evaluation of human character under the scrutiny of science. As was common among the ancients, he assimilates vice to sickness. A flawed character requires therapy. Just as one goes to a physician when one's body is sick, so too should one repair to a philosophical sage when one's soul is sick.[57] Indeed, one's soul may be so sick and one may be so habituated to that sickness that one may become unaware of how far one has fallen. One mistakes the foul for the fair. The normal equilibrium that constitutes health can elude self-inspection. An outside corrective is required. This is not quite an argument against privileged first personal knowledge. Rather, Maimonides, having inherited Aristotle's faculty psychology, sees the various parts of the soul in tension with each other. The passions, rooted in the appetitive faculty, can get the upper hand over reason. The goal of moral theory in the *Eight Chapters* is to give us tools to analyze this imbalance and to set it straight.

Virtues are dispositions or states of the soul equi-balanced between extremes of excess and deficiency. Thus, moderation is a mean between lust and insensitivity to pleasure; courage is a mean between rashness and timidity. Maimonides initially follows Aristotle's evaluation of virtue as a mean.[58] He seems convinced that there are objective measures for determining where one's disposition falls along the spectrum. These dispositions are acquired through long experience; one becomes habituated to either the mean or the extreme through repetition. When one has erred into the territory of the extreme, whether of excess or privation, one needs therapeutic correction. Thus, if one were to have become extremely miserly, he would be led to the mean of liberality by way of the opposite extreme, extravagance. He would be counseled to give lavishly and selflessly. Eventually, his disposition might be corrected and he could reach the mean state. Maimonides is clear that this therapy cannot be applied in a mechanical, textbook manner. Excesses may take more work to correct than deficiencies, or vice versa, depending on the vice in question. It is easier to get a person who is insensitive to pleasure receptive to pleasure than to dampen the lust of someone who has a voracious appetite for it. The mean is not the same for all persons; one must know the circumstances of one's patient. Medicine, he implies, is more an art than a science.

Unlike Aristotle, Maimonides does not present this analytic framework as a tool for self-inspection as much as he offers it as a metric for medical practice. Except for the pious ones (*Ḥasidim*), whom we will presently consider, these judgments of excess and deficiency are made by observers about "sick" individuals. The observers then compel these persons to behavioral routines with therapeutic consequences. The social setting for these transactions is nowhere spelled out. For Aristotle, the wise man, who knows himself and knows what balanced dispositions are like, may make judgments about others on the basis of their deviation from the mean. For Maimonides, one both judges *and* intervenes. Perhaps that stance reflects the taken-for-granted mutuality and solidarity of a covenantal community. The Aristotelian philosopher, although a political animal like all other human beings, aims at self-sufficiency and transcendence vis-à-vis the polis. But this is also a problem for Maimonides. Both Aristotle and Maimonides struggle with the proper balance between the political/ethical condition of humans and their potential for godlike transcendence of that condition. A tension or ambivalence about this balance marks the end of the *Guide* no less than the end of the *Nicomachean Ethics*.

Aristotle's analytic framework, which he does not apply consistently in his analysis of the virtues, may give rise to what Bernard Williams calls "a substantively depressing doctrine in favor of moderation."[59] Williams urges that the doctrine of the mean be forgotten. A similar criticism has been raised against Maimonides – does not Judaism sometimes require extremes?[60] Biblical heroes, such as Pinchas, who famously killed an Israelite man and his Moabite consort in a fit of righteous anger (Num. 25), are not models of moderation. Nor was Moses, who is described as the most humble of men. Well aware of this, Maimonides begins to stretch the concept of the mean almost as soon as he introduces it. Pious men (*ḥasidim*) *do* deviate from the mean in a self-aware and sensitive manner in order to perfect their own dispositions. Thus, they may fast, when the law permits them to eat, or refrain from sexual intercourse when they are otherwise permitted to do so. The common people, observing these apparently extreme actions, draw the false inference that the law encourages asceticism. Maimonides condemns asceticism as foreign to the spirit of the Torah. The pious ones were not acting like ascetics in other traditions in the sense that their entire way of life was devoted to *askesis*. Rather, they were engaged in strategic deviations from the mean for reasons of self-correction. Maimonides categorizes these actions as examples of the Talmudic principle of *lifnim me-shurat ha-din*: action within (or, some say, beyond) the limit of the law.

On this view, the Aristotelian mean still holds up as the criterion for appropriate moral action and disposition. Deviations from the mean are meant to bring one back to the mean. Indeed, Maimonides takes the Psalmist's praise of the Law – "the Law of the Lord is perfect, restoring the soul" (Ps. 19:9) – as testimony to the Law's conformity to the middle way. He goes on to analyze a number of mitzvot in terms of their pedagogic function as tutors to moderation. It would thus seem, on the evidence of the *Eight Chapters*, that Maimonides largely endorses the Aristotelian framework. The picture is complicated by the "Laws of Character Traits," however. He initially embraces the doctrine of the mean in the "Laws of Character Traits" in the *Mishneh Torah* but soon the departures from the Aristotelian position become radical. Aristotle, for example, sees anger as appropriate to the wise man under certain circumstances (*Ethics* 2.7 1108a5). At first, Maimonides agrees (*Character Traits* 1:4) – a man should "be angry only for a grave cause which rightly calls for indignation so that the like shall not be done again."[61] But then he appears to contradict himself and proscribe anger altogether at *Character Traits* 2:3. "There are some dispositions in which it is forbidden merely to keep to the middle path. They must be shunned to the extreme ... Anger, too, is an extremely bad passion and one should avoid it to the last extreme. One should train oneself not to be angry even for something that would justify anger."[62] Maimonides goes on to suggest that one might *feign* anger for pedagogic or corrective reasons when dealing with children, members of one's household, or political subjects, should the occasion require. But one's mind must be composed; one ought not really to *be* angry. Maimonides appears to be led here by Talmudic aphorisms about the inherent evil of anger. Maimonides reiterates the Talmudic claim that anyone who is angry is as if a worshipper of idols (*B. Shabbat* 115b). Furthermore, if a sage is angry, his wisdom departs from him; if a prophet is angry, his prophetic ability departs (*B. Pesachim* 66b). Nonetheless, Maimonides is always more than a homilist. He is not led by the text, at least in his philosophic work; he works in relation not subordination to it. Why his teaching on the role of the mean should differ from text to text and within one text itself remains puzzling. At any rate, it indicates a deep tension between his Aristotelianism and the pre-theoretical ethics of the rabbinic tradition. Maimonides does remark that the wise man (*ḥakham*) and the pious man (*ḥasid*) will differ over the extent to which they deviate from the mean (*Character Traits* 1:5). The *ḥakham* will deviate slightly; the *ḥasid* may deviate a great deal. One suggestion that has been proposed for reconciling his conflicting views is that the more strenuous ideal (no anger – and also extreme humility) is suitable for the *ḥasid* but not for the ordinary person, nor even for the wise man. The introduction of the pious man as the ideal Jewish type, however, pulls against the moderate *phronimos* of the Aristotelian tradition.[63] Here the Athens–Jerusalem tension breaks out anew.

Another point of tension between Maimonides' version of Aristotelianism and Aristotle per se is Maimonides' treatment of the virtuous man vs. the continent man. For Aristotle, the virtuous, in this case, temperate man ranks higher than the one who must struggle to control and contain wayward thoughts and impulses. The temperate man "craves the things he ought, as he ought and when he ought; and this is what rational principle directs" (*Ethics* 3:12 1119b). The continent man knows that "his appetites are bad" but "refuses on account of his rational principle to follow them" (*Ethics* 7:1 1145a). The non-conflicted man is more virtuous, more perfect than the conflicted but self-controlled person. He is more in harmony with his rational principle. A harmony between reason and desire, between the various parts of the soul, is better than an active conflict between them, the victorious outcome of the superior part notwithstanding. Maimonides inherits a rabbinic tradition which looks to be in conflict with the Greek moral anthropology, however. The rabbis say "Whoever is greater than his neighbor has likewise greater evil inclinations" (*B. Sukkah* 52) and "According to the labor, so is the reward" (*Avot* 5:23). Maimonides writes:

> Furthermore they command that man should conquer his desires, but they forbid one to say, "I, by my nature, do not desire to commit such and such a transgression, even though the Law does not forbid it." Rabbi Simeon ben Gamaliel summed up this thought with the words, "Man should not say, 'I do not want to eat meat together with milk; I do not want to wear clothes made of a mixture of wool and linen; I do not want to have illicit sexual relations,' but he should say, 'I do indeed want to, yet I must not, for my Father in heaven has forbidden it."[64]

On this view, the person who struggles against his impulses is, implicitly at least, more meritorious than the person in whom such impulses never (or no longer) arise. For the rabbis, repentance (*teshuvah*) is a major focus of the moral-religious life. The ideal is a constant wrestling with one's impulses and desires, a constant struggle to dedicate oneself to the correct goals by means of the correct path in the face of one's refractory human nature. No human being can ever be a finished product; God waits for every sinning person until the day of that person's death. The dynamism of moral life can know no stasis or *apatheia*. We cannot rest content with what we are or allow ourselves to be unresponsive to the insistent claim of holiness.

Maimonides reconciles these different tendencies by introducing, albeit critically, the categorical distinction of Saadya between "rational" and "traditional" laws. Maimonides believes, as readers of the *Guide* know, that all of the mitzvot are rational and equally so. There is no category of *ḥuqim* such that its laws are terminally resistant to rational explication. Rather, some laws, although completely rational, would not have been discovered or invented by reason were reason left to its own devices. These laws are revealed. God has given Israel laws to school them in holiness and to perfect them – such laws are not four-square with the "natural law" (not Maimonides' term but serviceable enough in this context) intuited by reason but they are no less rationally analyzable and justifiable for that. Maimonides' point here is that *both* Aristotle *and* the Rabbis agree that the person who has no desire to murder, to rob, to cheat, to harm, etc. *is* superior to one who does have those desires and suppresses them. There is no conflict on this score. Rather, the rabbinic ascription of greater merit to the continent man has only to do with that man's struggle to resist inclinations against performing the revealed commandments, that is, those commandments which would not be transgressions had the Law not established them. Maimonides sees this as virtually self-evident. Since these commandments add to nature, in a sense, there could be no merit in doing them (nor could there be demerit in failing to do them) for someone in a natural state. One must be commanded to do them. Aristotle is only talking about those fundamental matters of natural law or natural right which any human being must consider. Thus, the impression that the Sages and Aristotle disagree is based on a category mistake, in Maimonides' view. (And yet, couldn't one apply an Aristotelian analysis to a Jew's attitudes toward the revealed commandments? Why wouldn't someone who takes to them without inner conflict be superior to one who follows R. Gamliel's script? How can the superiority of struggle be justified against Aristotle's post-agonistic man?)

Aristotle, although a philosophical monotheist, is not a biblical monotheist. For a biblical monotheist, such as Maimonides, the distinction between the divine and the human is radical and categorical. Aristotle suggests at the beginning of his discussion of virtue, continence, and the as yet unnamed contrary of brutishness that that contrary is a kind of godlikeness. Brutishness is so savage and deformed that it is not analogous to the contraries of virtue (vice) or continence (incontinence). What is its contrary then? It is a form of divinity. For the gods cannot be said to be extraordinarily virtuous; they are beyond virtue insofar as they are gods. Similarly, the truly barbaric are beyond vice or incontinence. They form their own category of sub-humanity. For Aristotle, then, the divine and the human can be weighed on the same scale; the borders between them are fluid. Maimonides does not have this option. Aristotle can see the harmony, blessedness, equilibrium, and rationality of the gods as suitable models, goals, or norms for human attainment. Maimonides cannot. Even though human beings can emulate God's "attributes of action," their humanity will always confront them with their finitude, with the incompleteness and impermanence of their achievement. Considerations such as these may underlie Maimonides' deviation from Aristotle's characterization and ranking of the virtuous vis-à-vis the continent.[65]

As mentioned above, repentance is a major concern of Jewish moral thought. Maimonides systematized rabbinic teaching on repentance in a book of the *Mishneh Torah*, the "Laws of Repentance" (*Hilkhot Teshuvah*). He ensconces his teaching about the value and practicability of repentance in a philosophical argument on behalf of free will (or free choice, as medieval Jews framed it) and determinism, which is also discussed in the *Eight Chapters*. Without entering into an analysis of that problem here, we can simply say that Maimonides offered in both works a robust affirmation of the traditional rabbinic belief in the freedom of choice. Without freedom of choice – if, say, the determinism of the astrologers were true – "the commands and prohibitions of the Law would become null and void and the Law would be completely false."[66] (This is not, of course, much of an argument. When Maimonides mounts more of a real argument for freedom of choice in the *Guide*, things become more complex. It is not so clear that he holds to as strong a libertarian position as he seems to have done in the *Eight Chapters*.[67]) In the course of Maimonides' discussion in the *Eight Chapters*, he acknowledges that no human beings are born to virtue (or vice) anymore than they are born to skills and arts, which must be learned. Nonetheless, persons begin in different places. Some are inclined by their humors to quickness of mind, some to dullness; some are inclined toward cowardice and fear, others toward courage. Taking a basically "Greek," scientific stance, Maimonides wants to acknowledge the role of physiological determinants and of luck. But his point is that virtue, regardless of our starting point or unique constitutive challenges, can be learned. We are determined to some significant degree by factors beyond our control but, given the putative reality of freedom of choice, we have sufficient capacity for self-control to overcome our given natures. Maimonides has faith – a deeply Jewish faith – in the moral corrigibility of man.

Repentance, as a Jewish version of continence, is a crucial device of corrigibility. No matter what inner obstacles one faces, no matter how habituated one is to malign courses of action, Maimonides asserts the possibility of *teshuvah*.

> Let not the penitent suppose that he is kept far away from the degree attained
> by the righteous because of the iniquities and sins that he has committed. This

is not so. He is beloved by the Creator, desired by Him, as if he had never sinned. Moreover, his reward is great; since, though having tasted sin, he renounced it and overcame his evil passions. The sages say, "Where penitents stand, the completely righteous cannot stand." This means that the degree attained by penitents is higher than that of those who had never sinned, the reason being that the former have had to put forth a greater effort to subdue their passions than the latter ... Great is repentance, for it brings men near to the Divine Presence, as it is said, "Return, O Israel, to the Lord your God" (Hos. 14:2).[68]

The one who applies him or herself to *teshuvah* – which entails inter alia the moral discernment of one's faults, the articulation and confession of them, seeking the forgiveness of those one has offended, and a commitment to controlling oneself so as to break the malign pattern of behavior – is welcomed by God. "Repentance brings near those who were far away. But yesterday this person was odious before God, abhorred, estranged, an abomination. Today he is beloved, desirable, near [to God], a friend."[69] Even if we take this as a dramatic expression of moral motivation rather than the description of a metaphysical condition, it is far from Aristotle's outlook. The concern of a personal God for his creatures, his desire that they return to him and the covenantal framework within which these emotions, expectations, and possibilities are expressed, are alien to the Greek sources of Maimonides' ethics.

Repentance presupposes a dynamic moral cosmos in which corrigible human beings, equipped with moral reason, analyze and judge themselves and others and progress in the direction of increasing moral refinement. The course of ethical development which human beings are expected to undergo is not an end in itself, however. It is a necessary preparation and accompaniment for a higher stage: intellectual perfection. The Law, Maimonides tells us at *Guide* Part III, Chapter 27, aims at two things, the welfare of the body and the welfare of the soul. His formulation of these aims is public and political.

As for the welfare of the soul, it consists in the multitude's acquiring correct opinions corresponding to their respective capacity. Therefore some of them (namely, the opinions) are set forth explicitly and some of them are set forth in parables. For it is not within the nature of the common multitude that its capacity should suffice for apprehending that subject matter as it is. As for the welfare of the body, it comes about by the improvement of their ways of living with one another. This is achieved through two things. One of them is the abolition of their wronging each other. This is tantamount to every individual among the people not being permitted to act according to his will and up to the limits of his power, but being forced to do that which is useful to the whole. The second thing consists in the acquisition by every human individual of moral qualities that are useful for life in society so that the affairs of the city may be ordered. Know that as between these two aims, one is indubitably greater in nobility, namely, the welfare of the soul – I mean the procuring of correct opinions – while the second aim – I mean the welfare of the body – is prior in nature and in time.[70]

Maimonides has been broadly shaped by the Platonic teaching that the ideal polity is governed by a philosopher king and that, as Plato argues in Book X of the *Laws*, the ideal law must inculcate correct beliefs about the divine. Plato far more than Aristotle informs Maimonides' political theory, as is also true of his Muslim predecessors. Moses is roughly analogous to the philosopher king; the Torah is the only true claimant to an ideal, divine law. Maimonides' ethics, with its Aristotelian contours, needs to be situated within a largely Platonic political project.[71] The Torah secures the conditions for human communal flourishing in this world but also directs the focus of its philosophically attuned adherents to higher, meta-political and meta-historical concerns. It is clear from the citation above that the latter concerns have greater nobility and value than the former. It is also clear that one cannot rise to metaphysical, that is, theoretical knowledge without achieving the requisite prior perfection in moral, practical knowledge. The ultimate "perfection of the soul" requires the proximate "perfection of the body." And the latter cannot be achieved in isolation. "An individual can only attain all this through a political association, it being already known that man is political by nature."[72]

At the end of the *Guide*, however, Maimonides seems to subordinate ethics even further, diminishing its worth over and against pure metaphysics. At *Guide* Part III, Chapter 51 he writes "Thus it is clear that ... total devotion to Him and the employment of intellectual thought in constantly loving Him should be aimed at. *Mostly this is achieved in solitude and isolation. Hence every excellent man stays frequently in solitude and does not meet anyone unless it is necessary.*" (emphasis added)[73] He goes on to prescribe a regimen in which, although one is involved with other persons and the mundane tasks of household management, one's mind is completely abstracted, focused only on the intellectual love of God. "True human perfection" consists in operating at the highest level of theoretical knowledge: one acquires the rational virtues, "the conception of intelligibles, which teach true opinions concerning the divine things."[74] It is only in virtue of the perfection of theoretical knowledge that "man is man."[75] What immortality there is is found here – in the endurance of one's impersonal intellect cleaving to the impersonal, active intellect of God. A much lesser perfection is that of the moral virtues. "Most of the commandments serve no other end than the attainment of this species of perfection. But this species of perfection is likewise a preparation for something else and not an end in itself." And: "all the actions prescribed by the Law – I refer to the various species of worship and also the moral habits that are useful to all people in their mutual dealings – that all this is not to be compared with this ultimate end and does not equal it, being but preparations made for the sake of this end."[76] These concerns drive the perfected individual away from home, marketplace, and city. They draw him to asocial isolation, beyond the cave where the unenlightened dwell in darkness. What then of ethics as acting in imitation of God? What then of ethics as the imitation of God's attributes of action, the only "attributes" of God which we can, with suitable philosophical qualification, know?

The theory underlying this ranking replicates to some extent the Stoic view that value tracks what is most inalienable. Possessions are fully external to one; even bodily strength, vigor, and health are in a way external vis-à-vis that which cannot be removed from one without one's essence being destroyed, namely, the truly internal goods of the soul. Consequently, only these are fully to be valued. Maimonides offers the same argument although the costs are higher for him than for the Stoics. The cost for Maimonides would have to be paid in the complete subordination of ethics. In a perennially perplexing reversal, Maimonides shrinks from that cost in the final paragraphs of the *Guide*. He returns to the idea, developed at length in earlier sections of the *Guide*, that knowledge of God, the highest theoretical goal, cannot be severed from knowledge of God's ways. Knowledge of God's ways is practical knowledge, moral wisdom, which must be enacted not simply theorized. To know God theoretically entails that we act like God practically. "The way of life of such an [intellectually perfected] individual, after he has achieved apprehension, will always have in view loving-kindness, righteousness, and judgment, through assimilation to His actions, may He be exalted, just as we have explained several times in this treatise."[77]

It is tempting to see in this retreat from a pure endorsement of the *vita contemplativa* over the *vita activa* a belated triumph of the Hebraic over the Hellenic, but I don't think that is the right analysis. It is striking that Aristotle makes substantially the same move at *Nicomachean Ethics* X:8, where after arguing as Maimonides does for the superiority of the contemplative life on the basis of its greater self-sufficiency and inalienability, he endorses the practical life as a necessary dimension of human life. He thus sets the stage for his study of politics, without which the eudemonia of contemplative life cannot be secured. Perhaps Maimonides, in his return to practical life, albeit in a highly Judaic version, thereby shows his fidelity to Aristotle rather than any dissent from him. Perhaps Maimonides is taking Aristotle's moderate position as against extreme views of human independence from ordinary society. Such is an ethics that speaks both Greek and Hebrew, as it were.

This trio of thinkers theorized ethics in a self-consciously philosophical way, albeit more for purposes of piety, which is to say, of Jewish life, than for anything resembling twentieth-century metaethics. Given the disenchantment with modern metaethics in the Anglo-American world today, that is no strike against the medievals. Nonetheless, a genuinely scientific impulse was not lacking in their work. That is much less true of the popular and mystical ethics to which we now turn.

Notes

1   Good recent introductions to medieval Jewish thought may be found in Daniel Frank and Oliver Leaman, eds, *The Cambridge Companion to Medieval Jewish Philosophy* (Cambridge: Cambridge University Press, 2003) and Steven Nadler and Tamar Rudavsky, *The Cambridge History of Jewish Philosophy: From Antiquity to the Seventeenth Century* (Cambridge: Cambridge University Press, 2009). Three valuable studies focusing on medieval Jewish ethics are Hava Tirosh-Samuelson, *Happiness in Premodern Judaism: Virtue, Knowledge, and Well-Being* (Cincinnati: Hebrew Union College Press, 2003), Joseph Dan, *Jewish Mysticism and Jewish Ethics* (Seattle: University of Washington Press, 1986), and Joseph Dan, *Hebrew Ethical and Homiletical Literature: The Middle Ages and the Early Modern Period* (Hebrew) (Jerusalem: Keter Publishing, 1975).

2   For a philosophical discussion of this phenomenon, as well as citations of the relevant scholarly literature, see Kenneth Seeskin, *Autonomy in Jewish Philosophy* (Cambridge: Cambridge University Press, 2001), p. 59.

3   The Exodus version has its own motive clause at Exodus 20:11: "For in six days the LORD made heaven and earth and sea, and all that is in them, and He rested on the seventh day; therefore the LORD blessed the sabbath day and hallowed it." Deuteronomy's rationale is focused on human experience; the rationale of Exodus on reenacting the divine pattern. Deuteronomy's view, we might say, reflects the preoccupations of the Axial Age. Socrates' manner of philosophizing vis-à-vis the pre-Socratics, that is, by focusing on the human things, reflects an analogous shift.

4   The obligation to consent to what is right – and to see the concept of consent bound by a prior normativity – informs John Locke's understanding of consent to the social contract. See the discussion of Hanna Pitkin, "Obligation and Consent," *American Political Science Review*, Vol. LIX (December 1965), pp. 990–999, for analysis and sources. For a comparison of the Lockean view and Jewish political thought, see Mittleman, *The Scepter Shall Not Depart from Judah*, p. 94.

5   Isaac Heinemann, *Ta'amei Ha-Mitzvot be-Sifrut Yisrael* (*The Reasons for the Commandments in Jewish Literature*), Vol. I (Jerusalem: The Jewish Agency, 1966), p. 31. Heinemann's work is an invaluable guide to the theme of giving rational justification for the commandments in Jewish intellectual history. For an English translation, see Isaac Heinemann, *The Reasons for the Commandments in Jewish Thought: From the Bible to the Renaissance*, trans. Leonard Levin (Brighton: Academic Studies Press, 2008).

6   David Weiss Halivni, *Midrash, Mishnah and Gemara: The Jewish Predilection for Justified Law* (Cambridge, MA: Harvard University Press, 1986).

7   For an analysis of this oft-cited aggadah, see Barry L. Eichler and Jeffrey H. Tigay, eds, *Judah Goldin: Studies in Midrash and Related Literature* (Philadelphia: Jewish Publication Society, 1988), pp. 283–297. Goldin sees the story as a

confirmation of the adoption by the post-70 CE rabbis of majority rule. He notes that majority rule, however, was nothing to celebrate, given the tragic denouement of the tale.

8 For the notion of an "exclusive humanism" or "self-sufficing" (at least by its own lights) secularism, see Charles Taylor, *A Secular Age* (Cambridge, MA: Harvard University Press, 2007), p. 19.

9 Sifra 20:22 portrays human beings as wanting to follow what is natural, in this case eating pork and being promiscuous, but God has prohibited these and we cannot therefore follow our nature and satisfy our cravings. On this view, God's decree looks rather arbitrary yet this source also adduces a kind of reason for it: to separate Israel from the nations and allow it to be holy to God. God has a rational purpose, which can be explained instrumentally. The mitzvot in question, however, may still be less than rational, when considered intrinsically. Cited in Heinemann, *Ta'amei Ha-Mitzvot*, p. 22.

10 Yeshayahu Leibowitz, *Judaism, Human Values, and the Jewish State*, trans. Eliezer Goldman (Cambridge, MA: Harvard University Press, 1992), Chapter I.

11 For a strong argument against any trace of arbitrariness in the mitzvot, both among the Sages and in Saadya, see L. E. Goodman, "Rational Law/Ritual Law," in *A People Apart: Chosenness and Ritual in Jewish Philosophical Thought*, ed. Daniel H. Frank (Albany: SUNY Press, 1993). Goodman lessens the distinction between instrumental and intrinsic rationality by arguing that mitzvot with instrumental value – mitzvot whose purpose can be explained instrumentally – also have intrinsic worth. The way in which they refine us is not arbitrary; it is essential to the practice of the mitzvot per se. This is similar to the idea that virtue cannot be isolated from the practice of virtuous action. The good consequences to which, say, ritual mitzvot lead flow from the goodness of the actions themselves. Goodman advances a metaethical thesis about value; in brief, nothing can have instrumental value unless something has inherent value. He applies this view, developed at length in his *On Justice*, to the matter at hand.

12 The phrase "rules and laws" occurs frequently in the legal collections of the Pentateuch. The *mishpatim* may refer to case law and *ḥuqim* to statutes. The former adjusts and applies the latter to typical situations. For a thorough fleshing out of the ancient Near Eastern background, which is also of great interest to the biblical concern for public justice, see Moshe Weinfeld, *Social Justice in Ancient Israel and in the Ancient Near East* (Jerusalem: Magnes Press, 1995).

13 Heinemann, *Ta'amei Ha-Mitzvot*, p. 26.

14 Stanley Cavell, *Cities of Words* (Cambridge, MA: Belknap Press of Harvard University Press, 2004), p. 12.

15 Cavell, *Cities of Words*, p. 16. An exposition of Cavell's view of moral perfectionism may be found in Richard Eldridge, ed., *Stanley Cavell* (Cambridge: Cambridge University Press, 2003), pp. 36–43.

16 Medieval Jewish philosophy replicates the medical model of Greek and Hellenistic philosophy. For a study of philosophy qua therapeutic practice, see Martha Nussbaum, *The Therapy of Desire: Theory and Practice in Hellenistic Ethics* (Princeton: Princeton University Press, 1994). For an early expression of this view, see Phaedo 81–82d.

17 This text is often referred to as *The Book of Beliefs and Opinions* but scholars of medieval philosophical Arabic find this misleading. Saadya's terms intend to convey the basic harmony between doctrines held by the tradition and reasoned beliefs, which are the product of speculation and demonstration. Thus, translating the work as the *Book of Doctrines and Beliefs* indicates this progression in a way that the translation of the title as *Beliefs and Opinions* does not. "Opinions" is particularly misleading. See the discussion in the Translator's Introduction of the section on Saadya Gaon in Hans Lewy, Alexander Altmann, and Isaac Heinemann, *Three Jewish Philosophers* (New York: Atheneum, 1969), p. 19. All citations of Saadya are taken from Altmann's translation. (I wish to acknowledge here the role that Prof. Altmann played in my early education when I was an undergraduate at Brandeis University. Taking a course with him on Maimonides exposed me to the riches of medieval philosophy in a way that I could hardly appreciate at the time but have grown to esteem over the intervening decades.)

18 On Saadya's relationship to the Mutazila, see Sarah Stroumsa, "Saadya and Jewish kalam," in Frank and Leaman, eds, *The Cambridge Companion to Medieval Jewish Philosophy*.

19 Saadya's *Book of Doctrines and Beliefs* was translated from the original Arabic into Hebrew by Yehuda ibn Tibbon (1120–1190). He also translated other key works of medieval Jewish philosophy, such as Yehuda Halevi's *Kuzari*. His son, Samuel, translated Maimonides' *Guide for the Perplexed* from the Arabic, as well as some of Maimonides' other Arabic language works.

20 Saadya, *Book of Doctrines and Beliefs*, Altmann, ed. and trans., in Heinemann, *Three Jewish Philosophers*, pp. 95–96.

21 L. E. Goodman, "Rational Law/Ritual Law," p. 116.

22 Goodman continues: "We can see now why Saadya says, not that the objects of God's commandments are *deemed* fair or foul as a result of their being commanded, but that they *become* fair or foul as a result of their subsumption in a system of legislation. For that system has our perfection as its goal." L. E. Goodman, "Rational Law/Ritual Law," p. 119.

23 For a systematic exploration of the communally or socially assigned value of goods (in particular as a criterion for their just allocation), see Michael Walzer, *Spheres of Justice: A Defense of Pluralism and Equality* (New York: Basic Books, 1983).

24 One of the innovations of Saadya's philosophical project is the introduction of an epistemological apparatus and a theory of truth. Saadya argues that there are four sources of knowledge: sense perception, innate ideas, logical deduction, and, crucially for Jews, tradition. The rational mitzvot have a status akin to innate ideas; these entail epistemic cum practical norms without which thought per se is not possible. See the Prolegomena to *Book of Doctrines and Beliefs*, pp. 36–43.

25 Kant, *Groundwork of the Metaphysic of Morals*, trans. H. J. Paton (New York: Harper Torchbooks, 1964), p. 89. Saadya, *Book of Doctrines and Beliefs*, pp. 99–100.

26 Saadya, *Book of Doctrines and Beliefs*, pp. 99–100, cf. p. 41.

27 Saadya, *Book of Doctrines and Beliefs*, p. 102.

28 Saadya, *Book of Doctrines and Beliefs*, pp. 128–129.

29 Joseph Dan treats this chapter in his *Jewish Mysticism and Jewish Ethics* (Seattle: University of Washington Press, 1986), pp. 18–21. It is not clear to me

why Dan thinks that Saadya's ethics is mostly confined to the last chapter of *Doctrines and Beliefs*, nor is it clear to me why he isolates a "secular, even hedonistic" ethics from the whole of Saadya's book. Ethical considerations suffuse the entirety of the work. Its "secular" moments are no less anomalous than the worldliness of Proverbs and Ecclesiastes in the context of Scripture.

30 For Chapter 10, in English translation, one must consult Saadia Gaon, *The Book of Beliefs and Opinions*, trans. Samuel Rosenblatt (New Haven: Yale University Press, 1948), pp. 357–408. Unfortunately, a translation of this chapter was not attempted by Alexander Altmann in the selections found in *Three Jewish Philosophers*. For an analysis of this section of Saadya's teaching, see Hava Tirosh-Samuelson, *Happiness in Pre-Modern Judaism: Virtue, Knowledge and Well-Being* (Cincinnati: Hebrew Union College Press, 2003), pp. 145–160.

31 Saadya, *Book of Doctrines and Beliefs*, p. 103. In Prof. Altmann's view, the people who held this view were Indian philosophers, i.e. Brahmins. They advocated a version of "natural religion."

32 Saadya, *Book of Doctrines and Beliefs*, pp. 105, 112.

33 Saadya, *Book of Doctrines and Beliefs*, p. 45.

34 "Unless men had the confidence that there exists in the world such a thing as true report, no man would build any expectations on any report he might be told about success in any branch of commerce, or of progress in any art ... Nor would he fear what he should guard against, be it the dangerous state of a road or a proclamation prohibiting a certain action. But if a man has neither hopes nor fears all his affairs will come to grief. Unless it is established that there is such a thing as true report in this world, people will not pay heed to the command of their ruler, except at such time as they see him with their own eyes, and hear his words with their own ears; and when no longer in his presence, they will cease to accept his commands and prohibitions. If things were like this, all management of affairs would be rendered impossible and many people would perish." Saadya, *Book of Doctrines and Beliefs*, p. 110.

35 Note how the modern Enlightenment upends this typically Jewish medieval understanding of religion as politically formative revealed law. The Enlightenment transforms sacred law into religion in the sense of private belief, gathered voluntary community, church separated from state, etc. We shall briefly consider, in Chapter 5, Spinoza's contribution to the development of this modern, depoliticized concept of religion.

36 Saadya, *Book of Doctrines and Beliefs*, p. 113.

37 Saadya, *Book of Doctrines and Beliefs*, p. 45.

38 For a good introduction to Bahya's work, see the Introduction to Bahya ben Joseph ibn Pakuda, *The Book of the Direction to the Duties of the Heart*, trans. Menahem Mansoor (Oxford: Littman Library of Jewish Civilization, 2004). All excerpts from Bahya and all pagination refer to this edition. See also Julius Guttmann, *Philosophies of Judaism*, David W. Silverman (New York: Holt, Rinehart and Winston, 1964), pp. 104–110. Hava Tirosh-Samuelson locates Bahya within the courtier culture of educated Muslims (*adab*). She sees Bahya as a critic of those Jewish paladins who assimilated the values of that culture and neglected the inner spiritual values of their Judaism. See Tirosh-Samuelson, *Happiness in Pre-Modern Judaism*, pp. 172–189.

39   Baḥya, *The Duties of the Heart*, p. 89.

40   There is a major Talmudic discussion about which commandments, if any, require *kavannah* in order to be said to have fulfilled the commandment. See, e.g., *B. Berakhot* 13a–b, Eruvin 95b, Pesaḥim 114b. One principle that emerges from these discussions is that commandments that depend purely on intellectual focus or speech require *kavannah*. For a summary, see J. D. Eisenstein, *Otzar Dinim u'Minhagim* (New York: Hebrew Publishing Company, 1935) s.v. kavannah, p. 178.

41   Baḥya, *The Duties of the Heart*, p. 89.

42   Baḥya, *The Duties of the Heart*, pp. 91–92.

43   Baḥya, *The Duties of the Heart*, p. 95.

44   Saadya, *Book of Doctrines and Beliefs*, p. 95.

45   Baḥya, *The Duties of the Heart*, p. 178.

46   Baḥya, *The Duties of the Heart*, p. 181.

47   Baḥya, *The Duties of the Heart*, p. 183.

48   Baḥya, *The Duties of the Heart*, p. 195. A slight exception to this may be found in the politically oriented analysis at the end of Chapter Two, p. 172.

49   "Soul" is Mansoor's translation of the Arabic. Goodman suggests that a better translation would be "self" in the sense of ego or spirit (Lenn Goodman, private communication).

50   Baḥya, *The Duties of the Heart*, p. 199.

51   This is the subject of Chapter Nine of *The Duties of the Heart*.

52   Baḥya, *The Duties of the Heart*, p. 206.

53   Baḥya, *The Duties of the Heart*, p. 208.

54   Baḥya, *The Duties of the Heart*, pp. 211–212.

55   Translations of some portions of some of the chapters of the *Eight Chapters* may be found in Isadore Twersky, ed., *A Maimonides Reader* (West Orange: Behrman House, 1972). A full translation is found in Raymond L. Weiss and Charles Butterworth, eds, *Ethical Writings of Maimonides* (New York: Dover, 1983). Unless otherwise noted, citations used here are drawn from the Twersky volume. Portions of the medieval Hebrew translation may be found in Isaiah Tishbi and Joseph Dan, eds, *Mivḥar Sifrut Ha-Musar* (Jerusalem: M. Newman Publishing, 1970).

56   Twersky, *A Maimonides Reader*, pp. 365–366.

57   Twersky, *A Maimonides Reader*, p. 367.

58   *Nicomachean Ethics* 2.6 1106a. For an overview of Maimonides' appropriation of this doctrine, its Arabic sources, and current scholarly controversies about Maimonides' use of it, see T. M. Rudavsky, *Maimonides* (Oxford: Wiley-Blackwell, 2010), Chapter 8.

59   Bernard Williams, *Ethics and the Limits of Philosophy*, p. 36.

60   Steven Schwarzschild, "Moral Radicalism and 'Middlingness' in the Ethics of Maimonides," in Menachem Kellner, ed., *The Pursuit of the Ideal: Jewish Writings of Steven Schwarzschild* (Albany: SUNY Press, 1990).

61   Twersky, *A Maimonides Reader*, p. 52.

62   Twersky, *A Maimonides Reader*, p. 55.

63   Rudavsky, *Maimonides*, p. 170.

64 Twersky, *A Maimonides Reader*, p. 377. (I have changed the translation of *lavo 'al ha-ervah* from 'enter into an incestuous marriage' used in Twersky to 'have illicit sexual relations,' which better captures the range of *ervah*, following Weiss and Butterworth. The rabbinic aphorism of R. Gamliel is from *Sifra* Lev. 20:26.

65 One might, perhaps, see Maimonides taking a stance in some way reminiscent of Augustine in Book XIV of the *City of God*. Augustine criticizes the classical teaching about virtue. He sees the Christian as one who appropriately feels joy, pain, fear, and so on, as against the classical, here Stoic more than Aristotelian, teaching of apatheia. The classical teaching is subordinated to a biblically derived moral anthropology. There is something of this at work in Maimonides but he is more invested in keeping the Aristotelian project going than Augustine is vis-à-vis the Stoics.

66 *Eight Chapters*, chapter VIII, in Twersky, *A Maimonides Reader*, p. 380.

67 For an analysis of Maimonides' multifaceted views on this problem, see Alan Mittleman, "Free Choice and Determinism in Jewish Thought: An Overview," in Robert Pollack, ed., *Neuroscience and Free Will* (New York: Center for the Study of Science and Religion, Columbia University, 2009): http://www.columbia.edu/cu/cssr/ebook/FreeWill_eBook.pdf.

68 *Laws of Repentance*, chap. 7:4, 6 in Twersky, *A Maimonides Reader*, p. 79.

69 *Laws of Repentance*, chap. 7:6 in Twersky, *A Maimonides Reader*, p. 80.

70 Moses Maimonides, *The Guide of the Perplexed*, Vol. II, trans. and ed. Shlomo Pines (Chicago: University of Chicago Press, 1963), pp. 510–511.

71 Hermann Cohen gave prominence to Plato's influence on Maimonides, although from Cohen's point of view that influence has to do not with political theory but with a highly metaphysical value theory. Cohen objected to Aristotle's eudaimonism vis-à-vis Plato's theory of the good in *Republic*, Book VI. He wanted to associate Maimonides with the "higher" Platonic view. Leo Strauss picked up Cohen's association of Maimonides with Plato and restored the political significance of the connection. See Almut Bruckstein, trans. and ed., *Hermann Cohen: Ethics of Maimonides* (Madison: University of Wisconsin Press, 2003). We shall consider Cohen's thesis in Chapter 5. An important study of the impact of the Platonic motif of the philosopher king on Jewish thought is Abraham Melamed, *The Philosopher-King in Medieval and Renaissance Jewish Thought* (Albany: SUNY Press, 2003).

72 Maimonides, *Guide of the Perplexed*, p. 511.

73 Maimonides, *Guide of the Perplexed*, p. 621.

74 Maimonides, *Guide of the Perplexed*, p. 635.

75 Maimonides, *Guide of the Perplexed*, p. 635.

76 Maimonides, *Guide of the Perplexed*, p. 636.

77 Maimonides, *Guide of the Perplexed*, p. 638.

4
Medieval Rabbinic and Kabbalistic Ethics

In the century after his death, Maimonides' writings, as well as the derivative writings of his followers, were subjected to harsh criticism. The philosophical trend represented by Saadya, Baḥya, Maimonides, and others lost ground. Philosophical approaches to Judaism – in biblical exegesis, in law and ethics, in regard to nature and miracles, redemption and eschatology – lost ground to a traditionalist reassertion of rabbinic aggadah, to less rationalized, more willfully naïve constructions of Judaism. The Maimonidean controversy flared for over a century, dividing the rabbinic elite and exacerbating divisions within Jewish society.[1] The courtier class of Christian Spain largely favored philosophical learning, as had their predecessors in Muslim Spain. Some leaders of Jewish Provence were also loyal to philosophy and science. Against them, some leading rabbis found Maimonides' rationalism profoundly threatening, especially for the masses whose piety they feared would be undermined by philosophy. They were disturbed that Maimonides seemed, at best, to equivocate about resurrection; that he did not have a sufficiently miraculous view of miracles. His scientific predilection for the order and rationality of nature worked against a more supernatural, divinely driven physical world. Maimonides' view of immortality as the impersonal survival of the rational soul undercut more naïve, vivid presentations of the afterlife in Talmudic literature. The rabbis feared that if immortality was keyed to the intellectual comprehension of eternal truths, to the *intellectual* love of God, then the mitzvot might be viewed as inferior, subsidiary. Although there is no decisive proof that Maimonides' writings were burned, there were bans of excommunication against those who read them. There were also bans issued by sympathetic Maimonist rabbis against those who placed bans on them.

A Short History of Jewish Ethics: Conduct and Character in the Context of Covenant,
First Edition. Alan L. Mittleman.
© 2012 Alan L. Mittleman. Published 2012 by Blackwell Publishing Ltd.

One enduring, if sometimes ignored ban was promulgated by Rabbi Solomon ibn Adret in 1305. It prohibited the study of philosophy to anyone under 25 years old.[2]

The opposition to philosophy was both intellectual and political. Intellectually, some rabbis simply believed that philosophy was alien to Judaism, unnecessary and ultimately harmful. (Their opponents claimed that the Jews were philosophers in ancient times – Solomon after all was the wisest of men – but that philosophy had been lost among them due to the exile. The advocates of philosophy used the old Hellenistic Jewish legend that the Greeks imbibed philosophy originally from the Jews.[3]) Those who argued for the foreignness of philosophy thought it an insult to the omni-sufficiency of the Torah. What could justify going beyond the Torah to search for truth? Politically these rabbis thought that philosophy lowered the barrier between Jews and Christians; it created common ground in a way that might be detrimental to Jewish uniqueness. In the thirteenth century the Church had also banned (albeit without much success) the study of Aristotle in the universities. Some anti-philosophical rabbis turned to the Church for aid in combating the dissemination of Jewish philosophical culture. That outreach was to prove terribly unwise. In 1248, the Talmud was publicly burned in Paris. The Church's interest in the contents of Jewish books was spurred by its involvement in the Maimonidean controversy.[4]

The opponents of philosophy did not fully gain the upper hand until after the expulsion of the Jews from Spain at the end of the fifteenth century. By then, philosophy had declined and lay dormant until the modern period. The great project of synthesis, of reaching toward an understanding of Judaism in light of (what were thought) universal truths using universally valid methods, was discredited by the painful, particular fate of the Jews. In the thirteenth century, however, anti-philosophical animus and the reaffirmation of naïve traditionalism needed an intellectual basis. What provided that basis was an emerging, if esoteric trend: kabbalah.[5] This systematic expression of Jewish mysticism begins in Provence in the twelfth century and reaches a certain maturity with the emergence of the Zoharic literature toward the end of the thirteenth century in Spain. The non- or anti-philosophical rabbinic ethical works of the Middle Ages often come from kabbalistic circles. As kabbalah was intended to be esoteric, however, ethical works, which were meant to edify the Jewish masses, had to keep kabbalistic theosophical assumptions sub rosa. Thus, it may not immediately be apparent that an ethical work stems from a kabbalistic author. It is only later, by the sixteenth century, that the veil is removed and mystical theories of ethics become explicit.[6]

Far from the centers of kabbalistic activity in Spain and Provence, the Ashkenazi Jewish community of the Rhineland, devastated by massacres associated with the Crusades beginning in 1096, produced an ascetic movement of spiritual revival called German Hasidism (*Hasidei Ashkenaz*).[7] These pietists developed a mystical theology, based on the immanence of the divine, which underwrote a conception of life as a constant sacrifice for the sake of God. Ethical intention and action, using the commandments as a vehicle, was meant to procure transcendence and other-worldly salvation for the *hasid*. Theirs was a stern vision of constant struggle in a dark, demonic world. The commandments were in no way designed for human flourishing; they were designed to allow the Jew the chance – imposed through constant tests – to transcend his humanity. The culture of martyrdom, which took root in the age of the Crusades among Jews who willingly died to sanctify God's name, was to find application in every waking moment. The major work produced by these circles, the *Sefer Hasidim*, was to color much of the ethical literature of subsequent Ashkenazi Jewry.

In this chapter, we will analyze selections from several works of medieval ethical literature intended for popular consumption. Some of these works were written by kabbalists but mystical motifs come fully to the fore in only one of them, the sixteenth-century *Palm Tree of Deborah* (*Tomer Devorah*) by Moses Cordovero. Other works we will consider are Rabbi Moses ben Nahman's (Nahmanides) *Sermon on the Words of Ecclesiastes* (*Drasha al Divrei Kohelet*), Rabbi Jonah of Gerona's *Gates of Repentance* (*Sha'arei Teshuvah*), Rabbi Bahya ben Asher's *Jar of Flour* (*Kad ha-Kemah*), and Isaac Aboab's *Menorat Ha-Maor* (*The Lamp of Illumination*). These popular works all stem from the Iberian (Sephardic) stream of Jewish culture. While not philosophical, they exhibit a rational design. In some of them, topics are divided by chapter, concepts are analyzed in a logical fashion, and traditional materials are pressed into the service of a moral-spiritual vision of life. The works exhibit far greater coherence than ancient collections of aggadah or halakha. They reflect the ethical worldview of individual authors rather than the discrepant ideas of traditional collections. Thus, despite their often antagonistic stance toward philosophy, they do not reject the systematic, reflective character of philosophical writing.

Alongside these products of Sephardic moral reflection, we will also take a look at two Ashkenazi ethical texts, the *Sefer Hasidim (Book of the Pious)*, mentioned above, and the *Orhot Tzaddikim (Paths of the Righteous)*, which draws inspiration from German Hasidism, as well as from other medieval sources of *musar*.

Moshe ben Nahman

Rabbi Moshe ben Nahman, known as Nahma or by the acronym Ramban (1194–1270), was one of the major Jewish figures of the Middle Ages. He was distinguished as a leading biblical commentator, halakhic scholar, kabbalist, and communal leader. As a prominent rabbi, he had been called to defend Judaism in a famous disputation with a Jewish apostate before James I, king of Aragon. Although James guaranteed Nahmanides freedom of speech, both at the disputation and in Nahmanides' subsequent report on the disputation, he ran afoul of church authorities and James could not fully protect him. He was subsequently forced to flee the country, eventually settling in Jerusalem. In his old age he attempted to rebuild Jewish life in the holy city, founding a yeshiva and a synagogue there. Nahmanides revered Maimonides as a halakhist but opposed his philosophical writing, sometimes explicitly, often implicitly. He tried to take a moderate position in the Maimonidean controversy, refusing to condemn Maimonides or his writings but rejecting the study of philosophy per se. He did, however, use philosophical terminology and concepts in his own work. Mystical motifs are also present but kept below the threshold – Nahmanides did not want to publicize or promote kabbalah among the masses.

Among his many writings, he left an essay on the Book of Ecclesiastes. The essay was probably based originally on a sermon (*derasha*); it has a fluid, somewhat oral quality to it. Sermons are an important source for Jewish ethical teaching and reflection both in the medieval and in the modern period. The aspect of Nahmanides' sermon on Ecclesiastes, which has the greatest philosophical interest, is his attempt to domesticate Ecclesiastes' rather pessimistic view to a more typical, rabbinic perspective.

Ecclesiastes, or *Kohelet* in Hebrew, belongs to the genre of wisdom literature. Its alleged authorship by King Solomon secured it a place in the canon but its main ideas push, like Job, against the dominant biblical (and later rabbinic) theodicy of Deuteronomy. *Kohelet* repeatedly questions divine justice in the sense of desert being proportioned to moral performance. There might be a divine plan for nature and humanity, *Kohelet* believes, but we are unable to know what it is. If the righteous are rewarded for their actions and the wicked punished, that is not reflected in this life. And like the author of Job, the author of *Kohelet* does not seem to know of another life. All is futile (*hevel*). The best one can hope for is enjoying one's toil, accepting it as one's lot. *Kohelet's* assertion of the futility or vanity of human action, indeed, of the natural order, stands in stark contrast with the assertion of Genesis, chapter 1 that the world is good, indeed "very good." I have elsewhere argued that Genesis makes a strong, philosophically defensible claim on behalf of the goodness of being. A consequence of this is that the appropriate human response to the world, on the biblical and Judaic account, is to affirm its fundamental goodness and to manifest that goodness in human action.[8] Nahmanides wants very much to make such a claim and to read *Kohelet* such that the book can be pressed into agreement with it.

After an initial argument on behalf of the Solomonic authorship of *Kohelet*, Nahmanides expresses surprise that *Kohelet* claims the world is a vain and futile thing. Could it be the case that its divine Creator would do something useless and purposeless[9]? God Himself delights in the work of His hands (Jeremiah 27:8). It is fitting for us to question Solomon's judgment in this case! It might be possible to say that Solomon is only claiming that earthly matters are futile but that the heavenly spheres have value. But Nahmanides rejects that line of argument on philosophical grounds: phenomena that mark earthly existence such as day and night, summer and winter, and the generation of plants and animals are all contingent on the movement of the heavens. If earthly existence is vanity, then heavenly movement is in vain. Creation cannot be parsed in such a way: value must pervade all of it or none of it. Moses himself claims, at Genesis 1:31, that everything that God made is very good (*tov meod*). God saw what He had made and found goodness in it, even in those things, such as death, which from a human point of view do not seem good. This radical axiology is in conflict with Solomon's apparent dismissal of the value of being.

Nahmanides' resolution of this conflict makes use of a standard trope of medieval Aristotelianism, although he uses it in a non-standard way. All the wise men know, he claims, that all of the created things in the world are composed of matter and form (*homer v'tzurah*). Matter is permanently conserved and cannot be destroyed. In the celestial spheres, the permanence of matter is paralleled by the permanence of form. In the terrestrial sphere, however, matter is permanent but form is transient. (Nahmanides seems to mean by "form" something like "image," or "appearance," whereas for Aristotle and Maimonides form indicates that which makes a thing the thing it is and also renders it intelligible.) The outward appearances of things are constantly changing, both on their own and through human interaction with them. God is the source of forms. Nahmanides, with an imaginative sermonic flourish, uses the well-known verse from Deuteronomy (32:4), "The Rock, His work is perfect" (*ha-tzur tamim po'alo*) to claim that God (*tzur*) ultimately produces the forms (*tzurot*). Even though the forms of earthly things constantly change, the underlying process whereby they are produced is perfect; it is divine activity per se. Thus, Solomon's point is to call attention to the constant evanescence of form as over/against the enduring nature of matter – and to ascribe this process to a kind of divine justice. Nahmanides likens the transience of forms to hot breath on a winter day; one sees it for a moment before it vanishes, and yet it was real. So too individual creatures, including human beings, are real but their forms change and vanish when they come to an end. Their matter decomposes and returns to its constitutive elements.

Given this presumed metaphysics, Nahmanides reads *Kohelet's* claim of "vanity of vanities, all is vain" (*hevel havalim, ha-kol havel*) as making an ethical point. We are to take *Kohelet* on one level as a metaphysical account of change (via the composition and decomposition of matter and form) and on another level as an ethical injunction. Rather surprisingly, Naḥmanides states that "vanity of vanities" should not be understood in the biblical Hebrew as two nouns (in the construct state) but rather as an imperative! That is, the phrase commands us to understand things as vanities. We are to revise our conventional ideas of the value of pleasures and actions, and see them sub specie aeternitatis, as it were: as matters of no ultimate consequence. There is a great deal more to this text; Naḥmanides continues to interweave metaphysical analyses with ethical considerations. This brief treatment will have to suffice, however, to convey something of the flavor of the piece. As we can see, philosophical elements are not lacking, even in an "anti-philosophical" writer.

Jonah Gerondi

Naḥmanides' cousin, Rabbi Jonah of Gerona (or Jonah Gerondi as he is also known) (c.1200–1263), was also a key player in the Maimonidean controversy. He journeyed from Provence, where he lived and taught, to northern France to persuade the rabbis there to ban Maimonides' philosophical writings. Although the rabbis did not ban Maimonides' *Book of Knowledge* and *Guide*, they did criticize those who studied philosophy. They rebuked them for reading non-Jewish books of wisdom and for casting doubt on traditional understandings of biblical narrative and eschatology.[10] In addition to *The Gates of Repentance*, Gerondi also wrote commentaries on the biblical book of Proverbs and the rabbinic tractate *Avot*.

The Gates of Repentance is systematic.[11] It is divided into four "gates." The first concerns the basic principles (*ikkarim*) of repentance, which Gerondi counts as 20. The principles include such matters as regret (first principle), forsaking sin (second), sorrow at the implied rebellion of the sinner against God (third), various types of worry or fear arising from a sense of inadequacy in the work of repentance or from weakness of resolve (sixth), reordering one's desire toward suitable objects (ninth), etc. Each of these principles is analyzed in great detail. Desire is obviously a major category of concern for a traditional, rather ascetically oriented moralist. Gerondi invokes a familiar philosophical, ultimately Platonic trope, without any sense of its philosophic origins. Desire (*taavah*) needs to be governed by reason (*sekhel*). The would-be penitent needs to recognize that all sin is caused by desire for unworthy (especially for pleasant) things. Desire even for lawful permitted things (*devarim mutarim*) or persons must also be restrained. Thus, although Abraham was permitted sexual relations with his wife, Sarah, Abraham first *noticed* that his wife was beautiful years after their marriage. Such things didn't matter to him as he was a paragon of restrained desire. In the Genesis text, Abram (as he was still called at this point) is anxious about having to descend to sexually promiscuous Egypt, on account of the famine in Canaan, with a beautiful wife, Sarai. He tells Sarai to pretend that she is his sister, a perplexing, if not to say morally problematic tactic. "I am well aware," Abram says "that you are a beautiful woman" (Gen. 12:11). The Talmud (*B. Baba Batra* 16a) notes that Abraham had previously taken no account of his wife's beauty due to his sexual modesty, a point echoed by Rashi in his Genesis commentary. Gerondi seamlessly weaves together verses from Genesis and *Avot*, with the Talmudic aggadah in the background, to make the point that the righteous man, of whom Abraham is the paragon, must always restrain his desire.[12] Gerondi frequently gives practical examples of how to achieve the desired disposition, typically drawn from biblical characters as interpreted by the Sages. In the current case of restraining desire for permitted goods, for example, King David is adduced. David sequestered 20 concubines, providing for them but not engaging in sexual relations with them (II Sam. 20:3). Gerondi adds, citing the Jerusalem Talmud, that he would have them beautified every day so that he could look at them, feel aroused, and then subdue his desire, thus strengthening, through habituation, his ability to conquer his inclinations.[13]

The second "gate" explores the sources of motivation for repentance, the obstacles to repentance, and how to acquire the frame of mind to form and sustain the resolve to repent. There are six aspects to this quest. The last is developing a heightened consciousness of the limits of human life: none of us know when our end will come. We must be anxious to return the soul to God in the same state of purity in which God implanted the soul in us. The shortness of time should move us to repair the soul (*tikkun ha-nefesh*) and to acquire the virtues (*hasagat ha-ma'alot*) of love, fear, and cleaving to God.[14]

The third "gate" forms the longest section of the work. It deals with morally salient (as well as "purely ritualistic") commandments parsed into traditional categories such as positive and negative, action or thought oriented, light or heavy, biblical or rabbinic mitzvot. The schema which organizes the presentation of the commandments presents them in terms of the degrees of punishment attaching to their violation. Gerondi analyzes dozens of mitzvot with distinct moral content such as to lend to the poor, to pay a hired worker on the day of his labor, to rescue a neighbor and his property, to set up communal welfare systems, to rebuke one's neighbor for his immoral or illegal conduct, etc. He cites the source of the mitzvah in the Torah, adduces rabbinic texts that develop the commandment, and occasionally provides an argument on behalf of the commandment. Thus, in the case of institutionalizing a system in a city to provide for the general welfare, he argues that if the Torah commands us to rescue our neighbor's ox or sheep, how much more should we exert ourselves on behalf of the owner of those oxen or sheep.[15] If even non-Jews (in the Book of Jonah, chapter 1) wanted to find out who on their ship had angered God and caused the storm so that they could rebuke him, how much the more so should Jews, who are responsible for one another (*B. Shevuot* 39a), rebuke one another for infractions of the Torah.[16] This form of a fortiori argument, supported by examples from biblical and Talmudic texts, is typical. One imagines that it was an effective rhetorical technique in a homiletic setting, a genre close to medieval ethical texts.

Why be moral, on Gerondi's account? What motivates a traditional medieval moralist to advocate stringent observance of the commandments and ceaseless *tikkun ha-nefesh*? Although these questions may seem too obvious from the perspective of a traditional Jew to be worth asking, Gerondi does provide an answer of sorts.

> One who has been granted wisdom [*deah*] by the Blessed One will impress upon himself the fact that He sent him into this world to observe His charge, His Torah, His statutes, and His mitzvot, and will open his eyes only to discharge His commission; and, in the end of days, if he has faithfully executed His trust, he will return in song, crowned with everlasting joy, as a servant whose master has sent him across the seas, whose eyes and heart are entirely intent upon his mission, until he returns to his master. As Solomon, may Peace be upon him, said, "That you may put your trust in the LORD ... To let you know reliable words, that you may give a faithful reply to him who sent you (Prov. 22:19–21).[17]

The answer harks back to the covenantal origins and framework of biblical Israel and classical Judaism. Man is God's servant whose purpose is to fulfill his master's charge. God has sent us forth and eventually calls us back. We are to honor His will as we make our way through the world, as a knight bound by oath to a lord or as a servant in the faithful employ of a master. There is a covenantal relationship between the parties, albeit an immense disparity in power between them as well. Nonetheless, the weaker party has faith and trust in the goodness and benevolence of the stronger. The master wishes the servant's well-being in this world and the next.

Although this basic theological construct governs the whole project, ordering the invocations of punishment or reward in the afterlife for performance or malfeasance, a more subtle line of argument is also at work. Gerondi, like Saadya before him, claims that performance of the commandments with the proper intentionality and disposition increases the *virtue* of the performer. One's excellence as a human being grows with faithful devotion to God through the commandments (*mitzvot aseh*). Thus, the highest virtues (*ma'alot elyonot*) are given to us in the course of our dedication to the commandments. He cites biblical verses to ground the commandments, and then interprets these commandments as the communication of virtues. The virtue of freedom of choice is based on God's commandment to choose life (Deut. 30:9), for example. Gerondi's complete table of virtues includes learning (Torah), imitatio dei, trust, contemplation (of God's greatness), and remembrance (of God's grace).[18] The virtues, so enumerated, are not ends in themselves. They strengthen the ability to perform the commandments and enrich their meaning. The virtues are in turn strengthened by the practice of the commandments. Not hating one's brother in one's heart (Lev. 19:17) preserves the good that is in the heart, which would otherwise be lost, along with much else were the propensity for hatred to gain the upper hand. Gerondi envisions a mutual potentiation of the aretaic and deontic dimensions of the Torah within a broadly covenantal understanding of the relationship between the Jews and God.

Baḥya ben Asher

Baḥya ben Asher (thirteenth century), a student of Solomon ibn Adret who promulgated the ban noted above on the study of philosophy, was a highly influential commentator on the Pentateuch. His commentary has had enduring popularity over the centuries. Baḥya explicates the Torah in four ways: the way of commonly accepted meaning (*peshat*), the way of homiletic interpretation (*midrash*), the way of reason (*sekhel*), and the way of mystical interpretation (*kabbalah*). His commentary is one of the main vehicles by which kabbalistic interpretation became public. Baḥya's penchant for systematic, clearly organized exposition is also expressed in the *Kad Ha-Kemaḥ* (*Jar of Flour*). This work is an encyclopedia of fundamental Jewish concepts, ethical norms, and virtues. It proceeds alphabetically, treating such topics as *emunah* (faith), *ahavah* (love), *orhim* (guests), and *avel* (the mourner) under its first entry – all of these words begin with the letter *aleph* in Hebrew – and so on for the other letters of the Hebrew alphabet. Many of these entries are germane for a consideration of ethics. Let us consider two, Baḥya's treatment of purity of heart (*taharat ha-lev*) and of holiness (*kedushah*).

In keeping with the sermonic origin of the work, Baḥya typically begins his exposition with a biblical verse. He cites Psalm 51:12: "Fashion a pure heart (*lev tahor*) for me, O God; create in me a steadfast spirit." Baḥya reads "pure heart" as "purity of thought" (*taharat ha-maḥshavah*), which is an intellectual or rational virtue (*midah sikhlit*).[19] The virtues, he tells us, are divided into two categories, physical (*gufaniyot*) and rational (or, better in this context, "mental") (*sikhliyot*). The physical or bodily virtues are required to improve one's deeds; there can be no perfection of wisdom without the application of wisdom to action. Hence, for wisdom to flourish there must be the correction, improvement, and perfection of action. Baḥya relies, as is typical of homiletically derived ethics, on a verse: "The beginning of wisdom is the fear of the LORD; all who practice it gain sound understanding" (Ps. 111:9–10). The Talmud (*B. Berachot* 18a) had already observed that the text does not say "all who study it" but "all who practice it." Moral action is thus foundational to the achievement of wisdom. In Baḥya's view, the mental virtues must be cultivated *first*; they purify the mind so that right conduct may follow.[20] Wisdom, presumably, consists of the integration of purified mind with perfected conduct.

The mental virtues purify the mind so that one's thought may constantly be directed to the service of God. Baḥya cites Psalm 24:4, "He who has clean hands and a pure heart …" "Clean hands" allude to the physical virtues which shape action; a "pure heart" to the underlying intentionality of mind. Just as the verse from Psalms links the physical and the mental, the inner and the outer, Baḥya emphasizes their mutual dependence. He uses an ancient saying of Rabbi Akiva, which likens the Torah to glass. Just as glass permits one to see what is inside of it from the outside, so too must the disciple of the Sages show on his face all that is in his heart. There ought not to be a disparity between one's intention and one's action, one's thought and one's practice.[21] This utter lack of opposition, polarity, or dissonance between the "inside" and the "outside" of oneself is constitutive of the righteous person, the *tzaddik*. Such a person is blameless, flawless, and whole (*tamim*). Noah, Abraham, and Jacob were such men.

Until this point, it sounds as if such a state of moral excellence is achievable through human agency alone. But Baḥya shifts ground and introduces a somewhat mystical theme: an overflow (*shefa*) which emanates (*yitatzel*) from God onto one, such as David, who prays for divine assistance in achieving purity. The *shefa* renews one's inner spirit. Yet Baḥya does not leave the work of virtue to divine grace alone. In fact, he lays out a detailed path whereby one ascends a ladder of virtue, moving from one rung to another until purity of heart or mind is achieved. Indeed, one ascends beyond such purity into a state of contact with the holy spirit. The ascent entails a subtle balance between disciplined exertion and prayer, human effort and divine assistance. Baḥya builds on the famous rabbinic "ladder of virtues" in the Talmud at *B. Avodah Zarah* 20b.

> Rabbi Phineas b. Jair said: study leads to precision, precision leads to zeal, zeal leads to cleanliness, cleanliness leads to restraint, restraint leads to purity, purity leads to holiness, holiness leads to meekness, meekness leads to fear of sin, fear of sin leads to saintliness, saintliness leads to [the possession of] the holy spirit, the holy spirit leads to life eternal.[22]

The context in the Talmud for this saying is a discussion about the impermissibility of gazing at beautiful women (or their undergarments when they are drying outdoors after washing or at copulating animals). One must keep oneself from indulging in lewd thoughts during the day lest one fall into impurity, which presumably means a nocturnal emission, when one sleeps.

In the Talmudic context, the ladder seems to ascend from concern with lower things to concern for the highest things. Baḥya reads the text, however, to start with the *sikhliyot*, the mental virtues which purify the mind in order that the physical virtues, the *gufaniyot*, can then correct one's actions (*tikkun ha-ma'asim*).

Baḥya explicates the logic of this progression through a series of biblical verses where the terms are used and linked to one another. But he also uses philosophical arguments, defining the content of each virtue and the way one supports and enables the next. Homiletically, he asserts, for example, that saintliness (*ḥasidut*) leads to the holy spirit (*ruaḥ ha-kodesh*) because Psalm 89:20 states, "Then you spoke to your faithful ones (*ḥasidekha*) in a vision." The holy spirit connects precisely to those who have achieved *ḥasidut*, not to those who remain on a lower rung. Philosophically, he tries to show how one virtue underwrites another. Thus, the person who fears sin will keep silence in the face of taunts and insults (i.e. he fears to commit the sin of *lashon ha-ra*, hurtful speech) and this self-restraint leads to humility. Humility or meekness then leads one to restrain oneself from the full exercise of one's rights, say in a commercial transaction (*lifnim mi-shurat ha-din*), which is a mark of saintly behavior. Baḥya assumes if not the unity of the virtues then their complementary and mutually reinforcing nature. His comprehensive view is this. The first five virtues (precision, zeal, cleanliness, restraint, and purity) purify and focus the mind. They are the mental, rational, or intellectual virtues. The next four virtues (holiness, meekness, fear of sin, and saintliness) are the physical virtues which shape appropriate conduct.[23] Once this passage has been completed, it is appropriate that the holy spirit will come to rest on the saintly one (*ḥasid*).

Curiously, Baḥya seems to count the holy spirit both as God's emanation onto the perfected saint *and* as the final stage of virtue itself. This is puzzling. Is the holy spirit a metaphysical entity, existing apart from human beings, or is it a stage in the perfection of human character? The answer appears to be that it is both. Baḥya relies on an ontology that is familiar to a medieval reader but alien to a modern one. The virtue of purity of thought, he tells us, involves the rational soul (*nefesh sikhlit*). The rational soul has its root (*shoresh*) in an elevated, supernal source. Both thought (*maḥshavah*) and soul have a single underlying principle (*ikkar*). This principle acts as a power or potentiality (*koaḥ*) in man both to raise that which is low and to lower that which is elevated by means of thought. The basic idea here seems to be the ancient and medieval notion that like knows like. We know of the ultimate things because something of the ultimate dwells within us and bridges the chasm between us and that which is ultimate. Thus, Plato in *Phaedo* writes:

> But when it [the soul] investigates by itself [i.e. through pure thought], it passes
> into the realm of the pure and everlasting and immortal and changeless, and

being of a kindred nature, when it is once more independent and free from
interference, consorts with it always and strays no longer, but remains, in that
realm of the absolute, constant and invariable, through contact with beings of
a similar nature. And this condition of the soul we call wisdom. (*Phaedo* 79d)

The argument is similar although not identical. It is interesting that both
Bahya and Plato draw the same immediate conclusion from the likeness of
the soul to the highest things. The soul must be kept pure and uncontaminated
by its involvement with lowly things such as "uncontrolled desires" (*Phaedo*
81a). For Bahya, habituation to base thoughts and desires (*hirhurim raim*)
contaminates the soul and robs thought of its potential for purity. This leads
him to the counterintuitive (albeit Talmudic, see *B. Yoma* 29a) view that
sinful thoughts are more grievous than sinful actions. Sinful action, when
motivated by sinful thought, is much harder to correct than when action is
occasional or spontaneous. A mind accustomed to corrupt thought is prone
to rationalization; it lacks the capacity for inner correction and self-criticism.
It becomes so fixed on its inappropriate objects that nothing is allowed to
stand in its way. Bahya gives the rather extravagant example of a man who
is so focused on committing adultery with his neighbor's wife that he is
willing to assault or kill his neighbor to accomplish his desire. One is tempted
to dismiss such an example and its underlying thesis about motivation as
extreme, but a perusal of the daily headlines or local news gives Bahya's view
plausibility. It is easy for things to get out of hand.

Bahya's essay ends with the affirmation that one who tries to direct all of
his thoughts to God will be helped by God (*B. Yoma* 38b). God has given us
freedom to choose between the good way, the way of life, and the evil way
(Deut. 30:15). We will be punished not just for our actions but also for the
thoughts that inhibit us from doing good or that motivate us to do evil.
Precisely what the nature of that punishment is remains unclear. Perhaps we
relegate ourselves to a vicious circularity in a moral sense. Like Pharaoh, for
whom the hardening of the heart was his punishment, habituation to
corrupting thought alienates us from God who wishes to help us through
the emanation of his holy spirit. Mental impurity entrenches that alienation.

Isaac Aboab

Aboab (fourteenth century) sought to give systematic shape and prominence
to the aggadah, the non-halakhic or non-legal portions of the Talmudic and
midrashic literature. *Menorat Ha-Ma'or* was perhaps intended to organize
the aggada in a way comparable to how Maimonides organized the halakha
in the *Mishneh Torah*.[24] The book is constructed artfully upon the conceit of
a *menorah*, the seven-branched candelabrum used in the first and second

Temple (Exod. 25:37). Each lamp (*ner*) designates a chapter. The chapters are subdivided into principles, which are then subdivided into sections and then into subsections the number of which depends on how far Aboab continues his analysis. It is an orderly work, possibly designed for easy reference for preachers and ordinary readers.

Each "lamp" invokes a major moral concept or mitzvah. Thus, the first lamp/chapter is "not to pursue superfluous (or distracting, external) things," which is analyzed in terms of principles such as jealousy, lust, or appetite for, for example, wealth, luxuries, sex (these are sections, each further analyzed into subsections) and honor, through, for example, the rabbinate or the assumption of secular authority. The second chapter deals with the ethics of speech, analyzing topics such as flattery, gossip, embarrassment, foolishness, and keeping bad company, which would habituate one to these vices. While some of these topics are grounded in mitzvot in a narrowly legal sense, others arise from reflection on the ideals of character embodied in non-legal texts, such as the Psalms. In the third chapter, Aboab focuses on those mitzvot which straddle the presumptive line between ethics and ritual. He treats circumcision, prayer, honoring festivals and honoring parents, marriage, giving charity, giving persons respect in the form of gladdening a married couple, visiting the sick, accompanying the deceased to their interment, comforting mourners, and treating all persons with deference. He also explores truth-telling and the attitude that we bring to the performance of mitzvot in general. The treatment of "ritual" mitzvot in an ethical context and the seamless transition between formal ritual duties and more impeccably "ethical" topics, such as truth-telling, is typical, not only of Aboab, but of this entire literature. It harks back, as we have seen, to the conceptual interweaving of ritual, ethics, and law in the early biblical literature. The other chapters of *Menorat Ha-Ma'or* deal with the study of Torah (Chapter IV), with repentance (Chapter V), the ways of peace and love (Chapter VI), and with humility (Chapter VII).

The book is conceptualized in terms of another conceit as well. Aboab uses Psalm 34:15 ("Shun evil and do good, seek amity and pursue it") as an organizing principle. The first two chapters analyze the evil to be shunned; the next three chapters treat the good to be pursued; and the last two chapters deal with amity and its pursuit. Let us consider a section from Chapter VI. The chapter is concerned with walking in the ways of peace (*darkhei shalom*) and is divided into two sections: general standards of proper behavior (*derekh eretz*) and what it means to love one's friends (*ahavat ḥaverim*). Every chapter begins with an introduction. In this case, Aboab weaves together philosophically tinged motifs with verses from Proverbs, sayings from *Avot* and the Talmud, as well as aggadot. Aboab begins with the philosophical claim that the Active Intellect emanates a power which man acquires as a faculty of attraction to good and desirable objects and of repulsion from bad and undesirable ones.[25] This faculty (*sekhel naot*) properly draws us to the good and away from evil, and thus is in the end able to return to its source, the Active Intellect, only if its bearer has good traits of character (*middot tovot*), is whole or complete (*shalem*) in his comportment toward others (*derekh eretz*), and pursues love and peace toward other human beings. If a person is uninterested in virtue and proper comportment, however, he will neither have health of soul (*briyut nafsho*) nor be able to serve God – even if he is involved in Torah study and is able conceptually to grasp the highest, rational ideas (*muscalot*). Aboab seeks to reset the equilibrium between intellectual and moral claims, at least in comparison with the highly intellectualist approach of Maimonides. Without genuine devotion to character and conduct – concerns that fall within the penumbra of the system of formal, legally specifiable mitzvot – neither Torah study nor theoretical-rational endeavor avails. He backs this up with a familiar citation from *Avot* (3:21): If there is no proper conduct, there is no Torah. (It is interesting that he does not give the form that is standard in our Mishnah, "If there is no Torah, there is no proper conduct; if there is no proper conduct, there is no Torah." Perhaps he had a variant version or was simply quoting selectively to buttress his point.)

Aboab warrants the value of *derekh eretz* with several Talmudic sayings and stories that assert its worth. He then tries to derive *derekh eretz* from the formal mitzvah of neighborly love (Lev. 19:18). He states categorically that "All who want to be whole in their character traits, healthy in their service to their Creator, desirable in the eyes of other persons and clean before God and Israel, should learn the ways of proper comportment, should love all human beings, and even more so his friends, whose words should be dearer to him than his own. For this is the root of all of the ethical injunctions and practical commandments with respect to man and neighbor in the Torah. And all of them are comprised by the verse: 'Love your neighbor as yourself,' which the Sages took to mean: 'What is hateful to you, do not do to another.' This is what Hillel taught the gentile who came to convert to Judaism on the condition that Hillel teach him the entire Torah on one foot. One who is complete (*shalem*) in *derekh eretz*, who learns Torah, who is complete in his traits and who loves peace and pursues it, it will go well for him with God and with his fellowmen; he will be whole (*shalem*) in his body and in his property in this world and will be healthy in his service of God and meritorious of the world to come."[26]

The ways of proper comportment relate both to self and to others. *Derekh eretz* comprises a multitude of concerns. Aboab analyzes at great length how one should sleep, wake, wash, bathe, drink, eat, as well as what one should eat, in what position, how much or how little, the effects of different foods and the temperatures of different beverages. He discourses about sexual intercourse – all of this falls under the rubric of *derekh eretz*. The analysis is drawn from the medical science of the day, from Maimonides' medical views, but mostly from Talmudic material. Aboab shifts from relatively private matters of self-comportment to conduct between persons when he discusses what it is to be a guest in another person's home and what it is to be host. A person should always be deferential to the wishes of his host and the host should always be giving and self-sacrificial toward his guest. The guest should praise the host and bless him in the grace after meals. He should consider everything that the host has done as being done strictly for him and not, say, for members of the host's own family. The host should take the initiative, immediately putting food before a visitor, lest the visitor, hungry from his journey, be embarrassed to ask for food. Even if a person has many male and female servants, he should prepare the food for his guest himself. For who was greater than Abraham? And did not Abraham prepare the food for his (angelic) guests himself? One must pay special attention to welcoming guests with joy and making them feel relaxed and respected. "The welcoming of guests is greater than receiving the face of the Shekhinah."[27]

The second principle of the chapter is the importance of peace; it is further subdivided into how one pursues peace and the love of friends and associates. One who wants to pursue peace, Aboab writes, must distance himself from all things which cause strife and contention, the most grievous cause of which is anger.[28] One who lets his propensity toward anger rule over him (*moshel 'alav ka'aso*) will not have any peace, either "from above or from below." This is to say that anger will cause him to sin both against heaven and against other human beings. He cites a plethora of rabbinic texts, themselves citing *Avot* and Proverbs, which dwell on the corrupting and destructive consequences of anger and which assume that anger can be controlled and disciplined. Anger is viewed as the most dangerous passion, a kind of derangement which wrecks both the one who experiences it and his victims. Even the presence of the Shekhinah amounts to nothing for an angry man. Anger is tantamount to idolatry (*B. Shabbat* 105b). Aboab's approach is hortatory. As a good preacher, he vividly displays the disastrous consequences of indulging a passion. He does not sort out whether anger is its own punishment, whether it leads to punishment, whether it is bad for its consequences, or whether it is inherently bad. All of these possibilities are implicit in his treatment.

How would one effectuate this ideal of controlling anger? Aboab claims that the most praiseworthy characteristic of one who would pursue peace by controlling anger is learning not to reciprocate insults but to endure them. Indeed, not only to endure them but to forgive those who insult one. This is the way he asserts that God acts. The prophet Micah said of God, "Who is a God like You, forgiving iniquity and remitting transgression?" (Micah 7:18). The Talmud (*B. Rosh Hashanah* 17a) applies this divine standard to human beings. As cited by Aboab, the Sages instruct a person not to insist on strict justice, not to require recompense measure for measure. To "remit transgression" is literally, in the Hebrew, to pass by (*'over*). Thus, one should let another's hurtful acts toward one pass by one without resistance. Whoever allows such acts to pass by, who allows them not to stir up anger and a desire for recompense, even when justified by the strict letter of the law, is able to forgive. To do so is emulative of God's steadfast covenantal love toward his people. This explicit reference to imitatio dei in the matter of suffering insults and controlling anger is the point of the departure for the next work that we will consider, *The Palm Tree of Deborah*.

Moses Cordovero

Moses Cordovero (1522–1570) was a major exponent of kabbalah and a leading teacher of the mystical circle that flourished in the Galilean town of Safed in the sixteenth century. Cordovero – the name indicates his family's origin in Cordova, Spain – wrote enduringly important works on the doctrines of Jewish mysticism; he also embodied the distinctive mystical metaphysics of kabbalah into his ethics in an overt way.[29] That distinctive metaphysics is a teaching about the emanative nature of God. God is hidden *and* manifest, radically separate from the world and revealed within it through a sequence of hypostases known as *sefirot*. In classical kabbalah, there are 10 sefirot; they correlate with the God who is known by His actions in Scripture. Beyond these manifestations of divine attributes is an unknowable God, the source of the emanations. The unknowable God is called *'Ayn Sof* (the Infinite). The 10 sefirot tell a story of God leaving His inwardness and allowing His power to flow in stages into the universe. As such, kabbalah represents a massive incursion of myth – in the sense of a narrative about the life of the divinity – within Judaism.[30]

Each sefirah has its own essence, power, and significance; each enters into relations with the others, balancing the flow of divine energy from the Infinite to the immanent. The sefirotic order is both harmoniously balanced and subject to imbalance. The imbalance of forces among the sefirot leads to cosmic irruptions of evil. Evil ensues when God's own potentiality is unchecked, unbalanced by other aspects of His emanated nature. (Does this recall, within its own symbolic idiom, the dangerous eruptions of the divine which we previously noted in the Bible?) Human action can both upset the intra-divine equilibrium and restore it.[31] Thus, human agency has truly cosmic repercussions within this highly imaginative ontology. The human imitation of one or another feature of the divine, that is, the human instantiation of the character of a given sefirah, has theurgic consequences. The supernal world of the sefirot and the infernal world of the human are joined. Indeed, the system of 10 sefirot was often graphically depicted to correspond in outline to the human form; the world of the sefirot was called by the kabbalists

Adam Kadmon – the primordial man. Drawings of the sefirotic system were mapped onto the human form, reflecting the view that the divine macrocosm and the human microcosm were intimately connected to one another. The covenantal relation between God and Israel becomes an ontological one.

All human action has an impact on the ceaseless flow of energy emanating from *'Ayn Sof*. Ritual and ethical action, coupled with mystical intention, can restore the divine balance. Sexual coupling can awaken divine energies and actualize them in the order of time. Kabbalah adds an extravagantly imaginative dimension to the basic trope of imitatio dei. Cordovero's *Tomer Devorah* is an account of the workings of each sefirah and of how human beings can participate in and affect those reifications of divine immanence and power. Unlike non-kabbalistic exhortations to imitate the moral attributes of the divine, imitation here means ontological linkage. Human intention and action draw divine energies into the world from above or affect supernal realities through excitation from below. This metaphysics freights human agency with a significance far exceeding its mundane consequences within the framework of conduct *inter homines*. From a modern point of view, it is certainly implausible. Nonetheless, when interpreted charitably, it may enlarge the moral imagination.

The book begins with an extended meditation on the last verses of Micah (7:18–20):

> Who is a God like You,
> Forgiving iniquity
> And remitting transgression;
> Who has not maintained His wrath forever
> Against the remnant of His own people,
> Because He loves graciousness!
> He will take us back in love;
> He will cover up our iniquities,
> You will hurl all our sins
> Into the depths of the sea.
> You will keep faith with Jacob,
> Loyalty to Abraham,
> As You promised on oath to our fathers in days gone by.

It is fitting, Cordovero says, for man to imitate his creator in both likeness (*tzelem*) and image (*demut*), terms familiar from Genesis 1:26 and from Maimonides' classic treatment in the *Guide* (Part I, Chapter 1). But Cordovero takes a sharp turn away from Maimonides' intellectualizing reading of the nature of humanity's likeness to God. (Maimonides is emphatic in his denial of corporeality of God. Hence, these terms cannot refer to physical likeness.) He tells us that it is unfitting for us to resemble Supernal Form in our physical form (*b'gufo*) *alone*; we must resemble God in action as well. While the last claim is common, the prior claim is astonishing. It implies that it would be possible – although unworthy – for man to resemble God *physically*. The corporeal here alludes to Adam Kadmon, the primordial man whose form is limned by the system of sefirot. We are very far, indeed, from the rationalist tradition represented most consummately by Maimonides.

The Sages understood God to have 13 attributes (*B. Rosh Hashanah* 17b), based on their enumeration of God's traits in Exodus 34:6–7. Cordovero, however, finds the 13 attributes enumerated in the Micah verses to be superior to the attributes in Exodus, for the Micah text contains no hint of judgment, only of patience, forbearance, and grace. These latter 13 attributes are the characteristics of the first sefirah, *Keter* (Crown). The first chapter of the work gives a detailed analysis of each divine trait, corresponding to each line of the Micah text, followed by an explanation for how man can make the trait his own. Cordovero's analysis of the first stich is typical. The question – who is a God like You? – refers to God's forbearance in patiently tolerating the insults shown to Him by His creatures, a theme familiar from Aboab. The metaphysics here is novel, however. Cordovero claims that no one can exist for even a moment without a constant flow of divine energy (*koah elyon* or *shefa*) pouring into him. A God of strict justice might withhold the *shefa* when a man is about to use his infused energy for sin. God, however, continues to nourish man with His *shefa*, patiently bearing the insult that sinning man inflicts on the very source of his capacity for intentionality and action. Thus, man should also bear insults patiently and, like God, not fail to benefit even those who insult him with acts of kindness.

The metaphysical assumptions of kabbalah are similarly on display in Cordovero's explication of the next stich, "forgiving iniquity." The Sages taught in *Avot* that "he who commits one transgression acquires for himself one accuser" (*Avot* 4:13). Cordovero reifies the accuser (*kategor*) into a "destroying angel" who immediately comes before God and says, "So and so made me." God might have cast the *kategor* out of His presence, allowing him to descend and snatch the sinner's soul. But God rather sustains the destroying angel with His own energy so that it doesn't consume the earthly source of its existence; God bears the noxious presence of angelic evil until it is destroyed by the sinner's own repentance (or, if the sinner does not repent, by the sinner's eventual death and punishment). Tying this example of divine forbearance into a lesson for human virtue, Cordovero asserts:

> This is the greatest quality of tolerance (*middat savlanut gedolah*) that He nourishes and sustains the evil creature brought into being by the sinner until the latter repents. From which a man should learn the degree of patience in bearing his neighbour's yoke and evils done by his neighbour even when those evils still exist. So that even when his neighbour offends he bears with him until the wrong is righted or until it vanishes of its own accord and so forth.[32]

One sees here how a rather outlandish metaphysics may serve a salutary moral imagination.

The interplay of the metaphysical and the moral is even more apparent in Cordovero's commentary on the fragment, "[and remitting transgression ...] against the remnant of His own people." He takes "remnant" (*shearit*) to mean "relationship to my own flesh" (*shear basar li*): God and Israel are *physically* related to one another. Thus, "'What can I do to Israel since they are My relatives with whom I have a relationship of the flesh?' For they (the Community of Israel) are the spouse of the Holy One, Blessed be He. He calls her 'My daughter,' 'My sister,' 'My mother,' as our Rabbis of blessed memory have explained."[33] If God were to punish them, the "pain will be Mine." Cordovero goes on to give an application of this ontological claim to human responsibility. Taking the familiar rabbinic citation that all Jews are responsible (literally, a surety) for one another (*B. Shevuot* 39a), he claims that all Jews are literally related to one another insofar as their souls each have a portion of every other Israelite soul within it (*b'khol eḥad ḥalek eḥad me-ḥavero*). Thus, "since all Israelites are related to each other it is only right that a man desire his neighbour's well-being, that he eye benevolently the good fortune of his neighbour and that his neighbour's honour be as dear to him as his own; for he and his neighbour are one. This is why we are commanded to love our neighbor as ourself."[34]

The surprising claim that "he and his neighbour are one" (*she-herei hu, hu mamash*), obliterating individuation and therefore moral agency, is self-impeaching. It could not be sustained. Nonetheless, it is a vivid device for exhorting the reader to take the claims of the other with utmost seriousness and to view him or her with the same solicitude as he views himself. Scholars have long argued over whether Spinoza's monism drew some inspiration from the kabbalistic tradition, with which he was lightly acquainted.[35] Here is as good an example of metaphysical monism bent to a moral purpose as we are likely to find.

The succeeding nine chapters go on to deal with individual sefirot, what they reveal as to the nature of God and how human beings can imitate them. We are thus in an enchanted world where dispositions should be formed and actions should be performed not by reference to halakhic and moral norms alone but by reference to supernal sources of divine emanation. One must determine which emanated powers are dominant in the universe at a given point in time and how to relate to them. One must be a channel for the divine energy flow from the supernal worlds to the world below; one's receptivity to this flow in turn affects the internal dynamic of divinity itself. Although one should always strive to "draw near to the higher worlds," one should also accept that "it is impossible to conduct oneself in obedience to these qualities continually for there are other qualities in which a man has to be well-versed, namely, the lower qualities of Power ... But there are days when the Powers do not function and when men have no need of them ..."[36] One cannot always seek to instantiate the energy of *Keter* or *Hokhmah*. One must also live in a world where bodily concerns must receive their due. At stake here is what we might call a conflict of values. The text suggests that this can be resolved by time-sensitive attunement to the temporally dominant sefirah. It is not just our business to weight competing values, interests, or norms. We must also look to the balance of power on high and attune ourselves to it. Thus, bodily concerns, such as sexuality, can receive their due at certain times and, of course, in a certain manner. On the Sabbath, for example, sexual relations between man and wife are appropriate. The last sefirah, *Malkhut*, Sovereignty, is sometimes identified with the Shekhinah, the presence of God that is exiled (with Israel) into the world. A man, when separated from his wife, must strive to be in constant communion with this sefirah, which in turns acts as a divine female consort for him. (Man should be both "male and female," echoing Genesis 1:27. The sefirot are themselves divided into male and female; man as a microcosm must replicate the gendered order of the sefirotic system.) When man is again in the presence of his wife, after a week of work, travel, or Torah study, he should reunite with her – but not merely to do his "conjugal duty," let alone for the sake of pleasure, but to strengthen further his bond with the Shekhinah. If his bond is strong enough and the divine energy flows to him (and from him to his wife) at the proper time, he will be blessed with a righteous son. The borderline between what a man is to do for his wife and what he is to do for the Shekhinah is unclear. He owes his wife food, clothing, and sex; he seems to owe metaphorical versions of these goods to the Shekhinah in this text.[37]

Sexuality is a charged topic here and in kabbalah in general. There are echoes of primordial, mythic notions of the *hieros gamos*, the holy coupling of divine, cosmological forces reenacted by human agents for theurgic effect. There is also the traditional Jewish restriction of sexuality to marriage, to the cessation of the menstrual period, to a general depression of the value of pleasure. Thus, Cordovero is concerned that sexual thoughts, let alone activities, can awaken the evil inclination (*yetzer ha-ra*), separate man from the divine, and imbalance the supernal world of the sefirot. He has then to order the volatile potential of the *yetzer ha-ra*, which flows from the sefirah of *Gevurah*, Power, to the needs of the Shekhinah.

It is, therefore, proper not to bestir the evil inclination for man's own sake because this bestirs Power in Supernal Man and so destroys the world. Hence, every excitement of man towards Power and the evil inclination makes a flaw in Supernal Man ... In truth, the evil inclination should be bound and tied down so that it is not incited to any bodily act whatsoever, not for the desire of cohabitation, nor for the desire of money, nor towards anger, nor towards honor in any way. However, for his wife's sake he should gently bestir his evil inclination in the direction of the sweet Powers, to provide her with clothes and with a house, for example. And he should say: "By providing her with clothes I adorn the Shekhinah ..."[38]

The husband should in no way seek to derive pleasure from the evil inclination. Whatever benefit sexual intercourse provides for his wife, from his point of view, he is serving the Shekhinah and seeking to draw Her blessing onto him. Summing up the novelty of this work, Dan writes: "Jewish ethics in the Middle Ages and modern times is not concerned so much with the problem of what should be done in a certain set of circumstances, as with the question of why one should follow the ethical demands. To this question Cordovero presents the first clear and unambiguous mystical answer: ethical behavior should be adopted and followed not only because God says so, but because God is so; one should conform not only to the divine laws, but to the divine nature."[39] This view is amplified by the subsequent kabbalah of Isaac Luria. The thought of Cordovero and his followers, as well as Luria, comes to permeate the Jewish world, informing the ḥasidic movement of eighteenth-century Eastern Europe and, unexpectedly, contemporary North American Jewry's fascination with mysticism.

Ḥasidei Ashkenaz

Like the kabbalists, whose mystical thought quickly supplants theirs, the German pietists of the late twelfth and thirteenth centuries believed in a God who was both radically transcendent of the world and, in an important respect, sometimes immanent.[40] They believed in the emanated power of God, in God's glory (*kavod*) or presence (*shekhinah*), as an accessible force intruding into the natural world. Indeed, a dimension of God's immanence is present all the time. It shows itself in the regularity and stability of nature. But this immanence is so foundational as to be taken for granted. The natural order, stabilized by God, is only the background against which the human struggle for holiness occurs. What is consequential for this struggle is the occasional revelation of the glory of God, which makes itself felt in miracles and prophecy. God's providence, benevolence, and goodness are found in the exception, not in the natural norm. The naturalness of the world and of the human beings within it needs to be overcome. Spirit is sharply opposed to matter. A cultivated asceticism must prevail in order for the Jew to overcome his human nature and commune with the divine, both in the experience of transcendence in this life and in the eternal life to come. The mitzvot, far from allowing the Jew and the Jewish community to flourish within this world, are only means for transcending the shackles of the human condition. Each mitzvah is a sacrifice; each act is a struggle against our nature. Each occasion of worldly commerce is a temptation and a test. This vision, probably entertained by rather small circles of religious virtuosi, is animated by a desire to go beyond the rabbinic understanding of what is required of the Jew. God's will is an active force in the world, strengthening the "evil inclination" of the pietist and motivating him to understand the source of his ongoing trial in the divine will.[41] The pietist feels personally challenged and tested by God, typically through pain and suffering. To discern the divine will and to pass the test tips the balance of divine justice in the pietist's favor and beckons eternal reward (which will consist in basking in the light of the divine glory).

A sample of *Sefer Ḥasidim*'s ethics may be found in its treatment of a classic moral theme, *lashon ha-ra* (speech that damages another's reputation). The prohibition on uttering damaging speech (even if its content is true!) derives from Leviticus 19:16: "Do not deal basely with your countrymen." A more literal translation might be "Do not act as a merchant toward your own kinsman." The verse has often been translated, however, as "Do not go about as a talebearer among your countrymen." A contested word, *rakhil*, occasions these possibilities. *Rakhil* is thought to be similar to *merchant* (*rokhel*). Thus, according to Baruch Levine, "The idiom *lo' telekh rakhil* has been interpreted to mean that one should not move about in the manner of a merchant, who is presumed to be privy to secret dealings and gossip. This is how the sense of talebearing developed in postbiblical Hebrew."[42] So whether the verse implies "dealing basely" or "going about as a merchant" or "being a talebearer," all the possibilities indicate an injurious and inappropriate involvement in the lives of other persons. (With perhaps less etymological support but in the same vein, some medieval biblical commentators relate *rakhil*, from the root *r-kh-l*, to the word for spy (*meragel*), from the root *r-g-l*.) Thus, the rabbinic tradition takes the verse to mean that one should not gossip about others or spread detrimental rumors, even if based on truths, about one's fellows. This sort of behavior undermines fellowship and social trust. The definition, extent, logic, and broad significance of *lashon ha ra* are a major focus of traditional Jewish ethics, both philosophical and popular. Maimonides devoted the final chapter of his *Laws of Character Traits* (Chapter Seven) to the gradations and categories of malevolent speech. A major nineteenth-century treatment of the topic (the *Sefer Ḥafetz Ḥayim*) will be noted in the next chapter.

Sefer Ḥasidim engages the topic in paragraph 34.[43] As with the other texts we have considered in this chapter, the present work is comprised to some extent by sermonic material. The exposition builds on various biblical verses. It begins with Psalm 12:4: "May the LORD cut off all flattering lips, every tongue that speaks arrogance." "All who speak evilly (*lashon ha-ra*) it is as if they denied the existence of God (*kofer b'ikar*)." As support for this assertion, the author then cites the next verse from Psalms: "They say, 'By our tongues

we shall prevail; with lips such as ours, who can be our master?' (Ps. 12:5)."
The clear implication is that those who arrogantly trust in their own
eloquence repudiate the authority of their true master. Having established
the extreme venality of *lashon ha-ra*, the author turns to its destructive
potential. This may be gleaned from the incident of the spies in Scripture.
The spies spread a bad report (*motze shem ra*) about Canaan thereby
discouraging the Israelites from going up to conquer it right away (Num.
13:32). "If spreading a bad report about something [i.e. the land] that can
neither hear nor see nor become upset over the insult [is wrong], how much
more injurious is spreading a bad report about one's fellow, who is made in
the image and likeness of God!" Addressing the tongue rhetorically, the
author asks "What can you profit, what can you gain, O deceitful tongue?"
(Ps. 120:3). The tongue is now excoriated for its ingratitude. God reminds it
that all of the other limbs have been placed outside the body, but the tongue
has been secreted within, guarded by two "walls," a wall of bone, the teeth,
and a wall of flesh, the lips. In exchange for this special solicitude, the tongue
should be grateful. It should know its role, significance, and place and not
abuse its special status.

Against this background, the author now assays his major ethical point.
He cites Proverbs 10:19, "While there is much talking, there is no lack of
transgressing; but he who curbs his tongue shows sense." A man should
forever increase the amount of silence in his life, the author avers, speaking
rarely and then only about matters of wisdom or of bodily need. Did not the
Talmudic sage Rav speak of nothing superfluous or unnecessary all of his life
(*B. Yoma* 20b)? Indeed, one who speaks of worldly matters actually violates
a positive commandment. Deuteronomy 6:7, "Recite them [i.e. words of
Torah] when you stay at home and when you are away" implies for the
author that one should *recite them* – and nothing else; one shouldn't talk
about anything else.⁴⁴ This shunning of worldly speech accords with the
dictum of Solomon in Ecclesiastes (1:8), "All such things are wearisome, no
man can ever state them." Even permitted speech about bodily needs should
be kept to the minimum. For bodily needs themselves should be minimized,
providing little occasion for speech about them.⁴⁵ As if this extreme diminution
of the permissibility of speech were not enough, *Sefer Ḥasidim* applies it even
to speech about the Torah.

In matters pertaining to the Torah, one's speech should also be minimal
but one's thought should be expansive. The Talmud (*Pesaḥim* 3b) enjoins
that a sage should speak concisely and directly (*derekh ketzarah*) to his disciple. If one were to say much and think little, this would be foolish, a point
enforced by a citation from Ecclesiastes (5:2), "foolish utterance come[s]
with much speech." As *Avot* reminds us, "silence is a fence around wisdom"
(*Avot* 3:3). One should not therefore be in a hurry to respond; one should
be calm, measured, and deliberate, without vehemence and, above all, with

brevity. The discourse closes with another citation from Ecclesiastes (9:17), "Words spoken softly by wise men are heeded sooner than those shouted by a lord in folly."

Although building on a traditional suspicion of undisciplined, frivolous speech, *Sefer Ḥasidim* takes this in an extreme direction. It brings intention, focus, discipline, and awareness of every occasion of human intercourse as a potential hazard to a new level. The serious but pleasurable conversation of such Platonic dialogues as the Symposium or the Romantic enlargement of the role of speech found in modern Jewish philosophers such as Franz Rosenzweig or Martin Buber is poles apart from the stringent, restrained ethos offered here. *Sefer Ḥasidim* presents a rather gnostic world in which darkness, struggle, trial, and testing characterize the created order and human life. This peculiarly negative characterization of the world does not prevail, but its immense emphasis on the spiritual dimension of human action is to have a long afterlife.

An anonymous fifteenth-century work, the *Orḥot Tzaddikim* (*Paths of the Righteous*), takes up some of the emphases of German Ḥasidism and blends them with elements of Saadya, Baḥya, possibly Solomon ibn Gabirol, and others. In keeping with *Sefer Ḥasidim*'s praise of anonymity, the author of this work did not attach his name to it. Internal evidence suggests that it was written after the expulsion of the Jews from France (1306). The work first appeared in print, in a Yiddish translation and abbreviation, in 1542, followed by the full Hebrew version in 1581. The Yiddish version refers to the book, not as *Orḥot Tzaddikim* but as *Sefer ha-Middot* (the *Book of Qualities* or *Character Traits*), a name evocative of ibn Gabirol's *Tikkun Middot ha-Nefesh* (*Improvement of the Qualities of the Soul* or *Improvement of the Moral Qualities*).[46] After a somewhat philosophical introduction, the author arranges the relevant qualities or traits of the soul in contrasting pairs, a literary form found earlier in Gabirol. Thus, Chapters One and Two are "On Pride" and "On Modesty," Five and Six are "On Love" and "On Hatred." Twenty-eight traits are analyzed across a corresponding number of chapters, although the contrastive pair format is not always maintained. The author has a dialectical sensitivity. He sees that too much of a good trait can lead to the contrasting negative trait. Similarly, awareness of negativity can provide energy and motivation for a positive transformation. The soul itself is a field of oppositions and tensions. Let us briefly consider the introduction to the work, where the author develops his anthropology, and then look at his treatment of true and false speech, a topic that links to *Sefer Ḥasidim*'s treatment of *lashon ha-ra*.

Like Solomon ibn Gabirol's eleventh-century philosophical text, *The Improvement of the Moral Qualities*, our author grounds his moral anthropology on the five senses.[47] The five senses bring "every matter" to the mind, whose thoughts and deeds are then influenced by the deliverances of sense. The characteristics (*deot*) of the mind, such as pride, humility, memory, forgetfulness, sorrow, joy, shame, impudence, etc. are strengthened by sensory inputs. A blind man, for example, could not be proud of possessing those things which could only be known by sight.[48] (The work thus differs from Gabirol who tried, in a highly deterministic way, to ground dispositions and traits *on* the senses. Gabirol treats each sense as a "genus" with the traits to which it gives rise as "species." One way to take this is to think of the senses as the existence conditions for traits. The senses themselves are formed from the relative presence of the four humors of medieval medicine. While Gabirol introduces a "secular" or "scientific" system, *Orḥot Tzaddikim* is far from this sort of analysis but nonetheless gestures in its direction.) The Hebrew word which the author uses for sense or faculty (*koaḥ*) now allows him to make a comprehensive, teleological claim: human beings work with all of their strength or capability (*koaḥ*) to realize the ultimate good (*takhlit ha-tova*). (That is, the individual strengths (i.e. the senses) by which we perceive the world are ordered by a comprehensive capability to seek the true good.) The true or ultimate good is the "world of reward" (*olam ha-gmul*), the world to come. As there can be nothing higher than this, all of our actions are ultimately ordered to eternal reward.

The problem is that we are given very refractory material with which to work, namely ourselves. Our traits are always mixed, both good and evil, some inborn as dispositions, others acquired through bad choices, habits, and surroundings. Our given natures lead us toward some traits, both good and bad; no one is without natural advantages and disadvantages. All of the qualities, however, are subject to rational appraisal: we can and ought to learn how much of, say modesty, is required by a given situation or how little. One must exercise constant distancing from and analysis and supervision of one's self. And one must repair to the sages (*ḥakhamim*) who are healers of the soul (*rofe ha-nefashot*) to learn discernment and the ability of self-correction.[49] Some systematically fail in this quest for perfection because of a cognitive error: they remain confused about what is right and are unaware of the scope of their ignorance. Others fail through conative error: they know what is right but are hampered by laziness and weakness of will. The role of the book is then to instruct persons in how to diagnose themselves, discern the role of negative traits in their moral lives, and progress toward greater equilibrium and integration.

The linchpin of this system is the pure awe of God (*ha-yirah ha-tahorah*). No human action should be considered worthy without it. Everyone who wants to increase the dominance of the good qualities must focus on the awe of heaven as a motivating factor for – and accompanying thought of – every deed.

> For it is the fear of the Lord, reverence of God, that strengthens all of our qualities. And fear of the Lord or reverence of God is like the thread which we

run through the holes of pearls and then we tie a knot at its end so that it will firmly hold all the pearls. There is no doubt that if the knot should tear, all of the pearls will fall. Such is the reverence of Heaven. It strengthens all of the qualities and if you will undo the knot of reverence, then all your good qualities will depart from you, and when you have no good qualities within you, then you will have neither Torah nor Commandments. For the whole Torah depends on the constant improvement of the qualities (*kol ha-Torah teluyah b'tikkun ha-middot*).[50]

This citation shows how spiritualized the author's conception of action, including traditional Jewish religious behavior, is. Neither Torah nor mitzvot retain value without intentionality, specifically the awe or fear of heaven. Failure to cultivate a continuous awe-filled awareness of God both empties our actions of value and undoes our moral progress. In a manner reminiscent of *Sefer Ḥasidim* but taking up and strengthening many other interiorizing sources as well, the author emphasizes, to the greatest extent possible, what is at stake in the moral life. Here, the aretaic–deontic pattern is crystal clear. The commandments cannot endure without mindfully cultivated character.

Finally, let us consider the contrastive pair, falsehood and truth, essayed in Chapters 22 and 23. Some falsehoods, such as the statement that a wooden object is actually made of gold, are obviously wrong. But others, such as the claim that a copper object is made of gold, require close inspection. Wisdom and discernment are thus necessary for discriminating subtle lies from truth claims. But the problem is more complicated. Often, when matters are in doubt and there is evidence to support conflicting claims, we will choose the claim that best accords with our interests. Or, if we are lazy, we will habitually give up on following thought to its best explanation. Even the wise are prone to self-interest and premature abandonment of inquiry. The only salvation from falsehood then is the systematic cultivation of good qualities; we need to train ourselves to be both wise and persistent, to resist our own proclivity toward the arrest of inquiry.[51]

The author parses falsehood into nine categories. Some lies are comprised of blatant falsehoods that are meant to damage another; others are strategic communications meant to induce trust in the present for the purpose of damage in the future. Still others are couched in vagueness, as in the implication that one will help another in the future without making an explicit promise. All of these categories are elaborated conceptually, analyzed in terms of the harm they cause (to others, to the community as a whole, to oneself), and supported with citations from Scripture and rabbinic literature. Of special interest is the ninth category: telling a story that one has heard and taking poetic license with it. "Now there is no loss to any man in this, but he receives a bit of pleasure (*me'at hana'ah*) out of his lying, even though he does not gain any money out of it."[52] This is the sort of thing that modern persons would probably find innocent and playful, hardly a cause of concern when the social context is one of storytelling. But the author has a view of the gravity and significance of speech, which militates against casual embellishment. He bases his view on a Talmudic aggadah. In *Yevamot* 63a, we learn of the sage Rav who would ask his wife to prepare meals for him. Whenever Rav asked for lentils, his wife would make him peas; whenever he asked for peas, his wife would make him lentils. (Why his wife behaved in this curious fashion, we are not told.) Rav's son, Ḥiyya, inserted himself into this little family drama. If he knew that his father wanted peas, he would tell his mother to make him lentils (so that she would prepare peas) and vice versa. Ḥiyya did this for the honor of his father. Nonetheless, his father reprimanded him, invoking a verse from Jeremiah (9:4): "They will not speak truth; they have trained their tongues to speak falsely." The context here is not casual storytelling nor is Ḥiyya's lapse one of embellishment. He spoke quite strategically, attempting to manipulate his mother in order to honor his father. Nonetheless, the case can apply to the former problem of poetic license. In both cases, one consciously changes what one has heard to bring about some effect. One might argue that the speaker deforms the communication situation, treating the listener as a means to his end rather than an end in himself. The emphasis here, however, seems to be on the speaker's virtue or vice rather than on the effect of conduct on others. Nonetheless, the author is alive to the social consequences of lying. "For even when he speaks the truth, no one will believe him."[53]

Despite the perfectionist emphasis on the strict propriety of truth-telling, the author must cope with the fact that the rabbinic tradition does allow one to deviate from this standard when circumstances warrant. The Talmud enjoins Jews to praise a bride on her wedding day even if she is not praiseworthy (*B. Ketubot* 17a) and to refrain from praising a host who has been exemplary, lest he be deluged by future guests (*B. Arakhin* 16a). In both cases, the emotional or the social costs of strict fidelity to truth-telling would be unacceptably high. Similarly, if one is fluent in a Talmudic tractate, one should, out of modesty, deny one's learning if asked. If one is late to synagogue because one had sexual relations with one's wife, one should dissemble and invent a more socially appropriate excuse. Here the demands of modesty conflict with those of truth-telling. The author's judgment is that while indeed one is permitted to bend the truth, "if he can manage not to lie, that is preferable to lying." Lying is, in our idiom, excusable but not ultimately justifiable. Even where there is warrant, one should try to minimize the practice. This treatment does not sharply distinguish between the virtuous dimension of truth-telling, the deontological dimension of the intrinsic wrongfulness of lying, and prudential and consequentialist considerations of reputation or social trust. All of these are implicated in the author's analysis, although the emphasis on virtue (and vice) has the highest profile, given the overall character of the work.

The companion piece to the rigorous avoidance of misleading, embellished, or false speech is radical devotion to truth. In Chapter 23, the author grounds devotion to truth in a metaphysics.

> The soul is created from the place of the Holy Spirit, as it is said, "And breathed into his nostrils the breath of life" (Gen. 2:7). And it is hewn out from a place of purity, and it is created from the supernal radiance (*mi-zohar ha-elyon*), from the Throne of Glory. And in the realm above, in the place of the Holy of Holies, there is no falsehood. There everything is truth, as it is said, "But the Lord God is the true God" (Jer. 10:10).[54]

The imperative of truth-telling rests on fidelity to our own divinely designed nature. The soul descends from a world of truth – God's own seal is truth (*B. Shabbat* 55a). When persons act as the holy souls that they most essentially are, then the world below reflects the world above. The truth that God is the maker of heaven and earth is both on the lips and in the heart. A harmony between upper and lower reigns; when there is truth below, God looks down with justice.[55] It is within the scope of human agency to purify the heart so that man can serve God with truth. Such a soul will be upright and fulfill its Creator's intention and purpose.

All of the works that we have considered in the last chapter and in this one (with the possible exception of *Sefer Ḥasidim*) correspond to a structure of pre-modern moral reasoning which Alasdair MacIntyre describes as follows. In a pre-modern world, where thinkers could make confident assertions about what is essential to human nature and what the fulfillment of that nature portends, "there is a fundamental contrast between man-as-he-happens-to-be and man-as-he-could-be-if-he-realized-his-essential-nature. Ethics is the science which is to enable men to understand how they make the transition from the former state to the latter."[56] All of these traditional moral thinkers understand the meaning of our dispositions, traits, thoughts, desires, and capacities in terms of an image of divinely intended perfection. Indeed, that image is a distant copy of God's own image; with "image" understood as a paradigm for action, a guideline for self-transformation. Often this structure is interwoven with an etiological story about the soul, the link between the divine exemplar and the human material which needs to be reworked in the direction of perfection.

In modernity, the confidence drains out of this basic metaphysical/moral structure. True, strong traditionalists continue to write as if nothing has changed. But cumulatively the assaults of thinkers such as Spinoza and Kant take their toll. Modernity begins scarcely distinguishable from its predecessor epoch but in time reliance on old patterns of argument are thought by many Jews to be insufficient. Modernity is thus a time of the rebirth of Jewish philosophy, of new attempts to secure grounding for Jewish ethics. Modernity is also a time where tradition seeks to persist, to keep modern disenchantment and disconfirmation at bay; to set up social enclaves where traditionalist Jews can be immune from ill intellectual winds. We will consider all of these trends in the next chapter.

Notes

1 For a good overview of the Maimonidean controversy and references to the relevant scholarly literature, see Tirosh-Samuelson, *Happiness in Premodern Judaism*, Chapter 6.
2 For documentation of Adret's own thinking and correspondence between him and his opponents about the status of philosophy and the ban, see Franz Kobler, ed., *Letters of Jews Through the Ages*, Vol. I (New York: East West Library, 1978), pp. 248–259.
3 A full history of this idea is found in Abraham Melamed, *The Myth of the Jewish Origins of Science and Philosophy* (Hebrew) (Jerusalem: Magnes Press, 2010).
4 Tirosh-Samuelson, *Happiness in Premodern Judaism*, p. 274.
5 Dan, *Jewish Mysticism and Jewish Ethics*, Chapter 2. See also Dan, *Sifrut Ha-Musar v'ha-Drush*, pp. 146–149.
6 Dan, *Jewish Mysticism and Jewish Ethics*, p. 76.
7 For background relevant to the ethical productivity of this movement, see Dan, *Jewish Mysticism and Jewish Ethics*, Chapter Three, and Dan, *Sifrut Ha-Musar v'ha-Drush*, Chapter Seven. For an historical study, see Ivan Marcus, *Piety and Society: The Jewish Pietists of Medieval Germany* (Leiden: Brill, 1981).
8 See Alan Mittleman, "The Durability of Goodness," in Jonathan Jacobs, ed., *Judaic Sources and Western Thought: Jerusalem's Enduring Presence* (Oxford: Oxford University Press, 2011). My view is very much indebted to the work of Lenn Goodman. See his *On Justice* (Oxford: Littman Library, 2008) and *God of Abraham* (New York: Oxford University Press, 1996).
9 The text may be found in Chaim Dov Chavel, ed., *Kitve Rabbenu Moshe ben Maimon* (Jerusalem: Mossad Ha-Rav Kook, 1963), p. 183ff.
10 Tirosh-Samuelson, *Happiness in Premodern Judaism*, p. 269.
11 An overview of the schema and contents of the book may be found in Mayer Waxman, *A History of Jewish Literature*, Vol. II (New York: Bloch Publishing, 1943), pp. 273–274.
12 A wholesome counterpoint to this ascetic reading is found in *Genesis Rabbah* 40:4, where Abraham's astonished notice of his wife's beauty is explained by the fact that Sarah's good looks have been maintained despite the rigors of travel over the dusty roads of the Near East after many years. This "romantic" reading, alas, is not the final word of the midrash. The next interpretation has Abraham contrasting Sarah's beauty with that of the ugly, dark Egyptians among whom they are soon to settle. This is an unmistakably racist motif. For a discussion, see Abraham Melamed, *The Image of the Black in Jewish Culture: A History of The Other*, trans. Betty Sigler Rozen (London: Routledge-Curzon, 2003).
13 Rabbenu Yonah ben Avraham of Gerona, *Shaarei Teshuvah: The Gates of Repentance*, trans. Shraga Silverstein (Jerusalem: Feldheim Publishers, 1976), p. 47.

14 Rabbenu Yonah, *Shaarei Teshuvah*, p. 116. The term "tikkun ha-nefesh," repair of the soul, possibly alludes to Solomon ibn Gabirol's c.1045 book, *Tikkun Middot Ha-Nefesh* (*Repair of the Attributes of the Soul*). Maimonides also uses this phrase in "Laws concerning Character Traits."

15 Rabbenu Yonah, *Shaarei Teshuvah*, p. 191.

16 Rabbenu Yonah, *Shaarei Teshuvah*, p. 191.

17 Rabbenu Yonah, *Shaarei Teshuvah*, p. 109.

18 Rabbenu Yonah, *Shaarei Teshuvah*, p. 143.

19 *Kitve Rabbenu Baḥya*, ed. Hayyim Chavel (Jerusalem: Mossad Ha-Rav Kook, 1969), p. 188. To the best of my knowledge this work has not yet been translated into English. For a discussion of the work, see Joseph Dan, *Sifrut Ha-Musar v'ha-Drush*, pp. 160–162.

20 This is the opposite of Maimonides' ordering of the virtues. For Maimonides, the welfare of the soul can only be secured after the welfare of the body is established. See *Guide* Part III, Chapter 27.

21 Cf. Baḥya's Torah commentary to Exodus 25:11 for another version of this principle.

22 Text taken from the Soncino translation of the Talmud, ed. I. Epstein (London: Soncino Press, 1935) accessed online at http://halakhah.com/pdf/nezikin/ Avodah_Zarah.pdf. An older, slightly different version of this progression of virtues is found in the Mishnah, Sotah 9:15.

23 Baḥya's explication of the virtue of holiness (*kedushah*), which is the first of the *gufaniyot*, or bodily, physical virtues, is found in *Kitve Rabbenu Baḥya*, ed. Hayyim Chavel, pp. 350–354. Holiness is taken primarily in the sense of separation (*perishut*) from bodily desires, especially from the desire for those things which are permitted to us. We have seen this theme before in Yonah Gerondi.

24 There are two collections, similar in intent and overlapping in content, called *Menorat Ha-Maor*. The one we consider here is by Isaac Aboab. The other is by Israel al-Nakawa. It is unclear which came first and which influenced the other. For an analysis, see the entry on Isaac Aboab in *Encyclopedia Judaica*. See also the brief treatment by Joseph Dan, *Sifrut Ha-Musar v'ha-Drush*, p. 165.

25 Isaac Aboab, *Menorat Ha-Maor* (Jerusalem: Machon Meirav, n.d.), p. 586.

26 Aboab, *Menorat Ha-Maor*, p. 589.

27 Aboab, *Menorat Ha-Maor*, p. 614.

28 Aboab, *Menorat Ha-Maor*, p. 634. An earlier analysis of the corrupting effects of anger may be found in Naḥmanides' letter to his son. See the expanded facsimile edition of Israel Abrahams, ed., *Hebrew Ethical Wills* (Philadelphia: Jewish Publication Society, 2006), pp. 95–99.

29 For a translation of the *Tomer Devorah* with interpretive commentary and introduction, see Moses Cordovero, *The Palm Tree of Deborah*, trans. Louis Jacobs (London: Vallentine, Mitchell, 1960). Jacobs' Introduction has a useful overview of the doctrine of the sefirot, as related to Cordovero's work. A Hebrew–English edition is available in Rabbi Moshe Cordovero, *The Palm Tree of Devorah: Tomer Devorah*, trans. Moshe Miller (Southfield: Targum Press, 1993).

30 The sefirot in their order of emanation are *Keter* (Crown), *Ḥokhmah* (Wisdom), *Binah* (Understanding) – these higher sefirot instantiate God's thought; the seven lower sefirot instantiate His emotion and action. They are: *Ḥesed* (Mercy),

Gevurah (Power), *Tiferet* (Beauty), *Netzah* (Endurance), *Hod* (Majesty), *Yesod* (Foundation), and *Malkhut* (Sovereignty). There are many contemporary studies in kabbalah to which the reader could turn for background. One that I find helpful, as it speaks to the philosophical and theological problems motivating the construction of the conceptual system of sefirot, is Moshe Hallamish, *An Introduction to the Kabbalah*, trans. Ruth Bar-Ilan and Ora Wiskind-Elper (Albany: SUNY Press, 1999), esp. Chapter 9.

31   Hallamish, *An Introduction to the Kabbalah*, p. 171.

32   Cordovero, *The Palm Tree of Deborah*, trans. Louis Jacobs, p. 50.

33   Cordovero, *The Palm Tree of Deborah*, trans. Louis Jacobs, p. 51.

34   Cordovero, *The Palm Tree of Deborah*, trans. Louis Jacobs, p. 53.

35   For a history of the controversy surrounding Spinoza's alleged kabbalism – an influence that Popkin does not rule out – see, Richard Popkin, "Spinoza, Neoplatonic Kabbalist?" in Lenn E. Goodman, *Neoplatonism and Jewish Thought* (Albany: SUNY Press, 1992), pp. 387–410.

36   Cordovero, *The Palm Tree of Deborah*, trans. Louis Jacobs, p. 74.

37   Cordovero, *The Palm Tree of Deborah*, trans. Louis Jacobs, p. 120.

38   Cordovero, *The Palm Tree of Deborah*, trans. Louis Jacobs, p 103.

39   Joseph Dan, *Jewish Mysticism and Jewish Ethics*, p. 86.

40   This brief description of the theology underlying the *Sefer Hasidim* and related literature follows Dan, *Jewish Mysticism and Jewish Ethics*, pp. 49–63.

41   Marcus, *Piety and Society*, p. 12.

42   Baruch Levine, ed., *The JPS Torah Commentary: Leviticus* (Philadelphia: The Jewish Publication Society, 1989), p. 129.

43   No complete English translation of *Sefer Hasidim* exists. Hebrew readers may consult an annotated edition published by Mossad Ha-Rav Kook: Rabbi Judah the Pious, *Sefer Hasidim* (Jerusalem: Mossad Ha-Rav Kook, 1956), p. 96. The book is traditionally ascribed to Judah he-Hasid, although it is probably a composite collection. The book is arranged unsystematically in over 700 numbered paragraphs. For a critical literary analysis of its contents and genres, see Dan, *Sifrut Ha-Musar v'ha-Drush*, Chapter Seven.

44   This too is based on Talmudic precedent, see *B. Yoma* 19a.

45   This injunction seems to be based on the Talmudic story in *Hagigah* 5b, where the sage Rav is speaking tenderly to his wife during foreplay. His disciple, intent on learning proper conduct, is hiding under the bed. Rav criticizes him and tells him to leave the room. The gemara takes seriously the issue of whether such speech is permitted, the disciple's strange conduct notwithstanding. Rav himself had warned that God holds a person's superfluous conversation against him at the hour of his death and yet here Rav himself seems guilty of it. The gemara excuses him, however, as the circumstances warranted it. If he had no need to encourage his wife then his speech would not have been permissible. *Sefer Hasidim* wants to take this context-dependent example and generalize it to all profane speech.

46   For an overview of the work and speculation about its history, see *Encyclopedia Judaica*, Vol. 12, pp. 1458–1460.

47 Gabirol's work was translated from the original Arabic as Stephen S. Wise, trans., *The Improvement of the Moral Qualities*, Columbia University Oriental Studies, Vol. I (New York: Columbia University Press, 1902). The present work may be found in English translation with facing Hebrew text as Seymour J. Cohen, trans., *Orchot Tzaddikim: The Ways of the Righteous* (Jerusalem: Feldheim Publishers, 1969).

48 Cohen, trans., *Orchot Tzaddikim*, p. 5.

49 Cohen, trans., *Orchot Tzaddikim*, p. 11.

50 Cohen, trans., *Orchot Tzaddikim*, p. 15.

51 Cohen, trans., *Orchot Tzaddikim*, p. 369.

52 Cohen, trans., *Orchot Tzaddikim*, p. 377.

53 Cohen, trans., *Orchot Tzaddikim*, p. 379.

54 Cohen, trans., *Orchot Tzaddikim*, p. 383. Jeremiah 10:10 is used in the liturgy in the sense of "The LORD God is Truth." Perhaps that is what the author of Orchot Tzaddikim intended here.

55 Cohen, trans., *Orchot Tzaddikim*, p. 393.

56 Alasdair MacIntyre, *After Virtue* (Notre Dame: Notre Dame University Press, 1984), p. 52.

5

Modern Jewish Ethics

Alasdair MacIntyre sees the modern world, the world of the Enlightenment project, as a troubled time for ethics. Modern culture overreached. The Enlightenment teased morality out of a broad traditional context, segregating it from theology, aesthetics, and law and gave it a "cultural space" of its own.[1] It aimed to ground this newly discriminated morality on isolable first principles such as, in the empiricist tradition, the moral sentiments or, in the Kantian tradition, the moral law revealed by practical reason. But neither this deracinated morality nor the grounds adduced to justify it were coherent or sustainable. On MacIntyre's account, the failure of the Enlightenment project to provide rational justification for morality was exposed by Kierkegaard's *Either/Or*. Morality is an option which can but need not be chosen – and, to make matters worse, there are no grounds on which to choose it. There is no way to adjudicate between rival and deeply incommensurate ways of life; there are no rational grounds which independently prescribe for people how to live. There is only choice, a pure voluntarism unconstrained by any morally pertinent reality outside of the arbitrarily choosing subject. Values hang in the air, unrelated to facts, drawing their vitality only from the vagaries of the human preferences whose images they are. Thus, modernity becomes a time of immense but futile moral theorizing. In proportion to the futility of the project of grounding ethics is the human effort devoted thereunto. (There are good reasons for doubting this account, but let it stand as a heuristic portrayal of the modern condition.)

Could this same criticism be made of Jewish moral thought over the last few centuries? Do its values now hang fecklessly in the air? The answer depends in part on what we take modernity to be. If modernity stands only

A Short History of Jewish Ethics: Conduct and Character in the Context of Covenant,
First Edition. Alan L. Mittleman.
© 2012 Alan L. Mittleman. Published 2012 by Blackwell Publishing Ltd.

for a way of periodizing history, of mapping chronology, then it need not be seen as a time of upheaval, catastrophe, revolution, or rupture in Jewish moral thought. Traditional Jewish scholars continued to produce musar treatises and handbooks undergirded by pietistic and mystical assumptions. Halakhic analysis, continuing unabated, was applied to new challenges (such as electricity or automobiles and, lately, stem cells and cloning). There are still populations of Jews who take such guidance with utmost seriousness. One can find a good deal of continuity between the traditional works we have considered and nineteenth- or twentieth-century Jewish moral thought. Even those traditional moralists, who embraced some of the possibilities of modernity, worked hard to maintain conformity with traditional patterns. Responsa continued to be written; codes of law, with due attention to moral elements, continued to be produced. One need not see modernity as a caesura.

Modernity, however, is typically thought to portend much more than a segment of historical time. It indicates a set of distinctive intellectual, moral, and political cultures. It signals ways of thinking and being; not just a time in which persons live but a pervasive transformation of what it means to live. Although rumors of the death of religion have always been exaggerated, modernity is typically thought to be a secular age, an age of robust, self-sufficient secularity. From this point of view, Jewish ethics faced much the same challenge as Western thought overall. The challenges of grounding ethics in an age where traditional faith in God, both naïve and philosophical, became problematic were no less daunting for Jews than for others. Indeed, the vastly changed social and political circumstances of Jews in the European world of the eighteenth through the twentieth centuries gave these challenges their own sharp edge. For self-consciously modernist writers, the kind of ethics which sought continuity with earlier models had a bit of false consciousness or disingenuousness about it. Traditionalism was suspect. It emanated from Jewish groups which tried to keep modernity, in the culturally transformative sense, at bay or at least to minimize its thrust and bracket its disenchanting potential. Modernists embraced a tradition of the new, which took the Enlightenment and Emancipation as its point of departure. The stream of philosophically modernist ethics sought to face the modernist challenge head on, to break with the past, and radically reformulate a justificatory basis for the Torah's commandments and aspirations. Here it may be legitimate to speak of a real break with past patterns. The harbinger of this tradition of the new is Spinoza, the heretical Jew of Amsterdam. Spinoza lived during the early phase of the Enlightenment, albeit before European states emancipated their Jewish populations. Excommunicated by his Jewish community, he formulated a metaphysical, moral, and political philosophy along scientific lines. Nonetheless, Spinoza carried forward some of the central affirmations of previous Jewish ethics. Was Spinoza the last medieval or the first modern Jew? Or was he something else entirely, a secular man, neither Jew nor Christian, who philosophized for a world that did not yet exist? Even to raise these questions indicates the complex position of Judaism vis-à-vis emerging modernity.

One errs in drawing too stark a contrast between tradition and modernity. The two should be viewed as ideal types, polarities along a spectrum on which any given example will represent a mix of the two propensities. Spinoza, for example, doesn't just reject the Bible – nor did Hobbes, his influential predecessor. He reinterprets it. He takes pains to show why Maimonides' philosophizing hermeneutic is implausible. He domesticates biblical teaching, law, prophecy, and narrative to his naturalistic orientation. His polemical wrestling with Scripture and rabbinic interpretation, albeit in a modernist mode, at once bespeaks both continuity and rupture. Traditions are elastic – up to the point beyond which they can't be stretched. Then new ones begin, tradition itself being an inescapable category of the human condition. Whether Spinoza stretched or broke the bounds of Jewish philosophy remains an open question. Hermann Cohen, a profound student of Kant, Maimonides, and Plato, advanced a philosophy of Jewish ethics that in some ways breaks with prior tradition and in other ways builds on it. He rejected Spinoza for his putative pantheism. Is Cohen more modern or more traditional than Spinoza? It is hard to say. Rabbi Israel Salanter, the founder of the Musar movement, was a fervent – today we would say "ultra-Orthodox" – traditionalist, yet he sought reform of the exclusively Talmud-oriented curriculum of the Lithuanian yeshivot and advocated the teaching of secular subjects such as science. He was surely more traditional than Spinoza (or Cohen), yet he migrated from Eastern Europe to Berlin and affirmed its culture as fully compatible with his moral teaching. Easy distinctions between "tradition" and "modernity" are made more readily by ideologues than by scholars.[2] I am inclined to believe that drawing too sharp a dichotomy between modernity and its predecessor cultures, at least as far as Jews are concerned, is unwise. But this is not, of course, to claim that large and significant distinctions between the modern and the pre-modern traditional world are not in play.

One distinction, which bears on ethics, is revealed in a remark of Christine Korsgaard's. Reflecting on the post-Christian, "death of God," modernist mood in ethics, Korsgaard claims that the death of God

did not put us back into Plato and Aristotle's world. For in the meantime the revolution has completed itself. We no longer think [as we did under Christendom – A.M.] that we are what's wrong with the world. We are no longer at all puzzled about why the world, being good, is yet not good. Because for us, the world is no longer first and foremost form. It is *matter*. This is what I mean when I say that there has been a revolution, and that the world has been turned inside out. The real is no longer the good. For us reality is something *hard*, something which resists reason and value, something which is recalcitrant to form.[3]

That being per se is not good, but neutral or "hard"; that existence is not a gift, but a fact; that norms are no longer entangled with facts because, it was once believed, God infused creation with value – these demarcate the metaphysical horizon of modern ethics from that of traditional ethics, at least ideally. The Kantian project of discovering normativity in moral reason rather than in nature or in human nature, which being merely "hard" cannot support or justify distinctively moral claims, is essentially modern. Yet even this does not translate entirely well into Jewish thought. Cohen, an arch-Kantian, still organizes his ethics around imitatio dei. The divine will works like the Platonic form of the good. Spinoza, a founder of Jewish modernity, sees reality – as infinite divine substance – as the ground of value. His metaphysics would surely run afoul of Korsgaard's claim. Let us take these orientations, moral realism and moral anti-realism, as ideal types, with the latter signaling the purest affirmation of modernity and the former indicating the highest degree of continuity with traditional thought.

This chapter explores the endurance of traditional forms, however impinged by modern thought and social/political transition, as well as the growth of modernist forms of Jewish ethics. An early instance of this opposition may be found in Spinoza (1632–1677), on the one hand, and a traditional Jewish moralist of the next generation, Moses Ḥayim Luzzatto (1707–1746), on the other. One must be wary of fully embedding Spinoza into the context of Jewish thought, although a strong case can be made for seeing him not just as a (heretical) Jew who was a philosopher but as a Jewish philosopher, and hence as a Jewish moral philosopher. Whatever one makes of him, Spinoza raises the ante on what Jewish philosophy in general and Jewish ethics in particular must confront in modernity. My interest here is less in giving an adequate account of his thought than in establishing a baseline for what a bold confrontation with modernity entails. Luzzatto, by contrast, writes as if the eternal covenant between God and Israel were as durable as ever; the Law remains in full force, the traditional virtues remain as compelling as ever. He does not feel the need to transform his kabbalistic metaphysics into a post-Cartesian, post-Newtonian idiom. On the surface, nothing has changed. Yet beneath the surface, Luzzatto also inaugurates elements of the modern or proto-modern. Similarly, we will consider the moral productivity of Ḥasidism, an eighteenth-century movement of Jewish pietism and revival in Eastern Europe – a break from a disintegrating medieval order but still commensurate with medieval views about the ends of life and the conduct and character needed to realize them. The moral outlook of Ḥasidism's founder, Israel ben Eliezer, known as the Baal Shem

Tov (c.1698–1760), contrasts with the Enlightenment ethics of Moses Mendelssohn (1729–1786). These are contemporary phenomena but radically different in terms of the cultural norms they embody and with which they seek an accord. Later in the nineteenth century, we consider a Lithuanian traditionalist school of moral perfectionism, the Musar movement of Rabbi Israel Salanter (1810–1883), and the liberal, Enlightenment theorizing of Jewish ethics in the works of Moritz Lazarus (1824–1903) and Hermann Cohen 1842–1918).

We conclude with a brief look at some large-scale theoretical projects such as those of Franz Rosenzweig, Martin Buber, and Emanuel Levinas, as well as an overview of contemporary trends in Jewish ethics. Do these constitute a break or a renewal of the medieval tradition of high philosophy under the radically changed intellectual circumstances of modernity?

Baruch Spinoza

Baruch (later, Benedict) Spinoza was unlucky enough to have been born into a Jewish community which still had the power of excommunication. In 1656, the Jewish leaders of Amsterdam, after repeated warnings, banished Spinoza from the community, intending to terminate all contact between him and his family, friends, and other fellow Jews.[4] Had Spinoza lived earlier, he would have likely become a Christian in order to be able to survive. Had he lived a century later, when rulers were intent on weakening the autonomy of the Jewish community and with it the power to punish its members, he might have carried on within the community, shunned by its orthodox members but otherwise unmolested. (Indeed, that option was open to him but, perhaps out of intellectual integrity, he refused to publicly recant his offending views and carry on in quiet.) Perhaps based on his personal experience, as well as by revulsion toward theocracy-minded Calvinists in the Dutch Republic, Spinoza theorized a political society in which complete freedom of thought would be the highest value. Unlike Hobbes, who wanted a secular society based on a radical separation of church and state in order that a strong central political authority could rule unchecked, Spinoza's political thought aims at the freedom of citizens to pursue knowledge and thereby to achieve blessedness. Although beginning from a social contract account of political origins, as does Hobbes, his concern is for the life of the mind, the discipline of the heart, and the goods of community. These emphases also set him apart from his contemporary, Locke. Locke was acutely concerned about liberty but liberty for the sake of property rights and limited government. Spinoza, more than his contemporary political theorists, envisioned the bourgeois commercial republic enriched by trade and enlivened by the free marketplace of ideas.[5] Only Spinoza put in the foreground an essentially Maimonidean vision of a good society devoted to the love of God and thereby to the love of neighbor. There is an essential continuity with an earlier tradition of biblical, political thought, albeit under the sign of a metaphysics that opposed naïve, as well as Maimonidean, understandings of biblical faith.[6]

Spinoza's liberal, secularized political vision is supported by a debunking, naturalistic reading of the Bible (*interpretatio naturae*).[7] Spinoza ruled out midrashic, allegorizing, or philosophical readings of Scripture. He held that interpreting Scripture was similar to interpreting nature: both should be based only on the data which present themselves within their respective spheres. Both reveal their truths to the natural light of reason; no special revelation, inspiration, or prophetically founded traditions of interpretation are needed. Spinoza means to guard against eisegesis, that is, against importing ideas into the text rather than simply educing ideas from the text. (Of course, we have come to understand that the eisegesis/exegesis distinction is by no means straightforward. There is no presuppositionless reading of texts.) The Bible is no longer, as it was for Maimonides, a philosophical teaching about physics and metaphysics. It no longer originates in divine communication made known through prophets, whose intellects are perfected and cleave to God's own Intellect. The Bible reflects divine law, in the sense that divine law equals the eternal principles of ethics and human blessedness. These principles are present to the light of natural reason before they are conveyed by the text. Whatever is of genuine worth in the Bible accords with standards of rightness and goodness that are logically prior to the text; we judge and accept the text because we already know, through the natural light of reason, what God wants. As for the positive laws and rituals legislated by Moses in Scripture, their purpose is purely political. The ritual regulations, along with civil and criminal statutes, comprise the law of the ancient Hebrew republic. "From all these considerations," Spinoza writes, "it is clearer than day that ceremonies have nothing to do with a state of blessedness, and that those mentioned in the Old Testament, i.e. the whole Mosaic Law, had reference merely to the government of the Jews, and merely temporal advantages."[8] They had authority only in that political and social order. The attempt by the Jews to carry them forward in the absence of a state is perverse; it speaks to the otherworldly and emasculated character of the Jews. The attempt to implement these laws in a Reformed theocracy, such as the Geneva of Calvin and his later admirers in the Netherlands, is no less perverse. Spinoza's strong claim for a democratic republic based on freedom of thought and the separation of church and state relies on an argument for the time- and culture-bound obsolescence of God's (positive, scriptural) law.

For Spinoza, the prophets, including Moses, are demoted from receivers of divine revelation to political leaders with vivid imaginations and a capacity for rhetoric that moves and molds the masses. ("Thus, to suppose that knowledge of natural and spiritual phenomena can be gained from the prophetic books is an utter mistake …"[9]) Scripture is correlatively demoted from a disclosure of truth – that is, a set of assertions with truth-value – to a set of meaningful statements where "meaningful" indicates what the statement likely meant to its original author within its literary context.[10] In addition, Spinoza, although not the first to argue this view, was an early advocate of the composite, non-Mosaic authorship of the Torah. He sets the agenda for modern biblical criticism by promulgating the view that the various sections of the Pentateuch are of diverse authorship, reflect different milieus and attitudes, were synthesized late in Israel's history by Ezra, etc. Earlier exegetes, such as Abraham ibn Ezra whom Spinoza cites with approval, were well aware of differences in style throughout the Torah (for example, the use of different names for God), of Moses himself being a character in the narrative, or of the text describing its purported author's (Moses) own death. These factors stimulated midrashic creativity. Rather than defeat claims to divine dictation or inspiration and Mosaic authorship, they enriched them with dimensions of intellectual complexity. Much ink was spilled over the centuries, for example, on reconciling the order of creation in Genesis, chapter 1 with that of chapter 2. Spinoza and his intellectual descendants, however, consign this kind of activity to a limbo between superstition and sheer subjectivity.

Spinoza's approach to Scripture, I have suggested, was meant to serve primarily a political end: the reform of society in the direction of democratic republicanism where freedom of thought will prevail so that philosophers, such as Spinoza, will be left in peace to seek the highest ends. But what are the highest ends? His major work, the *Ethics*, published posthumously (the anonymous publication of the *Theological-Political Treatise* having caused an uproar that jeopardized his liberty) seeks to answer that question. Despite its title, *Ethics Demonstrated in a Geometrical Manner*, the book deals with far more than what we might take to constitute ethics. The work is a complete metaphysical system, articulated in a highly rationalistic, deductive manner. It starts with a naturalistic and monistic account of substance; there is only one substance God (or nature), instantiated in an infinitude of infinite attributes; these are in turn expressed by modes. God (or nature) is infinite, all-powerful, and necessary, operating according to eternal laws, the very laws which intellect discovers as laws of nature. The highest good is knowledge of God or nature, of which one can gain an adequate idea. The best way of life is conformity with the laws of God or nature, which entails pursuing the project requisite to the kind of being one is (*conatus*), and becoming, as far as possible, a knowing agent of one's actions rather than a passive reflex of the forces of nature. Since the highest form of knowledge is the knowledge of God or nature, the intellectual virtue of the knowing love of God (*amor dei intellectualis*) signals the highest form of life, as it does for

Maimonides. And as in Maimonides – a thinker he otherwise treats quite roughly – the life devoted to the intellectual love of God is not a solitary life, but a communal one. The highest virtue, knowledge of God which confers blessedness, is not in principle a scarce resource (although few attain it). It can be shared. The wise man desires nothing for himself that he does not desire for others. Genuine seekers after truth, which is what a society devoted to freedom of thought would nurture, will cooperate with one another. Love of one another, proper respect for oneself, joy in the attainment of knowledge, reason exercising control of the passions so as to increase one's agency – these are the goods of life. They are the basic teaching of the Bible, when it is approached through the proper hermeneutic lens.[11]

The Stoic element of Spinoza's thought – the background of metaphysical determinism against which rational apprehension of one's condition delivers a dimension of freedom – has echoes in prior Jewish thought. *Avot* (4:1) and Maimonides both propound the value of self-command, the latter against a keen understanding of the deterministic factors that condition human choice.[12] One can also argue that Spinoza's monism is similar to prior Jewish philosophy's affirmation that God's reality is, in a sense, the only true reality. Thus, Goodman writes:

> [Maimonides'] blueprint matches Spinoza's: Monism on the upper storeys opens out onto (and rests upon) a naturalistic scientific enterprise and an integrated ethical program. The style may differ. For Maimonides, like Baḥya, fills the space with the ethos and ritual of Halakha. Spinoza sets out the sparer furniture of a more generic life plan. Its cosmopolitan humanism only faintly suggests the biblical heritage that frames it.[13]

There is, thus, continuity between key dimensions of Spinoza's ethics and prior Jewish ethics. The emphasis on the virtues, particularly the intellectual virtues, points Spinoza toward the aretaic framework of traditional Jewish ethics. Although Jewish law plays no positive role within his own system, he nonetheless continues to conceive of ethics along deontic lines, that is, in terms of the obligation to treat one's fellows with respect, kindness, and generosity – arguably the heart of the Torah's moral vision. The liminal or transitional situation of Spinoza is captured in Wolfson's polar depiction of him as the last of the medievals or the first of the moderns. Subsequent Jewish ethics, in its modernist expression, remains, as we shall see, indebted to Spinoza.

Moses Ḥayim Luzzatto

Moses Ḥayim Luzzatto (known by his rabbinic acronym as Ramḥal) was, like Spinoza, a transitional, perhaps tragic figure. He too belongs in a way to an emerging modern world. Unlike Spinoza, Ramḥal remained a traditionalist, committed to the commandments and to a rabbinic way of life. Like Spinoza, however, he radically reinterpreted the meaning of the Torah and of the way of life that it enjoined; his theology was overtly kabbalistic, messianic, and theurgic. The prevailing traditional worldview of his day was already saturated with kabbalah, but Ramḥal drove this in a peculiarly messianic direction. His circle of young followers in his native Padua believed him to be a messiah, indeed, higher than the messiah – a kind of second Moses who would coordinate the activity of messianic subordinates. Each of his comrades had messianic roles to play in the unfolding of what they thought was an ultimate eschatological drama. Ramḥal's marriage contract (*ketubah*) portrays his marriage as an eschatological event; marriage and sexuality bring final reconciliation to the tensions among the sefirot which comprise the divine.[14] Like Spinoza, he was accused of heresy, in his case of being a follower of the seventeenth-century false messiah, Shabbetai Tzvi. (Repercussions and recriminations from that sad episode continued to reverberate into the eighteenth century.) He was ordered by the Padua Jewish community to cease writing kabbalistic tracts and to repudiate his claim to have received mystical revelations from a divine voice. He had to leave Padua, eventually making his way to Amsterdam, where he wrote his ethical works (and worked, like Spinoza, as a lens grinder). Eventually he moved with his family to the Land of Israel, where he thought that he could pursue kabbalah openly. Luck was not on his side, however. He died in a plague at age 40.

Like Spinoza, Ramḥal was steeped in the secular culture of his day. He knew classical languages and was conversant with Italian literature. His poems and plays based both on medieval Hebrew poetry and contemporary Italian literary culture made him a forerunner of the modernist movement of Jewish and Hebrew language revival (*Haskalah*) of the late eighteenth and nineteenth centuries. The "moderns" took him as a predecessor. But the "ancients" did as well. His ethical works were embraced by both the nascent hasidic movement and by their traditionalist opponents, the Mitnagdim. In the Lithuanian yeshivot of the latter, the Musar movement made Luzzatto's *Mesillat Yesharim* (*Paths of the Righteous*) basic reading. Although expelled by his native community of Padua, the accusation of Sabbatianism which dogged him during his lifetime was forgotten after his death and he was transformed into a saint by the various streams of Eastern European traditional piety. Indeed, historians of Hasidism find Luzzatto's kabbalistic emphasis on the mystical role of the leader to have informed Hasidism's elevation of the tzaddik, the charismatic leader. Thus, both emerging modernist and traditionalist Jewry claimed him as their own. Dan asserts that "Luzzatto stands as a central figure at the origins of all segments of modern Jewish movements."[15]

The *Mesillat Yesharim* is probably the most popular and influential work of traditional Jewish virtue ethics with the exception of Baḥya ibn

Pakuda's *Duties of the Heart*.[16] It is a highly systematic work, organized as a commentary and analysis of the statement of Rabbi Pinḥas ben Yair (*B. Avodah Zarah* 20b), which we earlier noted in Chapter 4. That statement suggests a "ladder of virtues" where one trait builds on another until, eventually, one achieves holiness and experiences the holy spirit (and, even more mysteriously, resurrection of the dead). A cluster of chapters is devoted to each trait. After a call to embrace the Torah, the ladder begins with the trait of cautiousness, care, or watchfulness (*zehirut*). Luzzatto provides a thematic overview of the significance of the virtue, followed by an analysis of its aspects and implications, followed by the cognitive and behavioral elements which enable one to acquire and strengthen the trait. He concludes with a study of factors that inhibit one from progressing in development of the trait and what to do about them. He follows this systematic method of exposition, analysis, and exhortation (although not always with separate chapters devoted to each set of concerns) for the other moral traits enumerated in the Talmudic saying, that is, zeal (*zerizut*), cleanliness (*nikiyut*), separation (*perishut*), purity (*taharah*), saintliness (*ḥasidut*), humility (*'anavah*), fear of sin (*yirat ḥet*), holiness (*kedushah*) and the holy spirit (*ruaḥ ha-kodesh*).

Let us get a sense of how Luzzatto conceives of his project by considering the Introduction to the work. Ramḥal, like many previous moralists, begins with a lament about the neglect of the virtues among his contemporaries. The virtues are neglected not only by the boorish or the worldly, he implies, but – explicitly – by men of reason (*anshe ha-sekhel*).[17] Rather than study saintliness (*ḥasidut*), they pursue the study of nature (*teva*), the study of astronomy and geometry (*handasa*) and other arts. Luzzatto is writing during the Enlightenment; perhaps he is responding to the new emphasis on learning and on the revival of the sciences. He laments as well that even the fine minds who continue to apply themselves to the study of Torah and halakha neglect *ḥasidut*. They do so because they think that the study of the virtues is an obvious thing – important in its way but not deserving of sustained attention. Consequently, the only persons who take the virtues seriously are simple people, who, their good intentions notwithstanding, do not have the intelligence to grasp the rational dimensions of *ḥasidut*. They mistake customs such as the recitation of Psalms, fasting, immersion in ice and snow and other ascetic practices as the heart of *ḥasidut*, but reason rejects this. The aim then is to give an account of the significance and essentiality of the traditional virtues which is compatible with reason. The study of *ḥasidut* should be elevated to its proper rank of intellectual and spiritual dignity.

Like natural tendencies such as sleep and wakefulness or hunger and satiety, the dispositions that are foundational for *ḥasidut*, such as fear and love (of God) and purity of heart, are rooted in a person's nature. But they are not as firmly rooted as other natural tendencies. They need to be fully acquired through discernment and cognition; their possession is an achievement, not an endowment. Thought and exertion are required. A method, means (*emtzaim*), must be applied to acquire them in an enduring way. (Is it possible to discern here an echo of the new emphasis on method in Descartes or Bacon?[18]) Luzzatto asks rhetorically "is it fitting that our intelligence exert itself and labor in speculations which are not binding upon us, in fruitless argumentation (*pilpul*), in laws (*dinim*) which have no application to us, while we leave to habit and abandon to mechanical observance our great debt to our Creator?"[19] Ramḥal here laments the neglect of musar as a neglect of duty. We are under an obligation, as Kant also thought, to perfect ourselves at least insofar as that is possible. For Luzzatto, we are bound to complete, as far as possible, the perfection of the work of creation. Continual mindfulness, rather than thoughtless and mechanical observance, is the coin in which our gratitude for our very being is to be paid.

Luzzatto does not shy away from putting the study of halakha into the same category as the study of philosophy, science, and the practical arts in the sense that all of these can defer or obstruct the proper endeavor of persons: knowing how to hold God in awe (*yirat ha-Shem*). This is a study in its own right. Fear of God is a kind, the highest kind, of wisdom. Nor can wisdom be achieved without true rational analysis (*iyyun*). Imagination and fallacious reasoning are the enemies of real wisdom and true perfection (*shleimut amiti*). Like Maimonides, Ramḥal leads with an intellectual orientation but the other dimensions of personhood are not neglected. The fear of God is not only a rational recognition of ultimate reality; it is also an attitude of humility, insignificance, and shame before the greatness of God. In addition to fear, the Jew must love God, must want to please God in the immediate and spontaneous way that one wants to please one's parents. One also needs to serve God wholeheartedly. One's motivation should be unified and singular as one applies oneself to the full observance of commandments. All the aspects of one's selfhood must be energized and enlisted in the loving, awe-filled service of God. The ladder of virtues is a kind of pilgrim's progress, an existential topography of ascent.

In the Introduction, we noticed the mingling of aretaic and deontic elements. We *ought* to pursue virtue and perfect ourselves. In the first chapter of *Mesillat Yesharim*, Ramḥal informs this basic theme with more detail. The chapter explicates the principle (*klal*) of man's duty (*ḥovah*) in the world. This is an intellectual inquiry. What are human beings for? What is the *summum bonum* toward which all human action should be directed? Luzzatto takes a rabbinic, traditionalist stance.

> Our Sages of blessed memory have taught us that man was created for the sole purpose of rejoicing in God and deriving pleasure from the splendor of His Presence; for this is the true joy and the greatest pleasure that can be found.

The place where this joy may truly be derived is the World to Come, which was expressly created to provide for it; but the path to the object of our desires is this world, as our Sages of blessed memory have said [Avot 4:16], "This world is like a corridor to the World to Come."[20]

The diminution of the importance of this world and the inflation of the significance of the world to come, i.e. of the sphere of post-mortem desert, is continuous with rabbinic teaching. (Albeit not without dissent. The very next mishnah in *Avot* (4:17) has the same teacher, R. Jacob, make a paradoxical claim: "Better is one hour of repentance and good works in this world than the whole life of the world to come; and better is one hour of bliss in the world to come than the whole life of this world." This arguably suggests a bit of ambivalence about a sphere in which, however blissful, moral action is no longer possible.) Luzzatto travels down well-worn paths in seeing this world as a place of trial and testing, of moral challenge and achievement without which entrance into the world to come would be meaningless. The commandments are the means with which one accrues moral merit; this world is the forum for that accrual. "Therefore, man was placed in this world first – so that by these means, which were provided for him here, he would be able to reach the place that had been prepared for him, the World to Come, there to be sated with the goodness which he acquired through them [i.e. the mitzvot]."[21]

Having based himself on a classical rabbinic teaching, Luzzatto tries to prove his point through argument. The core significance of the world to come is not pleasure in any material sense – it is perfection. And what is perfection if not cleaving to God (*devekut*)? This is the ultimate good, indeed, the only good (*ki rak zeh hu ha-tov*). Against this transcendent good, the purported goods which people choose are counterfeit. (They are the shadow goods of the Platonic cave, so to speak.) Nor can one realize good without labor. The good must be attained and the actions which conduce to the attainment of the good are the mitzvot. The world presses itself upon us, trying us with poverty and tempting us with riches. The human being must struggle for equilibrium, must strive to become a whole person (*ha-adam ha-shalem*), "who will succeed in uniting himself with his Creator, and he will leave the corridor [i.e. this world] and enter into the Palace, to glow in the light of life."[22] Becoming a "whole man," the person restores a primordial balance to the world. If one inclines toward sheer worldly desire one damages both self and world. If one takes command of one's desires and "uses the world only to aid him in the service of his Creator, he is uplifted and the world is uplifted with him."[23] Luzzatto hints here at the kabbalistic underpinnings of his metaphysics. The imbalanced divine cosmos is brought back to equilibrium through the human action of raising the divine sparks from their exile in materiality.

The "whole man" – the restored human being who has entered into communion with the divine – rights the cosmos and restores the world.

A second line of argument flows from the nature of the soul. We sense within ourselves a capacity to intuit perfection such that we are discontent with the imperfections of this world. We are never satisfied, not because we do not have sufficient quantities of goods or opportunities for pleasure but because we have an awareness of the limited, fragmentary nature of such experiences. The soul opens us to transcendence. It provides a criterion, however tacit or implicit, by which we relativize all worldly goods and weigh them against the transcendent good. Thus, the soul can come to despise the world and reject its pretensions to goodness. But Ramḥal is not a gnostic. The world is not despicable; it is problematic. The soul wants to recoil from the world and hold it in contempt but it may not. For the soul's task is to serve God in the world (in order to be worthy of the world to come) and therefore to affirm the world; the world is the scene of the service of God. It is not to be held in contempt or thought of as foreign. "And rather than the world's being despicable to the soul, it is, to the contrary, to be loved and desired by it."[24] For the world to lack ultimate value does not entail that it lacks all value. The mitzvot, which deal often with acutely mundane matters, keep the soul engaged in the world in a positive way. This is not a grim task. Luzzatto's appraisal of the world, the theme of trial notwithstanding, is not as dark as *Sefer Ḥasidim*'s. The pleasures of the world have a positive, non-sinister purpose: they give a person contentment and refreshment so that he or she can continue to serve God in a free and willing way. Only if these worldly pleasures were pried from their ultimate purpose and understood as intrinsic goods would they forfeit their claim to any positive value. In his validation of this world, his otherworldly aims notwithstanding, Luzzatto resembles Saadya Gaon.

Like Maimonides, for whom the prophet of the truly divine law is a perfect man (*Guide* Part II, Chapter 40), Ramḥal envisions human perfection as constant, close communion with the divine. One who is holy clings constantly to God; his soul passes among the true intelligible forms (*ha-muscalot ha-amitiyot*) that comprise ultimate reality.[25] He walks as perfectly before God as is it possible to walk in the land of the living. God's presence rests on him as if he were the altar of the Temple. Such perfection is not wholly a product of disciplined human agency. The righteous man initiates the process by setting upon the ladder of virtues but God completes it. Holiness begins as human labor, but ends as divine reward.[26]

This strong sense of the possibility of divine intervention is another marker of the distance between the ideal-typical tendency of traditional Jewish ethics and the modernist tendency. The idea of God as an active partner in the struggle for human obedience and perfection is lacking in modernist authors, where God is more likely to function as a normative ideal, a transcendental idea of perfection against which conduct can be judged and toward which aspiration may be directed. In Moses Mendelssohn, the traditionalist premise of divine lawgiving is wedded to the Enlightenment predilection for a non-agentic, deistic God.

Moses Mendelssohn

Mendelssohn is a unique figure – a great rarity in his time and an anomaly after his age. He achieved great fame as a leading German *Aufklärer*, an advocate of Enlightenment, a philosopher in the metaphysical tradition of Leibniz and the moral-political tradition of Locke. Mendelssohn won greater renown in general culture than any Jewish philosopher since Maimonides. But at no time did he neglect his Jewish compatriots. He inaugurated a parallel movement of Enlightenment (*Haskalah*) among German Jews, translating the Bible into High German, for example, so that Jews could begin to learn the language and hence the culture, arts, and sciences of the Central European lands in which they dwelt. Nor did Mendelssohn neglect traditional religious observance. His major Jewish work, *Jerusalem or On Religious Power and Judaism*, contains the first fully modern philosophical presentation and polemic on behalf of Judaism, yet its modernism is tied to an affirmation of full observance. Although the reformist movement of the nineteenth century claimed him as a progenitor, it could not do so entirely in good conscience. Mendelssohn's emphasis on observance of the commandments in their traditional guise, despite the modernist, deist tropes of his apologia, was unacceptable to his Reform-minded descendants. As such, Mendelssohn remains a crucial figure for historians of Jewish thought, as well as those of German intellectual history, but in a way an orphan in time. He left no school behind, founded no lasting movement. Later generations of Orthodox thought him, unfairly, the initiator of much mischief; later generations of Reform Jews claimed him, selectively and with violence to the complexity of his thought, as their own.

Much of Mendelssohn's work dealt with philosophical topics in vogue in the mid- to late eighteenth century – the moral sentiments, natural religion, the aesthetic sense.[27] There is nothing particularly Jewish about such work. His vast biblical translation project, with traditional, albeit modernizing Hebrew commentary, is another matter. The translation, known by the name of the commentary, the *Biur* (Hebrew for explanation or clarification), was co-authored by Mendelssohn and various friends and colleagues. Here we see Mendelssohn both continuing the project of medieval commentary by excerpting portions of the classical Jewish biblical commentators and steering his readers toward German linguistic competency and modern insights. The work which has drawn the most attention among students of

Jewish thought is *Jerusalem* (1783). Mendelssohn was loath to defend his Judaism in public but was forced to do so when an anonymous pamphleteer challenged him to explain how Judaism could be compatible with Enlightenment. Should he fail to do so, the writer believed that he would be honor-bound to convert to a modernized Christianity, which, presumably, was fully compatible with Enlightenment. Mendelssohn rose with great ingenuity to the challenge. He argued in the first section of *Jerusalem* for the incompatibility of religion with coercion and thus on behalf of, as we would put it, the separation of church and state. He offered an argument similar to Spinoza's and Locke's. The state deals with outward behavior, which is properly governed by law; religion deals primarily with inward conviction. Arraying the coercive apparatus of the state against the sanctity of conscience should not be within the competence of a lawful state. It also makes a mockery of religion. The churches should have no civil authority whatsoever – a point which led Kant to praise the work. They are voluntary societies made up of like-minded persons. Membership in them should neither advance nor detract from anyone's civil standing. The main implication of the argument was its Jewish interest. If the state should not be in the business of enforcing orthodoxies but rather of protecting the rights of conscience, then there can be no legitimate bar to the full enfranchisement of Jewish subjects. That they are not Christian should have no civil repercussions. The state's interest should be in law-abiding civility, not religious conformity. And there is no reason that Jews cannot meet the requisite standard of moral, civil behavior.

Although Mendelssohn would separate church and state – and subordinate the former to the latter – he sees both of them having a hand in the process of educating, civilizing, and moralizing human beings. Society and state have an immense educative role to play in bringing people from selfishness into concern for the common good. But "church" also has a hand in this since ultimate beliefs about God have direct moral consequences. Both state and church are concerned with the formation (*Bildung*) of human beings – with the enlargement of their sympathies, the consummation of their talents, and the enhancement of their capacity for benevolence.[28] The development of persons in the direction of benevolence leads to felicity, the ultimate goal of both the state and religion. While the state teaches through law, religion teaches through persuasion, love, and consolation. But Mendelssohn also allots religion a kind of soft power. Although religion does not have law in the civil sense, it does have commandments – and this is particularly the case with Judaism.[29] The commandments, indeed, the ancient framework of commandments qua law of a once coercive Jewish state, constitute a problem for Mendelssohn. The politicized embodiment of ancient – and to a much lesser extent medieval *kehilla* – Judaism seems to undermine his congenial Lockean dichotomy between the state as the sphere of coercion and religion as the sphere of consent and persuasion. Medieval

Judaism, although no longer host to the ancient sovereign state with halakha as its law, retained the power of the ban. It is here that Mendelssohn deploys his theory of Judaism with its broadly ethical conceptualization of Jewish law and practice.

Mendelssohn has to argue that residual coercive practices, such as the power of excommunication, are distortions of pure non-coercive Judaism. He marks out the biblical arrangement of commandment qua law as unique to those ancient circumstances and in no way a model for current arrangements.[30] Commandments served as law only when God was the direct ruler of the nation. But what exactly did these commandments command? Could ancient Jews properly be punished for inward opinions or were only outward actions punishable? Mendelssohn comes down firmly on the latter view: the commandments extend only to behaviors. The entire intellectual content of Judaism is compatible with (although not reducible to) the natural religion of right reason. Judaism prescribes no dogmas, teaches no esoteric truths, or enshrines any mysteries of the faith. In fact, it teaches nothing that rightly directed metaphysical and moral reason cannot already grasp. The commandments aim at *Bildung*: at educating and moralizing human beings. Mendelssohn proposes a sweeping theory of the commandments as a "living script" which trains persons through the imitation of normative cultural patterns. He offers a theory of language which argues that the rise of writing led ancient peoples to mistake signs for the realities they designate, leading to profound intellectual and moral confusions the most grievous of which was idolatry. God, by revealing commandments which require performance and enactment, mitigated the possibility of intellectual confusion while enhancing the likelihood of attention to moral awareness.

> Religious and moral teachings were to be connected with men's everyday activities. The law, to be sure, did not impel them to engage in reflection; it prescribed only actions, only doing and not doing. The great maxim of its constitution seems to have been: *Men must be impelled to perform actions and only induced to engage in reflection*. Therefore, each of these prescribed actions, each practice, each ceremony had its meaning, its valid significance; each was closely related to the speculative knowledge of religion and the teachings of morality, and was an occasion for man in search of truth to reflect on these sacred matters or to seek instruction from wise men.[31]

The intellectual search for truth was left to right reason and to face-to-face encounter with sages; the commandments trained the Jews to pattern their lives on principles embodying God's benevolence. Thus, in a manner somewhat reminiscent of Maimonides (and of Philo long before), Mendelssohn infuses the mitzvot with a pervasively moral purpose.

Mendelssohn follows Spinoza in the view that the revealed law of the Bible does not, contra-Maimonides, teach unique speculative truths.[32] Its thrust is moral. He differs from Spinoza in rejecting a primarily political function for the law. In place of Spinoza's politics, Mendelssohn enshrines ethics in the sense of comprehensive self-development and perfection – *Bildung*. Of course, crucially unlike Spinoza, Mendelssohn holds that the "ceremonial law" still has authority and requires observance: "no sophistry of ours can free us from the strict obedience we owe to the law."[33] And Mendelssohn sees immense value in the continuity of Jewish life, so much so that he would forgo any offer of emancipation that would require him to weaken or abandon his Jewish observance. These important differences notwithstanding, Mendelssohn shares a crucial likeness with Spinoza. They both want an end to a medieval order where the state is a Christian state and the Jew is an eternal outsider. Mendelssohn's prescription for a disestablishmentarian state is as radical as Spinoza's. And the price that he is willing to pay remains high. Judaism is to become a confession, a religion construed along Protestant lines, shorn of its political basis in theocracy, commonwealth, and republic. That Judaism should retain a divinely revealed "ceremonial" law – a massive fact which cannot be assimilated to a Protestant confessional paradigm – was necessary for Mendelssohn but unintelligible to his rationalist-reformist descendants. That part of his teaching was jettisoned by them. The primacy of the moral as the justification for continuing Jewish particularity gained ever-greater emphasis among modernist Jews.

Mendelssohn's distinctively Jewish views can be understood in the context of his general moral theory.[34] In his 1763 essay, "On Evidence in Metaphysical Sciences," which earned him the top prize of the Prussian Royal Academy of Sciences (beating, among others, Immanuel Kant), Mendelssohn argues on the basis of laws of nature. His approach reminds one of Spinoza's conatus. The first law of nature is "make your intrinsic and extrinsic condition and that of your fellow human being, in the proper proportion, as perfect as you can."[35] All beings pursue their own good. Beings endowed with reason and free will are exceptional in nature insofar as they can entertain false ideas of what constitutes their own good. So what is the highest good? It cannot be pleasure. Pleasure, he had earlier argued, points beyond itself toward perfection.[36] To identify the true good, we ought to be guided by the concept of perfection. Perfection is not coercive; it gives rise to a "moral necessity" to orient one's choices "to bring about as much perfection, beauty, and order in the world as possible." This is the "great final purpose of creation": to "become an imitator of the divinity whenever I render a creature, myself or another, more perfect."[37] Mendelssohn's view is basically aretaic although he tries to derive a "moral necessity," an obligation, from the cognition of the highest good. Although the language is Platonic, the conviction is Hebraic. The end state of felicity is impossible without benevolence. Loving one's neighbor as oneself is the imitation of God. Practically, one rises to proficiency in virtue through habituation. Mendelssohn's eventual stress on the commandments as a "living script" of actions is rooted in his philosophical emphasis on training in virtue via the inculcation of good habits. Rational reflection is possible and beneficial but for virtue truly to become second nature, one must follow an order of practice:

> Indeed, anyone who grapples with the highest stage of ethical perfection and strives for the blessed condition of bringing the subordinate powers of the soul into perfect harmony with the superior powers of the soul, must do this with the laws of nature just as the artist must do so with the rules of his art. He must continue practicing until, in the course of the exercise, he is no longer conscious of his rules, in other words, until his principles have turned into inclinations and his virtue appears to be more natural instinct than reason.[38]

This text has nothing overtly to do with Judaism but it is hard not to see in it a covert allusion to Mendelssohn's own way of life as an observant Jew. The theme of perfectionism, as well as the interweaving of obligation and virtue – the aretaic–deontic pattern – are familiar from the moral culture which nurtured Mendelssohn.

From Ḥasidism to Musar

As we have seen, the term *Hasidism* refers to the movement of Ashkenazi pietism in the Middle Ages. It also refers to what became a movement of spiritual and moral renewal, led by charismatic, popular kabbalists in southern Poland, Ukraine, and White Russia in the latter half of the eighteenth and the nineteenth centuries. Indeed, Ḥasidism remains a strong force in the Jewish world to this day, having recouped some of its immense demographic losses during the Holocaust and found ways to appeal, through the activism of one of its major communities, namely Chabad Lubavitch, to non-ḥasidic Jews. Ḥasidism might have spun off into numerous small heretical sects during its formative period. Part of why it did not is because of the essentially conservative medium in which its teachings were expressed – sermons and ethical literature. In Joseph Dan's view, the inherent traditionalism of its means of expression and propagation helped to neutralize the truly radical implications of some of its teaching.[39] Theologically, for example, some ḥasidic masters argued for a pantheistic God, immanent in, yet transcendent of, nature. Such a God gestures toward the God of Spinoza.

Ḥasidism draws from centuries of kabbalah, as well as from folk traditions of practical mysticism. The traditionalist Jews (*Mitnaggedim*) who opposed it, sensing a recurrence of the previous century's Shabbatean heresy, were no less mystically oriented. Mysticism per se is not what divided them. Ḥasidism offered a less ascetic, more joyous, more accessible path to the mystical goal of communion with God (*devekut*) than previous expressions of kabbalah. In Gershom Scholem's view, the emphasis on *devekut*, as well as its particular formulations of the concept, set Hasidism apart from its predecessor mystical cultures. The centrality of *devekut* goes back to the thought of Rabbi Israel Baal Shem Tov (known by the acronym Besht), the founder of the movement. Let us examine several sections of a compilation of the Besht's sayings, known as the *Testament of Rabbi Israel Baal Shem (Tzvaat Ha-Rivash)*. (It is well to bear in mind that the Besht did not actually write anything down himself. This compilation, first appearing in 1794, likely reflects the views of his followers as well as his own. Thus, the text presents a pastiche of views current in early Hasidism. For the sake of convenience, we will refer to the author as the Besht even though that is not strictly true.)

The *Testament* in many ways continues with prior expressions of Jewish ethical teaching. Fathers sometimes left written instructions ("ethical wills") for their children, as did rabbis for their students.[40] The *Testament* of the Besht is a collection of some 166 numbered paragraphs offering moral and spiritual instruction on Jewish life. It deals with the ritual dimensions of proper conduct, such as prayer, fasting, and study, in every instance seeking a mystical meaning for the practice and a mystical mode for correctly carrying it out. Unlike the ethical mysticism of *Mesillat Yesharim*, where *devekut* is thought to be the culmination of the mystic's path, the Besht takes *devekut* to be immediately accessible. Intimate communion with God, although arduous and impossible to sustain, is not a rare occurrence but an *expected* one; the hasid must work to keep strange thoughts and other threatening distractions from interrupting his communion. The ideal here is to maintain this close communion, which has a distinct experiential dimension – the experience of the light of God's immanent presence (*Shekhinah*) – under the circumstances of daily life. The hasid, although in the midst of the world and engaged in business, conversation, even Torah study, must cultivate an inner separation. The soul withdraws and actuates its connection to the upper world, the root of its being. Ordinary life is to be a dialectic of external action and inner withdrawal.

An example of this may be found in paragraph 45: "One should not look in the face of persons when one speaks with them if one knows that their thoughts are not continually cleaving to Hashem, may He be blessed. For gazing will inflict damage (*pagam*) on one's soul. But at persons, who are fitting, whose thoughts cleave continuously to Hashem, may He be blessed, one may gaze. And from the power of doing so one's soul will acquire additional holiness."[41] Continuous cleaving to God (designated in this text by the traditional locution, Hashem, literally, the Name) is normative. In the Besht's hasidism, *devekut* is primarily a solitary, private experience. Later teachers expand it into a shared, collective one.[42] The dialectic between presence and withdrawal, being fully engaged in the shared social world and being reserved, apart, and withdrawn at the same time, is an old one. It goes back at least as far as Plato's philosopher king, who would rather not descend into the cave to rule the benighted humans who, lacking his enlightenment, dwell there. It appears again at the end of Aristotle's *Ethics*. In Jewish literature it may be found in some of the prophets, who are acutely conscious of their own radical distinction from their countrymen. Their connection with God isolates them, yet they must dwell in the midst of the people and speak to them. Amos was taken by God from tending his sycamore trees; Jeremiah was designated as God's spokesman in the womb. This sublime aloneness in the midst of an active life appears, as we have seen, in Maimonides (e.g. *Guide* Part III, Chapter 51) and in the twentieth century was raised to thematic salience in Joseph Soloveitchik's *Lonely Man of Faith*. The mystics of Safed in the sixteenth century focused on *hitbodedut*, mystical isolation through solitary physical wandering. The idea of inner withdrawal is thus not new. What might be new is the expectation that this must be done all the time, given the constant norm of *devekut*. At *Guide* Part III, Chapter 51, Maimonides expresses doubt that anyone other than Moses was continuously able to maintain a connection with the divine in the midst of daily activity. For the Besht, this appears to be a serious possibility.[43]

An example of this may be found in the Besht's treatment of Torah study. Continuous study of the Talmud was the highest ideal of eighteenth- and nineteenth-century Eastern European Jewry. The fact that the Besht and his disciples subordinated Torah study to a yet higher concern, *devekut*, likely antagonized his opponents and galvanized the resistance to Ḥasidism.[44] In this teaching, the Besht, although he advocates constant study, also calls for study to be interrupted for the direction of thought toward *devekut*.

> In our generations, when we are poor in intellect, we need very much to hold fast to fear of God and to withdraw (*hitboded*) and direct thought constantly to fear and awe. Even during the time of Torah study (*limmud*), it is good to rest a little each time one studies and to withdraw his thought in order to adjoin himself to Hashem, may He be blessed.[45]

Nonetheless, one should study constantly, for "the Torah polishes the soul" and "if one doesn't study one will not have the mind to cleave to Hashem."[46] There is a necessary connection between the refinement of intellect and intention which Torah study engenders and the capacity for communion with God. But there are also some tensions or trade-offs between them.

The attitude that one ought to take toward the world has some resemblance to Stoic *apatheia*; one should be in it but not of it, ultimately indifferent to whatever distracts one's mind from communion with the ultimate. Citing Psalm 16:8 (I am ever mindful (*shiviti*) of the LORD's presence), the Besht claims "*Shiviti* means equanimity (*hishtavut*). In everything that happens to him, let it all be equal (*shaveh*) to him. Whether people praise him or shame him and in all other things ... let it all be equal in his eyes. For this removes his evil inclination bit by bit."[47] Furthermore, the continual preoccupation of seeking and sustaining *devekut* will depreciate the worth of all worldly occupations in his eyes. All will appear as "emptiness and vanity." Whatever pleasure he takes in the work of *devekut* must not be considered pleasure for its own sake but pleasure raised to its source in the Shekhinah.

Several moral implications flow from this attitude of inner withdrawal from, and corresponding depreciation of the value of, the workaday world. One is, as indicated above, a radical egalitarianism. Status, rank, and the opinion of others should cease to matter. The Besht urges:

> Let him not say in his heart that he is greater than his fellow; that he serves with greater *devekut*, for he is like all other creatures that have been created for the purpose of service to the Blessed One. Did Hashem not give his fellow a mind (*sekhel*) just as He gave him a mind? Is he more important than the worm? Does not the worm also serve its Creator, may He be blessed, with all of its capacities (*sikhlo v'koḥo*)? ... Had Hashem not given man his capacities he would not be able to serve Him even as the worm serves. He would not be more important than a worm, let alone than another man. Let him therefore think that he and the worm and all of the other small creatures are of equal importance and are as fellows in the world for all were created by Hashem, may He be blessed. And none of them have abilities beyond what the Creator, may He be blessed, graciously gave to them. And this word should always be in one's thought.[48]

At least at this stage the figure of the tzaddik, who takes on such central importance in the ḥasidic worldview, is not yet crucial. This radical egalitarianism in the eyes of God is an attractive feature.

The ḥasid should view all that goes on in the world, from the greatest events to the most negligible, as the direct work of God. As God's doings, they should be thought of as good, even though they may not appear to be good from the point of view of human assessment.[49] One should pray that God grant one a portion that is good from God's point of view. The theological imagination here supports fundamental moral attitudes. Far from encouraging a Stoic-like fatalism, this conviction of the intense reality of divine Providence liberates the ḥasid from fear and gloom. The text is full of exhortations to be energetic, enthusiastic, and joyous.[50] The fact remains, however, that one cannot be in a state of *devekut* all the time. How not then to succumb to fatalism? The Besht advances the categories of *katnut*, smallness and *gadlut*, greatness both to explain the emotional dynamics of bliss and despair and to cope normatively with them. For the Besht, Gershom Scholem writes, "*katnut* and *gadlut* are phases of life, everywhere and at all times, from purely natural and even artificial things up to the configuration of the divine *sefirot* where the same rhythm and same law prevail."⁵¹ In the state of *katnut*, human imperfection and the melancholy loss of *devekut* predominate; man must struggle against the sadness which follows from his awareness of estrangement from God. The ḥasid can discover in the midst of the sense of loss ways to direct his thought to God, to serve God, and to regain the connection of *devekut*, upon which he enters the state of *gadlut* once again. This cyclical but, the ḥasid hopes, upward spiraling movement is the necessary rhythm of human life. God is pictured as an active, covenantal partner in helping the Jew return from *katnut* to *gadlut*. It is as if the cyclicality of nature were reconciled with the agency of a personal, providential God. In later Ḥasidism, the tzaddik plays a key role in rescuing his followers from the melancholy of interruption.

Ḥasidism offers a charmed and charged universe in which human thought and action aim at and are believed to achieve a nurturing connectedness with an immanent divine reality. By the end of the nineteenth century, the modernized Jews of Central and Western Europe could no longer take such a metaphysics and its attendant moral vision seriously. The moral law, as enunciated by Kant, took the place of an active, mystically accessible providential God. We will see this in the work of Lazarus and Cohen. It was left to a radical neo-Romantic thinker of the next generation, Martin Buber, to attempt to restore the lived immediacy of ḥasidic *devekut* through his famous I-Thou encounter. Before considering these modern developments, however, we must look at the intense form of ethical piety that arose among the opponents of Ḥasidism, the Musar movement.

The ḥasidic movement did not succeed in penetrating the traditional Jewish world of Lithuania owing to the exertions of Rabbi Elijah ben Shlomo, known as the Vilna Gaon (1720–1797), and his disciples. The opponents of Ḥasidism (*Mitnaggedim*) began as advocates of time-honored, conservative traditionalism but soon became self-conscious and offered their own substantive theological-moral outlook. The Mitnaggedim shaped a culture of talmudic scholarship concentrated in yeshivot, where advanced, full-time rabbinic learning pursued for its own sake became the highest value. Rabbi Israel Salanter was a product of that culture. His scholarly lineage, traced through his teacher Rabbi Zundel of Salant, to his teacher, Rabbi Ḥayyim of Volozhin, goes back to the Gaon of Vilna. His emphasis on musar, on the cultivation of moral personality actuated by the yearning for moral perfection, was something of a new orientation, however. The traditional culture of talmudic study was, needless to say, concerned with musar. The leading disciple of the Vilna Gaon, Rabbi Ḥayyim of Volozhin (1749–1821), wrote a moral-theological treatise, *Nefesh ha-Ḥayyim* (*The Soul of Life*), which invokes a kabbalistic account of moral-legal action. The guiding thought of mitnaggedic piety, however, was that musar would flow naturally from the regular practice of Torah study; it need not become thematic. *Yirah* (the fear of God) would follow *talmud torah* (the study of Torah). Salanter disagreed. His writings, from the 1840s on, are full of zealous criticism of the traditional Jewish culture of his day for its moral laxity. The very same Jews who were scrupulous about kosher slaughter and eating could be promiscuous about *lashon ha-ra* or devious business practices. He contrasted Torah – the acquisition of authoritative traditional Jewish knowledge and the observant life that Torah supports – with *yirah*. Ideally, these two strengthen – and are radically incomplete without – each other. In practice, Salanter believed that *yirah* was widely neglected in Lithuania.[52] Salanter was perplexed that more Jews did not wish to devote themselves to moral improvement. He sought ways to address this problem directly.

One of the tasks of musar, then, is to awaken a more acute and continual sense of the fear and awe of God. Salanter's work was devoted to stimulating this awareness among both the ordinary householders and the rabbinic elite of Eastern Europe. He sojourned in Vilna and Kovno, the major centers of Jewish life. For the last two decades of his life, however, he lived in Germany and also travelled around Western Europe, preaching the musar doctrine. At once the product of a very traditional culture and a pioneer into the acculturated Jewish communities of the West, Salanter is a somewhat paradoxical figure. Although his musar orientation was opposed by some of the leaders of Lithuanian Jewry, after his death it came to dominate leading yeshivot.[53] The influence of the Musar movement is still felt in the successors of those institutions in the contemporary ultra-Orthodox world.

Although Salanter's teaching and the movement which he inspired seem in many respects to stand in opposition to modernization, his approach to musar is indebted to a modernist source. The Lithuanian yeshiva world, and the incipient Musar movement, opposed more than Ḥasidism; it opposed the Haskalah. The Haskalah, the Hebrew term for "Enlightenment," began in Berlin, in the circle of Moses Mendelssohn. It spread from Prussia to Eastern Europe. Haskalah proponents (*Maskilim*) advocated the modernization of schooling, for example, learning languages such as, in Eastern Europe, Russian. They wanted to splice science, geography, history, etc. into the traditional rabbinic curriculum. They worked to renew the Hebrew language and develop a modernist Hebrew literature. In the Russian Empire these initiatives were fraught. The Russian government under Czar Nicholas I in the 1840s wanted to forcibly acculturate its Jewish population; Maskilim were viewed as enablers and traitors by the traditional rabbinic elite. One *maskil*, a rabbi by the name of Menachem Mendel Lefin, wrote an Enlightenment-inspired tract on the improvement of moral character, *Sefer Ḥeshbon Ha-Nefesh* (*The Accounting of the Soul*), first published in 1808. Lefin had spent time in Berlin and was a friend of Mendelssohn; he brought the agenda of *Bildung* back to Eastern Europe and translated eighteenth-century psychology and philosophy into tradition-friendly terms. Curiously, Lefin's book owed much to Benjamin Franklin's autobiography, especially in its use of practical techniques for character development and transformation. Salanter knew of Lefin's work and even had it republished in 1844. Lefin's empirical, somewhat Lockean approach to the soul – that it accumulates sense impressions and that emotional states are formed almost mechanically out of impression-forming sensory stimuli – also carries into Salanter. Salanter's technique of arousal (*hitpa'alut*) of intense feelings through the study of musar works echoes psychological techniques advocated by Lefin.[54]

Salanter and his disciples offered a distinctive spiritual way that lent intensity and commitment to the life of the Mitnaggedim. Its main problem is how to awaken and strengthen the fear of God. Part of Salanter's preaching and writing is directed toward inspiring Jews to take heed of the day of reckoning. God is a righteous judge who will punish sinners for their violations of halakhic norms. Salanter is certainly not above what Kant condemned as sheer heteronomy. At his most interesting, however, Salanter proposed a set of practices that would transform heteronymous commands into imperatives that seem to flow from one's own conscience. He believed strongly in the cultivation of habits, which conduce to virtue by making habitual practices become one's second nature. His main innovation was emphasizing the study of classical musar texts. He and his disciples formed groups for the study of classics, such as Baḥya's *Duties of the Heart*, Cordovero's *Palm Tree of Deborah*, or Luzzatto's *Paths of the Righteous*. He advocated the creation of houses devoted to musar study (*beit musar*), near to but separate from traditional houses of Torah study (*beit midrash*). Never before had the study of the classics of Jewish moral thought been regularized and institutionalized. Salanter envisioned an educational program whose aim was moral perfection. Salanter's emphasis on studying this literature as part of the yeshiva curriculum awakened the opposition of those who believed in the omni-sufficiency of Talmud study. In addition to studying musar texts per se, he advocated Torah study for the sake of practice (*limmud l'ma'aseh*). If one became aware that one's major failing was improper speech, for example, one should strenuously and devotedly study the laws of speech, and so on for dishonesty in business, marital infidelity, etc. There is a highly intellectual orientation here, typical of the Mitnaggedim. Study, in the spirit of arousal (*hitpa'alut*), will transform the soul of the student. "Learning halakhot ... especially in order to observe them, bears fruit little by little, imparting courage to the soul ... One acquires a new nature ... Transgressions are distant by nature ... One would not even contemplate sin even under duress."[55]

Salanter has a dark view of human nature. In his moral anthropology, human beings are continually drawn to sinful behavior. The evil inclination or *yetzer ha-ra* predominates in them.[56] Their will, imagination, the deepest stirrings of the human heart are wild and almost ungovernable. Yet, if the good inclination (*yetzer ha-tov*), which is equivalent to holiness (*yetzer ha-kedusha*) and right rationality in Salanter's thought, is sufficiently cultivated, it can withstand the assault of its opposite number. This takes regular exertion and rational supervision.[57] In the *Musar Epistle*, the evil inclination has two sources: appetite (*taavah*) and the "impure spirit" (*ruḥaniyut ha-tumah* or *ruaḥ ha-tumah*).[58] Appetite signifies the desire to possess and enjoy what is momentarily pleasant. Such behavior precludes rational evaluation; one lives in the moment, heedless of consequences. Yet what is pleasant, for example certain foods that eventually cause disease, can be dangerous. Only from the standpoint of reason can pleasures be weighed and judged. But that capacity is precisely what is truncated in a person given over to appetite. The cure for restoring this deficit of reason, Salanter claims, is focusing on punishment in the afterlife. This thought has to be made vivid. The fear of divine retribution can reinstate the capacity for rational assessment. In this respect, Salanter is an otherworldly utilitarian.

Appetite has a personal or local instantiation. That is, different people have different inclinations, thresholds, and predilections for sin. (Cultures develop these idiosyncratic failings too). Appetite depends upon the particular physiology and upbringing of a person. It is otherwise with the impure spirit, which is a mysterious, pervasive, universal force. It leads to sin in which the sinner takes no pleasure. The pursuit of perverse objects of intention, such as worldly honor, can cause a great deal of pain. Furthermore, the very person who pursues such honor will neglect the honor that comes with performing mitzvot of the Torah.[59] What other than an irrational, non-hedonic "spirit of impurity" could account for such a mentality? The spirit of impurity is thus a profound and pervasive condition of confusion about proper ends.

The intellectual discipline of text study, wedded to a social support system of like-minded seekers of perfection, can contain the *yetzer ha-ra* and transform human nature. Although dark in his assessment of the, dare one say "fallen," state of that nature, Salanter is hopeful that deliberate, unrelenting human agency can initiate and sustain fundamental change. Such training in character is not supererogatory; it is of the very essence of halakhic obligation.[60] Rather unlike other perfectionists such as Luzzatto, Salanter does not leave a role for divine agency. God has created the disease of the *yetzer ha-ra* but He has also given us the cure, the *yetzer ha-tov* and the Torah. The holy spirit, another terminological variant for the *yetzer ha-tov*, is not an active divine principle, a gift as Luzzatto called it, provided to the seeker when God so wills. The holy spirit is a native endowment, which the Jew can choose to cultivate or to neglect. In this, Salanter reflects the naturalistic psychology of Lefin and the eighteenth-century

Enlightenment. He also resembles somewhat the modernists of Germany in whose midst he settled. For them, the "holy spirit" describes a strictly immanent capacity for moral transformation under the guidance of practical reason. One wouldn't want to overplay the likeness of such a post-Kantian view with Salanter's system, but one should not underestimate the modern tenor of his seemingly highly traditional program.

As mentioned, the Musar movement became firmly established in much of the mitnaggedic yeshiva world. Salanter's disciples, particularly Rabbi Simḥah Zissel Ziv, left important bodies of musar texts which continue to be explored and, more importantly, integrated into the daily practice of both Orthodox and non-Orthodox Jews. Although not technically associated with the movement, Rabbi Israel Meir Kagan (1838–1933), known popularly as the Ḥafetz Ḥayyim after the title of one of his works, wrote halakhic compendia which serve as moral codes. The text *Ḥafetz Ḥayyim* (*He Who Desires Life*) itself is an immensely detailed study of the laws of permitted and forbidden speech, that is, of *lashon ha-ra*, a classic topic of Jewish moralism. His *Ahavat Ḥesed* (*Love of Charity*) is a study of the laws of charity. These books contributed to the dense culture of halakhic learning and moral conscientiousness cultivated by traditional Jews down to the present day.

Lazarus and Cohen

Moritz Lazarus, a German-Jewish professor of psychology and a leader of Liberal (Reform) Judaism in the Second Reich, was immensely popular among his acculturated German coreligionists in the nineteenth century but is largely forgotten today. Lazarus represents an optimistic expectation of ever-greater acceptance of Jews by Germans – and this ensconced in a "basically unlimited faith in the strength and final victory of moral duty and of the peace-loving impulses in man."[61] He presents, far more sweepingly and robustly than Mendelssohn, a thorough ethicization of Judaism. Judaism is essentially, if not exclusively, ethics. Ethics becomes the master category to which all other aspects of Judaism are subordinated or, should that not succeed, discarded (as in the case of mysticism). His main work, *Die Ethik des Judentums* (*The Ethics of Judaism*) is the first modern systematic effort to interpret biblical and rabbinic religion entirely through the prism of ethics. From this distance, it is easy to dismiss Lazarus as an apologist for a failed project but, like Cohen, he is deeper than the outward trappings of his ideological uniform and deserves a closer look.[62]

Lazarus had a traditional education and was familiar with biblical and rabbinic sources in the original Hebrew. As a founder, with his brother-in-law, Heymann Steinthal, of the "psychology of nations," he sought to give scientific articulation to the widespread nineteenth-century idea that different peoples had characteristic ways of thinking, feeling, and valuing. Peoples participate in a "collective spirit" which unites them within a culture and affords them temporal continuity.[63] Lazarus constitutes the Jewish spirit as one of ethics and draws widely from the Bible, midrash and Talmud to exemplify the central values and orientations of the Jews. He systematically excludes the medieval philosophers such as Baḥya and Maimonides insofar as philosophy on his view is an elite practice and does not represent the authentic spirit of the people. For this he was roundly criticized by Hermann Cohen. Lazarus's reticence toward medieval Jewish philosophy is replicated in his cautious stance toward modern philosophy. He is concerned, on the one hand, to show that Judaism qua ethics is in broad accord with Kantian ethics. On the other hand, he is dismissive of those who would equate or subordinate Judaism to Kant.[64] He thus walks a narrow line between Judaism as a form of autonomous moral consciousness and Judaism as a heteronymous religious system. His attempt to preserve the naïve, authentic voices of traditional Jewish texts and to relate them to the most compelling contemporary intellectual voices did not issue into a methodologically coherent system. Cohen, once again, criticized Lazarus on this count.

As a psychologist rather than a philosopher, Lazarus seeks a more or less empirical basis for ethics. Ethical consciousness is not intuitive or naturalistic; it is informed by the "ought" not the "is," by reasons not causes, we might say. Ethics indicates the ideal sphere above natural existence toward which human beings, both on a personal level and socially, ought to strive. Nonetheless, Lazarus does not go in a fully Kantian direction and divorce moral imperatives from human drives, feelings, and desires.[65] Ethics arises from a drive toward the Good (*Trieb zum Guten*), from a feeling of obligation (*Gefühl der Verpflichtung*), which issues into rational assent.[66] But this is immediately problematic with respect to Judaism. If Judaism is equivalent to ethics and ethics arises from a sentiment of obligation, then the entire theistic framework of Judaism becomes irrelevant. Lazarus preserves the distinctive monotheistic assumptions of Judaism by making God, the author of ethics, pervasively moral. Lazarus, like Cohen after him, removes all traces of divine voluntarism. That God commands an imperative does not make it right; God commands it because it is right. God too is subject to moral law. For a human being, then, to will the moral law of one's free will is simultaneously to do God's will. "Morally good and pleasing to God; moral law and divine command – for Judaism these concepts are completely inseparable."[67] Inseparable but, he adds, not identical. God's command and the moral law are related through a third term, the concept of holiness.

Holiness plays a critical role in Lazarus's thought, as it does in Cohen's. For Lazarus, the biblical expression for the conjunction of divine command

and the moral law is "You shall be holy, for I the LORD your God am holy" (Lev. 19:2). God does not say "you shall be holy because I will it" or "... because I command it." God's own being as holiness is morality. "The fundamental teaching of Judaism runs: because the moral is divine, therefore shall you be moral and because the divine is moral, therefore shall you be become like God ... The highest form and the final end of all human life is imitatio dei (*Gottähnlichkeit*)."[68] The being or nature (*Wesen*) of God is not an object of biblical or rabbinic speculation. What we are given instead is God's holiness, and holiness is explicated by moral attributes. The call to holiness is a call to participate in the creative power of the moral world-order; a call to bring about the fulfillment of the purpose of creation.

Like Cohen, Lazarus wants to hold onto a traditional way of speaking but also to demythologize the texts he explicates. The holy God is the "primordial form of all morality" (*Urgestalt aller Sittlichkeit*). As much as he invokes "God" as the giver of the moral law, "God" also seems to be nothing more than the Jews' way of speaking about "the idea of the Good," "the Spirit of morality" (*Geist der Sittlichkeit*).[69] Similarly, the concept of revelation is deflated into the deliverances of moral reason. Long before the revelation of commandments at Sinai, Abraham kept the entirety of the law (*Mishnah Kiddushin* 4:14), which he attained through his own reason.[70] Autonomous moral reason is thus the source of moral instruction. Given his penchant for modernist demythologization, what role other than a notional one does Lazarus reserve for God and His holiness? The answer is that God and religion provide a conceptual framework which does not infringe the independence and self-sufficiency of ethics (*Selbstständigkeit des Ethischen*) but rather contributes a sharpening (*Einschärfung*) of its authority. Ethics does not derive its authority from God. We are, rather, to take the self-sufficient ethics which our reason discovers and dedicate our lives to the furtherance of ethics *for the sake of ethics*. We imagine this autonomous, self-sacrificial, total commitment as dedication to God, the highest possible object of our intentionality.[71] Our ethical intentions thereby never serve our mere self-interest. As a Kantian, Lazarus eschews any prudential or hedonistic ground for ethics, insofar as it would compromise the majesty and freedom of the ethical realm. Our moral aloofness from the pursuit of self-interest, which attests to the objectivity and universality of the moral law, is also given a vivid portrayal in the notion of a sovereign God.

The idea of holiness, the hallowing of all of life, is the master principle of Jewish ethics. "Holiness means nothing other than the complete ethicization [*Versittlichung*] of human society, of humanity as such."[72] The principle of holiness directs us to take life seriously and to identify those values which we ought to take with utmost seriousness. In Judaism's construal of holiness, we find two domains: the ritual and the ethical per se. For Lazarus, the ritual domain – expressed in the numerous biblical *ḥuqim*, which he calls, following nineteenth-century Reform usage, "ceremonial laws" – is not moral per se but nonetheless serves a moral telos. The ritual laws build a notional world on top of the natural world such that they remind the Jews that they belong both to the natural world and to something beyond. Insofar as the ritual laws order and transform natural human functions, such as eating or resting, they have a broad pedagogic role; they are pointers toward both nature and transcendence.[73] The ethical and the religious are inextricably intertwined. Neither concept is fully intelligible without the other in Judaism, although it is clear that the concept of the religious, of religious holiness, is dependent upon the concept of ethics, of ethical holiness. Ethical holiness has its own abstract self-sufficiency. An integrated, flourishing human life, however, requires that ethical holiness be enacted within the framework of religious holiness. Why? Because although we can give ourselves fully to the life of morality, we cannot fully cognize the sublime mystery (*erhabenes Geheimnis*), that is, the divine, at the heart of that life.[74] For Lazarus, it seems, the fully flourishing life is a life cognizant of that mystery. Religion, Judaism, brings us to the conceptual boundary at which the mystery can be acknowledged.

Mention has already been made of Hermann Cohen, a founder of the philosophical movement (Neo-Kantianism) which restored Kant to primacy in late nineteenth century Germany. (This in turn set the stage for Phenomenology, which in turn helped to produce, and was eclipsed by, Existentialism.) Cohen, unlike Lazarus, has had a long afterlife; works continue to be written about his thought and, more importantly, works are written that are inspired by his thought.[75] He is undoubtedly the more profound, systematic, and methodologically rigorous thinker of the two. Yet, from a distance, his basic tendency is not much different from Lazarus's. He too seeks to demythologize God, to deflate the idea of revelation, to intertwine religion as closely as possible with ethics. Like Lazarus, he seeks to give religion a qualified independence, an irreducible conceptual role to play, but the role serves an ethical telos. Like Lazarus, holiness is a pivotal concept for Cohen.

Cohen's approach, developed in Chapters VI and VII of the *Religion of Reason out of the Sources of Judaism*, completely eliminates the possibility of holiness as an empirical property. Following standard nineteenth-century biblical scholarship and anthropology, Cohen takes "holy" to designate the separation between some special (i.e. holy) objects and profane ones. The sense of holiness as separation, as Rudolf Otto and Mircea Eliade never tire of pointing out, is foundational to religious consciousness cross-culturally. For Cohen, holiness qua separation is available in polytheism as well as monotheism.[76] For Jewish monotheism, however, holiness means morality. It means a task. This makes it sound as if the holy is identical to the (merely) moral, but Cohen, far more than Lazarus, builds in a significant theological dimension. Holiness is the *being* of God and the task and action – the *becoming* – of man. To say that holiness is the being of God should not imply that, even for God, holiness is a static, inherent property. Rather, holiness is a mode of action – Cohen references here God's "attributes of action," Maimonides' term of art for the attributes enumerated in Exodus 34:6–7. Holiness refers not to God's "metaphysical causality" – something about which we cannot have any knowledge – but to his "purposive acting."[77] Holiness is the ensemble of all the attributes of action which form the purpose of God and hence of humanity.

Cohen draws from this a surprising, paradoxical implication: *God's holiness only exists because of man's task.* He thus takes to an extreme the theme of God's own holiness depending on man's instantiation of it in the world. Morality is a "correlation" of God and man (*not* a separation). Holiness qua morality is correlation, the exact opposite of the originally crude sense of the Hebrew root for "holy" (*k-d-sh*) as separation. In both cases, the root still designates a form of relation but Cohen turns the tables on the anthropologists, seeing the correlation with God, the transcendent ideal, as the primary meaning of "holy," and separation as a degenerate form of the concept. This accords well with Cohen's overall demythologizing strategy. "Primitive" religious contents are idealized by him and reclaimed for a pervasively ethical philosophical theology.

"Correlation" is a central philosophical term for Cohen. The concept of correlation functions for Cohen like God functions for Kant.[78] That is, God glues together the order of causality (nature) with the order of freedom (morality). Kant needs God to give some support to the law of freedom, to ensure that nature is ultimately a realm that can acknowledge our desert as pursuers of the moral law. We have and can have no proof that God created the world, but ethics, for Kant, requires that we adopt some crucial theistic views to support moral progress. Similarly Cohen needs correlation to support the transcendental objectivity of ethics. It is very important to Cohen that ethics has an objective (emphatically non-natural) basis.[79] The moral law originates in thought per se. (Cohen is, after all, a philosophical idealist.) Ethics has being – at the level of thinking – but not yet existence. Ethics is the "ought to be," that which must be brought into existence from its a priori original condition. Correlation designates a relationship between ideas, the ideas of God and man. To think of morality as emulation of the holiness of God gives morality, as in Lazarus, dignity and urgency. The idea that links the holiness of God with the task of humanity is the holy spirit.

Cohen devotes an entire chapter of *Religion of Reason* to the holy spirit. He equates the holy spirit with a capacity for continuous renewal within man such that man can overcome a burdensome sense of sin and progress infinitely in morality. This continuously renewing will to the infinite task is the holy spirit. It is precisely that which correlates man and God. "The holy spirit is fully as much the spirit of man as the spirit of God."[80] Holiness is reciprocal (that is, correlated): God is made holy through man; man is made holy through God. This is not about substance and property; it is about relation and status, an infinite process of becoming, of existentiation. The holy spirit, like ethics per se, is not factual. It is not a feature of nature or of a "spiritual" realm that apes nature without being natural. The being of the holy spirit is the being of value. These are transcendental ideas that originate and guide thought and action.

Cohen eschews any neo-Platonic, Christian, or mystical mediation or substantive connection between God and man through holiness. The holy spirit has no being other than the being of value. Cohen would find Luzzatto's system, as desirable as its applied ethics might be, deeply confused. Correlation has a purely conceptual sense. The link between the divine and the human is an idea; the idea of value. (Indeed, the divine per se is an idea.) Any sensuous or experiential link is polytheism and pantheism, which for Cohen signify the death of the objectively normative. Judaism, like Kant, entails the discovery of practical reason – of reason as the revelation of morality, which is categorically different from reason applied theoretically to nature.[81] Thus, to know God has nothing to do with knowing about a putative object in the world, however mysterious. Knowledge of God can only mean the knowledge of ethics.[82]

Holiness becomes human insofar as the holy spirit is the spirit of moral action. Ethics is the constitutive spirit of man. All conceptual problems of the divine become problems for ethics, for practical reason. God and man are unified, as it were, in the correlation that is holiness/ethics. Holiness is, in a way, completely mundane; one might even say profane. It is not an elevated state of knowledge or action; it is only the task and ideal of action, to be pursued in patience and humility daily. Cohen, like Lazarus, writes long after the age of miracles has passed. His work is premised on a thoroughly rational disenchantment of the world. The world is known through science. Philosophy, in its non-ethical deployment, is a theory of logic which explains how science is possible. Ethics is a transcendental inquiry that explains how moral normativity is possible. It explains how normativity comes to reside in cultural phenomena such as law and the state or, for our purposes, Judaism.

In Cohen's later years he was increasingly taken up by problems of religion. It is generally acknowledged today that Cohen's *Religion of Reason* does not break from his systematic, general philosophical *Ethics* in the way that Franz Rosenzweig thought that it did. Rosenzweig wanted to make Cohen rather more of an existentialist than he was. The claim was that the *Religion* gave prominence to the problems of the individual I, with its feelings of estrangement from God, yearning for acceptance by God, puzzlement at the fact of other individuals in the world and so on. For Cohen, one of the chief impulses of Jewish ethics is to turn the stranger, the one next to me (*Nebenmensch*), into a brother, a moral subject (*Mitmensch*). Furthermore, like Kant of the second *Critique* or of the *Groundwork of the Metaphysics of Morals*, Cohen insists on a teleological horizon for ethics – a kingdom of ends as a categorical, regulative idea of moral action. For Cohen, this is the messianic age. The prophetic discovery of the humanity and equality of all human persons and of the telos of history emerge from the "sources of Judaism" to substantiate Judaism's claim to be a religion of reason. These ideas are anchored in Cohen's earlier work and highlighted in the *Religion*.

Both Lazarus and Cohen are far from a naïve traditionalism which takes on faith the historical revelation of the Torah. They are children of an age post-Spinoza working arduously to rescue Judaism from cultured despisal and scientific illegitimacy. Lazarus builds ethics to a degree on natural sentiment, as is fitting for an early psychologist. Cohen repudiates any whiff of naturalism and builds ethics on self-originating, self-legislating rationality. Such idealism, however critical and anti-speculative, fell out of favor as the twentieth century progressed. Rationality per se, it is proposed today, is an evolutionary mechanism explicable along Darwinian lines.[83] Even so, one wants to assert the continuing distinction between causes and reasons. Whatever the origins of ethics in our primate past, the case for *justifying* the morality of one thought or act over another cannot be made on biological grounds.[84] It must be made on moral grounds. A morality may take naturalistic criteria (contra Cohen) into account but it is not reducible to them. A view like Cohen's or Kant's, which guards the distinction between causes and reasons, will always have a point but that point might be taken too far. Arguably, Cohen was guilty of just such an over-extension. Nonetheless, his work stands as a great monument to the aspirations of modern Jewry for a rigorously philosophical yet deeply reverent reappropriation of the Jewish ethical tradition.

Into Late Modernity

Already in Cohen's lifetime the torch of Jewish thought was being passed to a more romantic, experientially oriented generation of thinkers. The infamous trenches of the Great War brought more than the defeat of the Kaiser's Reich; it brought a vast disillusionment with the proud synthesis of faith and culture that constituted German-Jewish religious liberalism. Franz Rosenzweig scathingly called the intellectual products of the synthesis "atheistic theology."[85] What was proposed in its place was a new, less mediated encounter with the living God of Israel. Rosenzweig himself created a highly abstract system of philosophy which sought to overturn the speculative excesses and pretensions of German Idealism, albeit one which, despite its intentions, succumbs to some of them.[86] The timeless living encounter between God and the People of Israel entails a way for Rosenzweig to reclaim, at least in principle, the practice of Jewish law. Although Rosenzweig is not an ethical thinker as such, his work secures a theoretical grounding for normative Jewish practice. This has ethical consequences. Rosenzweig, as a modernist, does not affirm an historical revelation of the Torah at Sinai. (He too is a child of Spinoza.) But he does affirm an ongoing availability of the divine, a continuous revelation, which is constituted in the reality of love between God and Israel. The divine–human intimacy holds out the possibility that every law (*Gesetz*) of God can become a commandment (*Gebot*) for man in the sense of a personally felt, authentically enacted deed.[87] Although the observance of many of the commandments still waits under the sign of the "not yet," in principle all of them await fulfillment if only the individual Jew is open to the reality of divine presence. Rosenzweig's non-Orthodox traditionalism provided a powerful model for his compatriots, as well as for post-World War II Jewish existentialists who sought a way back to the tradition.

A different approach to the normative authority of the tradition was taken by Rosenzweig's older friend and collaborator, Martin Buber. His childhood among Ḥasidim notwithstanding, as an adult Buber never warmed to the practice of traditional rabbinic Judaism. As a theorist of religion, he saw law – or ethics for that matter – as an obstacle to an unmediated encounter with the divine. Law and morality are what remain of a living encounter after its momentary intensity has lapsed. Buber reclaims the Bible as a record of encounter (the so-called "I-Thou relationship") and urges a radical openness to the Bible as an antidote to the alienation of modern humanity.[88] But no ethic emerges from this stance. To be open to the other as a "Thou," to encounter the other's unique personhood, does not necessarily mean that one treats the other in a moral way after the moment of encounter. Indeed, there is a "sublime melancholy" to the human condition in that every Thou is destined to become an "it"; to elide back into the "It world," the world of ordinary use, exchange, and sociality. The I-Thou encounter is not a moral principle, like the second formulation of the Categorical Imperative to treat all persons as ends rather than as means. Nor is it precisely a description of an event. To an extent it is the invocation of a state of being. "I-Thou" in Buber's formulation is a "word" that one speaks with one's whole being. It is a deed or the quality of a deed. (I-It is a word that one speaks as a fragmented, non-integrated being.[89]) This says something about authenticity, about how to be authentically in the world which in turn suggests the normative valuation of ways of being. But this pulls against Buber's own categories.

Buber has perhaps what used to be called a situation ethics. With his emphasis on authenticity, one needs to be open to the situation in which one finds oneself. One must determine, situation by situation, the needs of the hour for oneself, for others, for God. Life is a "narrow ridge" where great poise and agility are required to keep from falling into inauthentic, dogmatic, inappropriate responses to the radical novelty of each situation.[90] Although this stance sounds entirely personal (and hence apolitical) and antinomian (and thus suitable only for the private and not the public realm), Buber often writes about social life. He was of a generation that was much impressed by Toennies's distinction between "community" and "society," a face-to-face realm that supports human flourishing vs. a mechanical mass-industrial society with all of its impersonal, presumably life-deadening woes. Buber's philosophy is always directed toward the rejuvenation of the public realm, not toward the personal ecstasy of the individual's transcendent I-Thou encounter. Along these lines, Buber mined the Jewish tradition for teachings that supported his vision of a good society marked by justice in human relations and openness to the Thou, both human and divine. His books on the Bible and imaginative translations of ḥasidic stories – the means by which many German-speaking Jews discovered something of the world of the Ḥasidim – are in this sense replete with moral perspective. Both Buber and Rosenzweig are good examples of thinkers who don't fit into the modern pigeon hole of "ethics" but whose works are pregnant with moral insight and imagination.

A thinker of the post-war period who deals with ethics much more forthrightly is Emmanuel Levinas. Levinas was born and raised in Kovno, Lithuania, a city in which Salanter had lived and worked. His upbringing was traditional, but not strictly Orthodox. He sought a university education in France, crossing the border into Germany to attend lectures by Edmund Husserl, with whom he became friendly, and Martin Heidegger. He was interned in a prisoner of war camp during World War II, his French army uniform having saved him from deportation to a death camp. Throughout his life, rather in the manner of Hermann Cohen, Levinas was engaged in both philosophical writing and teaching at the highest level of sophistication within his Continental philosophical idiom and in Jewish affairs. He gave a weekly lecture in his Paris synagogue, studied the Talmud regularly, lectured annually on the Talmud to a perennial conclave of French-speaking Jewish intellectuals, wrote on Jewish texts, themes, and affairs, and produced a philosophical oeuvre that fits within the traditions of both European thought and Jewish thought.

Levinas wants to make ethics "first philosophy." He wants to critique, somewhat like Rosenzweig, the entire Western tradition that runs, in Rosenzweig's phrase, "from Ionia to Jena" (Jena was the German city where Hegel lived for a time). Western thought has been riveted to questions of being, truth, and the rational cognition of the whole, to "totality," in Levinas's phrase. Its great scientific achievements notwithstanding, however, totalizing Western thought has done great damage to the human person.

There is a link between the aspiration to know the truth in its presumed rational totality and the great totalitarian schemes of subjugation and control which gave the twentieth century its peculiar menace. Levinas seeks a standpoint outside of totality, the standpoint of "infinity," and this he finds in ethics, in a good which we encounter with shattering immediacy in the face of the other. This is not a good to be conceptualized, to be subordinated to the scheme of totality; it is an infinite responsibility for the other to be lived. To get a sense of the radical depth of the role Levinas assigns to ethics, consider the words of one of his most acute scholars and followers, Richard Cohen:

> For Levinas … ethics is anything but abstract; indeed, it is an excessive immediacy and concreteness. It is the excessive immediacy and concreteness of human relationship, the face-to-face encounter. Levinas is careful not to say that humans first relate to one another and *then* can relate to one another ethically. Ethics is not a gloss on a prior reality, is not a second-order experience. What Levinas is saying, to the contrary, is that the *human* first emerges in the ethical face-to-face. The human emerges not as a genus or as the specification of a genus, but as responsibility for the other. Only in ethical relation does one encounter the other person as *other* and not as a role or mask in an historical play of behaviors. Thus the *real* also emerges from the ethical relation.[91]

There are echoes of Martin Buber here but Levinas criticizes Buber for the symmetry or mutuality held to obtain between the I and the Thou. For Levinas, the encounter with the other generates an infinite responsibility of the self toward the other. There is no mutuality, only, as Salanter's disciple Simḥah Zissel puts it, "bearing the yoke of one's friend" albeit ad infinitum.

Levinas's thought arises from a critique of Heidegger and Western ontology and metaphysics. That is its negative impulse. But it has a positive source and contribution as well; these issue from its Judaic side. Again, the words of Richard Cohen:

> Opposing the primacy of knowledge, Levinas opposes all that is Greek. Against intellectual history's various formulations of the Socratic dictum that "one must know the good to do the good," the ethical priorities of Levinas's thought recall the altogether different priority expressed in the famous response of the Jewish people at Mount Sinai: "We will do and we will listen." Thus Levinas's entire philosophy can be understood as but another layer of meaning attached to Sinai, another interpretation – the priority of the other, conscientiousness before consciousness, ethics before reason – exalting and penetrating to the heart of one of the greatest moments in the religious history of the world.[92]

It is appealing to see Levinas as a great avatar of the Jewish tradition of philosophical ethics. He both uses Western philosophy and strips it of its pretensions, domesticating reason to a revelation of moral value before which it must stand in humility and awe. This is thought to be the voice of Jerusalem, a call to ethical life that cannot quite be validated by reason alone. A revelation is needed, if not at Sinai then in the naked face of the other. Of course, as a modernist, Levinas breaks crucially with classical Judaism as well. He relativizes revelation, rejects theodicy, ethicizes election, and removes God, like Cohen and Buber, from the context of metaphysical discussion to a framework of radical ethics. Substantively, it is hard to reconcile Levinas's stress on our infinite responsibility to the other with the halakhic tradition of regulated responsibility to the other. Granted my obligation to give *tzedakah* (loosely translated as "charity") to support the poor – to care for the other who is before me – I have no halakhic obligation to impoverish myself on his behalf. There is a limit. How does Levinas's infinity relate to the bounded construction of responsibility in the halakha? It is also difficult to know what to make of the hard disjunction between reason and ethics. The covenant, which grounds the concrete responsibilities of Jews, was entered into on the basis of reasons. Levinas's global critique of rationality, a staple of modern Continental philosophy after Nietzsche, seems troublesome on Jewish, let alone philosophical, grounds. Nonetheless, one would not want to diminish Levinas's synthetic achievement or be blind to the infusion of energy into Jewish moral philosophy inspired by the study of his work.[93]

In the late twentieth and early twenty-first centuries, writing on Jewish ethics both popular and scholarly flourishes. There is a long and steady stream of books on diverse topics in applied ethics. Business ethics, biomedical ethics, the ethics of labor relations, gender, and sexuality attract the attention of popularizing Orthodox authors as well as Conservative, Reform, and other writers. The moral dilemmas attending modern medicine, such as the definition of death, the duties of doctors (and patients), use of life-prolonging equipment, organ transplantation, abortion, cosmetic surgery, and other topics, meet with halakhically oriented analyses from across the ideological spectrum. A literature is also emerging on cloning, stem cells, and other cutting-edge biotechnologies. A uniquely Israeli contribution to contemporary applied Jewish ethics may be found in an unfortunately inescapable topic in the Israeli reality, the ethics of war. This is a field that Jewish moral philosophy, with the exception of Maimonides, did not have much reason to treat. Works on the historic attitudes of Jews toward violence as well as on the ethics of contemporary battlefield conditions are now available. An immensely popular topic is the cluster of issues dealing with social inequality, income distribution, economic opportunity, health care equity, capital punishment, and such dimensions of public concern as environmental stewardship and political ethics. Within the Orthodox world, in particular, books continue to be written that extol and instruct in traditional values, social roles, family models, and character formation. In short, there is continuity with historic concerns and frameworks of Jewish ethics as well as expansion and application to new domains. In terms of sheer volume of publication, the contemporary period may be a golden age for Jewish ethics.

On the philosophical side, there has been a renewal of the kind of work pioneered by Hermann Cohen. The Jewish thought of the postwar decades was largely shaped by religious existentialism. With the passing of that paradigm, Jewish philosophers have gone back to figures like Maimonides and to the modern rationalists most determined to continue his project. Major figures in contemporary Jewish philosophical ethics include Lenn Goodman, David Novak and Kenneth Seeskin. Like Cohen, they are academic philosophers who work at the highest level of technical philosophical expertise, as well as Jewish erudition and commitment. Drawing more from the existentialist tradition is the Reform moral theologian, Eugene Borowitz. In the Orthodox world, serious moral philosophers include the late Walter Wurzburger, Michael Wyschogrod, David Hartman, and the Chief Rabbi of Britain, Lord Jonathan Sacks. The Conservative movement boasts Elliot Dorff, whose work addresses both academic and popular audiences. Theological and moral recasting of Judaism in the light of feminist concerns has also proliferated. The works of thinkers such as Judith Plaskow and Rachel Adler are notable contributions. In addition to these philosophically and theologically oriented contributors to Jewish ethics, one must note the work of Louis Newman, whose philosophical studies of Jewish ethics have tried to bring some conceptual clarity to the literature as a whole.

To think about ethics is to think about, Levinas notwithstanding, larger conceptual wholes of which ethics forms a part. As Hermann Cohen wrote, ethics is a "Lehre vom Menschen," a teaching about human beings. It is also, for Jews, a teaching about God, about the relationship between God and human beings, about the relationship among human beings at various levels, and about the relationship between human beings and the natural world that sustains them. Any inquiry into ethics branches out into unanticipated domains of ideas. Jewish thought, by refusing to segregate ethics into a discrete sphere, a "morality system," welcomes the intellectual adventure of moral inquiry. The one exception to this may be the rather positivistic, contemporary halakhic kind of writing that treats moral problems exclusively as legal ones, and that within a system that can generate definitive (although typically contested) answers. The spirit of pre-modern Jewish ethics, which wedded halakha to virtue and to reflective exploration of ultimate meanings and purposes, is much needed today. While treatments of biomedical problems, for example, abound, one meets with fewer truly philosophical explorations of the human significance of sickness, health, healing, and death. Profound thinkers such as Hans Jonas and Leon Kass bring a Jewish sensibility to such explorations but do not fully integrate their work into the Jewish moral tradition. A reappropriation of the whole tradition of Jewish ethics in its aretaic–deontic and narrative dimensions might advance a greater conceptual holism.

The concerns with which we began this chapter, whether values hang in the air and whether the world is "hard" and indifferent to our conviction of the ineluctable significance of value, cannot easily be resolved. Jewish thinkers in the modernist mode have tried to respond to these fundamental challenges. Jewish thinkers in the traditionalist mode sometimes ignore them. But perhaps they do not. Perhaps their very persistence as traditional Jews affirming a time-honored, morally rigorous way of life gives a tacit testimony to an imperishable moral vision. The vision is that of a covenantal partnership between what is ultimate and what is fleeting. The fleeting cannot perceive the ultimate, but is guided by it. That guidance, however we construe its nature, dictates, status, and implications, is what we mean by Jewish ethics.

Notes

1 Alasdair MacIntyre, *After Virtue*, p. 39.
2 For an entrée into scholarly treatments which make the facile opposition of tradition and modernity problematic, see S. N. Eisenstadt, "Post-Traditional Societies and the Continuity and Reconstruction of Tradition," *Daedalus*, Winter (1973), pp. 1–27 and Edward Shils, *Tradition* (Chicago: University of Chicago Press, 1981).
3 Christine M. Korsgaard, *The Sources of Normativity* (Cambridge: Cambridge University Press, 1996), p. 4.
4 The reasons for the expulsion from the community were nowhere stated and remain an object of scholarly inquiry. Nor was the ban as absolute as its promulgators might have hoped; Spinoza continued to have contact with Dutch Jews throughout his subsequent life. The community likely offered Spinoza multiple opportunities to save face, as they did to others accused of heresy. For a study of the incident and its aftermath, see Richard Popkin, "Spinoza's Excommunication," in Heidi M. Ravven and Lenn E. Goodman, eds, *Jewish Themes in Spinoza's Philosophy* (Albany: SUNY Press, 2002), Chapter X.
5 An excellent study of Spinoza's political thought – and of how his other works bear on his political thought – may be found in Steven B. Smith, *Spinoza, Liberalism and the Question of Jewish Identity* (New Haven: Yale University Press, 1997). For Spinoza's political distinctiveness vis-à-vis other modern founders, see Chapter V.
6 For the full complexity of Spinoza's relationship to Maimonides, a long-contested topic in scholarship, see Warren Zev Harvey, "A Portrait of Spinoza as a Maimonidean," *Journal of the History of Philosophy*, Vol. 19 (1981), pp. 151–172.
7 Smith, Spinoza, *Liberalism and the Jewish Question*, p. 60.

8 Benedict Spinoza, *Theological Political Treatise*, trans. R. H. M. Elwes, in *The Chief Works of Benedict de Spinoza*, trans. R. H. M. Elwes (New York: Dover Publications, 1951), Chapter V, p. 76.

9 *Theological-Political Treatise*, Chapter II, p. 27.

10 See, for example, *Theological-Political Treatise*, Chapter VII, p. 101: "We are at work not on the truth of passages, but solely on their meaning." Our effort to redeem biblical statements by justifying their truth content – the typical concern of a pious exegete – should be abandoned in favor of fixing the meaning of the statement in its ancient setting.

11 *Theological-Political Treatise*, Chapter XIII.

12 Lenn Goodman, "What does Spinoza's Ethics Contribute to Jewish Philosophy?" in Ravven and Goodman, *Jewish Themes in Spinoza's Philosophy*, p. 50.

13 Ravven and Goodman, *Jewish Themes in Spinoza's Philosophy*, p. 24.

14 Isaiah Tishby, *Messianic Mysticism: Moses Hayim Luzzatto and the Padua School*, trans. Morris Hoffman (Oxford: Littman Library of Jewish Civilization, 2008), Chapter 3.

15 Tishby, *Messianic Mysticism*. See the Introduction by Joseph Dan, p. xxiv.

16 Dan, *Sifrut Ha-Musar v'ha-Drush*, p. 249.

17 There are two English translations of *Mesillat Yesharim*. The text I am using here is Moshe Chayim Luzzatto, *The Path of the Just*, trans. Shraga Silverstein (New York: Feldheim, 1990), p. 5. An older translation by Mordecai M. Kaplan, with introduction by the translator, is Moses Hayyim Luzzatto, *Mesilat Yesharim: The Path of the Upright* (Philadelphia: Jewish Publication Society, 1966). Kaplan's Introduction is of some interest for his observations on the nature of Jewish ethics vis-à-vis philosophical ethics, as well as his consignment of Luzzatto to an irretrievable "Jewish medieval" past: "But, though the *Mesillat Yesharim* is not likely to be read for purposes of edification, it should at least be read among other books of a similar character for the purpose of acquiring a knowledge of the ethical ideals that actuated the inner life of the Jewish people in the past" (p. xiii). Kaplan's historicism is very much against the spirit of the present inquiry.

18 Note Leo Strauss's brief but penetrating analysis of the meaning of method in early modernity in Leo Strauss, "Progress or Return? The Contemporary Crisis in Western Civilization," *Modern Judaism*, Vol. 1, No. 1 (May, 1981), p. 25.

19 Luzzatto, *The Path of the Just*, p. 7. One difference between a traditional religious moralist and a modern moral theorist is surely the unquestioned faith in moral realism of the traditionalist. Luzzatto calls for a rational, introspective inquiry into one's moral motivation. Habit is not enough; awareness of one's divine source must be attained. A divine reality backstops norms. When this dimension falls out, as in Michael Oakeshott, for example, the call to inquire into conduct, to subject it to rational scrutiny, is rejected as an invitation to nihilism. Norms *ought* to be taken for granted because once one questions their normativity one sees that the emperor is no longer wearing any clothes. See Michael Oakeshott, "The Tower of Babel," in Michael Oakeshott, *Rationalism in Politics* (Indianapolis: Liberty Fund, 1991), pp. 465–487.

20 Luzzatto, *The Path of the Just*, p. 17.

21 Luzzatto, *The Path of the Just*, p. 17.

22 Luzzatto, *The Path of the Just*, p. 19.

23 Luzzatto, *The Path of the Just*, p. 21.

24 Luzzatto, *The Path of the Just*, p. 25.

25 Luzzatto, *The Path of the Just*, p. 329.

26 Luzzatto, *The Path of the Just*, p. 327.

27 For a selection of his general philosophical work in English, see Moses Mendelssohn, *Philosophical Writings*, ed. Daniel O. Dahlstrom (Cambridge: Cambridge University Press, 1997).

28 Moses Mendelssohn, *Jerusalem or On Religious Power and Judaism*, trans. Allan Arkush (Waltham: Brandeis University Press, 1983), p. 41.

29 Mendelssohn, *Jerusalem*, p. 45.

30 Mendelssohn, *Jerusalem*, p. 129.

31 Mendelssohn, *Jerusalem*, p. 119. By "speculative knowledge of religion" Mendelssohn means only the rational truths of natural religion.

32 Mendelssohn, *Jerusalem*, p. 23. This point is made by Prof. Alexander Altmann in the Introduction.

33 Mendelssohn, *Jerusalem*, p. 133.

34 For an approach that integrates Mendelssohn's Jewish work with his general philosophical theory, see Nathan Rotenstreich, *Jewish Philosophy in Modern Times: From Mendelssohn to Rosenzweig* (New York: Holt, Rinehart and Winston, 1968), Chapter I.

35 Moses Mendelssohn, *Philosophical Writings*, p. 296.

36 In the "Rhapsody," Mendelssohn states: "As far as pleasant sentiments are concerned, they are an effect of perfection, a gift of heaven inseparable from knowledge and from the choice of the good ... In the soul, a pleasant sentiment is nothing other than *the clear but indistinct intuiting of perfection* ..." Moses Mendelssohn, *Philosophical Writings*, p. 151.

37 Moses Mendelssohn, *Philosophical Writings*, p. 297.

38 Moses Mendelssohn, *Philosophical Writings*, p. 166.

39 Dan, *Mysticism and Ethics*, p. 116.

40 A classic anthology of original texts and translations of ethical wills, first published in 1926, remains in print. See Israel Abrahams, *Hebrew Ethical Wills* (Philadelphia: Jewish Publication Society, 2006).

41 *Tzvaat Ha-Ribash*, found in *Tzvaot v'Hanhagot me-Ha-Ribash v'Talmidav* (*Testaments and Manuals of Practice of the Ribash and his Students*) (Bene Brak: n.p., 1986), p. 19. All translations from this text are my own.

42 Gershom Scholem, "*Devekut* or Communion with God," cited in Gershon David Hundert, ed., *Essential Papers on Ḥasidism* (New York: New York University Press, 1991), p. 287.

43 An interesting constraint on the practice of *hitbodedut* is found in para. 65. "If he wants to practice *hitbodedut*, it is necessary for a companion to be with him. One person alone is in danger. There should be two persons in one room and each should be alone (*yitboded*) with the Creator, may He be blessed." Here withdrawal remains radically atomized but is also supported by a social structure.

44 Scholem, "*Devekut*," p. 287.

45 *Tzvaat Ha-Ribash*, p. 12, para. 29.

46   *Tzvaat Ha-Ribash*, p. 13, para. 30.

47   *Tzvaat Ha-Ribash*, p. 8, para. 5.

48   *Tzvaat Ha-Ribash*, p. 10, para. 13.

49   *Tzvaat Ha-Ribash*, p. 8, para. 7; cf. p. 25, para. 90.

50   See, for example, *Tzvaat Ha-Ribash*, para. 22 on *zerizut*, alertness or liveliness. On the avoidance of sadness and the imperative of joy, see para. 49.

51   Scholem, "Devekut," p. 291. For an example of the acceptance of *katnut* and a procedure to transcend it, see para. 154 in *Tzvaat Ha-Ribash*.

52   See the Introduction to Salanter's Musar Epistle (*Iggeret Ha-Musar*) written by his disciple, Rabbi Isaac Blaser, for a sharp enunciation of this critique. The epistle, in addition to Salanter's other published letters, may be found in Israel Lipkin Salanter, *Or Yisrael*, ed. Issac Blaser (Jerusalem: n.p., 1997), p. 2. A comprehensive English translation of Salanter's works may be found in Zvi Miller, trans., *Ohr Yisrael: The Classic Writings of Rav Yisrael Salanter* (Southfield, MI: Targum Press, 2004). Two excellent studies of Salanter's work and thought are Immanuel Etkes, *Rabbi Israel Salanter and the Mussar Movement: Seeking the Torah of Truth*, trans. Jonathan Chipman (Philadelphia: Jewish Publication Society, 1993) and Hillel Goldberg, *Israel Salanter: The Ethics and Theology of an Early Psychologist of the Unconscious* (New York: Ktav, 1982).

53   Etkes, *Rabbi Israel Salanter and the Mussar Movement*, p. 15. For an echo of the opposition to Salanter in the yeshiva world of the nineteenth century, see Rabbi Joseph Soloveitchik's principled, philosophical rejection of musar in Joseph Soloveitchik, *Halakhic Man*, trans. Lawrence Kaplan (Philadelphia: Jewish Publication Society, 1983), p. 74.

54   See Etkes, *Rabbi Israel Salanter and the Mussar Movement*, p. 132. Salanter discusses *hitpa'alut* in Letter Six of *Or Yisrael*.

55   From the Musar Epistle (para. 19), cited and translated in Goldberg, *Israel Salanter*, p. 84.

56   For a nuanced, thorough fleshing-out of Salanter's anthropology across all the periods of his creativity, see Goldberg, *Israel Salanter*, especially Chapter Two which explores Salanter's initial terminology and conception.

57   Salanter, *Or Yisrael*, Letter One, p. 63.

58   Salanter, *Or Yisrael*, p. 144; Musar Epistle, para. 20.

59   Salanter, *Or Yisrael*, p. 145 Musar Epistle, para. 21.

60   Goldberg, *Israel Salanter*, p. 83.

61   David Baumgardt, "The Ethics of Lazarus and Steinthal," *Leo Baeck Institute Yearbook*, 1957, Vol. 2, p. 216.

62   The secondary literature on Lazarus is scant, a sign of his neglect in favor of more rigorous philosophers like Cohen or more charismatic ones like Buber and Rosenzweig. On Lazarus, see Nathan Rotenstreich, *Jewish Philosophy in Modern Times*, Chapter III; David Baumgardt, "The Ethics of Lazarus and Steinthal," *Leo Baeck Institute Yearbook*, 1957, Vol. 2, pp. 205–217; and Heinz Moshe Graupe, *The Rise of Modern Judaism*, trans. John Robinson (Huntington, NY: Robert E. Krieger, 1978), pp. 239–242. For the original work under discussion here, see Moritz Lazarus, *Die Ethik des Judentums*, Vol. I (Frankfurt am Main: J. Kauffmann, 1898). This work was translated by Henrietta Szold and appeared in 1900 as Moritz Lazarus, *The Ethics of Judaism* (Philadelphia: JPS, 1900–1901).

63 Graupe, *The Rise of Modern Judaism*, p. 240.
64 As Baumgardt explains, Lazarus followed an early post-Kantian philosopher named Johann Friedrich Herbart. Herbart eschewed the speculative metaphysics of Fichte and Schelling. He provided a more congenial model for a moral philosophy, such as Lazarus's, that tried to remain anchored in empirical, psychological observation. See Baumgardt, "The Ethics of Lazarus and Steinthal," p. 205.
65 Rotenstreich, *Jewish Philosophy in Modern Times*, p. 46. The extent to which Kant divorces the noumenal moral law from the phenomenal condition of human psychology seems to me easy to exaggerate. See, for example, *The Metaphysics of Morals*, Part II, section XII where Kant discusses "concepts of what is presupposed on the part of feeling by the mind's receptivity to concepts of duty as such." See Kant, *The Metaphysics of Morals*, ed. Mary Gregor (Cambridge: Cambridge University Press, 1996), p. 159 ff.
66 Lazarus, *Die Ethik des Judentums*, Vol. I, p. 115.
67 Lazarus, *Die Ethik des Judentums*, Vol. I, p. 85. Translation my own.
68 Lazarus, *Die Ethik des Judentums*, Vol. I, p. 89. Translation my own.
69 Lazarus, *Die Ethik des Judentums*, Vol. I, pp. 89–90. Translation my own.
70 Lazarus, *Die Ethik des Judentums*, Vol. I, p. 91.
71 Lazarus, *Die Ethik des Judentums*, Vol. I, pp. 109–110.
72 Lazarus, *Die Ethik des Judentums*, Vol. I, p. 187 Translation my own.
73 Lazarus, *Die Ethik des Judentums*, Vol. I, pp. 191–192.
74 Lazarus, *Die Ethik des Judentums*, Vol. I, p. 196.
75 For the purposes of Jewish thought, Cohen's posthumous work, *Religion of Reason out of the Sources of Judaism*, is the most important text. See Hermann Cohen, *Religion of Reason out of the Sources of Judaism*, trans. Simon Kaplan, 2nd edn (Atlanta: Scholars Press, 1995). The introductory essays by Leo Strauss, Steven Schwarzschild, and Kenneth Seeskin are excellent guides to the study of Cohen. A translation of Cohen's monograph on the ethics of Maimonides is also available. See Hermann Cohen, *Ethics of Maimonides*, trans. Almut Bruckstein (Madison: University of Wisconsin Press, 2004). This volume also contains a helpful running commentary by Bruckstein, which relates Cohen's arguments to current philosophical concerns. The best single source for a study of the entirety of Cohen's work, general philosophical and Jewish, is Andrea Poma, *The Critical Philosophy of Hermann Cohen*, trans. John Denton (Albany: SUNY Press, 1997). On Cohen's untranslated systematic work, *Ethik des Reinen Willens* (Ethics of Pure Will), see Robert Gibbs, ed., *Hermann Cohen's Ethics* (Leiden: Brill, 2006). Contemporary Jewish philosophy in the spirit of Hermann Cohen can be found in the work of Kenneth Seeskin, e.g. in his *Autonomy in Jewish Philosophy*, noted in Chapter 3.
76 Cohen, *Religion of Reason*, p. 96.
77 Cohen, *Religion of Reason*, p. 96.
78 Cohen, *Religion of Reason*, p. 98.
79 Cohen is fiercely anti-Aristotelian (and pro-Platonic). He reads Maimonides, for example, to be informed by Plato's teaching about the form of the Good, which enshrines the objectivity and universality of ethics, rather than by Aristotle's doctrines of character-based virtues and the mean by which they are measured.

He finds all versions of eudaemonism incompatible with ethics and with Judaism. See Cohen, *Ethics of Maimonides*, pp. 123–125.

80   Cohen, *Religion of Reason*, pp. 102–103.

81   Cohen, *Religion of Reason*, p. 106.

82   Cohen, *Religion of Reason*, p.109.

83   See, for example, Robert Nozick, *The Nature of Rationality* (Princeton: Princeton University Press, 1993), Chapter IV.

84   For a contemporary attempt to "biologize" ethics, see Frans De Waal, *Primates and Philosophers: How Morality Evolved* (Princeton: Princeton University Press, 2006). This line of thinking is opposed by John Dupre, *Human Nature and the Limits of Science* (Oxford: Oxford University Press, 2005). For an eloquent statement against scientific reductionism in the matter of morality and religion, see Thomas Nagel, *Secular Philosophy and the Religious Temperament* (New York: Oxford University Press, 2010).

85   Franz Rosenzweig, *Philosophical and Theological Writings*, ed. and trans. Michael Morgan and Paul W. Franks (Indianapolis: Hackett, 2000), p. 10.

86   Benjamin Pollock, *Franz Rosenzweig and the Systematic Task of Philosophy* (Cambridge: Cambridge University Press, 2009). Pollock foregrounds Rosenzweig's intention to construct *The Star of Redemption* as a systematic work of philosophy.

87   Franz Rosenzweig, *On Jewish Learning*, ed. Nahum N. Glatzer (Madison: University of Wisconsin Press, 2002), p. 85.

88   Martin Buber, *Israel and the World* (Syracuse: Syracuse University Press, 1997), p. 89 ff.

89   Martin Buber, *I and Thou*, trans. Walter Kaufmann (New York: Touchstone, 1996) Part I.

90   For Buber's use of this term, see Maurice Friedman, *Encounter on the Narrow Ridge: A Life of Martin Buber* (New York: Paragon House, 1991) pp. 43–46.

91   Richard A. Cohen, *Elevations: The Height of the Good in Rosenzweig and Levinas* (Chicago: University of Chicago Press, 1994), p. 124.

92   Cohen, *Elevations*, p. 127. Cohen is referring to Exodus 24:7, where Israel proclaims that it will "do" and then "hear" what is to be done. This is a locus classicus, going back to the Talmud (*B. Shabbat* 88a) for emphasizing the merit of Israel and its trust in God, as well as the alleged priority of "doing" over "knowing." To derive these lessons from the verse, however, requires that one read it out of context from its narrative. Within the narrative, at Exodus 24:3, Moses has already told the people what God requires of them – knowledge precedes consent.

93   See, for example, the constructive philosophy of another Levinas scholar, Robert Gibbs. Robert Gibbs, *Why Ethics? Signs of Responsibilities* (Princeton: Princeton University Press, 2000).

Conclusion

Without trying to force the many texts which we have considered into the straightjacket of a single pattern, it is clear that there are common themes and motifs. An equal concern for virtue and obligation, a strong interest in perfectionism, and the embrace of a monotheistic metaphysics on which to ground these concerns mark the texts. Of these, the first concern has the most salience today, at least among secular moral philosophers.

Traditional ethics, not only among Jews, saw no divergence between virtue and obligation. The Platonic and Aristotelian idea that justice was a virtue is remote, not only in time, from the Rawlsian idea that justice is a set of institutional arrangements in which everyone is treated fairly. There is no need for virtue under that dispensation, nor do some of the advocates of virtue place any stock in constitutional and legal arrangements. They are suspicious of presumptive universals such as "human rights" and of the political and moral cultures that purport to sustain them. The advocates of justice and its obligations may also have little patience for virtue. Liberal societies ought not to pry into the private lives of their citizens. While no one wants to live in Mandeville's beehive, Kantian constructivists like Rawls have often treated virtue (unlike Kant) with indifference. The reconciliation of these different paradigms, which naturally fell together for ancient and medieval thinkers, as well as for the Jewish tradition, takes great philosophical ingenuity today. Perhaps the living example of the historic continuity of Jewish ethics holds lessons for that quest.

What likely stands as a bar to appreciating the Jewish moral tradition are its "strong" or "extravagant" metaphysical claims. For some of the leading contemporary philosophical ethicists, a theistic ethics is dead on arrival.

A Short History of Jewish Ethics: Conduct and Character in the Context of Covenant,
First Edition. Alan L. Mittleman.
© 2012 Alan L. Mittleman. Published 2012 by Blackwell Publishing Ltd.

I have tried to show that, if the main problem here is sheer incredulity at the idea of divine command, then this is much less a factor for Jewish ethics than it might appear at first glance. Divine command, for many but not all of the texts considered here, cannot be portrayed as an exercise in pure voluntarism. Our reason is as important as God's will. The sturdiest rationalists in the Jewish tradition see God as answerable to shared standards of value. Although that doesn't illumine the being of God, it describes what we can know of the divine and, in a sense, highlights why the divine should matter to us. Divine command remains an important feature of Judaism, but command is fully compatible with – and may even be said to require – autonomy in the sense of human appropriation and consent. For many contemporaries, however, the issue is not divine command but the divine per se. Atheistic critics think that theists are simply about the irrational belief in occult entities no different in kind from Greek gods, unicorns, and gremlins. It is beyond the scope of this book to address those charges with a theological argument. Nonetheless, by displaying the complexity of moral life from an historic Jewish point of view, I want to suggest that one should evaluate a culture in light of its complexity rather than through reductions and abstractions. To put Jewish ethics into a box called "religious ethics," to think that one knows in advance what is most important about the contents of the box, and to leave the box on the shelf is to forget the meaning of humanistic inquiry.

As Iris Murdoch reminds us, perfectionism is altogether too strenuous for much of modern ethics. Since many moderns are no longer able to speak of human nature in a thick, normative way, the perfection of such a putative nature sounds like an unpleasant detour into neurosis. The Jewish way depicted in many of these texts *is* hard. It is austere, demanding, and uncompromising. It assumes that life is a very serious business – and that the time is short. This is an ethic ill-suited to the age of high self-esteem and brief attention spans. Holding up a perfectionist ethic for humane consideration may enlarge our moral imaginations. It may open up new possibilities for what a flourishing, well-lived life entails.

There is another, more serious charge that one can make against perfectionism and perhaps against an emphasis on virtue altogether. A German-Jewish refugee, the philosopher Hans Jonas, held that all traditional moral outlooks might well be inadequate to the present cultural moment. All moralities, he believed, were able to take the existence of a habitable earth for granted. All could assume that as beastly as human beings might be to one another, they couldn't damage the ecosystem which could always be counted on to support human and all other biological life. That is no longer the case. For Jonas, this counted against the sufficiency of all inherited moral systems. To matter, a morality had to take account of this astonishing and shattering new fact: that we can damage the planet in a literally global way and imperil the future of our own and other species. From this point of view, there is something almost self-indulgent about the religiously oriented pursuit of virtuous self-perfection.

Or is there? The sources that urge us to pursue a sober, focused, attentive life rivet our awareness on our omnivorous appetites. The ideal Jew of the philosophical and popular musar traditions is not an ideal consumer. He or she may have the industriousness and capacity for deferred gratification of a proper early capitalist but he or she will not be animated by greed, or pleasure, or a lust to own more and more. This is a person who will make do with little, consuming less so that he or she can commune more. If the prospect of environmental disaster comes at least in part because of the way we have chosen to live in carbon-hungry societies, perfectionism might be exactly what we need. Taming our appetites, without killing our economies, will require self-restraint and reallocation of resources to worthy, and more sustainable, ends. The possible contribution of the Jewish moral tradition should not be discounted.

Leo Strauss wrote of progress and return. He was skeptical of the former and robust in his endorsement of the latter. Classical Judaism has no concept of progress. Its concept of return (*teshuvah*) is foundational to Jewish moral thought. To return is not to indulge in nostalgia for an idealized bygone time. To doubt the sway of progress is not to doubt that discrete advances have been and continue to be made. Rather, it is to take an attitude of attentiveness to the possibility of wisdom concealed in the texts of the past. That in the end is the best reason to undertake a study of the history of Jewish ethics.

Index